SPORT AND EXERCISE PSYCHOLOGY

Praise for the first edition

"The exploration of the co... ....p.. .. ..ise, the writing style is engaging and easily understandable without being patronising or simplistic ... a useful reference tool, a quick and user-friendly resource to be used to inform discussion, or [as] a source of illumination."

Higher Education Academy Psychology Network

Now including exercise psychology terms for the first time in its new edition, *Sport and Exercise Psychology: The Key Concepts* offers a highly accessible introduction to this fascinating subject, its central theories and state-of-the-art research. Over 300 alphabetically ordered entries cover such diverse terms as:

- adherence
- aggression
- emotion
- exercise dependence
- home advantage
- kinesiophobia
- left-handedness
- motivation
- retirement
- self-confidence.

Cross-referenced, with suggestions for further reading and a full index, this Key Guide contains invaluable advice on the psychology of sport and exercise. A comprehensive A–Z guide to a fast-moving field of inquiry, this book is an essential resource for scholars, coaches, trainers, journalists, competitors, exercisers—in fact, anyone associated with sport and exercise.

Ellis Cashmore is Professor of Culture, Media and Sport at Staffordshire University, UK, and author of *Making Sense of Sports* as well as biographies, such as *Beckham* and *Tyson: Nurture of the Beast*.

ALSO AVAILABLE FROM ROUTLEDGE

Fifty Key Thinkers in Psychology
Noel Sheehy
978-0-415-16775-8

Psycholinguistics: The Key Concepts
John Field
978-0-415-25891-3

SPORT AND EXERCISE PSYCHOLOGY

The Key Concepts

Second Edition

Ellis Cashmore

Routledge
Taylor & Francis Group

LONDON AND NEW YORK

First published 2002

This edition published 2008
by Routledge
2 Park Square, Milton Park, Abingdon, Oxon OX14 4RN

Simultaneously published in the USA and Canada
by Routledge
270 Madison Ave, New York, NY10016

Routledge is an imprint of the Taylor & Francis Group, an informa business

© 2002, 2008 Ellis Cashmore

Typeset in Bembo by
Taylor & Francis Books
Printed and bound in Great Britain by
TJ International Ltd, Padstow, Cornwall

British Library Cataloguing in Publication Data
A catalogue record for this book is available from the British Library

Library of Congress Cataloging in Publication Data
Cashmore, Ernest.
Sport & exercise psychology : the key concepts / Ellis Cashmore.
p. cm. — (Key guides)
Rev. ed. of: Sport psychology. 2002.
Includes bibliographical references and index.
1. Sports—Psychological aspects—Encyclopedias. 2. Exercise—
Psychological aspects—Encyclopedias. I. Cashmore, Ernest. Sport
psychology. II. Title. III. Title: Sport and exercise psychology.
GV706.4.C39 2008
796.0103—dc22
2007044039

ISBN10: 0-415-43865-9 (hbk)
ISBN10: 0-415-43866-7 (pbk)
ISBN10: 0-203-92809-1 (ebk)

ISBN13: 978-0-415-43865-0 (hbk)
ISBN13: 978-0-415-43866-7 (pbk)
ISBN13: 978-0-203-92809-7 (ebk)

CONTENTS

LIST OF KEY CONCEPTS

ability
achievement goal theory
achievement motive
action control
adherence
adrenaline rush
aerobic/anaerobic
affect
aggression
aggressiveness
aging
alcoholism
androgyny
anger
anger management
anorexia athletica
anorexia nervosa
ANOVA
anxiety
applied sport psychology
approach
arousal
assertiveness
athletic identity
attention
attribution
autogenic
automaticity
autonomic nervous system
   (ANS)
autotelic
avoidance

Bem sex role inventory
binocular rivalry
biofeedback
body dissatisfaction
body image
body language
body mass index
body shame
brainwaves
bulimia nervosa
burnout
catastrophe theory
catharsis
cause
celebrities
centering
character
choke
coach–athlete relationship
cognition
cognitive-behavioral modification
cognitive evaluation theory
cognitive load theory (CLT)
cognitive-motivational-relational
cohesion
comeback
commitment
competition
composure
concentration
concept
concordance

relational
relationship
relaxation
religion
REM
response
retirement
reversal theory
reward
Ringelmann effect, the
risk
rivalry
role model
sandbagging
schema
self
self-actualization
self-awareness
self-concept
self-confidence
self-determination theory
self-efficacy
self-enhancement
self-esteem
self-fulfilling prophecy
self-handicapping
self-protection
self-rating
self-regulation
self-serving bias
self-talk
sensation-seeking
sex
sex test
sex typing
sibling rivalry
skill
skill acquisition
skill execution
sleep

slump
social facilitation
social loafing
social physique anxiety
socialization
sociotropy
stereotype
stereotype threat
stimulus
streaks
stress
stress-inoculation training
stress-management training
superstitious behavior
talent
task/ego orientation
team player
telic dominance
temperament
theory
theory of planned behavior
therapy
transactional leadership
transformational leadership
transgendered
transsexual
transtheoretical model
2 × 2 achievement goal
    framework
Type A
vicarious agency
violence
visual perception
visuomotor
weight control
well-being
Yerkes-Dodson law
yips
yoga
zone

INTRODUCTION

What do we need to know about using this book?

This book is like a supermarket cart after a twenty-minute journey around the aisles: brimming with all manner of assorted products, some essential, others minor extravagancies, but all of which will get used at some point. Like the consumables from the supermarket, the contents of this book will not be enough to get the shopper through the whole week, and visits to other, more specialist stores will be needed. But there will be enough staples to get started, and many of the goods will be kept in the fridge and used at a later stage.

Purpose

The purpose of the book is quite simple: to provide a working A–Z of the key concepts in sport and exercise psychology. Why *working*? Because this reference source is not intended to sit on a bookshelf waiting in abeyance to be consulted every so often. It's meant to be carried around in a bag or a case, consulted daily, scrawled with handwritten notes and daubed with highlighter. Within six months of purchase, it should be dog-eared, battered and plastered with those Post-it index stickers. In other words, it's meant to earn its keep.

Organization

The shopping-cart metaphor works to an extent, though, of course, no one insists on arranging their goods on the check-out belt in alphabetical order: apples, aromatic candles, avocadoes, beer, burgers, and so on. Since this is a reference book, the alphabet offers a logical system of organizing the material, though this isn't quite as straightforward as it seems. For example, where does "EXERCISE IDENTITY" go? Under "E," or under "IDENTITY," with a subhead *exercise*? Or drugs? Should it be dope, DOPING, or even performance-enhancing drugs? And how about state anxiety? (Terms in SMALL CAPITALS have an entry of their own in the main text, by the way.)

My guide has been common sense. Exercise identity appears under "E," and there is an entry on DOPING, with a dummy entry for drugs. Dummy entries are signpost entries: They direct the reader to another or sometimes several other entries where the term is discussed and where its meaning will become evident. In the interests of precision, I have added a crisp usually one-sentence definition of what the term, in its most basic sense, means. The reader can then move to the other entries. State anxiety is subsumed under ANXIETY but reoccurs elsewhere, as a glance at the index will show. Similarly, sport commitment appears under COMMITMENT, so generic entries should be checked first.

Obviously, my central task has been to compile a book where all the key concepts in sport and exercise psychology are defined, but, even then, there may be some terms the reader can't find in the main text. In this case, the index should provide the reference to the appropriate page numbers. For example, you won't find headings on "depersonalization," or "lost move syndrome" in the main text, but you'll find them in the index and this will take you to the entries in which they appear.

Scope

I'm hesitant about being too prescriptive and including a "how to use this book" section. "What more do we need to know about how to use an A–Z?" readers might ask. Only this: There are three types of entries. The longest and most detailed types are what we might call gold key concepts. These are most valuable currency in sport and exercise psychology. They include "AGGRESSION," "AROUSAL," "EMOTION," "MOTIVATION," and "SOCIAL PHYSIQUE ANXIETY." Such is their value in the lexicon, it seems justified to allow extra space and detail to exploring their meanings and relevance, so there are many extended essays that will, I hope, stretch the imagination of the reader.

There is also a second category of very important concepts. Here I include terms that are habitually used though often without clear understanding. "CHOKE" is an obvious example. It crops up in newspapers and in sports commentary all the time, usually in a way that is not all illuminating. "DEPENDENCE" is another term we use, often interchangeably with addiction. Again, its use tends to obscure more than it reveals, particularly in the analysis of exercise. Everyday terms such as "RETIREMENT" fall into this category. There is nothing wrong with the way we use the term in everyday conversation, but there is an awful lot more that an explication of the term can tell us about what happens psychologically when people are either forced or choose to stop physical activities.

There are several different kinds of concept that occupy the third group. They range from general terms that are germane to scholarly analysis, like "MODEL," and "PHENOMENON"—again, terms commonly but carelessly used in sport and exercise studies—to terms that are specific to sport and exercise psychology, such as "PARALYSIS BY ANALYSIS," or "ZONE."

Are they all *key* concepts? In the sense that they are all essential for gaining access to understanding, yes. Obviously, there is always an arbitrary element to an A–Z reference book that aims to be comprehensive. In an effort to minimize this, the entry list has been reviewed and modified by a team of eight scholars from North America and Great Britain. The distillation of their appraisals is the current entry list. A skim through the pages will alert the reader to the scope of the book.

I've opted not to include the names of eminent psychologists, regardless of their contribution to the discipline. The book is much closer to a conventional dictionary than an encyclopedia and, as such, lists names only when they appear eponymously. For example, YERKES-DODSON LAW is named after Robert Yerkes and John Dodson, though the entry is about the theory they formulated and not about them. Similarly, Max Ringelmann is the man behind what we call the RINGELMANN EFFECT and David Premack gave us the PREMACK PRINCIPLE, but the men are less important than their contributions to knowledge—at least for the purposes of this book.

Shape and makeup

Although I've tried to avoid being overly schematic, consistency is always a virtue in reference books, and so I've ensured the book's contents are joined up, so to speak. Each entry starts with a shorthand definition, usually with an etymology, that is the origin of the word or phrase. I have tried to make clear how concepts apply to real situations, so, wherever possible, there are examples of how the concept is activated or comes to life. The reader should discover that there is vitality in even the most abstract concepts.

Learning a vocabulary is one thing. Understanding the uses of that vocabulary is another. To this end, I have provided examples of current research that employs the terms. Readers will find every entry garnished with studies, experiments, and other types of research that help make sense of how concepts are used in practical settings. In all cases, the full reference to the research follows the text of the entry in the further-reading guide. Here the reader will find full documentation of all work, whether theoretical or applied, cited in the text and, occasionally work that, while not quoted, is of direct relevance.

As with any A–Z, there are many, many connections between concepts and, in closing each entry, I've added suggestions as to where the reader might look next in the book. The see-also lists recommend other entries; they are not simply lists of entries in which the term appears but pointers to relevant items. Sometimes the connections between entries will be obvious from the text itself; other times, the reader might wonder why I have, for example, advised "See also depression," plus several other entries, after reading "PER-FECTIONISM." Their curiosity will be satisfied only after completing their reading. But their understanding will, I anticipate, be enriched.

I mentioned earlier that SMALL CAPITALS are used in the text to signal that there is a full entry dedicated to that word, or term elsewhere in the book. The capitals appear once only in the relevant entries.

Some readers will be familiar with the first edition of what was then *Sport Psychology: The Key Concepts*, which was published in 2002. The change of title reflects the opening out of the field of study to embrace a larger domain. Exercise psychology, it could be argued, is a field of enquiry in its own right and is taught that way in many educational institutions. I've deliberately integrated the enquiry in a way that allows the reader to see the areas of overlap, symmetry, and convergence. In a great many entries, there is a similarity of characteristics; where there is not, I've dedicated individual entries to, for instance, "EXERCISE MOTIVATION" or "APPLIED SPORT PSYCHOLOGY." But the overall shape of the book accommodates both sport and exercise psychology as facets of a unified field of study rather than distinct subfields.

SPORT AND EXERCISE PSYCHOLOGY

Second Edition

ABILITY

The capacity, competence, faculty, quality, or power that enables a person to achieve something with no further learning or training at a particular moment in a particular place is ability, or *an* ability, which is derived from the Latin *habilitas* for able. Ability is always context-dependent: because someone has ability to accomplish an action in one CONTEXT carries no implication that he or she can duplicate the same action in another. Coaches are often said to lose their ability to motivate players; yet, they often move to different clubs at which they regain that ability. Ability also waxes and wanes, increasing and decreasing in time. The ability to run a sub-three-hour marathon might be positively correlated to the amount of high-quality training. Over the years, that ability declines, regardless of the amount or quality of training.

In sport and exercise psychology, ability is frequently prefixed, as in, for example, George Rebok and Dana Plude's study of physical activity and memory in AGING adults, which included *cognitive ability* among its measures. By contrast, Molly Moran and Maureen Weiss assessed *athletic ability* and its links with various other characteristics. (Both studies used SELF-RATING as a method.)

Aptitude, while often used interchangeably with TALENT, is actually a *potential* to perform: latent qualities that might be developed into ability given the right conditions for training or learning. Without those conditions, aptitude might remain undeveloped.

Further reading

Ericsson, K. Anders and Charness, Neil (1994). Expert performance: its structure and acquisition. *American Psychologist*, 49, 725–47.
Moran, Molly M. and Weiss, Maureen R. (2006). Peer leadership in sport: links with friendship, peer acceptance, psychological character-istics, and athletic ability. *Journal of Applied Sport Psychology*, 18, 97–113.
Rebok, George W. and Plude, Dana J. (2001). Relation of physical activity to memory functioning in older adults: The memory workout program. *Educational Gerontology*, 27: 241–59.

See also: ACHIEVEMENT MOTIVE; AUTOMATICITY; DELIBERATE PRACTICE; GIFTED-NESS; INTELLIGENCE; LEADERSHIP; LEFT-HANDEDNESS; MASTERY CLIMATE; MENTAL TOUGHNESS; SELF-ACTUALIZATION; SELF-CONFIDENCE; SELF-EFFICACY; SKILL; SOCIA-LIZATION; STEREOTYPE

ACHIEVEMENT GOAL THEORY

Purports to explain MOTIVATION orientations in terms of how individuals define their goals.

See also: ACHIEVEMENT MOTIVE; APPROACH; AVOIDANCE; GOAL; GOAL ORIENTATION; GOAL SETTING; TASK/EGO ORIENTATION; 2 × 2 ACHIEVEMENT GOAL FRAMEWORK

ACHIEVEMENT MOTIVE

Striving for success is often seen as a manifestation of an achievement motive (or MOTIVATION), something that induces a person to direct his or her behavior toward the attainment of certain goals. Motive is from *motus*, Latin for move. The whole field of sport is guided by an achievement ethos, or climate: Victory is sought-after, and defeat is to be avoided in every endeavor. Competitors are energized by an achievement motive in the sense that they personally seek success rather than failure and are prepared to defeat others in their pursuit of that GOAL. Exercisers too are typically motivated to attain specific results.

The influential research of John W. Atkinson—especially with D. C. McClelland, J. W. Atkinson, R. A. Clark and E. C. Lowell, in *The Achievement Motive,* published in 1953—shed light on the composition of the achievement motive. It was the combination of two dispositional personality constructs: the motive to approach success and the motive to avoid failure. According to Atkinson, all humans have both; it is the way in which they combine that affects whether one person will be achievement-motivated. Atkinson's research involved testing subjects for both the motives to succeed and to avoid failure. For example, would they look for challenges, show persistence, remain unafraid to lose and blame themselves when making the attribution for success or failure? Or would they try to avoid failure, dodge challenges, preferring to compete against easy opponents, dislike being evaluated by others and attribute their performance to external factors, such as luck or hard opponents? Those who scored big on the first scale were said to have an achievement motive.

Situations also factor into Atkinson's model, which rates probability of success from 0 (no chance) to 1 (certainty) and builds in an incentive value (the lower the chance of success, the greater the incentive). An achievement-motivated football kicker faced with a 50-yard field goal chance to win a game and no time left on the clock would relish the opportunity. A kicker without a strong motive would prefer either an easier, more certain task, such as a 25-yard attempt, or an impossibly tough kick from outside field goal range— to avoid being blamed for the failure. So, the type of situation determines whether the behavioral tendencies of the achievement-motivated player will come to the fore. As many situations in sport have a midrange chance of success without a very high incentive value, the high achievement-motivated athlete is not always an asset; many situations demand a more conservative performer—a "safe pair of hands."

M. L. Maehr and J. G. Nicholls rejected many of Atkinson's assumptions about the invariance and objectivity of success and failure. Instead, they proposed that they are much more subjective, based on the perception of reaching or not reaching goals. There is, according to Maehr and Nicholls, "cultural variation in the personal qualities that are seen to be desirable." In other words: Success and failure will be viewed differently in different cultures. While they do not examine the relationship between the achievement ethic and the achievement motive, Maehr and Nicholls acknowledge that it is necessary to understand the meanings of achievement rather than assume there is a single definition that holds good for all. Their interest was in exploring how, for example, winning may be only criterion of achievement for some, while pleasing a coach by performing well may constitute achievement for others. Different goals give rise to different perceptions of success and failure. But, significantly, all individuals use goals of some kind to evaluate their achievements.

Achievement goals can be grouped into three kinds, according to Maehr and Nicholls: (1) to demonstrate ability; (2) to be task-involved (mastering a competence rather than assessing oneself against others); and (3) to seek social approval. The same competitor may have a different goal for each different sport, or at different times in his or her life, or even have several goals at once.

While much research has focused on achievement motives in sport, their relevance in exercise has been revealed in a number of studies in recent years, for instance Robert LaChausse's study of cycling offering an exploration of how cyclists who rode for fun differed markedly in their motives from competitive cyclists: "Non-competitive cyclists were more likely to endorse weight concerns and affiliation as motives. Road cyclists were more likely to endorse goal achievement and COMPETITION, while mountain bikers endorsed life meaning as a motivation for cycling."

Other studies have evidenced the presence of the achievement motive among exercisers but suggest, as does LaChausse's work, that there is a hierarchy of motives, and one which changes as exercisers progress through various stages of participation.

Further reading

LaChausse, Robert G. (2006). Motives of competitive and non-competitive cyclists. *Journal of Sport Behavior*, 29, 304–15.

Maehr, M. L. and Brascamp, L. A. (1986). *The motivation factor: A theory of personal investment*, Lexington, Mass.: Lexington Books.

Maehr, M. L. and Nicholls, J. G. (1980). Culture and achievement motivation: a second look. In Warren, N (Ed.) *Studies in Cross-Cultural Psychology*, pp. 221–67. New York: Academic Press.

McClelland, D. C., Atkinson, J. W., Clark, R. A., and Lowell, E. L. (1953). *The achievement motive*, New York: Appleton-Century-Crofts.

Schmalt, Heinz-Dieter (2005). "Validity of a short form of the achievement-motive grid (AMG-S): Evidence for the three-factor structure emphasizing active and passive forms of fear of failure. *Journal of Personality Assessment*, 84, 172–84.

See also: ABILITY; APPROACH; AVOIDANCE; COMMITMENT; COMPETITION; CONCORDANCE; CONTEXT; DOPING; EGOCENTRISM; EXERCISE MOTIVATION; EXTRINSIC MOTIVATION; FEAR OF FAILURE; GENDER; GOAL; GOAL ORIENTATION; HOPE; INCENTIVE; MOTIVATION; MOTIVATIONAL CLIMATE; TASK/EGO ORIENTATION; THEORY; 2 × 2 ACHIEVEMENT GOAL FRAMEWORK

ACTION CONTROL

An attempt to CONTROL intentional behavior.

See also: SELF-REGULATION

ADHERENCE

Behaving according to a plan is adherence, from the French *adhérer*, to stick. It should not be confused with compliance, as C. A. Shields et al. stress: "Adherence implies a more active or collaborative role in behavioral DECISION-MAKING for the participant, allowing for some choice and adjustment of plans." By contrast: "Compliance infers the participant is in a more passive role in which they either obey the recommended activity guidelines or they do not."

Explanation. 1: Intention and results. "Stickability" is a valuable quality in any athlete. "It is imperative," write Kerry Mummery and Leonard Wankel, "that an athlete conscientiously *adhere* to the prescribed program of training and preparation to gain maximum benefit from his or her efforts." The same can be said of exercisers. This raises questions, such as: What makes some people stick to their programs, while others shirk? Why do some people start exercising but quickly lose their resolve and others continue exercising into their advanced years?

While many people adhere to health-related exercise as a leisure-time activity, training for COMPETITION is different. Its goal is not to enrich body image or lifestyle but to improve performance. This is an instrumental objective, though participation sport also involves an emotional component—athletes enjoy competing, at least initially. At higher levels, a commitment to the utility of training is a more reliable predictor of adherence.

Consistent with the *theory of reasoned action* proposition that the main precursor of behavior such as exercise is intention, Mummery and Wankel's study of swimmers revealed that adherence to training (measured in terms of frequency, volume, and intensity) was greatest among athletes who held strong intentions to participate in and complete prescribed training. A combination of the attitudes held toward a specific behavior and subjective norms (what the subject thinks others think) affect intention. The THEORY OF PLANNED BEHAVIOR extends the previous theory and introduces behavioral CONTROL to the account. Volitional control in training for competitive sports is problematic: subjects do not actually choose to do 30×60 meter sprints, or nonstop crunches for three minutes or to get up at 4:00 a. m. to get to the training pool before it gets busy.

The swimmers in the study believed in the utility of their training: The outcome of their efforts would be improvements in performance. They also believed that other individuals who were important to them thought that they should complete their training. Swimmers who stuck to their regimens also perceived themselves as having the necessary abilities to complete the programs as required.

Should athletes fail to see any improvement in performance despite sticking to training schedules, then they may question the training's efficacy, the wisdom of their coach, or their own capabilities. In such circumstances, adherence is unlikely.

Tangible improvement and the SELF-EFFICACY that this promotes are often the result of GOAL SETTING, perhaps the most important intervention in enhancing exercise adherence, particularly among those rehabilitating from injury, according to Lynne Evans and Lew Hardy. Research by David Lombard et al. has shown that goal setting is especially effective among exercisers when supported by prompting. This ranges from providing participants with FEEDBACK on frequency, time, and distance, or telephone calls simply asking, for example, "How's your walking program going?"

But the limitations of goal setting have been exposed by the research of Cara Sidman et al. The "effort-adherence trade-off," meaning the PERCEPTION of strenuous physical or perhaps mental exertion required to maintain a program of activity, can take effect. Failing to attain generalized goals (for example, 10,000 steps of walking per day, using a pedometer) over time results in lowered MOTIVATION and a loss of adherence. Personalizing exercise goals allows for a greater rate of attainment among former sedentary exercisers and, hence, more lasting adherence.

Explanation 2: Social experience. Environmental factors can have a bearing on exercise adherence. For example, the combination of personal television and ambient music in gyms "promoted a more pleasurable exercise experience, which, in turn, promoted better adherence and longer, more intensive workouts," according to James J. Annesi. The effects of the iPod are, as yet, untested, though we can extrapolate from Annesi's work.

While much of the research on adherence is psychological, Miranda Thurston and Ken Green have added a sociological dimension, describing a "richness" of experience, meaning satisfaction and skills developed through lifestyle rather than competitive activities. While participation declines markedly among sports competitors after the age of forty-five, those who have engaged with three or more activities, not necessarily competitive, become *socialized* into exercise and become part of "social networks in which physical activity is customary [...] regular participation is mutually reinforcing."

Motivation, while conventionally understood as a precursor to participation in exercise, is, on this account, a consequence of the engagement and the resultant satisfaction associated with exercise.

SOCIALIZATION was also found to be an influential factor in the continuing participation in exercise programs of subjects with physical disabilities, the other main influence being the ABILITY of exercisers to perform activities of daily living as a result of their engagement, again highlighting the motivating potency of exercise consequences.

Further reading

Annesi, James J. (2001). Effects of music, television, and a combination entertainment system on distraction, exercise adherence, and physical outputs in adults. *Canadian Journal of Behavioral Science*, 33, 193–201.

Dirocco, Patrick J. (2005). Adherence to a physical fitness program by individuals with physical disabilities. *Research Quarterly for Exercise and Sport*, 76, A112.

Evans, Lynne and Hardy, Lew (2002). Injury rehabilitation: A goal-setting intervention study. *Research Quarterly for Exercise and Sport*, 73, 310–20.

Lombard, David N., Neubauer Lombard, Tamara and Winett, Richard A. (1995). Walking to meet health guidelines: The effect of prompting frequency and prompt structure. *Health Psychology*, 14, 164–70.

Mummery, W. K. and Wankel, L. M. (1999). Training adherence in adolescent competitive swimmers: An application of the theory of planned behavior. *Journal of Sport and Exercise Psychology*, 21, 313–28.

Shields, C. A., Brawley, L. R. and Lindover, T. I. (2005). Where perception and reality differ: dropping out is not the same as failure. *Journal of Behavioral Medicine*, 28(5), 481–91.

Sidman, Cara L., Corbin, Charles, and Rhea, Matthew (2003). An examination of the 10,000-step goal in sedentary women with different baseline step counts. *Women in Sport and Physical Activity Journal*, 12, 111–20.

Thurston, Miranda and Green, Ken (2004). Adherence to exercise in later life: how can exercise on prescription programmes be made more effective? *Health Promotion International*, 19, 379–87.

See also: ATTRIBUTION; COMMITMENT; CONTEXT; CULTURE; DISCIPLINE; EXERCISE BEHAVIOR; EXERCISE MOTIVATION; FEEDBACK; GOAL ORIENTATION; GOAL SETTING; IDENTIFIED REGULATION; INTEGRATED REGULATION; INTERNALIZATION; MOTIVATION; MOTIVATIONAL CLIMATE; OBEDIENCE; SELF-DETERMINATION THEORY; SOCIALIZATION; THEORY OF PLANNED BEHAVIOR

ADRENALINE RUSH

The sudden sensation of excitement and power that often occurs in stressful situations is described as an adrenaline rush, adrenaline (sometimes called *epinephrine*) being one of the two main hormones released by the medulla of the adrenal gland which covers part of the kidney—the word adrenaline derives from the Latin for "toward the kidney," *ad* meaning to and *renal* kidney. In COMPETITION, the rush of adrenaline into the system can act as a spur to athletes, often at unexpected moments. The reason is that adrenaline causes profound change in all parts of the body.

The release of the hormone effectively mobilizes the whole body for either *fight* or *flight*. By stimulating the release of glycogen (which serves to store carbohydrates in tissues) from the liver, the expansion of blood vessels in the heart, brain and limbs and the contraction of vessels in the abdomen. It diminishes fatigue, speeds blood coagulation and causes the spleen to release its store of blood. The eyes' pupils dilate. Sweat increases to cool the body and sugar is released into the bloodstream to provide more energy for vigorous muscular activity. The value of adrenaline release to the sports performer is obvious, which is why many often reflect on good performances as happening when the "adrenaline was pumping" or try to break a SLUMP during a competition by "getting some adrenaline going." The effects are similar to the stimulation of the sympathetic division of the autonomic NERVOUS SYSTEM—an advantageous state of AROUSAL.

Under certain, usually dangerous, conditions, the skeletal muscles might receive up to 70 percent of the cardiac output, that is, the blood pumped from the heart. More blood is fed to muscles that need it at the expense of the viscera, especially the abdomen, where the needs are not urgent. Feelings of PAIN and tiredness are minimized and the body is prepared for extraordinary feats.

The whole process is mobilized by the sympathetic division of the AUTONOMIC NERVOUS SYSTEM (ANS), which regulates heartbeat, breathing, digestion, and other internal processes. The sympathetic division stimulates the body and causes it to expend energy. Once the adrenaline rush subsides, the parasympathetic division of the ANS kicks in to bring the body's function back into balance; for example, breathing and heart rate slow down and digestion increases.

While competitors consciously hope for an adrenaline rush at some point during a flaccid performance, the surge typically occurs in the context of events that use natural conditions rather than synthetic environments, such as a stadium or an indoor arena. Long-distance swimming, orienteering, car rallying, and rock climbing are examples of sports in which the performers' lives may occasionally be in jeopardy. RISK creates perfect conditions for an adrenaline rush. The sense of exhilaration and might are difficult to reproduce artificially, of course; though part of the summer Olympics triathlon course in 2000 was held in Sydney harbor, and it was speculated that the sharks that habitually lurk in the waters might hasten triathletes to personal bests. One wonders what distances long jumpers could cover if 100-foot drops replaced sandpits!

Actually an answer of sorts comes from K. C. Hughes, writing for the military magazine *Armor*: "[I]n times of pure terror or crisis, the body might release ENDORPHINS [. . .] These chemicals cause soldiers to ignore pain and give the 'out-of-body' feeling that is described by many during traumatic events. This survival technique is called emotional numbing."

Athletes, particularly boxers, have reported similar desensitizing when enduring what might in noncompetitive circumstances be an unbearably painful injury and completing a contest.

Some coaches have preached the benefits of FEAR to sporting performance. For example, Cus D'Amato, who trained world heavyweight champions Floyd Patterson and Mike Tyson, among others, gave every boxer the same illustration of a deer crossing an open field. "Suddenly, instinct tells him danger is there," D'Amato related to writer Peter Heller, in his 1990 book *Tyson,* "and nature begins the survival process, which involves the body releasing adrenaline into the bloodstream, causing the heart to beat faster and enabling the deer to perform extraordinary feats of agility and strength."

Academic research by Pamela Smith and Jennifer Ogle reported how cross-country runners strove to achieve a similar awareness in their training: "The sensation of healthfulness was most discussed within the context of running and was described as a feeling of euphoria or an 'adrenaline rush' that a 'hard run' could incite."

One of the properties of the drug pseudoephedrine, which is found in many cold remedies and decongestants, is that it mimics the adrenaline rush. It is on most sports' list of banned substances. Five different types of the stimulant were found in the urine of Argentina's soccer player Diego Maradona when he was tested at (and subsequently banned from) the 1994 World Cup championships.

Further reading

Hughes, K. C. (2005). A lesson learned: Post traumatic stress disorder. *Armor,* July/August, 15–16.

Sandford, B. (1987). The "Adrenaline Rush". *Physician and Sportsmedicine,* 15, 184.

Smith, Pamela M. and Ogle, Jennifer Paff (2006). "Interactions among high school cross-country runners and coaches: Creating a cultural context for athletes' embodied experiences. *Family and Consumer Sciences Research Journal,* 34, 276–307.

See also: AEROBIC/ANAEROBIC; AGGRESSION; AROUSAL; DEATH WISH; ENDORPHINS; FEAR; GAMBLING; HEDONIC TONE; INSTINCT; MIMESIS; NERVOUS SYSTEM; RISK; SENSATION SEEKING; ZONE

AEROBIC/ANAEROBIC

These typically relate to types of exercise, aerobic denoting sustained activity that is designed to improve the efficiency of the body's cardiovascular system in absorbing and transporting oxygen; hence *aero*, meaning air, and *bic*, from *bios*, Greek for life. Aerobic exercise tends to be continuous, for twenty minutes or more. Anaerobic activity is that which does not involve oxygen: The exercise is typically short and episodic and conducted with high intensity. The maximum length of time is about three minutes, after which oxygen requirements are more than supply and a buildup of lactic acid in the muscles causes fatigue, which interferes with contraction.

The conventional measure of aerobic FITNESS is VO^2_{max}, this representing an individual's maximal ability to take in, transport, and use oxygen during exercise without reverting to anaerobic energy systems and building up an oxygen debt; it is used as a benchmark of aerobic fitness.

But, the benefits of what some researchers call chronic aerobic exercise (that is, ten or more weeks continuous) are not confined to physiological aspects: Sustained exercise has been shown to alleviate symptoms of, among other things, DEPRESSION, state ANXIETY, and STRESS.

The effect of aerobic exercise on cognitive function, especially of aging populations, has been subject to much study, the overall conclusion pointing to an improvement in EXECUTIVE CONTROL, that is, making voluntary decisions about where to direct ATTENTION and determining what the content of the short-term MEMORY should be.

Further reading

Anshel, Mark H. (1996). Effect of chronic aerobic exercise and progressive relaxation on motor performance and affect. *Behavioral Medicine*, 21, 186–99.

Dalgleish, J. and Dollerty, S. (2001). *The health and fitness handbook*. Harlow: Pearson Education.

Hall, Courtney D., Smith, Alan L., and Keele, Steven W. (2001). The impact of aerobic activity on cognitive function in older adults: A new synthesis based on the concept of executive control. *European Journal of Cognitive Psychology*, 13, 279–300.

See also: ADHERENCE; ADRENALINE RUSH; ALCOHOLISM; ANXIETY; BODY IMAGE; DEPRESSION; EXERCISE DEPENDENCE; EXERCISE IDENTITY; EXERCISE MOTIVATION; FITNESS; GOAL ORIENTATION; MOOD; OBESITY; PREGNANCY; REACTION TIME; SENSATION SEEKING; STRESS; THERAPY; WEIGHT CONTROL; WELL-BEING; YOGA

AFFECT

An umbrella CONCEPT that covers EMOTION, desire and feeling.

See also: EMOTION

AGGRESSION

While aggression has been used as an inclusive term to capture diverse behavior containing hostility, harm, and violation, there is so little common ground among scholars that we might profitably start by establishing what it is *not*, according to Diane Gill:

> An attitude, emotion or motive [. . .] Wanting to hurt someone is not aggression. ANGER and thoughts might play a role in aggressive behavior, but they are not necessary or defining characteristics [. . .] Accidental harm is not aggression [. . .] kicking a bench is not [. . .] sadomasochistic and suicidal acts [are not].

Yet, Burris Husman and John Silva contend that aggression is "an overt verbal or physical act that can psychologically or physically injure another person or oneself," meaning that sadomasochistic and suicidal acts would be, contrary to Gill, instances of aggression. In this definition, an abusive email that can "psychologically" injure its recipient counts as aggression. But, Richard Cox emphasizes that the aggressive "behavior must be aimed at another human being with the GOAL of inflicting physical harm [. . .] there must be a reasonable expectation that the attempt to inflict bodily harm will be successful."

A consistent feature appears to be *intention*. The 1996 position statement of the International Society of Sport Psychology stipulated: "Aggression [. . .] is reflected in acts committed with the intent to injure." Yet, even the inclusion of intention does not elicit complete agreement among scholars. Leif Isberg exchanges this for "the concept of *awareness* that an act will or could injure someone." Even, if a person did not intend to harm another, the fact that he or she was aware that it might makes their behavior aggressive. Isberg deviates from most definitions when he suggests that aggression is not behavior but rather "an unobservable starting point for potentially aggressive behavior."

There are other, deeper disagreements, but, for present purposes, we might propose that *aggression is behavior, or a propensity to behave, in a way that is either intended, or carries with it a recognizable possibility, that a living being will be harmed, physically or psychologically.* In this sense, aggression is quite different from what nowadays we call AGGRESSIVENESS, or assertiveness and conceptually distinct from VIOLENCE.

Conventionally, two types of aggression are specified: *hostile* (or reactive) and *instrumental.* The primary goal of hostile aggression is to cause harm to another: A football player might believe he or she has been unfairly tackled and retaliate by chasing and striking feet-first at the opponent's ankles with no intention of retrieving the ball. With instrumental aggression, there is a specific purpose beyond the aggression itself, and the intention to harm, or awareness that the action might cause harm to another, is incidental: The same player, later in the game, might jump for the ball, at the same time deliberately elbowing an opponent in the face—the goal is to reach the ball and the aggression is a way of deterring another player who might otherwise obstruct his path to the goal. In both cases, aggressive behavior inflicts harm.

Theory 1: Drives. The distinction between hostile and instrumental aggression is not always clear-cut: In sports, all aggression has a point, a purpose, in short, a GOAL. Even an enraged athlete who intentionally bites an opponent's ear à la Tyson does so in the context of a competition in which he or she has the overarching aim of victory. Tyson's action in 1997 was widely interpreted by the media as the escape of "the beast within," his aggressive instincts breaking through his civilized façade. Some schools of thought support this type of view, maintaining that aggression is a natural drive.

Ethologists (who study humans in the same way they would any other animal) contend that we are born with an aggressive instinct that has been quite serviceable in our survival as a species. So, we defend our "natural" territory when it is under threat. Konrad Lorenz wrote that human aggression is like other forms of animal aggression, only we have learned to route it into safe outlets, sports being an obvious one.

Sigmund Freud (1856–1939) too viewed sport as a way of discharging aggression. In his theory, we all have a DEATH WISH that builds up inside us to the point where it must be discharged, either inwardly (self-destructive acts), or outwardly. Because we do not always have socially acceptable opportunities for turning our aggression outward, we *displace* it into acceptable channels. Sports are perfect: we can get all our aggression out of our system either by participating or just watching; either way, we rid ourselves of the aggression.

On the other hand, "instrumental aggression is a reasoned behavior, strategically used to gain an advantage," as Geneviève Coulomb and Richard Pfister put it in their study of French soccer. "Cognitive processes are involved, and the players learn to use instrumental aggression at the right time and place to improve the ratio between cost (e.g. risk of being penalized by a referee) and profit (e.g. getting the ball directly or making the other team lose it quickly)." Their research indicated that "Hostile aggressive behaviors will become less frequent as players become more experienced and the level of COMPETITION increases."

Theory 2: Frustration-aggression. As if to prove that no research is without faults, the vastly experienced Zinedine Zidane, acknowledged as one of the finest footballers ever, contrived to get red-carded out of the 2006 World Cup Final—his farewell game—after a flagrantly hostile head-butt on a rival who had allegedly uttered insults immediately before the assault (interestingly, Barry Kirker et al.'s study of hockey and basketball found that, in a reversal of this, "player-to-player verbal aggression followed physical aggression").

Before the hostility, Zidane had been playing poorly (at least by his own standards), creating a CONTEXT in which he was likely to experience frustration. Sports, of course, are crucibles of frustration: individuals pursue aims while others try to stop them. Several theorists have argued that frustration creates a readiness for aggressive behavior: frustration–aggression theory, as it is called, hypothesizes that, when goal-oriented behavior is blocked, an aggressive drive is induced. Further frustrations increase the drive. On this account, all aggressive behavior is produced by frustration. The hypothesis was introduced as an alternative to theories of aggression based on innate characteristics. Scholars such as John Dollard rejected the notion of human behavior as programmed by nature and argued instead that the way we act is the product of stimuli in the world about us—frustration being the STIMULUS that produces aggressive behavior. Unlike Lorenz, Freud and others who portrayed sports competition as a cathartic experience, allowing all the aggressive energies to flow out, frustration-aggression theorists interpreted sports as heightening the possibility of aggression. Frustration of some order is inevitable in any competition.

Theory 3: Learning. The decisions of referees or officials are often a source of frustration to competitors, though physical aggression against officials is restricted. While attacks on referees and umpires are not unknown (for example, Roberto Alomar spat in the face of a baseball umpire in 1996; Paulo di Canio pushed a soccer referee to the ground in 1998; Rasheed Wallace was suspended by the NBA for threatening a referee in 2003), players often react in a verbally hostile way. In one notable instance, an animal was the source of frustration: In 2006, jockey Paul O'Neill was unseated by his horse during a race in England; after the race, the furious O'Neill head-butted the horse!

FANS too become frustrated by both refereeing decisions and the performance of players, and research indicates that they sometimes imitate the objects of their gaze. A 1987 study by Robert Arms et al., "Effects on the hostility of spectators of viewing aggressive sports," concluded that "the observation of aggression on the field of play leads to an increase in hostility on the part of the spectators." Why? If we are exposed to models who are rewarded for aggressive behavior as opposed to models who are punished, we are likely to imitate them. Research in the 1960s, much of it by Albert Bandura (1925–), revealed the powerful part played by imitation in shaping our behavior. Simply observing aggressive behavior can affect our own behavior, if that aggression was positively sanctioned in some way, or, we should add, if the person interpreted the aggression as being positively sanctioned.

Bandura's famous modeling experiment with Bobo dolls involved asking groups of children to watch a MODEL aggressively beating up a toy Bobo doll or treating it kindly. The tendency of the children was to copy the model they observed, especially when they witnessed the aggressive model being rewarded for the assault. Bandura concluded from this and other studies that we *learn* aggression, and, in this sense, it is a social rather than natural phenomenon. Clearly, this finding is totally at odds with the view of many coaches and players who believe (presumably, with Lorenz) that sports are a good way of letting off steam or getting our aggression out of our system. The aggression has never been in there, according to social-learning theorists: we acquire it during our interactions with others. (Crudely summarized, sport is an outlet for aggression in biologically based approaches, a mediating factor in the frustration–aggression hypothesis and an environment in which aggression is acquired in social-learning theory.)

This does not exclude frustration from the account: in social-learning theory, frustration is one of several experiences that lead to an emotional arousal. But, there may be others, including physical discomfort, or even pleasant circumstances, such as dancing in a club. Aroused by the physical exertion of dancing and a feeling of well-being, a person may be aggressive toward someone who accidentally bumps into them and makes them spill a drink. It may well be that the aggressor has learned this response through observing others at the same club, whose behavior was rewarded. Even if the person had been thrown out, his or her peers may have been suitably impressed. Several studies indicate that emotional arousal, regardless of the source, can increase aggression when the requisite stimuli are present. The consequences of, or the reaction to, the aggression can have decisive effects in shaping future behavior.

As noted before, most aggression in sport is instrumental, or goal-directed, with perhaps a modest amount of fear-induced aggression (when a normally meek athlete is threatened by an aggressive opponent, experiences an ADRENALINE RUSH and fights rather than flees). Whether one understands its source as lying in natural or social realms, the importance of CONTEXT is undeniable: aggression typically arises in the pursuit of objectives. Two athletes clashing aggressively during a contest may pass each other by or exchange banter when they to meet in a shopping mall or a bar. This also applies to fans. However aggression in sport is conceived, the significance of the context in which it is expressed should not be underplayed.

Further reading

Arms, R., Russell, G., and Sandilands, M. (1987). Effects on the hostility of spectators of viewing aggressive sports. In Yiannakis, A., McIntyre, T., Melnick, M., and Hart, D. (Eds.) *Sport Sociology*, 3rd edn (pp. 259–64). Dubuque, Iowa: Kendall/Hunt.

Bandura, A. (1977). *Social Learning Theory.* Englewood Cliffs, NJ: Prentice-Hall.

Coulomb, Geneviève and Pfister, Richard (1998). Aggressive behaviors in soccer as a function of competition and level and time: a field study. *Journal of Sport Behavior*, 21, 222–32.

Cox, R. H. (1998). *Sport Psychology: Concepts and applications*, 4th edn. Boston, Mass.: McGraw-Hill.

Dollard, J., Doob, J., Miller, N., Mowrer, O., and Sears, R. (1939). *Frustration and Aggression.* New Haven, CT: Yale University Press.

Gill, D. L. (2000). *Psychological dynamics of sport and exercise*, 2nd edn. Champaign, Ill.: Human Kinetics.

Husman, B. F. and Silva, J. M. (1984). Aggression in sport: definitional and theoretical considerations. In J. M. Silva and R. S. Weinberg (Eds.) *Psychological Foundations of Sport* (pp. 246–60). Champaign, Ill.; Human Kinetics.

Isberg, L. (2000). Anger, aggressive behavior, and athletic performance. In Y. L. Hanin (Ed.), *Emotions in Sport* (pp. 113–33). Champaign, Ill.: Human Kinetics.

Kirker, Barry, Tenenbaum, Gershon, and Mattson, Jan (2000). An investigation of the dynamics of aggression: direct observations in ice hockey and basketball. *Research Quarterly for Exercise and Sport*, 71, 373–87.

Tenenbaum, Gershon, Stewart, Evan, Singer, Robert N., and Duda, Joan (1996). Aggression and violence in sport: an ISSP position stand. *International Journal of Sport Psychology*, 27, 229–36.

See also: AGGRESSIVENESS; ANGER; AROUSAL; CATHARSIS; DEATH WISH; DEVIANCE; DRIVE; EMOTION; EMOTIONAL CONTROL; FEAR; GROUP DYNAMICS; HEDONIC TONE; MODELING; REINFORCEMENT; RIVALRY; ROLE MODEL; THEORY; VIOLENCE

AGGRESSIVENESS

Expressing assertive, forceful, offensive, dominant tendencies, a person with aggressiveness relentlessly pursues goals but without necessarily engaging in intentional harmful behavior. The root is *aggressio,* Latin for attack. In sport, aggressiveness is typically applauded and carries a positive connotation, unlike actual AGGRESSION, which is directed toward damaging others.

While Burris Husman and John Silva, in 1984, disapproved of the term aggressiveness as a "popularized" attempt "to legitimize behaviors that are illegal and injurious to opponents," their favored term "assertiveness" seems close, if not synonymous: "This goal-directed behavior may, and often does, involve the use of legitimate verbal or physical force [. . .] requires unusual energy and effort, which in most other social settings would appear to be aggressive behavior." According to the authors, assertive behavior "must be exhibited with no intent to harm or injure another person, nor may they violate the constitutively agreed upon rules of the sport."

Mental aggressiveness is a subcategory of "strategic interference" that is designed to "interfere with the performance of a game opponent. " Sean VanRoenn et al.'s 2004 study discovered that both female and male respondents regarded mental aggressiveness as acceptable. Athletes who show a ruthless disposition in their play are often praised for their desire to win at all costs. VanRoenn et al. argue that this is the "result of a SOCIALIZATION of acceptance toward certain behaviors and activities within sport."

Aggressiveness in sports is instrumental, in the sense that it is directed toward clear objectives; the goals may be specific (such as scoring in specific situations) or general (such as overall dominance in a COMPETITION). Tackling hard, but fairly, without flinching and without obvious regard for one's own safety would be an example of the former. Staring down, or PSYCHING out an opponent by some other means, would be an instance of the latter. In neither case, is any physical harm intended: The aggressiveness is intended to procure an advantage within the rules of the game. As Barry Kirker et al. specify, "the intent behind assertive behavior is not to hurt another, rather to be active, determined, and establish dominance."

But the demarcation is not always so clear-cut, and physical as well as psychological harm can result. While outright VIOLENCE is deterred in most noncombat sports, Jane Sheldon and Christine Aimar's study of ice hockey suggested that "performance does indeed benefit from aggressive behavior," adding the reminder, "sanctioned [that is, permitted or approved-of] behaviors in a sport can also be aggressive."

Whatever the CONTEXT, aggressiveness to be effective must be *displayed*: the competitor must make visible to opponents and spectators at the outset that he or she is intent on reaching the desired goals. Aggressiveness should be pre-emptive. As a pre-emptive strike is designed to prevent an attack by disabling a threatening enemy, so aggressiveness—at its most potent—inhibits opponents, making them indecisive and wary.

Further reading

Husman, B. F. and Silva, J. M. (1984). Aggression in sport: definitional and theoretical considerations. In J. M. Silva and R. S. Weinberg (Eds.), *Psychological Foundations of Sport* (pp. 246–60). Champaign, Ill.: Human Kinetics.

Kirker, Barry, Tenenbaum, Gershon, and Mattson, Jan (2000). An investigation of the dynamics of aggression: direct observations in ice hockey and basketball. *Research Quarterly for Exercise and Sport*, 71, 373–87.

Sheldon, Jane P. and Aimar, Christine M. (2001). The role aggression plays in successful and unsuccessful ice hockey behaviors. *Research Quarterly for Exercise and Sport*, 72, 304–9.

VanRoenn, Sean, Zhang, James, and Bennett, Gregg (2004). "Dimensions of ethical misconduct in contemporary sports and their association with the backgrounds of stakeholder. *International Sports Journal*, 8, 37–55.

Widmeyer, W. N., Dorsch, K. D., Bray, S. R., and McGuire, E. J. (2002) The nature, prevalence, and consequences of aggression in sport. In J. M. Silva and D. E. Stevens (Eds.), *Psychological Foundations of Sport* (pp. 328–51). Boston, Mass.: Allyn & Bacon.

See also: AGGRESSION; CATHARSIS; EMOTION; FEAR; MORAL ATMOSPHERE; RISK; SOCIALIZATION; TELIC DOMINANCE; TYPE A; VIOLENCE

AGING

The process of progressive, irreversible change in the body that occurs during the passage of time, aging, after a certain stage, results in a decline in task-performance abilities and in mental agility—though the latter may be offset by increased knowledge and experience. While often assumed to be an independent biochemical process, many believe aging is the product of an interaction with the social and physical environment and, as such, may vary across cultures and stages in history.

In sports, aging defines a kind of parabola in which the competitor rises to PEAK PERFORMANCE, usually somewhere between late teens and early thirties, then proceeds on a downward curve to the point where he or she can no longer perform at a competitive level. Degenerative changes guarantee that a sports performer cannot endure past a certain age: aging increases the probability that a competitor will lose with more frequency and more emphatically as his or her skill degrades and types of body cells die. There are huge variations between individuals and sports.

Variations 1: In sport. Examples of the variability of aging abound. At five, Steffi Graf had already played her first tournament and, by thirteen, she was playing professionally, winning all four Grand Slam single titles and an Olympic gold when aged nineteen. Fu Mingxia was twelve years old when she won the world diving championship in 1991. Nadia Comenici was fourteen when she was awarded six perfect scores of 10 for her winning performance on the asymmetric bars at the 1976 Olympics. The other famed gymnast of the period, Olga Korbut, was considered old when she won Olympic gold at the age of seventeen; by twenty-one, her career was over. Björn Borg, Stefan Edberg and John McEnroe were all dominant tennis champions, but none won a Grand Slam title after the age of twenty-five. Wilfred Benitez had his first professional fight two months after his fifteenth birthday, won the first of three world titles at the age of seventeen, lost to Thomas Hearns when aged twenty-three and slid into obscurity thereafter.

In contrast to athletes such as these who hit their peak early and, in sporting terms, aged early, there are others who peaked much later. Archie Moore was a professional boxer for twenty-eight uninterrupted years and did not win a world title until he was thirty-nine; he was almost fifty when he had his last fight (which he won by a third round knockout). Miruts Yifter won two gold medals on the track at the 1980 summer Olympics at the age of forty-three. Forty-two-year-old

Yekaterina Podkopayeva was the world's number-one-ranked female 1,500 meters runner in 1994. Linford Christie was an indifferent sprinter up to the age of twenty-five: from then until he was thirty-five, he won eleven major championship golds and, in the process, became the oldest man (at thirty-three) to win an Olympic 100-meters title. George Foreman turned professional in 1969 at the age of twenty, won a world title at twenty-three, another (after a ten-year retirement) at the age of forty-five and fought his final fight at the age of forty-nine.

It has been estimated that an adult human being produces 3–4 million cells per second; these replace a similar number of cells that have died. Some cells, such as muscle and nerve cells, do not undergo cell division at all in the adult being, while others, such as the cells in bone marrow that produce red blood cells, may divide twice in each twenty-four-hour period. Obviously, the muscle and nerve-ending cells that are not replaced will cause an athlete to decline physically, which makes Foreman's experience all the more remarkable.

Never a mobile fighter, Foreman was virtually stationary in his forties; his reactions were also relatively slow—no amount of training can improve reactions. But, he had compensating attributes, including punch power and a vast experience that enabled him to use timing, balance, and leverage to good effect. There is also evidence that some loss of sensitivity to pain comes with age, so Foreman may not have felt some of the body shots that would make younger men wince! Nevertheless, a sporting LIFE COURSE of almost thirty years is exceptional for boxing, as it is for most other sports, save those that are relatively sedate and carry little risk of serious INJURY. This is why Jack Nicklaus could tie for sixth place in the 1998 US Masters—ahead of favorite Tiger Woods—when he was fifty-eight.

Golf, like chess, bowls, snooker, and several other sports, is a sport that requires only limited physical prowess, a degree of "mental agility," but most importantly a great deal of judgment, anticipation, and tactical awareness. These are values that are acquired through experience. While "mental agility" as measured by intelligence tests, declines, experience increases, making the age of peak performance in these sports between thirty and fifty.

In other sports, speed is a factor and peaks typically arrive much earlier. John Elway's Super Bowl XXXIII win with Denver Broncos, at the age of thirty-eight, is a vivid exception, especially in a sport where the RISK of injury is constant. Elway exhibited no evident slowdown in simple aimed movements, or sensorimotor tasks, that is, making decisions about whether to pass, handoff, scramble, and so on (cognitive and intellectual rather than motor functions). Yet, research has shown that, while there is a loss of 10 percent in aimed movements between the ages of twenty and seventy, there is a loss of up to 25 percent in sensorimotor tasks, and this may increase to 50 percent on more complex tasks. While there are no definitive answers to why, the reason appears to be that the signals from the sense organs to the brain and from one part of the brain to another become weaker, while random neural activity in the brain tends to increase. The latter interferes with the former.

This is why, in some sports in which speed is not a factor, older players have no obvious disadvantage. The darts player usually takes time to settle, aim, and perfect the throw so it is accurate. A subtle, experienced player refuses to be rushed; there are no points to be gained for speed. Despite this, some loss of sensibility to the detection of fine movements of various joints will eventually hamper a darts player, as will a reduction of sensitivity to touch and vibration.

Variations 2: Physical change. Aging brings with it a loss of MEMORY, the reason being that the transfer of data from short to long-term storage is more troublesome and an amount of material is lost in the process. But material that has been safely stored is not forgotten more easily in later life; so, well-learned motor skills, including driving, playing bridge, or shooting, may be retained. New motor skills take longer to acquire. But, Formula 1 drivers do not usually drive into their forties. This is because, while they remain proficient in motor skill and judgment, their reactions may slow and their visual acuity may be reduced. There are other reasons, of course: Most have earned so much money by the time they reach their mid-thirties that they have no material need to continue in a sport where the risk of death is high.

Barring fatal injury, retirement is inevitable, and this poses problems for some athletes; faced with more time and opportunities to pursue interests, but perhaps restricted by changing capacities and delayed-onset injuries (such as osteoarthritis), ex-athletes sometimes become disoriented and go through profound PERSONALITY changes. Such changes are probably compounded by contemporary cultural values: youth, vigor, and athleticism are idealized, and individuals who once embodied all these but have since lost them may suffer. On the surface, this may appear to be more poignant for women than men, though female athletes often maintain training and dietary regimens to stay in shape. No doubt, several join the hundreds of thousands of women who attempt to counteract the visible signs of aging with face-lifts (rhytidectomy) and other forms of cosmetic surgery. There is some research that indicates that continuing sports activity and other forms of exercise in middle and old age has the potential to promote SELF-EFFICACY, though no causal relationship between the two has been demonstrated. A COMEBACK is always an option for an athlete who cannot cope without actual COMPETITION.

Variations 3: CULTURE. Aging certainly has many features of a universal process, though cultural variations alert us to the probability that types of diet and nutrition, standards of health care and sanitation and other environmental conditions can affect the pace at which aging proceeds. There are other cultural factors to consider, including the growth of an industry devoted to the postponement of aging (health clubs, health foods, surgery, and so on).

In cultures that venerate the aged, such factors may not be present, but, in those that elevate youth, the idea of aging is unlikely to be welcomed, and there will be strenuous efforts at counteracting it. While many opt for cosmetic surgery, a great many others extend, revive, or start activities. D. S. Tunstall Pedsoe records how septuagenarians have climbed Mount Everest and have swum the English Channel. City marathons, including the London and New York events regularly attract runners over eighty, and a ninety-two-year-old marathoner has completed the London course in 6 hours 7 minutes.

Tunstall Pedsoe issues the reminder that "death rates during sports participation increase dramatically with age as the incidence of coronary heart disease increases," though "the benefits of exercise even for the coronary prone are more generally appreciated."

The benefits of exercise for the elderly are not confined to coronary functions, as the research of, among others, Alessandra de Carvalho Bastone and Wilson Jacob Filho suggests. Involvement in an exercise program produced improvement in the participants' lower-limb function, gait velocity, joint mobility, and strength. It also improved depression symptoms and overall mental state, adding to the conclusion that physical activity in later life has benefits in both physical fitness and cognitive function, though not in a straightforward CAUSE–effect relationship. Health characteristics and social and environmental circumstances also enter the relationship.

Further reading

Austed, S. N. (1997). *Why we age: what science is discovering about the body's journey through life.* New York: Wiley.

Brown, D. R. (1992). Physical activity, ageing and psychological well-being: An overview of the research. *Canadian Journal of Sports Sciences,* 17, 185–92.

De Carvalho Bastone, Alessandra and Filho, Wilson Jacob (2004). Effect of an exercise program on functional performance of institutionalized elderly. *Journal of Rehabilitation Research and Development*, 41, 659–68.

Suthers, K., Jagger, C., and Simonsick, E. (2004). The relationship between cognitive function and physical activity in late life: A synthesis and overview. *The Gerontologist*, 44, 195.

Tunstall Pedsoe, D. S. (2004). Sudden death risk in older athletes: Increasing the denominator. *British Journal of Sports Medicine*, 38, 671–2.

See also: ABILITY; AEROBIC/ANAEROBIC; AUTOMATICITY; COGNITION; COMEBACK; CONTEXT; CULTURE; DECISION-MAKING; EXECUTIVE CONTROL; EXERCISE BEHAVIOR; FITNESS; INJURY; LIFE COURSE; MEMORY; MIMESIS; REACTION TIME; REHABILITATION; SELF-EFFICACY; SKILL; SKILL EXECUTION

ALCOHOLISM

Alcoholism refers to both the DEPENDENCE on the consumption of alcoholic drink and the compulsive behavior resulting from this. The term "alcohol use disorders" (AUD) is often used to capture the various ways in which alcoholism disrupts normal physical and mental functions. It is estimated that some form of AUD affects up to 20 percent of the population of the USA and several other developed countries.

While COGNITIVE-BEHAVIORAL MODIFICATION, skills training, psychopharmacological medications, and other interventions are used regularly to treat alcoholism, relapse rates range from 60–90 percent. Research has shown that physical exercise can be an effective adjunct to treatment.

Exercise is associated with favorable outcomes in the treatment of ANXIETY and DEPRESSION, as well as several other mood-related conditions. There is evidence that it can be applied to the treatment of and recovery from dependencies, including substance-based dependencies, smoking being the most obvious.

Studies in the 1980s, by D. Sinyor et al. and T. J. Murphy et al. suggested that AEROBIC exercise could play a role, particularly at early stages of recovery from alcohol dependence, when the possibility of behavior change is highest. Neither project considered ANAEROBIC exercise, or YOGA, both of which have been found to produce beneficial mental outcomes.

One of the persistent problems with most treatments of alcoholism is that, STRESS induced by abstention often inclines recovering alcoholics to smoke more, a trend reported by J. E. Martin et al. whose research concluded: "Post treatment abstinence rates [for both drinking and smoking] were significantly higher for the group receiving exercise maintenance (60 percent) than the ST [standard treatment] condition (31 percent)."

While the evidence suggests the positive impact of exercise in the treatment of alcoholism, the precise reasons for this are not clear: Exercise excites changes in MOOD states, which might precipitate lifestyle changes; or the exercise might form part of that package of lifestyle changes. Whatever the mechanism, Jennifer Read and Richard Brown's review suggests there is a significant correlation, though actually instigating the initial behavioral changes remains problematic: "Low MOTIVATION may be a substantial barrier to engaging in physical exercise among persons with alcohol and other substance use disorders."

While exercise can be used to counter alcoholism, the absence of exercise after a prolonged period of activity, combined with a loss of status can lead to dependence. As Jeff Pearlman points out: "Alcoholism is a significant problem among ex-athletes." Pearlman suggests how the drop in status experienced by sports performers, especially those who have occupied the attentions of the media during their competitive careers, can lead to alcohol abuse. The number of top-flight athletes who have drifted toward alcoholism both before and after RETIREMENT is legion, Northern Ireland's George Best and the USA's Joe Namath being famous examples.

There are several RISK factors that place athletes at a higher probability of developing an addictive disorder," write Thomas Miller et al., identifying "emotional distress," "inability to delay gratification," and "AGGRESSIVENESS/competitiveness" among them (we might add peer group influences and expectations of FANS). "Likewise there are protective factors that appear to insulate athletes from the susceptibility of developing an addiction," which include the COACH-ATHLETE RELATIONSHIP, "respect for authority, and the belief that they should be "trustworthy ROLE MODELS," according to Miller et al. Once these are removed, the likelihood of succumbing to alcoholism or other forms of dependency is heightened.

Further reading

Martin, J. E., Calfas, K. J., Patten, C. A., Polarek, M., Hofstetter, C. R., Noto, J., and Beach, D. (1997). Prospective evaluation of three smoking interventions in 205 recovering alcoholics: One-year results of Project SCRAP-Tobacco. *Journal of Consulting and Clinical Psychology*, 65, 190–4.

Miller, T. W., Adams, J. M., Kraus, R. F., Clayton, R., Miller, J. M., Anderson, J., and Ogilvie, B. (2001). Gambling as an addictive disorder among athletes: Clinical issues in sports medicine. *Sports Medicine*, 31, 145–52.

Murphy, T. J., Pagano, R. R., and Marlatt, G. A. (1986). Lifestyle modification with heavy alcohol drinkers: Effects of aerobic exercise and meditation. *Addictive Behaviors*, 11, 175–86.

Pearlman, Jeff (2004). After the ball. *Psychology Today, 37*(May/June). Available online at http://psychologytoday.com/articles/pto-20040514-000001.html.

Read, Jennifer P. and Brown, Richard A. (2003). The role of physical exercise in alcoholism treatment and recovery. *Professional Psychology: Research and Practice*, 34, 49–56.

Sinyor, D., Schwartz, S. G., Peronnet, F., Brisson, G., and Serganan, P. (1983). "Aerobic fitness level and reactivity to psychosocial stress: Physiological, biochemical, and subjective measures. *Psychosomatic Medicine*, 45, 205–17.

See also: AEROBIC/ANAEROBIC; DEPENDENCE; DEVIANCE; EXERCISE BEHAVIOR; GAMBLING; MOOD; OBSESSIVE-COMPULSIVE; REHABILITATION; RETIREMENT; STRESS; THERAPY; TRANSTHEORETICAL MODEL; TYPE A; YOGA

ANDROGYNY

From the Greek *androgunos*, a combination of *andros*, for man and *gune*, woman, androgyny is the condition of having certain male and female attributes. Androgen is the male hormone capable of developing and maintaining some male sexual characteristics. An androgyne is a human, or other kind of animal, possessing features of both males and females but who can usually be assigned to one biological SEX or another—as distinct from a hermaphrodite (from the name of the son of the Greek mythological figure who was the son of Hermes and Aphrodite and who was joined in one body with the nymph Salmacis) who cannot. In sports, female athletes who exhibit attributes typically associated with men as well as those associated with women have been called psychological androgynes.

Psychological androgyny is a term introduced in the 1970s when the feminist movement was in its ascendancy. Proponents disputed the deterministic notion that one's biology determines capability, competence, and aptitude; or, as a feminist slogan of the time expressed it, "biology is not destiny." Research indicated that female athletes, far from being limited by their biological sex, had a great many of the attributes traditionally assigned only to men.

The term came from the BEM SEX ROLE INVENTORY (BSRI), a sixty-item questionnaire designed in the early 1970s to test subjects' personality and relate these to biological sex. Twenty of the attributes on the scale reflected features popularly associated with masculinity in contemporary CULTURE: independence, athleticism, ASSERTIVENESS, and so on. Another twenty included affection, gentleness, nurturance, and other qualities often identified with popular conceptions of femininity. A further twenty were neither masculine nor feminine. Subjects who scored high on both masculine and feminine items were designated androgynous, while those who registered high scores on only one dimension or another were SEX typed as masculine or feminine (those who scored low on both were undifferentiated). The test concluded that androgynous athletes were more flexible and better able to adapt to changing circumstances than their sex-typed colleagues.

The concept of psychological androgyny indicated that humans could possess proportions of both types of characteristics traditionally associated with one sex or the other and SEX TYPING was meaningless. Later research on female athletes built on the BSRI conclusions, further undermining the notion that females have particular types of personalities and dispositions, which did not equip them for competitive sports.

Further reading

Bem, S. L. (1974). The measurement of psychological androgyny. *Journal of Consulting and Clinical Psychology*, 42, 155–62.

Del Rey, P. and Sheppard, S. (1981). Relationship of psychological androgyny in female athletes to self-esteem. *International Journal of Sport Psychology*, 12, 165–75.

See also: BEM SEX ROLE INVENTORY; GENDER; GENDER VERIFICATION; LEFT-HANDEDNESS; SEX; SEX TYPING

ANGER

The EMOTION of anger is typically a reaction to offense, outrage, displeasure or acute frustration; it manifests in facial expressions, BODY LANGUAGE, an AROUSAL of the sympathetic division of the AUTONOMIC NERVOUS SYSTEM and, at times, outright AGGRESSION. The word itself is probably drawn from Old Norse *angr*, grief, which, in turn may derive from the Latin for choke, *angere*.

In his essay, "Anger, aggressive behavior, and athletic performance," Leif Isberg breaks anger into four components. (1) *Cognitive and motivational*: Anger can enhance or impair COGNITION and hence judgment; it can also affect ACHIEVEMENT MOTIVATION. The social CONTEXT in which the emotion arises may reinforce or inhibit the expression of anger. (2) *Bodily-somatic*: Angry subjects have been shown to have an increased pulse rate and significantly high blood pressure (even suppressing anger may result in elevated blood pressure); there is contradictory evidence about the role of anger in the risk of cardiovascular disease, some studies suggesting that the opportunity to release anger facilitates heart recovery—but only in men. (3) *Behavioral*: Anger is typically expressed in the form of aggression, though, of course, AGGRESSIVENESS in sports is not always accompanied by anger. (4) *Affective*: There are situational determinants that affect whether or not anger will be expressed that is, a "person may let all anger out in one situation but keep a tight lid on it in another." According to Isberg, the INTENSITY and content of anger is determined by the environment in which it occurs.

Results 1: Uses. Like other emotions, anger has effects on athletic performance. "Anger focuses the athlete's ATTENTION on the past," write Heather Deaner and John Silva, "but sport demands a present and future orientation to respond quickly and anticipate play." On this account, anger distracts an athlete from "task-relevant variables (components of the game)" and toward "outside variables." Yet, is this true for all sports?

Andrew Roffman's research employed the phrase "anger-as-a-resource." This has two components: (1) anger as a signal, in the sense that it alerts a person that something of vital importance is taking place; and (2) anger as a pathway, allowing the person to retrace backward in time to discover the initial event or whatever phenomenon sparked the angry reaction. In this way, anger can be "coordinated."

A study published in 1989 by R. W. McGowan and B. B. Schultz disclosed that many athletes do use anger as a resource, except before a game rather than during or after it. McGowan and Schultz's research concluded that college football players performing relatively simple tasks used anger as a precompetition motivating strategy, a way of getting PSYCHED. "There's nothing wrong with getting a little angry as long as you use it positively," former tennis pro Virginia Wade once reflected, adding that John McEnroe could "orchestrate" so as to bring himself to his mettle.

Other research indicates that anger, in common with other strong emotions, often displaces reason completely and "is felt as controlling, swamping and engulfing," according to Virginia Eatough and Jonathan Smith. It can induce feelings of "powerlessness." In sports, no less than any other sphere of activity, this would seriously interfere with the rational prudence that is necessary to all but the most basic of tasks. So, a weight lifter, whose sole task is to raise a bar, may find anger beneficial in executing a basic lift. Similarly, a shot putter might put anger to good use. In these and some other events, technique has already been mastered and success depends on a brief, explosive response.

One of the purported effects of DOPING with anabolic steroids is the tendency for the user to undergo bout of "roid rage," which may enhance performance. On the other hand, fencers, rhythmic gymnasts, archers, and myriad other athletes who rely on SKILL, fineness of judgment, and a degree of composure would be disadvantaged by experiencing anger prior or during COMPETITION.

Results 2: Dependence. Several scholars, including Carol Tavris, have written of how subjects who are particularly prone to habitual bouts of anger develop a DEPENDENCE on the feelings associated with it. The physiological processes that accompany anger are not dissimilar to those accompanying sexual AROUSAL and, when supplemented with the empowerment reported by some angry subjects, this produces an agreeable emotional state—though not one with necessarily agreeable consequences, of course.

One of the most explosive fits of anger in the heat of competition came at the 1993 World Track and Field Championships. Leading the 10,000 meters at the bell, Moses Tanui became irritated by the near proximity of second-placed Haile Gebrselassie, who actually ran so close that he trod on the leader's heel, causing his shoe to come loose. Tanui exploded in rage, clapping his hands against his head before wildly kicking off the loose shoe and sprinting for home. His race plan abandoned and badly fatigued, Tanui was vulnerable to the patient Gebrselassie who reeled him in on the home bend and won the race.

Had Tanui managed his anger and stuck to his tactics, he might still have lost; he did, after all, have only one shoe properly fastened and his rival's finishing burst was deadly. Still, Tanui's failure to CONTROL his rage did not help him. Nor does it help many other athletes, though it would be mistaken to assume it does not serve functions: It is expressive of the need to avoid embarrassment and to maneuver another (living creature or object) so that a resolution of a negative feeling can be achieved. It is frequently used to intimidate another person, and this can have utility in sports where physical dominance is valued. On the other hand, containing or managing emotion is one of the assignments of the many athletes who make use of finesse and artfulness.

Results 3: Histrionics. In 1989, Leonard Berkowitz argued that feelings of frustration lead to anger and, ultimately, aggression. Sports, by definition, involve frustration: While one party strives to achieve a goal of some sort, another aims to prevent that happening—and vice versa. In the absence of a complete blowout, the competitive activity continually generates frustration. As person or team A pursues its clearly defined ambition—to win—person or team B does its best to frustrate that ambition. If ambitions were not frustrated, there would be no competition.

Anger is most likely to occur when the source of the frustration is seen as illegitimate: for instance, if foul play persistently impedes an athlete, he or she is more likely to experience anger, an anger which may either be diffuse or directed at the offenders. This is commonplace in contact and collision sports where physical impact is germane to the competition.

Anger is by no means confined to such sports. Witness, for example, tennis matches in which one player becomes frustrated at his or her own inability to execute shots. The anger is directed not at the opponent, but inwards; it manifests in truculent screaming and, occasionally, in smashing rackets. Penalties accrue to players who express their anger in this way, so it is in their own interests to contain, or manage their EMOTIONS as far as possible. The case of tennis is instructive in another sense: before the 1980s, racket-smashing was unheard-of. Yet, it became so prevalent that tennis authorities actually designated it racket abuse and introduced penalties to restrain it. The diffusion of angry histrionics culminating in racket breaking may well have owed something to MODELING.

Inspired perhaps by McEnroe, tennis players contrived theatrical performances, exaggerating their anger with displays of showmanship. It was almost as if a new script had been written for the expression of anger.

Further reading

Deaner, H. and Silva, J. M. (2002). Personality and sport performance. In J. M. Silva and D. E. Stevens (Eds.) *Psychological Foundations of Sport* (pp. 48–65). Boston, Mass.: Allyn & Bacon.

Eatough, Virginia and Jonathan Smith (2006). "I was like a wild wild person": Understanding feelings of anger using interpretative phenomenological analysis. *British Journal of Psychology*, 97, 483–98.

Isberg, L. (2000). Anger, aggressive behavior, and athletic performance. In Y. L. Hanin (Ed.) *Emotions in Sport* (pp. 113–33). Champaign, Ill.: Human Kinetics.

McGowan, R. W. and Schultz, B. B. (1989). "Task complexity and affect in collegiate football. *Perceptual and Motor Skills*, 69, 671–4.
Roffman, Andrew E. (2004). Is anger a thing to be managed? *Psychotherapy: Theory, Research, Practice, Training*, 41, 161–71.
Tavris, Carol (1989). *Anger: The misunderstood emotion*. New York: Touchstone.

See also: AGGRESSION; AGGRESSIVENESS; AROUSAL; BODY IMAGE; CATHARSIS; EMOTION; EMOTIONAL CONTROL; HEDONIC TONE; ICEBERG PROFILE; INTENSITY; INTERVENTION; MEDITATION; MOOD; PSYCHING; PSYCHOPATHOLOGY; REHABILITATION; RESPONSE; ROLE MODEL; STRESS-INOCULATION TRAINING; TEMPERAMENT; VIOLENCE

ANGER MANAGEMENT

The process of dealing with or controlling problematic emotion, anger management is a COGNITIVE-BEHAVIORAL MODIFICATION intervention that encourages subjects to "channel" their anger more productively or express it appropriately. Most anger-management programs are cognitively oriented and invite subjects to analyze their own anger, its causes, or at least antecedents, the rationale they invoked to express it (for example, "How did you justify it?") and the consequences of behaviors on others.

See also: AGGRESSION; ANGER; EMOTIONAL CONTROL

ANOREXIA ATHLETICA

The term "anorexia athletica" was introduced to describe a set of symptoms affecting a group of competitors in sports that emphasize the importance of physical appearance; these include gymnastics, ice dancing, and synchronized swimming. The term "anorexia" is from the Greek *an*, for not, and *orexis*, meaning appetite. "Athletica" is from the Greek *athletikos*.

While, in its original formulation, it referred specifically to a subtype of ANOREXIA NERVOSA, an EATING DISORDER, it has been broadened to encompass a compulsion to exercise, often to a point where normal body functions are impaired. Often confused with EXERCISE DEPENDENCE, anorexia athletica involves the use of exercise in a dysfunctional manner to reduce weight. For example, the subject might exercise severely after every meal in an effort to burn off calories as quickly as possible or exercise several times during a day to the point where he or she is debilitated.

The actual term was first used in 1980 (by N. J. Smith) but was provided with empirical referents in biologist Jorunn Sundgot-Borgen's 1994 study, which focused on eating disorders among female athletes. This study corroborated other research in finding that coaches actually recommend the use of pathogenic control methods, including vomiting, laxatives, and diuretics, to their charges. Coaches and trainers in weight-sensitive sports need to keep an eye on their charges' eating habits in preparation for COMPETITIONS. For example, lightweight rowers and jockeys must meet weight restrictions before competition. In their 1992 study, Diane Taub and Rose Benson found that: "Excess body fat and body weight in both males and females are widely considered by coaches, parents and participants to hinder performance."

The paradox is that the advantage of leanness and mobility that low body weight can confer is often counteracted. Research by K. Sudi et al. in 2004 confirmed that athletes often restrict calories and overexercise to achieve or maintain low body and fat masses, leading to metabolic and endocrinal disturbances.

Perhaps the most ironic conclusion from Sundgot-Borgen's early research is that the competitors most at RISK tend to be characterized by "high self-expectation, PERFECTIONISM, persistence and independence"—in other words, the very qualities that enable them to achieve in sports make them vulnerable to anorexia athletica.

Further reading

Loumidis, Konstantinos and Wells, Adrian (2001). Exercising for the wrong reasons: Relationships among eating disorder beliefs, dysfunctional exercise beliefs and coping. *Clinical Psychology and Psychotherapy*, 8, 416–23.

Sundgot-Borgen, Jorunn (1994). Risk and trigger factors the development of eating disorders in female elite athletes. *Medicine and Science in Sports and Exercise*, 26, 414–19.

Smith, N. J. (1980). Excessive weight loss and food aversion in athletes simulating anorexia nervosa. *Pediatrics*, 66, 139–42.

Sudi, K., Otti, K., Payeri, D., Baumgarti, P., Tauschmann, K., and Muller, W. (2004). Anorexia athletica. *Nutrition*, 20, 657–61.

Taub, Diane and Benson, Rose (1992). Weight concerns, weight control techniques, and eating disorders among adolescent competitive swimmers: The effects of gender. *Sociology of Sport Journal*, 9, 76–86.

See also: ANOREXIA NERVOSA; BODY DISSATISFACTION; BODY IMAGE; BODY SHAME; DEPENDENCE; DEPRESSION; EATING DISORDERS; EMOTIONAL CONTROL; EXERCISE DEPENDENCE; MUSCLE DYSMORPHIA; PERFECTIONISM; PHYSICAL SELF-PERCEPTIONS; SOCIAL PHYSIQUE ANXIETY; WEIGHT CONTROL

ANOREXIA NERVOSA

Anorexia nervosa, often shortened to just anorexia, was first documented medically in 1874, entering the popular vocabulary from the 1980s onward when cultural evaluations of fatness changed significantly. The value placed on being slim was promoted and maintained in popular CULTURE, particularly by a fashion industry that projected images of waiflike models as ideals. It was thought that an exaggerated sense of being fat impelled between 1 and 4 percent of the female population toward one of the two main EATING DISORDERS (with an increase in anorexia occurring primarily in white females between the ages of fifteen and twenty-four years). Only a small minority of men had eating disorders—an estimated 10 percent of the total reported cases.

Research has revealed no hereditary basis for eating disorders, and there appears to be no pattern in family background. Subjects with eating disorders commonly have disturbances of MOOD or EMOTIONAL TONE to the point where DEPRESSION or inappropriate elation occurs; but no causal link between the two has been found, only an association. The disproportionately high number of women affected has invited an interpretation of anorexia as a striving for empowerment: Women with such disorders are not usually high-achieving and financially independent professionals and, as such, have few resources apart from the ABILITY to CONTROL their own bodies. But, in this respect, they have total sovereignty.

Rachel Bachner-Melman has introduced the idea of VICARIOUS AGENCY into the debate, suggesting that parents set out to compensate for their "own lack of success by way of their children" and the children's PERCEPTION of their need to overachieve works as a predisposing factor.

Explanations of eating disorders in sports rely on the similar cultural factors, but include additional sports-specific constituents. Monitoring weight is normal in most sports: In some, leanness is considered of paramount importance. Sports that are subject to judge's evaluation, like gymnastics, diving, and figure skating, encourage participants to take care of all aspects of their appearance. About 35 percent of competitors have eating disorders and half practice what researchers term "pathogenic weight control."

In some sports, looking young and slender is considered such an advantage that competitors actively try to stave off the onset of menstruation and the development of secondary sexual characteristics or to counterbalance the weight gain that typically accompanies puberty. Menstrual dysfunction, such as amenorrhoea (abnormal absence of menstruation) and oligomenorrhoea (few and irregular periods), frequently result from anorexia. In endurance events, excess weight is generally believed to impair performance. Athletes reduce body fat to increase strength, speed, and endurance, though they risk bone mineral deficiencies, dehydration, and a decrease in maximum oxygen uptake (VO^2_{max}).

While it is not a recognized medical term, "orthorexia nervosa" was used by Stephen Bratman and David Knight to describe the obsession with fastidiously healthy eating. Orthorexia bears similarities to other eating disorders: Sufferers fixate on their food. The emphasis on ostensibly healthy food, including fresh, organic, and the avoidance of all food considered "bad" (fast food, pizzas, ice cream, and so on) leads to a pathology in its own right: a compulsion to eat pure and superior ingredients.

Further reading

Bratman, Stephen and Knight, David (2001). *Health food junkies—orthorexia nervosa: Overcoming the obsession of healthy eating.* New York: Bantam Doubleday Dell.

Bachner-Melman, Rachel (2003). Anorexia nervosa from a family perspective: Why did nobody notice? *American Journal of Family Therapy,* 31, 39–50.

Cooper, P. J. (1996). Eating disorders. In A. M. Colman (Ed.), *Companion Encyclopedia of Psychology* (Vol. I, pp. 930–49). London and New York: Routledge.

Hepworth, Julie (1999). *The social construction of anorexia nervosa.* London: Sage.

See also: ANOREXIA ATHLETICA; BODY IMAGE; BULIMIA NERVOSA; DEPENDENCE; DEPRESSION; EATING DISORDERS; EMOTION; EXERCISE DEPENDENCE; GENDER; MUSCLE DYSMORPHIA; OBESITY; OBSESSIVE-COMPULSIVE; OVERTRAINING SYNDROME; PERFECTIONISM; SEX; SEX TYPING; SOCIAL PHYSIQUE ANXIETY; VICARIOUS AGENCY; WEIGHT CONTROL

ANOVA

An acronym for analysis of variance, a statistical method in which the variation in a set of observations is divided into distinct elements for the purposes of identifying relationships between phenomena, such as the effects of exercise activity on mood states in different PERSONALITY types. The method has been in use since the 1960s. It is often used with "multivariate analysis of variance", or MANOVA. Variance, in statistical terms, is the measurable quantity equal to the square of the standard deviation. A MANCOVA is an abbreviation for multivariate analysis of COVARIANCE.

Further reading

Masters, K. S., Lacaille, R. A., and Shearer, D. S. (2003). The acute affective response of Type A behavior pattern individuals to competitive and noncompetitive exercise. *Canadian Journal of Behavioral Science*, 35, 25–34.
Sit, C. H. P. and Lindner K. J. (2006). Situational state balances and participation motivation in youth sport: A reversal theory perspective. *British Journal of Educational Psychology*, 76, 369–84.

See also: CONSTRUCT; COVARIATION PRINCIPLE; HEURISTICS; MODEL; PROFILE OF MOOD STATES

ANXIETY

There are several forms of anxiety, all related by a general emotional and cognitive reaction to a STIMULUS in which apprehension and trepidation are present. The term is from the Latin *anxius*, for CHOKE. While anxiety often involves the PERCEPTION of a threat, it should be distinguished from FEAR, which always assumes a person, event or object, AROUSAL which is usually understood as a physiological response to a stimulus, and stress which is also a physiological RESPONSE either to stimuli or to the absence of stimuli (known as hypostress).

Anxiety manifests itself at subjective, physiological, and behavioral levels, resulting in an increase in muscle tension and entropy (lack of order or predictability) so that "changes displayed under anxiety conditions reflect a regress to a movement execution also characteristic of earlier stages of SKILL ACQUISITION," according to research by J. R. Pijpers et al. This explains why even highly skilled performers are sometimes prone to beginners' mistakes.

The unpleasant sensations and physical changes result from a stimulus. But, as John Raglin and Yuri Hanin point out, the same stimulus "may be perceived as a beneficial challenge to one individual, threatening to another, and neutral to a third." So, in COMPETITION, anxiety, as Mark Anshel expresses it, "reflects the performer's feelings that something may go wrong, that the outcome may not be successful, or that performance failure may be experienced." To a different performer, the same competition may be an opportunity to demonstrate his or her mettle, or CHARACTER. Perhaps the most effective antidote to anxiety is, as will see below, SELF-CONFIDENCE.

Type 1: Trait anxiety is a relatively fixed behavioral disposition. Some athletes are disposed toward some anxiety regardless of the quality or level of the challenge; many top athletes confess to vomiting and other nauseous manifestations before a competition. These are known as TYPE A individuals, and their tendency is to appraise situations as threatening. *State anxiety* is a less permanent condition and affects competitors intermittently, depending on their PERCEPTION of the particular situation: It may subside, or increase, during the actual competition, or, as research by B. S. Hale et al. indicates, *after* exercise.

Research by, among others, Sheldon Hanton and Declan Connaughton, suggests that "experiencing anxiety symptoms is not necessarily debilitating to performance." SELF-CONFIDENCE is one of the most powerful resources for changing anxiety into a *facilitator* of enhanced performance. While competitors who experience anxiety and experience doubts about themselves are unlikely to persist, confident competitors respond to anxiety with a renewed effort, persisting in the face of the challenge. In other words, experiencing anxiety can have a positive influence on performance.

Presumably, the absence of anxiety would in itself be troublesome to top players: complacency can set in. The type of anxiety that can actually enhance performance is known as *somatic* state (pertaining to the body—increase in heartrate, sweating, muscle tension, and so on), and this ebbs and flows during a contest.

Type 2: Cognitive state anxiety (the mental dimension), on the other hand, usually has a negative effect on athletic performance. It can take the form of "pre-competition nerves" and may continue to affect performance throughout a competition, particularly at crucial moments. Athletes whose performances wither in critical situations are said to choke. State anxiety is by no means restricted to athletes, though vigorous training has been shown to be useful in reducing it across populations. "Cross-training [AEROBIC/ANAEROBIC training combined] can be effective for those who choose to exercise for mental health benefits," concluded Hale et al.

Interpretations. Anxiety typically results from the perception of some kind of threat, either to the physical SELF or reputation; it can also be precipitated by uncertainty or even a disruption of routine. While some athletes simply never suffer from trait anxiety, it would be unusual if they did not experience some sort of state anxiety. Even athletes known for their COMPOSURE are likely to approach a big contest or a comeback after INJURY with some anxiety. The "secret" of those who are able to overcome this is that they interpret their symptoms as propitious: They actually use it to their advantage, probably feeling anxiety and the physiological effects associated with it but interpreting this as normal in the circumstances. REVERSAL THEORY, as promoted by John Kerr, suggests that, while the symptoms may be interpreted positively or negatively, competitors sometimes transfer from one to another during a COMPETITION—a reversal. What matters is not so much the objective level of anxiety, but how the athlete interprets and responds to the situation.

The Competitive State Anxiety Inventory-2, devised by Rainer Martens et al., was one of several instruments designed to identify and measure anxiety levels in changing situations, though it yielded few definitive conclusions. There are few reliable indicators of when cognitive or somatic anxiety will take hold, nor when or how anxiety will impact athletic performance. Yuri Hanin believes the IZOF (INDIVIDUAL ZONES OF OPTIMAL FUNCTIONING) model offers promise: This attempts to isolate an ideal range of anxiety in which an athlete can reach PEAK PERFORMANCE. Hanin recognizes the significance of EMOTION, meaning that athlete's optimal anxiety zones are highly individual. On this account, general interventionist strategies to reduce—or induce—anxieties in athletes are unlikely to be successful; approaches should be sensitive to individuals and contexts.

Even excessive thinking about a task can induce what is known as PARALYSIS BY ANALYSIS. In other words, proficient performers can scrutinize their performance too carefully, trying to exercise conscious CONTROL over motions that, in other situations, they might have surrendered to unconscious control—AUTOMATICITY. The continuous-processing hypothesis, as it has also been called, suggests that, when athletes suffer from a decrement in performance, they sometimes respond by "trying too hard" and this has the effect of inducing even more anxiety.

Further reading

Anshel, M. H. (1997). *Sport psychology: From theory to practice*, 3rd edn, Scottsdale, Ariz.: Gorsuch Scarisbrick.

Hale, B. S., Koch, K. R., and Raglin, J. S. (2002). State anxiety responses to 60 minutes of cross training. *British Journal of Sports Medicine*, 36, 105–7.

Hanton, S. and Connaughton, D. (2002). Perceived control of anxiety and its relationship to self-confidence and performance. *Research Quarterly for Exercise and Sport*, 73, 87–97.

Kerr, J. H. (Ed.) (1999). *Experiencing sport: Reversal theory*, New York: Wiley.

Martens, R., Burton, D., Vealey, R. S., Bump, L. A., and Smith, D. E. (1990). Development and validation of the Competitive State Anxiety Inventory-2 (CSAI-2). In R. Martens, R. S. Vealey and D. Burton (Eds.), *Competitive anxiety in sports* (pp. 117–213). Champaign, Ill.: Human Kinetics.

Pijpers, J. R., Oudejans, R. R. D., Holsheimer, F., and Bakker, F. C. (2003). Anxiety performance relationships in climbing: A process-oriented approach. *Psychology of Sport and Exercise*, 4, 283–304.

Raglin, J. S. and Hanin, Y. L. (2000). Competitive anxiety. In Y. L. Hanin (Ed.), *Emotions in sport* (pp. 93–111), Champaign, Ill.: Human Kinetics.

See also: ALCOHOLISM; AVOIDANCE; BIOFEEDBACK; BODY DISSATISFACTION; BODY IMAGE; BODY SHAME; CHOKE; COGNITION; DEPRESSION; EMOTION; EMOTIONAL INTELLIGENCE; EXERCISE BEHAVIOR; FEAR; FITNESS; FOCUS; KINESIOPHOBIA; NERVOUSNESS; OUTPERFORMANCE; SELF-CONFIDENCE; SOCIAL FACILITATION; STEREOTYPE THREAT; SUPERSTITIOUS BEHAVIOR; YIPS

APPLIED SPORT PSYCHOLOGY

In contrast to theoretical or pure sport psychology, applied sport psychology is devoted to employing or making use of discoveries, insights, and knowledge. In a way, the description is implicit in the term: "applied" (from the Latin *applicare*, fasten to) means putting one thing to another and "psychology" is, of course, formed from *psych* (*psukhe* is Greek for soul, or life) and *logy* denoting a subject of study (*logos* is Greek for word).

Meaning. Frank L. Gardner distinguishes three types of roles for the sport psychologist today: (1) "using basic cognitive-behavioral and self-regulatory procedures and techniques to help athletes of all levels enhance their performance"; (2) "the delivery of psychological care and development of athletes above and beyond efforts at enhancing athletic performance [...] the development of life skills, coping resources, and care and attention to both clinical and developmental issues"; (3) "psychological testing in such areas as predraft selection and neuropsychological evaluation."

"One of the accepted tenets of applied sport psychology is the belief that thought precedes and influences athletic performance," writes Ralph Vernacchia. A science, however imperfect, of sport must be based on a body of existing and developing knowledge derived from rational research, judicious argument, and informed discussion. Its applied branch should properly extend these principles into practical settings, advocating the use of strategies and interventions that are themselves based on reason rather than, for example, superstition, custom or ungrounded beliefs.

Sport psychology's practical purpose lies in, as J. M. Williams and W. F. Straub usefully describe it, "identifying and understanding psychological theories and techniques that can be applied to sport and exercise to enhance the performance and personal growth of athletes." In fact, sport psychology was created in this spirit, the work of Bruce Ogilvie and Thomas Tutko in 1966 imparting this in its title *Problem Athletes and How to Handle Them.* Arnold Beisser's *The Madness in Sport* showed the virtues of the individual case-study approach—an approach that is still pursued today, though not exclusively.

History. The burgeoning of sport psychology in competitive sports settings has led to what might be regarded as a preeminence of the applied division. Sport psychologists are retained as consultants by sports clubs, Olympic squads and even in commerce and industry. This has not always been the case. David Wiggins traces the roots of discipline back to the nineteenth century, showing how much of the early research was not guided by practical imperatives. Wiggins identifies George Fitz's experiments on REACTION TIME in 1895 as the first significant academic study to have "ramifications for sport psychology."

Christopher Green pinpoints Coleman R. Griffith's appointment by the Chicago Cubs to improve the team's performance as a key moment in the development of professional applied sport psychology. Griffith, who had directed research in the University of Illinois' Athletics Laboratory in the 1920s and 1930s, filmed players, documented their motions, and quantified both their skills and attitudes in an attempt to build a "scientific" training program. He observed that the prevalent belief was that SKILL derived from instinct, a belief that was, he suggested, "a lazy, unimaginative and ignorant man's way of evading the demands of his job." In other words, skills were learned and should be improved. As Green puts it: "He [Griffith] broke new ground that would later grow into a whole industry."

Approaches. While, in recent years, applications have become crucial, sport psychology, like any other mature discipline has developed a NOMOTHETIC tradition dedicated to discovering "laws" or generalizations. This received a boost through the research and theorizing of Rainer Martens, who distinguished between applied knowledge and applied research, the former "sifting through all the research available on a problem, using one's tacit knowledge regarding the problem, and developing creative programs for how to solve it." In other words, while the separation between applied and academic sport psychology may appear distinct, the former cannot exist without the output of the latter.

A rather different approach, and one that leans toward IDIOGRAPHIC research, is proposed by David Cook in his preface to the volume edited by Mark Thompson et al.: "We believe that sport psychology is an art." It is an unusual but revealing reading of applied sport psychology: not as a science, but as an expression and application of human creative skill and imagination. While he does not elaborate, we might take Cook's point to mean that, while sport psychology itself may aspire to producing scientifically verifiable knowledge, employing that knowledge is more akin to an art. It requires resourcefulness, interpretation, design, and skilful execution if it is to have practical utility.

Further reading

Andersen, M. B. (2005). *Sport psychology in practice.* Champaign, Ill.: Human Kinetics.

Beisser, A. (1967). *The Madness in Sport.* New York: Appleton-Century-Crofts.

Gardner, F. L. (2001). Applied sport psychology in professional sports: The team psychologist. *Professional Psychology: Research and Practice,* 32, 34–9.

Green, C. D. (2003). Psychology strikes out: Coleman R. Griffith and the Chicago Cubs. *History of Psychology,* 6, 267–83.

Martens, Rainer (1987). Science, knowledge, and sport psychology. *The Sport Psychologist,* 1, 29–55.

Ogilvie, B. and Tutko, T. A. (1966). *Problem Athletes and How to Handle Them.* London: Pelham.

Thompson, M. A., Vernacchia, R. A., and Moore, W. E. (Eds.) (1998). *Case studies in applied sport psychology: An educational approach,* Dubuque, Iowa: Kendall/Hunt.

Williams, J. M. and Straub, W. F. (1998). Sport psychology: Past, present and future. In J. M. Williams (Ed.), *Applied sport psychology: Personal growth to peak performance,* 3rd edn (pp. 1–12). Mountain View, Calif.: Mayfield.

Wiggins, D. K. (1984). The history of sport psychology in North America. In J. M. Silva and R. S. Weinberg (Eds.), *Psychological Foundations of Sport* (pp. 9–22). Champaign, Ill.: Human Kinetics.

See also: CHARACTER; COACH–ATHLETE RELATIONSHIP; ETHICS; IDIOGRAPHIC; INTRO-JECTION; NOMOTHETIC; PREMACK PRINCIPLE; REACTION TIME; RINGELMANN EFFECT; SKILL ACQUISITION; STRESS-INOCULATION TRAINING; STRESS-MANAGEMENT TRAINING

APPROACH

In its broadest sense, approach describes a way of dealing with something that involves movement toward rather than away from; but there are several ways in which the word is used in sport and exercise psychology.

(1) *In relation to the application of theories.* For instance, in their study of soccer hooligans in the Netherlands, John Kerr and Hilde de Kock used REVERSAL THEORY, which they argued "provides an innovative APPROACH to understanding human motivation and personality."

(2) *To describe methods of analysis.* K. Anders Ericsson developed the "expert-performance approach," which forms part of his investigations into the cognitive mechanisms involved in DELIBERATE PRACTICE.

(3) *To define a response* to something that involves either: (a) moving nearer to a task in time or space; (b) speaking to someone or several people about something; or (c) starting to deal with an issue in a way that addresses rather than ignores potentially troublesome aspects. As a response, it is contrary to AVOIDANCE.

For example, a performance-approach GOAL focuses on the demonstration of competence and implies an engagement with achievement tasks, while a performance-AVOIDANCE goal would be to keep away from situations that demand such demonstrations.

Further reading

Elliot, Andrew J., Cury, François, Fryer, James W. and Huguet, Pascal (2006). Achievement goals, self-handicapping, and performance attainment: A mediational analysis. *Journal of Sport and Exercise Psychology*, 28, 344–61.

Ericsson, K. Anders (1996). *The Road to Excellence: The acquisition of expert performance in the arts and sciences, sports and games.* Mahwah, NJ: Lawrence Erlbaum.

Kerr, John H. and de Kock, Hilde (2002). Aggression, violence, and the death of a Dutch soccer hooligan: A reversal theory explanation. *Aggressive Behavior*, 28, 1–10.

Schmalt, Heinz-Dieter (2005). Validity of a short form of the achievement-motive grid (AMG-S): Evidence for the three-factor structure emphasizing active and passive form of fear of failure. *Journal of Personality Assessment*, 84, 172–84.

See also: ACHIEVEMENT MOTIVE; ATTRIBUTION; AVOIDANCE; DELIBERATE PRACTICE; EATING DISORDERS; EMOTIONAL CONTROL; FEAR OF FAILURE; GOAL; GOAL SETTING; HOPE; INJURY; KINESIOPHOBIA; LEARNED HELPLESSNESS; MENTAL TOUGHNESS; MOTIVATION; MOTIVATIONAL CLIMATE; OUTPERFORMANCE; REVERSAL THEORY; SKILL ACQUISITION; STEREOTYPE THREAT; TYPE A

AROUSAL

When stirred to activity, we experience a state of alertness, anticipation, and all-round readiness described as arousal. It is a diffuse pattern of activities, both physiological and cognitive, that prepares us for a task. The word itself is formed from *a* meaning on, up, or out and *rouse*, for startle or become active.

Processes. Typically, a high level of arousal involves the sympathetic AUTONOMIC NERVOUS SYSTEM: Metabolic rates increase, as does respiratory volume; blood vessels constrict, pupils dilate and sweat glands open. ATTENTION narrows and FOCUS sharpens as we approach the task. Whether a person experiences such changes as a desirable part of PSYCHING-up for a task, or a source of ANXIETY, apprehension, or downright FEAR, depends both on the individual and the CONTEXT, as well as the moment-to-moment changes in circumstances.

Some activation is needed for any task, whether watching a game on television or actually playing. Arousal might increase during any sports COMPETITION when a sudden, unexpected event occurs, no matter how minor: a plane passing overhead might arouse a tennis player preparing to serve, or a particularly rowdy fan may raise the arousal level of a football player, or, more seriously, a boxer leading comfortably on points might be knocked down by a speculative shot causing a sharp arousal.

All tasks have an optimal level of arousal: the aim of athletes is to calibrate that level to the vagaries of competition while maintaining COMPOSURE. The precise relationship between arousal and sports performance has occupied psychologists since the 1950s, when drive theory's equation *performance = arousal + skill level* held sway. A high level of arousal will assist a performance if the athlete has a high degree of skill; but it will hurt a performance by an athlete without skills. The formula was crude and unreliable and was superseded by others, one of the most influential being the INVERTED-U hypothesis.

Explanation 1: Inverted-U. If levels of arousal are imagined as the horizontal axis of a graph with "low" plotted to the left of "high" and performance plotted along the vertical axis, then we may think of arousal as defining an inverted U-shape. Performance is optimal between low and high and tapers off if either arousal is too low or too high. Several imperturbable athletes consistently operate with arousal levels inside the arc at the top of the inverted U. Other athletes seem to reach that state only occasionally.

Boxing, like football and sprinting, is a sport in which powerful gross motor behavior is crucial, but optimum performance in other sports relies more on fine-motor skills. So, darts and pool players would probably reach PEAK PERFORMANCE when their arousal levels are at lower levels. Imagine this as the arches of the McDonald's "M" with the left arch describing the arousal curve of darts, pool and other sport performers who need low arousal levels to hit peaks. Still others need to switch: the precision and fineness of judgment Tiger Woods used when putting probably required only a modest level of arousal; but a drive involved cognitive activity plus muscular activity and almost certainly required a much higher level of arousal.

While it has been a primary model for approaching the relationship between arousal and performance, the inverted-U hypothesis, as Shawn Arent and Daniel Landers remind us, "is simply a descriptive relationship; it is not a theoretical explanation." Arent and Lander's controlled experiment involving riding bicycle ergometers (apparatus that measures work or energy expended during a period of physical exercise), lent support to the inverted-U, but the authors admit it does not enable an understanding of how and why arousal influences performance.

How, for instance, can it explain Jana Novotna's extraordinary collapse in the 1993 Wimbledon final? Leading 4–1 in games and 40–0 up with serve in the final set, Novotna, who had exuded SELF-CONFIDENCE up to this point, seemed stricken with anxiety and disintegrated in the face of her opponent Steffi Graf's consistency. Novotna's reputation for CHOKING was boosted two years later in the French Open when she allowed Chanda Rubin to survive nine match points and crashed to defeat. Richard Cox gives a comparable example from the 1996 Masters when Greg Norman surrendered a six-shot lead with one round to go and lost to Nick Faldo (1998). In these instances, results suggest the onset of a catastrophe: performance did not decline smoothly as the athletes, sensing victory, became too aroused; but an abrupt descent—graphically, resembling an inverted-V.

Explanation 2: Catastrophe. To explain this, J. Fazey and L. Hardy argued that, if a competitor is highly physiologically aroused and experiences cognitive-state anxiety, then a sudden and often dramatic deterioration will occur; in other words, a catastrophe. High levels of physiological arousal do not in themselves CAUSE downfalls. Downfalls happen when high levels of physiological arousal are combined with increases in cognitive-state anxiety. The prospect of closing in on a victory can precipitate this kind of anxiety and, once the catastrophe has occurred, small reductions in arousal will do nothing to get the performance back to its former level. As most catastrophes happen toward the end of a competition, it is often too late for the aroused athlete to rescue the situation.

Explanation 3: Individual zones. The effort of many athletes, including distance runners, is to combine an optimum level of arousal with a degree of RELAXATION—the two are not at all incompatible, as Yuri Hanin's IZOF (INDIVIDUAL ZONES OF OPTIMAL FUNCTIONING) model shows. The IZOF model strays from theories that suggest general principles and stresses that each performer has individual levels of optimal intensity. Hanin used a self-report method, asking athletes to identify which types of positive and negative emotions they experience prior and during competition. Some level of anxiety is desirable. While arousal has physiological dimensions, Hanin is more interested in investigating its emotional side. The model might help explain improbable upsets. Presuming they have modest opposition, the favored individuals remain outside their IZOFs and fail to get sufficiently aroused, while the underdog functions effectively within their own zones.

Explanation 4: Contagion. Like the other theories discussed, IZOF works best when focusing on individuals. But many sports involve more complex, collective forms of arousal that may transmit throughout a team. Returning to catastrophes, we might mention the Houston Oilers in the 1992 NFL play-offs. Aroused to what appeared to be an optimal level, the Oilers ran up a seemingly unassailable 32-point third quarter lead against the Buffalo Bills. Confronted with an almost certain win, the whole Houston team seemed to tense up visibly, each player becoming affected by a contagion of negative anxiety. Houston contrived to lose 38–41.

The CONSTRUCT of SOCIAL FACILITATION is another factor that complicates studies of arousal. Operating at an optimal level of arousal in relatively mundane competitions is a different proposition to performing in front of large crowds in crucial games: some performers can rise to the occasion, reaching appropriate levels of arousal without becoming anxious; others become too aroused and fail to perform when the situation demands, often fearing the evaluations of others.

While arousal is clearly a vital CONCEPT in understanding the psychology of sports performance, generalizations about it are vitiated by mediating variables, including the individual, the task variables, and the CONTEXT in which the arousal takes place. Equally, generalizations about how best to manage arousal or harness it most effectively are notoriously difficult to formulate.

Further reading

Arent, Shawn M. and Landers, Daniel M. (2003). Arousal, anxiety, and performance: A reexamination of the inverted-U. *Research Quarterly for Exercise and Sport*, 74, 436–45.

Fazey, J. and Hardy, L. (1988). *The inverted-U hypothesis: A catastrophe for sport psychology?* British Association of Sports Sciences, Monograph No. 1, Leeds: National Coaching Foundation.

Hanin, Y. L (Ed.) (2000). *Emotions in sport.* Champaign, Ill.: Human Kinetics.

Hill, K. L. (2001). *Frameworks for sport psychologists.* Champaign, Ill.: Human Kinetics.

See also: ADRENALINE RUSH; AGGRESSION; ANGER; COMPOSURE; EMOTION; EMOTIONAL CONTROL; EUSTRESS; FEAR; FOCUS; INDIVIDUAL ZONES OF OPTIMAL FUNCTIONING; NERVOUS SYSTEM; PARALYSIS BY ANALYSIS; REVERSAL THEORY; SELF-AWARENESS; SELF-CONFIDENCE; SENSATION-SEEKING; SOCIAL FACILITATION; VICARIOUS AGENCY; VIOLENCE; YERKES-DODSON LAW; YIPS

ASSERTIVENESS

Showing a forceful or self-confident approach.

See also: AGGRESSIVENESS

ATHLETIC IDENTITY

"Athletic IDENTITY is [...] the degree to which an individual identifies with the role of an athlete and will look to others for confirmation of that role," according to Diane Groff and Ramon Zabriskie, whose research concluded: "Individuals who access their sense of SELF within the CONTEXT of sport more frequently and highly value this aspect of self, are likely to develop higher levels of athletic identity."

In a separate study, Elizabeth Daniels et al. observe: "Individuals with a strong athletic identity view statements such as 'I consider myself an athlete' and 'sport is the only important thing in my life' as highly representative of themselves." How athletes approached their sport was affected by their conceptions of themselves, whether as athletes or, for example, as people who just happened to be involved in sports.

Given the relative brevity of most sport careers, the transition to RETIREMENT is especially troublesome for those with strong athletic identities. "Diminished life satisfaction," was felt by several retiring athletes in a study by William Webb et al.: "Athletic identity was also strongly related to a sense of vagueness about the future."

Among the tools for measuring is the Athletic Identity Measurement Scale, or AIMS, introduced in 1993 by B. Brewer, and the Athletic Identity Questionnaire (AIQ) developed by Cheryl Anderson et al.

Further reading

Anderson, Cheryl B., Masse, Louise C., and Hergenroeder, Albert C. (2007). Factorial and construct validity of the Athletic Identity Questionnaire for adolescents. *Medicine and Science in Sports and Exercise*, 39, 59–69.

Brewer, B. (1993). Self identity and specific vulnerability to depressed mood. *Journal of Personality*, 61, 343–64.

Daniels, Elizabeth, Sincharoean, Sirinda, and Leaper, Campbell (2005). The relation between sport orientations and athletic identity among adolescent girl and boy athletes. *Journal of Sport Behavior*, 28, 315–32.

Groff, Diane G., Zabriskie, Ramon B. (2006). An exploratory study of athletic identity among elite alpine skiers with physical disabilities: Issues of measurement and design. *Journal of Sport Behavior*, 29, 126–41.

Webb, William M., Nasco, Suzanne, Rile, Sarah, and Headrick, Brian (1998). Athlete identity and reactions to retirement from sports. *British Journal of Sport Behavior*, 21, 338–62.

See also: BODY IMAGE; COACH–ATHLETE RELATIONSHIP; COMEBACK; EATING DISORDERS; EXERCISE DEPENDENCE; EXERCISE IDENTITY; FANS; IDENTITY; INJURY; PHYSICAL SELF-PERCEPTIONS; RETIREMENT; SELF; SELF-ACTUALIZATION; SELF-AWARENESS; SELF-CONCEPT; SOCIALIZATION

ATTENTION

The faculty of PERCEPTION that allows us to select and bring into focus some features of our environment while screening out others. Attention, as its root word *attentio* (Latin for take notice of) suggests, is directed: we *attend to* characteristics that lie outside us, or to aspects of ourselves, often consciously, but sometimes without being explicitly aware of the process. Effective sports performance demands that an athlete's attention be directed as selectively as possible at relevant persons, circumstances, and other factors, at the same time excluding irrelevancies.

Cricket captains must attend to a complex of factors, including weather, state of pitch, opponents and opponents' strengths, weaknesses and anticipated strategies as well their own team's qualities and the likely changes in physical environment over the period of the game (which can last five days). Hundred-meter freestyle swimmers, by contrast, must attend to their sport in a way that shuts out a great many environmental factors and focuses more narrowly on the execution of their own singular performance. Running on the gym's treadmill, while listening to music on the iPod, watching a television monitor and perhaps planning tomorrow's 9:00 a.m. meeting involves assigning priority to the latter, while still attending to other stimuli.

One way to think of attention is as a series of pools or spaces, each with separate resources for different senses, sight, hearing, and tactility. At times in a TASK-ORIENTED activity, a subject might need to watch very carefully and listen but without needing to touch, less still smell. At other times, the sense of touch may be paramount, as might sound and vision, so the subject deploys all three to attend to the task. For example, just after the snap, a quarterback will need breadth of vision to pick his receiver, touch to ensure the pass or handoff is just right, and sound to be able to listen for defense players from behind. Obviously, we do not have limitless attentional capacities. The same quarterback could not attend to all these and wave to his wife in the crowd—at least not without getting sacked. His particular job at that moment will require his entire attentional capacity. So, every sports performer must become adept attending selectively to relevant information, while screening out irrelevancies.

Because of the complexity of our powers of CONCENTRATION, we can either attend to an extremely restricted range of sensory material or innumerable stimuli in the environment simultaneously, while we also remain aware of our own thoughts, feelings, and behavior. So, attention can be broad or narrow; external and internal. This is the scheme of Robert Nideffer. Our quarterback will probably be using *broad* attention taking in a wide range of cues when finding his receiver, his attention also directed *externally* on objects and circumstances outside himself. A diver peering from a board over an Olympic pool will be attending very *narrowly*, probably only to his or her posture and balance, and *internally*, probably listening to the cadence of his or her breathing.

Attention, like many psychological concepts, is not directly observable and there is no absolute agreement on its ontological status, that is, the nature of its being. "It is fair to ask whether there is any unified, comprehensive concept of attention, or, rather, whether attention is a vague label that scientists from different orientations use to refer to distinct, disparate domains of cognitive activity," comment Diego Fernandez-Duque and Mark Johnson, who identify three main theoretical models of attention: (1) CAUSE theories, in which attention is presumed to a cause that modulates (regulates, adjusts or modifies) INFORMATION PROCESSING; a spotlight that scans items in a visual field is a popular metaphor; (2) effect theories, in which attention is considered as a by-product, or epiphenomenon, of information processing; the apposite metaphor in this case is that of a number of perceptual objects competing for a limited amount of processing resources; (3) hybrid theories that combine the two with competing stimuli *and* a modulating executive "template" that biases COMPETITION in favor of one stimulus over another.

Further reading

Eysenck, M. W. (1996). Attention. In A. M. Colman (Ed.), *Companion Encyclopedia of Psychology* (Vol. I, pp. 302–18). London and New York: Routledge.

Fernandez-Duque, Diego and Johnson, Mark L. (2002). Cause and effect theories of attention: The role of conceptual metaphors. *Review of General Psychology*, 6, 153–62.

Nideffer, R. M. (1976). Test of attentional and interpersonal style, *Journal of Personality and Social Psychology*, 34, 394–404.

See also: COGNITION; CONCENTRATION; DECISION-MAKING; EXECUTIVE CONTROL; FOCUS; GOAL; MEMORY; PEAK PERFORMANCE; PERCEPTION; REACTION TIME; REINFOR-CEMENT; SCHEMA; SELF-CONCEPT; SELF-TALK; SKILL ACQUISITION; SKILL EXECUTION; VISUAL PERCEPTION; YOGA; ZONE

ATTRIBUTION

The act of assigning or imputing a characteristic, or motive, to one-self or others is known as attribution; this is the exact meaning of its root term the Latin *attributum*. In sport and exercise, the attribution of causality is of special interest: when people explain the results of an activity, they attribute the causes either to personal factors, or to the actions of other people or aspects of the physical environment, or a combination of these. Wherever they believe the responsibility for the outcome lies is the locus of causality, or LOCUS OF CONTROL and it is one of what Tim Rees et al. identify as five dimensions of attri-bution, the others being *controllability* (whether the cause is con-trollable or not), *stability* (does the CAUSE remain over time?), *globality* (does it work in all situations?), and *universality* (does it apply to others?).

Attribution research built on the early work of Fritz Heider, who, in 1958, argued that everyone craves order in their lives and is con-stantly searching for ways of predicting and controlling the seemingly unpredictable and uncontrollable FLOW of life. In the 1970s and 1980s, Bernard Weiner argued that we attempt to understand success and failure in terms of ABILITY, effort, task difficulty, and LUCK, the latter two being out of our control, of course. Ability and task difficulty are stable in that they remain relatively consistent, while effort and luck are variable and, in the case of luck, random.

Marcia Wilson and Dawn Stephens found that "high EXPECTANCY athletes who perceived that they had performed to a high athletic standard had a greater internal locus of causality and a higher level of personal control." The internal locus is also crucial in exercise: A 2005 study by C. A. Shields et al. concluded that, "individuals who attribute their exercise setbacks or failure to internal, personally controllable causes may be more prepared for future attempts at exercise ADHERENCE."

For instance, joining a new gym in January with an express GOAL of losing 10 pounds by June and discovering on May 25 that only 5 pounds has disappeared might leave the exerciser attributing the apparent failure to her failure to train hard or consistently enough, or eating sugary foods—an internal locus. She would be more likely to resume her training than if she attributed the failure to a *force majeure*, an unforeseeable course of events that prevents her from reaching her goal.

All five dimensions are present: (1) the person may take responsibility for her failure (locus); (2) she understands that this was within her control and (3) will stay that way in the future (stability), (4) whatever the environment (globality); (5) the same goes for any other exerciser whose aim is to lose weight (universality). On the other hand, if she believes she is at the mercy of forces beyond her control—such as inclement weather that prevented her running as much as she had intended—the locus is *external* and unstable, dependent on circumstances and different for every exerciser.

Studies identify a SELF-SERVING BIAS in human COGNITION: We interpret reality selectively in a way that supports subjective needs, desires, and preferences. This is sometimes known as *hedonic* bias, "hedonic" meaning that it relates to pleasant sensations. The bias predisposes subjects to attribute successes in a relatively internal, stable, and controllable manner. Conversely, they attribute failures as externally caused, unstable, and uncontrollable. Peter De Michele et al.'s investigation of wrestlers is one such study. A wider-ranging, exhaustive review of other research on self-serving attribution across age, GENDER, and CULTURE by Amy Mezulis et al. concluded that "most people, most of the time, do attribute their successes to enduring, pervasive characteristics about themselves and discount their failures as unrelated to any enduring pervasive personal characteristics."

Other research has been done on how attribution patterns differ between men and women. The work is inconclusive, though women are found to locate causes externally more than men. Among the reasons offered for this difference are a FEAR of success that is more prevalent among women and the higher expectations of men. Neither is convincing. More certain is the finding that more skilled athletes, who have experienced success, attribute failure to unstable, external factors (incompetent officiating; bad luck) because they realize failure is temporary. Combined with a willingness to attribute success, whether individual or as part of a team, to effort, or other internal variables suggests a tendency to protect their SELF— which is obviously important in sustaining SELF-EFFICACY and, ultimately, SELF-CONFIDENCE. Less skilled athletes who have tasted defeat more often are likely to attribute failure to their own deficiencies; this leads to low future expectations, the likelihood of further defeats and a probable withdrawal from COMPETITION. Sometimes this group might experience a condition known as LEARNED HELPLESSNESS.

Further reading

De Michele, Peter E., Gansneder, Bruce and Solomon, Gloria B. (1998). Success and failure attributions of wrestlers: Further evidence of the self-serving bias. *Journal of Sport Behavior*, 21, 242–56.

Heider, Fritz (1958). *The Psychology of Interpersonal Relations*. New York: Wiley.

Mezulis, Amy H., Abramson, Lyn Y., Hyde, Janet S. and Hankin, Benjamin L. (2004). Is there a universal positivity bias in attributions? A meta-analytic review of individual, developmental, and cultural differences in the self-serving attributional bias. *Psychological Bulletin*, 130, 711–36.

Rees, Tim, Ingledew, David K., and Hardy, Lew (2003). Attribution in sport psychology: Seeking congruence between theory, research and practice. *Psychology of Sport and Exercise*, 6, 189–204.

Shields, C. A., Brawley, L. R., and Lindover, T. I. (2005). Where perception and reality differ: Dropping out is not the same as failure. *Journal of Behavioral Medicine*, 28, 481–91.

Weiner, Bernard (1972). *Theories of Motivation: From mechanism to cognition*. Chicago, IL: Markham.

Wilson, Marcia A. and Stephens, Dawn E. (2005). Great expectations: How do athletes of different expectancies attribute their perception of personal athletic performance? *Journal of Sport Behavior*, 28, 392–407.

See also: APPROACH; COGNITION; DEFENSIVE ATTRIBUTION; EXPECTANCY; LEARNED HELPLESSNESS; LOCUS OF CONTROL; LUCK; MIND ATTRIBUTION; RESPONSE; SELF-CONFIDENCE; SELF-EFFICACY; SELF-ENHANCEMENT; SELF-HANDICAPPING; SELF-PROTECTION; SELF-SERVING BIAS

AUTOGENIC

Formed from *autos*, Greek for self, and *gen* for produced, autogenic is often used synonymously with *autogenous* to describe actions that are self-initiated. In sports, autogenic RELAXATION techniques are practiced as part of training regimes. They were first introduced in the 1950s by Johannes Schultz, who, when working with patients under HYPNOSIS, discovered that his subjects reported a heaviness of limbs and a sensation of warmth. His version of autogenic training was designed to reproduce the two states.

Typically, autogenic RELAXATION involves self-initiated procedures in which the individual experiences progressive relaxation through sensations of weight and heat. IMAGERY is also used, as is SELF-TALK.

Further reading

Liggett, D. R. (2000). *Sport Hypnosis*. Champaign, Ill.: Human Kinetics.
Williams, J. M. and Harris, D. V. (1998). Relaxation and energizing techniques for regulation of arousal. In J. M. Williams (Ed.), *Applied sport psychology: Personal growth to peak performance*, 3rd edn (pp. 324–37), Mountain View, Calif.: Mayfield.

See also: BIOFEEDBACK; CENTERING; HYPNOSIS; IMAGERY; MEDITATION; PSYCHING; REINFORCEMENT; RELAXATION; SELF-TALK; YOGA

AUTOMATICITY

True to its root *automatos* (Greek for acting of itself) automaticity refers to the property of a process that operates independently of conscious CONTROL and ATTENTION. "Thinking that occurs without much awareness or effort is called automated," writes Michael Martinez. "When a skilled driver navigates a very familiar route, seemingly without effort, she is probably relying on automated thinking. In other words, she is exhibiting automaticity."

In sport and exercise, people, having mastered a basic SKILL, can often execute it *nonconsciously* (to use John Bargh and Tanya Chartrand's favored term), without CONCENTRATION, FOCUSING instead on other aspects of their performance, such as tactics, or their opponent's intentions. The process is associated with having an external focus of ATTENTION: Rather than being aware of the position and movement of parts of the body (the state known as *kinesthesia*), the performer typically focuses on external aspects, such as targets or goals.

Automaticity can be conceived as "overcoming resource limitations by the gradual withdrawing of deliberate attention," according to Robert N. Singer. Or, "the acquisition of a domain-specific knowledge base and the ABILITY to retrieve memory-stored instances." In either conception, sufficient quality practice is needed for automaticity to occur. So, for instance, inexperienced golfers are gradually discouraged from thinking about their swing. Once the basic technique is practiced, they should emulate proficient golfers and allow the swing to be automatic.

The same injunction applies to SKILL ACQUISITION generally. The arduous, conscious process of learning how to execute a move is eventually replaced by automatic operations. Skilled performers can surrender the information on how to consummate the skill to MEMORY and think not about what they are doing, but why they are doing it, for what overall purpose and what they will do if it does not work. Too much reflection on the mechanical elements of a SKILL will actually interfere with its smooth functioning. SELF-AWARENESS, or attention to skill execution can disrupt the normal processing of a task.

This stage in the skill acquisition process is often called the *autonomous* stage, when automatic processing takes over from controlled processing and the attentional demands of a task have decreased to a point at which there are sufficient processing resources available to be able to perform a previously learned activity concurrently with another, or several others. It is often visualized in terms of a continuum with controlled performance at one end and automaticity at the other. Research by James Bebko et al. on the learning of juggling, a complex motor task, offered a different interpretation.

For example, many of us have driving skills that are so automatic that we can think, plan, solve problems, or engage in other cognitive activities while driving. If a cat runs in front of the car, a new situation is suddenly presented and we swerve, brake or make another maneuver to avoid the animal while keeping the vehicle safely on the road. The controlled processing that enables us to do this is likely to be more effective if we are experienced. Our smooth adaptation to circumstances involved using higher levels of control that Bebko and his colleagues concluded are associated with higher levels of automaticity: "We found that control over those sorts of adaptation emerged concurrently with development of automatized skills."

Sometimes, even highly skilled athletes need to make conscious adjustments to style to accommodate either particular conditions, different batters, or, perhaps a loss of form. The same applies across the spectrum of sports performers. When skills erode, automaticity gradually disappears, and often retiring athletes rue that they have to think about what they once did automatically.

There is no single process that leads to automaticity. Coaches often use schedules of REINFORCEMENT designed to REWARD the appropriate behavioral skill. Approaches based on changing an athlete's COGNITION of situations and persons (included him or herself) have also been shown to be effective, as has COGNITIVE-BEHAVIORAL MODIFICATION which ushers athletes toward a position from which they can see the demonstrable effects of their skilled behavior and change their thinking about that behavior accordingly. The ultimate aim is to preclude any conscious thought about the skill at all.

Further reading

Bargh, John A. and Chartrand, Tanya L. (1999). The unbearable automaticity of being. *American Psychologist*, 54, 462–79.

Bebko, James M., Demark, Jenny L., Im–Bolter, Nancie, and MacEwn, Angie (2005). Transfer, control, and automatic processing in a complex motor task: An examination of bounce juggling. *Journal of Motor Behavior*, 37, 465–74.

Martinez, Michael A. (2006). What is metacognition? *Phi Delta Kappa*, 87, 696–9.

Singer, Robert N. (2002). Preperformance state, routines, and automaticity: What does it take to realize expertise in self-paced events? *Journal of Sport and Exercise Psychology*, 24, 359–75.

See also: AGING; ATTENTION; CHOKE; COGNITIVE-BEHAVIORAL MODIFICATION; CONCENTRATION; FLOW; FOCUS; MEMORY; MOTOR REACTION; PEAK PERFORMANCE; REINFORCEMENT; SKILL ACQUISITION; ZONE

AUTONOMIC NERVOUS SYSTEM (ANS)

A component of the nervous system responsible for bodily functions that are not under conscious control, for example, breathing and digestion.

See also: BIOFEEDBACK; NERVOUS SYSTEM

AUTOTELIC

As its name suggests, an autotelic experience is engaged in for its own sake, without any instrumental purpose. *Auto* is Greek for self and *telos* means goal. Behavior may be described as autotelic when, as Karen Lee

Hill puts it: "The activity itself is intrinsically motivated, and external rewards are reduced to a position of secondary motivators."

Sometimes, people's characteristics are described as autotelic, meaning that they are primarily oriented to their own aims and purposes, including self-protection. Mihaly Csikszentmihalyi even uses the term *autotelic personality* to describe a class of persons who habitually have enjoyably engrossing experiences "regardless of what they are doing."

Obviously, few of us do anything purely for autotelic reasons. Professional fitness instructors might exercise because they need to earn money to pay the mortgage, because they want to gain a reputation in the fitness industry, or because their SELF-CONCEPT depends on their popularity. These are what Ann Boggiano calls *exotelic* reasons. Pressure of others, or circumstances motivate the individual. But it is also probable that the instructor enjoys exercising for its own sake or, at least, began exercising for its own sake. So exercising was, and possibly still is, an autotelic activity.

Further reading

Boggiano, Ann K. (1998). Maladaptive achievement patterns: A test of a diathesis-stress analysis of helplessness. *Journal of Personality and Social Psychology*, 74, 1681–95.

Csikszentmihalyi. Mihaly (1999). If we are so rich, why aren't we happy? *American Psychologist*, 54, 821–7.

Hill, K. L. (2001). *Frameworks for Sport Psychologists*, Champaign, Ill.: Human Kinetics.

See also: CENTERING; EXERCISE MOTIVATION; EXTRINSIC MOTIVATION; FLOW; HEDONIC TONE; HYPNOSIS; INCENTIVE; INTRINSIC MOTIVATION; LOCUS OF CONTROL; METAMOTIVATION; MOTIVATIONAL CLIMATE; SELF-CONCEPT

AVOIDANCE

A movement away from, or to prevent something from happening, or to stop oneself from doing something is known as an avoidance, or an avoidance RESPONSE. While it often suggests an *active* physical motion away ("her avoidance of the health club became embarrassing"), or a *passive* absence of motion (her avoidance of driving after the crash suggested a lack of SELF-CONFIDENCE"), it can also involve metaphorical movement, such as an avoidance of all thoughts of exercise while on vacation. Avoidance can be prefixed with all manner of nouns, as in blame avoidance, harm avoidance, and arousal avoidance.

Avoidance-focused coping strategies are, as the term suggests, responses typically to ANXIETY or STRESS—especially when occasioned by social comparison—that involve keeping clear of, or ceasing from doing, or thinking about something.

The *avoidance ritual* is a term introduced by Erving Goffman to describe the series of actions performed regularly and according to a prescribed pattern to maintain formality in social interactions and to present a particular impression of the SELF.

Further reading

Goffman, Erving (1959). *The presentation of self in everyday life.* New York: Doubleday.

Kariv, Dafna and Heiman, Tali (2005). Task-oriented versus emotion-oriented coping strategies: The case of college students. *College Student Journal,* 39, 72–84.

See also: ANXIETY; APPROACH; ATTRIBUTION; CHOKE; COPING STRATEGIES; DEFENSIVE ATTRIBUTION; EATING DISORDERS; EMOTIONAL INTELLIGENCE; FEAR OF FAILURE; GOAL; GOAL ORIENTATION; KINESIOPHOBIA; LEARNED HELPLESSNESS; OUTPERFORMANCE; RESPONSE; 2 × 2 ACHIEVEMENT GOAL FRAMEWORK

AWARENESS

Consciousness or knowledge of a situation.

See also: PERCEPTION

BEM SEX ROLE INVENTORY

An index of sex-typed personality traits frequently used with adults. The scale is based on twenty items highly associated with the traditional view of masculinity, such as athleticism, dominance, and RISK-taking, and twenty items typically associated with femininity, such as gentleness, yielding, and nurturing. The inventory also has an ANDROGYNY scale to reflect the extent to which the respondent possesses a mixture of both masculine and feminine traits. Its name comes from its originator Sandra Bem (1944–).

Further reading

Bem, S. L. (1974). The measurement of psychological androgyny. *Journal of Consulting and Clinical Psychology,* 42, 155–62.

Bem, S. L. (1981). *Bem sex role inventory: Professional manual*. Palo Alto, Calif.: Consulting Psychologists Press.
Koivula, Nathalie (1999). Sport participation: Differences in motivation and actual participation due to gender typing. *Journal of Sport Behavior*, 22, 1–22.
McHale, Susan M., Kim, Ji-Yeon, Whiteman, Shawn, and Crouter, Ann C. (2004). Links between sex-typed time use in middle childhood and gender development in early adolescence. *Developmental Psychology*, 40, 5, 868–81.

See also: ANDROGYNY; EQUALITY; GENDER; GENDER VERIFICATION; INSTINCT; SEX; SEX TYPING

BINOCULAR RIVALRY

Occurring when two proximal stimuli presented to the two retinas cannot be resolved in a single object of PERCEPTION, that is, percept.

See also: RIVALRY; VISUAL PERCEPTION

BIOFEEDBACK

"One of the most powerful techniques for facilitating learning of AROUSAL self-regulation," is how Michael Bar-Eli et al. describe biofeedback (from *bios*, Greek for human life). It "uses instruments, usually with sensors and transducers, which provide information regarding the state of selected biological functions that typically are not under voluntary control."

This information is displayed to the person who learns to modify. The basic principle is that humans cannot sense the current state of, for example, heart rate and blood pressure, and so cannot alter them. By feeding back information about them, especially about the difference between desired and actual somatic functions, humans can minimize that difference.

Mathematician Norman Wiener (1894–1964), who subscribed to the philosophy that humans are complex machines, introduced the term "biofeedback." For Wiener, it was a method of controlling a system by "reinserting back into it the results of its past performance." Humans, as machines, can be controlled in the same way, he argued.

Some degree of biofeedback is essential to our survival, and we use biofeedback habitually. For example, when we walk into a dark room and grope forward until we feel something, kinesthetic FEEDBACK (that is, sensations of muscles, tendons and joints) tells us our arm's position so that we can make the next move. In other words, we use the information we receive through our bodies to adjust and regulate our behavior. This is made possible by our AUTONOMIC NERVOUS SYSTEM (ANS).

The ANS is a secondary system of nerves, many cell bodies of which lie outside the brain and spinal cords and receive information from receptors in the various organs of the body. After receiving the information, the bunches of cell bodies—known as ganglia—send out appropriate instructions to muscles, such as the heart, and to glands, such as salivary glands. As its name implies, the ANS is independent and self-regulated, whereas in fact the centers that CONTROL ANS activity are in the lower areas of the brain and usually below the threshold of conscious control. Devotees of YOGA try to bring the functions of the ANS under conscious control. Yogis have been able to slow heartbeat quite voluntarily, without corresponding changes in the rest of the body.

The appeal of such control in exercise and particularly sport is obvious. Many participants try to banish feelings of NEGATIVITY and establish feelings of inner calm or RELAXATION, which release tension and enable them to align body and mind on the proximate assignment. Some accounts suggest that the state of having this kind of FOCUS involves neural functions, principally the assembly of alpha brain waves. These are measurements of electrical activity in the brain and their graphic presentations as recorded on an ELECTRO-ENCEPHALOGRAM (EEG) show multiple patterns reacting to sensory information, which is fed through our senses. When the various brain waves emit synchronously, an alpha rhythm, or alpha state, is said to occur. On the other hand, when beta waves predominate, the subject is overexcited and aroused. There are two other types of brain waves: theta, when drowsiness occurs, and delta, during deep SLEEP.

By using the EEG, the subject can learn how to control his or her ANS under laboratory conditions and perhaps transfer the responses to competitive situations. Other methods that have been used to similar effect involve detecting and measuring galvanic skin responses, these being changes in the resistance of the skin caused by emotional stress and are detected by an instrument known as a galvanometer (perspiration is often an indicator of ANXIETY).

While biofeedback is mostly associated with attempting to reduce anxiety, Paul Davis and Wesley Sime argue that "applied practitioners should focus [biofeedback] interventions on methods to improve self-confidence rather than reducing anxiety." SELF-CONFIDENCE, they suggest, has a greater bearing on performance than anxiety.

There is also evidence of the efficacy of biofeedback in enhancing technique. Bar-Eli et al.'s study of eleven- to fourteen-year-old swimmers found a reduction in technical mistakes and improvements in head and body positions, leg strokes and breathing that regular training alone did not yield in the fourteen-week experimental period.

The most popular and accessible instrument for obtaining feedback and responding accordingly is the heart rate monitor, which both athletes and exercisers use principally in training. The device, comprising a chest-band transmitter and a wrist-worn receiver, indicates how fast the heart is beating. The principle of exercising within a certain percentage of maximum heart rate is not new, but the monitor enables wearers to train within precise limits.

Further reading

Bar-Eli, M., Dreshman, R., Blumenstein, B. and Weinstein, Y. (2002). The effect of mental training with biofeedback on the performance of young swimmers. *Applied Psychology: An International Review*, 51, 567–81.

Boutcher, S. H. and Zinsser, N. W. (1990). Cardiac deceleration of elite and beginning golfers during putting. *Journal of Sport and Exercise Psychology*, 12, 37–47.

Davis, Paul A. and Sime, Wesley E. (2005). Toward a psychophysiology of performance: Sport psychology principles dealing with anxiety. *International Journal of Stress Management*, 12, 363–78.

Petruzzello, S. J., Landers, D. M. and Slazar, W. (1991). Biofeedback and sport/exercise performance: Applications and limitations. *Behavior Therapy*, 22, 379–49.

See also: ANXIETY; ELECTROENCEPHALOGRAM; FEEDBACK; FLOW; MEDITATION; NERVOUS SYSTEM; PAIN; PROPRIOCEPTION; SELF-CONFIDENCE; SLEEP; YOGA

BODY DISSATISFACTION

Unhappiness with, or disapproval of one's own body.

See also: BODY IMAGE; BODY SHAME; SOCIAL PHYSIQUE ANXIETY

BODY IMAGE

The conceptions and evaluations we have of our own bodies, particularly our assessments of how others see us, are known collectively as body image, though some scholars divide this into two distinguishable facets: the non-evaluative PHYSICAL SELF-PERCEPTION and the evaluative PHYSICAL SELF-WORTH.

While T. F. Cash and T. Pruzinsky define body image as the "internal, subjective representations of physical appearance and bodily experience," we should recognize that these representations are filtered through popular portrayals of bodies, media depictions, and peer group expectations. In other words, the way in which we see our physical selves is not a "natural" process, but a culturally mediated one.

We learn how to recognize fatness, thinness, attractiveness, ugliness, and so on. We also learn how to associate these: thinness = attractiveness; fatness = ugliness. Rewards are available to those whose bodies measure up to cultural expectations; these include job opportunities and preferential treatment at school. Women and, to a lesser degree, men struggle to live up to cultural expectations and, as a result, become discontented with their own bodies. This is known as BODY DISSATISFACTION, and young women are especially prone. The EMOTION sometimes (though not inevitably) corresponding to this has been called BODY SHAME.

For young women, dissatisfaction with the body typically begins in puberty when rapid, though normal, weight gain provokes stress. Males, by contrast, have less concern with changes in physical appearance that arrive with the onset of maturity. Culturally, there is a different meaning for physical attractiveness in women than in men: "women tend to invest more in their physical appearance to attain a sense of well-being and SELF-ESTEEM," explain Tina Oates-Johnson and David A. Clark. There is what Ruth Henry et al. describe as a "self-inflicted need to achieve the perceived ideal body type," meaning that women consume television, magazines and movies, then respond to the images portrayed.

Research by, among others, Mary Pritchard and Gregory Wilson, has revealed a relationship between this and "physical ailments [such as colds, flu], negative health habits [smoking, drinking], STRESS fatigue [feeling overwhelmed], ANGER, tension, DEPRESSION, confusion, negative affect [moodiness], and the use of ineffective coping styles [including drugs]."

Even female athletes and frequent exercisers, who acknowledged that the "model skinny" ideal was unrealistic, "still expressed body dissatisfaction," in a 2005 study by Vikki Krane et al. This is especially prevalent among competitors in sports in what Paula Ziegler et al. call "aesthetic sports" in which "maintenance of the ideal body size and thinness has come to symbolize success."

Exercise has been shown to lead to improvements in body image, though the process may not be straightforward. Exercise can produce SELF-EFFICACY, thereby improving all aspects of self-esteem, including body image; or it may produce physical fitness that changes the body and, in turn leads to changes in body image.

Further reading

Cash, T. C. and Pruzinsky, T. (1990). *Body images: Development, deviance and change*. New York: Guilford.

Henry Ruth, Anshel, Mark A., and Michael, Timothy (2006). Effects of aerobic and circuit training on fitness and body image among women. *Journal of Sport Behavior*, 29, 281–303.

Krane, Vikki, Waldron, Jennifer, Michalenok, Jennifer, and Stiles-Shipley, Julie (2001). Body image concerns in female exercisers and athletes: A feminist cultural studies perspective. *Women in Sport and Physical Activity*, 10, 17–33.

Oates-Johnson, Tina and Clark, David A. (2004). Sociotropy, body dissatisfaction and perceived social disapproval in dieting women: A prospective diathesis-stress study of dysphoria. *Cognitive Therapy and Research*, 28, 715–31.

Pritchard, Mary E. and Wilson, Gregory S. (2005). Factors influencing body image in female adolescent athletes. *Women in Sport and Physical Activity Journal*, 14, 72–9.

Ziegler, Paula J., Kannan, Srimathi, Jonnalagadda, Satya S., Krishnakumar, Ambika, Taksali, and Nelson, Judith A. (2005). Dietary intake, body perceptions, and weight concerns of female US international synchronized figure skating teams. *International Journal of Sport Nutrition and Exercise Metabolism*, 15, 550–66.

See also: ANOREXIA ATHLETICA; ANOREXIA NERVOSA; BODY DISSATISFACTION; BODY SHAME; BULIMIA NERVOSA; CULTURE; EATING DISORDERS; MUSCLE DYSMORPHIA; PHYSICAL SELF-PERCEPTIONS; PHYSICAL SELF-WORTH; SELF-EFFICACY; SOCIAL PHYSIQUE ANXIETY; SOCIOTROPY; WEIGHT CONTROL

BODY LANGUAGE

Of the several forms of nonverbal communication, body language is perhaps the most obvious means through which humans express thoughts and emotions and so make representations of their experience visible to others. It involves gestures, facial expressions, EYE MOVEMENT, breathing patterns, skin color changes, muscle tone, interpersonal distance, and posture. Iain Greenlees and his colleagues examined all these in combination with clothing and assessed their impact among table-tennis players.

Some players might traipse languidly across the arena, shoulders drooping, head inclined downwards. The body language signals an acceptance of defeat. Other table-tennis players may stride impatiently to the table ahead of their opponents, repeatedly tapping their racket heads against their legs and staring intently ahead. They are alert, enthusiastic and eager to compete; their AROUSAL level is high. Other players fidget, their eyes darting, as they wait for their opponent to settle. Their actions betray lack of COMPOSURE. Those players who displayed "positive body language" were rated as "more assertive, aggressive, competitive, experienced, confident, positive, focused, relaxed, and fit than the models who displayed negative body language." Clothing did not make much difference.

The implication is that before and during a competition, every athlete communicates aspects of him or herself, sometimes intentionally but more usually unintentionally. Body language often reveals a representation at odds with the athlete's express intentions. No competitor wishes to communicate ANXIETY, resignation, FEAR, or any other form of NEGATIVITY; yet, they are frequently incapable of suppressing the nonverbal cues that communicate exactly these.

Body language, like other nonverbal communication, involves coding and decoding. People, not just athletes, may consciously encode their body movements and gestures in anticipation that teammates, opponents, and spectators alike all decode in accordance with their intentions. Or, they may be unaware that their actions are disclosing more than they wish. Worse still, they may encode significant information about themselves only for others to decode a completely different message.

In sport, almost all of the communicating is done by way of the body. Precompetition body language has become very much part of the spectacle. Players of virtually any contact sport will try to convey an impression of AGGRESSIVENESS during the preliminaries of a game, maintaining a stern facial expression, keeping muscles flexed and striding assertively. The research of Greenlees et al. indicates the efficacy of this style of body language on EXPECTANCY, which itself affects performance.

During a COMPETITION, body language has several functions. At the most explicit level, a handshake, a thumbs-up sign, or a clenched fist, may function as emblems communicating widely acknowledged meanings. There may also be nonverbal cues that CONTROL, guide, or regulate the flow of a competition. For example, a basketball or soccer player may extend arms downwards and turn palms outwards to indicate to a colleague that he or she should take possession of the ball. Body language may amplify speech: Coaches often grimace and point arms or punch the air as they issue instructions; team players frequently gesture flamboyantly as they encourage each other.

In each of these instances, the content of the message could have been communicated by speech. But, A. Kendon argues, gesture has different characteristics and functions to speech. As a silent but visible mode of communication, it can be useful in sport; for instance, by attracting the attention of a teammate but not a rival who may be looking in a different direction, or by transmitting a deliberately vague piece of information regarding tactics—this may be useful in making opponents wary that something is going to happen and possibly induce tension.

Seeing evidence of an opponent's uncovered competitiveness may also make athletes wary. "Players like [Lleyton] Hewitt and [Michael] Chang are obviously very competitive because they pump their fists," Pete Sampras once reflected on his tennis contemporaries, adding that his own body language reveals the same competitiveness, though in "a much more subtle way." "People who know me know when I'm fighting. You can see it in my eyes and my expression. I just do it in a more introverted way" (quoted in the *Independent on Sunday*, "Sportsweek" June 17, 2001, p. 3).

To return to Greenlees's work, participants reported lower SELF-CONFIDENCE in their ability to defeat an opponent when they viewed them portraying positive body language, suggesting the intimidatory potential of body language. So, celebrating every moment of success in a competition could carry this potential.

Perhaps the most interesting features of body language are the gestures, facial expressions, and body postures that change in the CONTEXT of a competition and occur without conscious awareness. Unlike most areas of life, in which speech and body movement complement each other in communication; sports harbor the potential for contradiction. Nonverbal cues can conflict with speech. A person may assure another, "I'm perfectly relaxed," while dilated pupils might suggest otherwise. "Honestly, it's the truth," may be accompanied by what P. Ekman and W. V. Friesen, in the 1960s, called "non-verbal leakage" in which information about a deception is transmitted through body movements (people try to control facial movements when trying to deceive others and are more likely to give themselves away with arm and torso movements). Sports competitors never intend to affirm to a rival that he or she has lost COMPO-SURE and is resigned to defeat. Yet, their body language may do precisely that.

Further reading

Ekman, P. and Friesen, W. V. (1969). Non-verbal leakage and clues to deception. *Psychiatry*, 32, 88–106.

Greenlees, Iain A., Bradley, Andrew, Holder, Tim P., and Thelwell, Richard C. (2005). The impact of opponents' non-verbal behaviour on the first impressions and outcome expectations of table-tennis players. *Psychology of Sport and Exercise*, 6, 103–15.

Greenlees, Iain, Buscombe, Richard, Thelwell, Richard, Holder, Tim, and Rimmer, Matthew (2005). Impact of opponents' clothing and body language on impression formation and outcome expectations. *Journal of Sport and Exercise Psychology*, 27, 39–52.

Kendon, A. (1985). Some uses of gesture. In O. Tannen and M. Saville-Troika (Eds.), *Perspectives on Silence* (pp. 215–34). Norwood, N.J.: Ablex.

See also: AGGRESSIVENESS; ANXIETY; ATTENTION; BODY IMAGE; COMPOSURE; EYE MOVEMENT; FEAR; NEGATIVITY; PHYSICAL SELF-PERCEPTIONS; PHYSICAL SELF-WORTH; RESPONSE; SELF-CONCEPT; SELF-CONFIDENCE

BODY MASS INDEX

A measure calculated by dividing a person's weight in kilograms by the square of their height in meters. There is an online calculator at http://www.bmiweightloss.co.uk/bmi_calculatior.cfm.

See also: OBESITY

BODY SHAME

Lisa Hallsworth et al. describe body shame as "the negative EMOTION that occurs when a person compares him- or herself to some internalized cultural ideal and perceives a discrepancy between this ideal and their body."

It can lead to, among other things, DEPRESSION, sexual dysfunction and EATING DISORDERS. Participants in sports and events that accentuate physical appearance, such as bodybuilding or ice dancing as well as performance, are likely to experience a painful feeling of embarrassment, humiliation, or distress caused by the consciousness of how their body differs from an ideal. The term shame comes from the German noun *Scham*.

While Hallsworth et al. do not specifically indicate how body shame differs from SOCIAL PHYSIQUE ANXIETY, we can presume that the former assumes an object—one's own body—while the latter lacks and object and is a diffuse, unpleasant state of apprehension. It is, as Peter Crocker et al. put it, the "ANXIETY an individual experiences as a result of perceived observation or evaluation of his/her physique." Body shame is a RESPONSE to one's own evaluation, though, inevitably, this is closely related to how one perceives others' reactions.

Further reading

Crocker, P. R. E., Sabiston, C. M., Kowalski, K. C., McDonough, M. H., and Kowalski, N. (2006). Longitudinal assessment of the relationship between physical self-concept and health-related behavior and emotion in adolescent girls. *Journal of Applied Sport Psychology,* 18, 185–200.

Hallsworth, Lisa, Wade, Tracey, and Tiggemann, Marika (2005). Individual differences in male body-image: An examination of self-objectification in recreational body builders. *British Journal of Health Psychology,* 10, 453–65.

See also: AVOIDANCE; BODY IMAGE; DEPRESSION; EATING DISORDERS; EMOTION; MUSCLE DYSMORPHIA; PHYSICAL SELF-PERCEPTIONS; PHYSICAL SELF-WORTH; RESPONSE; SELF-AWARENESS; SELF-CONCEPT; SOCIAL PHYSIQUE ANXIETY

BRAINWAVES

Electrical impulses in the brain.

See also: ELECTROENCEPHALOGRAM

BULIMIA NERVOSA

A subclinical EATING DISORDER, typically occurring among adolescent or early adult females, bulimia nervosa (from the Greek *boulimia,* meaning ravenous hunger) manifests in insatiable overeating, often followed by self-induced vomiting, fasting, and excessive use of laxatives. It usually involves a distorted BODY IMAGE, a corresponding BODY DISSATISFACTION and often DEPRESSION. (Note: *subclinical* means that it is a condition not severe enough to present readily observable symptoms.)

Research shows that bulimics have experienced changes in body weight and shape. Often, this occurs among young women after puberty when, as Sharon Thompson and Sohailla Digsby report in their study of cheerleaders, "changes in body shape affect female athletes' appearance and performance."

Typically, bulimics judge their actual body size to be larger and their ideal body size to be smaller. Their body image is labile, that is, liable to alteration. For example, after a meal, a bulimic may check her stomach size or the tightness of her clothing and subjectively interpret any kinesthetic FEEDBACK as an increase in fatness.

Binge episodes are often preceded by spells of dieting that lead to cravings. The impulsive overeating serves to reduce the negative mood relating to hunger but often leads to a worsening of negative affect. In other words, bulimics binge because they feel hungry but, having eaten, feel depressed about what they see as changes in their body. Their behavior becomes cyclical.

There is growing consensus about the status of bulimia nervosa as a syndrome. ANOREXIA NERVOSA, by contrast, is continuous with normalcy in the sense that it is an extreme form of dieting. Bulimia involves a distinct set of behaviors. As much as 4.2 percent of the female population may experience bulimia nervosa at some point in their lives, black females having less weight concern and so being less likely to suffer from eating disorders than their white counterparts. While bulimia nervosa commonly affects females, at least one study has shown that male competitors in weight-sensitive sports, in this case wrestling, engaged in behaviors that met the criteria for bulimia; these included bingeing, purging, and laxative and diuretic abuse.

Further reading

Baum, Antonia (2006). Eating disorders in the male athlete. *Sports Medicine*, 36, 1–6.

Osvold, Lisë Leigh and Sodowsky, Gargi Roysircar (1993). Eating disorders of white American, racial and ethnic minority American, and international women. *Journal of Multicultural Counseling and Development*, 21, 143–54.

Thompson, Sharon and Digsby, Sohailla (2004). A preliminary survey of dieting, body dissatisfaction and eating problems among high school cheerleaders. *Journal of School Health*, 74, 85–91.

Williamson, Donald A., White, Marney A., York-Crowe, Emily, and Stewart, Tiffany M. (2004). Cognitive-behavioral theories of eating disorders. *Behavior Modification*, 28, 711–38.

See also: ANOREXIA ATHLETICA; ANOREXIA NERVOSA; BODY IMAGE; BODY SHAME; DEPENDENCE; EATING DISORDERS; EXERCISE DEPENDENCE; GENDER; MUSCLE DYS-MORPHIA; OBESITY; OBSESSIVE-COMPULSIVE; OVERTRAINING SYNDROME; PERFEC-TIONISM; PSYCHOPATHOLOGY; SEX TYPING; SOCIAL PHYSIQUE ANXIETY; WEIGHT CONTROL

BURNOUT

Burnout is "a state of physical, emotional and mental exhaustion that results from long-term involvement in work situations that are emotionally demanding," according to W. B. Schaufeli and E. R. Greenglass. In the CONTEXT of sport, it has been defined as "a psychological, EMOTIONAL, and physical withdrawal from a formerly pursued and enjoyable sport as a result of excessive STRESS which acts on the athlete over time." This is the meaning offered by Daniel Gould et al. "It is the manifestation or consequence of the situational, cognitive, physiologic, and behavioral components of excessive stress."

Origins. Tage Kristensen et al. trace the origins of the concept to the mid-1970s, when studies of volunteer workers with underprivileged people revealed a prevalence of exhaustion, depersonalization, and, importantly, a reduced sense of personal accomplishment. The syndrome—this being a group of associated, recurring symptoms—was later found to affect employees in human service work, including nurses, social workers, and teachers.

While the symptoms of the sports version of burnout were the same, the conditions under which it occurs were different. Its popular use was to describe the condition typically affecting teenage sports performers whose rise is sudden, if not meteoric, but whose decline is premature and abrupt. Young tennis prodigies such as Tracy Austin and Andrea Jaeger were exemplars of burnout, both being top-class pros in their teens and seeming to be destined for long reigns at the top. Both were prolific achievers on the professional circuit but neither fulfilled their early promise. Recurring back and neck problems curtailed Austin's career when she was twenty-one; a chronic shoulder INJURY ended Jaeger's prospects before she was twenty.

Austin and Jaeger were well-publicized prodigies. There were and are countless others who burn out before even approaching their potential. At the time of the 1996 summer Olympics at Atlanta, a report was published that claimed that the rigors of competitive gymnastics amounted to child abuse. According to the 1996 report's authors, overambitious parents were pushing their children to succeed in sports out of selfish reasons. "Achievement by proxy" is how I. Tofler et al. described the manner in which parents drove their offspring toward an almost certain burnout.

Joan Ryan reached similar conclusions in her book *Little Girls in Pretty Boxes.* She chronicles the short-lived careers of Betty Okikino, practicing and competing with a broken neck, wearing a brace when resting; Kelly Garrison, pounding her ankle while waiting her turn until the pain of the stress fracture was numbed; Julissa Gomez, fatally snapping her neck in Tokyo; Christy Henrich, who should have made the 1992 Olympics, but died instead two years later, weighing less than 50 lbs (22.68 kgs). A combination of parental pressure and coaching tyranny contrived to bring a premature halt to many promising sporting careers. There are several theories that purport to account for burnout in sport.

Theory 1: Four stage. In 1986, Ronald E. Smith argued that there is a progression to burnout, with the child being placed under pressure to train and develop competitive approaches by significant others, including parents and coaches. The young athlete then begins to see the demands placed on her or him differently, some finding the situation threatening, and others not so. If the demand is perceived as threatening, the youth enters a third stage in which there is a physiological response, such as fatigue or insomnia. Finally, in a fourth stage, the physiological response leads to COPING STRATEGIES. These might manifest in decreased levels of competitive performance, interpersonal problems, or complete withdrawal from the sport. For Smith, PERSONALITY and motivational factors influence the four stages of the burnout process. The player's senses of SELF-ESTEEM, ambition, personal ANXIETY are all factors; so it is difficult to generalize from his theory. Some young sports performers might react positively, whereas others will feel the pressure.

Theory 2: Training stress. In 1990, John M. Silva identified "training stress" as the determinant in the burnout process. This is a physical characteristic: Sometimes the body becomes overloaded with the burden of training and COMPETITION; but, at other times, the young body becomes stronger and adapts to the rigors associated with higher levels of competition. The young competitors who are prone to burnout will experience a "psychophysiological malfunction" after their body's failure to respond positively to training. Their mental orientation is then affected and they become incapable of meeting the demands placed on their bodies. Again, emphasis on how individuals respond limits the applicability of the theory.

Lindsey MacDonald was a sixteen-year-old schoolgirl from Scotland when she reached the final of the 400 meters at the Moscow summer Olympics of 1980. Although she was beaten, she recovered three days later and helped the British team to bronze in the relay. The surprise performance spurred her to great ambitions, and she set herself a challenging and draining training schedule. INJURY and illness beset the rest of her career, and the promise shown in her teens was never fulfilled. She competed only until the age of twenty-five.

The importance of PERFECTIONISM in the burnout process should not be overlooked. Frequent worry about others' evaluations, uncertainty regarding one's own abilities and competitive state ANXI-ETY are all factors affecting young athletes striving and being encouraged to reach ever-improving level of performance. "Some youngsters have an 'at-risk' perfectionist personality that may predispose them to burnout," Gould and his coresearchers concluded. They also believed that many of those mistakenly identified as burnout cases in fact drop out not because of any stress but simply because their interests and ambitions change.

Theory 3: Powerlessness. Jay Coakley argues that the INTENSITY of competitive professional sports and the time-demands it places on promising young players denies the young person the opportunity to develop a normal multifaceted PERSONALITY. The youth is encouraged to focus totally on success in their sport and to exclude other experiences in their social life. The Jennifer Capriati case would fit perfectly with this MODEL. A young girl from Florida urged to play tennis at a very early age and provided with every manner of top-class coaching and facility, Capriati had endorsement contracts estimated to be worth $5 million before she hit a ball as a professional. She reached the final of her first tournament on the women's professional tour when she was only thirteen. Two months later, in her first Grand Slam event, she progressed to the semifinals of the French Open. The youngest-ever semifinalist at Wimbledon in 1991 (at fifteen years of age) and the youngest US Open semifinalist since Jaeger, in 1980, Capriati won a gold medal at the 1992 Olympics, beating Steffi Graf in the women's final. By this time, Capriati, though sound physically, was in the throes of psychological burnout caused by a conflict between public and parental expectations of her and her own desire to indulge herself as an "ordinary" teenager. She dropped out of the WTA tour and went back to school. Arrested for shoplifting and caught in possession of drugs in Florida, Capriati underwent drugs REHABILITATION and made an abortive COMEBACK in November 1994. Then she disappeared for two years, seemingly finished.

Coakley contends that a young phenom's ability to make decisions that affect her or his life are taken away, or minimized to the point where they feel powerless to influence the direction of their own lives. It is this sense of inability or disempowerment that creates the burnout. This gives rise to a further question: is burnout reversible? The tentative answer is, yes. In 1994, Capriati seemed certain to be linked with Austin and Jaeger as a brilliant tennis prospect who had burned out. But, at the age of twenty-four, Capriati resurfaced dramatically, beating world number one Martina Hingis to win the 2001 Australian Open.

Theory 4: Coaches. Perhaps the most overlooked group of burnout sufferers are coaches and trainers, who are often subject to stress and anxiety comparable to that of their charges. Among this group, the symptoms of burnout resemble those of the human-service workers mentioned earlier in the sense that the demands and experience of the workplace operate as causes: "Burnout has specific work-related causes and symptoms unlike the multifaceted physiological and bio-logical problems associated with depression," writes Alice McLaine in her "An Overview of Burnout in Athletic Trainers" (in *Athletic Therapy Today*, November, 2005, pp. 10–13).

It could be argued that the demands of sport increasingly resemble those of other kinds of work: they are routinized, frequently involve perfor-mance goals, and, perhaps, for some athletes, lack a sense of personal accomplishment. This is supported by Scott Cresswell and Robert Eklund's 2006 study in which athletes' "experiences were similar to those described by individuals in general work and human care settings."

Further reading

Coakley, J. J. (1992). Burnout among adolescent athletes: A personal failure or social problem? *Sociology of Sport Journal*, 9, 271–85.

Cresswell, Scott and Eklund, Robert (2006). The nature of player burnout in rugby: Key characteristics and attributions. *Journal of Applied Sport Psychology*, 18, 219–39.

Gould, D., Udry, E., Tuffey, S., and Loehr, J. (1996). Burnout in competitive junior tennis players: I. A quantitative psychological assessment and burnout in competitive junior tennis players: II. Qualitative psychological assessment. *The Sport Psychologist*, 10, 4, 322–40.

Kristensen, Tage S., Borritz, Marianne, Villadsen, Ebbe, and Christensen, Karl B. (2005). The Copenhagen burnout inventory: A new tool for the assessment of burnout. *Work and Stress, 19*(3), 192–207.

Ryan, Joan (1998). *Little Girls in Pretty Boxes: The making and breaking of élite gymnasts and figure skaters.* London: Women's Press.

Schaufeli, W. B. and Greenglass, E. R. (2001). Introduction to special issue on burnout and health. *Psychology and Health*, 16, 501–10.

Silva, J. M. (1990). An analysis of the training stress syndrome in competitive athletics. *Journal of Sport Psychology*, 8, 5–20.

Smith, R. E. (1986). Toward a cognitive-affective model of athletic burnout. *Journal of Sport Psychology*, 8, 36–50.

Tofler, I., Styer, B., Micheli, L., and Herman, L. (1996). Physical and emo-tional problems of elite female gymnasts, *New England Journal of Medicine*, 335, 281–3.

See also: ANXIETY; COACH–ATHLETE RELATIONSHIP; COMEBACK; COPING STRATEGIES; DEPRESSION; DROPOUTS; EMOTION; ETHICS; GIFTEDNESS; GOAL ORIENTATION; INJURY; LIFE COURSE; OVERREACHING; OVERTRAINING SYNDROME; PERSONALITY; SOCIALIZATION; STRESS; THEORY; VICARIOUS AGENCY.

CATASTROPHE THEORY

A theory purporting to explain unexpected discontinuities.

See also: AROUSAL

CATHARSIS

Katharsis is Greek for cleanse, purify or purge. Psychoanalysts use the term catharsis to suggest how "reliving" or recalling experiences that have prompted ANXIETY, but which have been repressed, can effect a cleansing discharge of tension. Some theorists have argued that playing and watching sports or exercising function as a catharsis, enabling participants and spectators to eliminate natural AGGRESSION that might otherwise build up and become destructive. Back in the 1920s, the psychiatrist A. A. Brill recommended attending a boxing show every month (quoted in Feshbach).

The ethologist Konrad Lorenz regarded sport as a kind of safety valve, a controlled mechanism for releasing innate behavioral tendencies, an INSTINCT (ethology is the study of behavior from a biological perspective). Because aggressive instincts were natural, nothing could be done about them. Human society had to devise ways to accommodate them or face continual VIOLENCE and devastation. Unlike other animals, humans had sufficient ingenuity to design measures that would allow the behavioral expression of aggressive instincts. Sport was the principal among them. It was a formalized, rule-bound order that licensed combative, violent, even warlike conduct but within a relatively secure framework. Competing in sports, either actually or vicariously (through watching others) allowed humans to rid themselves of aggressive instincts, usually without incurring, or doing, too much damage.

The theory of sport-as-catharsis was based on a model of the human being as a sophisticated animal, but an animal nevertheless, and so, to a large degree, at the mercy of instincts. While this may have intuitive appeal, research on the topic yielded mixed results. For example, the work of, among others, L. Martin published in 1976, lent some support to the concept of catharsis, concluding that athletes were less aggressive after competition. On the other hand, a succession of research projects, including those of E. Ryan, in 1970, and D. Zillman et al., in 1972, revealed that athletes were *more* aggressive after COMPETITION, leading to the suspicion that REINFORCEMENT might occur. Even if the aggressive behaviors were reduced, there remains the likelihood that they might recur. As Seymour Feshbach has pointed out, "if the cathartic aggressive responses are indeed successful in reducing aggressive impulses, the responses will be reinforced."

While it did not explicitly acknowledge it, the 1987 study by Robert Arms et al. implicitly recognized the role of reinforcement in shaping behavior, this time of spectators rather than competitors. It concluded that "the observation of aggression on the field of play leads to an increase in hostility on the part of spectators." This has been termed *vicarious catharsis.*

Further reading

Arms, R., Russell, G., and Sandilands, M. (1987). Effects on the hostility of spectators of viewing aggressive sports. In A. Yiannakis, T. McIntyre, M. Melnick, and D. Hart (Eds.) *Sport Sociology,* 3rd edn, pp. 259–64. Dubuque, Iowa: Kendall/Hunt.

Feshbach, Seymour (1984). The catharsis hypothesis, aggressive drive, and the reduction of aggression. *Aggressive Behavior,* 10, 91–101.

Lorenz, Konrad (1966). *On aggression.* New York: Harcourt, Brace & World.

Martin, L. (1976). Effects of competition upon the aggressive responses of college basketball players and wrestlers. *Research Quarterly,* 47, 388–93.

Ryan, E. (1970). The cathartic effect of vigorous motor activity on aggressive behavior. *Research Quarterly,* 41, 542–51.

Zillman, D., Katcher, A. H. and Day, K. D. (1972). Provoked and unprovoked aggressiveness in athletes. *Journal of Research in Personality,* 8, 139–52.

See also: AGGRESSION; ANGER; CONSTRUCT; CONTEXT; CONTROL; DEATH WISH; DRIVE; FLOW; HEDONIC TONE; INSTINCT; MIMESIS; MODELING; REINFORCEMENT; THEORY; VICARIOUS AGENCY; VIOLENCE

CAUSE

Something that gives rise to an action or chain of actions.

See also: RELATIONSHIP

CELEBRITIES

"Celebrities are well-known (through the media) for nothing in particular, whereas the truly famous are in some way *deserving* of individual recognition," writes David Giles in his 2000 psychological study of fame and celebrity. For Giles, the "truly famous" are acknowledged for their accomplishments while celebrities become widely known though not necessarily for great deeds and often not for very long. The word itself is from the French *célébrité*, which derives from *celebrare*, Latin for renown.

On this account, celebrity status is fragile and ephemeral and they do not have the longevity of, say, George Best, Joe DiMaggio, Muhammad Ali, or any number of other athletes whose accomplishments earned them recognition and long-lasting fame. Since Giles' analysis, however, the distinction between "well-knownness" and earned approval has been blurred by the appearance of, on the one hand, accomplished athletes who have been fêted as celebrities and afforded a status comparable with rock and movie stars, and, on the other, reality-television celebrities, who enjoy what might be called unearned fame, that is, their presence, rather than anything they have actually done, is rewarded by the attention of FANS and the endorsement contracts.

Fans' relationships with celebrities have been assessed on the Celebrity Worship Scale, which was designed to measure the intensity of IDENTIFICATION, that is, the strength with which they associate their own identity with that of the celebrity. The research team that devised it concludes that, at the end of the scale, there is *absorption*, which involves a total commitment of all available "perceptual, motoric, imaginative and ideational resources to a unified representation of the attention object" (motoric refers to movement; ideational refers to the capacity to form ideas). The fan might be motivated to learn more and more about their chosen celebrity, perhaps seeking out obscure sources of information that are not available to most fans, or they may resort to other behavior.

Skater Katarina Witt and tennis player Steffi Graf are among the many celebrity athletes to have attracted fans at this end of the scale. Witt was inundated with mail and unwelcome phone calls. Graf's absorbed fan stabbed her rival Monica Seles as a way of protecting Graf's status as the number-one player in the rankings. Several other celebrity athletes have been subject to similarly motivated fans, more popularly known as stalkers.

Further reading

Cashmore, Ellis (2006). *Celebrity/Culture*. London and New York: Routledge.

Giles, David (2000). *Illusions of immortality: A psychology of fame and celebrity.* New York: St. Martin's Press.

Maltby, John, Day, Liza, McCutcheon, Lynn E., Gillett, Raphael, Houran, James, and Ashe, Diane D. (2004). Personality and coping: a context for examining celebrity worship and mental health. *British Journal of Psychology,* 95, 411–28.

McCutcheon, Lynn E., Ashe, Diane D., Houran, James, and Maltby, John (2003). A cognitive profile of individuals who tend to worship celebrities. *Journal of Psychology,* 137, 309–14.

See also: CONTEXT; CULTURE; FANS; IDENTIFICATION; IDENTITY; IMPOSTOR PHENOMENON; MODELING; RELATIONSHIP; RELIGION; ROLE MODEL; SELF; VICARIOUS AGENCY

CENTERING

A mental skill to direct thoughts inwards before COMPETITION, introspectively checking whether ATTENTION is focused and AROUSAL is at the appropriate level. Athletes strive to become consciously aware of their entire bodies, trying to locate a center of gravity, while they eliminate thoughts of their immediate environment. Many athletes in all manner of sport can be seen to do this before COMPETITION: They close their eyes and remain motionless, sometimes for only a few seconds, sometimes longer. An athlete who is experienced at centering can execute the whole process in a few seconds, monitoring focal auditory and visual attention, and arousal, before seeming to snap out and attend to a task-relevant clue in readiness for competition.

Sprinters can often be seen seconds before they are called to the start line, their eyes closed, lying or standing perfectly still and breathing deeply, while they center. As soon as they hear the call, they leap to action, looking only at the track ahead of them to minimize distractions. Centering is one of the four techniques prescribed by Robert Nideffer for facilitating entry into the ZONE, the others being self-HYPNOSIS, improving CONCENTRATION and developing faith. It is "a breathing technique designed to produce physical balance and mental focus."

Centering, in this sense, involves a long, deep breath from the stomach (rather than the chest) followed by a maximum exhalation, leading to relaxation. The next step involves refocusing attention. Research by Lisa Rogerson and Dennis Hrycaiko into the effectiveness of centering in ice hockey found that is was "an important ingredient for improving performance," especially when combined with SELF-TALK.

While its significance is quite different, Jean Piaget (1896–1980) used the similar concept of *centration* when describing the tendency of children in the pre-operational stage of development (about eighteen months to seven years of age) to concentrate on only one aspect of a problem at a time. As a result, they could not solve problems that demanded attention to the whole, particularly involving conservation; for example, children did not comprehend that pouring liquid from a tall bottle into a flat tray does not decrease its volume. The similarity is that, in both the competitive situation and that of the child's problem-solving, centering on one feature necessarily means losing sight of the CONTEXT, or the properties surrounding that feature.

To avoid misunderstanding, mention should be made of *decentering*, which is not commonly used in sports, save for when an individual exhibits an unwavering belief that he or she is the FOCUS of everyone else's attention and this leads to ANXIETY. Decentering is the process of counseling designed to change this perception. Like centering, the term is associated with Jean Piaget and, in his theories, refers to a stage when children are able to see themselves in objective relationships with other persons and events in their environment.

Further reading

Nideffer, R. M. (1992). *Psyched to win*. Champaign, Ill.: Human Kinetics.
Nideffer, R. M. and Sagal, M.-S. (1998). Concentration and attention control training. In J. Williams (Ed.), *Applied sport psychology: Personal growth to peak performance*, 3rd edn (pp. 296–315). Mountain View, Calif.: Mayfield.
Rogerson, Lisa J. and Hrycaiko, Dennis W. (2002). Enhancing competitive performance of ice hockey goaltenders using centering and self-talk. *Journal of Applied Sport Psychology*, 14, 14–26.

See also: AUTOGENIC; AUTOTELIC; CONCENTRATION; FEEDBACK; FOCUS; HYPNOSIS; MEDITATION; MENTAL PRACTICE; PREPERFORMANCE; PSYCHING; RELAXATION; SELF-TALK; ZONE

CHARACTER

"Sport is one stage on which our moral character is acted out," writes Carwyn Jones. "Our deep-rooted moral dispositions, virtues and vices, are partly definitive of our character." Sport has popularly been regarded as a builder of character, which typically refers to the moral and mental qualities distinctive to an individual. The root of the term is the Greek *kharakter*, stamp or impress.

Character can be reduced to four constituents, the final two of which have moral dimensions: (1) the capacity to make great efforts to overcome adversity; (2) the competence to lead others; (3) the ABILITY to resist the temptation to transgress that is, break rules; and (4) altruism, the regard for others' interests and welfare above one's own. Does participation in sport instill these in a competitor?

Constituent 1: Striving. Studies, particularly those of Susan Harter, have drawn on White's concept of competence MOTIVATION. According to Harter, we are all innately motivated to be competent: Athletes whose perceptions of their own competence and self-control are high will exert more effort and persist at tasks in achievement situations. Success promotes feelings of SELF-EFFICACY and the athlete is encouraged to establish greater challenges and strive even harder. But, if an athlete's efforts result in failure, even perceived failure, then low-competence motivation will result and the athlete will probably drop out. Almost by definition, the athletes we watch and read about are in the first group: they have had to overthrow failure at some stage of their sports career and have redoubled their efforts to progress. Those who have not will have dropped out and disappeared. In this sense, sport does imbue in its participants the capacity to shrug off failure. But, there remains an unknowable mass of other, once-aspiring but now absent competitors for whom sport worked only to discourage and demoralize.

Constituent 2: LEADERSHIP. Leadership is integral to sports. Some figure or figures must exert authority and influence over others either through inspiration or by example, or both. Early psychological studies treated leadership as a PERSONALITY trait or a combination of features possessed by individuals. More sophisticated treatments have accentuated contingencies that are specific to situations and facilitate leadership skills. What is clear from the research is that effective leadership in sports needs flexibility: leaders need to adapt, switching, for example, from autocratic styles to more democratic approaches, depending on the circumstances and people involved. But, does involvement in sports equip athletes with the qualities and skills necessary for leadership? The answer is, yes and no. Obviously, the fact that there are managers and coaches or trainers who delegate leadership duties to captains who can respond to situational demands means that sports must equip some athletes with leadership qualities. Yet, for every captain, there is a team of players who either conform or else risk undermining team COHESION. In individual sports, the athlete is typically the one following instructions, not giving them. So, while it is reasonable to suggest that leadership skills are an inherent part of the sports experience for some, for others—probably the majority—the capacity to follow directions unquestioningly is a more useful SKILL.

Constituent 3: Fairness. Perhaps the most contentious part of the assertion that sport builds character concerns ethics: playing fair and square within the rules and accepting defeat without grumbling are popularly regarded as qualities of good character. (At the risk of simplifying the distinction, ETHICS refers to the principles that govern behavior, while *morals* are concerned with whether that behavior is right or wrong.) The values of fair play and abiding by rules were once central in sports, especially when the amateur ethos prevailed and reward of winning was subordinated to the joy of competing for its own sake. Professionalism introduced a more instrumental orientation, and qualities such as prudence and calculation have seeped into sport. According to some writers, such as William Morgan, rules have become little more than technical directives, and professional athletes will break every rule they can get away with and comply with every rule they cannot. In other words, pros follow rules not out of a moral commitment to their intrinsic rightness but because their calculations tell them that breaking them will lead to penalties. This approach does not seem confined to competitors. Administrators, managers, coaches, officials, and even presidents of major sports federations have all been guilty of fraud, corruption, or mendacity of one kind or another. Sport may once have been an institution that encouraged and infused a sense of fairness and obligation to obey rules. Now, the availability of extrinsic rewards has probably nourished a more instrumental mentality in which rules are not seen as inherently good or bad, but merely devices.

Constituent 4: Altruism. Intuitively, we might think that competing in sports, whether individually or as part of a team, compels us to act altruistically and to distribute credit for success among a variety of teammates or aides. On the other hand, we often hear athletes attributing their success to their own determination and hard work. There is a body of literature on ATTRIBUTION in sports. Various studies have shown that after success in a COMPETITION, athletes claim credit for themselves; while, after defeat, they cite external causes for their failure as a way of protecting their SELF-ESTEEM. Other research indicates that athletes often blame internal factors for defeats too, not wishing to be seen as making excuses for their failure. Ambiguous outcomes, however, are attributed to external factors. So, a tennis player on the wrong end of a tight call might interpret this as a "moral win" and blame inept judges for the ultimate defeat; the winner is likely to take credit.

There is little straightforward logic in blame/credit attribution. Some athletes prefer never to invoke self-serving strategies and take responsibility for their own fortunes, good and bad; while others spurn personal responsibility for failure. This does not exactly tell us much about athletes' altruism, but it tells us something about their EGOCENTRISM, which is, in many senses, its opposite. Rarely do athletes simply concede that a better opponent beat them. The opponent might be said to have been better "on the day" or having prevailed because of uncontrollable external factors ("our team was depleted by injuries"); these are unstable factors and susceptible to change. The reason is that, in sport, the LOCUS OF CONTROL must be understood as an internal state. For example, it would be ludicrous if coaches told athletes that their progress was determined by all manner of uncontrollable external factors, such as weather conditions, injuries, referees, judges, fate, or even pure LUCK. Athletes are taught that they hold the keys to their own success (or failure). If sports performers feel little or no CONTROL over competitive outcomes, they may veer toward learned helpless—and probable withdrawal. As if to underline their narrow ego orientation, athletes sometimes describe themselves in the third person, providing a phony objective perspective from which they presumably think they can escape the accusation of conceit. The ego protection/enhancement that is so central to progress in sports is hardly likely to lead to altruism—more likely a narrower, selfish approach that prioritizes personal success to the complete disregard of others.

Sport's capacity to engender character in its participants is not as self-evident as it appears. More likely, sport advocates the kinds of qualities and attributes that are, in many ways, inimical to character, as it is popularly defined. Those who once believed sport would provide a moral education for its participants confused two independent phenomena, as Jay Goldstein and Seppo Iso-Ahola point out: "Moral education has been defined as the 'deliberate and intentional activity of cultivating both moral growth and moral judgment'"; whereas moral training involves conformity to the social norms of a particular group. Maria Kavussanu et al.'s research indicates how conformity to group norms can function to absolve the individual of responsibility for intentions and behavior that would, in other contexts, embarrass or shame the competitor. This is an instance of the moral training Goldstein and Iso-Ahola have in mind.

Kavussanu et al. draw on the earlier research of D. L. Shields and B. J. L. Bredemeier to conclude: "The moral obligation to equally consider others' needs is temporarily suspended in favor of a more egocentric moral engagement, and this moral transformation is viewed as appropriate within the limits of sport."

Further reading

Goldstein Jay D. and Iso-Ahola, Seppo E. (2006). Promoting sportsmanship in youth sports: Perspectives from sport psychology. *Journal of Physical Education, Recreation and Dance*, 77, 18–25.

Harter, Susan (1981). The development of competence motivation in the mastery of cognitive and physical skills: Is there still a place for joy? In G. C. Roberts and D. M. Landers (Eds.) *Psychology of motor behavior and sport—1980* (pp. 3–29). Champaign, Ill.: Human Kinetics.

Jones, Carwyn (2005). Character, virtue and physical education. *European Physical Education Review,* 11, 139–51.

Kavussanu, Maria, Seal, Alistair R., and Phillips, Daniel R. (2006). Observed prosocial and antisocial behaviors in male soccer teams: Age differences across adolescence and the role of motivational variables. *Journal of Applied Sport Psychology*, 18, 326–44.

Morgan, William (1994). *Leftist theories of sport.* Urbana, Ill.: University of Illinois Press.

Shields, D. L. and Bredemeier, B. J. L. (1995). *Character development and physical activity.* Champaign, Ill.: Human Kinetics.

See also: ATTRIBUTION; COACH–ATHLETE RELATIONSHIP; COHESION; COMMITMENT; DEVIANCE; DOPING; EGOCENTRISM; LEADERSHIP; LEARNED HELPLESSNESS; LUCK; MENTAL TOUGHNESS; MORAL ATMOSPHERE; RISK; SELF-EFFICACY; SELF-ESTEEM; SELF-HANDICAPPING; SELF-SERVING BIAS

CHOKE

A choke is a sudden occurrence of severe ANXIETY at a critical stage of a COMPETITION. It is typically experienced by a performer who is approaching victory but becomes tense and apprehensive at the prospect and loses form. The term is, of course, taken from the original sense of the word "choke," which describes temporary or permanent suffocation, loss of breathing, or even paralysis due to a blockage of the throat. In sports terms, the choke is rarely temporary. The competitor suffers an acute attack and seldom has the chance to recover COMPOSURE before his or her rival capitalizes.

Individual and collective. "Suboptimal performance under pressure conditions," is how Roy Baumeister and Carolin Showers defined choking. Historically, the canonical event that became known as the Choke involved Jana Novotna, who led Steffi Graf 4–1 in games and

40–0 with serve in the third set of the 1993 Wimbledon singles final. Novotna, who had looked confidently in control of the game, crumbled and lost. A technically able player, Novotna choked again, this time in the French Open when leading 5–0 and 40–30 with serve against Chanda Rubin, in 1995. Her opponent survived nine match points.

This was an individual choke, though Baumeister and Showers argue: "To say that a team 'choked' in a championship series of games is to say that pressure interfered with their performance on many single occasions." Again, there is a canonical case when pressure interfered with a whole team's performance, in this instance during a critical NFL 1992 play-off game. Houston Oilers ran up what seemed an unassailable 32-point third quarter lead against the Buffalo Bills, suffered a series of decrements in performance and lost 41–38. The decrements alone were not enough to constitute a choke. As Jin Wang et al. warn, "performance decrements and choking are not always synonymous." There has to be the PERCEPTION of threat (in this case, the Bills' unexpected and sudden improvement).

As a specific form of anxiety that happens only at critical junctures of a competition, choking has unique features that are not shared with many other types of sports anxiety. For example, the choke may occur whenever athletes encounter a situation that seems beyond their CONTROL: an unfamiliar circumstance that has not been organized and integrated into their view of themselves. Novotna eventually assimilated the concept of her being a Grand Slam winner and, later, became a Wimbledon champion. Underdogs, especially inexperienced underdogs, frequently maneuver themselves into winning situations but eventually lose because they had not seriously entertained the CONCEPT of upsetting the odds. In other words, they did not really believe they could win.

Processes. What happens during a choke? When winning becomes an active possibility, AROUSAL levels may increase to the point where physiological functions interfere with performance. All athletes are told to guard against thinking too far ahead as this detracts from FOCUSING; but, with victory in sight, there may be a tendency to imagine the prospect of a victory. This thought in itself may prompt an increase in, for instance, metabolic rate and respiratory volume, a constriction of blood vessels and perhaps an abundant perspiration. Once these exceed optimum levels for athletic performance, they can lead to sharp decrements. As form deteriorates, the RELAXATION that would allow them to return to optimum becomes difficult, if not impossible to attain.

Sian Beilock and Thomas Carr's research found that individuals who used large capacities of working MEMORY were susceptible to pressure. Attending to the pressure had the effect of using up the memory capacity they relied on for their performance. The irony of their research findings is "that the individuals most likely to fail under pressure are those who, in the absence of pressure, have the highest capacity for success."

Contexts. There are also contextual factors to consider. Using archival baseball data, A. W. Heaton and H. Sigall, analyzed the "fear of failing" as a factor in "performance decrements under pressure." Interestingly, the study undermines the purported value of a HOME ADVANTAGE because the fear of failing is experienced more severely in front of a supportive home audience. The research concluded that home teams' frequency of fielding errors increased, contributed to their inability to maintain leads in decisive situations. The research was supplemented by Harry Wallace et al., who concluded that "people are more prone to choking when they must cope with high audience expectations."

"Are we our own worst enemies?" asked L. M. Leith in the subtitle of his 1988 research article which concluded that just talking about the possibility of choking before a COMPETITION may contribute to the probability of its happening. Research conducted with a basketball team revealed that talking about the choke works as an independent variable, the dependent variable in this study being free throws: Groups that did not discuss choking performed significantly better than groups that did.

Complicating the issue is the fact that choking is evident in some sports, yet not others. Tennis is a game that has to be won: leads cannot simply be protected. In other sports, they can: a boxer might begin to choke two-thirds of the way through a fight and still emerge a winner by decision, despite having lost the final four rounds. An entire basketball team can choke in the fourth quarter and see its points lead shrink but not disappear. The point is that only in certain sports does choking lead almost certainly to defeat. Golfers sensing victory, for instance, often report a spell of the YIPS when they become uncharacteristically tentative and inaccurate as their form deserts them. They may complete their final hole gracelessly but have enough of a lead to secure success.

Wang et al. argue that choking may be associated with inappropriate COPING STRATEGIES under pressure: "Approach coping strategies are likely to result in performers shifting their FOCUS from performance demands to problem solving and resolution" (APPROACH coping directs efforts toward reducing the threat, as opposed to *avoidance coping*, which directs activities away). Paradoxically, the additional efforts to execute well-learned skills that are ordinarily automatic, results in a further deterioration of form. In complete contrast, so-called "clutch" players actually become more focused and raise their performance to unprecedented levels when faced with daunting situations, though it is at least possible that they do not perceive the threat and hence do not feel pressure.

Further reading

Baumeister, R. F. and Showers, C. J. (1986). A review of paradoxical per-formance effects: Choking under pressure in sports and mental tests. *European Journal of Social Psychology*, 16, 361–83.

Beilock, Sian L. and Carr, Thomas H. (2001). On the fragility of skilled performance: What governs choking under pressure? *Journal of Experimental Psychology: General*, 130, 701–25.

Beilock, Sian L. and Carr, Thomas H. (2005). When high-powered people fail: Working memory and "choking under pressure" in math. *Psychological Science*, 16, 101–5.

Heaton, A. W. and Sigall, H. (1989). The "championship choke" revisited: The role of fear of acquiring a negative identity. *Journal of Applied Social Psychology*, 19, 1019–33.

Leith, L. M. (1988). Choking in sports: Are we our own worst enemies? *International Journal of Sport Psychology*, 19, 59–64.

Wallace, Harry M., Baumeister, Roy F., and Vohs, Kathleen D. (2005). Audience support and choking under pressure: A home disadvantage? *Journal of Sports Sciences*, 23, 429–38.

Wang, Jin, Marchant, Daryl, and Morris, Tony (2004). Coping style and susceptibility to choking. *Journal of Sport Behavior*, 27, 75–93.

See also: ANXIETY; AUTOMATICITY; COMPOSURE; CONTEXT; COPING STRATEGIES; EXECUTIVE CONTROL; HOME ADVANTAGE; NEGATIVITY; PARALYSIS BY ANALYSIS; RESPONSE; SELF-FULFILLING PROPHECY; SOCIAL FACILITATION; STEREOTYPE THREAT; YIPS

COACH–ATHLETE RELATIONSHIP

The word for a trainer or instructor is a figurative use of the noun popularly used to describe a vehicle used for transportation (the root of the word "coach" is *Kocs* a town in Hungary where they used to make wagons).

Similarly, the coach or fitness trainer is responsible for transferring trainees, clients, protégés or team members from one place to another destination, that being performance success, or some other defined

GOAL. As such, the process of coaching in any field of endeavor involves leading, making decisions, managing (or controlling) change and communicating.

David Peterson and Jennifer Millier write of "the alchemy of coaching" which involves: strategies to get to the desired destination; MOTIVATION, engagement and guidance; team building by the empowerment and enablement of individuals; accountability; and the assessment of results. "Alchemy" is an apt term as it originally described attempts to convert base metals into gold and nowadays refers to combining different elements to achieve a result.

Sophia Jowett and Artur Poczwardowski analyze coaches' relationships with athletes or clients in terms of their *effectiveness/ineffectiveness* and their being *successful/unsuccessful*. Ideally, a coach's RELATIONSHIP should be both effective and successful, the trainee maturing and improving his or her skills as well as achieving success. Should the coach promote personal growth and maturity but without tangible success, the relationship is characterized as effective but unsuccessful. Some coaches have uneasy, perhaps conflictual, relationships with their protégés; if the relationship is productive in terms of achieved goals, then this is ineffective yet successful. A relationship that fails both in terms of stated goals and interpersonal development is ineffective and unsuccessful.

While Jowett and Poczwardowski's research reveals, "Athletic success should not be a measure of harmonious, stable, and satisfying relationships," the CONTEXT in which the coach operates makes a significant impact. For example, a coach working with a mature, well-paid player who moves to his club from another for a cash INCENTIVE will be less concerned with effectiveness and more concerned with success. By contrast, a coach charged with the responsibility of developing a promising but untutored eleven-year-old gymnast might see success as contingent on effectiveness—if the young gymnast finds the relationship unrewarding or awkward, she might leave the coach completely.

In the latter case, the qualities of *closeness* (trust, liking) or *connectedness* (affinity) are important. A coach's amiable, approachable style might attract a similarly friendly and pleasant trainee, suggesting RECIPROCITY. On the other hand, a coach's authoritarian style might attract a trainee who is accommodating and compliant. Either way, there is a complementarity, though research by Geneviève Mageau and Robert Vallerand suggests the authoritarian, "controlling interpersonal style" is self-defeating and coaches have their most profound "impact on athletes' perceptions of autonomy, competence and relatedness [feelings of belonging to a group]." They suggest that the "autonomy-supportive style," in which coaches supply opportunities for choice, explain reasons and acknowledge feelings, is most beneficially influential in motivating a protégé *and* improving performance (that is, effective and successful).

Complicating this is the possibility that coaches who experience ineffective relationships with some members of a team might engender tolerance if success is achieved. In their study of cross country runners' interactions with their coaches, Pamela Smith and Jennifer Ogle found that runners prioritized unity over athletic performance, but "unity also was perceived by team members as a driving force that could create stronger team performances." Conversely, disunity was believed to impede success. Some individuals were not close or did not connect with the coach, but were prepared to subordinate their personal relationship to that of the group on the presumption that this was a "driving force" behind success.

The study reported "deferential AVOIDANCE" from athletes when they wanted to sidestep subjects they found painful or embarrassing when talking to coaches. Avoiding possible confrontations with the coach preserved team relationships and unity. Coaches too exercised deferential avoidance, suggesting that closeness was not valued invariantly. This provided coaches with the space from which to censure or, at times, condemn their protégés.

Perhaps the most interesting finding of this research was that the head coach, while "revered" as both "accomplished and influential," had misunderstandings about both the runners and "the broader sociocultural pressures that they faced" which led him to communicate "potentially dangerous and negative messages" to his athletes (for example, he expressed a preference for thin athletes and alluded to a relationship between thinness and sporting performance).

While coaches and trainers and their methods are often appraised in terms of their strengths or weaknesses, excellence or incompetence, insight or ignorance, research suggests that there are few stable qualities possessed by coaches that are effective and successful across all situations. Much more influential are the relationships the coach establishes with athletes and the context in which such relationships develop.

Further reading

Jowett, Sophia and Poczwardowski, Artur (2007). Understanding the coach–athlete relationship. In Sophia Jowett and David Lavallee (Eds.) *Social psychology in sport* (pp. 3–14). Champaign, Ill.: Human Kinetics.

Mageau, Geneviève and Vallerand, Robert J. (2003). The coach–athlete relationship: A motivational model. *Journal of Sports Sciences*, 21, 883–904.

Peterson, David B. and Millier, Jennifer (2005). The alchemy of coaching: "You're good, Jennifer, but you could be *really* good." *Consulting Psychology Journal: Practice and Research*, 57, 14–40.

Smith, Pamela M. and Ogle, Jennifer Paff (2006). Interactions among high school cross-country runners and coaches: Creating a cultural context for athletes' embodied experiences. *Family and Consumer Sciences Research Journal*, 34, 276–307.

See also: COHESION; CONTEXT; LEADERSHIP; PEER LEADERSHIP; RELATIONSHIP; ROLE MODEL; SOCIALIZATION; TEAM PLAYER; TRANSACTIONAL LEADERSHIP; TRANSFORMATIONAL LEADERSHIP; VICARIOUS AGENCY

COGNITION

The faculty for, or action of knowing is cognition, a term formed from the prefix *co*, meaning with other subjects or jointly, and *gnoscere gnit*, the Latin for attend, or apprehend. Cognition includes conceiving, perceiving and reasoning, as well as planning, remembering and DECISION-MAKING; it also embraces processes of an abstract CHARACTER, such as anticipation, problem-solving, complex rule use, and the construction of images and symbols. In sum, cognition defines the way humans use, process, and manage information to make sense of the world.

Cognition is a uniquely human capacity. For example, while a horses or dogs running around a track may behaviorally resemble human athletes, the horses run out of a combination of INSTINCT, training, and command, while humans are aware—they have cognition of objectives, tactics, anticipated outcomes, and an entire range of knowledge that contributes to the athletic performance. The CONCEPT of triumph is unknown to a horse, which simply runs without comprehension of rules or any concept of the meaning of a race.

Cognitive psychology, as its name suggests, focuses on how knowledge processing is organized and how it functions. It provides an alternative to psychological approaches, which explain human conduct in terms of STIMULUS input and behavioral output. By accentuating cognition, this branch of study explores how knowledge, both general and situational, is put to use in practical encounters. Underlying this is an assumption. As Karen Lee Hill puts it, "the cognitive model views the individual as an active participant in creating reality through information processing."

Hill's chapter "The Cognitive Model" is a serviceable introduction to cognition's role in sport psychology. Hill begins by outlining the difference between bottom-up and top-down INFORMATION PROCESSING. From the moment we are born, we are involved in gathering, storing, sorting, and assigning importance to data from the outside world. The data that we take in by way of the peripheral NERVOUS SYSTEM (the senses) and the central nervous system (spinal cord and brain) is processed by way of the bottom-up route. Top-down processing, by contrast, starts with us: we organize and relate pieces of data together, shaping knowledge that we can then use to guide future actions. This is how we make sense of the data and the world from which it came.

The patterns of processing are HEURISTICS: these are essentially quick-fire methods for finding elements of data, or for solving problems—techniques that enable reducing a huge range of possibilities to a managable number of probabilities. Heuristics may be provisional formulations that allow for testing, evaluation, and improvement of ideas or theories. They enable us to process information quickly and with less effort as we mature. As such, they are important in the SKILL PERFORMANCE when rapid assessments of situations and the selection of appropriate responses are critical.

Thoughts that are processed regularly are arranged into packets of three kinds, all of which have bearing on sports. Recent, accessible thought is *voluntary* and amenable to change, while *automatic* thought is more entrenched, though not as deeply entrenched as SCHEMA, which is the architecture of knowledge, beliefs, and expectations relating to a particular subject. It enables us to integrate new data into an existing structure of thoughts. The cognitive schema is what provides us with a sense of stability with relatively fixed conceptions of the world and our SELF. Yet, this does not suggest that cognitive content is completely unalterable: quite the opposite—thinking progresses and existing knowledge is open to challenge.

There is an interactive relationship between cognition and sport and exercise. Cognition affects every component of sports and exercise preparation and performance: the knowledge we have and how we use it guide conduct in and out of the competitive arena. Conversely, exercise has a positive impact on cognitive performance in both adults and children.

Often, athletes have performance-related problems that have no rational basis. Hill gives the example of choking when athletes are unable to perform to their maximum when the stakes are high. The CHOKE approaches as an athlete's confidence drains and apprehension not so much creeps, but rushes in, precipitating ANXIETY. The source of the problem lies in the athlete's cognition, how he or she sees and thinks about the predicament. According to Hill, this could be connected to the athlete's SCHEMA, which is difficult though not impossible to change.

Substandard athletic performance is a consequence of cognitive processes and can be addressed by examining those processes rather than the performance. Scott Cresswell and Robert Eklund's research with rugby players explored how players themselves experienced both the causes and consequences of playing: how they interpreted the heavy training, reacted to the perceived pressure to perform, understood the need to promote a positive image to the media and perceived the sometimes irreconcilable demands of professional sport—in other words, how they acquired their knowledge, thought it through (their cognitions) and responded to it.

The precise effect of exercise and training on cognition is the subject of debate, though research suggests strongly that cognitive performance is enhanced. One of the mechanisms through which the RELATIONSHIP works is cognitive inhibition: the suppression and/or removal of irrelevant information or stimuli from consciousness. This clearing out allows the brain to process information more efficiently, according to Benjamin Sibley and Jennifer Etnier.

Cognition is often contrasted to emotion, *conation*, which is concerned with willful action and *soma,* which relates to the body.

Further reading

Cresswell, Scott L. and Eklund, Robert C. (2006). The nature of player burnout in rugby: Key characteristics and attributions. *Journal of Applied Sport Psychology,* 18, 219–39.

Fiske, S. T. and Taylor, S. E. (1991). *Social cognition.* New York: McGraw-Hill.

Hill, K. L. (2001). *Frameworks for sport psychologists* Champaign, Ill.: Human Kinetics.

Sibley, Benjamin A. and Etnier, Jennifer L. (2005). Effects of an acute bout of exercise on inhibition and cognitive performance. *Research Quarterly for Exercise and Sport,* 76, A102.

See also: ANXIETY; ATTENTION; ATTRIBUTION; COGNITIVE-BEHAVIORAL MODIFICATION; COGNITIVE LOAD THEORY; CONCENTRATION; CONSTRUCT; DECISION-MAKING; EMOTION; HEURISTICS; INFORMATION PROCESSING; MEDITATION; METACOGNITION; NERVOUS SYSTEM; PERCEPTION; SCHEMA; SKILL ACQUISTION; SKILL EXECUTION; VISUAL PERCEPTION

COGNITIVE-BEHAVIORAL MODIFICATION

Combining techniques designed to restructure COGNITION with physical RELAXATION procedures is known as cognitive-behavioral modification, or intervention and sometimes THERAPY, and it is used to modify the manner in which people apprehend, interpret and respond to situations or specific stimuli. This is a technique for breaking down unwanted habits of thought and replacing them with more positive ones: cognitive restructuring.

Cognitive restructuring is intended to use intellectual and perceptual SKILL to alter the way people view situations, or stimuli in the environment. It is based on the premise that stimuli do not automatically imprint themselves on human senses: they are subject to interpretation. Responses to stimuli are the result of interpretations of them rather than the stimuli in themselves. The properties we infer or conjecture rather than the objective properties of the stimuli are crucial to the way we think and act toward them.

The two basic steps in cognitive-behavioral programs are to divide the unwanted thought or behavior into small managable sections and then systematically associate these with more positive, useful thoughts or emotions. The questions posed are, for example: Is this idea or mood rational or helpful? Is it too demanding of instant gratification to be valuable in the long term? Once the NEGATIVITY is recognized, the person links the thought or emotion to more positive states. Constant repetition of a positive association makes it eventually automatic.

For example, someone may be reluctant to return to a gym where she has witnessed a distressing incident (such as a fellow exerciser's collapsing and being administered emergency treatment). She might be reminded that the chances of a recurrence are small and that, at the gym, she enjoys the company of friends, becomes fit, and has other agreeable experiences.

Other examples of cognitive restructuring include COPING, SELF-TALK, and CENTERING, all of which are aimed at changing the athlete's response to stimuli, rather than the stimuli themselves. Like all types of cognitive restructuring, they assist in managing an athlete's interpretation of what might otherwise be perceived as threatening situations.

A related way of solving problems is by visualizing a problem, dissecting it into chunks, and then using our visuo-spatial capacities to put them all on paper in words or pictures. Then the person links them together in some ordered way, so that a pattern becomes evident. Individually, the problems may appear too many and large to solve, but by visualizing them as an entirety, novel solutions might arise.

Allying such restructuring with interventions to stabilize physiological AROUSAL may involve the use of REINFORCEMENT, applying the techniques of operant conditioning to reduce or eliminate problematic behavior or to encourage new behavior. While the approaches seem theoretically incompatible, in practice, they are less unsuited. Desired behavior is rewarded and unwelcome behavior punished. The basic principle encourages preferred responses to pertinent stimuli and, once the consequences are observed, a change in cognition may follow. Conversely, cognitive restructuring may be first: John Silva's study of a hockey player who retaliated against opponents as a way of regaining SELF-EFFICACY when dispossessed of the puck was persuaded that this was ineffective. He modified his behavior and witnessed a corresponding and, ultimately, reinforcing improvement in form.

MODELING is another related strategy, inviting subjects to imagine they are someone else or to behave as they believe another would behave in a particular type of situation. Breaking the association between an EMOTION and the presence of a certain STIMULUS can modify emotional behavior. For instance, a basketball player might freeze with ANXIETY when approaching free shots, or a soccer player may FEAR taking penalties. Separating the emotion from the stimuli is known as *desensitization*. Other behavioral techniques rely less on reinforcement and include relaxation training and skill rehearsal, though the upshot is similar—to instigate actual behavioral change to precede, or follow and complement cognitive restructuring.

Further reading

Cornelius, A. (2002). Introduction of sport psychology interventions. In J. M. Silva and D. E. Stevens (Eds.), *Psychological foundations of sport* (pp. 177–96). Boston, Mass.: Allyn & Bacon.

Silva, J. M (1982). Competitive sport environments: Performance enhancement though cognitive intervention. *Behavior Modification*, 6, 443–63.

See also: ALCOHOLISM; ANGER; APPLIED SPORT PSYCHOLOGY; CONTROL; COPING STRATEGIES; INTERVENTION; PSYCHOLOGICAL SKILLS TRAINING; RELATIONSHIP; STRESS-MANAGEMENT TRAINING; THERAPY

COGNITIVE EVALUATION THEORY

An account of motivation based on the premise that initial approaches to a task or a course of action involve an appraisal of its value and whether the subject believes he or she is capable of performing it successfully. The theory suggests that, if individuals believe the task lies within their capabilities, they will be intrinsically motivated to engage in the activity. But, if extrinsic rewards are offered, then the intrinsic MOTIVATION will decrease, even if they conclude the task falls within their sphere of competence.

For instance, a gym regular who enjoys regular workouts (INTRIN-SIC MOTIVATION) might be co-opted into a gym challenge, the prize for which is a week's vacation in the Caribbean. The workouts then become training sessions and, as the exerciser's cognitive evaluation of them changes, so does the motivational balance. Attendance at the gym then becomes more obligatory and the INCENTIVE of the vaca-tion (EXTRINSIC MOTIVATION) exerts a controlling influence.

It has been described by Edward Deci and Richard Ryan as a "subtheory" within SELF-DETERMINATION THEORY that has the aim of specifying factors that explain variability in intrinsic motivation, that is, attempting to identify conditions under which intrinsic motivation is facilitated or undermined. The introduction of extrinsic rewards, or incentives, can undermine intrinsic motivation by shifting the LOCUS OF CONTROL. In other words, a human senses a loss of choice and an encroaching CONTROL on behavior.

Further reading

Deci, E. L. and Ryan, R. M. (1991). A motivational approach to self: Inte-gration in personality. In R. Diestiber (Ed.), *Nebraska symposium on motiva-tion*, volume 38 (pp. 37–288). Lincoln, Nebr.: University of Nebraska Press.

See also: COGNITION; EXERCISE IDENTITY; EXPECTANCY; EXTRINSIC MOTIVATION; INCENTIVE; INTRINSIC MOTIVATION; LOCUS OF CONTROL; MOTIVATION; SELF-DETERMINATION THEORY; THEORY

COGNITIVE LOAD THEORY (CLT)

According to this theory of learning and SKILL ACQUISITION, the architecture of COGNITION consists of (1) a general purpose working MEMORY that has a limit capacity of only about seven chunks of information when holding information and just two or three when processing information; (2) a long-term memory that has a virtually unlimited capacity and holds information stored in schemas. Schemas reduce working memory load: once they have been acquired and automated, they can be handled in the working memory with little or no conscious effort.

A single SCHEMA can contain vast amounts of information, freeing up enough cognitive room to solve problems and perform complex tasks. But, unless schemas are created, chunks of information have to be kept in the working memory as separate items, possibly leading to a high demand on the working memory capacity. In other words, information is stored by way of encapsulation.

Actual experience in a domain, whether throwing a dart, playing a musical instrument, typing, or playing chess, is less relevant for acquiring a skilled performance than DELIBERATE PRACTICE: activities initially designed by a coach or instructor and set at a challenging level of difficulty to enable successive refinements.

In contrast to many other theories of SKILL acquisition, cognitive load theory (CLT) holds that important aspects of expert performance are not fully automated and the performer retains CONTROL over them, operating high levels of conscious monitoring. One of the implications of the theory is that the COACH–ATHLETE RELATIONSHIP is not one of dependence and that athletes design and monitor their own training activities. Another is that the (eventually self-guided) deliberate practice that underlies the acquisition of expertise is not intended to be enjoyable: it is repetitious and highly demanding. As the learner's knowledge base changes, schemas are reconfigured and greater CONCENTRATION and effort are needed to reach higher performance measures.

Further reading

van Gog, Tamara, Ericsson, K. Anders, Rikers, Remy M. J. P., and Paas, Fred (2005). Instructional design for advanced learners: Establishing connections between the theoretical frameworks of cognitive load and deliberate practice. *Educational Technology, Research and Development*, 53, 73–81.

Starkes, J. and Ericsson, K. A. (Eds.) (2003). *Expert performance in sport: Recent advances in research on sport expertise*. Champaign, Ill.: Human Kinetics.

See also: AUTOMATICITY; COACH–ATHLETE RELATIONSHIP; CONCENTRATION; CONCEPT; DELIBERATE PRACTICE; DEPRESSION; EXECUTIVE CONTROL; FOCUS; MEMORY; SCHEMA; SKILL; SKILL ACQUISITION; SOCIALIZATION; THEORY.

COGNITIVE–MOTIVATIONAL–RELATIONAL

This describes a conceptual MODEL developed by Richard Lazarus in his analysis of EMOTION and is adapted variously for examining, among other things, how athletes cope with competitive STRESS and whether men cope differently to women. Its premise is that emotions are, in themselves, meaningless; it is the person's specific interpretation of an AROUSAL that elicits an emotion. So, as Martin Hagger and Nikos Chatzisarantis explain, "Arousal is an intrapersonal variable that is likely to give rise to ANXIETY, but not all aroused individuals become anxious" (the prefix *intra* means within, or inside).

In this model, anxiety is a cognitive evaluation that includes: (1) primary appraisal, which is an initial assessment of the effect of a situation on one's well-being; there are four types—benefit, challenge, threat, and harm/loss; (2) secondary appraisal, which determines what the person should do to handle the perceived situation; (3) coping, which is the effort to manage, CONTROL, and balance the often competing demands that are taxing the person. Coping can be either emotion-focused or problem-focused, the latter is more appropriate in situations in which, for example, athletes have a measure of control over the sources of the perceived threat—that is, they can do something about it.

This indicates that emotions do not just exist but are subject to human appraisal and that athletes should be encouraged to make interpretations which are likely to render the emotions elicited by any event managable. Using the cognitive–motivational–relations approach to uncover whether men and women evaluate differently, Jon Hammermeister and Damon Burton discovered that "male and female endurance athletes tend to appraise competitive stress in similar ways, yet their preferences for coping exhibited many differences."

Further reading

Hagger, Martin and Chatzisarantis, Nikos (2005). *The social psychology of exercise and sport.* Maidenhead: Open University Press.

Hammermeister, Jon and Burton, Damon (2004). Gender differences in coping with endurance sport stress: Are men from Mars and women from Venus? *Journal of Sport Behavior,* 27, 148–65.

Lazarus, R. S. (1991). *Emotion and adaptation* New York: Oxford University Press.

Lazarus, R. S. (1993). From psychological stress to the emotions: A history of changing outlooks. *Annual Review of Psychology,* 44, 1–21.

See also: ANGER; ANXIETY; AROUSAL; ATTRIBUTION; COGNITION; COGNITIVE EVALUATION THEORY; COPING STRATEGIES; EMOTION; EMOTIONAL INTELLIGENCE; FEAR OF FAILURE; GENDER; PERCEPTION; RELATIONAL; STRESS

COHESION

When a team, squad or a roster of players has cohesion, or cohesiveness, its members are united in a common purpose. If they tend to stick together outside sport because similar tastes and interests attract them to each other, there may be total harmony, or *social cohesion*. But, even if the members do not like each other, they may join in the pursuit of shared goals and produce *task cohesion*. The two forms of cohesion operate independently of each other and, while social cohesion may be desirable, it is by no means as critical to success as task cohesion. The word is a compound of the prefix *co*, for jointly or mutually, and the Latin *haerere* meaning stick.

Cohesion is something of a Holy Grail for coaches and team managers. It is hard-to-find but almost magical in its effects, transforming an aggregation of individuals into a collective unit. Teams comprising outstanding individual athletes often underachieve, while teams of modest players exceed all expectations. The difference is that the latter is usually cohesive: its members selflessly work toward the aims of the team rather than their own personal ambitions. They might engage in what Harry Prapavessis and Albert Carron call "sacrifice behavior," giving up prerogative or privilege for the sake of another person. Prapavessis and Carron's research concluded that "individual sacrifice and teammates' sacrifice contribute to group cohesion."

It is possible to have both star players *and* cohesion. The Chicago Bulls team that won six NBA titles, 1991–3 and 1996–8, was full of stars, some of them—like Dennis Rodman—supreme individualists. Becoming a TEAM PLAYER did not mean losing one's individuality or suppressing one's personality. Coach Phil Jackson convinced his players that only within the framework of the team could their talents fully blossom. Jackson believed in what he called "the power of oneness instead of the power of one man." Jackson's accomplishment was in "making players connect with something larger than themselves."

Like Jackson, every coach strives to produce a *sui generis* entity, something that has unique properties over and above that of individual competitors. To do so requires subordinating the interests of individuals to that of the team. Even when this is achieved, cohesion can disappear quite suddenly. The reason for this is, as Carron pointed out, "[Cohesion is] a dynamic process, which is reflected in the tendency for a group to stick together and remain united in the pursuit of its goals and objectives." As a *process*, it cannot be presumed simply to be *there*; it has to be initiated and sustained. The question is, how?

Carron offered some answers in his 1982 article "Cohesiveness in Sport Groups: Interpretations and Considerations" in which he wrote of "determinants of team cohesion." *Situational factors*, such as living near each other, or rooming together on road trips, assist bonding, according to Carron. So does distinctiveness from other groups, dressing in a particular uniform or possessing a unique ritual contributes toward cohesion. The New Zealand rugby team's pregame *haka* ritual would be a fine example of this. *Personal* factors such as COMMITMENT and satisfaction also play a part, as do *leadership* factors: democratic styles of LEADERSHIP working more effectively than autocratic approaches. Carron also cited *team* factors, such as the clarity with which each member of the team understands his or her role and the manner in which he or she accepts it. Success in COMPETITION predictably increases cohesion. Carron later discovered that cohesion decreases as group size increases; so it would be harder to keep a football team cohesive than it would a volleyball team (especially a beach volleyball team).

Various scholars have emphasized the importance of developing unspoken standards or codes that are accepted by and adhered to by all members, a process known as *norming*. Members who challenge the norms challenge the cohesion of the whole group; so, methods must be found to exact conformity, but without using coercion or duress. Even if a player does not believe in the norms, he or she should still conform, if only out of a sense of obligation. Norms may relate to performance—for example, observing curfews and eating habits before a competition.

Sarcasm, teasing, and bragging might not appear to be of importance to team cohesion, but Paul Turman's research revealed that coaches used these as "inclusive strategies." For example, making the team laugh together allowed athletes to begin to develop interpersonal relationships with each other and the coach, and these eventually had a "dramatic" impact on the team.

Successful cohesive teams are likely to comprise players high on SELF-CONFIDENCE who do not blame themselves when their team loses and share in the credit following victory. Players who engage in behaviors that sabotage their own ABILITY to function provide a convenient ready-made excuse for failure ("I felt the flu coming on before the game"; "I never play well in cold weather"), but accept personal credit for success. This behavior is known as SELF-HANDICAPPING. Studies show that high levels of self-handicapping are associated with low task cohesion and low self-handicapping is related to high social cohesion. The problem is that, while a self-handicapper might fit into a task–cohesive team quite well, the expectations of the team may be quite moderate.

While it seems obvious that a task-cohesive team will be more effective, the effects of social cohesion on team performance are not clear. "For years coaches have assumed that positive feelings among team members result in better sport performance," writes Mark Anshel. "While this outcome is intuitively appealing, researchers aren't certain that it is true." He cites the example of teammates passing only to friends. We might add that historically high-achieving teams, such as the New York Yankees of the late 1970s or Manchester United of the 1990s had several players who refused to speak to each other. Despite the lack of social cohesion, both teams had sufficient task cohesion for success.

Further reading

Anshel, M. H. (1997). *Sport psychology: From theory to practice*, 3rd edn, Scottsdale, Ariz.: Gorsuch Scarisbrick.

Carron, A. V. (1982). Cohesiveness in sport groups: Interpretations and considerations. *Journal of Sport Psychology*, 4, 123–38.

Carron, A. V. and Dennis, P. W. (1998). The sport team as an effective group. In J. M. Williams (Ed.), *Applied sport psychology: Personal growth to peak performance* 3rd edn (pp. 127–41). Mountain View, Calif.: Mayfield.

Lazenby, R. (2000). *Mind games: Phil Jackson's long, strange journey*. New York: McGraw-Hill.

Prapavessis, Harry and Carron, Albert V. (1997). Sacrifice, cohesion and conformity to norms in sport teams. *Group Dynamics, Theory, Research, and Practice*, 1, 231–40.

Turman, Paul D. (2003). Coaches and cohesion: The impact of coaching techniques on team cohesion in the small group sport setting. *Journal of Sport Behavior*, 26, 86–104.

See also: COACH–ATHLETE RELATIONSHIP; CONTEXT; DECISION-MAKING; EQUALITY; GROUP DYNAMICS; LEADERSHIP; MENTALITY; MORAL ATMOSPHERE; OUTPERFORMANCE; RELATIONAL; RELATIONSHIP; RIVALRY; SELF-HANDICAPPING; SOCIAL FACILITATION; TEAM PLAYER; THEORY; TRANSFORMATIONAL LEADERSHIP

COMEBACK

The return of a once-retired athlete aiming to recapture his or her former position and status is, of course, a comeback. Recovery from long periods of incapacity caused by illness or INJURY sometimes warrants the term "comeback," though it is usually reserved for the resumption of a sports career that was considered over. Comebacks are legion in sports and, while the aphorism "they never come back" suggests that AGING competitors' attempts inevitably conclude in failure, several comebacks have been conspicuously successful.

Historical cases. Mario Lemieux came out of RETIREMENT in 2000 and, at the age of thirty-five, resumed his garlanded career with Pittsburgh Penguins and played hockey with same kind of brilliance as he had in the first phase of his career. George Foreman returned to the ring in the 1990s after a ten-year break at the age of forty-five and enjoyed considerable success until retiring for good at forty-nine. By contrast, Björn Borg dropped out of tennis at twenty-six, when still a top-five ranked player, only to come back ten years later. He suffered a series of ignominious defeats by modest players. George Best also retired in his twenties; this was the first of several "retirements," each followed by a comeback; the progressive decay of his once-formidable SKILL was evident in his every return to the soccer field. When he left soccer entirely, his progressive DEPENDENCE on alcohol contributed to his eventual death in 2005.

Clearly, every athlete takes risks when deciding to come back; the more prestigious the athlete, the greater the RISK. For them, the possibility of a humbling is accentuated: witness the embarrassment suffered by multiple gold medalist Mark Spitz, his gray hair colored to conceal his age but his physical decline painfully revealed in a sequence of defeats in the pool. Spitz won seven gold medals at the 1972 Munich Olympics and worked as a television analyst at the 1984 Los Angeles Olympics. The experience of watching others compete frustrated him so much that he made his unfortunate comeback several years later.

Motivations. The MOTIVATION behind some comebacks may be obvious. Borg, for example, had become involved in disastrous business ventures and needed money. Best too was lured by the temptation of riches. Most retirees need to work and are poorly prepared to do so, having spent fifteen or so years in competitive sports. Lacking preparation for any occupation outside sports, many return simply to make a living. But, in the case of successful athletes who clearly have wealth enough to sustain them through several lifetimes, the motivation is less certain.

Journalist Blake Morrison suggested an interesting possibility in speculating on the much-discussed comeback of Michael Jordan: "The obvious explanation is that he misses the buzz, the adrenalin and applause [. . .] when a man's celebrity is based on something he no longer does, he can feel very strange about it—exiled from himself." Jordan was thirty-eight at the time of the conjecture about his return, older than most athletes who stage a comeback. Morrison argued that many men (he did not mention women) venture toward some way of "confirming and vindicating" themselves as they approach forty. Harley Davidson motorcycles have a large market comprising males of that age group.

The *midlife crisis* supposedly accounts for many fortyish men embarking on unexpected and often dangerous pursuits, presumably as a way of endorsing their credentials as active and dynamic agents rather than listless, middle-aged residues of people whose vitality and youth have long gone. For athletes, the predicament is arguably more acute. For a substantial part of their maturity they are engaged in pursuits that demand vitality and youth, as well as many other physical attributes. Their sense of SELF as well as their public persona is based not so much on wisdom, sagacity, insight, or soundness of judgment, but on performance. When they are no longer able to perform to appropriate levels, managers, coaches, critical FANS, and the media rudely remind them of this. There is no room for self-delusion in sports. Retirement may be the result of conscious decision, but that decision is usually affected by the judgment of others, or, in some cases, serious injuries. Once the echoes of others' criticisms have faded and the injuries have healed, fresh perspectives appear and the athlete may sense the chance of proving him- or herself all over again.

Ray Leonard's comeback seems to fit into this model. Regarded as a suitable inheritor of Sugar Ray Robinson's mantle, Leonard led a triumphant amateur and professional career, establishing himself as one of finest pound-for-pound boxers in history. A detached retina forced him out of the sport. Surgery repaired the injury, and Leonard plotted an outrageous comeback, moving up a weight class to middleweight to challenge—and beat—Marvelous Marvin Hagler (who promptly retired himself and refused several lucrative offers to come back). Leonard's critics were silenced as he regaining his finest form, making several successful defenses, at one point stepping up a further weight class. The present writer interviewed Leonard at his camp while he prepared for what was to be his final fight (a defeat to Terry Norris) and sought the sources of Leonard's attachment with his sport. "This is the only place I feel who I really am," said Leonard. (Leonard actually made two comebacks, the first—before the Hagler fight—lasting only one fight.)

Sport was the context for establishing Leonard's SELF-EFFICACY, for validating himself, both through public approval and intrinsic gratification:

He had an ATHLETIC IDENTITY. Deprived of his ability to fight, Leonard believed he could no longer be who he truly was. Like Lemieux, Foreman, and several other athletes who came back after long, prosperous careers (Leonard had already earned an estimated $30 million when he first "retired'), Leonard returned to sport because he felt *deprived*. Stripped of opportunities to perform to an audience, to demonstrate their worth and to draw acclaim, athletes lose a facility that has been with them for most of their adult lives and which actually forms part of their lives.

Other factors contributing toward the comeback derive from the sports SOCIALIZATION—the learning process through which athletes acquire particular values, ambitions, and designs. Athletes are usually immersed in sports culture by the time they reach eleven; in many sports (such as gymnastics and tennis), competitors are training hard and cultivating ambitions from about the age of six (Chris Evert was one such athlete who did not come back and famously declared "there *is* life after tennis"). By the time any sports performer is thirteen, he or she will have started to formulate plans. As ambitions in sports take priority, so athletes discard other career aims and involve themselves in an environment in which significant influences include coaches, managers, scouts, and, perhaps, agents. These form a type of protective enclosure, shielding the athlete from the travail and irritation that affect most people—like procuring a mortgage, paying bills, investing for the future. Unless the athlete prolongs his or her involvement in sport after retirement (as a manager, or television commentator, for instance), he or she is likely to lose the enclosure and become part of a different environment. Coming back may be a way of re-entering what was once a comfortable environment.

Those who populate the enclosure continually dispense advice, and one of the first caveats a prospective athlete hears is that a career in sport is relatively short. As Billie-Jean King once said: "When athletes reach their thirties [. . .] everybody keeps telling them they should quit. They start to think they are slowing down because everybody asks, 'Are you slowing down?'" (King made a money-motivated comeback at forty and made it to the Wimbledon singles semi-finals). In other words, athletes often retire prematurely because of mere convention, and, when they sense that other, perhaps older athletes have resumed their careers, they are inspired to follow suit. Athletes staging a comeback who APPROACH or even surpass their previous form provide living proof that the comeback trail is not always a dead end.

Competitiveness also comes, or is at least heightened, through socialization in sports and, once an active career is over, challenges

97

disappear. Sometimes, they are replaced by new challenges, but what greater challenge is there than to relaunch a sports career?

Socialized into rising to meet challenges, no matter how awesome, a retired athlete may construe the comeback as the ultimate challenge. This seems to account for the comeback of rower Steve Redgrave, who, in 1996, after winning his fourth Olympic gold, ordered the media: "Shoot me if I go near a boat again." Four years later, he returned to win a fifth gold medal.

Martina Hingis also relished the comeback challenge. "Winning [tournaments] is twice as sweet this time around," she said after her Pan Pacific Open title win in 2007. Between 1997 and 1999, Hingis won five Grand Slam titles, then sustained recurring foot and ankle injuries, which precipitated her retirement at the end of 2002. She came back in 2006, still only twenty-five. "It used to be so normal for me in 1997 and 1998," she remarked of winning. "I never thought I'd have the chance to win tournaments again."

Her motivation resembled that of Matt Biondi, who retired from competitive swimming after the 1988 Olympics, having amassed six gold medals. "I realized that it was ridiculous to give it up because I still enjoyed it" (he won two more golds and a silver in his comeback). Competitive sports are a way of earning a living for professional athletes, but the initial interest in the activity was intrinsic. It is at least possible that, despite the years of arduous training interspersed by injury, the joy of COMPETITION lingers long enough to motivate a comeback.

Further reading

Lainson, S./Sportstrust (1997). Comebacks. *The Creative Athlete*, 18, 1–2. Available online at http://www.onlinesports.com/sportstrust/creative18.html.
Morrison, B. (2001). Jordan, me, and the lure of the comeback. *Independent on Sunday*, Focus section, April 20, p. 15.

See also: AGING; ATHLETIC IDENTITY; CHARACTER; CONTEXT; DEPENDENCE; EXTRINSIC MOTIVATION; IDENTITY; INCENTIVE; INJURY; INTRINSIC MOTIVATION; LIFE COURSE; MOTIVATION; RETIREMENT; REWARD; RISK; SOCIALIZATION

COMMITMENT

Any engagement or involvement that restricts freedom of action is a commitment. The sense in which the term is used in sport and exercise is actually not so different from its other meanings: to deliver someone officially to custody (of, for example, a psychiatric treatment program), or the pledge to obligate oneself to another person; it has been described as the attitudinal component of loyalty. All, in some way, implicate people in a course of action from which there are limited escape routes. The word is a compound from the Latin *com*, for together, and *mittere*, entrust.

Clearly, continuance in sport and exercise requires some level of commitment, whether it is in terms of time dedicated to training or abstinence from other fulfilling endeavors. T. K. Scanlan et al. conceived of a "sport commitment model" and argued that commitment was "a psychological CONSTRUCT representing the desire and resolve to continue sport participation." The inclusion of "desire"—which is not defined, but can be taken to mean a strong, positive feeling for something—suggests that there is an intrinsic element present. As Konstantinos Alexandris et al. write, "Pleasure, fun and excitement have been shown to be important motives for exercise participation," though, in competitive sport, extrinsic factors are likely to feature in the attachment.

E. Guillet et al. argue for a tighter definition of commitment: "This construct must clearly be distinguished from its antecedents and consequences." Antecedents or causal conditions might include enjoyment, liking or even love of an activity, or perhaps the degree to which alternatives are more or less attractive. Its consequences can be actual behavior, like persistence, or perhaps barriers prohibiting the termination of the activity, but the commitment, the "desire and resolve" continue. This might be in adversity. E. Guillet et al. argue that: "Enjoyment has been consistently found to be one of the strongest predictors of commitment," but add that the sources of enjoyment are diverse. In their study of handball players, autonomy was critical to satisfaction. In professional sport, autonomy might be similarly valued, with money the means of gaining it.

The scope of commitment is variable. Exercisers combine other commitments with their workouts; some athletes have a much narrower scope, their training occupying more of their time and energy than other pursuits. While many elite performers prioritize their sports, Mark Thompson argues that, "sport is not and should not be the only avenue in which they [athletes] derive a sense of self-worth." Commitment, in this view, is not the same as *monomania* (an inflexible fixation on one thing) but an adaptable orientation that allows the athlete to pursue task-related objectives—but not to the exclusion of other potentially fulfilling pursuits.

Sports may not be the only avenue from which many athletes can "derive a sense of self-worth," but, for the minority who succeed consistently at the highest possible levels, it seems to be precisely that. Commitment is a variable concept: Its meaning for those seeking pleasure, SELF-EFFICACY, and, perhaps, some measure of SELF-CONFIDENCE, is more flexible than for those driven by an ACHIEVEMENT MOTIVE and for whom alternatives are not readily available.

Further reading

Alexandris, Konstantinos, Zahariadis, P., Sorbatzoudis, C. T., and Grouios, George (2002). Testing the sport commitment model in the context of exercise and fitness participation. *Journal of Sport Behavior,* 25, 217–30.

Guillet, E., Sarrazin, P., Carpenter, P. J., Trouilloud, D., and Cury, F. (2002). Predicting persistence or withdrawal in female handballers with social exchange theory. *International Journal of Psychology,* 37, 92–104.

Scanlan, T. K., Simons, J. P., Carpenter, P. J., Schmidt, G. W., and Keeler, B. (1993). The sport commitment model: Measurement development for the youth-sport domain. *Journal of Sport and Exercise Psychology,* 15, 254–65.

Thompson, M. A. (1998). The charge. In M. A. Thompson, R. A. Vernacchia, and W. E. Moore (Eds.), *Case studies in applied sport psychology: An educational approach* (pp. 257–60). Dubuque, Iowa: Kendall/Hunt.

See also: ACHIEVEMENT MOTIVE; ADHERENCE; CONSTRUCT; DELIBERATE PRACTICE; DISCIPLINE; DROPOUTS; GOAL; INTENSITY; INTERNALIZATION; LIFE COURSE; MASTERY; MASTERY CLIMATE; OBEDIENCE; OVERTRAINING SYNDROME; RETIREMENT; SELF-DETERMINATION THEORY

COMPETITION

Although competition invariably suggests a contest against others, the concept's original meaning is wider. From the Latin *com,* meaning for, and *petere,* seek, it defines a search or endeavor for superiority in some quality or qualities, either *with* or against others. The term shares a common source with *competence.*

Competition is, of course, the "essence" of sports, though it carries no necessary connotation of opposition or RIVALRY. This property has been added by cultures that encouraged contest as part of the struggle to demonstrate competence. In 1976, Rainer Martens defined competition as "a process in which comparison of an individual's performance is made with some standard in the presence of at least one other person who is aware of the criterion for comparison and can evaluate the comparison process" (quoted in Gill 2000). The "comparison" is typically understood as a contest.

The question germane to competition is: Does there have to be a necessary bifurcation of winners and loser, victors and vanquished? Karen Lee Hill, in examining the "humanistic model" of sports offers a conception that is close to the original meaning of the term: "Rather than conceptualizing competition as a 'war' with one's adversary, it is looked upon as a cooperative venture in which 'associates' [. . .] agree to provide each other with the necessary resistance to catalyze development of each other's potential."

In other words, opponents in a competition are not trying to eliminate or destroy their opponents but are providing legitimate resistance sufficient that their opponents can develop potential and demonstrate capabilities. There is, of course, only one winner, though both parties profit from the encounter in the sense that they have both exercised SKILL and demonstrated SELF-EFFICACY. This conception of competition seems at odds with commonsense interpretations which STRESS winning as the end point. While this may seem to be the case, competitors are actually helping each other reach individual goals by forcing them to produce their best effort and perhaps improve their performance. Without stern opposition, this may not be possible. The rules of any competition define the conditions under which human excellence may be realized and advanced.

In this conception, final scores, results, standings, and other measures of success are linear and misleading. All parties, winners and losers, are beneficiaries of the competitive experience. Hill's humanistic interpretation of competition contradicts conventional notions of competition, most of which are predicated on "winning is the only thing," or similar slogans. Interestingly, it is compatible with the orientation of many sports performers.

Research by Diane Gill and her associates indicates that highly skilled athletes gauge success not by the outcome of a contest but by their evaluation of their personal performances. Obviously, they strive toward victory in competition, but competitive orientation, defined as "desire to strive for success in competition," is only one element of their overall MOTIVATION: The quality of their own accomplishment is integral to the sports experience.

While competition, as conceived today, involves an interaction between two or more parties in pursuit of the same GOAL and the ultimate failure of one or more or more of the parties to attain it, the term should properly be understood in its original form. Even in contemporary competition, it seems, defeat is not a synonym for failure; it is one of several criteria used to evaluate the competitive experience.

A related term is *competitiveness*, which is a characteristic of some-one or something. A person might have or display a strong desire to be more successful than others. Athletes, almost by definition, possess this, as might those in business or industry. Cultures and markets can be described as competitive too.

Further reading

Gill, D. L. (2000). *Psychological Dynamics of Sport and Exercise*, 2nd edn. Champaign, Ill.: Human Kinetics.

Gill, D. L., Dowd, D. A., Williams, Beaudoin, C. M. and Martin, J. J. (1996). Competitive orientation and motives of adult sport and exercise participants. *Journal of Sport Behavior*, 19, 307–18.

Hill, K. L. (2001). *Frameworks for sport psychologists.* Champaign, Ill.: Human Kinetics.

See also: ACHIEVEMENT MOTIVE; CHARACTER; GOAL ORIENTATION; INTRINSIC MOTIVATION; MASTERY; MOTIVATION; RIVALRY; SELF-CONFIDENCE; SKILL

COMPOSURE

Composure is the quality of calmness possessed by people who can arrange their thoughts, behavior, and even expression, for a specified purpose and refuse to be fazed (disconcerted, perturbed) by activities around them. It derives from the Latin *com*, together, and *ponere*, put, and its meaning in sport and exercise stays true to its origins: a composed athlete or exerciser remains organized and together regardless of changing circumstances.

Achieving and retaining composure is a function of AROUSAL control. Every physically active individual needs a level of arousal to execute a sporting performance; those who are able to master the level required remain composed, or *poised*—a related term that describes someone's sense of balance (for example, weighing up the urgency of trailing with only five minutes left of a football game with the need to avoid panicking). Composure invariably facilitates effective performance in the face of pressure.

While some athletes are said to be GIFTED with natural poise, the composure exhibited during activity is more likely to be the result of learned technique. Richard Gordin relates the findings of case studies in which various interventions were tested for effectiveness. The "treatments" for performance ANXIETY included: learning COPING SKILLS—keeping CONTROL over how the performer reacts to the changing circumstances of a COMPETITION; SELF-TALK—maintaining an *inner dialogue* throughout the competition; CONCENTRATION training—focusing on the process of performing, not the outcome of the performance; *simulation* (or MODEL) training—facing FEAR and doubt as a way of strengthening oneself.

By employing techniques such as these, Gordin was able to demonstrate that, far from being a natural trait, composure can be acquired. In one interesting case, a swimmer practiced techniques that actually impeded his performance rather than inducing composure. A perfectionist, the swimmer focused externally, that is, on a wide range of cues outside himself—a technique more appropriate to team players. He also engaged in SELF-TALK, which was "virtually all negative" because of the high expectations he had of himself. The swimmer effectively sabotaged his performance. He was recommended COPING STRATEGIES which involved recognizing the destructive effects of his PERFECTIONISM; he was also advised to remove himself mentally from the pool environment before a race. Gordin believed that, by using these and other techniques, the swimmer would control anxiety and build composure before and during races.

Further reading

Gordin, R. D. (1998). Composure: arousal and anxiety dynamics. In M. A. Thompson, R. A. Vernacchia and W. E. Moore (Eds.), *Case studies in applied sport psychology: An educational approach* (pp. 37–62). Dubuque, Iowa: Kendall/Hunt.

See also: ANXIETY; BODY LANGUAGE; CENTERING; CHOKE; CONCENTRATION; CONTROL; COPING STRATEGIES; EMOTION; EMOTIONAL CONTROL; EMOTIONAL INTELLIGENCE; PREPERFORMANCE ROUTINES; RELAXATION; SELF-TALK; SUPERSTITIOUS BEHAVIOR; ZONE

CONCENTRATION

Concentration is the means through which ATTENTION is engaged and managed, attention referring to the mental process that allows us to focus on some features of our environment, at the same time excluding, at least partially, several others. In short, concentration employs, directs, and controls all of one's attention, usually in the pursuit of a definite GOAL or assignment. In sports, as in other aspects of life, the distinction between concentration and attention is not always clear: Being urged to "pay attention," for example, means, for all intents and purposes, to concentrate by bringing together all attentional capacities to convergence on a central image or task. In this sense, its application in sports is not so different in meaning from its Latin foundations, *cum* for with or together, and *centrum* for center.

A tennis player preparing to serve must use concentration to FOCUS his or her attention narrowly on executing the task, ignoring or GATING out irrelevant sensory data in the environment, such as murmurs in the crowd or planes passing overhead. The position of his or her opponent is, of course, relevant and must be attended to. By contrast, opponents are irrelevant to a sprinter, who needs to concentrate attention even more narrowly, selecting only cues that are essential to the immediate assignment. Even in the gym, a weight trainer needs to prepare by focusing on what he or she is going to try to do: "I'll go for eight reps," he or she might tell the spotter, at the same time attending to the immediate task.

Usually, the more adept athletes become at their sport, the more able they are to concentrate efficiently. For example, a beginning judo player will need a great amount of conscious thought in accomplishing a shoulder throw, as would a novice fencer in mastering a thrust. They need to be aware of their own body movements (PROPRIOCEPTION) as well as their opponents', processing input and output information and responding to perceptual and motor demands. More experienced athletes perform these skills seemingly without thinking, or even much effort, the reason being that input and output information is so quickly processed that it has become reflexive, or automatic.

Learning new skills requires attending to a great many features and, correspondingly, needs strenuous mental effort. Having gained the skills, the athlete can lessen the mental effort and concentrate on other aspects of the environment, relating, for example, to tactics and changes in circumstances; this is a form of *attentional narrowing*, often known as focusing.

Imagine attention as a light beam with concentration being the flash lamp that controls it. Early in an athlete's development, the beam will be broad, illuminating a range of materials that need attention. Later, when the basic and even more complex skills are acquired, the beam narrows so that it sheds light only on more analytical matters, such as planning moves and reading situations as they develop. The experienced athlete need not concentrate on the more elementary tasks that once demanded so much effort.

They can accomplish several different tasks at the same time, as easily as an experienced driver can drive, listen to the CD player, and have phone conversations, while concentrating only on the route ahead. Similarly, players of team sports need to concentrate on several contingencies of the game so they are ready to respond to a wide range of situations.

Yet, even experienced athletes can have their concentration shattered. As the motorist's concentration might be broken by a fellow motorist running a red light and causing a near miss, the athlete's concentration can be disrupted by a bad decision from an official, or foul play from an opponent—which is why trailing players often foul their opponents, attempting to break their concentration and divert their attention away from the COMPETITION. Elite athletes who know the importance of concentration will sometimes make special efforts to interrupt their opponents'. Consider Martina Hingis' attempts at the 1999 French Open final against Steffi Graf: Hingis demanded that the umpire inspect a mark on the clay surface after her forehand landed next to the baseline, took a five-and-a-half minute restroom break and even served underarm when facing match point on two occasions. Graf's concentration remained unperturbed, and she went on to win.

Internal diversions can also redirect concentration, as Aidan Moran points out: "Typical distractions in this category include wondering what might happen in the future, regretting what has happened in the past, worrying about what other people might say or do and/or feeling tired, bored or otherwise emotionally upset."

Among the more ingenious theories of the causes of concentration loss is that of D. M. Wegner who argues that trying to control thought processes actually increases the probability that they will be interrupted. This is essentially a derivation of shouting in a crowded room: "Do *not* think of an elephant!" In trying to prevent the formation of the thought, everyone has an image of an elephant. "In other words, the intention to suppress a thought activates an automatic search for that very thought in an effort to monitor whether or not the act of suppression has been successful," writes Moran about Wegner's argument.

Similarly, Wegner suggests that willfully trying to concentrate inadvertently makes us vulnerable to irrelevancies. So-called "powers of concentration" may appear to be "givens"—taken-for-granted abilities—but sport psychology regards them as acquired through practice and has developed procedures for removing the enemies of concentration, the principal ones being, distractions, ANXIETY and inappropriate focus, according to Jeff Simons.

Further reading

Moran, Aidan P. (1996). *The psychology of concentration in sport performers: A cognitive analysis.* Hove: Psychology Press.

Moran, Aidan P. (2004). *Sport and exercise psychology: A critical introduction*. London and New York: Routledge.

Simons, Jeff (1998). Concentration. In M. A. Thompson, R. A. Vernacchia and W. E. Moore (Eds.) *Case studies in applied sport psychology: An educational approach* (pp. 89–14). Dubuque, Iowa: Kendall/Hunt.

Wegner, D. M. (2002). Thought suppression and mental control. In L. Nadel (Ed.), *Encyclopaedia of cognitive science*, (Vol. IV, pp. 395–7). London: Nature Publishing.

See also: ATTENTION; AUTOMATICITY; CENTERING; COGNITION; EMOTIONAL CONTROL; EYE MOVEMENT; FOCUS; GATING; GOAL SETTING; INTENSITY; MEDITATION; PREPERFORMANCE ROUTINES; SELF-CONFIDENCE; SKILL EXECUTION; ZONE

CONCEPT

An abstraction, idea or mental representation, the word "concept" derives from the Latin *conceptum*, for something conceived. While all concepts are abstractions, they range from abstractions of something tangible to complete abstractions. For example, the concept of a football is in our heads, but there are obviously tangible objects that have all the properties of footballs and are called footballs. The concept of a university, by contrast, is intangible: A university is not just the bricks and mortar, plus the ground on which the campus stands and all the people working and studying on it, but rather the complex of all these consolidated with a unifying concept.

Andrew Roffman writes of the concept of ANGER, R. Lazarus and B. Lazarus refer to the concept of EMOTION, both terms being familiar to us through their behavioral expression. While David Smith analyzes the less familiar "concept of training impulse," "which is determined as the product of training duration and intensity where the average heart rate is multiplied by a non-linear metabolic adjustment factor that is based on the classically described blood lactate curve and the duration of a training session." So, some concepts we can grasp intuitively; others need detailed explication of their meaning.

In sport and exercise psychology, there are many terms prefixed by the adjectival form of "concept". For example, Tom Pyszczynski et al. claim "sociometer theory lacks the conceptual apparatus." *Conceptual apparatus* refers to the equipment a THEORY carries for explaining a phenomenon. One of the first questions we ask about a theory is: Does it provide us with the tools to be able to apply it in research? (Note: Sociometer theory is an attempt to understand

SELF-ESTEEM as providing information regarding one's FITNESS for inclusion in social groups.)

Readers will also find references to conceptual *frameworks* (the supporting structure of a theory) conceptual *properties* (attributes or characteristics of a concept) and conceptual *differences* (dissimilarities between concepts) as well as many more terms beginning with conceptual. They will also encounter the verb *conceptualize*, which means to form a concept, idea or theory, and *reconceptualize*, meaning thinking over again.

Further reading

Lazarus, R. S. and Lazarus, B. (1994). *Passion and reason: Making sense of our emotions.* New York: Oxford University Press.

Pyszczynski, T., Solomon, S., Greenberg, J. Arndt, J., and Schimel, J. (2004). Why do people need self-esteem? A theoretical and empirical review. *Psychological Bulletin*, 130, 435–68.

Roffman, Andrew E. (2004). Is anger a thing to be managed? *Psychotherapy: Theory, Research, Practice, Training*, 41, 161–71.

Smith, David J. (2003). A framework for understanding the training process leading to elite performance. *Sports Medicine*, 33, 1103–26.

See also: CATHARSIS; COGNITION; CONSTUCT; EQUALITY; IDIOGRAPHIC; NOMO-THETIC; RELATIONAL; THEORY

CONCORDANCE

An agreement. In sport and exercise psychology, concordance, which is from the Latin, *concordant*, for being of one mind, often involves PERCEPTION. For instance, David Bergin and Steven Habusta found a concordance of parents' and young hockey players' perceptions of goals. C. A. Shields et al. use concordance to capture a harmony between perceptions and actuality, a "concordance between perceptions and ADHERENCE type," (and, conversely, "nonconcordance" in some circumstances). It can also refer to motives, as in Todd Thrash and Andrew Elliot's study of implicit and self-attributed achievement motives. When there is agreement between the two types, there is "motive concordance."

Further reading

Bergin, David A. and Habusta, Steven F. (2004). Goal orientations of young male hockey players and their parents. *Journal of Genetic Psychology*, 165, 383–98.

Shields, C. A., Brawley, L. R., and Lindover, T. I. (2005). Where perception and reality differ: Dropping out is not the same as failure. *Journal of Behavioral Medicine*, 28, 481–91.

Thrash, Todd M. and Elliot, Andrew J. (2002). Implicit and self-attributed achievement motives: Concordance and predictive validity. *Journal of Personality*, 70, 729–55.

See also: ACHIEVEMENT MOTIVE; EXPECTANCY; GOAL; IDENTIFICATION; IDENTIFIED REGULATION; IDENTITY; PERCEPTION

CONFIDENCE

Feeling of assurance, or conviction in someone, or something.

See also: SELF-CONFIDENCE

CONSTRUCT

In psychology, a construct refers to the conceptual equivalent of a physical thing that is deliberately built for a purpose. It is an idea or series of associated ideas designed and built for analysis. Typically, it is not based on empirical evidence, at least not initially, but can be operationalized to perform a function in research. Often a construct is related to a theoretical MODEL, which is an abstract representation of reality. For example the TRANSTHEORETICAL MODEL (TTM) represents behavior change. Ralph Maddison and Harry Prapavessis observe, "the TTM constructs of SELF-EFFICACY, decisional balance, and processes of change [...] significantly predicted exercise stage transition."

Similarly, Sophia Jowett and Melina Timson–Katchis analyze the specificities of interactive properties: "RELATIONSHIP quality of the coach–athlete dyad has been defined here in terms of three interpersonal constructs: closeness, COMMITMENT and complementarity."

Seymour Feshbach uses the term in a slightly different and broader way to describe something that appears in several different models or accounts: "The construct of CATHARSIS has been used as a generic term to describe a process which is believed to be common to all of these suggested AGGRESSION-reducing activities."

Catharsis is, of course, not a physical phenomenon, but its reality is inferred and evidenced through observed physical behaviors. AROUSAL can also be studied through the ways in which bodily changes occur.

In this context, Yaniv Hanoch and Oliver Vitouch have introduced the term "meta-construct": "One can view the arousal construct as a meta-construct, since it serves as a rubric for a wide range of physiological changes." In this sense, the term is a kind of umbrella for several other constructs used in the analysis of the changes associated with arousal.

A great many other psychological constructs have empirical referents, though some constructs are HEURISTIC, that is, they are abstract, technical devices that enable discovery or facilitate learning but have no observable reality in themselves.

Further reading

Hanoch, Yaniv and Vitouch, Oliver (2004). When less is more: Information, emotional arousal and the ecological reframing of the Yerkes-Dodson Law. *Theory and Psychology*, 14, 427–52.

Feshbach, Seymour (1984). The catharsis hypothesis, aggressive drive, and the reduction of aggression. *Aggressive Behavior*, 10, 91–101

Jowett, Sophia and Timson-Katchis, Melina (2005). Social networks in sport: Parental influence on the coach–athlete relationship. *Sport Psychologist*, 19, 267–87.

Maddison, Ralph and Prapavessis, H. (2006). Exercise behavior among New Zealand adolescents: a test of the transtheoretical model. *Pediatric Exercise Science*, 18, 351–63.

See also: AROUSAL; CATHARSIS; COACH–ATHLETE RELATIONSHIP; CONCEPT; IDIO-GRAPHIC; INDIVIDUAL ZONES OF OPTIMAL FUNCTIONING; MENTAL TOUGHNESS; META-ANALYSIS; MODEL; NOMOTHETIC; PHENOMENON; SCHEMA; THEORY; TRANS-THEORETICAL MODEL

CONTEXT

The circumstances in, or conditions under which an event happens and which assist in fully understanding it. Knowledge of context assists in accounting for and evaluating the meaning of an event. The origins of the term are revealing. From the Latin *contextus*, from *con*, toge-ther, and *texere*, to weave, it suggests the reconstruction of something.

Contexts include both time and place and, as such, involve events preceding and following, surrounding objects and people (including their beliefs), and other background factors that are pertinent. The analyst needs to establish what level of context is relevant.

For example, Seymour Feshbach distinguishes between the *inter-personal context*, that is, the immediate situation in which an interaction takes place, *historical context*, meaning the broader background factors that impinge on the interaction, and *dramatic context*, in which "the individual may be alone." We might add that the *global context* is often regarded as relevant to many events. The term "social context" is used in a variety of ways but always making reference to the characteristic features of a particular social group, CULTURE, or wider society. These can include all or some of the following: people, values, beliefs, mores, institutions, conventions and other organized activities specific to a particular place during a particular period.

Some research, such as Maria Kavussanu's studies of moral atmosphere, uses context as its central focus, then tightens or widens the lens to examine *achievement contexts* within specific sports, or *competitive contexts* that pervade several sports. In all cases, the accent is on how the surrounding complex of beliefs—or *ethos*—affects individuals' values and behavior: "It is not surprising therefore, that in such a context athletes are inclined to engage in unfair play to achieve success as defined in their team."

IDIOGRAPHIC research is reliant on context, especially when assessing subjective experiences. Chris Harwood's analysis of achievement goals illustrates "the greater sensitivity that can be achieved at a contextual level."

Further reading

Feshbach, Seymour (1984). The catharsis hypothesis, aggressive drive, and the reduction of aggression. *Aggressive Behavior*, 10, 91–101.

Harwood, Chris (2002). Assessing achievement goals in sport: Caveats for consultants and a case for contextualization. *Journal of Applied Sport Psychology*, 14, 106–19.

Kavussanu, Maria (2006). Motivational predictors of prosocial and antisocial behaviour in football. *Journal of Sports Sciences*, 24, 575–88.

See also: ACHIEVEMENT MOTIVE; COMPETITION; CULTURE; EXERCISE BEHAVIOR; FANS; GAMBLING; GENDER; IDENTITY; IDIOGRAPHIC; LEARNED HELPLESSNESS; MASTERY CLIMATE; MORAL ATMOSPHERE; SOCIAL FACILITATION; SOCIAL LOAFING; SOCIALIZATION; VICARIOUS AGENCY; YERKES-DODSON LAW

CONTROL

The power to guide, command, restrain, regulate, or manage is control (from the Latin *contra*, against, and *rotulus*, roll). In a sense, sport and exercise psychology aims to control by modifying or changing thought and behavior in a way that is conducive to improved performance and enriched physical experience. It does so by assuming charge of a situation or, more often, enabling a person to assume charge of his or her own experiences; this typically involves changes to both behavior and COGNITION.

Control is most popularly associated with branches of psychology that systematically use REINFORCEMENT to reward desired responses to stimuli and punish unwanted behavior. Yet, control is implicit in all psychology interventions, even those that aspire to "unlocking potential," or "liberating" subjects through CATHARSIS and analogous expedients. To achieve a successful outcome, some measure of control must be attained, whether over a participant or the CONTEXT in which they operate.

Most strategies available to the psychologist are predicated on control: COGNITIVE-BEHAVIORAL MODIFICATION, COPING STRATEGIES, STRESS-MANAGEMENT TRAINING and STRESS-INOCULATION TRAINING all address the regulation of either behavior or EMOTION.

Physical techniques designed to facilitate self-control include BIO-FEEDBACK, progressive RELAXATION, and breathing control, while cognitive operations consist of AUTOGENIC procedures, HYPNOSIS, IMAGERY, and meditation. In practice, many of these are combined. Cognitive restructuring and SELF-TALK are thought-modification techniques designed to allow individuals to appraise themselves and situations differently so as to create a capacity to guide action with authority rather than let situations slip away. Perhaps the most abundant form of control practiced by athletes, especially elite athletes, is intended to restore some measure of command over the near-ubiquitous STRESS that affects competitors.

Further reading

Dawson, K. A., Brawley, L. R. and Maddux, J. E. (2000). Examining the relationships among concepts of control and exercise attendance. *Journal of Sport and Exercise Psychology*, 22, 131–44.

Kauss, D. R. (2001). *Mastering your inner game: A self-guided approach to finding your unique sports performance keys*. Champaign, Ill.: Human Kinetics.

See also: AUTOGENIC; BIOFEEDBACK; COGNITION; COGNITIVE-BEHAVIORAL MODIFICATION; COPING STRATEGIES; EMOTION; EMOTIONAL CONTROL; EMOTIONAL INTELLIGENCE; REINFORCEMENT; RELAXATION; SELF-TALK; SKILL EXECUTION; STRESS

COPING STRATEGIES

To cope is, of course, to deal successfully with a person, a predicament or some other kind of unwelcome situation; the term comes from the Greek word *kolaphos*, later anglicized to *cop*, meaning a strike with the fist. A coping strategy is a deliberate, rationally planned program for contending with persons or circumstances that might otherwise produce ANXIETY and STRESS. Usually, the coping strategy is aimed at the source of the anxiety, unlike *defensive* strategies, which are directed at the anxiety itself.

Some people use coping strategies in preparation for a particular event, while others employ them on a continuing basis; still others have no need for planned strategies. "There are numerous situations that athletes may find challenging, threatening, or harmful," write Nikos Ntoumanis et al., "avoiding or recovering from INJURY, playing an important game, media attention, poor refereeing, bad weather conditions, provocative opponents."

Whatever strategy is used, it must be focused, whether on the upcoming affair, an ongoing condition, or a personal state. *Problem-focused* strategies, for instance, are directed at trying to change the conditions under which anxieties or stresses occur. Enhanced planning, more information, greater effort, or new SKILL ACQUISITION may be in the repertoire of strategies that will enable someone to contend with a situation or an opponent more effectively and thus reduce anxiety. Concern for personal safety, for example, is a pervasive source of mental or emotional strain (a stressor) for many women, and developing a competence in physical self-defense can be "a transformative experience that enhances women's overall sense of their capabilities," according to Julie Weitlauf et al.

By contrast, *emotion-focused* coping implicates the athlete in trying to identify the specific EMOTION or set of emotions that lie at the source of his or her anxiety. EMOTIONAL CONTROL begins way before an event when athletes start to turn thoughts inwards, scrutinizing their own case histories to recognize specific persons, events, and situations where a sudden emotion has been experienced before. They can then rehearse appropriate responses.

Controlling an emotion means being sensitive to cues, so that an emotion like ANGER can be recognized before it displaces rational thought and leads to unreasonable responses, such as AGGRESSION and perhaps VIOLENCE.

AVOIDANCE coping strategies are typically organized around the decision to withdraw from the immediate task or to engage with an alternative task. A jogger, who is embarrassed when she runs in a group and struggles to keep up with the pace, might opt to run alone, or switch to biking, for example. Unlike problem-focused strategies, avoidance coping does not involve a direct attempt to deal with the source of the challenge but tries to divert attention away from it or even change its meaning ("What's so special about running? You can achieve the same results from biking.")

While avoidance has been a strategy typically favored by women, not only in sport and exercise but in all manner of stressful environments, Dafna Kariv and Tali Heiman's 2005 study of college students yielded contrary findings, "with men reporting a significantly higher usage of avoidance as a coping tool."

Further reading

Kariv, Dafna and Heiman, Tali (2005). Task-oriented versus emotion-oriented coping strategies: The case of college students. *College Student Journal*, 39, 72–84.

Lazarus, R. S. and Lazarus, B. (1994). *Passion and reason: Making sense of our emotions*. New York: Oxford University Press.

Ntoumanis, Nikos, Biddle, Stuart J. H., and Haddock, Geoffrey (1999). The mediating role of coping strategies on the relationship between achievement motivation and affect in sport. *Anxiety, Stress and Coping*, 12, 299–327.

Smith, R. E. (2000). Generalization in coping skills training. *Journal of Sport and Exercise Psychology*, 20, 358–78.

Weitlauf, Julie C., Cervone, Daniel, and Smith, Ronald E. (2000). Generalization effects of coping-skills training: Influence of self-defense training on women's efficacy beliefs, assertiveness, and aggression. *Journal of Applied Psychology*, 85, 625–33.

See also: AGGRESSION; ANGER; ANXIETY; AVOIDANCE; COGNITION; COGNITIVE-BEHAVIORAL MODIFICATION; DEPRESSION; EATING DISORDERS; EMOTION; EMOTIONAL CONTROL; EMOTIONAL INTELLIGENCE; GENDER; LOCUS OF CONTROL; MOOD; MOTIVATIONAL CLIMATE; SELF-EFFICACY; STRESS; STRESS-INOCULATION TRAINING; STRESS-MANAGEMENT TRAINING; WEIGHT CONTROL

CORRELATION

Mutual RELATIONSHIP between two or more phenomena.

See also: RELATIONSHIP

COVARIATION PRINCIPLE

Covariation refers to a RELATIONSHIP between two events in which the variation in one is always accompanied by the same variation in the other, the conclusion being that they are causally linked.

Tim Rees et al., apply the covariation principle to ATTRIBUTION. The original covariation principle, which was formulated in the 1960s, posited that people use three types of information to link outcomes to causes: *consistency, distinctiveness*, and *consensus*. Rees et al. give the example of a despondent tennis player, who, having lost a match, concludes, "I'm just no good. I feel like giving up." This might be challenged by prompting the players to reassess the initial postmatch reaction with information derived from distinctiveness (What were the good aspects of your game?), consistency (Have you ever played as poorly, yet still pulled through?), and consensus (Do you know others who have played as badly, felt the same way after the game, yet still continued successfully?).

In this CONTEXT, the covariation principle is used as a "source of support for helping to generate information about a client's unrealistic or dysfunctional attributions." "By focusing on consistency, distinctiveness, and consensus information one can help people to better understand the CAUSE of an event."

(Note: covariation is stronger than *co-occurrence*, which suggests that events happen at the same time.)

Further reading

Rees, Tim, Ingledew, David K., and Hardy, Lew (2005). Attribution in sport psychology: Seeking congruence between theory, research and practice. *Psychology of Sport and Exercise*, 6, 189–204.

See also: ATTRIBUTION; CAUSE; COACH–ATHLETE RELATIONSHIP; COGNITION; CONSTRUCT; FEEDBACK; NEGATIVITY; RELATIONAL; RELATIONSHIP

CULTURE

The learned component of human experience, including values, customs, lifestyles, language, and heritage, as well as the expressive representations of these in art, architecture, music, and so on.

See also: CONTEXT; SOCIALIZATION

DEATH WISH

While the popular use of the term "death wish" owes much to the five Charles Bronson movies between 1974 and 1994, it is accepted in some psychological circles as representing the motivational state of SENSATION-SEEKING persons who habitually seek out hazardous situations. Freudians prefer to interpret the behavior of such persons in terms of Thanatos, or the death INSTINCT (often contrasted with Eros, the life instinct), which inclines individuals away from gratification, and toward denial, restraint, and expiation (Thanatos was the Greek god of death; Eros the god of love). Some athletes, especially those in sports in which there is a considerable RISK of harm, are often thought to be possessed of a death wish.

Every sport involves the risk of death or serious INJURY. Boxing draws the wrath of American and British medical associations because of the physical punishment incurred in virtually every fight by virtually every boxer. Statistically, however, motor racing and air sports have far more victims than other sports, with accidents claiming the lives of competitors in what are clearly high-risk endeavors involving elaborate items of technology. Research by R. C. Cantu and F. O Mueller indicated that American football, ice hockey, gymnastics, and wrestling (not WWE) were sports in which competitors were at greatest risk. Less obviously dangerous sports include running and cycling. In these, athletes are typically killed in road accidents while training, or by training too zealously in middle age. Even sedentary competitions, such as chess or bridge, harbor unseen perils (such as the onset of deep vein thrombosis after remaining stationary for long periods!)

While the notion of a death wish has a superficial plausibility, it remains in the realms of hypothesis: There is no empirical research to consolidate its status as anything but a popular phrase. Further, there are no known athletes who resemble Bronson's death-dealing urban vigilante who hurtles into treacherous situations at every opportunity. Even Formula 1 drivers, whose professional *raison d'être* is to travel at unsafe speeds, are motivated by more tangible incentives than the chance to cheat death—like the prospect of earnings of over $30 million per year.

EXTREME SPORTS devotees are also considered to be driven by a death wish: they readily acknowledge nurturing a DEPENDENCE on the ADRENALINE RUSH that typically accompanies high-risk activities. Technically, it is possible to become dependent on an activity that elicits a particular type of sensation, though the term "adrenaline junkies" may not be completely appropriate.

Matt Jarvis suggests another utility for the CONSTRUCT: "Our death instinct leads us to be aggressive. Freud proposed that although the instinct for AGGRESSION is always with us, we can to some extent exert conscious CONTROL over it." The expression of aggression in sport, on this account, has the effect of *sublimating* the behavioral aspects of the instinct (that is, modifying or diverting them into a culturally acceptable activity).

Matt Pain and Matthew Pain express the opposite view: "In direct contrast to the Freudian position, we put ourselves at risk not because we have a death wish, but because we wish to confront and overcome our deepest fears."

Further reading

Cantu, R. C. and Mueller, F. O. (1999). Fatalities and catastrophic injuries in high school and college sports, 1982–97: Lessons for improving safety. *Physician and Sports Medicine*, 27, 35–48.

Jarvis, Matt (2006) *Sport psychology: A students' handbook*. London and New York: Routledge.

Pain, Matt T. G. and Pain, Matthew A. (2005). Essay: Risk taking in sport. *The Lancet*, 366, S33–S35.

See also: ADRENALINE RUSH; AGGRESSION; CATHARSIS; DEFENSIVE ATTRIBUTION; DRIVE; ENDORPHINS; FEAR; HEDONIC TONE; INSTINCT; RELIGION; RISK; SENSATION-SEEKING

DECISION-MAKING

The process of making a choice between alternatives when the outcome cannot be known in advance, is decision-making. It involves often complex deliberations, such as predicting probable consequences, balancing moral and technical considerations, and attending to the likely impact of the decision on others. As such, decision-making is a cognitive SKILL.

In sport and exercise, decisions are made about which activities to start, whether or not to pursue them fulltime, when, if ever, to stop and, possibly, when to make a COMEBACK. In COMPETITION, decisions are constantly made from an array of options, many of them tactical in nature, others based on the employment of skill. No successful athletic performance relies exclusively on the CONTROL of movement. Decisions on what motor response to produce are crucial.

Decision-making is performed in conditions of uncertainty. Those making the decisions will try to maximize expected utility, utility being the subjective value of the outcome. Every decision involves a degree of COMMITMENT: a choice leads to some outcomes and closes out others. Choices are made in anticipation that the consequences of them will be more valuable than the ones that would have resulted from the options eschewed. But, the choice has to be ranked in some order of probability.

A cricket batsman facing a spin bowler has about 0.2 of a second to make a choice whether to attack the ball and try for a boundary or to defend. He must rapidly rate his chances of achieving a boundary against those of only snicking the ball and getting caught in the slips. Baseball batters face similar decisions: go for a big run-earning slug, but one that carries with it a chance of total failure, or perhaps just bunt. To minimize the uncertainty, athletes try to recognize consistent patterns in opponents' deliveries or identify movement idiosyncrasies associated with the environment. In such situations, it is always possible that the cognitive task will cause a disruption of motor activities, especially in less skilled performers. Research by J. M. Poolton et al., indicated that table-tennis players experienced difficulty in executing motor performances in situations demanding decisions of high complexity, meaning those involving a storage and retrieval of information, rather than a straightforward STIMULUS– response; for example, batters attend to the sequence of previous deliveries to predict the speed and direction of the next incoming ball.

"Executing a motor skill and decision complexity may make an impact on one another," concluded Benjamin Sibley and Jennifer Etnier in another study, this time of volleyball. "Making several decisions simultaneously or decisions that require the processing of multiple stimuli-situations common in real sport environments-may seriously impact skill performance." Both studies underline the cognitive demands of practically any sport in which competitors must make decisions that require immediate motor responses.

No athlete, or exerciser (indeed, no human being) makes the appropriate choice every time. Good athletes make them more consistently than average athletes. Experienced athletes, in particular, use their MEMORY as a resource in decision-making. Of course, making decisions and having the ability to execute them are not the same and, while AGING athletes frequently know the right choice, they also know that their chances of executing them exactly as they wish grow slimmer through the years.

Reliable and consistent decision-makers are often credited with LEADERSHIP roles. Sound decision-making contributes to team COHESION and individual SELF-CONFIDENCE. Yet, there is no single blueprint adopted by all dependable decision-makers and every decision is influenced by seven factors, according to P. Chelladurai: (1) time pressure; (2) importance (when there are several options); (3) information location (a team captain might have a better grasp of the immediate situational demands than a coach standing away from the action); (4) problem complexity; (5) group acceptance (a unilateral decision could be resented by a team); (6) coach's power; (7) group integration.

Factors (6) and (7) have a crucial bearing on decision-making styles. At one extreme, the autocratic type of decision-maker takes decisions on his or her own, without seeking input from other team members; at the other, the democratic decision-maker solicits the views of all other members. Researchers V. H. Vroom and A. G. Jago, in 1988, concluded that each style required different skills. The autocrat needs to appraise various options before deciding on the best, while the democratic decision-maker needs to be participative, involving others in discussion and negotiation. The latter may take longer, but produces more innovative decisions.

Factor (1) also has a significant impact on style. In the heat of competitive action, time is a valuable resource, and a democratic style may not be practicable. Members of a football team must place their faith in the decisions of a leader, such as the quarterback. A boxer must listen to the advice of his or her corner in the sixty-second break between rounds. Rally drivers simply react to the decisions called by their navigator. Rowers attend to every instruction of their cox. In each case, the decisions must not only be made quickly, but they must be communicated lucidly with no room at all for misunderstanding.

Further reading

Chelladurai, P. (1993) Leadership. In R. N. Singer, M. Murphey, and L. K. Tennant (Eds.), *Handbook of Research in Sport Psychology* (pp. 647–71). New York: Macmillan.

Poolton, J. M., Masters, R. S. W., and Maxwell, J. P. (2006). The influence of analogy learning on decision-making in table tennis: Evidence from behavioural data. *Psychology of Sport and Exercise*, 7, 677–88.

Sibley, Benjamin A. and Etnier, Jennifer L. (2004). Time course of attention and decision-making during volleyball set. *Research Quarterly for Exercise and Sport*, 75, 102–7.

Vroom, V. H. and Jago, A. G. (1988). *The new leadership: Managing participation in organizations.* Englewood Cliffs, N.J.: Prentice-Hall.

See also: ATTENTION; COGNITION; COHESION; DISCIPLINE; EXECUTIVE CONTROL; GOAL ORIENTATION; INFORMATION PROCESSING; INTELLIGENCE; LEADERSHIP; MASTERY; OBEDIENCE; PERCEPTION; REACTION TIME; SELF-CONFIDENCE; SKILL EXECUTION; TRANSTHEORETICAL MODEL

DEFENSIVE ATTRIBUTION

Defensive attribution of responsibility refers to undeserved victimization. For example, a spin-class enthusiast who observes a fellow spinner fall off her machine exhausted and being taken out on a gurney might maintain a sense of self-security "by distorting their perceptions of the victim's causal role in his or her own victimization," as Bill Thornton put it. So they might reduce the threat to themselves by deciding the casualty had not eaten for hours before the session or tried too hard to show off. This defends them from imagining that similarly capricious misfortunes could befall them. The pertinence of this in dangerous sports, especially where there are fatalities, are obvious.

Further reading

Thornton, Bill (1984). Defensive attribution of responsibility: Evidence for an arousal-based motivational bias. *Journal of Personality and Social Psychology, 46*(4), 721–34.

See also: ATTRIBUTION; DEATH WISH; MIND ATTRIBUTION; RISK; SELF-SERVING BIAS; SENSATION-SEEKING

DELIBERATE PRACTICE

Conscientious, intentional, and repeated application of a performance activity or SKILL so as to acquire and retain proficiency in it, deliberate practice has been identified as the single most important predictor of an individuals' capacity to improve and perform tasks habitually. The practice is self-directed (at least, after initial instruction), and levels of challenge are systematically raised. The activities should also contain the element of FEEDBACK, enabling the exerciser, athlete, or whoever practices, to monitor progress. SKILL ACQUISITION and improvement is likely to be maximized.

For proponents of deliberate practice, actual COMPETITION is a less effective framework for skill improvement. If opponents are weaker, they will not challenge one to exert maximal or even near-maximal effort when making tactical decisions, and problems or weaknesses in one's play are unlikely to be exploited. "The opportunity for learning is also attenuated during matches against much stronger opponents," argue Neil Charness and his colleagues, "because no amount of effort or concentration is likely to result in a positive outcome."

Nor is repetition effective without the graduated challenges or feedback. Deliberate practice activities are not intrinsically rewarding and may be joyless affairs conducted in isolation for several thousand hours.

There is neither a "magic bullet" nor innate TALENT that allows the attainment of expert levels of skill performance, according to K. Anders Ericsson, with whom the CONCEPT of deliberate practice is associated: "Even for the most 'talented' individuals, the road to excellence takes many years of daily deliberate practice to acquire the complex mechanisms and adaptation that mediate expert performance and its continued maintenance and improvement."

Further reading

Ericsson, K. Anders and Charness, Neil (1994). Expert performance: Its structure and acquisition. *American Psychologist*, 49, 725–47.

Charness, Neil, Tuffiash, Michael, Krampe, Ralf, Reingold, Eyal, and Vasyukova, Ekaterina (2005). The role of deliberate practice in chess expertise. *Applied Cognitive Psychology*, 19, 151–65.

Schraw, Gregg (2005). An interview with K. Anders Ericsson. *Educational Psychology Review*, 17, 389–412.

See also: ABILITY; COGNITIVE LOAD THEORY; COMMITMENT; CONSTRUCT; DISCIPLINE; FEEDBACK; GIFTEDNESS; INTRINSIC MOTIVATION; MEMORY; MODEL; SKILL; SKILL ACQUISITION; SKILL EXECUTION; TALENT; THEORY

DEPENDENCE

When individuals have a strong, compelling desire continually to use a drug or other substance, or engage in an activity excessively, they are said to have dependence. The term "dependence" is favored over "addiction," which was originally used only for dependence deriving from physiological changes (themselves resulting from repeated administrations of the drug or substance). But the line between purely physiological addiction and dependence, which may be psychological, is not clear. Dependence can be the result of a craving for a substance or activity that provides relief or euphoria but does not produce basic biophysical changes such that further intake of the substance or prolongation of the activity is needed for normal functioning. The term stems from the Latin *pendere*, meaning hang down, as in sus*pend* or *pend*ant.

Addiction. Few substances that are widely used have genuinely addictive properties. Prolonged use of heroin induces physiological changes in the user—which is why addicts need to be weaned off it or given the substitute analgesic, methadone. Long-term use of alcohol is capable of affecting the functions of the central NERVOUS SYSTEM, and the sudden cessation of its use can cause withdrawal symptoms; further ingestion of alcohol alleviates these temporarily. But studies have shown that most heavy drinkers do so to experience its positive effects rather than escape the aversive experiences produced by its absence. Some scholars, such as Geoffrey Lowe, argue that the CONCEPT of addiction can be expanded to encompass the "total experience involving physiological changes in individuals (some of whom may be genetically and/or psychologically predisposed). These changes are interpreted and given meaning by the individual within the sociolocultural CONTEXT in which the addictive behaviour occurs."

It also possible to acquire a dependence on a substance that has no tolerance potential, meaning something that does not lead the body to adapt in such a way that ever larger doses are needed to get the same effect. So, while addiction is still used popularly to describe, for instance, cravings for chocolate, or caffeine habits, dependence more accurately describes the psychological dynamic behind continued use of substances. Serena Williams acknowledged dependence on online shopping, sometimes spending up to three hours before a game surfing the net with her credit card at the ready.

Athletes. Reports of athletes with dependence, or addictions, particularly on alcohol and narcotic DRUGS, are legion. Mickey Mantle and Daryl Strawberry had two of the best-known dependences in sports history, Mantle's on alcohol, Strawberry's on crack cocaine. Paul Merson and Tony Adams, both members of the successful Arsenal soccer team of the 1990s, admitted to having alcohol dependence (Merson was also a habitual cocaine user). Nicotine dependence is less prevalent, though not totally absent from sports. In 1997, New York Mets pitcher, Pete Harnisch, was placed on the disabled list while he tried to overcome his dependence; he was the first player to be incapacitated by withdrawal symptoms resulting from his attempts to quit tobacco.

Analgesics are commonly used in sports, especially collision sports, such as football and soccer, where painful injuries are customary but often not serious enough to prevent an athlete's performing. Pain-killers are administered regularly, and have been for decades. Brett Favre's well-publicized dependence on painkillers in the late 1990s may be but one of an unknown number of similar conditions among athletes or ex-athletes who carry injuries beyond their playing careers.

Given the demands of particularly professional sports and the pressure under which athletes perform, it would be unusual if many did not seek relief through antidepressants or other psychoactive drugs. Benzodiazepines, such as diazepam (for example, Valium) and nitrazepam (Mogadon) were reported to have been popular in the 1970s, Paul Hoch reporting that athletes were "tranquilized to get their eyeballs back in their head—to even get a night's sleep," in his *Rip Off the Big Game*. It also likely that there is a high incidence of antidepressant dependency among sports performers. An estimated 40 million people have taken Prozac alone since it was introduced in 1988. Whether or not antidepressants can lead to addiction is open to debate. Some argue that long-term use of Prozac and similar drugs may pose a significant risk of neurological side effects, while other dismiss such claims. Clearly though, the risk of dependence is palp-able; the greater the dose and duration of consumption, the greater the RISK. This rule holds good for any type of dependence, though cocaine taken in the form of crack or freebase is known to have high "addiction potential" and can accelerate its occasional users to become compulsives or addicts rapidly.

While dependence is often used synonymously with substance dependence, certain activities, for example, GAMBLING, are known to have dependency potential. Relevant to this subject is EXERCISE DEPEN-DENCE, which involves a craving for excessive and often deleterious exer-cise activities. Symptoms of exercise dependence include withdrawal effects, such as ANXIETY and DEPRESSION, when unable to exercise, an inability to conduct interpersonal relationships, and difficulties in holding down jobs (because of the time demands of exercising).

Reasons. There is no unequivocal answer to the question of why people become dependent on a substance or activity. While some approaches prefer to treat each form of dependence uniquely, others view dependence and addiction more inclusively. Genetic arguments center on the hereditarian principle that we are born with the potential to become dependent on something and that CULTURE merely supplies triggers. There is some support for this, especially in the area of ALCOHOLISM. But there is less support for the related view that dependence is a consequence of an "addictive PERSONALITY." Both approaches focus on individuals rather than social contexts.

The social-learning MODEL, by contrast, accentuates the role of learning in the "sociocultural CONTEXT," as Lowe calls it. This includes MODELING behavior on that of others or responding to the pressures of a cultural milieu that values indulgence in alcohol, drugs, or other substances and responding positively to the temporary sensation of empowerment supplied by the substance (for example, avoiding responsibility or the feeling of STRESS). This APPROACH holds more promise for understanding dependence in sports. Typically, athletes have long intervals in their weeks or months when training is over but COMPETITION not yet begun; they also spend periods traveling, staying in hotels away from their family and close friends. This may be an ideal context for developing habits that develop into dependence. The situation is often accentuated when athletes retire from competition and find an even greater amount of free time available to them. Countless sports performers have developed sometimes chronic dependence in their RETIREMENT.

Further reading

Hausenblas, Heather A. and Symons Downs, Danielle (2002). Relationship among sex, imagery, and exercise dependence symptoms. *Psychology of Addictive Behaviors*, 16, 169–72.

Lowe, Geoffrey (1996). Alcohol and drug addiction. In A. M. Colman (Ed.), *Companion encyclopedia of psychology* (Vol. II, pp. 950–68). London and New York: Routledge.

Stainback, R. D. (1997). *Alcohol and sport*. Champaign, Ill.: Human Kinetics.

See also: ALCOHOLISM; ANOREXIA ATHLETICA; ANOREXIA NERVOSA; ANXIETY; BULIMIA NERVOSA; DEPRESSION; EATING DISORDERS; EXERCISE DEPENDENCE; GAMBLING; HYPNOSIS; MODELING; MUSCLE DYSMORPHIA; OVERTRAINING SYNDROME; ROLE MODEL; STRESS

DEPRESSION

Depression is a MOOD typified by a sense of insufficiency, dejection, sadness, hopelessness, fatigue, or acute lack of MOTIVATION. It may arise in response to a specific incident or set of circumstances, or it may be part of a complex or syndrome of related symptoms. Women are twice as likely as men to suffer from depression. The term stems from the Latin for press, *pressio*, prefixed with *de* for down.

Tina Oates-Johnson and David Clark identify "excessive concern for social approval and relatedness" as possible factors in precipitating depression, especially among women: "Heightened concerns with physical appearance, body weight and image have also been implicated, along with low SELF-ESTEEM."

The effects are manifold. Gloria Balague and James Reardon's case study of an athlete whose mother had died illustrates how depression can rapidly affect an athlete's form. The athlete reported "lack of energy, low MOTIVATION to perform and several recurring injuries" which were later revealed to be symptomatic of depression. The athlete grew irritable with peers and isolated himself from them.

Severe depression is often treated with antidepressant drugs, though, in the above case, the athlete used a COGNITION-based INTERVENTION that included new GOAL SETTING procedures and PREPERFORMANCE ROUTINES.

Research on the relationship between depression and physical exercise has generally highlighted the role of exercise in alleviating the symptoms of STRESS. In the early 1990s, T. P. LaFontaine et al. found aerobic exercise was useful in relieving depression as well as other forms of NEGATIVITY. Several other small studies (including that of John Bartholomew et al. in 2005) offered support to the idea that moderate-to-intensive exercise (for example, thirty minutes on a treadmill or brisk walking at 60 mph) was a promising treatment for depression.

On the other hand, Kerry Mummery pointed out that heavier training loads accompanied by overly ambitious GOAL SETTING that has not been appropriately adjusted to a particular environment can make the trainer vulnerable: "Depression and depressive symptoms in athletes might be related to high volumes and intensities of training, to maladaptive COGNITION in relation to sport and combination, or to a combination of both."

While one might intuitively expect people attempting to alleviate depression through exercise to experience difficulties in maintaining ADHERENCE, this is not the case, and, once in a program, those with symptoms of depression have no need of special considerations. The social support provided by a gym combines with the feeling of WELL-BEING that comes through exercise to maintain the individual's attachment.

Further reading

Balague, Gloria and Reardon, James P. (1998). Case studies of a clinical nature. In M. A. Thompson, R. A. Vernacchia, and W. E. Moore (Eds.), *Case studies in applied sport psychology: An educational approach* (pp. 227–44). Dubuque, Iowa: Kendall/Hunt.

Bartholomew, John B., Morrison, David, and Ciccolo, Joseph T. (2005). Effects of acute exercise on mood and well-being in patients with major depressive disorder. *Medicine and Science in Sport and Exercise*, 37, 2032–7.

LaFontaine, T. P., DiLorenzo, T. M., Frensch, P. A., Stucky-Ropp, R. C. Bargman, E. P., and McDonald, D. G. (1992). Aerobic exercise and mood: A brief review, 1985–90. *Sports Medicine*, 13, 160–70.

Mummery, Kerry (2005). Essay: Depression in sport. *The Lancet*, 366, S36–S38.

Oates-Johnson, Tina and Clark, David A. (2004). Sociotropy, body dissatisfaction and perceived social disapproval in dieting women: A prospective diathesis-stress study of dysphoria. *Cognitive Therapy and Research*, 28, 715–31.

Oman, Roy F. and Oman, Kimberley K. (2003). A case-control study of psychosocial and aerobic exercise factors in women with symptoms of depression. *Journal of Psychology*, 137, 338–50.

See also: AEROBIC/ANAEROBIC; ANXIETY; BODY IMAGE; COGNITION; COGNITIVE-BEHAVIORAL MODIFICATION; EATING DISORDERS; ENDORPHINS; EXERCISE BEHAVIOR; FITNESS; GOAL SETTING; INJURY; MENTAL HEALTH MODEL; MOOD; MOTIVATION; NEGATIVITY; PREGNANCY; STRESS; WELL-BEING.

DEPTH PERCEPTION

The state of awareness of the relative distance of objects in one's particular field of vision.

See also: PERCEPTION; VISUAL PERCEPTION

DEVIANCE

Formed from the Latin *de*, from, and *via*, way, deviance describes the manner in which society responds to behavior that has been defined, usually in some official way, as unusual, irregular, and, in some extreme cases, threatening. Deviance, it should be emphasized, does not describe behavior, or any properties of it; nor does it characterize particular individuals or groups. It refers to the process in which a label is stuck onto people designated as rule-breakers and their actions nominated as transgressions. So, deviance is a relative CONCEPT. What constitutes rule breaking in one CULTURE at a certain stage in history may not in another culture or at a different time. In other words, deviance is CONTEXT-sensitive: The reaction of society to behavior determines whether or not that behavior will be designated deviant, as the example of drugs illustrates.

Rule breaking 1: Drugs. DOPING was originally designed to enhance athletic performance and was practiced systematically in many countries, both in and out of the Soviet sphere of influence, particularly from the late 1950s, when the utility of anabolic steroids became well known. A great many athletes took drugs with impunity. The introduction of rules prohibiting doping (from 1972) officially changed the status of this behavior and of the athletes engaging in it. So, the enactment and enforcement of the rules created the conditions under which this piece of deviance came into being. Progressively strict testing procedures and punishment for violators aided by an occasionally hysterical media were all features of a reaction that defined doping as deviance and those discovered taking drugs as deviants.

Even once the rules are introduced, it is perfectly possible to break them habitually and not be caught. Only after the behavior is known publicly can what many call the "labeling process" click into motion. The classic example in sport is Ben Johnson. Once hailed as the fastest man in the world, he was labeled the "world's greatest cheat" following his expulsion from the 1988 summer Olympics.

Doping is example of how a behavior defined as a serious violation of rules in one context may be permissible in another. The types of substances typically taken by athletes are often legally available either on prescription or over the counter of any pharmacy. The reverse is also true: behavior tolerated and, in some cases, approved of in sport would be harshly punished outside the context of sport. Imagine what would happen if a violent incident from a typical NHL game took place in a shopping mall. In some circumstances, perpetrators of violent behavior in, for example, hockey, rugby, and soccer, has been held accountable through civil and criminal courts.

Rule breaking 2: Control. The MOTIVATION to break rules lies in the desire to win at any cost, a desire that has been nurtured by the copious amount of money available in professional sports. This may not be the only factor, but it combines with, for example, PERSONALITY characteristics, ACHIEVEMENT MOTIVATION, and a cluster of situational variables to produce a propensity to transgress.

Various theories have been advanced to explain why people become deviant. Earlier models based on genes, skull characteristics, and other individual endowments have given way to theories that accentuate the role of social processes, including the background of the rule-breakers, their investment in society, and their peer-group associations on the one hand and enforcement agencies, the courts, and the entire criminal justice system on the other. In other words, accounts of deviance need to take account of the whole context in which rule violation is defined and processed as well as produced.

Some theories hold that a certain amount of deviance is *functional*, its punishment serving to remind society where the boundaries between right and wrong lie. Others insist that deviance is about a relationship between groups who have economic and political power and the ability to write the rules (law) and groups who have neither power nor access to resources. The incessant *conflict* between them brings about deviance, with the powerful framing law in a way that reflects their best interests and penalizes the powerless for breaking it. And still other theories maintain that deviance is a question of interaction between rule-breakers and the *social reaction* to them, which is essentially the framework used in this entry. Studies using this frame of reference tend to focus on agents of CONTROL (police, courts, and so on) rather than the rule breakers.

Rule breaking 3: Motivational climate. Much play has been made about the impact of sports participation on young people's tendencies toward deviant behavior. The rehabilitative consequences of participating in sport for young offenders and potential offenders has been widely assumed, though a fusillade of research on this subject since the 1930s has failed to make a direct hit. Some studies found that sports curbed rule-breaking tendencies, or perhaps subordinated them to the greater GOAL of succeeding athletically. Others unearthed a bonding subculture among athletes, which promoted the kinds of attitudes and values that commissioned rule breaking. Some studies have found that a disproportionate amount of athletes are accused of sexually related offenses, yet only a tiny minority are convicted, suggesting that the status associated with being a sports performer may be a valuable resource in escaping conviction.

This has been the subject of several studies, all highlighting the importance of motivational GOAL ORIENTATION on an athlete's propensity to violate rules, engaging in violent behavior, or verbally abusing opponents to intimidate them. Athletes whose primary FOCUS is to win justify these kinds of actions by reference to the competitive context, or motivational climate. A climate in which achievement goals are emphasized and winning is valued by significant others, such as managers, coaches, or parents, is an ego-involving climate (as opposed to a MASTERY CLIMATE, in which success is defined as skill MASTERY and individual improvement). Respect for rules and conventions, officials and other players are likely to lower amid a climate that accentuates performance goals.

A GENDER difference has also been reported, females disapproving of deviant behavior during COMPETITION less than their male counterparts. This could be explained by historical lag, sport being a traditionally male domain, with women rising to elite levels of professional sport only in recent decades. Ego-involving motivational climates are, of course, likely to be encountered more at the higher echelons of competitive sport where EXTRINSIC MOTIVATION often propels athletes and winning is of paramount importance. In such climates, ends are likely justifications for rule-breaking.

Further reading

Benedict, J. and Klein, A. (1997). Arrest and conviction rates for athletes accused of sexual assault. *Sociology of Sport Journal*, 14, 86–94.

Coakley, J. J. (2001). *Sport in society: Issues and controversies*, 7th edn. New York: McGraw-Hill.

Kavussanu, Maria (2008). Morality in sport. In Sophia Jowett and David Lavallee (Eds.), *Social Psychology in Sport* (pp. 265–78). Champaign, Ill.: Human Kinetics.

See also: AGGRESSION; ALCOHOLISM; CHARACTER; CONTEXT; DOPING; EATING DISORDERS; EXERCISE DEPENDENCE; GAMBLING; MASTERY CLIMATE; MORAL ATMOSPHERE; MOTIVATIONAL CLIMATE; PERSONALITY; VIOLENCE

DISCIPLINE

The maintenance of ordered conduct in the pursuit or preservation of a standard is discipline, a term derived from the Latin for learn, *discipulus*. Its connotations of learning still hold: discipline is usually practiced with the intention of cultivating a SKILL, proficiency, competence, or qualification for entry to a higher realm. In sport and exercise, as in other areas, discipline is of two kinds: (1) exercised by an authority over subordinates; or (2) exercised by oneself—self-discipline.

Discipline is often enforced by the use of *punishment*, a term with which it is sometimes confused. For example, order is maintained over schoolchildren, prisoners or soldiers who operate within a framework of rules and norms, deviation from which is punishable. CONTROL of behavior is facilitated by a transparent system known to all; if the rules or norms are transgressed, then transgressors are liable to punishment and DEVIANCE occurs. Although this is effective in the structured environments of institutions, it is less effective in more permissive milieus, like gyms, where the rules are not so clear and punishments are not appropriate. In such circumstances, desirable conduct can be rewarded; this type of REINFORCEMENT serves to maintain discipline without resort to castigation.

To be effective, punishment must also function as what Michel Foucault (1926–84), in his *Discipline and Punish: The Birth of the Prison* called a "fable": it conveys a moral message, explaining and justifying itself. Punishment contains a "lesson" not just to recipients but all others in the institution. Football, baseball, basketball, and other kinds of sports clubs are institutions, and athletes as well as other staff are subject to rules. Violators are punished with fines and suspensions. Discipline is not maintained through surveillance, but by athletes' awareness that surveillance is possible without knowing whether it is actual. This principle is based on the late-eighteenth-/early nineteenth-century philosopher Jeremy Bentham's concept of the *panopticon*, his ideal prison in which cells were arranged around a central watchtower in which a concealed authority figure could inspect without being inspected. (Bentham would have approved of speed cameras on highways: drivers can see them but do not know if they have film in them.)

Many other sports lack the formal structure of club-based team sports. Cyclists and motor-racing drivers, for example, compete for a team, but not within the structure of a club. Surveillance by the media is always possible, of course. Players are often exposed gambling, partying, or indulging in other types of disreputable pleasures. The punishment typically entails embarrassment or humiliation. This may work as a negative reinforcer (life without embarrassment is less painful), though more effective is INCENTIVE: rewards for virtuous behavior.

Other athletes operate outside any formal structure of CONTROL. Boxers, tennis players, and the majority of Olympic athletes may, on occasion, compete as part of a team but operate, for the most part, without any rigid structure. COMMITMENT requires that the individual arranges his or her conduct according to a regimen (that is, a prescribed course of exercise and diet) involving a degree of abstinence. Recall the scene from the first and fifth *Rocky* movies when Balboa rises before daylight, swallows raw eggs, and grinds out his miles through the streets of Philadelphia in subzero temperatures. There is no one to punish Rocky if he skips a day or eases up on his pace; his discipline is imposed and sustained by himself, his behavior reinforced by the prospect of the title fight.

Robert Rinehart's study of a swim school includes the observation, "The swimming body has discipline imposed from both outside and inside: it is inscribed by others, including coaches and parents, and it is inscribed by itself." Rinehart describes how, working as a coach at the school, he was urged to train according to a prescribed method, and all disciples (he does not use this word, but it seems appropriate) were inculcated accordingly. Young swimmers, who were initially attracted to the sport because of the "love of water" or the sheer joy of swimming, had soon surrendered any notion of enjoyment and accepted that competitive success would only come through regular, predictable systematic training. There was, writes Rinehart, "an ironically abnegating yet self-absorbed discipline" that pervaded the school. The initial INTRINSIC MOTIVATION was replaced by an EXTRINSIC MOTIVATION.

Drawing on Foucault, Rinehart argues that punishment convinces potential transgressors why they should stick to the regimen. The "relative freedoms of swimming," as Rinehart calls them, are gradually eroded "to be replaced by a disciplinary system both insidious and tenacious." Movements are broken down into minute fragments, each analyzed and subject to electronic surveillance; attendance is checked, progress is monitored, goals are set—"a form of panopticism within swimming," Rinehart calls it. The study illustrates how the denial that is so important to discipline in competitive sports is not simply imposed: it is *internalized*.

INTERNALIZATION has been defined by Jemma Edmunds et al. as "an inherent tendency possessed by all humans to integrate the regulation of extrinsically motivated activities that are useful for effective functioning in the social world, but that are not inherently interesting." Edmunds and her colleagues studied involvement in exercise programs, observing that external regulation was predictably ineffective. Creating social environments that promoted feelings of competence and autonomy, as well as personal development and well-being were a more effective strategy for keeping exercisers involved because, "in order to partake in strenuous exercise behaviors, which necessitate considerable physical and mental exertion and stamina, individuals must place some value on the exercise and recognize its importance in terms of health and well-being."

Edmunds et al. concluded that, "promoting high levels of both intrinsic motivation and identification would be most beneficial to optimal and continued behavioral engagement in exercise." While the study's approach is very different to Rinehart's, the results are similar: that, while discipline in training can be externally imposed, it is a more effective predictor of practice activity when it is internalized by the subject.

Further reading

Edmunds, Jemma, Ntoumanis, Nikos, and Duda, Joan L. (2006). A test of self-determination theory in the exercise domain. *Journal of Applied Social Psychology*, 36, 2240–65.

Foucault, M. (1977). *Discipline and punish: The birth of the prison.* New York: Pantheon.

Rinehart, Robert (1998). Born-again sport: Ethics in biographical research. In Rail, Geneviève (Ed.), *Sport and postmodern times* (pp. 33–46). Albany, N.Y.: State University of New York Press.

See also: ADHERENCE; COMMITMENT; EXTRINSIC MOTIVATION; INTERNALIZATION; INTRINSIC MOTIVATION; MENTAL TOUGHNESS; MOTIVATION; OBEDIENCE; REINFORCEMENT; SELF-DETERMINATION THEORY; SKILL; SKILL ACQUISITION; WEIGHT CONTROL

DOPING

"Doping is defined as using forbidden substances or methods in order to increase physical and/or mental performance. Doping is regarded as the use of drugs and chemical substances to increase the performance in an artificial and illegal way, or the use of physiological substances in large amounts during or out of COMPETITION," according to Mehmet Unal and Durisehvar Ozer Unal.

The substances usually refer to DRUGS, though foodstuffs and other materials, such as enriched or even artificial blood may also qualify as "dope" (the word itself deriving from the Dutch *doop* for sauce). *Gene doping* refers to the nontherapeutic use of genes, genetic elements and/or cells that have the capacity to change athletic performance. Thus, the purpose of doping is typically to enhance performance; though, in exercise, the reasons are typically esthetic— to improve muscular appearance. In horse racing, doping may be intended to slow down an animal, making it easier for less-favored horses to win—and thus help knowing betters make a killing.

In sport, human beings take dope or are provided with dope to: (1) gain a competitive advantage over opponents; (2) deny opponents suspected of doping from gaining an advantage. With only rare exceptions, sports forbid doping and penalize infractions with suspensions and fines, citing the possible harmful consequences on the health of the athlete and the violation of fair play as reasons for the ban. Yet, athletes disregard such bans. "Despite the many dangers associated with performance-enhancing chemicals, their use continues and even increases," writes D. Stanley Eitzen in his *Fair and Foul: Beyond the Myths and Paradoxes of Sport*, adding that: "The motive is obvious—an extreme desire to excel."

This may be a simple, but accurate summary of the MOTIVATION behind doping in sport, though it prompts a further question: Why should competitors transgress rules, RISK long-term suspensions, jeopardize their careers, and possibly endanger their health not only to excel but to surpass all others in their pursuit of a GOAL? To uncover this motive, we need to understand changes in the meaning of competitive sport and in the CULTURE of which it is part.

Change 1: Motivations. The need to achieve is a cognitive factor related to ATTRIBUTION: the achievement MOTIVATION, as it is called, refers to a subject's propensity either to APPROACH success or avoid failure. Those who have a need to succeed are usually high achievers while those who try to avoid failure are not. It follows that an athlete prepared to engage in doping will be driven by a motivation to achieve. Typically, such people relish a challenge, even when the odds are stacked against them. The most highly motivated achiever will also be inclined to take chances, perhaps even encourage situations when RISK-taking is necessary. This type of "win-at-all-costs" mentality has been fostered by an environment in which winning has been afforded a pre-eminent value and merely competing or even excelling have been assigned lesser values. In this sense, as J. Savulescu et al. note: "Performance enhancement is not against the spirit of sport; it is the spirit of sport."

The value of winning in sports has always been recognized, though not accentuated in the way it has been since the 1960s. The period saw the onset of professionalization in all major sports, including tennis and track and field, both old traditional sports that had embodied the amateur ethos. Both spurned professionalism for decades, maintaining that the essence of sporting competition lay in participating, not winning. While the conception of athletics as paid work goes way back to the 1860s—when the Cincinnati Red Stockings became the first salaried baseball club and the English instituted the "gentlemen *vs.* players" distinction to ensure that the working-class players who were paid were not genuine sportsmen—professionalism in sports picked up MOMENTUM from the 1960s. By the end of the century, no mainstream sport was still completely amateur. Amateurism crumbled under the weight of the money heaped on sport in the last few decades of the twentieth century.

As the achievement ethic permeated practically all sports, competitors became more task-oriented. Instead of understanding their ABILITY as a stable personal feature, they saw it as dynamic, changeable, and responsive to their own efforts. The very CONCEPT of having a coach to supervise or assist in training and other forms of preparation is evidence of an orientation that places onus on achievements wrought from work and perseverance rather than god-given "gifts" or natural TALENT. (Training itself was regarded as tantamount to cheating by English gentlemen cricketers of the nineteenth century.) Athletes developed in a sports culture that encouraged them to take control of their own destiny and not to look outside themselves in their ATTRIBUTION of success and failure.

Change 2: Substances. The use of substances to improve performance is as old as sport itself: There is evidence of competitors in Ancient Greek games and Roman COMPETITION either side of the Christian era, ingesting animal parts, especially testicles, in the belief that they could acquire characteristics of, for example, bulls (strength) or dogs (ferocity). Research in the first half of the twentieth century disclosed the potential of certain types of pharmaceutically produced materials as aides to athletic performance. In particular, an anabolic steroid Dianobol, first manufactured by the Ciba company in 1958, aroused interest among strength-based sports performers in both the USA and the Soviet Union.

In 1960, the former East Germany (then a communist state) introduced Program 1425, which provided for the induction of about 10,000 young people into sports academies where they were trained, conditioned, and supplied with performance-enhancing drugs. Far from being the restorative discipline it is today, sports medicine was originally conceived to advise on appropriate substances to improve athletic performance. As Ivan Waddington writes in his 1996 article "The Development of Sports Medicine": "It is not possible to separate out the development and use of performance-enhancing drugs from the development of sports medicine." Drug testing was not introduced until 1968 and even then it was designed for research purposes rather than to root out "cheats."

At the Munich Olympics of 1972, a more systematic approach to drug-testing was taken, though there was no reliable way of differentiating anabolic steroids from oral contraceptive steroids. A way had been found by 1976, though a test for testosterone proved elusive until 1982, by which time a protein hormone that confused results was available. Every four years, it seemed the International Olympic Committee introduced new tests designed to identify new drugs.

Signpost events indicated that anabolic steroids, amphetamines, and other substances were progressively becoming part of sports: the death of Tommy Simpson during the 1967 Tour de France, the disqualification of Ben Johnson from the 1988 summer Olympics, the expulsion of Diego Maradona from soccer's World Cup of 1994. The insistence of coaches that athletes were responsible for their own accomplishments or downfall appeared less plausible amid a culture in which doping was prevalent. Even the most task-oriented athletes must have entertained the suspicion that their defeats were attributable not entirely to their lack of preparation, exertion, or desire, but to the fact that their rivals were on dope of some sort. One way of rescuing the internal LOCUS OF CONTROL—that is, the sense of agency for controlling one's own fortunes—was to improve one's own performance by similar means.

It is possible that much of the doping that grew out of post-1988 (that is, Johnson) period was a product of a "If you can't beat 'em, join 'em" resignation, rather than a willful attempt to gain an unfair advantage; though there is scant evidence to support this, and, even then, the evidence is inferential. For example, surveys of young athletes suggest that, given the opportunity to take a banned substance that guarantees (1) it cannot be detected, and (2) success in every event entered for five years, followed by a certain death, more than half the athletes said they would take the drug, according to a report by Michael Bamberger and Don Yaeger in 1997.

Change 3: Environment. In 2002, the World Anti-Doping Agency (WADA) organized a conference, at which the applications of gene therapy in sport were highlighted. Gene-doping is not the same as gene therapy: it includes indirect genetic technologies, such as biosynthetic drugs designed specifically to enhance athletic performance. Because athletes are injected with copies of genes naturally present in the body (such as those encoding growth factors or testosterone), gene-doping is undetectable unless by inference. It has been called "unpredictable and of unproven safety" (see Unal and Unal 2004).

The willingness to sacrifice long-term health in the pursuit of victory seems perfectly consistent with the achievement ethic of contemporary sports, but why would healthy achievement-oriented athletes be prepared to risk disqualification, shame, and the stigma that typically attaches to athletes found to be using dope? The tentative answer is that they are aware or at least suspect that a great many of their rivals are using dope and that "the minority of athletes who are natural are at a *disadvantage*," as the Olympian discus thrower Werner Reiterer put it in his autobiography *Positive* (2000). Reiterer reflected on his own reluctant decision to take dope: "You must adapt to an environment as it is, not as you think it should be." If this view is taken, athletes who have been suspended for dope violations and who are labeled "cheats" probably have powerful achievement orientations and devotion to retaining an internal locus of control; they may also feel compelled to abandon any ideals as they "adapt to an environment" in which drug-taking is common. This may sound a charitable interpretation, but the role of the sports scholar is to examine and comprehend rather than make pronouncements.

Further reading

Bamberger, Michael and Yaeger, Don (1997). Over the edge. *Sports Illustrated*, 86, 60–8.

Eitzen, D. Stanley (1999). *Fair and foul: Beyond the myths and paradoxes of sport*. Lanham, Md.: Rowman & Littlefield.

Reiterer, W. (2000). *Positive: An Australian Olympian reveals the inside story of drugs and sport*. Sydney: Pan Macmillan Australia.

Savulescu, J., Foddy, B., and Clayton, M. (2004). Why we should allow performance enhancing drugs in sport. *British Journal of Sports Medicine*, 38, 666–70.

Unal, Mehmet and Unal, Durisehvar Ozer (2004). Gene doping in sports. *Sports Medicine, 34*, 357–62.

Waddington, I. (2000) *Sport, health and drugs: A critical sociological perspective*. London: E&FN Spon.

See also: ACHIEVEMENT MOTIVE; ATTRIBUTION; BODY IMAGE; CHARACTER; COMMITMENT; DEPENDENCE; DEVIANCE; EXTRINSIC MOTIVATION; GOAL; OBSESSIVE-COMPULSIVE; PERFORMANCE ENHANCEMENT; RISK; ROLE MODEL; WELL-BEING

DRIVE

A motive force, whether instinctual or learned, that impels a subject in a certain direction (usually toward a GOAL) is a drive. There are two main kinds of drive: *primary* and *acquired*. The first arises from deviations from a state of homeostasis, meaning the body's tendency to maintain a constant internal environment. Prolonged deprivation of a needed substance, or excessive temperature can activate a drive to restore homeostasis, as can the need to avoid PAIN or loud noise. The second type of drive is learned through SOCIALIZATION and is usually associated with a primary drive. Money is an example, and, while this may function as an acquired drive in sports, there are others, such as winning titles, breaking records, and setting new standards of excellence. The adjective "driven" is often applied to athletes who exhibit especially high levels of COMMITMENT. An Old Norse word *drífan*, meaning chase or urge in a direction, is the probable source.

Drive theory is associated with Clark Hull (1884–1952), who, in the 1940s and 1950s, formulated an influential equation $B = HS \times D$, with B standing for behavior, HS habit strength and D drive. There are primary and secondary elements: how people behave is a consequence of primary drive and how they have learned best to reduce it. The higher the drive, the more likely they are to behave in a certain way, what Hull called the "dominant response," or the behavioral response that has the greatest habit strength. Habit strength is learned through conditioning, a process in which repeated REINFORCEMENT plays a central role.

The dominant response is not always the most appropriate one, and this is glaringly obvious to sports FANS who have witnessed dramatic switches in style during COMPETITION. A boxer who is a decent brawler may, in preparation for a particular fight, work assiduously at perfecting long-range tactics. For most of the fight, he may execute the plan, but, with two rounds remaining and the fight poised, drive may rise, and he will switch to the dominant response, which is to brawl. A tennis player's greatest habit strength may be to run around their weaker backhand to return with her stronger forehand (HS) but practice returning with backhand when playing a left-handed opponent. At tie-break in the fourth and trailing 1–0 in sets, a high drive is evoked (D), and she may start running around the serve (B) again. In line with the prediction of Hull's theory, AROUSAL increases the dominant response, even though it may not be the preferred or even correct one in the circumstances.

In a different CONTEXT, the concept of drive has been used to explain AGGRESSION, the hypothesis being that, when goal-directed behavior is obstructed in some way, an aggressive drive is induced, which then manifests aggressive behavior. In this view, all aggression is the result of frustration, with drive as the motivating force. As with Hull's theory, this was seminal in producing research and related theories, but both accounts are now dated.

Being watched by others can increase an individual's drive arousal and increase the likelihood of a dominant response. This will prove effective for a skilled athlete, especially if the tasks are relatively straightforward. The performance is less likely to be effective if the task is complex or the subject is not skilled.

Further reading

Dollard, J., Doob, J., Miller, N., Mowrer, O. and Sears, R. (1939). *Frustration and aggression*. New Haven, Conn.: Yale University Press.
Hull, C. L. (1943). *Principles of behavior.* New York: Appleton-Century-Crofts.

See also: AGGRESSION; AROUSAL; CATHARSIS; CHOKE; HOME ADVANTAGE; INSTINCT; MOTIVATION; NERVOUS SYSTEM; SOCIAL FACILITATION; VIOLENCE

DROPOUTS

Athletes and exercisers who abandon their participation after disagreeable experiences are known as dropouts. Both types of dropout suffer a drop in MOTIVATION, though research indicates that sport dropouts leave with feelings of rejection, their SELF-CONFIDENCE lowered. Exercise dropouts do not enjoy their experiences and are occasionally embarrassed in the company of others.

According to Robert Vallerand and Paule Miquelon, passion is a factor in determining whether or not someone drops out: "Obsessively passionate athletes should be less likely to drop out of sport than harmoniously passionate athletes." The former are those people who feel compelled to engage in a sport or regular exercise; in other words, they experience being controlled and cannot envision their lives without their sport or exercise activities, which become part of their identities. Those who are harmoniously passionate do not feel controlled and are thus likely to drop out should they experience conflict or perhaps just inconvenience.

Studies in the 1970s reported that young dropouts left sports because they disliked the competitive emphasis, or they did not have enough time, or they just hated their coach. Some jumped from one sport to another, while others were remitting—in other words, taking time out. Only a minority of dropouts were victims of negative experiences, though it strains credulity to think that young people would leave a sport in which they have favorable or positive experiences.

This suggests that the MOTIVATIONAL CLIMATE in which athletes or exercisers work out is an important factor. For example, an ego-involving climate (perhaps cultivated by a coach), in which performance and results are measured against those of others, is likely to promote dropping out. If experience in some activity is rewarded, if not by winning, by camaraderie, valuable interaction, and some semblance of learning, then a person does not willingly leave. Dropping out, almost by definition, implies an unpleasant encounter, like a spate of disappointing defeats, a series of injuries, a total loss of MOTIVATION. Jennifer Capriati recalled that, despite her early career success (in 1990, she reached the semi-final of the French Open at the age of fourteen and had made her first million), she was exhausted, even in her teens: "Mentally, I'd lost it. I wasn't happy with myself, my tennis, my life, my coaches, my friends," she told Brian Viner, of the *Independent* (Review section, June 22, 2001, p. 7).

Capriati, like many other dropouts, returned to her sport renewed and restored. Jay Coakley concludes that many others who appear to leave sports actually stay involved, usually not in actual COMPETITION. He also regards dropping out as transitional. Young people get married, or start a new job, or have children and prioritize these over sports; this is backed up by Konstantinos Koukouris's research on "disengagement" from sport. In Coakley's view, dropping out may actually be a sensible decision. Sticking with sports brings with it all manner of problems, especially for "those who have no IDENTITY apart from sports or who lack the social and material resources they need to make transitions into other careers" (that is, the obsessively passionate).

While the term "dropout" is popularly associated with competitive sport, research on dropouts from exercise programs has yielded interesting results. C. A. Shields et al. challenge the idea that dropouts are a homogeneous group and suggest that among those who initiate then discontinue physical activities are those who see themselves as "successful dropouts." Perceived success is crucial: if a person leaves an activity, perhaps with an intention of resuming later, believing that they have enjoyed it and put effort into it, and with a sense of enhanced competence, then they regard themselves as successful. The study removes connotations of failure from the term "dropout."

Further reading

Coakley, J. J. (2001). *Sport in society: Issues and controversies*, 7th edn. New York: McGraw-Hill.

Koukouris, K. (1994). Constructed case studies: Athletes' perspectives of disengaging from organized competitive sport. *Sociology of Sport Journal*, 18, 114–39.

Sarrazain, P. Vallerand, R., Guillet, E., Pelletier, L., and Cury, F. (2002). Motivation and dropout in female handballers: A 21-month prospective study. *European Journal of Social Psychology*, 32, 395–418.

Shields, C. A., Brawley, L. R., and Lindover, T. I. (2005). Where perception and reality differ: Dropping out is not the same as failure. *Journal of Behavioral Medicine*, 28, 481–91.

Vallerand, Robert J. and Miquelon, Paule (2007). Passion for sport in athletes. In Sophia Jowett and David Lavallee (Eds.) *Social psychology in sport* (pp. 250–63). Champaign, Ill.: Human Kinetics.

See also: ADHERENCE; BURNOUT; COACH–ATHLETE RELATIONSHIP; COMMITMENT; CONTEXT; DISCIPLINE; IDENTITY; INTRINSIC MOTIVATION; MOTIVATION; MOTIVATIONAL CLIMATE; SELF-DETERMINATION THEORY

DRUGS

Substances that have physiological and, sometimes, cognitive effects when introduced into the body.

See also: DOPING

DYSPHORIA

Extreme discontentment with life, or, aspects of life.

See also: BODY IMAGE; BODY SHAME; DEPRESSION; MUSCLE DYSMORPHIA; SOCIO-TROPY

EATING DISORDERS

When unusual eating habits become health-threatening, they are known as eating disorders, the two most common being ANOREXIA NERVOSA, a condition characterized by an obsessive avoidance of food, and BULIMIA NERVOSA, a syndrome that involves binge-eating followed by self-induced vomiting or use of laxatives and diuretics. *Binge-eating disorder*, while closely related to bulimia diagnostically, is now considered to have a separate etiology (set of causes) and is common among those enrolled on weight-loss programs. A less common condition is *pica*, eating material not considered nutritious.

Among the several effects of eating disorders are: menstrual dysfunction, such as amenorrhea (absence of menstruation) and oligomenorrhoea (few and irregular periods), PERSONALITY changes, including increased moodiness, depression and impulsivity, and a decrease in SEX drive.

Apart from pica, all types of eating disorders are typically driven by dissatisfaction with one's own body and are attempts to correct imagined defects in appearance or composition (eating, in some cases, is tantamount to contaminating the body and restricting intake or purging is regarded as a purification). But why is dissatisfaction with the body so widespread? The answer involves cultural as well as psychological factors.

"Many women in Western society internalize the thin body cultural ideal as a standard of beauty for themselves," observe Tina Oates-Johnson and David Clark: "This thin body shape preference provides an ideal that women may strive for regardless of their actual body shape and weight." Discrepancies between the ideal and the actual can lead to BODY DISSATISFACTION, a preoccupation with WEIGHT CONTROL, dieting, depression, and even exercise DEPENDENCE (or ANOREXIA ATHLETICA).

This cultural idealization of thinness complements what Donald Williamson et al. call "FEAR of fatness." This is an important cognitive bias: "The person's standard for an ideal body weight/shape/size becomes increasingly more thin as weight loss occurs." The cognitive impact of eating less and less motivates the subject to want to become progressively thinner. Hence the eating disorder continues. The cognitive association between thinness and life satisfaction and happiness is crucial. The exaggerated concern for body size and eating is a key feature of all forms of disordered eating.

Research has revealed no hereditary basis for eating disorders, and there appears to be no pattern in family background. Subjects with eating disorders commonly have disturbances of mood or EMOTIONAL tone to the point where DEPRESSION or inappropriate elation occurs, but no causal link between the two has been found, only an association.

Nor has research identified similarities in personality styles, according to Konstantinos Loumidis and Adrian Wells, whose studies revealed that exercise can, for some, "become a maladaptive behavior and may contribute to the development of eating disorders." Exercisers are, on this account, "a particularly vulnerable group." Both exercise and disordered eating are COPING STRATEGIES, or safety behaviors.

Exercise and a reduced food intake are often seen as positive problem-focused coping strategies in improving one's health when weight loss is desirable on health grounds. Yet, they are also associated with emotion-focused and AVOIDANCE-coping strategies rather than attempts to solve the objective problem. For example, a preoccupation with food might effectively displace another kind of STRESS. In other words, the eating disorder (and exercise) might be an inadequate adjustment to the situation that is, a maladaptive coping strategy.

On the other hand, research has also shown that exercise can be an effective part of treatment for eating disorders, particularly binge-eating disorder. "Health-related quality of life, depression, BODY IMAGE and SELF-ESTEEM are all positively affected by participation in physical activity," write Crandall Jason and Patricia Eisenman.

While exercise may be a maladaptive behavior contributing to or perhaps precipitating an eating disorder or an effective treatment for it, competitors in sport are certainly at risk. In some sports, looking young and slender is considered such an advantage that competitors actively try to stave off the onset of menstruation and the development of secondary sexual characteristics; or to counterbalance the weight gain that typically accompanies puberty.

Competitors in sports that emphasize the importance of physical appearance, such as gymnastics, ice dancing and synchronized swimming are especially inclined to eating disorders. A 2004 study found that the lifetime prevalence of eating disorders might reach 3.7 percent for anorexia nervosa and 4.2 percent for bulimia among cheerleaders, an activity that has 3.7 million participants in the USA. (Estimates of the prevalence of eating disorders across the sporting population vary widely between 3 and 22 percent.) The motivation of participants in these sports is similar to that of non-athletes: to achieve a particular type of BODY IMAGE rather than to enhance competitive performance.

The extreme restriction of food intake and the induced purging characteristic of eating disorders among athletes are "based on the premise that a thinner or leaner body can enhance performance (for example, lightweight rowing, distance running)," according to Roberta Trattner Sherman and Ron Thompson. This suggests that eating disorders are prevalent among men as well as women. "Eating disorders are an underrecognized problem in male athletes" writes Antonia Baum whose study indicates that: "Sports in which there is a need to make weight are notorious for encouraging the development of, sustaining, or attracting those with a vulnerability to eating disorders." To those mentioned above, we might add wrestling, martial arts and horse racing, which are all sports in which men are active.

Further reading

Baum, Antonia (2006). Eating disorders in the male athlete. *Sports Medicine*, 36, 1–6.

Jason, Crandall, K., and Eisenman, Patricia A. (2001). Physical activity: A treatment option for binge eating disorder? *Women in Sport and Physical Activity*, 10, 95–103.

Loumidis, Konstantinos and Wells, Adrian (2001). Exercising for the wrong reasons: Relationships among easting disorder beliefs, dysfunctional exercise beliefs and coping. *Clinical Psychology and Psychotherapy*, 8, 416–23.

Oates-Johnson, Tina and Clark, David A. (2004). Sociotropy, body dissatisfaction and perceived social disapproval in dieting women: A prospective diathesis-stress study of dysphoria. *Cognitive Therapy and Research*, 28, 715–31.

Trattner Sherman, Roberta, and Thompson, Ron A. (2006). Practical use of the international Olympic Committee medical commission position stands on the female athlete triad: A case example. *International Journal of Eating Disorders*, 39, 193–201.

Williamson, D. A., White, M. A., York-Crow, E., and Steward, T. M. (2004). Cognitive-behavioral theories of eating disorders. *Behavioral Modification*, 28, 711–38.

See also: ANOREXIA ATHLETICA; ANOREXIA NERVOSA; BODY DISSATISFACTION; BODY IMAGE; BODY SHAME; BULIMIA NERVOSA; DEPENDENCE; DEPRESSION; GENDER; OBESITY; OBSESSIVE-COMPULSIVE; PERFECTIONISM; PREGNANCY; SOCIAL PHYSIQUE ANXIETY; STRESS; WEIGHT CONTROL

EGOCENTRISM

Ego is Latin for "I," and, as the term suggests, egocentrism, or ego-centricity (as it is sometimes known) refers to a preoccupation with the SELF and insensitivity to others. This should not be confused with *egotism*, which is usually equated with conceitedness and selfishness. Nor with *egoism*, which is an ethical theory based on the conception of self-interest as the central MOTIVATION of humans. But it does share a great many features with what sports and exercise psychologists call *ego orientation,* which is used to describe the state of individuals who define success as relative to the performance of others.

An ego-oriented runner may return a poor time in a 1500-meter race, but, as long as she finishes in front of the field, it counts as more of a success than if she had run a personal record but finished second.

A football player may have a nightmare game, but, if his team won, it will be evaluated as far greater triumph than if he had played the game of his life but ended up on the losing side. Even in gym culture, an ego-oriented spinner might evaluate his or her performance in comparison with other class members. Their counterparts, who FOCUS on the process of performing, are called task-oriented. The exercisers have ample MOTIVATION but have starkly different goals.

One of the most canonical instances of egocentrism came at the Nürburgring Grand Prix of Europe, in 2001. Michael Schumacher all but squeezed his younger brother Ralf into the pit wall to defend his pole position. While technically permissible, it was a potentially perilous maneuver and one that accented the self-absorption so integral to Schumacher's quest for success. It could be argued that some degree of egocentrism is required of all athletes with the ambition to succeed at elite professional levels. At some stage in any sport, an athlete must be ruthless (which, incidentally, is from the Old English word *hreow*, for "compassion," and "less").

Leniency, sympathy, and sensitivity to others may be in evidence during the formative years of an athletic career, but athletes who progress to the higher echelons typically become relentless. The adage "nice guys finish last" has a resonance that extends beyond any one particular sport. But, as Matt Jarvis points out, "a task orientation has the advantage of greater persistence in the face of adversity." Marathon enthusiasts are largely task-oriented in the sense that they often seek personal-best times or aim to compete in the major city marathons around the world. Their finishing place is of incidental importance only. Jarvis notes cultural influences too. He gives the examples of martial arts aikido and wing chun, both of which are practiced in task-oriented environments. In contrast, judo and taekwondo encourage an ego-orientation in competitive training.

There is some debate over whether egocentrism is an integral part of an athlete's PERSONALITY or a quality that is acquired progressively as the subject moves into the higher realms of COMPETITION. Are successful athletes the ones who actually learn to be egocentric, or did they simply have the right kind of personality for sports? If the former, then environment or MOTIVATIONAL CLIMATE plays a pivotal part.

Further reading

Duda, J. L. (1993). Goals: A social-cognitive approach to the study of achievement motivation in sport. In R. N. Singer, M. Murphey, and L. K. Tennant (Eds.) *Handbook of Research on Sport Psychology* (pp. 421–36). New York: Macmillan.

Jarvis, Matt (2006). *Sport psychology: A students' handbook*. London and New York: Routledge.

See also: ACHIEVEMENT MOTIVE; GOAL ORIENTATION; MASTERY; MENTALITY; MOTIVATION; MOTIVATIONAL CLIMATE; PERSONALITY; SELF; TASK/EGO ORIENTATION; TEAM PLAYER; TYPE A

ELECTROENCEPHALOGRAM (EEG)

From the Greek *en*, for "in," *kephale*, "head," and *gramme*, "line," the electroencephalogram (EEG, which is used almost interchangeably with electroencephalograph, or EEC) is an instrument for visually recording the changes in the electrical discharges of the brain. The graphic presentations of the discharges as recorded by the EEG are called brainwaves.

Brainwaves are of several types. Alpha waves are high-amplitude waves with frequencies of 8–12 Hertz and are characteristic of relaxed subjects, whose ATTENTION is directed toward a relevant task and who have shut out other distracting stimuli. These are perfect conditions for an athlete to get focused. When a person is under some kind of STRESS or in a state of high AROUSAL, the EEG will usually record a predominance of beta waves. Drowsiness is typified by theta waves, and delta waves are very low frequencies of 1–3 Hertz, high amplitude, that occur during deep, dreamless SLEEP.

EEGs have applications in sports, especially in what is known as brainwave training. This entails attaching electrodes to the scalp and observing one's own brainwaves, the purpose being to set up a BIO-FEEDBACK loop in which the participant can monitor his or her own output with a view to aligning it with a desired state, for instance, an alpha-wave rhythm. This has been used to good effect, promoting SELF-CONFIDENCE, training visual attention, and assisting recovery from injury. In one research project, EEG was used in conjunction with visual IMAGERY. "The EEG biofeedback gave the hitter [a baseball player participating in the program] an understanding of what it meant to concentrate maximally and attain a state of heightened level."

Further reading

Davis, Paul A. and Sime, Wesley E. (2005). Toward a psychophysiology of performance: Sport psychology principles dealing with anxiety. *International Journal of Stress Management, 12*(4), 363–78.

Demos, John N. (2004). *Getting started with Neurofeedback*. New York: Norton.

Rael Cahn, B. and Polich, John (2006). Meditation states and traits: EEG, ERP, and neuroimaging studies. *Psychological Bulletin*, 132, 180–211.

See also: ANXIETY; ATTENTION; AUTOGENIC; BIOFEEDBACK; CONCENTRATION; EXECUTIVE CONTROL; IMAGERY; INFORMATION PROCESSING; MEDITATION; NERVOUS SYSTEM; SELF-CONFIDENCE; SLEEP

EMOTION

A subjective state, or sensation that momentarily interrupts otherwise steady functioning with sudden and unexpected physiological, experiential and behavioral changes. Derived from the French *émotion* (from *émouvoir*, to excite, after *mouvoir* to move), the term is used loosely and frequently conflated with AFFECT, which is a broader, less focused concept that covers both emotion and *feeling*, itself a more diffuse sensory impression, and *sentiment*, a more permanent disposition. All lead to particular courses of action.

Composition. Emotions are complex and episodic; thoughts, perceptions, and feelings contribute to them; they manifest and disappear, often quite quickly. They are integral to sports. FANS are excited to EMOTIONAL extremes such as euphoria and despondency when watching COMPETITION. Athletes deliberately try to induce emotions in rivals. They may try expressing intimidating emotion to try to force rivals into experiencing dread or outright FEAR; or they may try to make them angry enough to lose COMPOSURE and perhaps become violent. In these and other ways, emotion affects performance. Competitive sports are emotional: without emotion, sports would lose their *raison d'être*.

More precisely, we should identify distinguishing features. An emotion is: (1) *ephemeral*—it is always a short-lived transitory state; (2) *intentional*—it is always directed at a person, event, or object, so that there is a RELATIONSHIP between the state and whatever it is intended toward or about (embarrassed by, proud of); (3) *evaluative*—it is always good, bad, or a mixture of the two, never neutral; (4) *disturbing*—it interrupts and agitates mental states; (5) unexpected—its arrival and impact can rarely, if ever, be anticipated; (6) *irrational*—it often displaces reason and rational thought, leading to erratic action; (7) *subjective and objective*—it is experienced subjectively but involves bodily changes that are observable.

Love, hate, horror, relief, happiness, sadness, ANGER, serenity: these are labels we apply to the complex, kaleidoscopic expanse of emotions experienced in sport. The behaviors they instigate are referred to collectively as emotionality, and these can be measured by, for example, heart rate and galvanic skin response, or observed by emotional responses, such as crying, trembling, shouting, or AGGRESSION.

Theory 1: James–Lange. The attempt to explain emotion dates back to the 1880s when two independent publications advanced a similar proposition: when events or persons in our environment produce sudden bodily responses, particularly in the AUTONOMIC NERVOUS SYSTEM, we feel these changes and *that* is the emotion. In other words, the bodily changes that come about as a result of something unexpected or shocking act as a signal which we pick up, and our PERCEPTION of them is the emotion. This was the answer to the question William James (1842–1910) posed himself in his "What is an emotion?" article, and his answers were approved by Carl Georg Lange (1901–76). Hence the title, the James–Lange theory of emotion. One implication of the theory was that every particular emotion is originated by a unique set of bodily and visceral (relating to abdominal cavity and organs) responses.

Theory 2: Cannon. The theory was challenged in the late 1920s by Walter B. Cannon (1871–1945) who found, among other things, that all the major emotional states, such as anger and fear, were accompanied by the same general emergency response that prepares the body for activity. The response was sympathetic AROUSAL and was based on the sympathetic system of the AUTONOMIC NERVOUS SYSTEM (ANS), leading to an increase in metabolic rate and energy mobilization (the centers that CONTROL ANS activity are in the lower centers of the brain and usually below the threshold of conscious control). Increase in heart rate and blood pressure, heightened respiratory volume, constriction of blood vessels in the skin, and sweating were among the characteristic responses. Whereas James and Lange argued that we experience emotion because we feel our bodies in a particular way, Cannon held that there were common emotional patterns that respond to occurrences in the environment and then trigger bodily and visceral expressions. For James and Lange, we feel embarrassed because we experience a hot flush; for Cannon, we flush because we feel embarrassment.

Theory 3: Schachter. Neither theory recognized the part played by cultural factors in initiating and shaping the experience of emotion. In an effort to do so, Stanley Schachter (1922–97) drew on James's idea that emotion depends on FEEDBACK from changes in the body but also accepted that different emotions share the same bodily response, as

Cannon had insisted. Schachter affixed the positions with his own view that information from the surrounding context in which the experience takes place modifies the way an emotion is appraised or interpreted. A single physiological arousal state can result in dozens of different, possibly conflicting, emotions, depending on how the individual interprets the situation—whether pleasant/unpleasant, benign/dangerous, joyful/scary, glad/sad, and so on.

A series of experiments by Schachter and J. E. Singer supported this APPROACH. They concluded that situational factors not only played a part in modifying the expression of an emotion but in actually constituting that emotion. In this view, COGNITION was vital: the precise manner in which we interpret a state of arousal affected both the quality and the effect of the emotion. "If you believe your state of arousal is caused by an wild animal that is chasing you, then you are likely to experience the state as fear," suggests Bryan Parkinson to illustrate the point, adding "if you think that your AROUSAL is triggered by the close presence of somebody attractive, you might well come to feel your reaction as love, or at least as lust, for that person." Emotion, in Schachter's theory, hinges on the ATTRIBUTION of arousal to the events, persons or other factors in the immediate context.

Emotions in action. Of course, attributions do not *cause* emotions, but they explain a limited amount of variance. For example, a team wins an important game but an individual player feels he or she played poorly, so the success is attributable to others. If the team had lost, the player might feel shame, the defeat being attributable in large part to his or her performance. In success, the player experiences elation, though perhaps not as much pride as teammates, and may even experience guilt. This configuration of emotions results from a *reflective appraisal.* After a heavy defeat, an athlete might decide the competition was not important; whereas, if the same player had won, he or she might have viewed it as important. The appraisal will alter the INTENSITY, type, and possibly duration of the emotions experienced.

Readiness for action is obviously vital to any successful athletic performance, and active emotions, such as fear and fury facilitate this. By contrast, more passive emotions like anguish and gloom will not. Research supports the link between action readiness and involuntary and sometimes impulsive emotions. N. H. Frijda uses the term CONTROL *precedence* to indicate that the urge to behave, or refrain from behaving, in a certain way is often not willful, it just comes over people, like the well-known red mist that descends in moments of rage.

Interpreting a situation in one way might arouse one to an optimal state in which sensations of anger, if not outright rage, will facilitate a determined and vigorous athletic performance; interpreting the same situation another way may result in awe, in which case the performance may be tentative and irresolute. Trying to identify the optimal emotional state for competitive performance is the task of much research deriving from the INDIVIDUAL ZONES OF OPTIMAL FUNCTIONING model. For example, Claudio Robazza et al. studied archers. "Emotions are thought to influence performance through generation and utilization of psychophysical energy needed to execute the task," they write after observing how "debilitating emotions" immediately before competition resulted in "a reversal of energy generation function" and, ultimately, a poor performance.

The CAUSE of a failure to achieve the optimum emotion is varied. Competing in front of a roaring crowd, for example, may appear to confer HOME ADVANTAGE on players, but when the fans start encouraging attacking play, the players begin to swell with SELF-CONFIDENCE and see offensive opportunities where, objectively, there are none. In other words, emotion can momentarily blind athletes to important cognitive clues. Equally negative for athletes are situations when emotion displaces reason. Emotion is often contrasted with rationality, of course. Every sport has instances of competitors "losing it": tennis rackets are smashed, opponents are punched, officials are abused—all involve transgressions that, ultimately, prove detrimental to athletic performance. Mike Tyson's biting Evander Holyfield's ear is a dramatic example.

While competitive sport elicits emotional responses with detrimental consequences, participation in exercise has been found to improve what Sarah Donaldson and Kevin Ronan call "emotional well-being." More formal organized sports requiring discipline, teamwork, and sustained involvement were more effective than less structured activities.

It is not only participants who experience emotional change during competition: fans too, especially highly identified fans, are sensitive to fluctuations, as research by, among others, Charles Hillman et al. indicates: "During the course of sporting events, identified fans often demonstrate strong emotional and behavioral responses, (both pleasant and unpleasant)." It might be argued that without such emotional responses, the experience of being a fan would be less attractive.

Further reading

Cannon, W. B. (1927). The James–Lange theory of emotions: A critical examination and an alternative theory. *American Journal of Psychology*, 39, 106–24.

Cannon, W. B. (1929). *Bodily changes in pain, hunger, fear and rage*, 2nd edn. New York: Appleton.

Donaldson, Sarah J. and Ronan, Kevin R. (2006). The effects of sports participation on young adolescents' emotional well-being. *Adolescence*, 41, 369–94.

Frijda, N. H. (1986). *The emotions*. Cambridge: Cambridge University Press.

Hillman, C. H., Cuthbert, B. N., Cauraugh, J., Schupp, H. T., Bradley, M. M., and Lange, P. J. (2000). Psychophysiological responses of sport fans. *Motivation and Emotion*, 24, 13–28.

James, W. (1884). What is an emotion? *Mind*, 9, 188–205.

Parkinson, B. (1996). Emotion. In A. M. Colman (Ed.), *Companion encyclopedia of psychology* (pp. 485–505), 2 volumes. London and New York: Routledge.

Robazza, Claudio, Bortoli, Laura, and Noughier, Vincent (2000). Performance emotions in an elite archer: A case study. *Journal of Sport Behavior*, 23, 144–64.

Schachter, S. (1964). The interaction of cognitive and physiological determinants of emotional state. In L. Festinger (Ed.), *Advances in experimental social psychology*, (Vol. I, pp. 27–48). New York: Academic Press.

Schachter, S. and Singer, J. E. (1971). Cognitive, social and physiological determinants of emotional state. *Psychological Review*, 69, 379–99.

See also: ANGER; AGGRESSION; AGGRESSIVENESS; ANXIETY; AROUSAL; CHOKE; COPING STRATEGIES; DEPRESSION; FANS; FEAR; FLOW; INDIVIDUAL ZONES OF OPTIMAL FUNCTIONING; MEDITATION; MIMESIS; MOOD; NERVOUS SYSTEM; PERCEPTION; POSITIVE AFFECT; RISK; SENSATION-SEEKING; TELIC DOMINANCE; VICARIOUS AGENCY; WELL-BEING; ZONE

EMOTIONAL CONTROL

Designating a state or reaction as emotional indicates that it is, in some measure, affected by an underlying EMOTION. In sport and exercise, there is a class of expressions prefixed by emotional, perhaps the most significant being emotional CONTROL.

Jack Lesyk uses the term "emotional control" to characterize situations in which, "The sudden, powerful emotion compels attention away from appropriate stimuli, and CONCENTRATION is lost." This may be the case when an official's call goes against expectations or after a provocation by an opponent. Lesyk's prescription is to maintain FOCUS on the task at hand and on immediate matters that can be controlled; this may include SELF-TALK, articulating statements such as "Just let it go; plan your next action."

Emotional CONTROL begins before COMPETITION: athletes examine their own case histories to identify specific hot spots, including persons, events, and situations where a sudden emotion has been experienced. They can then rehearse appropriate responses. Controlling an emotion means being sensitive to cues, so that an emotion can be recognized before it displaces rational thought and leads to unreasonable behavior.

When athletes persistently fail to control emotion, they are said to have emotional *instability*, meaning that they exhibit inappropriate behavior in and, possibly, away from a competitive CONTEXT. Their behavior is variable and possibly unpredictable. Often emotional instability threatens an athlete's competitive career. The intrusion of intense subjective experiences interferes with their ABILITY to perform complex tasks competently. The inability is sometimes known as *emotional blocking*, where emotions overwhelm all other states.

This is but one of several conditions in which emotions induce behavioral reactions that are inappropriate to the immediate task; they are known collectively as emotional or affective *disorders* and include the oft-quoted emotional *immaturity*—which is used to describe athletes who regularly throw temper tantrums or challenge officials. At the other extreme, there are athletes who never display emotion during competition. While it is unlikely that such athletes have a disorder, there is actually a condition known as emotional *anesthesia*. As the name indicates, there is an unusual amount of insensitivity or numbness related to this condition: subjects react indifferently to circumstances and persons who might be expected to arouse them.

Further reading

Biddle, S. (2000). Exercise, emotions and mental health. In Hanin, Y. L. (Ed.), *Emotions in sport* (pp. 267–92). Champaign, Ill.: Human Kinetics.
Lesyk, J. L. (1998). *Developing sport psychology within your clinical practice: A practical guide for mental health professionals.* San Francisco, Calif.: Jossey-Bass.

See also: AGGRESSION; ANGER; CONCENTRATION; CONTROL; DRIVE; EMOTION; EMOTIONAL INTELLIGENCE; FEAR; INSTINCT; MENTAL TOUGHNESS; NERVOUS SYSTEM; OBSESSIVE-COMPULSIVE; SELF-TALK

EMOTIONAL INTELLIGENCE

"A set of interrelated abilities for identifying, understanding, and managing emotions, both in the self and in others," is how Gerald

Matthews et al. define this concept. John Mayer et al. add that it includes the ABILITY "to reason and problem-solve on the basis of them [emotions]." The term is popularly associated with Daniel Goleman.

INTELLIGENCE itself has been the subject of several competing definitions, though most include the capacity to learn and abstract from actual experiences and to adapt to the environment. Emotional intelligence (EI) suggests a faculty, expertise, or SKILL in recognizing and assimilating information about one's own and others' emotions and being proficient at managing them. Managing, in this sense, means taking charge, organizing, or handling rather than wielding CONTROL over or suppressing emotions. In other words, using emotions effectively rather than reacting to them, or being at their mercy.

A great many claims have been made for EI: it has been related to life satisfaction and WELL-BEING, successful interpersonal RELATIONSHIPS, academic achievement, occupational stress, work performance, and LEADERSHIP, according to Ioannis Tsaousis and Ioannis Nikolaou, whose own research supports the claims that increased levels of EI are related to physical health and a reduction of STRESS. "People with high control of emotions will not resort to unhealthy solutions when facing difficulties, but on the contrary, they will proactively seek for techniques to cope with distressed situations that might CAUSE them health difficulties," they conclude, pointing out that there is a relationship between EI "and health-related behaviours, such as drinking, smoking and exercising."

EI correlates negatively with smoking and drinking and positively with RELAXATION and planned exercising.

Research designed "to elicit evaluative ANXIETY, seen in educational, sports, and social contexts," found an association between EI and less worry and AVOIDANCE coping during the performance of an anxiety-inducing task, yet only limited support for the view that EI is a reliable predictor of responses to all stressful situations. But, the authors suggest that EI might become a more important factor "in performance environments requiring interaction with other people, such as teamwork situations [. . .] than [in] the solo performance contexts."

The ability to recognize and respond to the emotions of others is one of the properties of EI, and this a promising quality in any team player, especially those in DECISION-MAKING positions.

Further reading

Goleman, Daniel (1995). *Emotional intelligence*. New York: Bantam Books.

Matthews, G., Emo, A. K., Funke, G., Zeidner, M., Roberts, R. D., Costa, P. T., and Shulze, R. (2006). Emotional intelligence, personality and task-induced stress. *Journal of Experimental Psychology*, 12, 96–107.

Mayer, John D., Caruso, D. R., and Salovey, P. (1999). Emotional intelligence meets traditional standards for an intelligence. *Intelligence*, 27, 267–98.

Tsaousis, Ioannis, and Nikolaou, Ioannis (2005). Exploring the relationship of emotional intelligence with physical and psychological health functioning. *Stress and Health*, 21, 77–86.

See also: ANXIETY; COPING STRATEGIES; DECISION-MAKING; EMOTION; EMOTIONAL CONTROL; FITNESS; INTELLIGENCE; LEADERSHIP; MOOD; NEGATIVITY; PERSONALITY; RELAXATION; REVERSAL THEORY; STRESS; STRESS-MANAGEMENT TRAINING; TEAM PLAYER; WELL-BEING.

EMOTIONAL TONE

This describes an overall favorable quality in either a RELATIONSHIP or an individual RESPONSE to a situation. For instance, "Our results suggest that positive reactions from parents are associated with greater levels of inter-dependence between the coach and the athlete, particularly as it pertains to the emotional tone of the relationship (that is, closeness)" (Jowett and Timson-Katchis). Or it can describe an individual's response to changing conditions: "Irrespective of the type of sport, participation produced positive changes in emotional tone with increases in excitement and decreases in negative emotions" (The Digest). Both suggest favorableness.

Further reading

Digest, The (2006). Telic dominance and emotional response in basketball and running. *Journal of Sport and Exercise Psychology*, 28, 409–10.

Jowett, Sophia and Timson-Katchis, Melina (2005). Social networks in sport: Parental influence on the coach–athlete relationship. *The Sport Psychologist*, 19, 267–87.

See also: AGGRESSION; EMOTION; EMOTIONAL INTELLIGENCE; FITNESS; HEDONIC TONE; MOOD; NERVOUS SYSTEM; OVERTRAINING SYNDROME; REINFORCEMENT; TELIC DOMINANCE; VIOLENCE; WELL-BEING

ENDORPHINS

The body manufactures its own natural painkillers, known as endorphins. These are neurotransmitter chemicals that bind with a certain kind of neuron called an opiate receptor and have a powerful effect on sensation, MOOD, and behavior. The "natural high" often reported by exercisers exhilarated by a hard workout has been popularly attributed to the secretion of endorphins—the name being a compound of *end*, from endogenous, meaning originating within, and *orphins*, from morphine, the pain-suppressing derivative from opium.

The effects of plant extracts containing opiates are well documented, though it was not until the 1970s that it was discovered that the body produced its own compounds that worked on receptors in response to PAIN or STRESS. Opiate receptors work to reduce pain sensations, and many pain-reducing drugs, especially derivatives of opium (including morphine, of course), are administered to stimulate these opiate receptors.

The exact mechanisms of the endorphin production process are not clear. Studies of animals have shown that the application of continuous stress or pain activates the process. In humans, it has been speculated that endorphins inhibit the release of excitatory substances for neurons carrying information about pain.

The therapeutic potential of exercise is well documented, and even ten minutes of vigorous exercise can raise endorphin levels for an hour. But evidence for a direct RELATIONSHIP between intense exercise and the secretion of endorphins is scant. Endorphins represent only one of many neurotransmitters involved in pain modulation. Serotonin and dopamine, which facilitate communication between parts of the brain, are associated with pleasurable feelings, and the release of these can be activated as the temperature of the brain rises. There are also more apparent reasons. Working out at a gym offers opportunities for conviviality and enjoyable interactions, for example; and improvements to BODY IMAGE resulting from exercise can also contribute to feelings of satisfaction.

Further reading

Hoffmann, P. (1997). The endorphin hypothesis. In W. P. Morgan (Ed.), *Physical Activity and Mental Health* (pp. 163–77). Washington, D.C.: Taylor & Francis.

Keiley, Lynn (2006). The secret to stress relief. *Mother Earth News*, June/July, 216. Available online at http://www.motherearthnews.com/Natural_Health/2006 _June_July/The_Secret_to_Stress_Relief.

Kraemer, R. R., Dzewaltowskj, D. A., Blair, M. S., Rinehardt, K. F., and Castracane, V. D. (1990). Mood alteration from treadmill running and its relationship to betaendorphine, corticotrophine, and growth hormone. *Journal of Sports Medicine and Physical Fitness, 30*(3), 241–6.

Springen, Karen (2004). The serenity workout. *Newsweek*, 144, 68–71.

See also: ADHERENCE; ADRENALINE RUSH; BODY IMAGE; DEPRESSION; MEDITATION; PAIN; RELAXATION; STRESS; WEIGHT CONTROL; WELL-BEING

EQUALITY

From the Old French *egalité*, which, in turn derives from Latin *æqualis*, meaning even, equality describes a condition of sameness in value, degree, rank, status, standing, or position between two or more subjects. It is sometimes confused with *equity*, which refers to fairness and principles of justice, which is quite different. It is possible to have a COMPETITION that upholds principles of equity but which is also unequal. All entrants compete under a system of rules and conditions that apply indiscriminately; yet, the competition is designed to ensure, or at least maximize the chances of, inequality of outcomes. Ties, draws, and dead heats notwithstanding, there will be winners and losers. In this sense, the whole point of sporting competition is to establish and verify inequality.

On the other hand, *equal treatment* is actively encouraged at all levels. Research by, among others C. Ames and J. Archer, highlighted how a transparent lack of preferentiality underpins a task-involving MOTIVATIONAL CLIMATE. Similarly, team sports emphasize equality of status and rights as a way of encouraging the cooperation that is vital to teamwork and COHESION.

Gestalt psychology has a second meaning for equality. As more than one STIMULUS in a perceptual field become similar, they will tend to be perceived as a single unit. This is known as the *law of equality*.

Further reading

Ames, C. and Archer, J. (1988). Achievement goals in the classroom: Students' learning strategies and motivation processes. *Journal of Educational Psychology*, 80, 260–7.

Morgan, W. J. (2000). The philosophy of sport: A historical and conceptual overview and a conjecture regarding its future. In J. Coakley and E. Dunning (Eds.), *Handbook of sports studies* (pp. 204–12). London: Sage.

See also: COHESION; COMPETITION; CONTEXT; GOAL; GROUP DYNAMICS; INCENTIVE; LEADERSHIP; MASTERY CLIMATE; TEAM PLAYER

ETHICS

Codes or rules based on moral precepts that are intended to govern a person or group's behavior. An ethic sometimes refers to a set of guiding principles related to a *specific* field of conduct, such as the Protestant Ethic, which prescribed that a person's duty was to achieve success through hard work, thrift, and abstention from forms of indulgence.

Professional practice PARAMETERS are intended both to CONTROL the behavior of professionals and assist them in resolving dilemmas in a manner that appropriately matches client expectations and needs. According to Zella Moore, there are six key areas or "primary topics" in the ethical standards of sport psychologists.

(1) *Confidentiality*: Information that passes between the psychologist and the client is "privileged" in the sense that it has special rights and immunities and should not ordinarily be shared with others, at least not without the explicit agreement of the client.

(2) *Use of informed consent*: The client has to give his or her permission for something to happen or for the psychologist to do something. The consent should be "informed," meaning that all information necessary for an educated decision about the likely benefits and risks of an intervention must be made available. Typically, the onus is on the practitioner to explain in language appropriate to the client and invite all parties to sign a written contract, which may function as a legal RISK-management document.

(3) *Practicing within areas of competence*: In this instance, competence is based on education, training, supervised experience, consultation, study, or professional experience and not one area of interest. For example, a consultant might recognize the symptoms of an eating disorder. If he or she does not possess the qualifications to treat this, then a referral rather than an INTERVENTION is appropriate.

(4) *Terminating the practitioner–client relationship*: Given the nature of sport, a professional relationship is likely to be transient, so practitioners have a responsibility to provide clients with continuity of care, despite changes in circumstances. Even if a sport psychologist is abruptly dismissed, he or she must secure other resources to meet the needs of the client.

(5) *Multiple roles*: The psychologist often functions in more than one professional relationship at a time, and he or she may engage in various roles with the client. As well as being an adviser, he or she might become a genuine friend, for example. Loss of objectivity, damage to the therapeutic alliance and even exploitation of the client are some of the dangers in fulfilling multiple roles that conflict with each other.

(6) *Multiple organizational demands*: Professionals are frequently employed by a club and work with individuals who are members of that club. This can raise dilemmas, such as if an athlete reveals information to the psychologist within the confidential relationship but which the psychologist believes should be brought to the attention of the club (for example, that the athlete is using performance-enhancing dope).

Further reading

Andersen, Mark B., Van Raalte, Judy L., and Brewer, Britton W. (2001). Sport psychology service delivery: Staying ethical while keeping loose. *Professional Psychology: Research and Practice,* 32, 12–18.
Moore, Zella E. (2003). Ethical dilemmas in sport psychology: Discussion and recommendations for practice. *Professional Psychology: Research and Practice*, 34, 601–10.
Whelan, J. P., Meyers, A. W., and Elkins, T. D. (2002). Ethics in sport and exercise psychology. In Judy L. Van Raalte and Britton W. Brewer (Eds), *Exploring sport and exercise psychology,* 2nd edn (pp. 503–23). Washington, D. C.: American Psychological Association.

See also: APPLIED SPORT PSYCHOLOGY; BURNOUT; COACH–ATHLETE RELATIONSHIP; DEPRESSION; DOPING; EATING DISORDERS; MORAL ATMOSPHERE

EUSTRESS

The delight, elation, or blissfulness experienced after an especially satisfying event is known as eustress, *eu* being Greek for good or pleasant (as in *eu*phoria, *eu*thanasia and *Eu*reka!) While the term "STRESS" has negative connotations, the state of AROUSAL elicited by eustress is agreeable, moderate, and usually interpreted as beneficial.

Galen Trail and Jeffrey James have identified eustress as one of the appealing factors that motivate FANS to follow sport, and Daniel Wann et al. argue that it heightens the attraction of actually being a fan. In the latter's study, experiencing eustress was a pleasant alternative to the tedium of some types of work and the excessive physiological or mental stimulation of some others. Anxiously awaiting a penalty shoot-out or a game-deciding field GOAL attempt or just laughing in despair about an inept performance can all be sources of eustress.

Further reading

Berk, L. S., Felten, D. L., Tan, S. A., Bittman, B. B., and Westengard, J. (2001). Modulation of neuroimmune parameters during the eustress of humor-associated mirthful laughter. *Alternative Therapies in Health and Medicine*, 7, 62–76.

Kremer, J. and Scully, D. (1994). *Psychology in sport*. London and New York: Routledge.

Trail, Galen T., and James, Jeffrey D. (2001). The motivation scale for sport consumption: Assessment of the scale's psychometric properties. *Journal of Sport Behavior*, 24, 108–28.

Wann, Daniel L., Allen, Beverly, and Rochelle Al R. (2004). Using sport fandom as an escape: Searching for relief from under-stimulation and over-stimulation. *International Sports Journal,* 8, 104–10.

See also: EMOTION; ENDORPHINS; FANS; NERVOUS SYSTEM; NERVOUSNESS; PSYCHING; STRESS; TELIC DOMINANCE; VICARIOUS AGENCY; WELL-BEING

EXECUTIVE CONTROL

A high-level cognitive function that is used in DECISION-MAKING, attending to more than one object, and determining the content of short-term MEMORY, among other complex tasks. *Executivus* is Latin for "carry out," as in execute an order. Karen Springen puts it simply, when she describes executive control as, "the ABILITY to FOCUS on important things and tune out distractions."

Executive control is associated with the brain's frontal lobe, which is used "where more than one concurrent stimulus allows multiple and conflicting actions," as Courtney Hall et al. put it. They continue: "In such situations, goals or instructions provide additional constraint, a constraint called executive control." As such, executive control is crucial in competitive activity.

While the overall effects of aerobic exercise on declining cognitive function in the elderly is unproven, there is evidence to suggest that regular physical activity can improve executive function in particular.

Further reading

Hall, Courtney, D., Smith, Alan L., and Keele, Steven W. (2001). The impact of aerobic activity on cognitive function in older adults: A new synthesis based on the concept of executive control. *European Journal of Cognitive Psychology*, 13, 279–300.

Hillman, C. H., Belopolsky, A. V., Snook, E. M., Kramer, A. E., and McAuley, E. (2004). Physical activity and executive control: Implications for increased cognitive health during older adulthood. *Research Quarterly for Exercise and Sport*, 75, 176–85.

Springen, Karen (2004). The serenity workout. *Newsweek*, 144, 68–71.

See also: AEROBIC/ANAEROBIC; AGING; ATTENTION; COGNITION; COGNITIVE LOAD THEORY; CONCENTRATION; DECISION-MAKING; KNOWLEDGE OF RESULTS; MEMORY; NERVOUS SYSTEM; REACTION TIME

EXERCISE BEHAVIOR

While the term suggests a description of the way in which people conduct themselves in RESPONSE to activities requiring physical effort (usually carried out to sustain or improve WELL-BEING), there are actually several facets to exercise behavior that are open to investigation. The word "exercise" derives from the Latin *exercitium*, meaning to keep busy, or practice.

Exercise readiness, for instance, is the state of willingness or preparedness to engage in exercise. This can include physical indices, such as the ability to transport and use oxygen efficiently (VO^2_{max}), or psychological, for example, perceived SELF-EFFICACY or belief in the capability of successfully completing the exercise. *Exercise transition* is another aspect. This defines the process of change either instigated by or affecting the exerciser. Again, this can involve physical changes, like weight reduction, or psychological ones, including changes in SELF-CONFIDENCE and a sense of MASTERY—which are themselves often associated with physical changes.

Exercise ADHERENCE, as the name suggests, describes whether or not the exerciser sticks fast to a program or routines. Prolonged involvement in exercise can give rise to what has been known as EXERCISE IDENTITY, when an adherent integrates the activity into his or her own conception of self. This affects practically every other aspect of a person's being.

Not all effects of sustained engagement with exercise are beneficial. The incidence of EXERCISE DEPENDENCE and ANOREXIA ATHLETICA indicate how what is initially a physically and psychologically favorable pursuit can become a source of maladaptive behavior and even psychopathology. The use of exercise IMAGERY (visualizing oneself with a leaner body, or being exhilarated by running, for example) was discovered to be a positive predictor of exercise dependency symptoms, by Heather Hausenblas and Danielle Symons Downs.

A SOCIALIZATION process takes place in the environment surrounding exercise activities. The gym in itself can be conducive to a MASTERY

CLIMATE, which encourages the preparedness to accept new challenges. The exercise milieu can serve as a source of social support.

Much recent work on exercise revolves around the questions, why or why not—as Jemma Edmunds et al., advise: "Examining the motivational determinants of exercise behavior has become a prominent topic in exercise psychology."

Christopher Lantz et al., for example, discovered that concern over BODY IMAGE manifesting as SOCIAL PHYSIQUE ANXIETY was a powerful inhibition. People did not want to exhibit their bodies. And, while INTRINSIC MOTIVATION seems an obvious reason for becoming involved in exercise, other studies have shown that this is not the case. "People are unlikely to maintain regular exercise behavior, with all the organization and COMMITMENT that it entails, purely for the intrinsic reasons of fun and enjoyment," Edmunds et al. point out.

The key to understanding prolonged MOTIVATION to exercise is not INTRINSIC MOTIVATION, but IDENTIFIED REGULATION. As Edmunds et al., conclude: "In order to partake in strenuous exercise behaviors, which necessitate considerable physical and mental exertion and stamina, individuals must place some value on the exercise and recognize its importance in terms of health and well-being." Improved fitness, weight reduction, and good looks are relevant to active engagement in the exercise setting. This finding suggests a degree of INTERNALIZATION is necessary.

Other research has found that the self-efficacy mentioned earlier as a consequence of exercise behavior can also function as a determinant. "A person with greater self-efficacy to overcome barriers to exercise is more likely to be active, and greater activity is, in turn associated with greater self-efficacy," conclude Ralph Maddison and Harry Prapavessis. A complementary study by Jennifer Linde et al. indicated an association between self-efficacy beliefs and exercise programs, as well as weight-loss trials.

Besides the manifold physiological benefits of exercise, many claim there are significant psychological advantages. The attenuation of DEPRESSION, state ANXIETY and STRESS are documented effects; research is now directed at identifying the precise mechanisms through which exercise works in these areas.

Further reading

Anshel, Mark H. (1996). Effect of chronic aerobic exercise and progressive relaxation on motor performance and affect. *Behavioral Medicine*, 21, 186–99.

Edmunds, Jemma, Ntoumanis, Nikos, and Duda, Joan L. (2006). A test of self-determination theory in the exercise domain. *Journal of Applied Social Psychology*, 36, 2240–65.

Hausenblas, Heather A. and Symons Downs, Danielle (2002). Relationship among sex, imagery, and exercise dependence syndrome. *Psychology of Addictive Behaviors*, 16, 160–72.

Lantz, Christopher D., Hardy, Charles J., and Ainsworth, Barbara E. (1997). Social physique anxiety and perceived exercise behavior. *Journal of Sport Behavior*, 20, 83–93.

Linde, Jennifer, A., Rothman, Alexander J., Baldwin, Austin S., and Jeffrey, Robert W. (2006). The impact of self-efficacy on behavior change and weight change among overweight participants in a weight loss trial. *Health Psychology*, 25, 282–91.

Maddison, Ralph, and Prapavessis, Harry (2006). Exercise behavior among New Zealand adolescents: A test of the transtheoretical model, *Pediatric Exercise Science*, 18, 351–63.

See also: ADHERENCE; EXERCISE DEPENDENCE; EXERCISE IDENTITY; IDENTIFIED REGULATION; INTERNALIZATION; INTRINSIC MOTIVATION; SELF-CONFIDENCE; SELF-DETERMINATION THEORY; SELF-EFFICACY; WEIGHT CONTROL; WELL-BEING.

EXERCISE DEPENDENCE

Also known as exercise addiction, and closely associated with—though not the same as—ANOREXIA ATHLETICA, exercise dependence is "a craving for exercise that results in uncontrollable excessive physical activity and manifests in physiological symptoms, psychological symptoms, or both," according to Heather Hausenblas and Danielle Symons Downs, who differentiate between *primary* and *secondary* exercise dependence. The former physical activity is an end in itself, whereas, in secondary exercise dependence, CONTROL, and manipulation of the body shape and composition is the ultimate GOAL, and exercise is a means of achieving this.

D. Smith and B. Hale's research on bodybuilders indicated that a low level of life satisfaction is a common antecedent condition. The typical dependant is "single, childless, of intermediate or low socioeconomic status, and will have a relatively low level of subjective WELL-BEING." Trainers frequently take up bodybuilding to compensate for dissatisfaction elsewhere. But their resulting obsessive approach to training leaves them with a "psychologically dysfunctional and undesirable state of mind."

The strength of their attachment to bodybuilding means that they cannot easily cut down the amount of time spent at the gym. Like other forms of DEPENDENCE, it involves compulsive behavior, and exercisers feel that they are unable to control themselves. The fact that this form of dependency can persist often for several years suggests that it does not necessarily lead directly to physical debilitation and the dependent person *may* operate functionally in a behavioral sense.

Further reading

Hausenblas, Heather A. and Symons Downs, Danielle (2002). Relationship among sex, imagery, and exercise dependence symptoms. *Psychology of Addictive Behaviors*, 16, 169–72.

Munroe-Chandler, K. J., Arvin J. and Gammage, Kimberley L. (2004). Using imagery to predict weightlifting dependency in men. *International Journal of Men's Health*, 3, 129–39.

Smith, D. and Hale, B. (2005). Exercise-dependence in bodybuilders: Antecedents and reliability of measurement. *Journal of Sports Medicine and Physical Fitness*, 45, 401–9.

Szabo, A. (2000). Physical activity as a source of psychological dysfunction. In S. J. Biddle, K. R. Fox and S. H. Boutcher (Eds). *Physical activity and psychological well-being* (pp. 130–53). London and New York: Routledge.

See also: ALCOHOLISM; ANOREXIA ATHLETICA; ANOREXIA NERVOSA; BODY IMAGE; BULIMIA NERVOSA; DEPENDENCE; EATING DISORDERS; GAMBLING; GENDER; OBSESSIVE-COMPULSIVE; OVERTRAINING SYNDROME; SELF-ACTUALIZATION; SOCIAL PHYSIQUE ANXIETY; WEIGHT CONTROL

EXERCISE IDENTITY

This CONSTRUCT serves to establish to what extent exercise forms a characteristic of who or what a person believes him or herself to be. "As exercise identity may be influenced by significant others, reinforcements, and attributions for one's own behavior, the manner in which social-cognitive influences and interventions designed to promote and encourage physical activity should continue to be examined," observe Bradley and Marita Cardinal, whose research draws on earlier work that examined how involvement in exercise programs affects how participants think about themselves.

Further reading

Cardinal, Bradley J. and Cardinal, Marita K. (1997). Changes in exercise behavior and exercise identity associated with a 14-week aerobic exercise class. *Journal of Sport Behavior*, 20, 377–87.

Anderson, D. F. and Cychosz, C. M. (1995). Exploration of the relationship between exercise behavior and exercise identity. *Journal of Sport Behavior,* 18, 159–66.

See also: AGING; ATHLETIC IDENTITY; COGNITION; COMEBACK; DROPOUTS; EXERCISE DEPENDENCE; IDENTITY; SELF-ACTUALIZATION; SOCIALIZATION

EXERCISE MOTIVATION

While both sport and exercise are elective forms of physical activity, exercise is, as Marcus Kilpatrick and his colleagues put it, "engaged in to gain, maintain or improve fitness." Criteria for success in exercise is different from those in sport. They are likely to be more task-oriented, with personal success measured in terms of improvement rather than the more ego-oriented winning. Effort and persistence are accentuated rather than results alone. As such, motives for participating might be expected to vary.

Yet, there are congruencies. Both exercise and sport offer the opportunity for assessing success and competence in tangible or even measurable terms, whether physical strength, weight loss, aerobic fitness, or appearance. The latter is especially important in exercise and introduces the possibility of more ego-involved orientations: Research on SOCIAL PHYSIQUE ANXIETY indicates that self-presentational motives lie behind much exercise. A comparison of competitive and noncompetitive cyclists disclosed that, while all cyclists endorsed GOAL achievement and health as reasons for participating, noncompetitive exercisers, especially female exercisers, were motivated by weight concerns, affiliation, and SELF-ESTEEM. Mountain-bike riders cited "life meaning" as a primary motivation for cycling.

Further reading

Kilpatrick, Marcus, Bartholomew, John, and Riemer, Harold (2003). The measurement of goal orientations in exercise. *Journal of Sport Behavior,* 26, 121–7.

LaChausse, Robert G. (2006). Motives of competitive and non-competitive cyclists. *Journal of Sport Behavior,* 29, 304–15.

See also: ACHIEVEMENT MOTIVE; BODY IMAGE; ENDORPHINS; EUSTRESS; GOAL ORIENTATION; IDENTIFIED REGULATION; INTERNALIZATION; MOTIVATION; MOTIVATIONAL CLIMATE; SELF-ESTEEM; SOCIAL PHYSIQUE ANXIETY; ZONE

EXPECTANCY

The state of anticipating the probability of an outcome is expectancy. It is formed from *ex*, meaning "out," and *spectare*, Latin for "look." Expectancy bears heavily on how athletes evaluate the significance and consequences of a COMPETITION and how they respond in an EMOTIONAL sense to situations arising once that contest is under way.

An example of how this works in practice is given by Peter Crocker et al., who hypothesize a basketball player who has been injured during a game: "Initially she is very angry if she believes that the other person was responsible." The ANGER subsides as she realizes that she may be out for the rest of the season, paving the way for "unhappiness" to set in. Then, she examines the INJURY to discover it is not so serious and that she will receive top medical treatment. "Her expectancies are that the situation will get better." As the extent of the injury becomes clear, she anticipates that she will still be able to pursue her goals after all. "This will change the emotional state of unhappiness into a different emotional state, such as relief."

In this example, expectancies change as appraisals of immediate situations change and the athlete modifies her anticipation of the future. Expectancy is part of a general appraisal process. The precise way in which expectancy is understood depends on a theoretical approach. For instance, a behaviorist interested in the REINFORCE-MENT value of contingencies will study expectancy through such objective features as muscular tension, eye dilation, and, perhaps, other indicators of AROUSAL, while a researcher focused on COGNITION will wish to study expectancy through the perceptions, states of awareness, and general subjective apprehension of the subject. There are two basic applications of the concept in sport and exercise psychology:

Application 1: Expectancy value. Expectancy is one of three different types of belief that contribute to MOTIVATION, according to a 1964 book by V. H. Vroom, the others being *instrumentality* (the belief that a performance will be rewarded) and *valence* (the perceived value of the reward to the individual). A person who never receives reinforcement when practicing a SKILL may have a low expectancy level such that, no matter how hard they try, they will not achieve a higher level and may not try too hard. Even if they do work hard and still receive little or no REWARD, motivation is likely to recede. If and when the rewards do arrive, they have to be appropriate. For instance, there is no point in rewarding a child learning a new skill with a new bike if they were longing for a PlayStation. This is, of course, an unlikely scenario. In practical terms, the adult offering the reward would probably exert a socializing influence on the child, shaping the child's values and ambitions to the point where there would be symmetry between the expectancy and the valence.

Application 2: Expectancy effects. This is associated with the SELF-FULFILLING PROPHECY and refers to the manner in which beliefs formed before an activity can affect the actual outcome of the activity in a way that confirms the initial expectancy. The process has a self-validating efficacy. Information available to athletes, their opponents, judges, officials, coaches, and so on may be partial, distorted or plainly false, but it can still be used to form a set of expectations about others. This can guide the way in which a subject perceives, considers, and interprets further information. The subject filters through information, discovers, then pays attention selectively to items of information that are encoded in a way that supports the expectancy, and remembers them. In actual encounters, this information affects both the subject's judgment and hence behavior toward the object of the expectancy.

The reputations of figure skaters, or gymnasts performing last, have been shown to be factors leading to expectancy effects, judges tending to award higher scores to last-appearing gymnasts or to "name" skaters. But the research does not show conclusively "that pre-event expectancies can influence the evaluation of performances," according to Richard Buscombe et al., whose own research on tennis players' pre-match BODY LANGUAGE and dress highlighted how information early in a competitive encounter is used to influence the way future information is used and their perceived likelihood of success.

This does not suggest a guarantee, however, and, as Kristina Diekmann and her colleagues point out: "Individuals will fail to accurately predict how they will behave when faced with a competitive opponent." There is a "disconnection" between desirability (our ideal representation of future events) and feasibility. "People rarely accurately perceive the situational constraints that will propel their behavior and do not make adequate allowance for the uncertainties of situational constraints," Diekmann et al. conclude. Those situational constraints can include practically anything.

Diekmann et al.'s research also reveals how "the target of the competitive expectancy" can change as a result of the original forecast, especially if the holder of the belief has failed to consider the motivations inspired in the opponent by a competitive situation. There is a tendency to FOCUS on the foreground rather than the

"situational background" or the "larger CONTEXT." Targets of a competitive expectancy came to see themselves as more competitive and behave
more aggressively. The study highlights the influence of expectancy,
though not necessarily in bringing about a desired outcome.

Further reading

Buscombe, R., Greenlees, I., Holder, T., Thelwell, R., and Rimmer, M. (2006).
Expectancy effects in tennis: The impact of opponent's pre-match non-verbal
behaviour on male tennis players. *Journal of Sports Sciences*, 24, 1265–72.

Crocker, P. E., Kowalski, K. C., Graham, T. R. and Kowalski, N. P. (2002).
Emotion in sport. In J. M. Silva and D. E. Stevens (Eds.), *Psychological
foundations of sport* (pp. 107–31). Boston, Mass.: Allyn & Bacon.

Diekmann, Kristina A., Tenbrunsel, Ann E., and Galinsky, Adam D. (2003).
From self-prediction to self-defeat: Behavioral forecasting, self-fulfilling
prophecies and the effect of competitive expectations. *Journal of Personality
and Social Psychology*, 85, 672–83.

Vroom, V. H. (1964). *Work and motivation*. New York: John Wiley.

See also: ATTENTION; BODY LANGUAGE; CELEBRITIES; COACH–ATHLETE RELATION-
SHIP; COGNITION; CONSTRUCT; CONTEXT; FEAR; HALO EFFECT; HOME ADVANTAGE;
KNOWLEDGE OF RESULTS; LEARNED HELPLESSNESS; SELF-CONFIDENCE; SELF-ESTEEM;
SELF-FULFILLING PROPHECY; SOCIALIZATION; THEORY

EXPERTISE

Supreme SKILL in or knowledge of a specific domain.

See also: SKILL; SKILL ACQUISITION; SKILL EXECUTION

EXTREME SPORTS

Physically dangerous pursuits, including paragliding, skydiving, and
bungee jumping.

See also: DEATH WISH; RISK; SENSATION-SEEKING

EXTRINSIC MOTIVATION

If the reason or reasons for action are not part of its character and lie
outside it, the motivation for engaging in it are said to be extrinsic, a

word that derives from the Latin *extrinsecus*, meaning outward. In much the same way, extrinsic factors are those that operate from the outside (for example, extrinsic factors affect domestic industry) and extrinsic rewards are separated from an achievement (for example, an industrial worker is rewarded for several hours of overtime with a cash bonus).

Most people's initial MOTIVATION for becoming involved in sport and exercise is intrinsic—contained within the activity—and might typically include, for example, pleasure in performing the exercise or the fun of competing. Extrinsic motivation usually follows prolonged involvement in an activity. A professional athlete might eventually be motivated by money, or a habitual exerciser might visit the gym strictly to lose weight or because of health concerns. In both cases, something outside the activity is the reward.

While the distinction between extrinsic and INTRINSIC MOTIVATION is a conceptual one, in practice there is often considerable overlap. There is also evidence of a sliding relationship between the two. For example, offering cash rewards to engage in an activity that was previously regarded as just for fun can have the effect of decreasing intrinsic motivation. One account of this is offered by COGNITIVE EVALUATION THEORY, which suggests basically that, when approaching a task, people assess or form an idea of its value in terms of how it meets their needs to feel competent.

For example, if someone concludes that he or she is capable of completing the task, they will be intrinsically motivated and need no further motivation. If, on the other hand, the person concludes that the task falls outside his or her sphere of competence, then extrinsic factors will be needed to induce participation. In the latter case, the extrinsic rewards will have a controlling effect.

This is complicated by the fact that, even if a person enjoys performing a task and relishes the challenge of attempting a task that they have not successfully completed before, the presence of an extrinsic motivation will still make that person feel controlled in some measure. This will diminish the intrinsic motivation.

Further reading

Deci, E. L. and Ryan, R. M. (1991). A motivational approach to self: Integration in personality. In R. Diestiber (Ed.), *Nebraska symposium on motivation*, volume 38 (pp. 37–288). Lincoln, Nebr.: University of Nebraska Press.

Ryan, R. M. and Deci, E. L. (1989). Bridging the research traditions of task/ego involvement and intrinsic/extrinsic motivation: Comment on Butler (1987). *Journal of Educational Psychology*, 81, 265–88.

EYE MOVEMENT

Because the PERCEPTION of others' intentions and behavior is so crucial in sports, eye movement is important, both to communicate visual information and to deliver/receive social signals. So much of sport is conducted in the absence of speech that alternative means of communication are habitually employed. Eye movement is one element of a whole repertoire of BODY LANGUAGE that comes to the fore in any contest.

The pattern of glances in everyday life is closely coordinated with speech; whereas in sports it is often coordinated with nonverbal gestures. A tennis player may raise an arm in apology for a winning let-cord shot, but the import is lost unless it is accompanied by eye contact for a few seconds. During a game, staring directly downwards or glancing only occasionally at an opponent is coded—along with hunched posture and a sagging head—as negative body language. Maintaining eye contact with an opponent for prolonged periods of time is an integral part of positive BODY LANGUAGE, according to research on tennis players by Iain Greenlees et al.

Teammates in many sports use glances to collect information from each other and to make affiliative contact through the course of a contest. In any sport, a glance, followed by an exaggerated blink and a turn away signals contempt or ridicule.

Perhaps the most interesting eye movement in sports is the mutual *fixation*, better known as "eyeball–to–eyeball," or just "eyeballing," the latter sometimes meaning a one-way stare. This involves two rivals simultaneously orienting their eyeballs so that the projection of the viewed object—in this case, the other's pupils—falls on the fovea (the tiny depression at the back of the eye) and stays in focus. If we could draw lines from both subjects' pupils to the objects of their gaze, there would, in theory be just two lines rather than four, as the fixation point for each would be the other's pupils.

Mutual fixations, or "mutual gazes," occur during everyday conversation, though rarely for more than 30 percent of the interaction and hardly ever for more than five seconds. More typically, eyes dart over the other's facial features, dwelling for about 0.3 seconds on each, perhaps longer on the mouth; this jerky screening movement is known as a *saccade*. Fixation contact, by contrast, is for several seconds, demonstrates interest and an increase in AROUSAL, suggesting that an important message is being communicated. In sports, the fixation is a barely coded social signal: a threat designed to elicit agitation, FEAR, and alarm in the opponent. A rival who does not or cannot respond by fixing eyes will be "stared-down" and forced to concede a perhaps small, but symbolic defeat either before or during a contest. In boxing, it became a popular PSYCHING technique.

There is no empirical evidence that dominance in an eye-movement encounter necessarily translates into competitive dominance, and its value may be concomitant rather than direct. For example, the opponent who breaks off the fixation and looks at a rival's shoulders or away completely may do so because of an unwillingness to break CONCENTRATION on the actual COMPETITION and not because of intimidation. The dominant eye-mover, on the other hand, may interpret this as a significant victory in the psychological battle that accompanies the actual competition; that interpretation will enhance his or her SELF-CONFIDENCE. Today, when eyeball-to-eyeball fixations are so commonplace as to be ritualistic, some athletes refuse to engage in them and, instead, grin mockingly, sending out another signal: "I'm not getting involved in this nonsense; I just want to get on with the business."

The question remains: Why should eye movement carry the potential to evoke such powerful behavioral and EMOTIONAL reactions? Human infants respond to fixed eye contact as young as four weeks, allowing the parents to employ a gaze or stare as a simple yet effective form of CONTROL and DISCIPLINE. Through maturity, the child learns to decode other meanings for fixed eye contact. He or she learns that paying ATTENTION is accompanied by mutual gazing: "Look at me when I'm talking to you!" Later, the value of mutual fixation in demonstrations of affection may appear: "They stared deeply into each other's eyes." The STIMULUS properties of eyes in signaling sexual attraction are, of course, great. Winking, staring and even self-consciously averting one's gaze are all strategies of courting rituals, though they are used in different ways in different cultures—as are eye movements generally.

Referees also look for eye movements in athletes. In boxing, referees famously look into a fighter's eyes to ascertain his (or her) condition. This is a spurious technique: there are no reliable ocular indicators for determining the boxer's overall physical condition. Referees rarely disclose what they are looking for, though they sometimes report a "glazed look." A boxer under pressure is likely to fix his sights on the opponent rather than the referee, perhaps misleading the official to conclude that he or she cannot FOCUS. In soccer, players can be cautioned for "dissent" if a referee interprets a look as signaling disagreement with a decision. Baseball umpires are less sensitive and habitually engage in mutual fixations with managers.

Further reading

Bull, P. and Frederikson, L. (1996), Non-verbal communication. In A. M. Colman (Ed.) (1996). *Companion encyclopedia of psychology* (Vol. II, pp. 852–72). London and New York: Routledge.

Greenlees, Iain, Buscombe, Richard, Thelwell, Richard, Holder, Tim, and Rimmer, Matthew (2005). Impact of opponents' clothing and body language on impression formation and outcome expectations. *Journal of Sport and Exercise Psychology*, 27, 39–52.

Rakos, R. F. (1991). *Assertive Behavior*. London and New York: Routledge.

See also: AROUSAL; ATTENTION; BODY LANGUAGE; CENTERING; CONCENTRATION; FEAR; FOCUS; PERCEPTION; PSYCHING; RIVALRY; SELF-CONFIDENCE; SKILL EXECUTION; VISUAL PERCEPTION

FANS

There are two versions of the source of the word "fan," which today refers to an enthusiast, devotee, or supporter. One traces it to the adjective fanatic, from the Latin *fanaticus*, meaning "of a temple"; so the fan is someone who is excessively enthusiastic or filled with the kind of zeal usually associated with religious fervor. The term crept into baseball in the late 1880s, but as a replacement for the more pejorative "crank," according to Tom Sullivan, writing for the *Sporting Life* of November 23, 1887. The alternative is even older: the "fancy" was the collective name given to patrons of prize-fighting in the early nineteenth century. There are references in Pierce Egan's 1812 classic *Boxiana*. Whatever its etymology, "fan" lost its religious and patrician connotations and became a description of followers, or admirers of virtually anybody or anything in popular CULTURE.

Fandom refers to the condition in which whole congregations of people devote parts of their life to following, or just admiring a rock star, a sports team, or virtually anything ("dom" means a collective domain in which subjects share common practices, manners and elements of lifestyle, like king*dom*, official*dom* or free*dom*).

"The history of fandom is full of parallels with the history of RELI-GION," writes David Giles, who describes fans' relationships with the objects of their devotion as PARASOCIAL INTERACTION, a term introduced in 1956 by D. Horton, and R. R. Wohl. Meaningful as the RELATIONSHIPS are for the fans, "they can never be more than unilateral." In other words, the club, the celebrity, or the show cannot enter the relationship, which is always destined to be one-way. This is clear when we recognize that fans do not restrict the objects of their ATTENTION to sports. Pop music, soaps, and old television shows, like *Star Trek* and *The X-Files*, develop followings of devotees, who occasionally exhibit obsession with their chosen genres or icons.

In a revealing study published in 1991, Neil Alperstein wrote of "Imaginary social relationships with celebrities appearing in television commercials." The "artificial involvement," as Alperstein called it, in the lives of people viewers have never met paradoxically helps them "make sense of reality." A later piece of research by Benson Fraser and William Brown yielded similar conclusions, though this time about one celebrity in particular. In their "Media, celebrities, and social influence: identification with Elvis Presley," Fraser and Brown wrote, "Fans develop self-defining relationships with CELEBRITIES and seek to adopt their perceived attributes, resulting in powerful forms of personal and social transformation." Fraser and Brown argue that the CONCEPT of parasocial relationship can't adequately cope with the bilateral, or two-way character of this kind of fan–celebrity interaction. It precipitates affective and behavioral changes in the fan that they describe as IDENTIFICATION, meaning that fans "reconstruct their own attitudes, values, or behaviors in response to the images of people they admire, real and imagined, both through personal and mediated relationships." While these studies were not about sports fans, their conclusions concur with those of Daniel Wann, who has examined the psychology of fans, specifically how being a highly identified fan has "strong implications for their feelings of SELF-WORTH," and how identification is a form of escape from "the stress and boredom in one's life."

For Mark Dechesne et al., documenting how fans identify with a figure or a team and how this contributes to self-worth is insufficient. "Sports has become an important source of social IDENTITY," they agree. But why? Their research provides an answer: "People bask in the reflected glory of particularly successful groups and individuals, including sports teams and well-known athletes, to feel valuable and special, which in turn ameliorates their concerns about morality."

This study (conducted in the Netherlands and USA) derived its theoretical approach from terror-management theory, which proposes that reminders of mortality increase the tendency to affiliate with some person, group, or institution as a defense against existential concerns.

Another attempt to specify the causal factors behind fan identification is that of Cheryl Harris who interprets fandom "as a PHENOMENON in which members of subordinated groups try to align themselves with meanings embodied in stars or other texts [that is, things that have meaning to the fan] that best express their own sense of social identity." For Harris, this signals a powerlessness that is in some way negated by following the exploits of others and perhaps displacing one's own inadequacies in the process. Being a fan confers a power on subjects who have little material power.

Sometimes, fans are excited to action. For example, in 1949, a fan shot Philadelphia Phillies player Eddie Waitkus. In the 1990s, tormented admirers harassed Katarina Witt and Steffi Graf. Graf's fan, who kept a shrine to her in his aunt's attic, ran onto a tennis court to stab Graf's rival Monica Seles. Similarly obsessed fans have pestered celebrity athletes, such Anna Kournikova and David Beckham and are known to suffer from *erotomania*, meaning a delusion that the object of their passion reciprocates the emotion. This extreme form of identification can induce fans to transfer their cognitions into practical actions, which are invariably unwelcome and might eventually become threatening.

Further reading

Alperstein, Neil M. (1991). Imaginary social relationships with celebrities appearing in television commercials. *Journal of Broadcasting and Electronic Media*, 35, 45–58.

Dechesne, Mark, Greenberg, Jeff, Arndt, Jamie, and Schimel, Jeff (2000). Terror management and the vicissitudes of sports fan affiliation: The effects of mortality salience on optimism and fan identification. *European Journal of Social Psychology*, 30, 813–35.

Fraser, Benson P. and Brown, William J. (2002). Media, celebrities, and social influence: identification with Elvis Presley. *Mass Communication and Society*, 1, 183–207.

Giles, D. (2000). *Illusions of immortality: A psychology of fame and celebrity*. New York: St. Martin's Press.

Harris, C. (1998). A sociology of television fandom. In C. Harris and A. Alexander (Eds.), *Theorizing fandom: Fans, subculture and identity* (pp. 41–54). Cresskill, N.J.: Hampton Press.

Horton, D. and Wohl R. R. (1956). Mass communication and parasocial interaction. *Psychiatry*, 19, 215–29.

Wann, Daniel L. and Grieve, Frederick G. (2005). Biased evaluations of in-group and out-group spectator behavior at sporting events: The importance of team identification and threats to social identity. *Journal of Social Psychology*, 145, 531–46.

Wann, Daniel L., Allen, Beverly, and Rochelle A. R. (2004). Using sport fandom as an escape: Searching for relief from under-stimulation and over-stimulation. *International Sports Journal*, 8, 104–10.

See also: CELEBRITIES; CONTEXT; EUSTRESS; HEDONIC TONE; HOME ADVANTAGE; IDENTIFICATION; IDENTITY; LUCK; RELIGION; RIVALRY; ROLE MODEL; SELF-ACTUALIZATION; SELF-CONCEPT; SOCIAL FACILITATION; SUPERSTITIOUS BEHAVIOR; VICARIOUS AGENCY; VIOLENCE

FEAR

Unlike ANXIETY, which is usually regarded as an apprehension or anticipation of something unwelcome, or *phobia*, which is a persistent, irrational aversion to something, fear is an EMOTION associated with an actual impending danger or evil. It is often characterized by the subjective experience of discomfort and AROUSAL and, sometimes, sympathetic physiological responses, such as those accompanying an ADRENALINE RUSH. The relevance of fear to sports is equivocal. Fear can induce a kind of paralysis in some competitors so that they "freeze" in the face of a forbidding rival. It can also act as what Mike Tyson's first trainer Cus D'Amato called "a friend," causing exhilaration that facilitates optimum performance.

In both types of situation, fear may be experienced similarly, the analogous physiological changes may be close, and the outward expressions of fear will almost certainly be disguised (most athletes are trained not to show fear). The behavioral responses, on the other hand, are different. The first is a type of AVOIDANCE, while the second encourages an AGGRESSIVENESS if not outright AGGRESSION. Repeated exposure to formidable opposition and fear-inducing situations will benefit competitors with a tendency to freeze, though athletes who thrive on fear and eventually become desensitized to it may experience difficulty in PSYCHING up for opponents.

The former's fearlessness should result in greater SELF-CONFIDENCE, while the latter's will lead to insensibility. The third possibility is that it will lead to persistent anxiety and perhaps even some form of PSYCHOPATHOLOGY, as the research of Giulia Buodo et al., suggests:

"In the face of a potential threat, the experience of fear is appropriate, but there are many instances and conditions in which fear is disproportionately great or persists long after the removal of the threat."

Some sports, by their very nature, are bound to bring about the experience of fear in all but the most desensitized competitors. Formula 1 racing, for example, carries ever-present risks of DEATH, as do air sports, skiing, surfing, and EXTREME SPORTS. All forms of motor racing, including NASCAR, are dangerous, but the financial incentives are very high, and one presumes these persuade competitors of the need to live with their fear. Yet, the other high-RISK sports are not so rewarding financially and require some explanation.

Frank Furedi argues that we actually seek out fearful situations because we find them agreeable. Furedi's argument is that the apparent lust for danger is a product of a safety-first CULTURE in which personal security, public protection, and environmental management have become priorities. As the search for safety gains MOMENTUM, the ways to escape it become more ingenious. Established practices, like mountain climbing, stunt cycling, and potholing continue as newer adaptations flourished. Zorbing, bungee jumping, and whitewater rafting contain ersatz dangers. They offer thrills, though under controlled conditions. Other responses, such as hang gliding, or kayaking off waterfalls, are less amenable to CONTROL and so have genuine life-threatening potential.

While we avoid risks that lie outside our control, we are quite prepared to take voluntary risks. The so-called "lifestyle risks" such as smoking, drinking, and driving are examples of this. But sports present us with something quite different: manufactured risks that are actually designed in such a way as to preserve natural dangers or build in new ones and so elicit fear in us. Michael Bane, author of *Over the Edge: A Regular Guy's Odyssey in Extreme Sports*, agrees that, "In our personal lives, we accept the government's (and the legal system's) position that life should be free of risks." For Bane, fear-inducing sports are a RESPONSE to an increasingly safe environment.

Since the days of Ivan Pavlov (1849–1936), behaviorists have experimented with fear conditioning, pairing an ordinarily neutral environment or sound with a harmful or unpleasant STIMULUS (like an electric shock). Following exposure to the conditional stimulus, rats exhibit a conditioned defense response—they freeze. This automatic behavior is established through classical conditioning. John Broadus Watson (1878–1958) managed to condition a child to fear, though, for ethical reasons, this is not an experiment that has been replicated.

The point is that, if fear can be conditioned—and behaviorists would insist that fear is no more than a conditioned response—then presumably it can be eradicated through training too.

Finally, a study by David Baruch et al. concluded that physical exercise alters hippocampal function (the hippocampus is thought to be the brain's center of emotion, MEMORY, and the AUTONOMIC NERVOUS SYSTEM) and learning. The investigation was conducted on rats, which were subject to fear conditioning. Exercised rats froze after being exposed to shock, suggesting that physical exertion enhances learning, in this case learning fear.

Further reading

Bane, Michael (1997). *Over the edge: A regular guy's odyssey in extreme sports.* London: Gollancz.

Baruch, David E., Swain, Rodney A., and Helmstetter, Fred J. (2004). Effects of exercise on Pavlovian fear conditioning. *Behavioral Neuroscience,* 118, 1123–27.

Buodo, Giulia, Sarlo, Michela, and Palomba, Daniela (2002). Attentional resources measured by reaction times highlight differences within pleasant and unpleasant, high arousing stimuli. *Motivation and Emotion,* 26, 123–38.

Furedi, Frank (1997). *Culture of fear.* London: Cassell.

See also: ADRENALINE RUSH; AGGRESSION; ANXIETY; APPROACH; AROUSAL; BODY LANGUAGE; CHOKE; EMOTION; EYE MOVEMENT; FEAR OF FAILURE; KINESIOPHOBIA; NERVOUSNESS; RISK; SENSATION-SEEKING; THERAPY; VICARIOUS AGENCY; YIPS

FEAR OF FAILURE

Athletes who are overwhelming favorites to win a COMPETITION are sometimes disabled by an unwelcome EMOTION prompted by the belief that they are likely to fail. Stricken by the high expectations of others, they fail to perform to their best.

In terms of achievement GOAL theory, fear of failure disposes people to adopt particular types of achievement goals. As well as needing to achieve, they will be motivated to avoid failure and will behave in a way that reduces the likelihood of experiencing failure. This may take a passive form (feigning INJURY to remove themselves from being evaluated by others) or they may perhaps try too hard to exhibit competence to others.

In terms of causal priority, there has been debate about whether fear of failure, as a disposition, logically precedes (that is, antecedes)

achievement goals or vice versa. The conundrum has been likened to that of the chicken and egg by David Conroy and Andrew Elliot. Their research concludes, "Fear of failure antecedes and increases the likelihood that individuals will adopt AVOIDANCE achievement goals." In other words, fear of failure functions as a potent energizer, inclining subjects toward the pursuit of avoidance achievement goals.

Fear of failure has often been linked with the IMPOSTOR PHENOM-ENON, which refers to a condition in which subjects harbor doubts about their own capabilities, even when presented with evidence of these. High-achievers, not only in sport but in any sphere of activity, believe others overestimate them and will eventually expose them as phonies—impostors (from the French *imposteur*, meaning one who passes him or herself off as someone else). Impostors' concerns are underpinned, justified, and, if Conroy and Elliot's findings are to be accepted, anteceded by fear of failure.

Although the term "fear of failure" suggests a single, uniform PHE-NOMENON, it manifests in various ways and at different levels of intensity. Those with fear of failure can experience shame or embarrassment and will be obnoxious to others; they can experience others as being overcritical, neglectful, and unsupportive. FEAR of failure can also be transient and susceptible to interventions.

Heinz-Dieter Schmalt distinguished between active and passive forms, the former of which equates to the conventional conception of fear of failure as an inhibiting tendency. But the active form is, surprisingly, a facilitating tendency, "which gets activated when individuals have learned to master a challenge to avoid an impending punishment."

Some athletes seem disposed to CHOKE at crucial stages in competitions they are poised to win. This may be because of an ANXIETY, in this case a *fear of success*, a term coined by Matina Horner to describe the horror some people experience at the prospect of actually accomplishing their goals or of succeeding in other people's eyes.

Horner's much-criticized 1972 work argued that women are more afflicted by this, not only in sports but in society generally. Women fear that if they succeed in a domain traditionally dominated by men, others will deduce a lack of femininity. As a consequence, they perform modestly at a level below their optimum. Research has not supported Horner's argument.

Further reading

Conroy, David E. and Coatsworth, J. Douglas (2004). The effects of coach training on fear of failure in young swimmers: A latent growth curve analysis from a randomized controlled trial. *Journal of Applied Developmental Psychology*, 25, 193–214.

Conroy, David E. and Elliot, Andrew J. (2004). Fear of failure and achievement goals in sport: Addressing the issue of the chicken and the egg. *Anxiety, Stress and Coping*, 17, 271–85.

Horner, M. S. (1972). Toward an understanding of achievement-related conflicts in women. *Journal of Social Issues*, 28, 157–76.

Schmalt, Heinz-Dieter (2005). Validity of a short form of the achievement-motive grid (AMG-S): Evidence for the three-factor structure emphasizing active and passive forms of fear of failure. *Journal of Personality Assessment*, 84, 172–84.

Kumar, Shamala, and Jagacinski, Carolyn M. (2006). Imposters have goals too: The imposter phenomenon and its relationship to achievement goal theory. *Personality and Individual Differences*, 40, 147–57.

See also: ACHIEVEMENT MOTIVE; ANXIETY; AVOIDANCE; FEAR; HOPE; IMPOSTOR PHENOMENON; MOTIVATION; OUTPERFORMANCE; SCHEMA; SELF-FULFILLING PROPHECY; SELF-HANDICAPPING

FEAR OF SUCCESS

The fright experienced at the prospect of succeeding in the eyes of other people.

See also: FEAR OF FAILURE; OUTPERFORMANCE

FEEDBACK

The modification or CONTROL of a process or system by returning information about its results, output, or effects is known as feedback. Originally an electrical term (referring to the return of a fraction of an output signal from one stage of a circuit), feedback in sport and exercise describes the process of trying to minimize the difference between desired and actual results by relaying data about the results of performers' actions back to the performers. In this way, a SKILL is honed and perfected.

As a thermostat monitors temperature and feeds this information back into the heating system it regulates, so information about the outcome of skilled action feeds back to the performer and provides the basis for modification or stability. *Extrinsic* feedback is the observation of the results of an action (possibly by others, including coaches), while *intrinsic* feedback is the subjective feelings the performer gets. For example, boxers sometimes say they know when they have scored a knockout by the sensation they get at the point of impact of their punch; baseball sluggers claim they know they have hit a home run as soon as they make contact with the ball. The terms used to cover the sensory systems involved in providing information about position, location, orientation and movement of the body are PRO-PRIOCEPTION, or *kinesthesia*. The information received operates as a basis for future action. The nature of the event dictates what type of feedback is available. For example, show jumpers or motor racers can instantly see the results of their actions and have both forms of feedback available to them, whereas divers rely on proprioceptive information, at least until they have the chance to view a video or talk to their coaches.

Feedback is part of the mechanics of SKILL ACQUISITION. For example, an unskilled person may be able to produce what appears to be a skilled piece of behavior on a one-off, or even occasional basis. A football fan might kick a 30-yard field goal; a tennis fan might serve an ace; an archer might score a bull's-eye. The possessor of a skill, on the other hand, can produce the behavior time and again. In other words, skilled behavior has a consistent outcome. An NFL kicker will make the field goal eight times out of ten; a tennis pro will serve a quota of aces in every game; an Olympic archer can find the bull's-eye regularly.

This does not mean that the skilled athlete uses exactly the same combination of muscle contractions and skeletal movements on every occasion; the results, however, are very similar. KNOWLEDGE OF RESULTS provides the performer information about the outcomes of his or her actions. The novice kicker will adapt his movements as a result of the flight of the ball. Coupled with this is the advice of coaches and teammates who will proffer further information that aid the performer in refining the kicking skill; this is known as *knowledge of performance.*

Feedback operates in different ways at different levels of an athlete's development. A beginner might rely heavily on what is known as closed loop control, concentrating on the feedback he or she receives during the execution of a particular skill and consciously attending to as many features as possible. At more advanced stages, when skills have been mastered, feedback is less important, though it serves the purpose in adapting skills to particular environments (as a golfer might toss grass in the air to assess the direction and force of the wind). In some situations, no feedback is necessary at all: this is known as open-loop control, and athletes can complete a skill without paying ATTENTION to information, either intrinsic or extrinsic. The expression "as easy as riding a bike" applies perfectly to skills subject to open-loop control.

A less familiar CONTROL system is known as *feedforward*. If the thermostat is the exemplar for feedback, then the washing machine is feedforward's equivalent. As a wash sequence is controlled by a program, so muscular activity is controlled by a particular set of instructions or advice from the brain, though the ultimate output is influenced by local conditions. Whereas feedback monitors the divergence between actual and desired output, feedforward anticipates the relation between the environment and the organism (or system) to determine a course of action.

Further reading

Adams, J. A. (1971). A closed loop theory of motor learning. *Journal of Motor Behavior*, 3, 111–50.

Annett, J. (1969). *Feedback and human behavior*. Harmondsworth: Penguin.

Stillman, Barry C. (2002). Making sense of proprioception: The meaning of proprioception, kinaesthesia and related terms. *Physiotherapy*, 88, 667–76.

See also: AROUSAL; AUTOGENIC; AUTOMATICITY; BIOFEEDBACK; CENTERING; CONCENTRATION; CONTROL; ELECTROENCEPHALOGRAM; FLOW; KNOWLEDGE OF RESULTS; MENTAL PRACTICE; NERVOUS SYSTEM; REINFORCEMENT; SKILL ACQUISITION; THEORY OF PLANNED BEHAVIOR; VISUOMOTOR

FITNESS

There are three related meanings of fitness.

(1) A condition of physical WELL-BEING, with associated connotations of strength, hardiness, and lack of disease.
(2) Suitability for a duty, obligation, or challenge; that is, fit for purpose.
(3) An organism's ability to survive and reproduce in a particular kind of physical environment.

The last meaning is the one Charles Darwin (1809–82) used—as a way of explaining how some species adapted successfully to change, while others perished.

Inclusive fitness describes the organism's success in passing its genes to the next generation. This incorporates one's own personal fitness in transmitting genes and kin selection strategy, that is, the shared genes passed on by close relatives.

Fitness (1) is, of course, a motive in explaining EXERCISE BEHAVIOR, though much research in sport and exercise psychology centers on the effects of changes in the level of fitness: for example, Ruth Henry et al. found that engaging in a combined aerobic and interval circuit-training program resulted in a significantly improved BODY IMAGE and several fitness PARAMETERS.

The RELATIONSHIP between fitness and SELF-ESTEEM has also been widely researched, Marcus Kilpatrick et al., revealing how fitness, or, more accurately, perceived fitness was one of the criteria by which people rate their own self-esteem. For Tom Pyszczynski et al. self-esteem is a buffer against ANXIETY: People's fitness intentions could be manipulated by reminding them of their mortality. There is also research indicating the positive effects of physical fitness on MOOD; though the perfectionistic pursuit of ever-increasing levels of fitness has been found to be a contributory factor in EXERCISE DEPENDENCE.

Further reading

Hansen, Cheryl J., Stevens, Larry C., and Richard Coast, J. (2001). Exercise duration and mood state: How much is enough to feel better? *Health Psychology*, 20, 267–75.

Hausenblas, Heather A. and Symons Downs, Danielle (2002). Relationship among sex, imagery, and exercise dependence symptoms. *Psychology of Addictive Behaviors*, 16, 169–72.

Henry Ruth, Anshel, Mark A., and Michael, Timothy (2006). Effects of aerobic and circuit training on fitness and body image among women. *Journal of Sport Behavior, 29*(4), 281–303.

Kilpatrick, Marcus, Bartholomew, John, and Harold Riemer (2003). The measurement of goal orientations in exercise. *Journal of Sport Behavior*, 26, 121–9.

Pyszczynski, T., Solomon, S., Greenberg, J., Arndt, J., and Schimel, J. (2004). Why do people need self-esteem? A theoretical and empirical review. *Psychological Bulletin*, 130, 435–68.

See also: ADHERENCE; AEROBIC/ANAEROBIC; ANXIETY; BODY IMAGE; EMOTIONAL INTELLIGENCE; EXERCISE BEHAVIOR; EXERCISE IDENTITY; INJURY; KINESIOPHOBIA; PERFECTIONISM; SELF-ESTEEM; SOCIAL PHYSIQUE ANXIETY.

FLOW

Coined originally in 1990 by Mihaly Csikszentmihalyi to describe the state many call the "natural high," flow has been studied systematically over the years with a view to identifying its characteristics and the conditions under which it can be achieved. The term's origin is the Germanic *Flo*, meaning flood.

In everyday parlance, of course, flow refers to a smooth procession or movement, a yielding, stream-like pouring, or a gushing, abundant supply of something, such as blood, money, or electric current. Essentially, this is its meaning in physical activity: a mental state in which a performance seems to move by itself without any undue effort from the individual, who experiences a number of sensations, all of which combine to produce a flow. In many senses, the experience closely resembles what athletes call the ZONE.

Paul Silvia emphasizes how flow experiences involve a reduction of SELF-AWARENESS: "Flow states usually involve feelings of competence, unawareness of time, blurring of boundaries between SELF and environment, and pleasant affective states."

Features 1: Conceptual. Csikszentmihalyi later collaborated with Susan Jackson to formalize the concept in *Flow in Sports: The Keys to Optimal Experiences and Performances.* As the title suggests, there is a relationship with experience and performance: if one is optimal, the other should correspond. Jackson and Csikszentmihalyi delineated nine features of flow. These are:

(1) A balance between a performer's PERCEPTION of challenge of a situation and the performer's SKILL (the C–S balance): The task must extend the performer without being impossibly difficult.
(2) Merging of action and awareness: Consciousness of one's own body results in a sense of totality or union of body and mind.
(3) Clear goals: The immediate ambition is so explicit that the performer can visualize him or herself accomplishing it throughout the whole physical performance.
(4) Unambiguous FEEDBACK: Kinesthetic feedback from the athlete's own body and outcome feedback from the performance itself (and perhaps coaches and spectators) enables the individual to monitor progress.
(5) CONCENTRATION on the immediate task: Alertness to the here-and-now is crucial and the performer must be able to pick up clues from the environment.

(6) Sense of CONTROL: There is no forcing from individuals, who should experience utter SELF-CONFIDENCE and sense an effortless MOMENTUM carrying them along.

(7) Loss of self-consciousness: Doubts, criticism, and judgments do not concern the performer who does not entertain negative thoughts at all.

(8) Transformation of time: Perceptual distortions often accompany flow states, joggers experiencing long runs as gone in "a flash," or tennis players seeing the tennis ball as big as a beachball.

(9) AUTOTELIC experience: The flow experience is totally agreeable in its own right, so that it is intrinsically valuable to the performer.

The ninth feature is interesting because sports are, by definition, competitive and, as such, have aims or goals to which all endeavor is directed. It is possible to watch tapes of Roger Federer in the 2000s and understand his often exquisite performances as completely autotelic, as if he were involved in a display of skill rather than a contest. Of course, the point about Federer's apparently flow-like states is that they were made possible precisely because they were organized around achieving a prescribed objective. It is the concept of challenge that elicits the flow—as Jackson and Csikszentmihalyi recognize in (1) the C–S balance. So, flow will evade a noncompetitive exerciser unless he or she is rising to meet a challenge.

Features 2: In practice. Even allowing for this apparent contradiction, the MODEL provides empirical as well as conceptual information, much of it gleaned from Jackson's 1996 research with elite athletes on the constitution of flow. Subsequent research published in 1999 by Jackson and another team concluded that, "it does appear that cognitive, rather than physiological processes may be related to the flow experience." In other words, the flow's origins might lie in ATTENTION narrowing, heightened CONCENTRATION, CENTERING, or some other cognitive process.

The problem with flow is how to replicate it. For example, in 1982, David Moorcroft unexpectedly broke the world's 5,000 meters record in 13 minutes and 0.41 seconds. There was nothing in Moorcroft's form to indicate he was capable of such a time: he had never approached the mark before and, indeed, never approached it again. It was strictly a once-only performance, on which Moorcroft reflected that, once he took the lead in the race, he seemed to be carried along almost independently of his own efforts—AUTOMATICITY. His description squared almost perfectly with the Jackson-Csikszentmihalyi criteria.

Similarly, Bob Beamon offered no explanation for his logic-defying, record-shattering long jump of 29 feet 2 inches (8.90 meters) at the 1968 Olympics in Mexico. He reported a sensation of unprecedented power as he soared through the air for a barely believable record— and collapsed, probably in disbelief, shortly afterward.

By contrast, Federer seemed to be able to produce flow-like states at will, and 79 percent of the elite athletes Jackson studied in 1995 reported that flow was, for them, a controllable state. Jackson related this to the level of skill attained by the athlete. William Russell confirmed this in his 2001 study, in which he noted, "flow is perceived as more controllable for elite versus non-elite populations." The more skilled a performer is, the more controllable the flow state becomes.

Interestingly, in 2000, Csikszentmihalyi broadened his concept to the point where it became a synonym for other satisfying states of mind. In the essay "Positive psychology: an introduction" (co-authored with Martin Seligman), he paired flow with "happiness," and "insight." He also wondered: "What are the neurochemistry and anatomy of flow, good cheer, realism, future mindedness, resistance to temptation, courage, and rational or flexible thinking?" This suggests the originator of the concept suspected that the sources of flow and analogous states lay in either the properties or structure of the NERVOUS SYSTEM.

Further reading

Csikszentmihalyi, Mihaly (1990). *Flow: The psychology of optimal experience.* New York: Harper & Row.

Jackson, S. A. (1995). Factors influencing the occurrence of flow in elite athletes. *Journal of Applied Sport Psychology,* 7, 138–66.

Jackson, S. A. and Csikszentmihalyi, M. (1999). *Flow in sports: The keys to optimal experiences and performances.* Champaign, Ill.: Human Kinetics.

Jackson, S. A., Ford, S. K., Kimiecik, J. C., and Marsh, H. W. (1999). Psychological correlates of flow in sport. *Journal of Sport and Exercise Psychology,* 20, 358–78.

Russell, William D. (2001). An examination of flow state occurrence in college athletes. *Journal of Sport Behavior,* 24, 83–107.

Seligman, Martin E. P., and Csikszentmihalyi, Mihaly (2000). Positive psychology: An introduction. *American Psychologist,* 55, 5–14.

Silvia, Paul J. (2002) Self-awareness and emotional intensity. *Cognition and Emotion,* 16, 195–216.

See also: AUTOTELIC; CATHARSIS; CENTERING; COGNITION; EUSTRESS; FOCUS; MEDITATION; NERVOUS SYSTEM; PEAK PERFORMANCE; REVERSAL THEORY; SELF; SELF-AWARENESS; STREAKS; TELIC DOMINANCE; ZONE

FOCUS

The term "focus" is popularly used to describe a state of AROUSAL, in which the subject is paying ATTENTION. In psychology, there is no consensus about its precise meaning. Aidan Moran, for example, equates focus with CONCENTRATION, "the ABILITY to focus effectively on the task at hand [. . .] while ignoring distractions." Jasmin Hutchinson and Gershon Tenenbaum use *attention focus* to describe the manner in which attention is allocated. For example, during prolonged, intense exercise, attention is focused on body sensations but, during a COMPETITION, attention is toward external stimuli, such as rivals or a projectile. Combining the two senses, we can establish that being focused means screening out all *irrelevant* stimuli in the environment and selecting only auditory and visual information that is pertinent to the immediate task. The word *focus* was originally Latin for fireplace, or hearth.

Processes involved. Being focused in the lead-up to an event is actually a different process to being focused during the event itself. For instance, a high jumper may claim to be focused for up to four years, insisting that he or she is focused on winning an Olympic gold medal and that all endeavor over that period is a form of preparation for a single, ultimate competition. The athlete means that intervening competitions, like the International Association of Athletics Federations World Championships or the Pan American Games, will be subordinate challenges and that training schedules will be designed to ensure he or she peaks for the Olympics. In this sense, "focused" describes a pattern of activities organized around a grand plan. The athlete may be preoccupied with the Olympics to the point where they pay less attention to what they regard as less important affairs, but they are unlikely to wreck their car or burn down the house because attention focus was so narrow. Yet, in the actual Olympic competition, focused attention will be strictly on a single task and a process of sensory GATING will have begun; extraneous stimuli, both external (in the environment) and internal (thoughts), will be shut out.

During training, *internal association* occurs, which means that a participant monitors internal states, focusing on sensations, whether PAIN, fatigue, or arousal. Noncompetitive trainers at a gym might daydream while on the treadmill, and this process is known as *internal dissociation* (task-irrelevant thoughts occupying the attention focus), while those who prefer to jog outdoors might focus on scenery in a process of *external dissociation*.

This is in contrast to the *external association* that occurs during COMPETITION, when the individual attends to task-relevant stimuli, such as tactics, opponents, or the flight of a ball, and not to sensations (unless there is an INJURY, of course). These can change during a competition. A team member, say a midfield soccer player, needs a broad focus when appraising attacking options but may need to narrow focus when passing or involved in a tackle. The direction of the focus will be external, spotting cues from other players and, of course, the movement of the ball. A weightlifter, by contrast, will maintain a narrow focus and internal association, attending the cues from their own body. A boxer's focus will be narrow because there is only a single opponent, and the direction of the focus will be mainly external, though, of course, internal cues, such as tiredness and INJURY will also become part of the focus as the fight progresses.

Visual and auditory focus. In some sports, like high jumping, or swimming, or boxing, visual attention is sharply focused: visual stimuli falling in the central area of vision is processed much more thoroughly than those further away from the central area. A well-focused athlete will extract little information from the peripheral areas of the visual attentional spotlight—VISUAL PERCEPTION resembles a car headlight with everything at the center of the beam visible with clarity, but objects lying at the edge or outside the beam, only imperfectly, if at all. Auditory information, from the crowd for example, will be ignored as far as possible.

Formula 1 places unusual attentional demands on drivers. While their visual focus falls on the track ahead, they are constantly receiving instructions through their helmets from their pit crew and must respond alertly and accurately; focusing for them is a matter of dividing visual and auditory attention.

Competitors in team sports, on the other hand, must focus in a different way. Both visual and auditory foci must be broader to take account of movement and sounds. Athletes must be able to integrate information, including instructions from teammates and the actions of opponents in peripheral vision. So, the scope of both attentional channels must be wider. A. M. Williams and K. Davids suggest that allocating attention focus in this way is "visual scanning behavior." This does not mean the soccer player is any less focused than a high jumper: to be an effective TEAM PLAYER, the subject must learn to divide his or her focal attention selectively. Maintaining a high level of performance in team sports depends on combining often complex tasks, and this demands the development of AUTOMATICITY, which makes little or no demands on attentional resources. So, for example, the high jumper can attend to the run-up, the take-off position and the height of the bar (external), and the manner in which they will make their approach and execute their flight (internal); the mechanics of the jump itself will be so well practiced that they will not need to attend to them.

Factors that inhibit focusing include distractions and the arrival of multiple stimuli. Athletes frequently introduce distractions, appealing to umpires or referees or behaving theatrically to direct opponents' attention to a new STIMULUS. Returning focused attention to the target stimulus then becomes difficult. Multiple stimuli can include virtually any auditory or visual information not absolutely relevant to the immediate task. So, a football player in a team engaged in a crucial game that determines whether that team makes the playoffs may be interested in the score of another game featuring a rival team that kicked off at the same time. But, the player's focus will be inhibited if the score comes through to the bench during the game. Crowds are often thought to confer a HOME ADVANTAGE, though players who heed the crowd do so to the detriment of their focus and, probably, their performance. Being focused should not be confused with related but distinct experiences, such as achieving PEAK PERFORMANCE, being in a FLOW state, or entering the ZONE.

Further reading

Hutchinson, Jasmin C. and Tenenbaum, Gershon (2006). Attention focus during physical effort: The mediating role of task intensity. *Psychology of Sport and Exercise*, 8, 233–45.

Moran, Aidan P. (2004). *Sport and exercise psychology: A critical introduction*. London and New York: Routledge.

Williams, A. M. and Davids, K. (1998). Visual search strategy, selective attention, and expertise in soccer. *Research Quarterly for Exercise and Sport*, 69, 111–29.

See also: ANXIETY; AROUSAL; ATTENTION; AUTOMATICITY; BIOFEEDBACK; CENTERING; COGNITION; COGNITIVE LOAD THEORY; CONCENTRATION; CONTROL; INTENSITY; FLOW; MEMORY; MENTAL PRACTICE; NERVOUSNESS; PARALYSIS BY ANALYSIS; PEAK PERFORMANCE; PROPRIOCEPTION; SKILL; SKILL EXECUTION; ZONE

GAMBLING

Any enterprise that involves risking losing something of value with the chance of making a profit or becoming successful is gambling, a term that derives either from the Italian *gambetto*, a practice of sacrificing something minor to secure a larger advantage, or the Old Saxon *gamen*, meaning amusement. For many, gambling has little amusement value and can become a compulsion that disrupts and perhaps harms other aspects of personal and social life. In this case, we speak in terms of problem gambling, pathological gambling, gambling addiction, or gambling DEPENDENCE. All have the same import: the gambling behavior is disordered.

Athletes, particularly male athletes, are renowned gamblers, their risk-taking endeavors in COMPETITION often reflected in their penchant for games of chance or SKILL (a crap game, which is played with a pair of dice, being an example of the former; a game of golf with a side wager, an example of the latter). Thomas Miller and his research colleagues suggest that there is often *comorbidity*, meaning that gambling disorders are simultaneously present with other conditions, such as ALCOHOLISM or drug dependencies.

Miller et al. list a number of "risk factors" that make sport performers vulnerable to gambling, and these include a desire for instant gratification and a reluctance to defer this, a penchant for SENSATION-SEEKING, and competitiveness. These are many of qualities that contribute to a successful outlook in an athlete, of course. They are buffered by what Miller et al. call "protective factors" such as a respect for authority, a sense of DISCIPLINE and an awareness that athletes should behave as "trustworthy role models." On this account, athletes with "poor impulse CONTROL" are likely to become involved in a "cycle of addiction" that can lead to debts, desperation, and DEPRESSION.

Dave Clarke's research among gamblers in New Zealand concurred that impulsiveness and depression were prevalent among problem gamblers. Clarke argues that problem gamblers are motivated to experience stimulation by gambling. Motivations figured prominently in this work and, while it did not FOCUS on athletes, its findings are redolent of sport. For example, the "external motivations" driving gamblers were to relieve tension and guilt and prove oneself to others. Money was not a factor. Athletes often operate in competitive environments replete with strains, restlessness, and apprehension. An unforced error or naïve mistake during training or, worse, COMPETITION, can burden an individual with feelings of shame and culpability. As such, athletes are consistently challenged to prove their worth, both in and out of competition. Timidity and caution are rarely rewarded. RISK-taking is a more effective method of proving one's mettle.

Some of sport's greatest heroes have been known to gamble frequently, often with vast amounts of money; some have acknowledged their own compulsions. Among the most notorious is Pete Rose who bet on baseball games while he was the manager of the Cincinnati Reds between 1985 and 1987. English football player Paul Merson checked himself into REHABILITATION while still a player-manager. In a sense, sport itself provides a CONTEXT for gambling, and, as central players in such a context, athletes are responding to the often-conflicting situational demands of, on the one hand, behaving as exemplary citizens and, on the other, establishing their credentials as fearless and venturesome risk-takers.

Further reading

Clarke, Dave (2004). Impulsiveness, locus of control, motivation and problem gambling. *Journal of Gambling Studies*, 20, 319–45.

Ginsburg, D. E. (2003). *The fix is in: A history of baseball gambling and game-fixing scandals*. Jefferson, N.C.: McFarland.

Miller, T. W., Adams, J. M., Kraus, R. F., Clayton, R., Miller, J. M., Anderson, J., and Ogilvie, Bruce (2001). Gambling as an addictive disorder among athletes: Clinical issues in sports medicine. *Sports Medicine*, 31, 145–52.

See also: ADRENALINE RUSH; ALCOHOLISM; AROUSAL; COACH–ATHLETE RELATIONSHIP; CONTEXT; DEPENDENCE; ENDORPHINS; INTRINSIC MOTIVATION; LOCUS OF CONTROL; LUCK; MORAL ATMOSPHERE; MOTIVATION; OBSESSIVE-COMPULSIVE; REHABILITATION; RISK; ROLE MODEL; STREAKS; SUPERSTITIOUS BEHAVIOR; TELIC DOMINANCE; VICARIOUS AGENCY

GATING

Gating, sensory gating, or gating out, means excluding, disregarding, or filtering features of the environment that are not relevant to the immediate task. Think of a gate: whether preparing for exercise, training, or competition, a subject must allow it to open only just wide enough to let in the sensory input he or she needs, shutting out the other, possibly distracting, pieces of information. At the same time, an onlooking instructor or coach is also gating: keeping out the potentially diverting influences of loud music, or cold weather, or a growing hunger, while maintaining concentration. In all instances, the individual is paying selective ATTENTION to relevant materials.

When spectators watch sport on television from home, they may pay attention to, for example, a ringing phone, a thirst for a drink, or the need to go to the bathroom, all of which might elicit a RESPONSE.

These are distractions but not necessarily pernicious ones—they will not ruin enjoyment. If an athlete in a COMPETITION is unable to gate out inessential data, he or she may be in trouble. Any kind of distraction can prove costly. These can range from a jeering crowd to the lingering MEMORY of an error, even one from several years before.

Depending on the sport, performers often need to open and shut the gate to suit circumstances: A soccer goalkeeper will open the gate only a sliver when facing a penalty kick, but he or she may push it wider during open play and, if trailing 0–1 with seconds remaining and needing to play upfield may thrust the gate open to take in a broad range of situational factors. Golfers are known to gate tightly, especially when putting. The distraction of a cellphone ringing is particularly unwelcome.

Further reading

Cox, R. H. (1998). *Sport psychology: Concepts and applications*, 4th edn. Boston, Mass.: McGraw-Hill.

See also: ATTENTION; CHOKE; CONCENTRATION; FOCUS; INFORMATION PROCESSING; NERVOUSNESS; PSYCHOLOGICAL SKILLS INVENTORIES; SELF-TALK; ZONE

GENDER

In contrast to SEX, which describes the binary classification of animals according to biological criteria, gender refers to the manner in which a society responds to those biological differences. In this sense, the way societies designate roles, styles, and institutional arrangements determine the boundaries of gender differences. These in turn are accepted and internalized by people so that we may speak of gender identities—the ways in which people think about themselves and, indeed, about others. The word is from the French *gendre*, which derives from the Latin *genus* meaning class or kind (of animals or plants). Used since the fourteenth century, though primarily to refer to classes of noun in Latin, Greek, and other languages that designate nouns as masculine, feminine, or neuter, "gender" gained popular currency in the mid-twentieth century.

Boundaries 1: Construction. Sports, like the rest of society, are organized around gender differentiation. Few sports are "mixed," or co-ed, while most are organized into male and female competitions. The reasons for this are historical and cultural, based on prevailing beliefs, practices, and codes that mirror assumptions about the basic differences between men and women. It has been argued that the entire institution of sports is established on a gender division. Established by men, for men, organized sport was intended to validate masculinity at a stage in history (late nineteenth century) when the factory system was superseding human labor, making men's physical input less important than at earlier stages in industrialization. There was also, what Timothy Chandler and John Nauright call "the need for an arena to provide a sense of traditional masculinity, which the development of an increasingly urban-industrial society was eroding."

Competitive sport was an arena in which men could exhibit and develop their physical prowess. Women's roles were confined to that of spectators. The only sports they were permitted to participate in were "ladylike" pastimes, such as croquet or a gentle game of tennis, a game that had no resemblance to the explosive type of activity witnessed today. Gender was inscribed in sport from its inception. Women were excluded from the first Olympic games, though four years later, in 1900, they were allowed to compete in a restricted number of events. So, the Victorian era saw the start of what is often called the "gendering of modern sport."

Medical opinion solidified the gendering, cautioning that vigorous physical activity, while acceptable for men, was actually dangerous for women, who were too frail to participate in competitive sports and risked all manner of side effects (including the loss of reproductive functions and the transformation of sexual characteristics) if they did so. Helen Lenskyj's study pays particular attention to the ways women's achievements in sports were discredited, typically by accusations of impropriety or unnatural status.

Boundaries 2: Masculinity. It should not be assumed that sports were merely repositories of society's prejudices against women. Nancy Therberge argues that gendered sports advanced a particular type of gender arrangement: "What is critical about the contribution of sport to the construction of gender is that sport provides an image of idealized, or 'culturally exalted' [...] masculinity." In other words, the material and cultural dominance of men has been reproduced in some part by sports. *Hegemonic masculinity* is the phrase used to describe the manner in which a whole range of women's attributes and activities, including sports, are devalued, while men's equivalents are elevated.

While Victorian ideals of masculinity and femininity have been considerably modified and women's accomplishments in sport have assisted this, challenges are often thwarted. The denigration of gay female as well as gay male athletes has served as a bulwark for traditional gender arrangements. Women's exposé of the myth of frailty through their achievements has not persuaded everyone. Marathons are still split into separate races; women tennis players are often ridiculed as incapable of beating a man ranked in the top 100.

The media-assisted accentuation of the physical appearance of women, as opposed to the athletic performance of men persists. Female athletes, especially tennis players, are "sexualized," that is, turned into objects of the male gaze.

Boundaries 3: Classification. This has effected what many call a *gender typing,* or SEX TYPING in sport and, for that matter, exercise. Nathalie Koivula's 1999 study built on research findings that indicated that women's motives for participating in sport and exercise revolve around appearance issues, such as WEIGHT CONTROL and BODY IMAGE, or social factors, such as conviviality and peer-group support. For men, COMPETITION and physical competence are strong motives. Individuals can be classified according to whether they report or exhibit attitudes and behavior congruent with these findings. So, for example, some men could be gender-typed, others cross-gender-typed, still others androgynous (having features of both types) and still others undifferentiated. "The whole process of differential SOCIALIZATION and experience with sport can be interpreted as a part of the social construction of female–male relations which works to maintain, strengthen and naturalize gender differences," concludes Koivula.

Research in 1996 by Susan Wilkinson et al. concurred with this. "Many parents, teachers, coaches, and peers continue to behave as if girls should not exercise and participate in sport to the same degree and level that boys should," their study concluded. "This attitude and expectation results in the SELF-FULFILLING PROPHECY: girls participate, perform, practice, compete, and behave exactly as society expects. The result is reduced levels of physical activity and practice, in turn resulting in lower levels of health-related physical fitness and sports skills."

A third study conducted in the 1990s, this time commissioned by the Australian Bureau of Statistics concluded that, while the overall rates of participation in sports is about the same for women (72 percent) and men (74 percent), women's motives are different. For example, almost half cited their parents and coaches, or to win trophies. Males were overwhelmingly motivated by the prospect of competing and beating others. Predictably, the difference affected women's ADHERENCE and, while over a third of males continued into organized sport, barely a quarter of women progressed (http://www.sportrec.gov.au/zone files/organizational development/whydon'tgirls playsport.co, 2001).

While this body of research is of historical interest, it gives little indication of the cultural changes that have affected gender-typing in the twenty-first century. The task-oriented female athlete seeking social approval initially but lacking the necessary motivation or persistence to set herself higher-level achievement goals has become a STEREOTYPE, a *redundant* stereotype. Research on MOTIVATIONAL CLIMATE has revealed the impact of collective CONTEXT on individual cognitions, particularly perceptions of SELF and of objectives (for example, Heuzé et al., 2006). Because gender is a cultural property rather than a fixed, biological state, it is susceptible to changes.

Further reading

Chandler, Timothy J. L. and Nauright, John (1996). Introduction: Rugby, manhood and identity. In John Nauright and T. J. L. Chandler (Eds.), *Making men: Rugby, and masculine identity* (pp. 1–12). London: Cass.

Heuzé, J.-P., Sarrazin, Philippe, Masiero, Manuel, Raimbault, Nicolas, and Thomas J.-P. (2006). The relationships of perceived motivational climate to cohesion and collective efficacy in elite female teams. *Journal of Applied Sport Psychology,* 18, 201–18.

Koivula, Nathalie (1999). Sport participation: Differences in motivation and actual participation due to gender typing. *Journal of Sport Behavior,* 22, 1–22.

Lenskyj, Helen (1986). *Out of bounds: Women, sport and sexuality.* Toronto: Women's Press.

Therberge, Nancy (2000). Gender and sport. In Jay J. Coakley and Eric Dunning (Eds.) *Handbook of Sports Studies* (pp. 322–33). London: Sage.

Wilkinson, Susan, Williamson, Kay M., and Rozdilsky, Ruth (1996). Gender and fitness standards. *Women in Sport and Physical Activity,* 5, 1–11.

See also: ANDROGYNY; ANOREXIA NERVOSA; BULIMIA NERVOSA; COPING STRATEGIES; EATING DISORDERS; GENDER VERIFICATION; IDENTIFICATION; IMPOSTOR PHENOMENON; LEARNED HELPLESSNESS; OBESITY; OUTPERFORMANCE; SELF-CONCEPT; SELF-EFFICACY; SEX; SEX TYPING; SOCIALIZATION; STEREOTYPE; WEIGHT CONTROL

GENDER VERIFICATION

The process of establishing the GENDER of a person, gender verification, was previously known as SEX testing and has been used in sports competitions since the 1966 European track and field championships. There had been demands for some form of test since 1946, when three female medal winners came under suspicion due to their facial hair and ambiguous genitalia. Chromosomal tests suggested they were men.

Certificates from the athletes' countries were accepted as proof, though innuendo and anecdotal evidence of similar irregularities became more commonplace in the years that followed, prompting the requirement for all female participants to parade naked before a panel of female doctors to validate their femininity at the 1966 games in Budapest. Shortly after, a chromosomal test was introduced. Eva Klobukowaska, a Polish sprinter, who passed the physical inspection examination at the Budapest games, was found to have one chromosome too many to be declared a woman: she had a rare chromosomal condition that gave her no advantage (she had internal testicles) and was forced to return all her medals.

The summer Olympics of 1968 employed a histological test for the presence of a Barr body. This is a small, densely staining structure in the cell nuclei of female mammals, consisting of a condensed, inactive X chromosome and is thought to be diagnostic of femaleness. In 1977, the New York Supreme Court ruled that the insistence of the United States Tennis Association (USTA) that Renée Richards should take a Barr body test was "grossly unfair, discriminatory, and inequitable, and violative of her rights." Richards had earlier undergone sex-reassignment surgery, having played as Richard Raskind on the men's circuit.

The Barr body test was replaced in 1992 by polymerase chain reaction (PCR) determination, which was intended to identify uniquely male DNA sequences. But, as J. C. Reeser points out, "The attempt to rely on genetic testing methods of sex determination had opened up a veritable Pandora's box of problems."

Reeser means that athletes who were female in terms of their observable characteristics (that is, phenotype), sometimes appeared be male in terms of their genetic constitution (that is, genotype). "The most common of these 'intersex states' is the condition of androgen insensitivity," writes Reeser. Androgen insensitive syndrome is a congenital condition in which individuals are externally female but have the Y male-sex chromosome; it affects 1 in 60,000 males. Seven of the eight athletes with non-negative PCR gender verification results at the 1996 Atlanta Olympics were ultimately permitted to compete, highlighting the ambiguity surrounding sex-testing.

By 2000, most international sports federations had dropped attempts at gender verification, though doubts remained about how to respond to TRANSSEXUAL athletes, who had undergone surgery and hormone treatment to acquire the physical characteristics of the opposite sex. (Note: A person born with the physical characteristics of one sex but who aligns him- or herself psychologically with the opposite sex, without surgery is more usually known as TRANSGENDERED, a term that also encompasses intersexed persons, as outlined above, and others who do not conform to popular types.)

Following the Richards controversy, a Canadian mountain-bike racer, Michelle (formerly Michael) Dumaresq competed as a female for Canada at the World Championships, having undergone reassignment surgery in 1996. This sparked debate with the International Olympic Committee (IOC), and, in 2003, its medical director Patrick Schamasch announced: "We will have no discrimination [. . .] the IOC will respect human rights [. . .] after certain conditions have been fulfilled, the athlete will be able to compete in his or her new sex" (the "conditions" related to length of hormone treatment and timing of surgery).

The admission of transsexuals to the Olympic competition of their "new sex" did not remove doubts over the fairness of this change in protocol. During the earlier-mentioned *Richards* v. *USTA* case, the World Tennis Association and the US Open Committee opposed Richard's right to compete on the women's circuit because "there is a competitive advantage for a male who has undergone 'sex-change' surgery as a result of physical training and development as a male."

It remains possible that, as Reeser puts it, "residual testosterone induced attributes could influence performance capacity [for male-to-female athletes]." Of course, an athlete found with exogenous testosterone in his or her system would fail a drugs test and be liable to disqualification.

Finally, mention should be made of the case of Heidi Krieger, of the former German Democratic Republic, who won the shot gold medal at the 1986 European championships, when aged twenty and later revealed that she had been on a DOPING program that included anabolic steroids for the previous three years. In 1997, Krieger underwent surgery to have her female sex organs, including breasts, ovaries, and womb removed. Krieger legally changed her name to Andreas and became officially a man, though he did not continue his athletic career.

Further reading

Australian Sports Commission (n.d.) *Women and sport: Issues*. Available online at http://www.feminist.org/news/news_search.html.

Birrell, S. and Cole, C. (1990). Double fault: Renée Richards and the con-struction and naturalization of difference. *Sociology of Sport Journal*, 7, 1–21.

Reeser, J. C. (2005). Gender identity and sport: Is the playing field level? *British Journal of Sports Medicine*, 39, 695–9.

Simpson, J. L., Ljungqvist, A., Ferguson-Smith, M. A., de la Chapelle, A., Elsas, L. J., Ehrhardt, A. A., Genel, M., Ferris, E. A., and Carlson, A. (2000). Gender verification in the Olympics. *Journal of the American Medical Association*, 284, 1568–9.

See also: ANDROGYNY; BEM SEX ROLE INVENTORY; DOPING; FEAR OF FAILURE; GENDER; SEX; SEX TYPING

GIFTEDNESS

Conventionally defined as having exceptional talent, INTELLIGENCE, or natural ABILITY, giftedness is an adjective of the noun "gift," something willingly given to, or bestowed on someone. It suggests the individual has not had to cultivate or work at developing the gift: they are endowed with it.

The gift is thought to become manifest during childhood. At seven, Chopin was composing and performing for Europe's aristocracy; Paganini performed his first concert at the age of twelve; Stevie Wonder played keyboards and harmonica and was writing and recording hit records at thirteen; at five, Steffi Graf had already played her first tennis tournament and, by thirteen, she was playing professionally; Ruth Lawrence graduated from Oxford when aged thirteen and was a junior fellow at Harvard at nineteen.

The THEORY or doctrine that capacities are innate rather than acquired or learned is known as *nativism* (from the Latin *nativus*, for born). The contrary view, that the primary influence on the development of an individual comes from outside, is often known as *environmentalism*, though, of course, the more popular meaning of this is a person who is concerned with the protection of the environment. The debate between the two approaches is known as nature versus nurture.

Those favoring the role of nurture include K. Anders Ericsson who maintains: "Based on research on gifted students, it is clear that a considerable portion of their superior performance related to mechanisms that were acquired in extended practice activity akin to DELIBERATE PRACTICE" (quoted by Schraw). "I have found no evidence that innate biologically determined capacities constrain people from attaining expert levels of performance beyond the exception of height and body size." The two exceptions are, of course, extremely relevant in sport.

David Shanks' review of contemporary research buttresses the importance of practice: "Innate talents play a minimal role in the development of exceptional performance," he argues, adding, "It is not only in specific abilities such as MEMORY, music, chess, or sports that the effects of the environment can be seen. It is now clear that even INTELLIGENCE, that traditional favorite of psychologists, can be dramatically influenced by changes in the environment."

Wolfgang Amadeus Mozart (1756–91), who is often seen as an archetype of giftedness, and whose extraordinary accomplishments are popularly attributed to natural TALENT, grew up in an unusual environment. His father was an outstanding musician and strongly encouraged—some might say pressured—his son to enhance his musical ability. Writing for the *Daily Telegraph*, Vicki Greer notes: "Mozart was a celebrity and the breadwinner for his family. Mozart's success and growing reputation fuelled his father's ambitions and eye for publicity. Dubbing his [seven-year-old] son 'The Little Miracle,' Leopold ensured legendary stories [...] were widely published" ("A career composed of hits and mysteries," January 27, 2006).

Opponents of the environmentalist APPROACH remain unimpressed. "Despite attempts to account for giftedness in terms of nurture, no evidence allows us to rule out the necessity of an innate [natural, inborn] component" states Ellen Winner, who accepts the efficacy of learning and deliberate practice, but identifies among gifted children an "intense DRIVE" and exceptional MOTIVATION allied to a pronounced task orientated adaptation to learning environments. "They work for hours with no parental prodding or external reinforcement [...] they pose challenges for themselves [...] make discoveries on their own."

This "rage to master," as Winner calls it, accompanies the cognitive and physical development of many individuals who are credited with being gifted and indicates the strength of the role played by learning. But it is possible that there is a genetic source to the motivation to engage in sustained, unsupervised learning.

Winner's research explores "different domains of giftedness." Studies indicate that some individuals gifted in music or art may have unremarkable IQs; those with outstanding mathematical ability often have limited verbal competence. Ludwig van Beethoven (1770–1827) is an exemplar: often credited with being a musical genius, he had poor verbal skills and practically no mathematical ABILITY at all.

Savants are gifted people, usually in the field of science, but an *idiot savant* is someone who is considered disabled mentally (occasionally autistic), yet possesses one brilliant SKILL, usually involving encyclopedic MEMORY or exceptional ability at numerical calculation. For Winner, idiots savants suggest that general intelligence is unrelated to high levels of achievement in particular domains and the wider implication of this is that at least some part of giftedness is naturally endowed.

Further reading

Gardner, Howard (1997). *Extraordinary minds: Portraits of exceptional individuals and an examination of our extraordinariness*. New York: Basic Books.

Roth, Stephen (2007). *Genetics primer for exercise science and health*. Champaign, Ill.: Human Kinetics.

Schraw, Gregg (2005). An interview with K. Anders Ericsson. *Educational Psychology Review*, 17, 389–412.

Shanks, David R. (1999). Outstanding performers: Created, not born? *Science Spectra*, 18, 18–34.

Winner, Ellen (1996). *Gifted children: Myths and realities*. New York: Basic Books.

Winner, Ellen (2000). Giftedness: Current theory and research. *Current Directions in Psychological Science*, 9, 153–6.

See also: ABILITY; BURNOUT; DELIBERATE PRACTICE; INSTINCT; INTELLIGENCE; LEFT-HANDEDNESS; PHENOMENON; SKILL ACQUISITION

GOAL

An aim, objective or result that a person plans for, or intends to achieve is, of course, a goal (a word whose origins are obscure, but which may be a version of *gol*, a Middle English term for "boundary"). The concept should not be confused with a *dream*, which is a mental image, or *fantasy* that carries no necessary assumption that action will follow, or *purpose*, which is a purely internal target that guides behavior. A goal is external to the subject (though goals cannot, in practice, exist without an internal purpose).

An aspiring player may say her dream is to win the US Open, yet fail to practice enough to make the necessary improvements. Another athlete may have a purpose that motivates her to train hard to improve but may have no clear specific goal that will strengthen her COMMITMENT and narrow her ATTENTION. But, an athlete with a GOAL ORIENTATION will have a practical program designed to enable the attainment of tangible objectives. So, a goal is a level of performance proficiency that a person intends to reach within a timeframe.

To be effective, goals have to incorporate: (1) a clearly defined level of performance proficiency, which includes a minimum standard; (2) a timeframe inside which the level should be reached; and (3) a direction (for behavior). Goals allow an individual, or group to devote full ATTENTION to implementing intentions and, once they are achieved, supply the SELF-CONFIDENCE to make key decisions.

Todd Thrash and Andrew Elliott distinguish two types of goals: "MASTERY goals are focused on the development of competence or task mastery, whereas performance goals are focused on the attainment of competence relative to others." Goals FOCUS either on approaching a positive outcome or avoiding a negative consequence, and this is known as their valence. This produces four distinct goal types, three of which the authors delineate: (1) mastery goals that focus either on developing competence or mastery of tasks; (2) performance-APPROACH goals that focus on outperforming others; and (3) performance-AVOIDANCE goals that focus on not performing worse than others. (We can assume the fourth is mastery or competence avoidance.)

Aidan Moran argues that, "a goal which is stated positively tells the person what to do, whereas a negatively stated goal does not provide such explicit guidance." So, for example, "I am going to do two-hours at the gym, at least three times a week" is a more efficient goal than, "I won't get involved in phone conversations when I'm about to leave work for the gym."

It is impossible to entertain the idea of an athletic career without goals. COMPETITION demands that proficiencies, standards, and accomplishments are achieved, and achieving them is inconceivable without goals to orient the athlete. A common strategy to direct athletes is GOAL SETTING, in which each specific objective reached works as REINFORCEMENT, conferring SELF-EFFICACY and encouraging further progress. Similarly, exercise entailing goal-directed strategies, whether weight loss, measurably improved cardiovascular efficiency, improved running speed, and so on, promises to increase behavioral engagement with programs. But, as Martin Hagger and Nikos Chatzisarantis point out, "people's execution of their intentions may be interrupted because other competing goal-directed behaviors take priority over the original intended behavior."

Conflicting goals (leaving the gym early to pick up the children from school) or *supervening goals* (needing to visit a family member who unexpectedly falls sick and is hospitalized) typically disrupt or change a situation. There are several other factors affecting the implementation of goals, including proximity (short-term goals mobilize effort most effectively), degree of difficulty (moderately challenging, but achievable goals elicit most MOTIVATION and application), and specificity (clearly stated and attainable goals).

Further reading

Burton, D. (1992). The Jekyll/Hyde nature of goals: Reconceptualizing goal setting in sport. In T. S. Horn (Ed.), *Advances in sport psychology* (pp. 267–97). Champaign, Ill.: Human Kinetics.

Hagger, Martin and Chatzisarantis, Nikos (2005). *The social psychology of exercise and sport*. Maidenhead: Open University Press.

Moran, Aidan P. (2004). *Sport and exercise psychology: A critical introduction*. London: Routledge.

Thrash, Todd M. and Elliot, Andrew J. (2002). Implicit and self-attributed achievement motives: Concordance and predictive validity. *Journal of Personality*, 70, 729–55.

See also: ACHIEVEMENT MOTIVE; ADHERENCE; EXPECTANCY; GOAL ORIENTATION; GOAL SETTING; KNOWLEDGE OF RESULTS; MENTAL TOUGHNESS; MOTIVATION; OBEDIENCE; SKILL ACQUISITION; TASK/EGO ORIENTATION; 2 × 2 ACHIEVEMENT GOAL FRAMEWORK; TYPE A; WEIGHT CONTROL

GOAL ORIENTATION

The stable tendency to position oneself in the direction of a GOAL is known as a goal orientation. It is an underlying, long-term inclination that guides a person and so exerts a significant influence on his or her MOTIVATION, not only in sports but in any enterprise that requires task MASTERY or SKILL ACQUISITION.

There are two types of goal orientation: (1) *performance* goal orientation: an athlete's perceived mastery of new tasks, or all-round improvement in SKILL; and (2) *outcome* goal orientation: objective, measurable confirmation of improvements, such as winning and beating others. Mastery of skills is a means to the end of winning, not an end in itself, though the goals to be set typically concern performance, rather than outcome.

In (1), athletes or exercisers tend to gear their thoughts and efforts to quality of performance and the satisfaction they derive from this. The actual outcome of a COMPETITION is of secondary importance. By contrast, in (2), competitive athletes would prefer to perform badly as long as they win, and exercisers will not mind how much they have strayed from original plans as long as they achieve the desired outcome (such as a routine completed in a set time, or a drop in body weight). The result is what matters.

Sometimes, one can be mistaken for the other. For example, during Jennifer Capriati's COMEBACK year, 2001, it was widely assumed that she harbored an outcome goal orientation, having won the Australian and French Opens. The outcome in question was the Grand Slam. Only after her defeat at Wimbledon did she reveal that: "Everybody was making a big deal out of the Grand Slam except me. I'm pretty happy the way the year has gone so far." Even allowing for a degree of rationalization in her verdict, it seems fair to assume that, after her troubled career interval, her goal orientation was geared to holding her own on the circuit rather than winning titles.

"In many cases task and ego orientations are not mutually exclusive, but are present at varying levels simultaneously," write Brenda Riemer and Jeanne Thomas. "Furthermore, these are not the only goal orientations possible," they infer from their 2005 study of dog obedience-show competitors. While Riemer and Thomas do not specify how the multiple-goal orientation works, an earlier study by Gregg Steinberg et al. emphasized the effectiveness of coexisting goal orientations.

As well as the two main goal orientations, the study included a *mastery/competitive* goal group, meaning that performers might initially develop proficiency in mastery oriented situations then enter more competitive environments to test their skills, before re-establishing task orientations to improve or acquire new skills, which equip them better to compete. Those who progressed through this interactive sequence "had the flexibility to garnish competence information from both the demonstration of superiority as well as personal improvement."

There is also a social aspect to goal orientations. Among the influences are peers, coaches, the competitive structure (league, ladder and so on), and potential rewards. David Bergin and Steven Habusta's research uncovered a congruence between parents' and young hockey players' task orientations: "Even though hockey has a STEREOTYPE of competitive AGGRESSION, parents and sons agree that they are more interested in learning and mastering hockey skills."

While the expected predominance of task orientation in exercise is supported by evidence, Marcus Kilpatrick et al. found that self-presentation was also salient, suggesting that an ego orientation was present: "A likely strategy to maximize one's image is to outperform others in the environment, particularly when physical strength and aerobic FITNESS are important domains of physical SELF-ESTEEM."

Further reading

Bergin, David A. and Habusta, Steven E. (2004). Goal orientations of young male hockey players and their parents. *Journal of Genetic Psychology*, 165, 383–97.

Kilpatrick, Marcus, Bartholomew, John, and Harold Riemer (2003). The measurement of goal orientations in exercise. *Journal of Sport Behavior*, 26, 121–9.

Nicholls, J. G. (1984). Achievement motivation: Conceptions of ability, subjective experience, task choice and performance. *Psychological Review*, 91, 328–46.

Riemer, Brenda A. and Thomas, Jeanne L. (2005). Achievement goal orientations in competition dog obedience participants. *Journal of Sport Behavior*, 28, 272–82.

Steinberg, Gregg M., Singer, Robert N. and Milledge, Murphey (2000). The benefits to sport achievement when a multiple goal orientation is emphasized. *Journal of Sport Behavior*, 4, 407–23.

See also: ACHIEVEMENT MOTIVE; ADHERENCE; BODY IMAGE; BODY LANGUAGE; BURNOUT; COMEBACK; COMMITMENT; DROPOUTS; GOAL; GOAL SETTING; MASTERY; MOTIVATION; RELATIONAL; SELF-ACTUALIZATION; SOCIALIZATION; TASK/EGO ORIENTATION

GOAL SETTING

The process of establishing a level of performance proficiency which should be reached within a prescribed time period is known as goal setting. It has proven effectiveness in enhancing performance and productivity in several contexts, including employee exercise programs, competitive sport, and industrial organizations, and provides a basis for both increasing a person's SELF-EFFICACY and for instilling a task with intrinsic worth. A gym habitué who finds twenty minutes on the treadmill tedious, for example, might set goals in terms of distance covered, and keep resetting targets as he or she reaches them. The twenty minutes become a directed, focused and inherently satisfying race against an invisible adversary. While the advantages of goal setting are manifold, it also has disadvantages, which we itemize after clarifying its qualities and purpose.

The type and duration of goals set vary appreciably, as does the manner in which they are set. An aspiring athlete may set goals intuitively at the outset of a career, for example, to execute a decent pass, sustain a rally, or just finish a race. As a career progresses, athletes typically define specific goals, sometimes establishing a long-term

GOAL that can be broken into less ambitious short-term goals, setting up a kind of hierarchy of goals to be achieved one by one. An office worker might enroll in a company FITNESS program, setting goals related to a broad class of health-related behaviors, so exercise goals are related to complementary dietary aims and objectives such as walking instead of driving to work four times a week and taking the stairs every morning.

In other words, effective goal setting involves prescribing particular and challenging but realistic objectives, which, once met, lead to further objectives—which again should be particular and precise rather than general and vague. Tiny, gradual, but progressively demanding objectives provide intrinsic value most effectively. The goals should also be made "public": harboring "private" goals secretly may be satisfying but making known the goals at which athletes are aiming is more efficient in yielding performance improvements.

Multiple-goal strategies involve a kind of portfolio of goals, each set of goals being pertinent to a particular context. Krista Munroe-Chandler et al.'s research provides an illustration: "A golfer may set a goal to win the tournament, a goal to increase the salience of practice, and a goal to aid in concentration." It is also possible that a person might have several goals set for each CONTEXT and arrange them in order of priority. The practicing golfer might rank CONCENTRATION as an initial priority and, once this is fixed, move to improving swing, then putting, and so on. Each goal is set within its own timeframe, though allowance must be made for the occasional failure.

Mark Anshel reports on a strategy of grouping goal setting so that a single poor performance does not invalidate the overall goal. This is known as *interval goal setting* and may take an average time from a cluster of five time trials, not every single one. The average times may themselves be intervals in a more ambitious long-term goal, such as an end-of-season personal record, a placing at a major championship, or completing 5 miles on the treadmill. This approach emphasizes the observable outcome type of goal orientation not the subject's interpretation of progress, the effort he or she sinks into pursuing the goal or, indeed, the participant's own experience of personal success or failure. In other words, it lacks a subjective dimension, which would allow an athlete's ANXIETY, confidence, GOAL ORIENTATION, and, in general, COGNITION a role in the process and these can vitiate, or impair, the usefulness of goal setting.

For example, a company concerned with rising absenteeism due to sickness might start its own health-promotion scheme by setting exercise goals for workers and providing facilities for reaching them. According to David Harrison and Laurie Liska, these are effective, but only when there is "sufficient employee commitment." The goals must be linked to some other "positively valenced outcomes" (that is, with perceived value to the individual). COMMITMENT is one of four "moderator variables". Highly committed athletes may strive to reach their goals, regardless of whether they are hard or easy; so highly demanding goals work for this type of participant. Other moderators are important to goal setting in less competitive environments: the person's ability, FEEDBACK from others (monitoring), and task complexity. As variables, they are factors that are liable to vary or change, depending on the individual and context. There are other drawbacks.

Disadvantages. Gary Latham and Edwin Locke describe goal setting as "first and foremost a discrepancy-creating process, in that the goal creates constructive discontent with our present performance." While their 2006 research was concerned with commercial and industrial organizations, the ten possible disadvantages Latham and Locke identify are generalizable.

(1)   If people lack the requisite basic knowledge and skill to attain a goal, they may perform less adequately than if they had been told "to do their best."

(2)   Setting goals for groups can have a detrimental effect if there is conflict among members and individuals regard their own personal goals as unrelated to those of others.

(3)   Goals can be threatening.

(4)   People curb RISK-taking behavior too much.

(5)   Having attained goals, achievers continue to employ the same strategies in their efforts to reach more demanding goals and become conservative in their practices.

(6)   Cheating: People tend to overstate their performance, especially if there is a cash incentive attached to the goal.

(7)   People can become "over-committed" to goals, which leads to a reluctance to abandon them even when it becomes rational to do so.

(8)   Behavior that does not entail goals is ignored in favor of goal-directed pursuits (why bother going for a drink with friends when you could be on the treadmill chasing goals?).

(9)   Goals can induce STRESS, especially if there are multiple goals to be achieved.

(10)   The tendency to continue setting evermore challenging goals will inevitably lead to punishing failure and perhaps decreases in SELF-CONFIDENCE.

An eleventh problem is in evidence in Robert Weinberg et al.'s study of National Collegiate Athletic Association coaches, who, with their athletes, negotiated goals that included enjoyment and fun as well as perfor- mance outcomes. A discrepancy opened up when coaches focused exclusively on performance goals. There was only limited value in goals that were either imposed or changed, however slightly, once set. To be effective, goals need to be negotiated and accepted by both the people trying to reach them and those guiding them toward the goals.

Further reading

Anshel, M. H. (1997). *Sport psychology: From theory to practice*, 3rd edn. Scottsdale, Ariz.: Gorsuch Scarisbrick.

Fry, Mary D. and Newton, Maria (2003). Application of achievement goal theory in an urban youth tennis setting. *Journal of Applied Sport Psychology*, 15, 50–66.

Harrison, David A. and Liska, Laurie Z. (1994). Promoting regular exercise in organizational fitness programs: Health-related differences in motiva- tional building blocks. *Personnel Psychology*, 47, 47–71.

Latham, Gary P. and Locke, Edwin A. (2006). Enhancing the benefits and overcoming the pitfalls of goal setting. *Organizational Dynamics*, 4, 332–40.

Munroe-Chandler, Krista J., Hall, Craig R., and Weinberg, Robert S. (2004). A qualitative analysis of the types of goals athletes set in training and competition. *Journal of Sport Behavior*, 27, 58–75.

Weinberg, R., Butt, J., Knight, B., and Perritt, N. (2001). Collegiate coaches' perceptions of their goal-setting practices: A qualitative investigation. *Journal of Applied Sport Psychology*, 13, 374–98.

See also: ACHIEVEMENT MOTIVE; ADHERENCE; ATTRIBUTION; BIOFEEDBACK; COG- NITION; COGNITIVE-BEHAVIORAL MODIFICATION; COMMITMENT; GOAL; GOAL ORIENTATION; INCENTIVE; MOTIVATION; WEIGHT CONTROL

GROUP DYNAMICS

Processes that generate change in groups of people are known as group dynamics, a concept that insinuates that, as the maxim goes, "the whole is more than the sum of the parts." The word "dynamic," from the Greek *dunamikos*, for power, refers to energizing or motive force, and the dynamism's source lies in the emergent properties of the group. Rather than being a mere aggregation of individuals, the group generates properties over and above those of the individual members: they *emerge* during the interactions of the individuals. This is especially important in sports, not only in team sports in which factors such as COHESION and LEADERSHIP are pivotal but in individual sports when the right kind of "chemistry" between an athlete and his or her coaching staff can yield significant changes in performance.

The concept of group dynamics is often associated with Kurt Lewin, who was influenced by early twentieth-century Gestalt psychology (*Gestalt* is German for structure, or configuration), which examined the dynamism of the PERSONALITY holistically (that is, as a structured whole). Groups are approached as entities in their own right rather than as compositions of individuals. Once a group is formed, it generates characteristics of its own quite independently from its members. The term used to describe this independent character is *sui generis*.

Group dynamics are evident in practically any situation in which individuals interact on a meaningful basis: when they have awareness of each others' presence, an insight into others' MOTIVATION, and an expectation of what the outcome of their interaction with others might be. In sports, groups, whether teams, squads, rosters, or even partnerships, come together with a GOAL—to succeed at some level. That unity of purpose introduces dynamic processes that affect DECISION-MAKING roles, the collective MOTIVATION of the group, the methods of communication and other features that cannot exist at an individual level.

Conflicts, tension, and, especially, power struggles frequently characterize group dynamics. Often, the CONTEXT of the group allows a blossoming of personality styles or other characteristics that are not evident outside the group. Even perceptual changes are possible. Solomon Asch's 1955 research concluded that forces to conform to others overpowered a person's ability to make simple sensory judgments. This and other studies highlighted the influence of collectivities in affecting both the thought and behavior of individuals, even in the face of often bizarre, conflicting evidence. The prison experiments of Philip Zimbardo (1935–) in 1971, in which participants were randomly split into two groups, "prisoners" and "guards" and instructed to act out role appropriate behavior in a specially constructed prison at Stanford University, edged toward catastrophe as guards tormented the captives, imposing punishments cruelly and arbitrarily. Their behavior was inconsistent with their behavior outside of the experiment.

The bridge between group dynamics and sport psychology was SOCIAL FACILITATION research, according to Julie Partridge and Diane Stevens; we should also highlight the importance of the RINGELMANN EFFECT and SOCIAL LOAFING, all of which suggest the preeminence of

RELATIONAL processes over that of individuals in certain settings. Partridge and Stevens emphasize the emergence and maintenance of group norms in encouraging predictability, highlighting central values and minimizing DEVIANCE. As group norms (that is, informal rules that govern the manner in which the group is organized) are created, formal rules are needed less and less and OBEDIENCE becomes unproblematic, as the earlier Asch study had indicated.

Physiological changes can also be a consequence of group dynamics, as Marc Jones et al. point out: "The presence of others can increase an individual's drive AROUSAL [and] may substantially affect motor performance." "Others" in this context, can be surrounding team members, or observers. In both cases, their presence can lead to changes.

Further reading

Asch, Solomon (1955). Opinions and social pressures. *Scientific American*, 193, 31–5.

Haney, C., Banks, W. C., and Zimbardo, P. G. (1973). Interpersonal dynamics in a simulated prison. *International Journal of Criminology and Penology*, 1, 69–97.

Jones, Marc V., Bray, Steven R., and Lavallee, David (2008). All the world's a stage: Impact of an audience on sport performers. In Sophia Jowett and David Lavallee (Eds.), *Social psychology in sport* (pp. 103–13). Champaign, Ill.: Human Kinetics.

Lewin, K. (1948). *Resolving social conflicts* New York: Harper.

Partridge, J. and Stevens, D. E. (2002) Group dynamics: The influence of the team in sport. In J. M. Silva and D. E. Stevens (Eds.) *Psychological Foundations of Sport* (pp. 272–90). Boston, Mass.: Allyn & Bacon.

See also: AGGRESSION; APPLIED SPORT PSYCHOLOGY; AROUSAL; COACH–ATHLETE RELATIONSHIP; COHESION; LEADERSHIP; MODEL; MORAL ATMOSPHERE; MOTIVATIONAL CLIMATE; RELATIONAL; RELATIONSHIP; RINGELMANN EFFECT; SOCIAL FACILITATION; SOCIAL LOAFING; SOCIALIZATION; SOCIOTROPY; TEAM PLAYER; THEORY

HALO EFFECT

Tendency to base an overall judgment of someone or something on a single outstanding characteristic. A halo is a circle of light above the head of a saint and is associated with an idealized person.

See also: BODY LANGUAGE; EXPECTANCY; HOME ADVANTAGE

HAWTHORNE EFFECT, THE

A change in people's behavior resulting from their awareness of being studied. Hawthorne was the name of the Western Electric Company's Chicago plant where, in the 1920s, a study demonstrated this PHENOMENON.

See also: SELF-TALK; SOCIAL FACILITATION

HEDONIC TONE

Hedonic tone is the subjective quality of an experience, measured in terms of the pleasure or displeasure it brings. The term is from two Greek words: *hedone* for "pleasure," and *teinen*, "to stretch"; tone often refers to a favorable overall quality, as in *muscle tone*, which describes firmness or a slightly contracted state of muscles.

In sport and exercise, hedonic tone is often used to describe an emotional response among FANS or competitors. For instance, John Kerr and Hilde de Kock attempted to understand the emotional attraction of being football hooligans: "They can experience feelings of satisfaction and pride associated with the mastery state, maximizing their rewards in terms of positive affect of hedonic tone."

In a different context, Claudio Robazza et al. discovered:

> Athletes experienced pleasant emotions as more pleasant when they were perceived as helpful [...] A competitor who experiences a high level of ANGER as beneficial for performance may also label it as pleasant, but if any further increase in anger intensity is detrimental to performance the athlete can subsequently label it as unpleasant.

The Italian research team concluded that, "increments of hedonic tone would be more pronounced when associated with optimal-pleasant rather than dysfunctional-pleasant emotional intensities."

This has some application to exercise: if exercise behavior is geared specifically to an outcome, such as WEIGHT LOSS or improved cardio-vascular performance, then its impact on hedonic tone would be expected to be modest. Conversely, exercising for the sake of the experience without particular outcome goals might provide a degree of pleasure. Increases in hedonic tone would occur when the latter involves the former, for example, when a gym session is enjoyable in its own right *and* entails a loss of weight.

Further reading

Kerr, John H. and de Kock, Hilde (2002). Aggression, violence, and the death of a Dutch soccer hooligan: A reversal theory explanation. *Aggressive Behavior*, 28, 1–10.

Robazza, Claudio, Bortoli, Laura, and Hanin, Yuri (2006). Perceived effects of emotion intensity on athletic performance: A contingency-based individualized approach. *Research Quarterly for Exercise and Sport*, 77, 372–86.

See also: ADRENALINE RUSH; AGGRESSION; ANGER; AUTOTELIC; CATHARSIS; DEATH WISH; EMOTIONAL TONE; FANS; INDIVIDUAL ZONES OF OPTIMAL FUNCTIONING; MIMESIS; MOOD; PAIN; REVERSAL THEORY; TELIC DOMINANCE; VIOLENCE; ZONE

HEURISTICS

Mental shortcuts for solving problems by reducing the range of possibilities for the solution.

See also: SKILL EXECUTION

HOME ADVANTAGE

Competing in front of a home crowd is popularly thought to confer benefits on a team, or an individual, those benefits being known as home advantage, or, sometimes home field or court advantage. Intuitively, it might be thought that the advantage derives from the comfort of competing in a familiar environment, the freshness of not having to travel, or the boost of a partisan crowd. Research suggests differently. It also suggests less obvious variables, including the impact of crowds on officials and the role of the SELF-FULFILLING PROPHECY.

Reason 1: Familiarity. Some teams would seem to have an obvious edge by virtue of familiarity. For example, playing in Buffalo in midwinter would appear to present the Bills with a distinct advantage, especially against teams, such as Tampa Bay Buccaneers, which practice and play in warm climates (and, for long, had a reputation for never winning games when the temperature was 40 degrees Fahrenheit (4.4 degrees Celsius) or lower. Similarly, playing at home on artificial turf would be an advantage when playing teams used to playing on grass.

Reason 2: Travel. A long, draining flight across time zones from Australia to the Caribbean would seem to leave a visiting cricket team exhausted, jetlagged, and with less time to prepare in the new environment. But a review by K. S. Courneya and Albert Carron concluded that, in themselves, these could not account for the tendency for teams playing at home to win (over 50 percent of the time across several sports, according to the review).

Reason 3: Hormones. A study of hockey players by Justin Carré et al. indicated that: "Pre-game testosterone levels and SELF-CONFIDENCE are higher at home and somatic anxiety is higher when players are in their opponents' venue." The researchers also point out that raised testosterone levels may be related to AGGRESSION, assertiveness, and dominance, though their results did not reveal an association between higher pre-game testosterone and better performance, probably, they anticipate, because of the social STRESS induced by the pressure "to perform in front of friends and family who are more likely to be present in the home venue."

Reason 4: Crowd. There is a considerable body of research on the effects of audiences on performance. While early SOCIAL FACILITATION research dating back to the early twentieth century suggested that the mere presence of the other was enough to arouse competitors or increase the motivational state known as DRIVE, more recent studies have been more ambivalent about the role of crowds. For instance, in 2005 Harry Wallace et al. argued that audience support can prove beneficial when the task at hand needs effort or in climates that might otherwise be unmotivating. But, when skill is needed, a home crowd can create an experience of pressure, and a competitor may opt for failure avoidance or, worse, CHOKE. "Supportive audiences are often beneficial to performance, but we have also provided evidence that sometimes they can be detrimental to performance," they conclude, complementing research inspired by the YERKES-DODSON LAW that highlights the problems associated with too much AROUSAL.

Research by Emily Pronin et al. revealed that FANS themselves often perceive that they can influence the performance of their team when they harbor positive thoughts and visions of success. This helps explain why some fans are deliberately antagonistic to visiting teams, chanting, banging drums, and blowing horns to create a deafening cacophony.

Another disadvantage of performing in front of a home crowd is known as *evaluation apprehension.* Athletes performing in front of a crowd that is judging them in some way may experience ANXIETY and distraction. So, while a baying, partisan home crowd is popularly assumed to be an unqualified advantage, the research is conditional, and this invites a further question: if the supportive crowd does not influence the competitors in a uniformly positive way, does it influence the referee?

Reason 5: Officiating. A research letter in *The Lancet* (April 24, 1999, p. 1416) reported a small study involving eleven soccer referees, coaches and players who were split into two groups and asked to make calls on fifty-two incidents as they watched a video of a game of soccer. One group watched the recording with background noise, the other with the "mute" button on. "Observers had a greater tendency to award a foul when viewing challenges by away players in the presence of the crowd noise," related the research team headed by A. M. Nevill. Officials did not referee objectively, "but referred to the crowd for guidance" (the letter did not state whether the refs, coaches or players were more or less influenced, or whether there was any pattern). The same research team studied the winter Olympic games over ninety years and unearthed "significant evidence of home advantage," most of it explicable in terms of "subjective assessment by officials." The findings reflected "the way judges respond to the reactions of the crowd."

While this research did not address Varca's 1980 findings that visitors display "dysfunctional assertive behavior" and commit more fouls, it implicitly cast doubt on them. Perhaps away players are simply penalized more by referees who are "guided" by crowd noise. On this view, it is likely that home advantage is as much to do with the crowd's effect on the officials as it is on the competitors.

Reason 6: self-fulfilling prophecy. The counterpart to home advantage is away disadvantage, and at least one project concluded that home teams did not necessarily raise their game when playing at home, but visitors' standards of performance declined so markedly that it *appears* the home teams play better. Statistical research using historical data disclosed a pattern of underachievement by away teams, while home teams' statistics remained constant. One inference from this is that traveling players lack confidence, while players performing at home gain a boost. This is supported by 2000 research by S. R. Bray and W. N. Widmeyer. While the researchers do not mention it, their research throws up the possibility of a self-fulfilling element. If, when on the road, players believe they will be at a disadvantage, their decrements in confidence may contribute to their performance which, in turn, affects their team's performance and facilitates a defeat, thus confirming the players' original suspicions.

A study of English soccer by Fiona Carmichael and Dennis Thomas added some weight to this type of explanation by showing statistically that teams changed their style of play when playing away, tending to more defensive tactics.

Further reading

Bray, S. R. and Widmeyer, W. N. (2000). Athlete's perception of home advantage: An investigation of perceived causal factors. *Journal of Sport Behavior*, 23, 1–10.

Carmichael, Fiona and Thomas, Dennis (2005). Home-field effect and team performance: Evidence from English Premiership football. *Journal of Sport Economics*, 3, 264–81.

Carré, J., Muir, C., Belanger, J., and Putman, S. K. (2006). Pre-competition hormonal and psychological levels of elite hockey players: Relationship to the "home advantage." *Physiology and Behavior*, 89, 392–8.

Courneya, K. S. and Carron, A. (1992). The home advantage in sport competitions: A literature review. *Journal of Sports Exercise Psychology*, 14, 13–27.

Nevill, A. M., Balmer, N. J., and Williams, A. M. (2002). The influence of crowd noise and experience upon refereeing decision in football. *Psychology of Sport and Exercise*, 2, 261–72.

Pronin, Emily, Wegner, Daniel M., McCarthy, Kimberly, and Rodriguez, Sylvia (2006). Everyday magical powers: The role of apparent mental causation in the overestimation of personal influence. *Journal of Personality and Social Psychology*, 91, 218–31.

Varca, P. (1980). An analysis of home and away game performance of male college basketball teams. *Journal of Sport Psychology*, 2, 245–57.

Wallace, Harry M., Baumeister, Roy F., and Vohs, Kathleen D. (2005). Audience support and choking under pressure: A home disadvantage? *Journal of Sports Sciences*, 23, 429–38.

See also: BODY LANGUAGE; CHOKE; COGNITION; DRIVE; EXPECTANCY; FANS; FEAR OF FAILURE; HALO EFFECT; PARALYSIS BY ANALYSIS; SANDBAGGING; SELF-FULFILLING PROPHECY; SELF-HANDICAPPING; SOCIAL FACILITATION; STEREOTYPE THREAT; SUPERSTITIOUS BEHAVIOR; YERKES-DODSON LAW

HOOLIGANISM

Violent PHENOMENON associated with soccer crowds. "Hooligan" is probably from the apocryphal nineteenth-century London-Irish family, Houlihan, renowned for fighting.

See also: RELIGION; REVERSAL THEORY; RIVALRY; VIOLENCE

HOPE

A feeling of expectation and desire for a particular outcome, hope can help sustain MOTIVATION. Someone goes to the gym in the hope of easing painful joints or has hopes of making the Olympic team. Hope often provides grounds for believing something can happen. A team on a losing STREAK after losing several players to INJURY has hope for the future when those players return.

There are two cognitive components in hope: (1) *agency*: someone must have a goal and be prepared to act in a way to meet that particular goal; (2) *pathways*: he or she must be able to think of one or several routes to achieving the GOAL. "Any sport involves a focusing upon a desired goal, which in and of itself is motivating and serves to shut out possible outside interferences," observe Lewis Curry et al. "The thoughts about how one is going to produce the pathways to secure the coveted goal provide a mental plan of action that is focused upon to the exclusion of possible interfering forces."

Inevitably, in sport or, for that matter, any type of endeavor, there will be "interfering forces," and these include injuries, superior opponents, insufficient time to train, and several other kinds of setbacks. Curry et al.'s study indicated that ultimately successful athletes quickly developed new pathways as part of their overall plan. So, their hopeful thinking was not damaged. The study concluded that sustained hope is a more reliable predictor of academic as well as athletic performance than, for example, SELF-CONFIDENCE, amount of time spent practicing or even what they call "natural athletic TALENT."

The findings are complemented by those of Heinz-Dieter Schmalt who identifies what he calls "hope of success." This is a motivating tendency "composed of positive evaluations of efficacy, the stated need to achieve, and the initiation of actions designed to master difficult tasks."

While their research considered academic achievement, Elizabeth Alexander and Anthony Onwuegbuzie offer a way of understanding the function of hope as a COPING STRATEGY in the face of procrastination (defined as the postponement of goals "to the point where optimal performance becomes highly unlikely").

Students in the research shared many of the misgivings typically experienced by athletes: evaluation ANXIETY, low SELF-EFFICACY, and the maladaptive PERFECTIONISM that typifies FEAR OF FAILURE. Those who "exhibited higher levels of hope were less likely to procrastinate [. . .] than were those with lower hope scores."

Further reading

Alexander, Elizabeth S. and Onwuegbuzie, Anthony J. (2007). Academic procrastination and the role of hope as a coping strategy. *Personality and Individual Differences*, 42, 1301–10.

Curry, L. A., Snyder, C. R., Cook, D. L., Ruby, B. C., and Rehm, M. (1997). Role of hope in academic and sport achievement. *Journal of Personality and Social Psychology*, 73, 1257–67.

Schmalt, Heinz-Dieter (2005). Validity of a short form of the achievement-motive grid (AMG-S): Evidence for the three-factor structure emphasizing active and passive form of fear of failure. *Journal of Personality Assessment*, 84, 172–84.

See also: ACHIEVEMENT MOTIVE; APPROACH; COPING STRATEGIES; EXPECTANCY; FEAR OF FAILURE; PERFORMANCE ENHANCEMENT; POSITIVE AFFECT; SELF-EFFICACY; SELF-FULFILLING PROPHECY; SELF-HANDICAPPING; STREAKS; WELL-BEING

HYPNOSIS

From the Greek *hupnos*, for "sleep," and the suffix *osis*, denoting an action or condition, hypnosis describes a process of inducing extreme suggestibility in humans. The precise mechanism through which this is achieved is not clear, some theorists believing that a different state of consciousness is attained, while others argue that the peculiar interaction between participant and hypnotist facilitates changes in PERCEPTION and awareness.

Origins. The eighteenth-century medic Franz Anton Mesmer (1734–1815), from whose name the term "mesmerism" derives, experimented with hypnotism, though its first systematic application came with Manchester physician James Braid. Braid's ideas were developed by the American psychologist Ernest Hilgard (1904–2001), who argued that there are several systems of cognitive CONTROL, all monitored and governed by the executive ego of a central structure.

But, when a subject is hypnotized, the hypnotist removes much of the normal monitoring and control functions—so much so that the subject experiences motor movements as involuntary, memory and perceptions as hazy, and hallucinations as real. Hilgard introduced the term "hidden observer" to describe a part of the mind that is not within awareness yet seems to be watching the subject's whole experience; that is, a mental structure that monitors everything that happens, including events that the hypnotized subject is not consciously aware of perceiving at the time. Hilgard's experiments in the relief of PAIN revealed how hypnotized subjects were able to describe the pain felt, at the same time responding to the hypnotist's suggestions that they should be relieved of the pain. This process is called *dissociation* and has been influential. Hypnotized subjects have allegedly been able to undergo operations without anesthetic, regress to childhood memories, temporarily lose sensory functions, and experience imaginary phenomena as "real."

Yet, others have doubted whether hypnotized subjects are transported to another type of consciousness, the altered state suggested by this line of work. In contrast, they insist that, while hypnosis exists, it is best understood not as a special state but as a label for a context. The research of, among others, Graham Wagstaff suggests that the involuntary behavior of hypnotized subjects is not automatic at all but may be retrospectively interpreted by subjects as nonvolitional. In other words, the RELATIONSHIP between the subject and the hypnotist creates a CONTEXT ripe for compliance, or even faking. This is not to deny that subjects have a heightened susceptibility: they are certainly susceptible to the influence of the hypnotist. But, according to this view, they do not enter a separate state of consciousness.

While explanations of hypnosis differ, there is no dispute about its effects, some of which are measurable in terms of physiological RESPONSE. Changes in the electrical potential of the brain, respiration rate, skin temperature, and blood pressures have been recorded, though there is not a unique correlate of the hypnotic state; many of the quantifiable changes resemble those achieved through progressive RELAXATION. This is complicated by the fact that hypnotized subjects may engage in vigorous physical activity.

Some writers argue that such subjects may remain relaxed in a cognitive sense even while exerting themselves physically. But, even if the physiological profiles of subjects under hypnosis and progressive relaxation are very similar, there remain interesting differences in the experiences of subjects. For example, accounts of hallucinations and amnesia seem to suggest that hypnotized subjects become involved in what has been called "trance logic" in which normal expectations of consistencies in time and space are nullified. There are also claims that subjects are able to perform feats quite beyond normal expectations.

Hypnotic analgesia has obvious application in sports, though, again, claims are disputed: Subjects reporting relief from painful injuries when hypnotized have been interpreted by followers of Hilgard as surrendering the actual PAIN to a separate cognitive subsystem. Detractors argue that humans have a capacity to CONTROL and tolerate pain without chemical analgesics, but we learn thresholds of tolerance and how to express pain, according to cultural imperatives.

Whatever the interpretation of hypnotic experiences, the results are undeniable. Hypnotized subjects' ATTENTION is extremely selective, and they receive instructions without challenging them from one source. Post-hypnotic responses are sometimes strong, and subjects frequently observe suggestions about behavioral or cognitive habits—sometimes without knowing why (hypnotic amnesia occurs where a subject cannot recall what he or she has been told). Whether this is the product of an altered state or merely an extreme state of suggestibility in subjects who are susceptible to influences, anyway, is open to doubt.

Applications. The uses of hypnosis in sport and exercise are various: by suggesting specific modes of thought and behavior to a hypnotized person, desired post-hypnotic responses may be evoked. Hypnotism has been used to dispel dependences. Recovery from INJURY can also be accelerated through hypnotism, especially when used in conjunction with MEDITATION, GOAL SETTING, and SELF-TALK, Marcia Milne et al. suggest. There are also claims that hypnosis has been used effectively in the treatment of several maladies, including irritable bowel syndrome and various allergies, according to Sarah Pressman and Sheldon Cohen, who note its role in producing POSITIVE AFFECT, defined as "a level of pleasurable engagement with the environment."

B. Rael Cahn and John Polich include hypnosis with RELAXATION and trance-induction techniques as altered states that can be facilitated by meditation practices. Whether athletes can regularly employ this is a matter of debate. J. H. Edgette is emphatic: "Hypnosis allows the majority of athletes to enter the ZONE regularly and predictably." He writes of "eyes open, talking and walking hypnosis" that can be employed by, for example, a golfer who can "dip seamlessly and easily into the 'zone'."

Support for this remains inferential. For example, the first well-known use of hypnotism in sport was that of Ken Norton who fought three tough fights with Muhammad Ali in the 1970s. A rank underdog in the first of the series, Norton sought hypnotic help to convince him that he could upset the odds and beat Ali—which he did. There are dangers for boxers and other athletes in sports where the RISK of injury is high: Hypnotically induced sense deceptions can render an athlete less sensitive to PAIN and so more open to serious punishment.

Yet, favorable applications of hypnosis in sports are available: Nervous athletes who may be proficient in training yet suffer ANXIETY in COMPETITION have benefited from newfound SELF-CONFIDENCE or perhaps just an ABILITY to relax. Other sports performers have acquired a hitherto elusive ability to concentrate in clutch situations.

Further reading

Edgette, J. H. (2004). Zone in: Using hypnosis in sport psychology. *European Journal of Clinical Hypnosis*, 5, 31–43.

Gafner, George (2004). *Clinical applications of hypnosis*. New York: Norton.

Liggett, D. R. (2000). *Sport hypnosis*. Champaign, Ill.: Human Kinetics.

Milne, Marcia, Hall, Craig, and Forwell, Lorie (2005). Self-efficacy, imagery use, and adherence to rehabilitation by injured athletes. *Sport Rehabilitation*, 14, 150–67.

Pressman, Sarah D., and Cohen, Sheldon (2005). Does positive affect influence health? *Psychological Bulletin*, 131, 925–71.

Rael Cahn, B. and Polich, John (2006). Meditation states and traits: EEG, ERP, and neuroimaging studies. *Psychological Bulletin*, 132, 180–211.

Wagstaff, G. F. (1996). Hypnosis. In A. M. Colman (Ed.), *Companion Encyclopedia of Psychology*, (Vol. II, pp. 991–1006). London and New York: Routledge.

See also: AUTOGENIC; AUTOTELIC; BIOFEEDBACK; CENTERING; ELECTRO-ENCEPHALOGRAM; FOCUS; MEDITATION; MENTAL PRACTICE; MIND ATTRIBUTION; PEAK PERFORMANCE; PSYCHING; REHABILITATION; RELAXATION; SLEEP; VISUO-MOTOR; YOGA; ZONE

ICEBERG PROFILE

This is a graphic representation of the MOOD states of athletes during performance. The "iceberg" refers to the outline, or shape of the representation, rather than an expression of coolness. For example, if we imagine a classic iceberg shape, the visible tip would represent vigor, with ANGER, DEPRESSION, tension, fatigue, and confusion submerged beneath the water. Vigor, obviously, is associated with good performance, and strong athletes have an abundance of this; correspondingly, they have below-average scores in the other moods. Athletes have exhibited the iceberg profile across a wide spectrum of sports, suggesting a continuity of PROFILE OF MOOD STATES.

Further reading

Morgan, W. P. (1980). Test of champions: The iceberg profile. *Psychology Today*, 39, 92–108.

See also: ANGER; IDIOGRAPHIC; INDIVIDUAL ZONES OF OPTIMAL FUNCTIONING; INJURY; PEAK PERFORMANCE; PERSONALITY; PROFILE OF MOOD STATES; PROFILING

IDENTIFICATION

This describes a process in which individuals, as Benson Fraser and William Brown put it, "reconstruct their own attitudes, values, or behaviors in response to the images of people they admire, real and imagined, both through personal and mediated relationships."

While Fraser and Brown are referring specifically to FANS (in this case, of Elvis Presley), their description can be appropriated to fit any type of identification in which one attributes to oneself—not necessarily deliberately—one or more characteristics of another person, or even group. Daniel Wann and Frederick Grieve looked at the consequences of identification with one such group (a team, actually) and concluded, "one's level of group identification plays a vital role in social PERCEPTION." Fans of the same team, who identified though at different levels, saw the same thing—for example, a game—completely differently.

The process involves establishing, perhaps just imagining, a link between oneself and the object of the identification, whether an iconic figure or a local football club. This is a stronger link than in, for example, a straightforward *affiliation* (which means attaching oneself to or joining a collection of similarly devoted others). It means conceptually creating an equation between the SELF and the object by highlighting similarities or changing the self to become more like the object. In a highly identified state, a person might change his or her own name or undergo cosmetic surgery to accentuate the likeness. Fraser and Brown's work indicated that self-concepts were affected in some cases, fans actually striving for the VICARIOUS AGENCY of "living through" someone else.

Susan Boon and Christine Lomore were interested in the peculiar identification fans have with CELEBRITIES. Part of their 2001 research required participants to list current or historical celebrities, who they felt affected their lives. Apart from Elvis, several other influential figures were long gone, Jim Morrison, Albert Einstein, and John Wayne included.

Highly identified fans expressed strong feelings, suggesting that they had thought about what they believe some celebrities embodied and found a CONCORDANCE with their own values. Boon and Lomore concluded that "as changing social and demographic patterns continue to weaken and fragment social networks," identifications such as these are likely to become commonplace.

Further reading

Boon, Susan D., and Lomore, Christine D. (2001). Admirer–celebrity relationships among young adults: Explaining perceptions of celebrity influence on identity. *Human Communication Research*, 3, 432–65.

Fraser, Benson P. and Brown, William J. (2002). Media, celebrities, and social influence: Identification with Elvis Presley. *Mass Communication and Society*, 1, 183–207.

Wann, Daniel L. and Grieve, Frederick G. (2005). Biased evaluations of in-group and out-group behavior at sporting events: The importance of team identification and threats to social identity. *Journal of Social Psychology*, 145, 531–45.

See also: ATHLETIC IDENTITY; CELEBRITIES; FANS; GENDER; IDENTITY; MENTALITY; MORAL ATMOSPHERE; OBSESSIVE-COMPULSIVE; RELATIONSHIP; SELF; SELF-CONCEPT; SELF-CONFIDENCE; SUPERSTITIOUS BEHAVIOR; TEAM PLAYER; VICARIOUS AGENCY

IDENTIFIED REGULATION

According to Geneviève Mageau and Robert Vallerand: "*Identified regulation* refers to behaviours that are performed by choice because the individual judges them as important. They are self-determined because the person has fully endorsed the values underlying these behaviours."

For example, if the exerciser believes in the benefits of working out and values the positive outcomes but still finds the actual activities of running on the treadmill, or doing Pilates or spin classes tedious, then there is identified regulation. The results are regarded as worthwhile, but the methods of achieving them do not provide satisfaction in themselves.

Identified regulation is often compared with INTEGRATED REGULATION which refers to "behaviours that are so integrated in a person's life that they are part of the person's SELF and value system. They are highly self-determining because they are concordant with the person's self," according to Mageau and Vallerand.

Further reading

Mageau, Geneviève and Vallerand, Robert J. (2003). The coach–athlete relationship: A motivational model. *Journal of Sports Sciences*, 21, 883–904.

Ryan, Richard M. and Deci, Edward L. (2000). Self-determination theory and the facilitation of intrinsic motivation, social development, and well-being. *American Psychologist*, 55, 68–78.

See also: ADHERENCE; ATHLETIC IDENTITY; COACH–ATHLETE RELATIONSHIP; CONCORDANCE; EXERCISE IDENTITY; EXTRINSIC MOTIVATION; IDENTIFICATION; INTEGRATED

REGULATION; INTERNALIZATION; INTRINSIC MOTIVATION; METAMOTIVATION; MOTI-
VATION; PARTICIPATION MOTIVATION; REVERSAL THEORY; SELF; SELF-ACTUALIZATION;
SELF-DETERMINATION THEORY; SELF-ESTEEM

IDENTITY

The stable conception a person has of him or herself as an individual
is an identity. There are two major components. *Personal identity* is the
continuous awareness of distinctness and uniqueness, while *social
identity* is a conception reflected from the images others have of a
person. In practice, there is a close relationship if not CONCORDANCE.
The conception we have of ourselves is, in large part, a mirror of
how others see us (the word itself is taken from the Latin *identitas*,
meaning "same"). This is especially interesting in terms of athletes, as
Elizabeth Daniels et al. point out:

> ATHLETIC IDENTITY reflects the importance and exclusivity of the
> athlete role within individuals' constellation of other identities
> [...] Individuals with a strong athletic identity view statements
> such as "I consider myself an athlete" and "sport is the only impor-
> tant thing in my life" as highly representative of themselves.

In other words, some athletes, both amateur and professional, think
of themselves is as, in essence, athletes. "They establish this identity
through the development of skills, CONFIDENCE, and social interaction
in sports contexts," Daniels et al. observe. When this is no longer so
(after a career-ending INJURY, or voluntary RETIREMENT), FANS, peers
and significant others, who have for years supported and sustained
that conception, stop seeing them as such. The resulting lack of
congruence may trigger an athletic identity crisis—a mismatch
between how the individual regards him or herself and how others
see him or her, leading to a loss of continuity.

A study by William Webb et al. discovered that even in their teens,
"highly successful athletes have internalized the ATHLETIC IDENTITY,
frequently at the expense of other possible social roles. As a result, an
internalized athlete identity likely dominates the individual's overall
SELF-CONCEPT." A career-ending injury, an abrupt loss of form or an
enforced departure from sport can have far-reaching consequences.
As Webb et al. point out: "When retirement subsequently denies
opportunities to foster and maintain this identity, the individual with
such a strong, centralized athletic identity is presumed to lack the
flexibility necessary for redefining the self-concept."

A similar crisis of identity may occur when athletes who think of themselves as proficient or exceptional experience a loss of form and are forced to confront the uncomfortable actuality that they may not be as accomplished as they thought. One of the identity-protecting mechanisms often used by athletes is to rationalize a poor performance with "that wasn't the *real me* out there, tonight."

Wolf-Dietrich Brettschneider and Rüdiger Heim believe that: "Individuals can only regard themselves as unmistakable, distinct, or unique (identity) when they are able to sufficiently describe themselves (self-concept)." In their view, self-concept is multidimensional, composed of aspects of ourselves, including GENDER, political ideology, personal philosophy, leisure activities, and so on. "Identity, on the other hand, represents the complete integration of different self-perceptions and values and their reflexive processing." The reflexive processing refers to the way we interpret others' perceptions of us. So, identity is a coherent totality of particles of knowledge about ourselves.

Because the development of a person's identity involves not only being different from others, but a sense of coherence and an apprehension of how one appears to others, the body is central. PHYSICAL SELF-WORTH is a constituent of the self-concept and, hence, identity, according to Brettschneider and Heim, who studied young athletes involved in sports with a view to understanding how the body impacts on identity formation. In all sports, BODY IMAGE and body-maintenance activities are crucial factors in athletes' self-concepts.

Perceptions of the body are also crucial to what Bradley and Maria Cardinal call EXERCISE IDENTITY. This is not as susceptible to the vagaries of COMPETITION as athletic identity but still forms a powerful component of self-concept. The Cardinals' study examined the social and cognitive effects of regular exercise behavior, measuring on a nine-item *Exercise Identity Scale* (taken from Anderson and Cychosz's 1994 study). This measure determines "the extent to which exercise is descriptive of one's concept of self." For example, an item is, "I would feel a real loss if I were forced to give up exercising."

Besides *athletic* and *exercise identity*, we should note *fan identity*, which, Daniel Wann and Frederick Grieve argue, is fostered by "both in-group favoritism and out-group derogation." A strong sense of attachment to other fans can be a salient part of fans' identities. As the other forms of identities can be threatened by injury, retirement or poor performance, so the fans' identity is vulnerable too, for instance, by the results of the team they support, the behavior of rival fans, or sheer geography (that is, traveling to away games).

Further reading

Anderson, D. F., and Cychosz, C. M. (1994). Development of an exercise identity scale. *Perceptual and Motor Skills*, 78, 747–51.

Brettschneider, W.-D. and Heim, R. (1997). Identity, sport and youth development. In K. R. Fox (Ed.), *The physical self: From motivation to well-being* (pp. 205–27). Champaign, Ill.: Human Kinetics.

Cardinal, Bradley J., and Cardinal, Marita K. (1997). Changes in exercise behavior and exercise identity associated with a 14-week aerobic exercise class. *Journal of Sport Behavior*, 20, 377–477.

Daniels, Elizabeth, Sincharoean, Sirinda, and Leaper, Campbell (2005). The relation between sport orientations and athletic identity among adolescent girl and boy athletes. *Journal of Sport Behavior*, 28, 315–32.

Wann, Daniel L. and Grieve, Frederick G. (2005). Biased evaluations of in-group and out-group behavior at sporting events: The importance of team identification and threats to social identity. *Journal of Social Psychology*, 145, 531–45.

Webb, William M., Nasco, Suzanne A., Riley, Sarah, and Headrick, Brian (1998). Athlete identity and reactions to retirement from sports. *Journal of Sport Behavior*, 21, 338–62.

See also: ANOREXIA NERVOSA; ATHLETIC IDENTITY; BODY IMAGE; COACH–ATHLETE RELATIONSHIP; COMEBACK; EATING DISORDERS; EXERCISE DEPENDENCE; EXERCISE IDENTITY; FANS; IDENTIFICATION; INJURY; RETIREMENT; SELF-ACTUALIZATION; SELF-AWARENESS; SELF-CONCEPT; SOCIALIZATION

IDIOGRAPHIC

"An Idiographic APPROACH is committed to the detailed examination of a PHENOMENON as it is experienced and given meaning in the lifeworld of a person," state Virginia Eatough and Jonathan Smith: "It emphasizes the importance of the individual as the unit of analysis."

The name is taken from the Greek *idios*, meaning "own," the idea being that the results of a piece of research relate only to that phenomenon—they are its own. As such, the findings of idiographic analysis resist generalization.

Peter Hassmén et al. used an idiographic method to investigate state ANXIETY and SELF-CONFIDENCE among golfers. They discovered what they termed "intra-individual" variability. "Not only do athletes differ from one another in the level of anxiety experienced before a given COMPETITION, they also are likely to exhibit differences in the range of variability of precompetition anxiety across competitions," they concluded after asking individual players to complete trait inventories immediately before games, the intention being to capture in CONTEXT (time and place) the subjective states of individual players. The research suggests other approaches are too broad ranging and lack the insights idiographic research is capable of generating.

Autobiographies, case studies, and personal histories all constitute raw material for idiographic research. In the context of health psychology, Sarah Baker asked participants in her study to complete a baseline self-appraisal form, then a daily diary, providing "reports of positive and negative MOOD, hassles and uplifts." Baker writes that, with the subjective recording process, "participants' experience of daily events were assessed." (Baker augmented her results with a quantitative element to produce what she calls "an idiothetic understanding.")

George Howard and Paul Myers aimed for similar subjective results with a "Daily Rating Sheet that contained scales on three variables that each participant believed to have the greatest impact on his or her ABILITY to exercise." In this study, "the choice of three idiographic predictor variables was left to each participant, and the variables differed from subject to subject." In all cases of idiographic research, *individual experiences* are crucial to the method and this contrasts with NOMOTHETIC approaches, which strive for general results.

Further reading

Baker, Sarah R. (2006). Toward an idiothetic understanding of the role of the social problem solving in daily event, mood and health experiences: A prospective daily diary approach. *British Journal of Health Psychology*, 11, 513–31.

Eatough, Virginia and Smith, Jonathan (2006). "I was like a wild wild person": Understanding feelings of anger using interpretative phenomenological analysis. *British Journal of Psychology*, 97, 483–98.

Hassmén, Peter, Raglin, John S., Lundqvist (2004). Intra-individual variability in state anxiety and self-confidence in elite golfers. *Journal of Sport Behavior*, 27, 277–90.

Howard, George S. and Myers Paul R. (1990). Predicting human behavior: Comparing idiographic, nomothetic, and agentic methodologies. *Journal of Counseling Psychology*, 37, 227–37.

See also: APPLIED SPORT PSYCHOLOGY; CONCEPT; CONSTRUCT; CONTEXT; INDIVIDUAL ZONES OF OPTIMAL FUNCTIONING; LIFE COURSE; META-ANALYSIS; NOMOTHETIC; PHENOMENON; SELF-CONFIDENCE; SELF-RATING; THEORY

IMAGERY

From the Latin *imago* (imitate), imagery involves creating a mental picture of an event as vividly as possible with the intention of duplicating that event in actuality. As a technique used before COMPETITION, it is predicated on the idea that mentally rehearsing a desired outcome enhances the probability that the desired outcome will materialize. There are three main forms of imagery, according to K. J. Munroe-Chandler et al.

(1) *Technique imagery.* The user needs to be able to construct clear and real images, controlling their content and action. There are two possible perspectives: Individuals can either try to simulate experience of, for example, traveling over the high-jump bar or executing a perfect dive, or imagine they are viewing themselves from the vantage point of an outsider, like a photographer. For example, an athlete might recall a previous performance with which he or she was satisfied and imagine him or herself repeating the exact movements involved in the SKILL.

(2) *Energy imagery.* While imagery is popularly thought to work at the level of COGNITION, research by K. A. Martin and C. R. Hall, in 1995, indicated that it can also operate at the levels of MOTIVATION. Through imagining competitive situations, subjects can become energized in a way that readies them for the fray.

(3) *Appearance imagery.* This involves images associated with a leaner, fitter, and healthier appearance and is used more by women than men, according to Kimberley Gammage et al. It is popular in exercise. The exercise can be structured in terms of scripts, so that the participant is guided through a series of imaginary maneuvers.

The evidence about whether this actually results in performance improvements is equivocal. In reviewing several studies, Karen Lee Hill concludes that there have been "mixed findings," though the weight of evidence favors the view that imaging does contribute to improved performance, especially in basketball, darts, golf, gymnastics, and tennis. These are, mostly, sports that require an element of DECISION-MAKING. Imagery enables athletes to think through possible scenarios. Elite athletes are more accomplished at imagery, if only because they are more likely to visualize technically correct procedures. For example, Melanie Gregg and Craig Hall's study of golfers indicated that the regular and effective use of imagery was significantly related to skill level, as measured by golf handicap. But imagery can also aid novices in SKILL ACQUISITION, for example, by MODELING their performance on that of an experienced athlete.

Imagery immediately following a competition has also been reported as beneficial, enabling someone to become more efficient at imaging vividly based on proximate experiences, according to Claire Calmels et al.

This begs an important question: How does imagery work? Allen Cornelius pulls together four groups of explanation.

(1) *Psychoneuromuscular* a.k.a. "muscle memory": Imaginary movements produce muscle innervation similar to those used in actual movement. For example, a swimmer visualizes performing the backstroke, these images produce a low-level activation of the nerves and muscles involved in swimming sufficient to affect the motor pattern in the motor cortex responsible for the execution of the movement. There is only weak support for this theory.

(2) *Symbolic learning*: Imagery works like a mental blueprint that we can use later; that is, a symbolic coding of information. Again, only weak support.

(3) INFORMATION PROCESSING: An image is an organized set of propositions in the brain and, when imaging, we activate STIMULUS propositions that describe the content of the image as well as RESPONSE propositions. Cornelius gives the example of a basketball player who "may imagine the crowd noise, sweaty palms, and NERVOUSNESS before stepping to the foul line with 0.5 seconds left and the score tied (stimulus proposition)." He also imagines shooting and watching the ball fall clean through the net, which is the response proposition.

(4) *Triple-code*: This has three components: (a) the imagery which facilitates (b) somatic responses (such as optimal ATTENTION and/ or AROUSAL); and (c) the meaning of the image to the subject. The meaning component is crucial because one athlete's image of a situation may evoke ANXIETY and STRESS, while another's image of the same situation evokes CONFIDENCE.

Even though the mechanisms through which imagery works are not clear and there are doubts about whether it does in fact affect performance, there is no evidence that it damages performance (though, as Hill points out, imagining a negative outcome in sport can lead to deterioration in SKILL EXECUTION).

Further reading

Calmels, C., Holmes, P., Berthoumieux, C, and Singer, R. (2004). The development of movement imagery vividness through a structure intervention in softball. *Journal of Sport Behavior*, 27, 307–22.

Cornelius, A. (2002). Intervention techniques in sport psychology. In J. M. Silva and D. E. Stevens (Eds.) *Psychological Foundations of Sport* (pp. 197–223). Boston, Mass.: Allyn & Bacon.

Gammage, Kimberley L., Hall, C., and Rodgers, W. (2000). More about exercise imagery. *The Sport Psychologist*, 14, 348–59.

Gregg, Melanie and Hall, Craig (2006). The relationship of skill level and age to the use of imagery by golfers. *Journal of Applied Sport Psychology*, 18, 363–75.

Hill, K. L. (2001). *Frameworks for Sport Psychologists*. Champaign, Ill.: Human Kinetics.

Martin, K. A. and Hall, C. R. (1995). Using mental imagery to enhance intrinsic motivation. *Journal of Sport and Exercise Psychology*, 13, 149–59.

Morris, Tony, Spittle, Michael, and Watt, Anthony P. (2005). *Imagery in sport*. Champaign, Ill.: Human Kinetics.

Munroe-Chandler, K. J., Kim, Arvin J., and Gammage, Kimberley L. (2004). Using imagery to predict weightlifting dependency in men. *International Journal of Men's Health*, 3, 129–39.

See also: ANXIETY; AROUSAL; AUTOMATICITY; BIOFEEDBACK; BODY IMAGE; COGNITION; CONCENTRATION; DECISION-MAKING; EMOTIONAL INTELLIGENCE; EXPECTANCY; GOAL SETTING; INFORMATION PROCESSING; MENTAL PRACTICE; NEGATIVITY; NERVOUS SYSTEM; PROPRIOCEPTION; REINFORCEMENT; SELF-CONFIDENCE; SELF-FULFILLING PROPHECY; VISUOMOTOR

IMPOSTOR PHENOMENON

A condition in which people have thoughts or feelings of doubts about their own proficiencies, which they believe to be overestimated by others. These individuals FEAR that others will expose them as incompetent, if not complete fakes. The term derives from the French *imposteur*, someone who strives to be accepted or taken for someone else. In English, this becomes impostor, or imposter.

In the 1988 study in which the term was introduced, there were both male and female impostors, though men were better able to cope with their fears because of group support in working environments. A 2006 study by Shamala Kumar and Carolyn Jagacinski supported the original Clance and O'Toole study in this respect and added that improvement at a task does not produce feelings of competence for women who have impostor fears: "Instead they must outperform others to feel competent [...] the potential buffering effect of task goals is not operational for women."

Further reading

Clance, P. and O'Toole, M. (1988). *The impostor phenomenon: An internal barrier to empowerment and achievement.* Binghamton, N.Y.: Haworth Press.

Kumar, Shamala, and Jagacinski, Carolyn M. (2006). Imposters have goals too: The imposter phenomenon and its relationship to achievement goal theory. *Personality and Individual Differences*, 40, 147–57.

Thompson, T., Davis, H., and Davidson, J. (1998). Attributional and affective responses of imposters to academic success and failure outcomes. *Personality and Individual Differences*, 25, 381–96.

See also: ACHIEVEMENT MOTIVE; FEAR; FEAR OF FAILURE; GENDER; GOAL; OUTPERFORMANCE; PHENOMENON; SANDBAGGING; SELF-CONFIDENCE; SELF-FULFILLING PROPHECY

INCENTIVE

Any incitement or provocation that motivates behavior is an incentive, from the Latin *incentivus*, meaning setting the tune. Incentives in sport and exercise are varied, including trophies with little extrinsic worth, and measurable levels of FITNESS improvement. Underlying them all is the supposition that incentives are objects or conditions that are perceived as fulfillers of needs. In this sense, an incentive both encourages and controls behavior.

Incentive has links with concepts of DRIVE in the sense that the level of the drive state determines its utility and effectiveness. Water has incentive value for a dehydrated castaway; a million dollars may have no incentive value for a basketball player who already owns two Gulfstream jets. The money would be an *extrinsic* incentive. The player might respond more readily to an *intrinsic* incentive, for example, to achieve a personal milestone.

Incentives may improve the effectiveness of a performance, but they do not necessarily improve the underlying efficiency with which tasks are performed: "The individual may try to compensate for any actual or anticipated decline in performance by directing more effort at the task at hand or changing strategies" in their efforts to take the reward, according to Nickolas Smith et al. So, the performance might be successful in achieving a desired result (effectively), but might achieve it with too much wasted energy or other kinds of resources (inefficiently).

Establishing incentives that motivate workers to greater output by offering supplemental rewards (that is, "incentivizing") is common in a CULTURE that rewards the reaching of targets. Many industries adopt a practice used in sports, perhaps since before the Christian era, inducing desired behavior rather than trying to force it—carrot rather than stick. A combination of the two was favored by Livia, the wife of Augustus, in *I, Claudius*, the Robert Graves (1895–1985) novel. Disgusted by the lack of effort of some the gladiators, she decides, "These Games are degraded by more and more professional tricks to stay alive [. . .] I won't have it. So put on a good show and there'll be plenty of money for the living and a decent burial for the dead. If you let me down, I'll break this guild and I'll send the lot of you to the mines."

The prospect of being condemned to slaving in mines, in this sense, acts as a *disincentive*, this being a factor that discourages a certain activity (that is, not fighting to the death!). Similarly, it might be argued that the balance of world power rests on some nations' having nuclear capabilities, while others do not. Non-nuclear powers are effectively provided with an incentive not to engage in warfare; if they do so, they risk the possibility of nuclear retaliation.

Further reading

Smith, N. C., Bellamy, M., Collins, D. J., and Newell, D. (2001). A test of processing efficiency theory in a team sport context. *Journal of Sports Sciences*, 19, 321–32.

Smith, R. E. (1998). A positive approach to sport performance enhancement: principles of reinforcement and performance feedback. In J. M. Williams (Ed.), *Applied sport psychology: Personal growth to peak performance*, 3rd edn (pp. 28–40). Mountain View, Calif.: Mayfield Press.

See also: ACHIEVEMENT MOTIVE; ADHERENCE; AROUSAL; ATTRIBUTION; CONTROL; DISCIPLINE; DRIVE; EXTRINSIC MOTIVATION; IDENTIFIED REGULATION; INTEGRATED REGULATION; INTRINSIC MOTIVATION; MOTIVATION; OBEDIENCE; REINFORCEMENT; REWARD; SELF-DETERMINATION THEORY; SOCIAL LOAFING

INDIVIDUAL ZONES OF OPTIMAL FUNCTIONING (IZOF)

The theoretical MODEL, or approach to study, known as IZOF, is based on the view that, as its originator Yuri Hanin puts it, "to understand why and how outstanding performers achieve consistent excellency [sic], one needs to focus primarily on their unique experiences." In contrast to NOMOTHETIC theories, which seek abstract or general principles, Hanin favored an IDIOGRAPHIC approach that treats individuals singularly and which relies on SELF-RATING. His claims for it are many, including to "describe, predict, explain, and CONTROL athlete's [sic] optimal and dysfunctional experiences related to individually successful and poor performances."

Devised in part to challenge the popular INVERTED-U theory of AROUSAL, itself nomothetic, IZOF is based on the view that the optimal performance occurs when individually meaningful emotional states are in specific zones. Both the state and the ZONE differ from athlete to athlete. So, empirical testing is the only way to ascertain the precise zone an athlete should be aiming for. Athletes describe their own emotional states as positive, such as "happy," "vigorous," or "daring," and negative, such as "angry," "worried," "afraid."

For each of these, there is a zone of optimal intensity that is associated with PEAK PERFORMANCE. The emotions are rated in terms of their intensity. Poor performances are also associated with emotions, positive or negative, and their INTENSITY: dysfunctional states are identified. Athletes who rate their COMPETITION performances as successful are more likely to be closer to their optimal facilitating zones and outside their dysfunctional states.

For every facilitating EMOTION there is a zone of optimal intensity. Given the idiographic emphasis, each individual has a different zone. So, it is possible for one athlete to produce peak performances when he or she experiences, say, very intense eagerness, while another athlete experiencing the same emotion with the same intensity may not. The latter might perform optimally when feeling eager, but only mildly eager; too much intensity may hinder the performer (over-eagerness). The IZOF model holds that emotions have both facilitating and debilitating effects on performances, depending on the athlete's individual optimal zone.

While devotees of IZOF believe that it is a path-breaking and enlightening THEORY full of potential applications, critics are not so sure. Its resistance to generalizations obviously limits its utility as a theory. There are also several key questions left not only unanswered, but also unasked, according to Peter Crocker et al. For example: How are specific emotions produced in athletes? Why would the same emotional state produce individual differences in performance (that is, what are the mechanisms)? As the model has only been tested on elite athletes, does it have validity for younger, less experienced athletes?

Further reading

Crocker, P. E., Kowalski, K. C., Graham, T. R., and Kowalski, N. P. (2002). Emotion in sport. In J. M. Silva and D. E. Stevens (Eds.), *Psychological foundations of sport* (pp. 107–31). Boston, Mass.: Allyn & Bacon.

Hanin, Y. L. (Ed.) (2000). *Emotions in sport*. Champaign, Ill.: Human Kinetics.

Hanin, Y. L. (2003). Performance related emotional states in sport: An analysis. *Forum: Qualitative Research*, 4, 1–29. Available online at http://www. qualitative-research.net/fqs-texte/1–03/1–03hanin-e.htm.

Russell, William D. and Cox, Richard H. (2000). A laboratory investigation of positive and negative affect within individual zone of optimum functioning theory. *Journal of Sport Behavior*, 23, 164–81.

See also: AROUSAL; EMOTION; EMOTIONAL CONTROL; HEDONIC TONE; ICEBERG PROFILE; IDIOGRAPHIC; INTENSITY; INVERTED-U; MENTAL HEALTH MODEL; META-ANALYSIS; MODEL; MOOD; NEGATIVITY; NOMOTHETIC; PEAK PERFORMANCE; PROFILE OF MOOD STATES; SELF-RATING; ZONE

INFORMATION PROCESSING

In the 1950s, a series of papers by Nobel Prize winner Herbert A. Simon (1916–) suggested that psychological phenomena could be simulated using the computer and that traditional psychological problems could be envisioned in terms of information processing. In this MODEL, the human being was a processor of information, the senses providing an input channel for information and the MEMORY operating as a mental repository for the transformed input that would, in turn, generate responses. The *information*, in this sense, refers to any knowledge that is capable of being received, and *processing* is organizing, interpreting and responding to incoming stimulation (that is, information).

Richard Cox provides the example of a quarterback who "stores thousands of pieces of information about offenses and defenses." Just before the snap, he notices a late change in the opposition's defense, decides on a new play and calls an audible (a change in the offensive play). Cox explains what has happened in information processing terms: "Previously stored information about the opposing team was retrieved from memory and used to initiate a different but appropriate RESPONSE."

The stored information "may be based on previous encounters or reports from others (for example, teammates, coaches, the media)," as Iain Greenlees points out. In any sport and, indeed, any field of endeavor where choices are necessary, information processing like this is going on constantly. In information processing, the same rules that govern how the quarterback encodes, stores, and recalls bits (units of information, in computing terminology; *bi*nary+di*git*) about defenses apply to all other situations. While people and physical stimuli, whether rival football players, motorcycles, people who work on the supermarket checkout, and so on, have strikingly different features that attract ATTENTION, once one pays attention to the player, the machine, or the sales assistant, processing is likely to be the same. So, information processing offers a general, or NOMOTHETIC, model that holds good regardless of individual or CONTEXT.

Information processing has been used to explain how IMAGERY works, the idea being that an image is an organized cluster of propositions, or plans, in the brain that comprise STIMULUS propositions and response propositions. The basic processes of encoding, storing, and recalling apply. Similarly, information processing has been applied to ANXIETY and AROUSAL in sports, the conclusions supporting the predictions of the YERKES-DODSON LAW: At a particular level of arousal, the information-processing capacity of the system is at its maximum and performance will be optimal.

In information-processing models, all human cognitive and perceptual operations proceed. They move forward in stages, information being inputted, stored, retrieved, and outputted. SKILL ACQUISITION and performance can be explained in these terms, an experienced and proficient operator being able to proceed through the stages at great speed.

There are, however, limitations. "The issue of *automatic processing,* for example, is not explained," points out Matt Jarvis. "If a stimulus can be responded to without conscious attention, the model fails to explain at what point in the system it is filtered from consciousness and what precisely happens to this information."

Further reading

Cox, R. H. (1998). *Sport psychology: Concepts and applications*, 4th edn. Boston, Mass.: McGraw-Hill.

Greenlees, Iain (2007). Person perception and sport performance. In Sophia Jowett and David Lavallee (Eds.), *Social psychology in sport* (pp. 195–208). Champaign, Ill.: Human Kinetics.

Jarvis, Matt (2006). *Sport psychology: A student's handbook.* London and New York: Routledge.

INJURY

Any involuntary, physically disruptive experience constitutes an injury. At its mildest, an injury interrupts or restricts, while, more seriously, it can harm, damage, and, sometimes, terminate a sports career or an active exercise life. Like other forms of illness, an injury has both physical and psychological consequences and, according to some research, it may have psychological causes too.

Athletes experience loss after an injury. Not only do they lose a physical capability; they also lose a salient part of their SELF. "The integrity of the self is assaulted and threatened," writes Andrew Sparkes: "Earlier taken-for-granted assumptions about possessing a smoothly functioning body are shaken, previous assumptions about the relationships between body and self are disturbed, and the sense of wholeness of body and self is disrupted." Because many athletes shape their lives around the performance of their body in sports, an injury has manifold effects. Studies have shown that DEPRESSION, ANXIETY, and low SELF-ESTEEM frequently accompany an injury. Similarly, persons who have what some researchers call an EXERCISE IDENTITY, experience a change in MOOD states following an injury.

The impact of knee injury on, say, someone who serves coffee at Starbucks, may not appear to be profound; a similar injury for a squash player may be traumatic. Anyone is affected by an injury to a limb and, in many instances, may experience a loss of work. The player may experience an added sense of failure, followed by a fragmentation of self. Athletes rely on a unity of body and self to accomplish their deeds; the DISCIPLINE they practice is designed to subordinate their bodies to conscious CONTROL. When their body no longer responds to their commands, the unity is broken. The proficient squash player, whose speed of reaction is aligned to anticipation, may experience his or her injured body as alien, as something that stands in opposition to his or her wishes.

A. C. Sparkes and other researchers have applied the idea of a narrative, or storyline, to make sense of how athletes respond to injury. This is a framing device that shapes athletes' understanding of their progress in sport. Injury ruptures the narrative, forcing the athletes to recognize the limitations of their bodies. As well as constraining the competitors' mode of expression, the injury, according to J. Heil, "raises uncertainty about return to COMPETITION." Of course, some athletes never do, while others are forced to make adjustments to their style to return. Like patients with terminal illnesses, athletes can go through "denial," refusing to accept the extent of their injury. Problematic as denial is, it can, on occasion, be functional when it "protects the athlete from being overwhelmed by negative emotions."

Ramón De Heredia et al. studied how a self-restoring return to activity competition involved a reunification of body and IDENTITY and a re-emergence of the ICEBERG PROFILE of mood states. Other injured athletes fail to restore themselves fully and settle for a contingent personal identity: never quite the competitor they once were, but still adept. Those who accept they have no chance of resuming their former selves try to salvage some part of their previous identities. How athletes respond to injury psychologically is as crucial to their REHABILITATION as their physical RESPONSE though, in a practical sense, the two are not separable.

Athletes may respond to injuries rather differently from others. Research by H. L. Nixon concluded that, because they are inculcated into a CULTURE in which RISK, PAIN, and injuries are regarded as commonplace, athletes tend to interpret these as features of their working lives. The sports media convey messages that affirm this, inclining athletes toward the view that they should accept injuries that most would understand as serious as quite normal.

While injury and, indeed, other kinds of illness are often attributed to accidents, some research indicates that athletes' perceptions of situations are contributory factors. For example, if competitors respond to what they regard as threatening situations with muscle tension and a narrowing of visual fields, then they will become vulnerable. This is what is known as a STRESS response and, together with other factors, such as previous injuries or general life stress, can enhance the athlete's chances of getting injured. This may help explain why some athletes, most famously Michael Jordan, led a almost injury-free career, while others gain reputations for being "injury-prone." The problem with this is that it bases too much expectation on the personal qualities of individual performers; a more satisfactory account would require more detail on, for example, the state of fatigue, the difficulty of the SKILL being attempted at the time of the injury, the importance of the occasion and other circumstantial factors.

On the other hand, research into the recurrently injured athlete may show a clear antecedent history and suggest that the behavior leading to the injury is predictable. For example, rugby fly half Jonny Wilkinson was forced into 1,167 days of inactivity for the treatment of eleven separate injuries, including serious damage to both knees, both arms, neck, groin, appendix, and kidney. Returning at twenty-seven, Wilkinson was considered jinxed, especially when he was hurt again during his COMEBACK. A more logical appraisal would be that the collisional nature of rugby was a contributory factor. Players are exposed to injury both in competition and training, and Wilkinson's reputation as a key player made him something of a target for rivals.

Further reading

De Heredia, Ramón Alzate Sáez, Muñoz, Amaia Ramírez, and Artaza, Juan Luis (2004). The effect of psychological response on recovery of sport injury. *Research in Sports Medicine*, 12, 15–31.

Heil, J. (2000). The injured athlete. In Y. L. Hanin (Ed.), *Emotions in sport* (pp. 245–65). Champaign, Ill.: Human Kinetics.

Nixon, H. L (1993). Accepting the risks of pain and injury in sport: Mediated cultural influences on playing hurt. *Sociology of Sport Journal, 10*(2), 183–96.

Sparkes, A. C. (2000). Illness, premature career-termination, and the loss of self: A biographical study of an elite athlete. In R. L. Jones and K. M. Armour (Eds.), *Sociology of sport: Theory and practice* (pp. 14–32). Harlow: Longman.

See also: AGING; ANXIETY; ATHLETIC IDENTITY; COACH–ATHLETE RELATIONSHIP; COPING STRATEGIES; DEPRESSION; EXERCISE IDENTITY; IDENTITY; LIFE COURSE; MENTAL TOUGHNESS; PAIN; REHABILITATION; SELF-ESTEEM; THERAPY

INSTINCT

An inborn propensity to behave without conscious intention but with apparent rationality under appropriate conditions is an instinct—a word that derives from the Latin *instinctus,* meaning "incite," "instigate," or "impel." Being innate, instincts are biological and cannot be learned: they are patterns of behavior fixed from birth by hereditary factors and usually responses to simple stimuli. Sport is full of athletes described as "instinctive players" or those who, on occasion, "play by instinct alone." Neither possibility is plausible.

Before the publication of Charles Darwin's *On the Origin of the Species by Means of Natural Selection* in 1859 and, indeed, for a long time after, nonhuman animal behavior was attributed to instincts. Devoid of intellect and the power to reason, animals were considered fundamentally different from humans. Darwin (1809–82), in revealing continuity in evolutionary adaptations, cast serious doubt on the assumed distinction between humans and other primates. This suggested to some, particularly the British-born American psychologist William McDougall (1831–1938), that humans, like other animals, were guided by instinct rather than rational thought. While McDougall believed that inherited instincts were susceptible to modification through experience and social learning, the sources of behavior were biological. He even went so far as to identify the compelling instincts; these included "acquisition," "flight," "pugnacity' and "self-assertion." His model left no room for DECISION-MAKING and reasoned interpretation, or, indeed, for the role of COGNITION or REINFORCEMENT; the MOTIVATION behind behavior was instinctive. As such, the human being was at the mercy of innate forces.

Darwin himself had regarded instincts as complex reflexes that were made up of inherited units and were subject to change through evolutionary adaptations to the environment. His work influenced, among many others, the Austrian zoologist Konrad Lorenz (1903–89) who maintained that animal behavior included a number of fixed-action patterns that were characteristic of species and largely genetically determined. Each instinct was a *fixed-action pattern*.

In a different way, Sigmund Freud (1856–1939) believed that inner forces determined human conduct by two opposing instincts, *Eros*, which enhances life, and *Thanatos*, the DEATH WISH. The energy of *Eros* is libido, which revolves primarily around sexual activities. *Thanatos* can be directed inward in the form of suicide or other self-destructive behavior, or outward in the form of AGGRESSION toward others. Freud believed that SEX and aggression were two basic motives of human behavior. During 1920s, instinct theory was replaced by concept of DRIVE—a state of AROUSAL that results from a biological need, for example, for water, sex, or the avoidance of pain.

Studies of sport based on this, as Matt Jarvis puts it, "have viewed sport in general as a healthy way of expressing our death." Few contemporary theorists cling to instinct theories and, though many allow that there is a biological predisposition behind many behaviors, few consider genetic factors solely responsible for human conduct. Discredited as instinct THEORY is, it is tempting to interpret sport in instinctual terms. Much of the aggression and VIOLENCE in sport appears to be a manifestation of destructive instincts, or Lorenz's fixed-action patterns. The instinctive "play" of certain types of animal bears a resemblance to human forms of sport and leisure activities. Even the bonding, particularly of males, in team sports has counterparts among other animals. From this perspective, sports constitute a healthy and socially acceptable outlet for instinctive behavior. Despite this, the perspective is not a current one. Most contemporary analysts of sport FOCUS on the institution of sport as a cultural construction and the MOTIVATION of athletes as the product more of the interaction between circumstances and individuals than of immanent forces.

Further reading

Atkinson, R. L., Atkinson, R. C., Smith, E. E., Bem, D. J., and Hilgard, E. R. (1990). *Introduction to psychology,* 10th edn. New York: Harcourt, Brace, Jovanovich.

Jarvis, Matt (2006). *Sport psychology: A student's handbook.* London and New York: Routledge.

MacFarland, D. J. (1987). Instinct. In R. L. Gregory (Ed.) *The Oxford companion to the mind* (pp. 374–75). Oxford: Oxford University Press.

Roth, Stephen (2007). *Genetics primer for exercise science and health.* Champaign, Ill.: Human Kinetics.

See also: ADRENALINE RUSH; AGGRESSION; AROUSAL; CATHARSIS; DEATH WISH; DRIVE; GIFTEDNESS; INCENTIVE; MOTIVATION; TALENT; VIOLENCE

INTEGRATED REGULATION

A form of MOTIVATION that shares many qualities with INTRINSIC MOTIVATION but is considered extrinsic because, as Richard Ryan and Edward Deci put it, "they [the resultant behaviors] are done to attain separable outcomes rather than for their inherent enjoyment." The behavior is maintained regularly without guidance and eventually becomes combined with the rest of a person's lifestyle. Often compared with IDENTIFIED REGULATION.

Further reading

Ryan, Richard M. and Deci, Edward L. (2000). Self-determination theory and the facilitation of intrinsic motivation, social development, and well-being. *American Psychologist,* 55, 68–78.

See also: EXTRINSIC MOTIVATION; IDENTIFIED REGULATION; INTRINSIC MOTIVA-
TION; MOTIVATION; SELF-DETERMINATION THEORY

INTELLIGENCE

Intelligence may be described as the capacity to comprehend, understand, and reason in a way that enables successful adaptations to changing environments. This is a distillation of several, often widely differing, definitions offered over the decades of a term that stems from the Latin *intellectus*, for PERCEPTION. In a famous project in 1921, the editors of the *Journal of Educational Psychology* solicited definitions from fourteen eminent psychologists. The responses ranged from the crisp "ABILITY to carry on abstract thinking" (Lewis S. Terman) through the pragmatic "capacity to learn or to profit from experience" (W. F. Dearborn) to the rather cryptic "capacity to acquire capacity" (H. Woodrow). Common to many offerings was the capacity to learn and abstract from actual experiences and to adapt to the environment. Contemporary psychologist Robert Sternberg brings these together in his definition: "the ability to make sense of and function adaptively in the environments in which one finds oneself."

Sternberg's definition is well suited to sports, in which there is often thought to be a specific form of intelligence. Journalists often praise "intelligent play" and compare intelligent athletes to their cruder counterparts who trade on raw power. The athlete who has the ability to make sense of and to play effectively and/or adaptively under competitive conditions (environments) has intelligence that is specific to sports.

"Adaptively" also has a variety of meanings. A rookie learning a certain type of play in a football team, a boxer modifying his or her style to accommodate a cut that opens up during a fight, a basketball player traded from another club who tailors his or her game to fit in with new colleagues, a baseball pitcher who alters every pitch to inconvenience different batters, a cricket captain who changes the field to discomfort batsmen: these are examples of adaptive play that occurs regularly in COMPETITION. The responses are instances of sporting intelligence.

Many of the colossal disputes over intelligence and, particularly, attempts to measure it with IQ tests, revolve around how conceptions of intelligence differ from CULTURE to culture. Whether or not the capacity we call intelligence actually is the same across or even within cultures, we should acknowledge that it is not universally regarded in precisely the same way. What is intelligence in one culture may not be in another. So, while sport carries "jock" connotations and criticisms of its anti-intellectual leanings, it should not be dismissed as unintelligent. A particular type and quality of intelligence operates in sport and, though, it has not been measured by conventional tests, evidence of it is abundant in any competition where tactics and good sense are required.

John Eisenberg writes of a "creative athletic performance as intelligent, as involving the highest functioning of the mind in conjunction with a highly skilled body." Eisenberg's argument is a robust refutation of INFORMATION PROCESSING approaches and begins from the observation that any athlete is "confronted by an intrinsic indeterminacy, an indeterminacy that precludes total, even substantial, understanding and CONTROL of our destinies."

Once competition begins, performers must be "receptive to indeterminacy"—in other words, the situation is uncertain and can never be known in advance. So the athlete needs to use "transformative creativity" to try to use knowledge in a way that brings the contest under control. In some contexts, this may need accuracy and technique, while, in others, it will require innovation and originality. Eisensberg gives examples of transformative athletes, including Muhammad Ali, Dick Fosbury, the Canadian figure skater Toller Cranston, and the Bulgarian wrestler Valentin Jordanov, all of whom introduced technical innovations that reflected "bodily kinesthetic intelligence," as Eisenberg calls it; though the implication of his thesis is that *all* athletes are involved in a form of creative thinking, if only by virtue of the uncertain circumstances of competition.

This observation is supported by Daniel Gould et al.'s NOMETHIC study, which revealed among some athletes, "the ability to analyze, being innovative relative to one's sport technique, being a student of the sport, making good decisions, understanding the nature of elite sport, and being a quick learner." The researchers described this as *sport intelligence*.

Further reading

Eisenberg, John (with Levin, M., Eben, M., Katz, M., Cheifetz, D., Hanna, M., and Moffat, B.) (2004). *The triumph of the imagination: Creativity in sport*. Toronto: Chestnut Publishing.

Gould, Daniel, Dieffenbach, Kristen, and Moffett, Aaron (2002). Psychological characteristics and their development in Olympic champions. *Journal of Applied Sport Psychology*, 14, 172–204.

Sternberg, Robert J. (1987). Intelligence. In R. L. Gregory (Ed.) *The Oxford companion to the mind* (pp. 375–9). Oxford: Oxford University Press.

Sternberg, Robert J. (1996). Intelligence and cognitive styles. In A. M. Colman (Ed.), *Companion encyclopedia of psychology* (Vol. II, pp. 583–601). London and New York: Routledge.

See also: ABILITY; AGING; COGNITIVE–MOTIVATIONAL–RELATIONAL; DECISION-MAKING; EMOTIONAL INTELLIGENCE; FITNESS; GIFTEDNESS; INFORMATION PROCESSING; MENTAL TOUGHNESS; RACE; SKILL EXECUTION; SOCIALIZATION

INTENSITY

The amount or quality of eagerness, ardor, effort, or sheer passion a subject either contributes or experiences is intensity, a word that has evolved from *intensus*, Latin for strain, stretch, or direct. Arthur Reber advises that the term is borrowed from physics: "Hence, physical stimuli will be characterized in terms of intensity, for example, of a light, a tone, an electric current, and so on."

Assessing intensity renders a property or qualities measurable. Often, in psychology, the effort is to quantify subjective experiences or states by way of SELF-RATING methods; the degree to which, for example, a sensation or EMOTION is felt is then recorded on a scale of intensity. For example, De Heredia et al. report on the "intensity of the injured person's RESPONSE to STRESS," Feshbach on "a continuum of affective intensity," Eatough on "emotional intensity, Smith on "mental intensity," and Exline and Lobel on "sensitivity about being the target of a threatening upward comparison intensity." In all instances, intensity is a single dimension along which some feeling or experience can be expressed.

In accounts of MOTIVATION, intensity is frequently, though simplistically, identified as one of the two major dimensions, the other being direction: motivation = direction + intensity of behavior. Laura Finch points out that this is not constant. For instance, if an athlete is attracted toward a sport, he or she is likely to exhibit high intensity (defined as "how much effort an athlete puts forth in particular situations") in pursuing it. But, this is not always the case, and a competent athlete may appear listless and unmotivated. Changing coaches, switching to a different club, or league, or new types of GOAL SETTING can increase the competitor's intensity. So, intensity of both experience and effort is not fixed and can be changed by altering environments. The athlete would not only intensify input, but he or she would presumably experience more intensity from playing in a more challenging environment.

Further reading

De Heredia, Ramón Alzate Sáez, Muñoz, Amaia Ramírez, and Artaza, Juan Luis (2004). The effect of psychological response on recovery of sport injury. *Research in Sports Medicine*, 12, 15–31.

Eatough, Virginia and Smith, Jonathan (2006) "I was like a wild wild person": Understanding feelings of anger using interpretative phenomenological analysis. *British Journal of Psychology*, 97, 483–98.

Exline, Julie Juola and Lobel, Marci (1999). The perils of outperformance: Sensitivity about being the target of threatening upward comparison. *Psychological Bulletin*, 125, 307–37.

Feshbach, Seymour (1984). The catharsis hypothesis, aggressive drive, and the reduction of aggression. *Aggressive Behavior*, 10, 91–101.

Finch, Laura (2001). Understanding individual motivation in sport. In J. M. Silva and D. E. Stevens (Eds.), *Psychological foundations of sport* (pp. 66–79). Boston, Mass.: Allyn & Bacon.

Reber, A. S. (1995). *Dictionary of psychology*, 2nd edn, Harmondsworth: Penguin, pp. 380–1.

Smith, N. C., Bellamy, M., Collins, D. J., and Newell, D. (2001). A test of processing efficiency theory in a team sport context. *Journal of Sports Sciences*, 19, 321–32.

See also: ANGER; AROUSAL; BURNOUT; COMMITMENT; CONCENTRATION; CONCEPT; EMOTION; FLOW; FOCUS; INDIVIDUAL ZONES OF OPTIMAL FUNCTIONING; MIMESIS; MOTIVATION; NEGATIVITY; OVERTRAINING SYNDROME; PEAK PERFORMANCE

INTERNALIZATION

The incorporation, acceptance, or adaptation of values, beliefs, attitudes, practices, standards, or activities which derive from the outside and which are valuable for effective functioning in the social world. This is different to "borrowing" attitudes for convenience, adopting values without actually believing in them, or enacting behavior ritualistically without COMMITMENT. Internalization suggests that, while the sources of the attitudes or behavior lie outside the individual, they become part of the individual. An exerciser might internalize the kind of habits associated with FITNESS and WELL-BEING, eating well, sleeping adequately, and working out at regular intervals. Initially, these may be externally imposed, though, after a while, the individual may internalize the activities together with the values and beliefs that underpin them. Eventually, there is no element of regulation, compulsion, or imposition. The exerciser enjoys participating and believes in the value of his or her behavior.

"Providing a meaningful rationale for an uninteresting behavior, along with supports for autonomy and relatedness, promote[s] its internalization," report Richard Ryan and Edward Deci, who also point out that CONTROL (or attempts to control) "thwart" internalization.

If the exerciser believes in the benefits of working out and values the positive outcomes but still finds the actual activities of running on the treadmill, or doing Pilates or spin classes tedious, then the term IDENTIFIED REGULATION describes the MOTIVATION. The results are regarded as worthwhile, but the methods of achieving them do not provide satisfaction in themselves. So, exercise needs either internalization or identified regulation if it is to be sustained.

These terms should be distinguished from INTROJECTION, which is usually used in the CONTEXT of psychoanalysis and refers to the process in which an individual unconsciously adopts attitudes, values or beliefs from others, typically, parents.

Further reading

Deci, E. L., Eghari, H., Patrick, B. C., and Leone, D. (1994). Facilitating internalization: The self-determination theory perspective. *Journal of Personality*, 62, 119–42.

Edmunds, Jemma, Ntoumanis, Nikos, and Duda, Joan L. (2006). A test of self-determination theory in the exercise domain. *Journal of Applied Social Psychology*, 36, 2240–65.

Ryan, Richard M. and Deci, Edward L. (2000). Self-determination theory and the facilitation of intrinsic motivation, social development, and well-being. *American Psychologist*, 55, 68–78.

See also: COMMITMENT; CONTROL; DISCIPLINE; EXERCISE IDENTITY; IDENTIFIED REGULATION; INTRINSIC MOTIVATION; MOTIVATION; OBEDIENCE; POSITIVE AFFECT; RELATIONAL; SELF-DETERMINATION THEORY; SOCIALIZATION

INTERPERSONAL RELATIONSHIP

The manner in which two or more people regularly associate and communicate with each other.

See also: GROUP DYNAMICS; RELATIONSHIP

INTERVENTION

An intervention is the action of coming between so as to interrupt, prevent, or modify a result; from the Latin *inter*, "between," and *venire*, "come." The intervening agent is extraneous, that is, having origins external to whatever process is being changed. Intervention techniques are systematic procedures aimed at changing existing processes. They are used in surgery, for example, to stop PAIN; in psychotherapy, they are typically designed to arrest behavior patterns; in education, they are intended to enhance learning competencies. While there are many types of psychological interventions designed to assist physically active persons with their performance, they all share basic features: They involve detailed evaluation, or assessment, some element of education, or retraining and practical attempts to modify both COGNITION and behavior.

According to Allen Cornelius, all sport and exercise psychology interventions progress through four phases.

(1) *Assessment phase.* This involves accumulating detailed knowledge of an performer's SKILL, resources, past experience, and problems. The assessment typically takes the form of an examination with structured interviews, objective tests, and performance PROFILE, yielding the data needed to inform the intervention. Structured and semistructured interviews are valuable in gathering information about someone's experiences and his or her GOAL, or goals. Objective tests are also used, one of the best-known being the PSYCHOLOGICAL SKILLS INVENTORY for sport, which measures six cognitive abilities. A related test is the Test of Performance Strategies, which measures the frequency of behaviors of athletes in training and in COMPETITION. Sixty-four items are used to assess eight strategies: GOAL SETTING, IMAGERY, SELF-TALK, RELAXATION, EMOTIONAL CONTROL, attentional CONTROL, SELF-CONFIDENCE, and AUTOMATICITY.

(2) *Education phase.* This involves SKILL ACQUISITION or perhaps, more accurately, *new* skill acquisition—athletes who already possess skill are retooled to equip them more fully. In this phase, techniques such as BIOFEEDBACK are employed to enable an athlete to gain more control and self-discipline. Relaxation techniques are also used to engineer appropriate levels of AROUSAL in the athlete. Alternative educative techniques are based on REINFORCEMENT and involve rewards as incentives for desired responses and punishment for unwanted responses. COGNITIVE-BEHAVIORAL MODIFICATION is predicated on the assumption that it is the athlete's specific interpretation of stimuli in the environment that is crucial, rather than the stimuli per se.

(3) *Practice phase.* Proficiency is never immediate and, once new skills are acquired, a period of systematic practice follows with

monitoring of progress in situ being vital. For example, a newly acquired ABILITY to relax may serve an athlete well in many practice situations, but will he or she be able to replicate this in the middle of competition, or will ANXIETY creep in? Interventions are usually away from the competitive arena, but, to be effective, they must translate into practical action when they are needed.

(4) *Evaluation and modification phase.* The question that informs this phase is simply whether or not the intervention has worked/is working. The evaluation may be subjective, soliciting the perspectives and opinions of athletes involved. Or, it may be objective, scanning the performance of someone to assess the quantifiable improvements, if any. This is a crucial phase, as interventions must work: they should be geared to the enhancement of physical performance. While enriching the subjective experience of participation in sports is valued, the effectiveness of interventions is graded on the actual performance of the subjects. It is assumed that there is a close relationship between the two.

Many of the techniques covered elsewhere in this book are interventions; these include GOAL SETTING, IMAGERY, and STRESS-INOCULATION training; interventions are used for the treatment of, among other problematic conditions, EATING DISORDERS, MUSCLE DYSMORPHIA, and OBSESSIVE-COMPULSIVE behavior.

Systematic exercise is often cited as a valuable intervention. "The assumption is becoming popular that involvement in physical activities and improvement in skill, knowledge, FITNESS, or health will enhance self-perceptions," as Kenneth Fox points out, specifying mental WELL-BEING, holistic health and, in general, self-enhancement. Being able to display physical competencies is linked to conceptions of SELF-EFFICACY and how positively we feel about ourselves. Fox concludes: "Programs designed for skill and fitness improvement can have a positive impact on SELF-ESTEEM."

Further reading

Cornelius, A. (2002). Introduction of sport psychology interventions. In J. M. Silva and D. E. Stevens (Eds.), *Psychological foundations of sport* (pp. 177–96). Boston, Mass.: Allyn & Bacon.

Fox, K. R. (1997). Introduction: Let's get physical. In K. R. Fox (Ed.), *The physical self: From motivation to well-being* (pp. vii–xiii). Champaign, Ill.: Human Kinetics.

Thompson, M. A., Vernacchia, R. A., and Moore, W. E. (Eds.) (1998). *Case studies in applied sport psychology: An educational approach.* Dubuque, Iowa: Kendall/Hunt.

See also: ANGER; ANXIETY; APPLIED SPORT PSYCHOLOGY; BODY IMAGE; COGNITIVE-BEHAVIORAL MODIFICATION; DEPRESSION; GOAL SETTING; MEDITATION; PSYCHOLOGICAL SKILLS TRAINING; REHABILITATION; RELAXATION; SELF-TALK; STRESS-INOCULATION TRAINING; STRESS-MANAGEMENT TRAINING; THERAPY

INTRINSIC MOTIVATION

In contrast to EXTRINSIC MOTIVATION, which entails incitement from outside an activity (such as money or a prize), intrinsic motivation refers to propellants of behavior that are actually part of the character of that behavior; from the French *intrinsèque*, meaning "inner." There is, according to Jemma Edmunds et al., "an inherent tendency possessed by all humans to seek out novelty and challenges, to extend and exercise their capabilities, to explore and to learn." "Inherent" suggests it is a permanent part of human nature, or essence. On this account, it follows that humans naturally pursue activities that are enjoyable or provide relief, pleasure, or amusement.

"People who are intrinsically motivated tend to engage in activities for the interest and enjoyment inherent in engaging in the activity itself. They think of themselves as competent and self-determining, and they feel that the locus of causality for their behavior is internal," observes Kailas Nath Tripathi.

Many people start playing a sport or working out because they are gratified or fulfilled by the activity, though exercises might be motivated by extrinsic factors too (a bet on how much weight they can lose or whether they can complete a marathon, for example). Their MOTIVATION can remain intrinsic or it may change over time, perhaps because of changes in circumstances or personal factors.

The introduction of extrinsic motivational factors can stimulate greater effort in the activity, but it can also lead to the loss of intrinsic motivation, as the person feels obliged to perform the activity. This occurs when the reward is seen as controlling. After signing a professional contract, a young man who once played basketball for pleasure might feel he is now under obligation and senses his loss of self-determination. This is a valued resource. The conviction that one is controlling one's own behavior, acting on the basis of personal beliefs and values, rather than those of external agencies is crucial in upholding intrinsic motivation. SELF-DETERMINATION THEORY is predicated on this expectation.

Several studies have confirmed the predicted relationship between intrinsic motivation and sustained exercise participation. So, establishing conditions that support autonomy and facilitate intrinsic motivation enhance the development of WELL-BEING and promote the likelihood of exercise ADHERENCE.

Further reading

Deci, E. L., Betley, G., Kahle, J., Abrams, L., and Porac, J. (1981). When trying to win: Competition and intrinsic motivation. *Personality and Social Psychology Bulletin*, 7, 79–83.

Edmunds, Jemma, Ntoumanis, Nikos, and Duda, Joan L. (2006). A test of self-determination theory in the exercise domain. *Journal of Applied Social Psychology*, 36, 2240–65.

Hagger, Martin and Chatzisarantis, Nikos (Eds.) (2007). *Intrinsic motivation and self-determination in exercise and sport*. Champaign, Ill.: Human Kinetics.

Papaioannou, A., Bebetsos, E., Theodorakis, Y, Christodoulidis, T., and Kouli, O. (2006). Causal relationships of sport and exercise involvement with goal orientations, perceived competence and intrinsic motivation in physical education: A longitudinal study. *Journal of Sports Sciences*, 24, 367–82.

Tripathi, Kailas Nath (1992). Competition and intrinsic motivation. *Journal of Social Psychology*, 132, 709–19.

See also: ADHERENCE; COGNITIVE EVALUATION THEORY; EXTRINSIC MOTIVATION; GOAL; IDENTIFIED REGULATION; INCENTIVE; INTEGRATED REGULATION; INTERNALIZATION; LOCUS OF CONTROL; MOTIVATION; REWARD; SELF-DETERMINATION THEORY

INTROJECTION

The adoption of ideas or values of others without knowing it.

See also: INTERNALIZATION

INVENTORY

From *inventorium*, Latin for things discovered, which comes from *invenir*, for "find." An inventory is a detailed, ordered list or catalog of items designed to assess or measure a stock of goods. PSYCHOLOGICAL

SKILLS INVENTORIES are used to take stock of aptitudes, attitudes, beliefs, coping SKILLS, opinions, PERSONALITY traits, or other psychological attributes. They are usually administered by way of questionnaire.

In sports, one of the best-known inventories is the Psychological Skills Inventory for Sports, a forty-five-item register that measures ANXIETY, CONTROL, CONCENTRATION, CONFIDENCE, mental preparation, MOTIVATION, and team orientation. The Athletic Coping Skills Inventory extrapolates from information on coping skills to predict athletic performance.

Further reading

Ostrow, A. E. (1996). *Dictionary of psychological tests in the sport and exercise sciences*. Morgantown, W.Va.: Fitness Information.

See also: MOTIVATION; PERSONALITY; PROFILE OF MOOD STATES; PROFILING; PSYCHOLOGICAL SKILLS INVENTORIES; SELF-CONFIDENCE

INVERTED-U

A CONSTRUCT explaining states of AROUSAL for optimal performance.

See also: AROUSAL; YERKES-DODSON LAW

KINESIOPHOBIA

Pain-related fear of body movement. From the Greek *kinesis* for movement (kinesiology is the study of the mechanics of body movements). While there is disagreement whether the range of fears relating to PAIN form a simple phobia (that is, an extreme or irrational dread or aversion), there is consensus over the importance of FEAR and fear-avoidance beliefs in explaining disabilities and the transition from acute to chronic musculoskeletal pain.

Specifically, the fear that physical activity will cause INJURY or reinjury has consequences for exercise behaviors. Someone who, as R. M. A. Houben et al. put it, "catastrophizes about pain (that is, who is convinced that his/her body is extremely vulnerable, weak, and must be carefully protected from overstrain) is likely to be fearful of movement/(re)injury, when experiencing pain."

Such fearful responses are associated with AVOIDANCE and, in the long term, can lead to disuse, DEPRESSION, and, perhaps, even disability. By contrast, someone who experiences pain, possibly though not necessarily through injury, and does not catastrophize is more likely to assume or resume exercise activities which will either aid a recovery or be conducive to WELL-BEING in other ways.

Further reading

Houben, R. M. A., Leeuw, M., Vlaeyen, J. W. S., Goubert, L., and Picavet, H. S. J. (2005). Fear of movement/injury in the general population: Factor structure and psychometric properties of an adapted version of the Tampa scale for kinesiophobia. *Journal of Behavioral Medicine*, 28, 415–24.

See also: AVOIDANCE; CAUSE; DEPRESSION; EXERCISE BEHAVIOR; EXERCISE MOTIVATION; FEAR; HYPNOSIS; INJURY; NEGATIVITY; PAIN; RESPONSE; SELF-HANDICAPPING; THERAPY

KINESTHESIA

Awareness of the position and movement of parts of the body by means of sensor organs.

See also: PROPRIOCEPTION

KNOWLEDGE OF RESULTS

Knowledge of results (KR) is a form of FEEDBACK used by the learner to adapt responses to the MODEL specified by a trainer or coach. While the term applies across a variety of settings in which learning takes place, it has particular relevance to SKILL ACQUISITION in sports. KR is usually measurable in terms of, for instance, lap times, number of shots on target, speed of serve, and so on. This information should form the basis of future responses to similar situations and thus contribute toward MASTERY of skills. (We might also note that KR is sometimes used in a therapeutic CONTEXT, to apprise clients about progress, and occasionally in laboratory settings to feed back responses to participants in an experiment.)

A novice will typically receive advice and tuition in the form of information about the appropriateness of his or her RESPONSE to a given situation. This is known as *knowledge of performance*, or KP, and is issued directly by a coach, trainer or manager, in the form of advice and tuition.

Both forms of feedback are extrinsic in the sense that they are transmitted by sources external to the individual. Intrinsic feedback refers to the sensations received by the individuals as they execute actions. Athletes use both forms to modify their movements and develop skills. Feeding back knowledge of results typically yields the most rapid mastery of SKILL, though there is debate on the long-term benefits of KR on SKILL ACQUISITION.

Some research has found that a DEPENDENCE on KR can result from its provision. This can lead to inferior performance when KR is not available and sometimes even when it is. It has been suggested that KR encourages the learner to make too many corrections during practice, which leads to an inability to recognize and produce stable behavior across all situations. There is also the possibility that valuable KR can lead skill learners to ignore intrinsic sources of sensory feedback, such as PROPRIOCEPTION.

Further reading

Anderson, D. I., Magill, R. A., Sekiya, H., and Ryan, G. (2005). Support for an explanation of the guidance effect in motor skill learning. *Journal of Motor Behavior*, 37, 231–8.

Liu, John and Wrisberg, Craig A. (1997). The effect of knowledge of results delay and the subjective estimation of movement form on the acquisition and retention of a motor skill. *Research Quarterly for Exercise and Sport*, 68, 145–53.

Salmoni, A. W., Schmidt, R. A., and Walter, C. B. (1984). Knowledge of results and motor learning: A review and critical appraisal. *Psychological Bulletin*, 95, 355–86.

See also: AUTOMATICITY; BIOFEEDBACK; FEEDBACK; IMAGERY; INFORMATION PROCESSING; MASTERY; MEMORY; MODEL; NERVOUS SYSTEM; PROPRIOCEPTION; SKILL; SKILL ACQUISITION; SKILL EXECUTION; THERAPY

LEADERSHIP

The deployment of power, authority or influence to guide others' thought and/or behavior and induce them to follow, willingly or not, is leadership, a word that evolved interestingly from *lædan*, an Old English word for someone or something that takes the load. Leadership describes not so much the quality of a person as the process of a social group in which power relations are asymmetrical, or levels of influence are hierarchical.

In sports, occupants of leadership positions—managers, coaches, captains—lack authority over how others think, feel, and relate to one another. Managers and coaches, in particular, influence, or at least try to influence others' behavior, the assumption being that good performances will yield positive relations between themselves and their charges or between members of a team. Effective leadership inspires or directs competitors, though, in some situations, coercion and CONTROL can yield beneficial results. TRANSFORMATIONAL LEADERSHIP describes the former, TRANSACTIONAL LEADERSHIP the latter.

Model 1: Traits. Some approaches involve studying leaders and distilling their key characteristics, or traits. More sophisticated approaches emphasize how situations factor into the equation. For example, an authoritarian PERSONALITY might be an effective leader in highly structured situations where rules are clear and rigid, but the same person may be laughed at and disrespected in another CONTEXT. Identifying which combination of traits is effective in which situation was the task of the *contingency model*. Its chief proponent, F. E. Fiedler concluded that "situational favorableness" affects leadership, so that a task–oriented leader (who concentrates strictly on performance) will work best in situations that are either favorable or unfavorable that is, where the leader has very little or lots of control and influence. In situations of only moderate favorableness, a RELATIONSHIP-oriented leader, who stresses good interpersonal relationships with athletes, is likely to be more effective. In other words, the fit between the type of leader and the context is crucial.

Model 2: Life cycle. Other approaches to leadership move even further away from leaders themselves and focus on followers. Life cycle approaches suggest that the maturity level of the subjects determines the effectiveness of the style of leader. Young and immature individuals have low levels of ABILITY to set and achieve goals, accept responsibility and experience; a more task-oriented leader, who brings structure, would find them responsive. According to this THEORY, a more relationship-oriented leader who builds trust and fosters mutual respect will reap rewards among more mature subjects who have experience and knowledge and do not need so much structure. Hersey and Blanchard's 1977 research using this approach found that neither group at each end of the continuum—very young/immature and vastly experienced—responded well to leaders who emphasized task structure.

Model 3: Path-goal. This conceives of leaders as figures who illuminate, guide, and assist followers in the pursuit of their goals. Leadership is less to do with any qualities the leader might possess, more to do with the aspirations and preferences of the subjects. The leader merely facilitates (or retards) progress. Leadership lies not with either party but in the changing relationships between them. This has some similarity to the sociologist Max Weber's conception of a *charismatic leader*, someone to whom special qualities are attributed regardless of whether the leader actually possesses them; again, the STRESS is on the relationship.

Model 4: Multidimensional. P. Chelladurai and colleagues tried to formalize the leadership relationship in a MODEL, comprising three interacting components: (a) stable factors that precede leader behavior—characteristics of the situation, leader, and members; (b) leader behavior—required, actual, and preferred (by members); (c) consequences of combining (a) and (b) on team members' satisfaction and performance. Coaches who are autocratic or domineering are effective in some sports, such as basketball, because team members prefer this and the sport is compatible with a bossy approach; this would be the case with football, rugby, and combat sports. Would it work with other sports? Maybe not tennis, certainly not golf, and probably not in several other sports that demand individual judgment and initiative.

An interesting feature of this model is its inclusion of cultural preferences. Leadership styles that are effective in one CULTURE may backfire badly in another, even in the same sport. The point is brought out in Fred Schepisi's 1992 film *Mr. Baseball* in which experienced Major League Baseball pro Tom Selleck opts to play out his career in the Japanese league where he finds his new coach a disciplinarian, completely unlike his former coaches. Inevitably, clashes follow.

Succession of leadership is a problem that faces any sport: replacing a successful manager or coach. Drafting in a successor with an outstanding track record with other teams or clubs is never a guarantee of continuity because player preferences and expectations as well as other situational contingencies change. It is possible that the "Rebecca Myth" may take effect, as in the Daphne du Maurier book *Rebecca* (in which the housekeeper idolizes her late mistress and refuses to accept her employer's new wife). Team members may fail to show their new manager/coach proper deference or respect; they resist the newcomer as a "legitimate heir" to the position once held by someone they knew and trusted. In sport, there are countless examples of coaches with solid credentials transferring to new clubs and failing. Leaders may move, but leadership is not always portable.

There is also the possibility of informal yet influential types of informal PEER LEADERSHIP developing in groups, and these can sometimes threaten to undermine formal modes of leadership. In the study by Todd Loughead et al., this was not the case, and the two types of leadership played complementary roles in effective group functioning, peer leaders assisting group members by "making sense of ambiguous scenarios" (for example, clarifying coaches' instructions).

Further reading

Chelladurai, P. (1993). Leadership. In R. N. Singer, M. Murphey, and L. K. Tennant (Eds.) *Handbook of research in sport psychology* (pp. 647–71). New York: Macmillan.

Fiedler, F. E. (1967). *A theory of leadership effectiveness.* New York: McGraw-Hill.

Hersey, P. and Blanchard, K. H. (1977). *Leadership and the one minute manager.* New York: William Morrow.

Loughead, Todd M., Hardy, James, and Eys, Mark A. (2006). The nature of athlete leadership. *Journal of Sport Behavior*, 29, 142–58.

See also: COACH–ATHLETE RELATIONSHIP; DISCIPLINE; GROUP DYNAMICS; LIFE COURSE; MOTIVATIONAL CLIMATE; OBEDIENCE; PEER LEADERSHIP; TRANSACTIONAL LEADERSHIP; TRANSFORMATIONAL LEADERSHIP

LEARNED HELPLESSNESS

This describes a state produced by repeated exposure to unpleasant, negative situations from which there seems to be no escape; persons experience helplessness as an unavoidable condition, their failure to reach goals seen as the result of inevitable, uncontrollable forces.

The term was introduced by J. B. Overmier and Martin E. P. Seligman in 1967 study, but was adapted by Carol Dweck who argued that "learned helpless" children attributed failure under competitive conditions to such things as lack of ABILITY or LUCK—factors over which they have no CONTROL. They show a tendency to concede defeat and opt out of sports after initial failures because they see no prospect of improvement. They avoid challenges, believing that they can do nothing to influence the course of events. Failure is certain, in their eyes.

Early experiments were conducted with dogs, which were systematically subjected to unpleasant treatment. Even when the dogs were presented with the opportunity to escape the painful treatment, they did not take it; thus, their helplessness was a learned, not natural, state. Further research by Donald S. Hiroto, published in 1974, indicated: "Learned helplessness can be experimentally produced in man," using "moderately aversive events as well as the more traumatic events used in animal studies."

Obviously, humans search for explanations, so attributions and the establishment of LOCUS OF CONTROL and particularity all became relevant. For example, humans, when faced with an aversive experience will ask themselves: "Why did that happen?" and "Whose fault was it?" They will also wonder whether it was a one-off event and likely to happen repeatedly, not just to them but to anybody who behaves similarly.

In sport, failure in itself matters far less than how athletes interpret that failure. For example, if they believe it is because of their inability to improve or continually poor refereeing, they are likely to learn helplessness and drop out. But, if they assign the CAUSE of their defeats to lack of practice, experience, or adequate coaching, they may well persist. Those who see success as a matter of personal performance improvement, rather than sheer win-or-lose results are likely to sink more effort into their preparation, believing that their fate is in their own hands.

A critical assumption of learned helplessness THEORY is that, after an uncontrollable event (for example, a defeat by a superior rival, or an unavoidable injury), an inference might be made that effort is unrelated to the desired outcome, producing a PERCEPTION of having *no contingency* (a contingency is a provision for a future circumstance that can't be forecast with certainty; for instance, "allow an extra thirty minutes travel time for contingencies").

People whom the competitor respects can influence such inferences; a gymnast who is consoled in defeat by a former Olympic champion who assures her that she was judged too harshly might not be deterred. A young decathlete whose coach assures him that a slight modification in pole-vault technique will yield positive results will probably try strenuously to change his technique. An absence of this kind of input or, worse, negative responses ("You didn't deserve to win," "You're useless with that pole") is likely to promote learned helplessness.

Attributional retraining is designed to empower subjects with the feeling that they can CONTROL performance outcomes. Success or failure are not predetermined, but in their own hands. Success or failure do not always equate to wins and losses: Participation in itself may be viewed as success. Steering athletes clear of learned help-lessness involves convincing them that outcomes are not inevitable and that they can assume a degree of SELF-EFFICACY, influencing the course of future events in a way they desire.

Further reading

Dweck, Carol S. (1980). Learned helplessness in sport. In C. H. Nadeau, W. R. Halliwell, K. M. Newell, and G. C. Roberts (Eds.) *Psychology of Motor Behavior and Sport—1979* (pp. 1–11). Champaign, Ill.: Human Kinetics.

Hiroto, Donald S. (1974). Locus of control and learned helplessness. *Journal of Experimental Psychology*, 102, 187–93.

Overmier, J. B. and Seligman, M. E. P. (1967). Effects of inescapable shock upon subsequent escape and avoidance responding. *Journal of Comparative and Physiological Psychology*, 63, 28–33.

Seligman, M. E. P. (1975). *Helplessness: On depression, development and death*. San Francisco, Calif.: W. H. Freeman.

See also: ANXIETY; ATTRIBUTION; CHARACTER; COGNITIVE-BEHAVIORAL MOD-IFICATION; FEAR OF FAILURE; FEAR OF SUCCESS; GENDER; ICEBERG PROFILE; INJURY; KINESTHESIA; LOCUS OF CONTROL; MENTAL TOUGHNESS; NEGATIVITY; SELF-CON-FIDENCE; SELF-EFFICACY; SELF-HANDICAPPING

LEFT-HANDEDNESS

Handedness describes the favoring of one hand rather than another for performing tasks. "Handedness is probably a continuous measure and certainly not a homogenous one," argue Nicolas Cherbuin and Cobie Brinkman. In other words, there are degrees of handedness. People whose left hands are more serviceable than their right are known, of course, as left-handed, though the more formal term is *sinistral*, deriving from the Latin for "left," *sinister*, which also means an evil omen (for example, sinister-looking person), or something malignant (sinister motive). Historically, there was little difference: left-handed people were associated with malevolence. As the belief receded, it was replaced by more enlightened empirical research.

Michel Raymond et al. found that, compared to their proportion in the total population (about 10 percent of men and 8 percent of women), left-handers are over-represented in particular sports, those in which opponents are confronted directly, such as baseball, boxing, and fencing. This applies at all levels of COMPETITION. The closer the interaction between competitors, the greater the prevalence of left-handers. Raymond et al.'s conclusions strongly favored the view that left-handed athletes enjoy an advantage in confrontational sports.

Explanations. The reasons for handedness are not clear. It is a distinctly human trait: other animals show no bias or preference in claws, paws, hoofs, fins, and so on. Human populations have a predominance of right-handedness, or dextrality, that has remained stable for centuries. Most theories are based on the lateralization of the brain, that is the degree to which the right and left cerebral hemispheres of the brain differ in specific functions. The human brain is divided into two hemispheres, the left side often being described as the dominant half because that is where the centers of language and speech and of spatial perception are located in most people. Nerves on the two sides of the body cross each other as they enter the brain, so that the left hemisphere is associated with the right-hand side of the body. In most right-handed people, the left hemisphere directs speech, reading, and writing, while the right half is responsible for emotion.

It was thought that left-handedness was the result of a reversal of the more usual pattern, with the main functions of the brain being on the right. But, in the 1970s, research showed that, in fact, most left-handers are still left-brain dominant and have their centers of language, speech, and spatial perception in the same place as right-handers. Only a minority of left-handers are reversed.

N. Geschwind and A. M. Galaburda proposed that there was an association between left-handedness and immune or immune-related disorders, and this stemmed from birth-related problems. Left-handedness was also related to disabilities, such as stammering and dyslexia. S. Coren and D. F. Halpern claimed that left-handers die sooner than right-handers. The mean age of death for lefties was sixty-six compared with seventy-five for dextrals. Coren and Halpern gave two explanations for this. First, environment: we live in a world that has been designed and built with right-handed people in mind. Door handles, telephones, cars: the construction of these and countless other technological features reflects right-handedness. So, when left-handed people perform even the simplest of functions, they find them slightly more awkward and so have a higher risk of accidents (and accident-related injuries). Several subsequent studies confirmed that lefties were more prone to accidents.

Second, birth problems: referring back to Geschwind and Galaburda studies, Coren and Halpern hypothesized that exposure to high fetal testosterone at birth may lead to developmental problems for left-handed people. This particular aspect and, indeed, the whole early-death theory did not go unchallenged by other studies. For instance, Warren Eaton et al. took one strand of Coren and Halpern's research and argued that "Indirect evidence for an association between sinistrality [left-handedness] and maturational lag can be found from the fact that males, who are more likely to be left-handed, are less advanced in language and skeletal development than are females."

Advantages in sport. This body of research raises a question: If, as most of the evidence suggests, left-handers are disadvantaged in these ways, why do so many excel in sports? Every sport has at least one exceptional left-handed athlete: Babe Ruth, Rod Laver, Marvin Hagler et al. Raymond's research found that, over a six-year period, about 16 percent of top tennis players were left-handed as were between 15 and 27 percent of bowlers in international cricket and pitchers in Major League Baseball. For close-quarter sports, the difference is more pronounced: 33 percent of competitors in the men's World Foils Championships, increasing to 50 percent by the quarterfinal stage of the competition. Remember, this is a group that represents about 10 percent of the total male population. The pattern was less marked for women, though there was still over-representation at the fencing championships.

One possible explanation for this is an association between handedness and differences in the morphology and structure of the *corpus callosum* (the band of nerve fibers joining the hemispheres of the brain), as well as functional lateralization. Cherbuin and Brinkman's work on differences in REACTION TIME and visual field capacity—both germane to sporting performance—revealed an increasing efficiency of hemispheric interactions with increasing left-handedness. Their findings were consistent with others that showed non-right-handed subjects performing significantly better than right-handed equivalents in motor, tactile, and coordination tasks.

This suggests that differences in cerebral architecture might be the source of advantages in areas of development and functionality, such as hand-to-eye coordination, quick reflexes, and perhaps even astute judgment. Or, it could simply mean that the sheer fact of favoring one's left arm in a CONTEXT geared to right-hand biases lends the southpaw a strategic advantage. Because of the frequency of right-handers in any given population, sports performers are habituated in training and in competition to facing other dextrals. So, left-handers, because of their relative scarcity, have an edge of sorts: they hit, run and move in unexpected ways.

Certainly, sports are full of stories of orthodox (left leg forward) boxers who detest fighting southpaws because of the special problems they pose. These include having to jab along the same path as the opponent's jab and constantly having one's front foot trodden on. Baseball hitters swing at the ball in such a way that their momentum carries their bodies in the direction they want to move to get to first base; saving fractions of a second can be vital in a game where fielding is crisp and accurate. Pitchers, like cricket bowlers, can deliver at unfamiliar angles. Returning serve against left-handers is known to be difficult for a right-hander, especially defending the advantage court; lefties are known for their ability to cut the ball diagonally across the body of the receiver. In basketball, a portsider typically tries to pass opponents on the side they least expect; there is barely time to determine whether the opponent is left-handed or not.

The strategic advantage of playing against opponents who are used to a different pattern of play seems to be the answer to the preponderance of them in some sports. In others, where being left-handed counts for little, their prevalence is about the same as in the general population. According to Raymond et al., 9.6 percent of goalkeepers in soccer are lefties; and left-handed field-eventers account for 10.7 percent of all competitors. At the top levels of darts, snooker, bowling, and gymnastics, southpaws are actually under-represented. Somehow, they gravitate toward the sports in which they possess a natural advantage (Will Knight reviews this research).

An anonymous journalist with *The Economist* magazine adds an evolutionary level to this argument: over the years, the strategic advantage enjoyed by lefties outweighed the other possible disadvantages uncovered by the previously mentioned research. Natural selection, of course, favors the best physically equipped (fittest) species, which survived and were able to pass on their genes to their children. This would account, though in a crude way, for the persistence of left-handed people in an environment built largely by and for right-handers and in which social pressures (such as associating sinistrality with wrongdoing) might reasonably have been expected to pressure lefties to change their biases.

Further reading

Anonymous (1997). "Sinister origins" *The Economist*, 342 (February 15), 80–1.

Cherbuin, Nicolas and Brinkman, Cobie (2006). Hemispheric interactions are different in left-handed individuals. *Neuropsychology*, 20 (6), 700–7.

Coren, S. and Halpern, D. F. (1991). Left-handedness: A marker for decreased survival fitness. *Psychological Bulletin*, 109, 90–106.

Eaton. W. O., Chipperfield, J. G., Ritchot, F. M., and Kostiuk, J. H. (1996). Is a maturational lag associated with left-handedness? A research note. *Journal of Child Psychology and Psychiatry and Allied Disciplines*, 37, 613–17.

Geschwind, N. and Galaburda, A. M. (1987). *Cerebral lateralization.* Cambridge, Mass.: MIT Press.

Knight, Will (2004). Left-handers win in hand-to-hand combat. *NewScientist. com.* Available online at http://www.newscientist.com/article/dn6773-lefthan ders-win-in-handtohand-combat.html.

Raymond, M., Pontier, D., Durfour, A., and Moller, A. P. (1996). Frequency-dependent maintenance of left-handedness in humans. *Proceedings of the Royal Society of London*, Series B, 263, 1627-33.

See also: ABILITY; ANDROGYNY; CULTURE; GIFTEDNESS; NERVOUS SYSTEM; REACTION TIME; SKILL; SOCIALIZATION; VISUAL PERCEPTION

LIFE COURSE

This describes the process of change brought about as a result of the interaction between an organism and the environment. The term "course" (as in onward movement, or direction, from the Roman *cursa*, "run") suggests than, unlike many other living forms, humans do not experience their lives according to a strict chronological sequence of stages. It is often used instead of *life cycle*, which describes the pattern of phases every living organism passes through from birth to death.

In the 1960s, Erik Erikson's approach to development was influential: life proceeded through eight *psychosocial* stages from cradle to grave. Each stage has its own particular problems or crises that need to be confronted and its own significant social relationships. So, for example, in adolescence, or stage five, the psychosocial crisis involves confusion over IDENTITY and the significant social relationships are with peer groups and outgroup. At stage seven, middle adulthood, Erikson wrote of *generativity* which is a concern with guiding and providing for the next generation, and the feeling of despair that the GOAL or goals that were set earlier in life will not be achieved.

Later approaches rejected the idea that human life conforms to stages of growth and degeneration in the fixed pattern of, say, a plant. "People construct and reconstruct their lives continuously to give meaning to life events and to integrate new experiences," argued Johannes Schroots, who identified turning points or transformations, which are "those changes in the life of the individual which direct the life-course distinctly, and which are separated in time by one or more affective, important or critical life events, experiences, or happenings."

The life course is a narrative, or more accurately series of narratives "from birth to (expected) death [...] From this perspective, growth should be interpreted as the lifelong process of development, measured in years from birth, and decline as the lifelong process of aging, which is traditionally defined in terms of survival and measured in years of residual lifespan."

Contemporary research on health, exercise and the life course has tended to align with this fluid and subjective APPROACH. The work of Brent Roberts et al., for instance focuses on the pivotal role of *conscientiousness* ("propensity to follow socially prescribed norms and rules regarding impulse CONTROL and to be GOAL directed, planful, and able to delay gratification"), showing how this features more prominently as a result of life experiences: "The behaviors people exhibit and the life paths they follow are dictated in part by being conscientious, in turn facilitating increased conscientiousness. This continues through the life course and affects all manner of health-related behavior [including exercising], so affecting development."

While much research identifies the life course as an object to be explained, other studies use the life course as an explanatory instrument. For example, Anthony Papathomas and David Lavallee's study attempts to understand how the expansion of choice and change corresponds to what they call normative transitions and sometimes implicates athletic youth in EATING DISORDERS. Exercise can be both part of a perfectionist complex, or a source of REHABILITATION, depending on the experiences. The life course, in this research, is converted into "life history methodology [that] enables the relationships among the person, the sport, and the eating disorder to be viewed in a longitudinal development fashion." Longitudinal research involves gathering information about an individual or groups over a long period. The IDIOGRAPHIC method enables "the intricacies and idiosyncrasies" of unique cases to be brought into view.

Further reading

Erikson, Erik (1963). *Childhood and society.* New York: Norton.

Papathomas, Anthony and Lavallee, David (2006). A life history analysis of a male athlete with an eating disorder. *Journal of Loss and Trauma,* 11, 143–79.

Roberts, Brent W., Walton, Kate E., and Bogg, Tim (2005). Conscientiousness and health across the life course. *Review of General Psychology,* 9, 156–68.

Schroots, Johannes J. F. (2003). Life-course dynamics: A research program in progress from the Netherlands. *European Psychologist,* 8, 192–9.

See also: AGING; ATHLETIC IDENTITY; BURNOUT; COMEBACK; COMMITMENT; CULTURE; EATING DISORDERS; EXERCISE IDENTITY; IDENTITY; IDIOGRAPHIC; INJURY; MODEL; PERFECTIONISM; REHABILITATION; RELATIONSHIP; SOCIALIZATION

LOCUS OF CONTROL

The perceived location of the source of CONTROL over one's behavior. The word *locus* is Latin for place. So, if someone perceives that the forces that CONTROL what happens in his or her life lie outside them, perhaps with other people or with abstract forces over which they have little or no influence, then there is an external locus of control. Alternatively, the person might see themselves as an agent of his or her own destiny, believing in their own ABILITY to control events. In this case, there is an internal locus of control or locus of *causality.*

Evidence from the 1990s suggests that the locus of control is more multidimensional and that a person might perceive themselves as having an ability to control matters to a certain degree, at the same time believing that there are other factors that will exert influence, such as other, more powerful groups, institutional forces, or just LUCK. Dave Clarke's 2004 study of gamblers reinforced this, while exposing the error of assuming that problem gamblers (who may have a DEPENDENCE) would perceive an external locus of control more strongly than casual gamblers. Even if they are do not have an OBSESSIVE-COMPULSIVE disorder, the likelihood seems to be that they would feel less in charge of their GAMBLING habit than other kinds of punters.

Additionally, operant conditioning theory would suggest that the intermittent REWARD of winning money should initially reward gambling behavior: Gamblers who regard their fate as being out of their hands have that PERCEPTION reinforced by losing more often than winning. So, external loci should be found among problem gamblers. Clarke found otherwise. In fact, locus of control was not a reliable indicator of problem gambling at all. Problem gamblers and nonproblem gamblers differed on the frequency with which they gambled, their parents' gambling behaviors, impulsiveness, propensities to DEPRESSION, and, most significantly, MOTIVATION. But not on locus of control. Gamblers may attribute success to internal factors, skill being the main one, and losses to factors beyond their control. Locus of control, on this view, a combinational concept.

Further reading

Clarke, Dave (2004). Impulsiveness, locus of control, motivation and problem gambling. *Journal of Gambling Studies*, 20, 4, 319–45.
Lefcourt, H. M. (1991). Locus of control. In J. P. Robinson, R. R. Shaver and L. S. Wrightsman (Eds.), *Measure of personality and social psychological attitudes*, 2nd edn (pp. 413–98). San Diego, Calif.: Academic Press.

See also: ATTRIBUTION; CHARACTER; COGNITIVE EVALUATION THEORY; COPING STRATEGIES; DEPENDENCE; DOPING; DROPOUTS; GAMBLING; LEARNED HELPLESSNESS; MENTAL TOUGHNESS; MOTIVATION; OBSESSIVE-COMPULSIVE; PERCEPTION; PERSONALITY; REINFORCEMENT; RELATIONSHIP; SELF-HANDICAPPING; SELF-SERVING BIAS; SUPERSTITIOUS BEHAVIOR

LUCK

When success or failure is the result of chance rather than skilful action, we attribute it to luck, a term that has origins in the Middle High German *gelücke*, modernized to *Glück*, which translates as happiness or good fortune. There is, however, a difference between luck and fortune. If something agreeable happens to a person in the normal course of events, then he or she is fortunate; luck intervenes when something agreeable happens despite the odds against its happening.

Luck is ubiquitous in sports; it is this that preserves sports from the domesticating influences of rational management, at the same time maintaining fans' fascination with the unpredictability that COMPETITION always creates. No matter how well prepared an athlete or team may be, the best-laid plans are often at the mercy of circumstances beyond the CONTROL of anyone or anything. As the philosopher Nicholas Rescher observed: "Competence alone is not enough to secure success in a chancy world."

For Rescher, luck involves three elements: (1) a beneficiary or maleficiary (recipient of harm); (2) a development that is benign (positive) or malign (negative) from the standpoint of the interests of the affected individual; (3) unforseeability, that is, it must not be expected. The first two elements have clear relevance in sports. A World Cup cricket team might lose the toss and be put in to bat, accumulating a modest score that their opponents begin to chase before a thunderstorm interrupts play after 14 overs. The Duckworth/Lewis rule cannot be used before 15 overs, so "no result" is recorded and the team that was the beneficiary of the toss then becomes the maleficiary of the weather, which denies it the opportunity of winning a match.

The third element also occasionally appears. A football striker's shot hits a teammate's leg, which deflects the ball into the net. This is fortuitous: the second player never intended to score and could not have expected the ball to hit him. Research by S. R. Clarke and P. Allsopp examines some of these vagaries, concluding, "Luck can play a big part in tournament success and progress is not necessarily the best measure of performance."

This last point is absolutely crucial to the enduring appeal of COMPETITION. Much of sport is founded on the CONCEPT of merit. Yet, the fascination of sport lies in the very fact that, if talent + work = merit, merit is not always rewarded. Otherwise, all of sports competition would be calculable. This is clearly not the case. Research by Michael Cantinotti et al., found that, while luck was largely discounted by gamblers who tended to attribute their winnings and losses to judgmental skills and perspicacity, "The results of this experiment suggested that the so-called 'skills' of the sports bettors are indeed cognitive distortions. Expert bettors did not achieve better monetary gains than chance."

No matter how calculable a competition appears to be, it is not. Yet, recognition of this does not necessarily equip competitors well. Patrick Thomas et al. studied ten-pin bowlers and discovered, "Luck and uncontrollability characterize the attributions of less skilful bowlers more than highly skilled bowlers. Attributions such as these are often associated with LEARNED HELPLESSNESS and negative MOOD states, including DEPRESSION."

A congruence of attributions and reality is, on this account, a less reliable predictor of success than incongruence. In other words, skilful competitors believe all events are potentially within their control and that luck will not be a factor. This is the gist of the saying, "The harder you try, the luckier you get."

While coaches remind athletes of the perils of relying on good luck, they are probably aware that it is a part of any contest. For this reason, SUPERSTITIOUS BEHAVIOR is rife in sports. Typically, athletes stumble across a particular piece of behavior that precedes an exceptionally good performance and then repeat the behavior before every contest. No matter how elaborate the ritual or how fastidiously it is followed, their benefit is always subjective. Performing them imbues competitors with SELF-CONFIDENCE. If, as competitors suggest, their aim is to bring good luck, they must fail. Luck can never be invoked—if it could be, it would not be luck.

Further reading

Cantinotti, Michael, Ladouceur, Robert, and Jacques, Christian (2004). Sports betting: Can gamblers beat randomness? *Psychology of Addictive Behaviors*, 18, 143–7.

Clarke, S. R. and Allsopp, P. (2001). Fair measures of performance: The World Cup of cricket. *Journal of the Operational Research Society*, 52, 471–9.

Rescher, Nicholas (1995). *Luck: The brilliant randomness of everyday life* New York: Farrar, Straus & Giroux.

Thorkildsen, Theresa A. and White-McNulty, Lisa (2002). Developing conceptions of fair contest procedures and the understanding of skill and luck. *Journal of Educational Psychology*, 94, 316–26.

Thomas, Patrick, R., Schlinker, Paul J., and Over, Ray (1996). Psychological and psychomotor skills associated with prowess at ten-pin bowling. *Journal of Sports Sciences*, 14, 255–68.

See also: ATTRIBUTION; DEPRESSION; EXPECTANCY; FANS; GAMBLING; LEARNED HELPLESSNESS; MOMENTUM; OUTPERFORMANCE; SELF-FULFILLING PROPHECY; STREAKS; SUPERSTITIOUS BEHAVIOR

MANOVA

Multivariate analysis of variance.

See also: ANOVA

MASTERY

The accomplishment or application of a SKILL is known as mastery, a term taken from the Old French word *maistre*, in turn from the Latin *magister*, a commanding superior. The derivations of the term are clear, for example, magistrate, maestro, master bedroom, and so on. While its use in sports is common, particularly in the CONTEXT of SKILL EXECUTION ("...she demonstrated complete mastery of the crosscourt backhand"), it is a contestable concept. Is it a GENDER-neutral term or does it carry sexist connotations?

Certainly, historical uses of "master" and "mastery" suggest male dominion. A ship's master was invariably male, as was the master of a house, a master-at-arms and Master of the Lodge. The masters of a house or schoolmasters were contrasted to the female mistresses. These and myriad other uses of master intimate an equivalency of

maleness and superiority and femaleness and subjection. The historical reasons for this have been removed to a large degree and, in some
cases the word has been replaced with more neutral appellations, like
head teacher. On the other hand, there are still Masters degrees, Old
Master works of art and master craftsmen.

The extensive use of the term mastery in sports suggests the term
has been "neutralized," uncoupled from its sexist origins or perhaps
used in the same way as master key, master switch, or masterstroke. Its
cognate adjectives, masterful and masterly—highly skilful—have lost
much of their gender specificity, though perhaps not quite all. Arthur
Reber, in his *Dictionary of psychology* has no qualms in defining mastery as simply: "The achieving of some pre-set (and usually high)
level of functioning on some task."

While reservations about the unqualified use of mastery remain, it
has yet to be replaced in sport and exercise psychology's lexicon and, it
seems safe to assume that its continued use will further sever its links with
its patriarchal and SEX-specific meanings. Of the possible alternatives,
"grasp" seems somehow insufficient, and "command," while technically adequate, fails to convey the innovation, creativity or "flair" that
excellence in a SKILL EXECUTION often elicits. "Apprehension," like
"grasp," indicates a subject's hold over a skill but without communicating the high level of functioning included in Reber's definition.

Further reading

Reber, A. S. (1995). *Dictionary of psychology*, 2nd edn. Harmondsworth:
Penguin.

See also: COGNITIVE LOAD THEORY; COMMITMENT; DELIBERATE PRACTICE;
KNOWLEDGE OF RESULTS; MASTERY CLIMATE; OVERTRAINING SYNDROME; PEAK PER-
FORMANCE; PSYCHOLOGICAL SKILLS TRAINING; SKILL; SKILL ACQUISITION; SOCIALI-
ZATION; TALENT; ZONE

MASTERY CLIMATE

"A motivational climate conducive to the development of independence, SELF-CONFIDENCE, and SELF-ESTEEM," is how Richard Cox defines
a MASTERY climate. He equates the concept with "task environment"
and reminds readers that "mastery orientation" and "task orientation"
are "identical" (*sic*). (Note: Task orientation, in J. G. Nicholls' 1984
formulation, is the tendency to perceive ABILITY based on personal

improvement rather than how others perform, the concept being part of the MODEL of GOAL ORIENTATION.)

In contrast to an ego-oriented climate, the mastery climate, or mastery environment, as it is sometimes called, is conducive to the development of skills that remain under the CONTROL of the athlete. Ego-oriented, or performance climates encourage comparison with others as a way of assessing one's own competence. As the primary goal of a mastery environment is the cultivation of SKILL, defeating others is of little consequence. Criteria of success can be self-referenced.

Consistent with this use of mastery as an adjective, rather than its more usual employment as a noun, there are *mastery approaches* (to, for instance, coaching and parenting) and the *mastery stage* of an athletic career, which, as Paul Wylleman et al. write, "reflects the athlete's participation at the highest competitive level."

Mastery imagery has been defined by Allen Cornelius as a method of "imagining executing the proper technique and movement of a free throw [and potentially any other skill]." IMAGERY is a much-favored technique used in the SKILL ACQUISITION process.

Further reading

Cornelius, A. (2002). Intervention techniques in sport psychology. In J. M. Silva and D. E. Stevens (Eds.), *Psychological foundations of sport* (pp. 197–223). Boston, Mass.: Allyn & Bacon.

Cox, R. H. (1998). *Sport psychology: Concepts and applications*, 4th edn. Boston, Mass.: McGraw-Hill.

Nicholls, J. G. (1984). Achievement motivation: Conceptions of ability, subjective experience, task choice and performance. *Psychological Review,* 91, 328–46.

Wylleman, P., De Knop, P., Verdet, M.-C., and Sasa, C.-E. (2007). Parenting and career transitions of elite athletes. In Sophia Jowett and David Lavallee (Eds.), *Social Psychology in Sport* (pp. 233–47). Champaign, Ill.: Human Kinetics.

See also: ATTRIBUTION; COACH–ATHLETE RELATIONSHIP; COMMITMENT; CONTEXT; DECISION-MAKING; DEVIANCE; EGOCENTRISM; EQUALITY; EXERCISE BEHAVIOR; GOAL; GOAL ORIENTATION; HEDONIC TONE; IMAGERY; MASTERY; MODELING; MOTIVATION; MOTIVATIONAL CLIMATE; PARTICIPATION MOTIVATION; OBEDIENCE; OVERTRAINING SYNDROME; PERFECTIONISM; RELATIONAL; SELF-ACTUALIZATION; SELF-CONFIDENCE; SELF-REGULATION; SOCIALIZATION

MEDITATION

The practice of concentrating on a single mental or sensory activity for a period to aid RELAXATION, contemplation, or some other type of mental development. Meditation (from the Latin *meditare* for measure) is typically conducted in silence or to the accompaniment of chanting or repetition of words, for example, mantras. Like progressive relaxation, HYPNOSIS and trance induction, meditation tries to regulate ATTENTION. Varieties of mediation include Vipassana, which involves CONCENTRATION on the body or its sensations, and the more widely known Zen, the aim of which is to achieve enlightenment (*sartori*) by transcending rational thought.

Zen, which is a Japanese school of Mahayana Buddhism, treats the mind as a facility that can be trained for specific purposes. This is in contrast to conventional Western conceptions of the mind as a motor of COGNITION and PERCEPTION.

In the 1977, James Malec and Carl Sipprelle were unimpressed by the results of Zen meditation exercises, which included breath control, MODELING, and graduated relaxation. Their research indicated that Zen meditation helped lower muscle tension and respiration rate but, overall, produced only "small physiological changes in naive, unpracticed subjects."

Almost thirty years later, B. Rael Cahn and John Polich, after completing an exhaustive META-ANALYSIS of other studies, reported "no clear consensus about the underlying neurophysiological changes from meditation practice has emerged."

Rael Cahn and Polich found, "the most widely found state effects of meditation—periods of alpha and theta enhancement—overlap significantly with early drowsing and SLEEP states."

Despite such reservations, meditation has been popularized both through martial arts, such as the Korean taekwondo and Chinese t'ai chi chuan, which incorporate mediation, and most conspicuously YOGA, many varieties of which are now practiced in gyms around the world.

Further reading

Burke, D. T., Al-Adawi, S., Lee, Y. T. and Audette, J. (2007). Martial arts as sport and therapy. *Journal of Sports Medicine and Physical Fitness*, 47, 96–102.

Malec, James and Sipprelle, Carl N. (1977). Physiological and subjective effects of Zen meditation and demand characteristics. *Journal of Consulting and Clinical Psychology*, 45, 339–40.

Rael Cahn, B. and Polich, John (2006). Meditation states and traits: EEG, ERP, and neuroimaging studies. *Psychological Bulletin*, 132, 180–211.

See also: ATTENTION; AUTOGENIC; BIOFEEDBACK; CENTERING; CONCENTRATION; ELECTROENCEPHALOGRAM; FLOW; HYPNOSIS; MENTALITY; RELAXATION; SELF-ACTUA-LIZATION; SLEEP; YOGA; ZONE

MEMORY

Not so much a single PHENOMENON, but a portfolio, which contains several different but related mental processes through which we retain, or encode, information, store it and, later, retrieve it. This is made possible by short-term and long-term memories.

Capacities 1: Types. In some situations, we need to store material for only the briefest of moments. For instance, a rugby player glimpses and hears one of his teammates running to his right. He makes use of this memory seconds later when he delivers a lateral pass to that teammate. Once the pass has been completed, he has no further need of the memory. But to make the pass at all, he needs to have a vast bank of knowledge of how to play rugby at all, so that he can draw on aspects of that store at any time.

In making the pass, the athlete makes use of a series of *sensory* memory systems, including a brief visual image, or iconic memory, as it is known, and a momentary sound, or *echoic* memory. The sounds and images may last for only up to two seconds before they are discarded. *Short-term,* or *"working" memory* describes the functions at work during these moments. So, we can usually finish the sentence we started or retain a seven-digit phone number after looking it up in our phonebook.

Rita Atkinson et al. once used the metaphor of a "mental box with seven slots" to describe short-term memory: "So long as the number of items does not exceed the number of slots, we can recall the items perfectly," they wrote in 1983. In practice, we are always introducing new items into the box, so existing ones have to make way or, if they are important enough, get dispatched to the *long-term memory* for storage.

The way information is filed away in the *long-term memory* is often through chunking, which means clustering information together in familiar forms that can be readily retrieved. If a person were asked to remember ten letters OSDEWRTGOI, it would prove difficult; unless they chunked them into two words, Tiger Woods, in which case it would be easy. Athletes do similarly during SKILL ACQUISITION, rendering complex instructions more accessible by reframing them in sequences that can be laid down and retrieved quickly and frequently.

For instance, if we learn the motor skills involved in serving a tennis ball correctly, we watch someone else, then serve and serve repeatedly. Throughout the process, we are only partially conscious of the vast amount of data gradually being absorbed (in the cerebellum, the part of the brain which functions to coordinate muscular activity). Initially, we will concentrate on what we are doing, focusing on foot positions, height of the toss, arc of the swing, and so on, but, ultimately, we serve automatically.

The long-term memory itself involves materials that may have been retained for intervals of only a few minutes or as long as a lifetime. Specific pieces of information are usually encoded in terms of meaning rather than content. Someone might vividly recount the plot of Nick Hornby's *High Fidelity*, but they will not be able to recite the text line by line. No one recalls every instruction given to him or her by their first coach, but most athletes will be able to recollect the meaning of them. The obvious analogy is that of a library. Trying to locate a certain book is a huge task unless you understand the cataloging system, or the ways in which the books are organized, either in terms of subject or author's surname and so on. Once the ordering scheme is meaningful to the person looking for the book, the task is simplified and retrieval is possible. The more information we organize in terms of its meaning, the greater our chances of a successful retrieval.

Long-term memory is much more than a vast repository of meanings. It is a convenient term for several types of information and the processes by which they are stored and recovered. Altering an example from Endel Tulving, there are differences between a memory of watching a particular football game on television and remembering how many players are in a football team. Both require memory, but, while Tulving argued that they reflect the operation of distinct and separate systems in the brain, others, such as Alan Baddeley, suggest it may be the same system operating under different conditions.

For Tulving, *episodic* memory refers to the conscious recollection of personally experienced events, while *semantic* memory involves factual knowledge. I might remember that Zinedine Zidane headbutted Marco Materazzi in the 2006 World Cup Final (semantic), but I have no memory of the events leading up to the incident—that episodic memory is exclusively Zidane's.

Capacities 2: Encoding/decoding. Retrieval of information from long-term memory is affected by the way in which we originally encoded the material. The obvious analogy is that of a library: as we noted above, the more information we organize in terms of its category, or class, the greater our chances of a successful retrieval.

The CONTEXT in which we originally encode information also affects retrieval. A context may be a physical environment, such as a place or a certain type of situation or even someone's face, or it may be a subjective state, such as an EMOTION felt at the moment the information was first encountered. That same EMOTIONAL state facilitates subsequent retrieval of the information from the long-term memory. Even induced states, such as those experienced under the influence of alcohol or drugs, can affect retrieval. Research has shown that a drunken person may, for example, hide something, then completely forget where once they are sober. The next time they are drunk, they remember! The memory, in this case, is *state dependent*.

Emotions are important in several ways. The term "flashbulb memory" was coined to describe memories that are sharp, moving and frequently evoke details of the context in which the information was encoded. "Where were you when you heard about the attack on the World Trade Center?" is a question that typically draws a comprehensive answer from people who can recount accurately where they were, with whom, doing what and so on. New and startling information that excites a high level of emotional AROUSAL can be expected to become the material of flashbulb memories.

The ultimate retrieval failure is also influenced by EMOTION, in this case elicited by a traumatic experience that functions to block access to target memories. Women who have been raped, for example, may not be able to recollect the specifics of the rape nor, indeed, the rapist. There are various views on the mechanism behind this repression. Some believe that the ANXIETY brought about by the experience does not cause the memory failure: it is associated with other incidental thoughts that are not germane to the rape itself but that serve to interfere with retrieval.

Exceptional performance, whether in sport, medicine, music, or any other sphere, requires extensive knowledge and cognitive mechanism acquired through extensive practice. Research has focused on whether the superior memory associated with higher levels of performance is a product of brain anatomy or repeated application. Brain imaging has failed to show unequivocally that difference in brain structure and electrical activities can account for top-level performances in, for example, chess and memory contests.

K. Anders Ericsson argues that the encoding methods used by exceptional performers are qualitatively different, and this helps explain differences in brain activation but is acquired through deliberate practice, a technique that Ericsson and his followers use to account for superior memory. Mnemonic processing, similar to the previously mentioned Tiger Woods example, is shown to be especially effective. Chess, a sport that makes exacting demands on the memory, offers an interesting case and a body of research has examined the way in which chess players acquire their expertise. Neil Charness et al. reveal how: "Several thousand hours of concentrated analysis and memorization of chess tactics and positions" enable the retrieval of memory-stored instances of play.

Capacities 3: Exercise effects. Memory processing is affected by the slowing of cognitive function that results from aging, though exercise has been linked to improvements in elderly people. The research tends to be equivocal, however. For example, studying a small sample of aging adults, George Rebok and Dana Plude found a link but warned, "the findings are correlational and do not address questions about directionality of effects." In other words, they realized that more cognitively able persons might be more likely to participate in what the researchers called a memory workout program. A CORRE-LATION is a RELATIONSHIP or association rather than anything more conclusive, such as a causal connection.

The assumption is that exercise programs improve cardiovascular fitness, which, in turn, stimulates blood flow to the brain, improving cognitive functions. Research by Courtney Hall et al. gave guarded support, advancing a positive role for exercise, not so much in improving memory but in curtailing loss in older adults. The argument was that aging brings a decline in cerebral blood supply and exercise ameliorates this by stimulating blood to flow to the site of EXECUTIVE CONTROL, the frontal lobe. This is the part of the brain that lets us make voluntary decisions about where to direct ATTENTION and determines what the content of the short-term memory should be. While Hall et al. do not discuss this specifically, we might add that, if the executive control is defective, then a person can shift attention continuously, shifting between myriad stimuli that compete for attention. "Age-related declines in cognition and their remediation by exercise are most prominent for executive function," they conclude.

Further reading

Atkinson, R. L., Atkinson, R. C., and Hilgard, E. (1983). *Introduction to Psychology*, 8th edn. New York: Harcourt, Brace, Jovanovich.

Baddeley, A. (1996). Memory. In A. M. Colman (Ed.), *Companion encyclopedia of psychology* (Vol. I, pp. 281–301). London and New York: Routledge.

Charness, Neil, Tuffiash, Michael, Krampe, Ralf, Reingold, Eyal, and Vasyukova, Ekaterina (2005). The role of deliberate practice in chess expertise. *Applied Cognitive Psychology*, 19, 151–65.

Ericsson K. Anders (2003). Exceptional memorizers: Made, not born. *Trends in Cognitive Sciences*, 7, 233–5.

Hall, Courtney D., Smith, Alan L., and Keele, Steven W. (2001). The impact of aerobic activity on cognitive function in older adults: A new synthesis based on the concept of executive control. *European Journal of Cognitive Psychology*, 132, 279–300.

Rebok, George W. and Plude, Dana J. (2001). Relation of physical activity to memory functioning in older adults. The memory workout program. *Educational Gerontology*, 27, 241–59.

Tulving, E. (1972). Episodic and semantic memory. In E. Tulving and W. Donaldson (Eds.), *Organization of memory* (pp. 381–403). New York: Academic Press.

See also: ABILITY; AEROBIC/ANAEROBIC; AGING; ATTENTION; AUTOMATICITY; CHOKE; COGNITION; DECISION-MAKING; DELIBERATE PRACTICE; EXECUTIVE CONTROL; FOCUS; IMAGERY; MODELING; MOTOR REACTION; PEAK PERFORMANCE; PERCEPTION; REACTION TIME; RELATIONSHIP; SCHEMA; SKILL; SKILL ACQUISITION; SKILL EXECUTION; VISUAL PERCEPTION

MENTAL HEALTH MODEL

Originally formulated by W. P. Morgan, this suggests that athletes with poor-to-average mental health should, generally, perform worse than athletes with good mental health. The model predicted that athletes scoring high on such measures as trait ANXIETY, DEPRESSION, neuroticism, confusion or exhibiting other signs of PSYCHOPATHOLOGY would tend to be unsuccessful compared with athletes scoring in the low-to-normal range on these measures. Successful athletes should have low trait anxiety and emotional stability. The MODEL has been damaged by scholarly evidence and the occasional biographies of successful sports performers who have experienced DEPRESSION and other psychopathological conditions.

Further reading

Morgan, W. P. and Johnson, R. W. (1978). Psychological characteristics of successful and unsuccessful oarsmen. *International Journal of Sport Psychology*, 11, 38–49.

Raglin, John S. (2001). Psychological factors in sport performance: The mental health model revisited. *Sports Medicine*, 31, 875–90.

See also: ANXIETY; DEPRESSION; DROPOUTS; EMOTIONAL CONTROL; EMOTIONAL INTELLIGENCE; INDIVIDUAL ZONES OF OPTIMAL FUNCTIONING; OVERTRAINING SYNDROME; PERSONALITY; PERSONALITY ASSESSMENT; PSYCHOLOGICAL SKILLS TRAINING; PSYCHOPATHOLOGY; STRESS

MENTAL PRACTICE

When thought processes are used as part of the SKILL ACQUISITION process, the term "mental practice," or sometimes, mental preparation, describes the collection of techniques available for covert or symbolic rehearsal in the absence of any observable muscular movement. Understandably contrasted to actual behavioral practice, mental practice frequently involves IMAGERY (not usually precompetition imagery), though, as Richard Cox points out: "Mental practice implies that an individual is practicing a physical task in some covert way, although actual images of the task may or may not be present."

It is equally possible that athletes or serious exercisers use imagery without visualizing a SKILL PERFORMANCE (they may imagine themselves on the victory rostrum, or fitting into a particular pair of jeans, for example). In other words, mental practice, while often used synonymously with imagery, is actually distinct.

The term itself is not entirely unproblematic. "Mental," which is from the Latin *mentalis*, for "mind," is not a word that elicits universal approval. The age-old debate over the status, or even existence, of the mind is unlikely ever to reach a conclusion, and this has implications for the way in which the adjective "mental" is used. In popular use, mental refers to functions that reflect INTELLIGENCE or the lack thereof. In another sense, mental processes are those that mediate between physical stimuli and the observable responses of a human being. Mental may also be said to be a general rubric under which elements of COGNITION are drawn together. In mental practice, mental is contrasted with physical: the individual is not spinning or shooting hoops, but he or she is thinking about performing those tasks.

Mental practice is typically done when in repose, possibly, though not necessarily, at an advanced state of RELAXATION. As such, it can be done when far away from the sports field or gym: at home, on a plane, virtually anywhere an athlete can establish a degree of solace.

Practiced exponents are sometimes able to GATE out distractions and mentally practice even in crowded, noisy places.

Intuitively, the idea of mentally practicing a technical skill or some facet of a SKILL EXECUTION or even an entire sequence of tasks has appeal. But, does it work? The balance of research results tends toward a tepid "yes." Robert Weinberg, in 1981, and D. L. Feltz and D. M. Landers, in 1983 agreed that there is a beneficial effect on performance, but it is not nearly as effective in SKILL acquisition as physical practice, though it is better than no practice at all. In 1992, S. M. Murphy and D. P. Jowdy confirmed what common sense suggests: that a combination of mental and actual practice is most effective, one complementing the other. J. S. Hird et al. concluded that mental practice is not uniformly effective across the board. It works best with tasks, and, hence, sports that lay the accent on cognitive skills as well as purely physical ones, which is presumably why, as Paul Lloyd and Sandra Foster report, it is also used in commercial and industrial organizations.

Also, sequence is important: mental practice before physical practice is more effective than after, according to a 1996 study by J. L. Etnier and D. M. Landers. More experienced and skilled athletes will extract more benefit from mental practicing than novices. Despite the reservations and qualifications, mental practice is accepted as an accessible INTERVENTION and one that is used almost universally by contemporary athletes.

Further reading

Etnier, J. L. and Landers, D. M. (1996). The influence of procedural variables on the efficacy of mental practice. *The Sport Psychologist*, 10, 48–57.

Feltz, D. L. and Landers, D. M. (1983). The effects of mental practice on motor skill learning and performance: A meta-analysis. *Journal of Sport Psychology*, 5, 25–57.

Hird, J. S., Landers, D. M., Thomas, J. R. and Horan, J. J. (1991). Physical practice is superior to mental practice in enhancing cognitive and motor task performance. *Journal of Sport and Exercise Performance*, 13, 281–93.

Lloyd, Paul J. and Foster, Sandra L. (2006). Creating, health, high-performance workplaces: Strategies from health and sports psychology. *Consulting Psychology Journal: Practice and Research*, 58, 23–39.

Murphy, S. M. (1994). Imagery interventions in sport. *Medicine and Science in Sports and Exercise*, 26, 486–94.

Murphy, S. M. and Jowdy, D. P. (1992). Imagery and mental practice. In T. Horn (Ed.) *Advances in sport psychology*, 2nd edn (pp. 405–39). Champaign, Ill.: Human Kinetics.

Suinn, R. M. (1997). Mental practice in sport psychology: Were we have been, where do we go? *Clinical Psychology: Science and Practice*, 4, 189–207.

Weinberg, R. S. (1981). The relationship between mental preparation strategies and motor performance: A review and critique. *Quest.* 33, 195–213.

See also: BIOFEEDBACK; CENTERING; DELIBERATE PRACTICE; GOAL SETTING; HYPNOSIS; IMAGERY; INTERVENTION; KNOWLEDGE OF RESULTS; RELAXATION; SKILL ACQUISITION; SUPERSTITIOUS BEHAVIOR; VISUOMOTOR; ZONE

MENTAL TOUGHNESS

Mental toughness describes a bundle of qualities that include an unusually high level of resolution, a refusal to be intimidated, an ability to stay focused in high-pressure situations, a capacity for retaining an optimum level of AROUSAL throughout a COMPETITION, an unflagging eagerness to compete when injured, an unyielding attitude when being beaten, a propensity to take risks when rivals show caution and an inflexible, perhaps obstinate insistence on finishing a contest rather than concede defeat.

In contrast to *physical* toughness—which is durability, an exceptionally high threshold of PAIN or a rugged APPROACH to competition—*mental* toughness suggests qualities of mind or intellect (*mentalis* being Latin for "mind," toughness from the Old English *töh,* strong or hard to break).

"Mentally tough athletes respond positively to adversity and are able to persist in the face of disappointment and setbacks," states Ronald E. Smith. "They often exhibit PEAK PERFORMANCE in pressure situations, and they tend to more consistently perform in accordance with their SKILL level." Jean Côté observes: "Mentally tough athletes are able to keep their emotions in CONTROL and are calm and relaxed under pressure situations."

Smith adds that they encode demanding situations as challenges, have high SELF-EFFICACY, positive expectancies and "a distinctive motivational structure." This means they actually seek out difficult situations with uncertain outcomes and do not require external pressure to work hard at achieving goals. "Mentally tough athletes know how to develop action plans, how to learn, and how to improve."

Côté's review of research on "Coach and Peer Influence on Children's Development through Sport" draws on 1996 work by Smith and Smoll, who describe mental toughness for children as "the ability to keep physical AROUSAL within manageable limits." The relevance of this work is that it challenges popular notions that mental toughness is simply an innate quality that some athletes have and others do not.

Côté discusses some procedures designed to "enhance children's mental toughness."

(1) Change aspects of situations that place unnecessary STRESS on young athletes. This might include practicing away from spectators or even changing rules to suit the SKILL level of the athlete.

(2) Increasing resources for dealing with pressure situations. This involves working on technical SKILL ACQUISITION so that the young athlete acquires the SELF-CONFIDENCE to be able to execute the skills in competitive situations.

(3) Help children develop a positive attitude toward competition. At the outset, young athletes should be taught that ANXIETY is "not produced solely by a situation but rather by the way one interprets that situation" and that COGNITION is the key to responding appropriately to even the most taxing situations.

(4) Rehearse RELAXATION: Côté, along with several other scholars, encourages MENTAL PRACTICE at an early age, particularly teaching children the skills needed to relax and the ability to use IMAGERY.

The techniques are a stock-in-trade of sport psychologists and several other types of INTERVENTION, for example, GOAL SETTING, complement them. The interest in the present CONTEXT is in how Côté and others, such as Stephen Bull et al., believe that mental toughness may be *taught* in childhood, the presumption being that it will carry through to adulthood.

Outdoor adventure education would seem to be an ideal environment for learning mental toughness, though Michael Sheard and Jim Golby's study discovered that the psychological benefits were not as significant as they promised. "Individuals high in mental toughness are disciplined thinkers who respond to pressure in ways that enable them to remain relaxed, calm, and energized," they argued. Yet, they concluded the rough-and-tumble experiences of an outdoor adventure did not yield significant changes in levels of mental toughness, nor SELF-ESTEEM, SELF-EFFICACY, dispositional optimism ("a general tendency to expect things to go one's way"), and positive affectivity (the disposition to be "energetic, enthusiastic and enjoy life").

While mental toughness is a positive attribute both in competitive sport and ADHERENCE to exercise programs, its value in recovery from sport- or exercise-related INJURY is less unequivocal. Andrew Levy and his colleagues studied its effects on enduring PAIN, adhering to a REHABILITATION program and, generally, coping with the unwelcome interruption to activity. Mentally tough patients were able to withstand physical pain, though this did not necessarily assist their recovery; they would often appraise their injuries to be less severe than they actually were.

Despite the popularity of the term, some scholars are reserved about the utility of mental toughness. Graham Jones et al., for example, suggest "a general lack of conceptual clarity and consensus as to its definition, as well as a general failure to operationalize the CONSTRUCT in a consistent manner."

Further reading

Bull, S. J., Shambrook, C. J., James, W., and Brooks, J. E. (2005). Towards an understanding of mental toughness in elite English cricketers. *Journal of Applied Sport Psychology*, 17, 209–27.

Côté, J. (2002) Coach and peer influence on children's development through sport. In J. M. Silva and D. E. Stevens (Eds.), *Psychological foundations of sport* (pp. 520–40), Boston, Mass.: Allyn & Bacon.

Jones, Graham, Hanton, Sheldon, and Connaughton, Declan (2002). What is this thing called mental toughness? An investigation of elite sport performers. *Journal of Applied Sport Psychology*, 14, 205–18.

Levy, A. R., Polman, R. C. J., Clough, P. J., Marchant, D. C., and Earle, K. (2006). Mental toughness as a determinant of beliefs, pain, and adherence in sport injury rehabilitation. *Journal of Sport Rehabilitation*, 15, 246–54.

Sheard, Michael and Golby, Jim (2006). The efficacy of an outdoor adventure education curriculum on selected aspects of positive psychological development. *Journal of Experiential Education*, 29, 187–209.

Smith, Ronald E. (2006). Understanding sport behavior. *Journal of Applied Sport Psychology*, 18, 1–27.

Smith, Ronald E. and Smoll, F. L. (1996). *Way to go, coach*. Portola Valley, Calif.: Warde.

See also: ADHERENCE; APPROACH; CHARACTER; COACH–ATHLETE RELATIONSHIP; COMMITMENT; CONSTRUCT; DISCIPLINE; EMOTIONAL CONTROL; EMOTIONAL INTELLIGENCE; INJURY; INTELLIGENCE; LOCUS OF CONTROL; MORAL ATMOSPHERE; NEGATIVITY; PERSONALITY; REHABILITATION; SELF-CONFIDENCE; SELF-ESTEEM; STRESS; TASK/EGO ORIENTATION

MENTALITY

Often used interchangeably with *mindset*, mentality refers to a set of attitudes or a way of thinking characteristic of a particular group. Its root is the Latin *mentalis* for "mind."

The term is used frequently in sport and exercise, often to capture changes in the overall frame of mind of the enterprise. For example, in his analysis of the development of mutual trust as a source of sports team COHESION, Paul Turman describes what he calls "a you help me, I'll help you mentality" among team members.

This is unusual; more prevalent is what Sean VanRoenn et al., along with many other writers call "the 'win-at-all-costs' mentality." Such an outlook is encouraged even among adolescents, particularly in contact sports, as Maria Kavussanu observes. She describes the emergence of an "informal combat mentality, which discourages altruistic interaction and encourages a negative view of others."

Leslee Fisher and Craig Wrisberg suggest that qualities of mind are pervasive, affecting relationships across the whole spectrum of sport. There is, they detect, "a mentality of avoiding closeness in the future [that] has obvious ramifications for relationships between athletes and those they interact with, including athletic trainers."

Further reading

Fisher, Leslee A., and Wrisberg, Craig A. (2005). The "Zen" of career-ending-injury rehabilitation. *Athletic Therapy Today*, 10, 44–5.

Kavussanu, Maria (2008). Morality in sport. In Sophia Jowett and David Lavallee (Eds.), *Social psychology in sport* (pp. 265–77). Champaign, Ill.: Human Kinetics.

Turman, Paul D. (2003). Coaches and cohesion: The impact of coaching techniques on team cohesion in the small group sport setting. *Journal of Sport Behavior*, 26, 86–104.

VanRoenn, Sean, Zhang, James, and Bennett, Gregg (2004). Dimensions of ethical misconduct in contemporary sports and their association with the backgrounds of stakeholders. *International Sports Journal*, 8, 37–65.

See also: ATHLETIC IDENTITY; COACH–ATHLETE RELATIONSHIP; COMPETITION; EGOCENTRISM; PERSONALITY; SCHEMA; SOCIALIZATION; TEAM PLAYER

META-ANALYSIS

"Meta-analytic reviews are more likely to lead to summary statements of greater thoroughness, greater precision, and greater inter-subjectivity or objectivity," writes R. Rosenthal. He refers to the fact that, by combining the findings of several studies, the meta-analyst is able to spot trends, consistencies, and patterns that assist investigations. *Meta* means "beyond," and that is precisely what meta-analysis strives for: to reach beyond the conclusions of any single study and present an exhaustive, comprehensive, NOMOTHETIC review, or retrospective survey of existing research with a view to presenting a critical assessment of an entire field of study. It is not primary research because it does not involve the sourcing of primary material, such as interviews, or archives. It is based on research conducted by others.

Further reading

Ashford, Derek, Bennett, Simon J. and Davids, Keith (2006). Observational modeling effects for movement dynamics and movement outcome measures across differing task constraints: A meta-analysis. *Journal of Motor Behavior*, 38, 185–205.

Mezulis, Amy H., Abramson, Lyn Y., Hyde, Janet S. and Hankin, Benjamin L. (2004). Is there a universal positivity bias in attributions: A meta-analytic review of individual, developmental, and cultural differences in the self-serving attributional bias. *Psychological Bulletin*, 130, 711–36.

Rosenthal, R. (1991). *Meta-analytic procedures in social research*. Newbury Park, Calif.: Sage.

See also: ATTRIBUTION; CONSTRUCT; IDIOGRAPHIC; INDIVIDUAL ZONES OF OPTIMAL FUNCTIONING; METACOGNITION; METAMOTIVATION; MODEL; MODELING; NOMOTHETIC; REVERSAL THEORY; SELF-DETERMINATION THEORY; THEORY OF PLANNED BEHAVIOR

METACOGNITION

The monitoring and CONTROL of thought.

See also: AUTOMATICITY; SKILL EXECUTION

METAMOTIVATION

According to Kurt Frey, metamotivation is the "way in which a person's motives can change and fluctuate during the course of activities and daily life." The state in which the person finds him or herself "sets" what that person wants and these are liable to change as an interaction progresses.

Frey gives the example of an informal game of basketball at a local gym. A player may start simply wanting to have fun, dribbling, showboating, and trash-talking fellow players. In contrast, he or she may also be in a more serious frame of mind, anxious about personal performance and determined to win, however insignificant the game. "These opposite states are operative in everyone and entail distinctive motives, perceptions and emotions," writes Frey, an adherent of REVERSAL THEORY.

Reversal theory states that metamotivational states occur in couples of opposites, or dyads, so that when one state is active, its opposite is inactive. There are four dyads: (1) telic-paratelic (serious vs. fun); (2) conformist-negativistic (fitting in vs. challenging); (3) autic-alloic (SELF-oriented vs. other-oriented); and (4) MASTERY-sympathy (competitive vs. caring). Humans alternate or reverse back and forth between these oppositions, and this affects their behavior. Each pair of states is mutually exclusive; individuals can only experience one of the two opposing states at a given time. Environmental stimuli trigger reversals between the states.

The perspective challenges more conventional accounts of MOTIVATION, which typically claim that motives revolve around a single optimal point. The prefix *meta*, from the Greek for "beyond" and meaning, in this instance, a change of position or condition to another order (as in metabolism), suggests how the CONCEPT of a single energizer of action is replaced by a duality, a duality that changes through a course of action. At the heart of this lies a MODEL of the human being as inconsistent, self-contradictory, and endlessly capricious, devoid of a stable PERSONALITY and animated by competing states rather than a single DRIVE or impulsion.

Cindy Sit and Koenraad Lindner used the metamotivational MODEL to study the motives for sport and physical activity among fourteen- to twenty-year-olds in Hong Kong:

> Participants who were strong in a particular state balance in each dyad subscribed to different participation motives [...] for example, the conformist-balanced individuals, who tend to fit in and comply with group norms within the sports contest, perceived team/friend as a more important sport motive than the negativistic-balanced group.

Further reading

Frey, K. P. (1999). Reversal theory: Basic concepts. In J. H. Kerr (Ed.), *Experiencing sport: Reversal theory* (pp. 3–17). London: Wiley.

Sit, Cindy H. P. and Lindner, Koenraad J. (2006). Situational state balances and participation motivation in youth sport: A reversal theory perspective. *British Journal of Educational Psychology*, 76, 369–84.

See also: AUTOTELIC; DRIVE; EMOTION; EXTRINSIC MOTIVATION; IDENTIFIED REG-
ULATION; INTRINSIC MOTIVATION; META-ANALYSIS; MODEL; MOTIVATION; PERSON-
ALITY; REVERSAL THEORY; TELIC DOMINANCE; THEORY

MIMESIS

Mimesis is a representation or imitation of an actual process. It might
be expressed through art and literature or through the actions of
humans deliberately imitating the behavior of others. Its source is the
Greek *mimesis*, for "imitation." *Mimetic activities*, according to Joseph
Maguire, "provide a 'make-believe' setting which allows emotions to
FLOW more easily and which elicits excitement of some kind, imitating that produced by real-life situations, yet without its dangers or
risks."

All sports are, in effect, mimetic activities. They create tensions and
drama and evoke EMOTION of high INTENSITY; and, while they sometimes involve the actual rather than imagined RISK of harm or even
DEATH, this is deliberately minimized. The ethologist Desmond
Morris believes precursors of what we now call sports "filled the gap
left by the decline of the more obvious hunting activities." In his
view, all sports are mimetic hunts and competitors are what he calls
"pseudo-hunters." (Ethology is the study of human behavior from a
biological perspective.)

In this sense, every COMPETITION is a stylized hunt and, as such,
involves strategy, fitness, CONCENTRATION, stamina, vision, and imagination. Many others have argued that sports resemble warfare.
Greek and Roman competitions either side of the Christian era were
explicitly designed to prepare competitors for combat and often
concluded in death or wounding. The CONTROL of VIOLENCE that
accompanied the civilizing process ensured that sports incorporated
measures to minimize hazards, though Patrick Murphy et al. point
out that the medieval and early modern British "mock fights," bore
"a greater resemblance to real fighting than their modern-day
equivalents."

Obviously, the moods elicited by participation in sports are different from those elicited by actual situations. Yet, there is resemblance.
The ADRENALINE RUSH experienced in flight-or-fight situations is
often replicated in sports, particularly high-risk activities such as
EXTREME SPORTS. States of AROUSAL and, indeed, ANXIETY achieved
through sports bear resemblance, at least in a quantitative sense, to
states experienced in stressful predicaments. The point of sport is to

stimulate what Maguire calls the "pleasurable excitement" that comes from "achievement sports."

A *mimetic* describes a habitual practice that has the same effect as something else. Exercise, for example, can be a mimetic. As Steven Joyal, writes on the treatment of OBESITY: "Physical exercise may function as a calorie restriction mimetic and this may help explain, in part, the positive associations between calorie restriction/ moderate physical exercise and improvements in surrogate markers of AGING."

Further reading

Joyal, Steven V. (2004). A perspective on the current strategies for the treatment of obesity. *Current Drug Targets—CNS and Neurological Disorders*, 3, 341–56.

Maguire, Joseph (1992). A sociological theory of sport and the emotions: A process-sociological perspective. In E. Dunning and C. Rojek (Eds.), *Sport and leisure in the civilizing process: Critique and counter-critique* (pp. 96–120). Basingstoke: Macmillan.

Morris, Desmond (1981). *The soccer tribe.* London: Jonathan Cape.

Murphy, P., Sheard, K., and Waddington, I. (2000). Figurational sociology and its application to sport. In J. Coakley and E. Dunning (Eds.), *Handbook of sports studies.* London: Sage.

See also: ADRENALINE RUSH; AGGRESSION; AROUSAL; CATHARSIS; COMPETITION; EMOTION; EUSTRESS; HEDONIC TONE; INTENSITY; MODELING; MOOD; OBESITY; RISK; TELIC DOMINANCE

MIND ATTRIBUTION

Directly assessing the minds of others is known as mind attribution, or *mentalizing*, and incorporates inferring emotions and intentions. The opposite is *dementalizing*, and this involves explaining a person's behavior in terms of physical events, pre-existing disposition or causal chains that do not involve COGNITION. Sport requires both. Outguessing or out-strategizing an opponent necessitates a capacity for deducing their aims and motives, while, under certain circumstances—for example, immediately after scoring a knockdown in a boxing match—the aggressor might feel compelled to see the fate of his opponent in his own hands regardless of his opponent's intentions.

Further reading

Kozak, Megan N., Marsh, Abigail A., and Wegner, Daniel M. (2006). What do I think you're doing? Action identification and mind attribution. *Journal of Personality and Social Psychology, 90*(4), 543–58.

See also: ATTENTION; ATTRIBUTION; COGNITION; DECISION-MAKING; DEFENSIVE ATTRIBUTION

MODEL

A representation that approximates or reflects a series of relationships either observed in reality or statistics. Its purpose is to assist comprehension or guide future research. "We have mental models for how we think and perceive our world," writes Richard Gerson. "We have theoretical models to help us understand and describe how things work. And we have performance models to help us make things better."

Further reading

Gerson, Richard F. (2006). The missing link in HPT. *Performance Improvement*, 45, 10–19.

See also: CONSTRUCT; DELIBERATE PRACTICE; KNOWLEDGE OF RESULTS; NOMO-THETIC; RELATIONSHIP; ROLE MODEL; SCHEMA; STEREOTYPE; THEORY; TRANS-THEORETICAL MODEL

MODELING

Observing another's behavior, retaining an image of it and, later, attempting to imitate it is known as modeling; from the Latin *modulus*, meaning "exemplary" or "ideal." In physical activity, as in many other realms, modeling is a significant means of learning and, as such, is a basic component of the SOCIALIZATION process. Obviously, the process is not automatic: the conditions under which the observation takes place, the characteristics of the model being observed, and other situational factors affect how effectively the behavior is learned. As such, modeling suggests an alternative to theories predicated on the importance of INSTINCT or DRIVE in learning behavior and those stressing a passive role for humans in reacting to STIMULI in the environment. COGNITION plays a crucial part in modeling: the person can think and represent situations, anticipate probable consequences of behavior and interpret stimuli rather than just react to them.

Modeling, or *vicarious learning* (as it is sometimes called), is not confined to the literal imitation of behavior, but is associated with the acquisition of information from another person, visually or verbally. EMOTION can also be learned by watching the EMOTIONAL responses of others as they undergo painful or pleasurable experiences. A child who observes another child contorting and screaming in a dentist's chair may feel FEAR when he or she approaches a dental appointment.

One of the classic experiments in modeling by Albert Bandura and Richard Walters involved nursery-school children who observed an adult express various forms of aggressive behavior toward an inflated doll. After watching the adult, both boys and girls mimicked the adult, punching, kicking, and striking the doll with a hammer. Subsequent research indicated that children were most likely to imitate the behavior when they observed models being positively reinforced for their behavior, a process called vicarious REINFORCEMENT. The consequences of behavior played an important part in shaping the behavior of the children. Relatively new behaviors could be acquired with this method.

Similar processes operate during other types of learning, including SKILL ACQUISITION. Bandura advanced a four-stage theory in which: (1) a person *attends* to a performance, taking note of key features; (2) he or she *retains*, or remembers vital material, coding and storing information to the MEMORY; (3) the person attempts to *reproduce* the SKILL EXECUTION, perhaps recruiting help from others initially; (4) he or she must have requisite MOTIVATION to keep repeating the performance and, in this respect, positive REINFORCEMENT is important. While Bandura's process was somewhat linear, later research embellished it, adding that the SEX of the model being imitated made a difference; same-sex modeling works most effectively. Also, observing a peer performing a task more proficiently than oneself can underline a SKILL discrepancy and demotivate a learner.

Learning through modeling is cumulative, building from simple to more complex tasks. Playing hockey, for instance, requires basic skills, such as skating and controlling the puck, but the proficient player must integrate these and other learnt behaviors into a more complex repertoire. In this way, a beginner develops SELF-EFFICACY and the confidence that grows from repeated SKILL performance. This, in itself, is not sufficient to account for creativity and the imaginative use of skill, but the point about modeling is that it is generalizable:

once basic units of skill are augmented by the repertoires, learners can extend and enlarge skills that were not initially observed.

While there is widespread agreement about the efficiency of modeling as a learning tool, especially when combined with other instruments such as IMAGERY, there is no consensus about precisely how it works. A 2006 META-ANALYSIS by Derek Ashford et al. outlined the VISUAL PERCEPTION perspective that suggests, "modeling involves the transformation of information associated with observed movements into a reference of correctness against which subsequent movement attempts can be compared."

A motor learning perspective proposes that, during observation, a new movement is acquired as the learner perceives and imitates a motor pattern, after which the learner *scales* (that is, controls) those motions to meet the demands of the task. Modeling aids the early acquisition, but not the scaling of the motor action. DELIBERATE PRACTICE is of greater consequence, if only because of the anatomical, morphological, and situational differences between model and learner, as work by Spencer Hayes et al. points out.

This makes modeling especially effective during the early stages of skill acquisition. But Derek Ashford et al. discovered that the results on movement outcomes, such as being able to throw a basketball through a hoop consistently or score goals, are less convincing.

Modeling has been used to account for the learning of sports-related skills, yet, it has also been demonstrated to affect the type of long-term goals and the GOAL ORIENTATION adopted by young athletes. The research of Sam Carr and Daniel Weigand suggests how sporting heroes can unwittingly become significant others and models for aspirations. (In this CONTEXT, "significant others" are persons who are influential in affecting an individual's development of SELF-CONCEPT, norms and values).

Further reading

Ashford, Derek, Bennett, Simon J., and Davids, Keith (2006). Observational modeling effects for movement dynamics and movement outcome measures across differing task constraints: A meta-analysis. *Journal of Motor Behavior*, 38, 185–205.

Bandura, A. (1977). *Social learning theory*. Englewood Cliffs, N.J.; Prentice-Hall.

Bandura, A. and Walters, R. H. (1963). *Social learning and personality development*. New York: Holt, Rinehart & Winston.

Carr, Sam and Weigand, Daniel A. (2002). The influence of significant others on the goal orientations of youngsters in physical education. *Journal of Sport Behavior*, 25, 19–39.

Hayes, S. J., Hodges, Nicola J., Scott, M. A., Horn, R. R. and Williams, A. M. (2006). Scaling a motor skill through observation and practice. *Journal of Motor Behavior*, 36, 357–66.

See also: AGGRESSION; ATHLETIC IDENTITY; DELIBERATE PRACTICE; DRIVE; EMOTION; EXERCISE IDENTITY; GOAL; GOAL ORIENTATION; IMAGERY; KNOWLEDGE OF RESULTS; LEADERSHIP; MASTERY CLIMATE; MIMESIS; MOTIVATION; ROLE MODEL; SELF-CONFIDENCE; SELF-EFFICACY; SKILL ACQUISITION; SKILL EXECUTION; SOCIALIZATION; VICARIOUS AGENCY; VISUOMOTOR

MOMENTUM

Used originally in mechanics to describe the quantity of motion (mass + velocity) and the impetus gained by movement, momentum (the word is actually from the Latin for "move," *movimentum*) in sport and exercise refers to shifts in the FLOW of a contest or challenge that affect the perceptions of the contestants and, perhaps, the outcome of the COMPETITION.

According to Scott Kerick et al., momentum in psychological terms arises from a PERCEPTION associated with a sense of CONTROL in the pursuit of a GOAL and can lead to increased SELF-CONFIDENCE, MOTIVATION, focusing ABILITY, and "mind-body synchrony." Yet, there are other scholars who doubt its existence at all and liken it to a myth.

Proponents of momentum include many coaches, including tennis's Alistair Higham: "Momentum acts like water—flowing backwards and forwards, sometimes faster or slower, or at times not moving at all." As a stone thrown into water makes ripples, a precipitating event initiates psychological momentum (PM). A break of serve at 4–4 in the fourth set to lead for the first time in the match, a flash knockdown, a late equalizing goal, a fielding error; a mishit—potentially any event can introduce or change momentum on this account. An event works as a catalyst, prompting a response from competitors. There are three accounts of what happens.

(1) *Multidimensional model*. J. Taylor and A. Demick proposed that cognitive, physiological, and behavioral changes combine to produce a driving force that affects the athlete's behavior and, in turn, elevates his or her performance. Change in perceptions (in particular, of SELF-EFFICACY and CONTROL) and AROUSAL, translates into performance. Conversely, losing momentum, or experiencing negative momentum, can prove detrimental to performance,

especially if a lead has been depleted and one's opponent is coming from behind.

(2) *Antecedents–consequences theory.* Antecedents, like an improbable catch in the field or a freakish goal, affect perceptions, which can lead to an improved performance, or the opposite process if one is on the receiving end of the event. PM can influence performance, though this depends on circumstances, according to R. J. Vallerand et al. For example, in a sport requiring low levels of AROUSAL, such as putting or free throw shooting, psychological momentum may be of no benefit, though R. M. Adams' study of pool concluded that improvements in CONCENTRATION followed momentum shifts.

(3) *Projected performance model.* In contrast to the first two approaches, Allen Cornelius et al. suggest that momentum has little impact on performance. Perceptions of momentum are typically short-lived and can encourage a competitor to coast; this is known as "positive inhibition." Also, a player who has performed poorly and witnessed his or her opponent catch up or go into a lead, may be stung into action and become more energized than ever, a process known as "negative facilitation."

Stéphane Perreault et al. conducted experiments that gave partial support to all three theories, finding evidence that coming from behind "can have a profound effect on perceptions of PM," and this facilitates competitive performance, particularly in sports that need a great deal of effort. They also discovered that the negative facilitation suggested by Cornelius could work to influence the performance of athletes who have seen their initiative slip away.

While changes in perceptions of momentum may influence competitors during contests, the question of sustained momentum's impact on the future of successive contests is open to doubt. Roger Vergin's 2000 research on winning and losing STREAKS, for example, undermined the "almost universal belief by athletes, sports fans and media observers that a winning (or losing) sequence affects future results." Vergin questions the status of momentum as an objective causal agent in the outcome of contests:

One is strongly tempted to conclude that while momentum is widely accepted as a PHENOMENON by sport participants, fans and observers, it is more myth than reality. If it does exist at all, it is of such a low strength that it is almost equally balanced by the phenomena of positive inhibition and negative facilitation.

Further reading

Adams, R. M. (1995). Momentum in the performance of professional tournament pocket billiards players. *International Journal of Sport Psychology*, 26, 580–7.

Cornelius, A., Silva, J. M., Conroy, D. E. and Petersen, G. (1997). The projected performance model: Relating cognitive and performance antecedents of psychological momentum. *Perceptual and Motor Skills*, 84, 475–85.

Higham, Alistair (2000). *Momentum: The hidden force in tennis*. Leeds: Meyer & Meyer.

Kerick, S. E., Iso-Ahola, S. E.m and Hatfield, B. D. (2000). Psychological momentum in target shooting: Cortical, cognitive-affective, and behavioral responses. *Journal of Sport and Exercise Psychology*, 22, 1–20.

Perreault, S., Vallerand, R. J., Montgomery, D. and Provencher, P. (1998). Coming from behind: On the effect of psychological momentum on sport performance. *Journal of Sport and Exercise Psychology*, 20, 421–36.

Taylor, J. and Demick, A. (1994). A multidimensional model of momentum in sports. *Journal of Applied Sport Psychology*, 6, 51–70.

Vallerand, R. J., Colavecchio, P. G., and Pelletier, L. G. (1988). Psychological momentum and performance inferences: A preliminary test of the antecedents-consequences psychological momentum model. *Journal of Sport and Exercise Psychology*, 10, 92–108.

Vergin, Roger C. (2000). Winning streaks in sports and the misperception of momentum. *Journal of Sport Behavior*, 23, 181–5.

See also: AROUSAL; CHOKE; COGNITION; FEAR; FLOW; FOCUS; LUCK; PEAK PERFOR-MANCE; PERCEPTION; RELIGION; SELF-CONFIDENCE; SELF-EFFICACY; SLUMP; STREAKS; THEORY

MOOD

Unlike EMOTION, mood is a pervasive, lingering subjective state that is usually diffuse, in the sense that it has no FOCUS. A mood is not necessarily evaluative: for example, a person may simply be in a good or bad mood, without being pleased or angry with anyone or anything. The word is from the Old English *mod* meaning "mind" or "thought."

Mood *swings* usually refer to relatively swift and unexpected vacillations between DEPRESSION and elation, irritability and good humor, without obvious antecedents. When such swings become so excessive that they interfere with normal functioning, they become *bipolar* mood disorders, or the less extreme *cyclothymic* disorders in which the swings occur in relatively consistent cycles.

The beneficial mood effects of exercise have been established by several studies, including that of Cheryl Hansen et al., in 2001, and William Russell et al., whose 2003 work showed how moods could be enhanced by exercise, as long as the exercise is "self-selected" (that is, chosen by the exerciser rather than imposed).

This does not establish that exercise in itself affects mood. Other mediating factors might include: the interaction with other exercisers; the SELF-EFFICACY that emerges from training; and the distracting effects of exercise in taking a person's ATTENTION away from their mood. Still other possibilities are that the increased secretion of neurotransmitters has a positive effect on mood and the production of ENDORPHINS improves feelings of well-being.

Not everyone benefits from the mood-enhancing effects of exercise. Kevin Masters et al. disclosed exceptions. Individuals exhibiting TYPE A behavior patterns (TABPs) reaped benefits, but only under strictly noncompetitive exercise conditions, such as being allowed to work out alone on a step machine for a fixed period. Under more competitive conditions, such as being set a target in the presence of others on similar machines, the TABPs are likely to seek out a challenge and approach the task as if they are in COMPETITION with others. The research highlighted how situational as well as PERSONALITY factors influence the impact of exercise on mood.

Other research has been directed at the effect of mood, particularly precompetition mood, on performance. For example, an IDIOGRAPHIC study by Andrew Lane and Robert Chappell began from the popular supposition that negative mood states are potential indicators of poor competitive performance. The research found no evidence to support this, showing only that mood had negligible impact on performance.

Further reading

Hansen, Cheryl J., Stevens, Larry C., and Coast, J. Richard (2001). Exercise duration and mood state: How much is enough to feel better? *Health Psychology*, 20, 267–75.

Lane, Andrew M. and Chappell, Robert C. (2001). Mood and performance relationships among players at the World Student Games basketball competition. *Journal of Sport Behavior*, 24, 182–96.

Masters, Kevin S., Lacaille, Rick A., and Shearer, David S. (2003). The acute affective response of Type A behavior pattern individuals to competitive and noncompetitive exercise. *Canadian Journal of Behavioral Science*, 35, 25–34.

Russell, W., Pritschet, B., Frost, B., Emmett, J., Pelley, T. J., Black, J., and Owen, J. (2003). A comparison of post-exercise mood enhancement across common exercise distraction activities. *Journal of Sport Behavior*, 26, 368–83.

See also: ADHERENCE; AEROBIC/ANAEROBIC; ALCOHOLISM; ANGER; BODY IMAGE; COGNITIVE-BEHAVIORAL MODIFICATION; DEPRESSION; EMOTION; EMOTIONAL TONE; ENDORPHINS; EUSTRESS; EXERCISE IDENTITY; FEAR; FITNESS; FLOW; HEDONIC TONE; INDIVIDUAL ZONES OF OPTIMAL FUNCTIONING; NEGATIVITY; PROFILE OF MOOD STATES; REHABILITATION; SELF-EFFICACY; STRESS; TELIC DOMINANCE; TEMPERAMENT; TYPE A; WELL-BEING

MORAL ATMOSPHERE

"Shared group norms define the moral atmosphere of a group," writes Maria Kavussanu, who built on earlier research in school and prison environments to study how sports groups or clubs generate "a set of collective norms regarding moral action on the part of group members."

Moral atmosphere can exert influence not only on the behavior but also on the intention and judgment of group members. Together, they can combine to produce unsportsmanlike actions, such as deliberately trying to injure an opponent, playing recklessly and consciously flouting rules. While an individual might find such actions inappropriate and perhaps repugnant in others, he or she might engage in them nevertheless if, for example, he or she perceives the coach as encouraging them or teammates willing to do so.

Group norms do not accurately reflect individual norms of conduct or thought. A *performance climate*, in which, for instance, mistakes are not tolerated and winning is highly valued, has a significant effect on the preparedness of players to provoke others, rough them up or cheat. As Kavussanu concludes: "The moral atmosphere of the team appears to have a profound influence on athletes' moral functioning."

Further reading

Kavussanu, Maria (2007). Morality in sport. In Sophia Jowett, and David Lavallee (Eds.), *Social psychology in sport* (pp. 265–77). Champaign, Ill.: Human Kinetics.

Kavussanu, Maria and Spray, Christopher M. (2006). Moral atmosphere, perceived performance motivational climate and moral functioning in male youth footballers: An examination of their interrelationships. *The Sport Psychologist*, 20, 1–23.

MOTIVATION

Formed from a Latin source *motus*, for "move," motivation refers to prompting movement. Beyond this elementary definition of motivation, there is little agreement on the precise meaning of a CONCEPT that is absolutely central to sport and exercise psychology. A sample of the various interpretations available includes: "the intensity and direction of behavior" (Silva and Weinberg); "processes involved in the initiation, direction, and energization of individual behavior" (Green); "the forces that initiate, direct, and sustain behavior" (Beaudoin); "an intervening process or an internal state of an organism that impels or drives it to action" (Reber); "the tendency for the direction and selectivity of behavior to be controlled by its connections to consequences, and the tendency of this behavior to persist until a GOAL is achieved" (Alderman); and "the desire to engage and persist in sport, often despite disappointments, sacrifice, and encouragement" (Hill). Distilling these, we are left with *an internal state or process that energizes, directs and maintains goal-directed behavior.*

While some analysts prefer to APPROACH motivation as a generalized DRIVE, others, particularly those concerned with sports, argue that motivation is specific to particular objectives and directions. Motivation functions as a kind of mainspring for action, directing it toward identifiable ends; obviously, the resulting behavior is intentional, though the consequences of the behavior may not be. Where there is no link between action and outcome, there is usually no motivation (captured in the term *amotivation*—if weight training has no connection with improving chess skills, the chess player will have no motivation to lift weights, unless for another purpose). The anticipated outcomes, effects, or consequences of a motivated behavior are vital to the maintenance of motivation. This is illustrated in Mark Anshel's breakdown of motivation in a sport and exercise CONTEXT.

Anshel's treatment is inspired by Alderman's conception and involves five component parts: (1) direction of motivation—"the motivated athlete is energized to engage in a purposeful and meaningful task"; (2) selectivity of behavior—behavior is rarely automatic or random and needs direction, often selected by a coach; (3) connections to consequences—the tangible results of motivated action must be available for inspection; (4) goals—these provide "the incentive to persist at a task until a new SKILL or performance mastery has been achieved"; (5) expectancy—for motivation to continue to energize, there must be an reasonable expectation that efforts will lead to desired results.

Theory 1: DRIVE. While this anatomy is useful, it leaves an important question unanswered: What induces a person to act? In other words, from where does motivation come? Abraham Maslow's answer in the 1950s was based on his celebrated *hierarchy of needs*, which was a structure based on human imperatives, the primary one of which was biological (hunger, thirst, temperature maintenance, and so on). Above the basic needs were tiers of ever-more cultivated needs, including the need for affiliation with others, aesthetic needs and the need for SELF-ACTUALIZATION, to find fulfillment in realizing one's own potential. For Maslow (1908–70), our initial motivation derives from the satisfaction of needs at the lower end of the hierarchy and, once these are met, we ascend upwards, striving to satisfy the more sophisticated needs. Motivation, in this model, has origins in human needs, or drives, some of which have organic sources.

Sigmund Freud (1856–1939) also believed humans are motivated by primal drives, in his case SEX and AGGRESSION. In childhood, parents forbid the free expression of sex and aggression and these become repressed, remaining in the unconscious. For Freud, these unconscious motives manifest in later life, exercising an influence over conduct, though in disguised ways, such as in illness, accidents, mannerisms, or Freudian slips (of the tongue). The motive, or the power behind the behavior, is not immediately available to the senses, as it lurks in the unconscious. In their different ways, Maslow and Freud offered canonical accounts of motivation, both premised on the presence of drives or instincts that govern human conduct.

McClelland et al. distinguished between *implicit motives*, which reflect the phylogenic (that is, evolutionary development) of the human species (and which humans share with other animals) and *self-attributed* motives, which represent values, principles, or ethical codes and are uniquely human. The former motives are responsive to natural incentives in the environment, while the latter are responsive to social incentives and are comprehensible to us. In other words, we know exactly why we are doing some things.

Theory 2: Self. Action is governed not by unconscious or unknown forces, but by the way we envisage the consequences. This approach diverges from not only drive-based, or INSTINCT theories, but also those of behaviorists, most of whom avoid all reference to consciousness, subjectivity, ideas, or other cognitive processes (that is, activities concerned with thinking, knowing, reasoning, insight, intention, and so on). There are several variants of this approach, all in some way subscribing to the view that people are motivated to action in areas of their lives in which they are likely to experience positive feelings of competence and esteem. The opposite is also presumed: that motivation is reduced in activities that yield feelings of NEGATIVITY.

SELF-based approaches fall within the framework of cognitive theory in the sense that they explore the ways in which behavior is motivated and, indeed, shaped by self-evaluations. If a person desires to look like a supermodel and they see themselves as overweight, then their motivation may be to exercise and eat less as a way of closing up the discrepancy between what they are now like and what they want to be. Competence is not high, but the desire to improve competence, or, in this case, appearance is sufficient to provide the motivation. Whether or not the equation is accurate is not relevant; in fact, many EATING DISORDERS are precipitated by flawed judgments of this kind. What counts is the person's subjective evaluation of their likely success. In this sense, the desire for SELF-EFFICACY, perceptions of personal CONTROL and SELF-CONFIDENCE in ability are likely to feature. There is no presumption that we are rational decision-makers.

Working in this vein, Susan Harter, in 1978, argued that we are motivated in domains in which we feel we can demonstrate our competence, especially if we also feel intrinsically attracted toward that domain and discern an internal locus of control in our attribution of success of failure. Many of the approaches to motivation that focus on COGNITION engage with the ACHIEVEMENT MOTIVE debate, which was originally started by the argument that we are all impelled by the motive to achieve success and the motive to avoid failure.

Jacquelynne Eccles et al.'s expectancy-value model uses "value" which bears resemblance to Harter's intrinsic motivation and, for that matter, to the concept of FLOW. Utility value is determined by how well a task relates to current and future goals, such as career goals. For example, a pupil who takes tennis lessons after school, even though she might not enjoy them, might do so because she wants to please her parents or be with friends. Her behavior might appear to be extrinsically motivated. But she also has a long-term GOAL to be a tennis professional, so the task has value for her. But there are inhibiting costs. Performance ANXIETY and FEAR OF FAILURE as well as the effort involved and the lost opportunities (she could be out with her friends) are among the potential costs.

The difference between *intrinsic* and *extrinsic* motivations is not absolutely distinct in this sense, but the conventional definition is that the former derives from feelings of satisfaction and fulfillment, the latter from factors that involve reward or punishment (or both) from outside forces. Edward Deci's work with children who were set puzzle-solving tasks indicated that those who received a reward spent less free time working on puzzles than those who received no reward. In other words, being paid for an intrinsically interesting activity decreased INTRINSIC MOTIVATION. This has obvious relevance for professional athletes, all of whom will have been originally motivated by intrinsic factors but whose motivation probably becomes purely extrinsic once they begin to earn money from sports: Extrinsic incentives undermine intrinsic rewards—which helps explain why an NFL or Premier League player might choose to sit out his contract, even though ten years before, he would probably play football endlessly for pure enjoyment.

In line with cognitive approaches, Deci assumed that we are motivated by the urge toward self-MASTERY and competence in dealing with the environment. So, individuals are intrinsically motivated to perform activities that enhance their sense of accomplishment. "Any event that enhances perceived competence will tend to enhance intrinsic motivation," declared Deci and Ryan in 1985.

When extrinsic rewards displace intrinsic factors as the primary reason for engaging in an activity, individuals experience a loss of CONTROL. Instead of determining for themselves how and when to participate in an activity, they feel controlled. This is not confined to professional spheres. For example, young athletes are sometimes pressured by parents to participate in a sport, so that the line between intrinsic and EXTRINSIC MOTIVATION is blurred: While they may enjoy competing, they may also feel the burden of having to respond to parents' imploring them to succeed. The conflict helps account for the high rate of BURNOUT among young tennis pros; they sense a loss of control—and a corresponding loss of self-efficacy—from an early age, rarely enjoying the intrinsic satisfactions of their sport. Extrinsic rewards carry with them the potential to wrest control from the individual. Turning pro often implies surrendering part of one's ABILITY to decide one's own destiny.

Perhaps the starkest illustration of this in sports is corruption. The bribe is an extrinsic REWARD that motivates an athlete *not* to perform to the best of his or her ability and so not exhibit competence. Any residual intrinsic motivation to engage in a sport is sacrificed in the interests of pursuing money and COMPETITION is reduced to exhibition.

Theory 3: Reversal. While the cognitive approach to motivation in many ways supplanted earlier theories, which rested on assumptions that drives lay at the source of motivations, they also made untestable assumptions, particularly about the human endeavor to demonstrate competence and aspire to self-determination and esteem. Reversal theory's alternative account replaces motivation with the term "METAMOTIVATION," which is intended to capture the sense of a constant movement in and out of different psychological states. There is no single motivation: individuals' motives change before and during activities, *reversing* back and forth. This fluidity makes theories of motivation based on a single drive or a desire to improve and demonstrate competence too linear, according to reversal theory. Action is propelled by the interplay between several, often conflicting, motives.

Psychological theories of motivation abound, and there are several others not mentioned here but which are neatly summarized by Jacquelynne Eccles and Allan Wigfield. These include SELF-EFFICACY theories, FLOW theories, and theories based on ATTRIBUTION and the LOCUS OF CONTROL, all of which are given their own entries elsewhere in this book.

Further reading

Alderman, R. B. (1974). *Psychological behavior in sport.* Philadelphia, Pa.: Saunders.

Anshel, M. H. (1997). *Sport psychology: From theory to practice,* 3rd edn, Scottsdale, Ariz.: Gorsuch Scarisbrick.

Beaudoin, Christina M. (2006). Competitive orientations and sport motivation of professional women football players: An internet survey. *Journal of Sport Behavior,* 29, 201–12.

Biddle, S. J. H. (1997) Cognitive theories of motivation and the physical self. In K. R. Fox (ed.), *The physical self: From motivation to well-being* (pp. 59–82). Champaign, Ill.: Human Kinetics.

Deci, E. L. and Ryan, R. M. (1985). *Intrinsic motivation and self-determination in human behavior.* New York: Plenum Press.

Eccles, Jacquelynne S. and Wigfield, Allan (2002). Motivational beliefs, values, and goals. *Annual Review of Psychology,* 53, 109–32.

Green, R. G. (1996). Social motivation. In A. M. Colman (Ed.), *Companion encyclopedia of psychology* (Vol. I, pp. 522–41). London and New York: Routledge.

Harter, Susan (1978). Effectance motivation reconsidered: Toward a developmental model. *Human Development,* 21, 94–104.

Hill, K. L. (2001). *Frameworks for sport psychologists: Enhancing sport performance.* Champaign, Ill.: Human Kinetics.

McClelland, D. C., Koestner, R., and Weinberger, J. (1989). How do self-attributed and implicit motives differ? *Psychological Review,* 96, 690–702.

Reber, A. S. (1995). *Dictionary of psychology,* 2nd edn. Harmondsworth: Penguin.

Silva, J. M. and Weinberg, R. S. (1984). Motivation. In J. M. Silva and R. S. Weinberg (Eds.), *Psychological foundations of sport* (pp. 171–6). Champaign, Ill.: Human Kinetics

See also: ACHIEVEMENT MOTIVE; ATTRIBUTION; DRIVE; EXERCISE MOTIVATION; EXTRINSIC MOTIVATION; FEAR OF FAILURE; FEAR OF SUCCESS; FLOW; GOAL ORIENTATION; GOAL SETTING; INCENTIVE; INTRINSIC MOTIVATION; LOCUS OF CONTROL; METAMOTIVATION; MOTIVATIONAL CLIMATE; PARTICIPATION MOTIVATION; REVERSAL THEORY; REWARD; SELF-ACTUALIZATION; SELF-CONFIDENCE; SELF-DETERMINATION THEORY; SELF-EFFICACY

MOTIVATIONAL CLIMATE

This refers to the type of social atmosphere prevailing in a CONTEXT of sport or physical activity over a period. There are two climates. A MASTERY CLIMATE is a setting in which learning and skill development is conspicuous and valued and the prospect of outperforming others is of no direct interest. In contrast, a *performance climate* is one in which success and failure are noticeably emphasized.

Motivational climates are likely to be linked with GOAL ORIENTATION, as the research of, among others, Nikos Ntoumanis and Stuart Biddle revealed. Perceptions of a mastery climate encourage task orientations, while perceptions of a performance climate are likely to be related to an ego's GOAL orientations.

A coach exerts influence in establishing and perpetuating the climate and the type of achievement goals accentuated in each. Mary Fry and Maria Newton's 2004 study revealed the importance of tennis professionals in creating what they call "a positive climate" that determined the types of experiences of young athletes in a tennis program. In this study, Fry and Newton noted how "moral growth" is facilitated, meaning that the climate encouraged "sportspersonship" (what used to be called sportsmanship: holding high principles for proper conduct).

Research by a Norwegian research team led by Blake Miller endorsed these findings, adding that a strong mastery climate was positively associated with COMMITMENT, respect for social conventions, and respect for rules and officials. A strong performance climate was negatively associated with these, but positively associated with respect and concern for opponents. A GENDER difference also surfaced, males being more likely to embrace sportsmanlike values than females.

Further reading

Fry, Mary D. and Newton, Maria (2004). Application of achievement goal theory in an urban youth tennis setting. *Journal of Applied Sport Psychology*, 15, 50–66.

Miller, Blake W., Roberts, Glyn C., and Ommundsen, Yngvar (2004). Effect of motivational climate on sportspersonship among competitive youth male and female football players. *Scandinavian Journal of Medicine and Science in Sports*, 14, 193–202.

Ntoumanis, Nikos and Biddle, Stuart (1998). The relationship between competitive anxiety, achievement goals, and motivational climates. *Research Quarterly for Exercise and Sport*, 69, 176–87.

See also: ACHIEVEMENT MOTIVE; CHARACTER; COACH–ATHLETE RELATIONSHIP; CULTURE; GOAL ORIENTATION; INTERNALIZATION; MASTERY CLIMATE; MORAL ATMOSPHERE; MOTIVATION; SOCIALIZATION; TASK/EGO ORIENTATION; 2 × 2 ACHIEVEMENT GOAL FRAMEWORK

MOTOR REACTION

This refers to a reflex-like action or series of actions produced without significant observable components. When the word "motor" is used, it relates to muscular movement, or, sometimes, the nerves activating that movement. Motor is from the same Latin root as MOTIVATION, *motus*, for "move." Motor reactions are commonplace in competitive situations: evading a punch, returning a serve, catching or even blocking a ball all involve muscular processes. But, while they require perceptual and cognitive processes, they are typically made in time-pressured situations that allow very little, if any, time in which to deliberate. In other words, there is no apparent DECISION-MAKING behind the muscular movement.

Athletes playing in goal are often said to make "reflex saves" when playing reactively; other athletes are said to possess intuitive skills or instincts, though these descriptions shed little light on the learning processes that enable motor reactions in competitive action contexts. It has been argued that motor responses are the results of an extraordinarily fast INFORMATION PROCESSING of incomplete information, some based on a proprioceptive awareness of internal physiological states.

The concept of *priming* has also been suggested. Priming describes the process of presenting an event, episode, or occurrence to someone in such a way that he or she is more sensitive and responsive to a wider range of stimuli in future. This priming can take place outside conscious awareness; so nonconscious associations between perceived stimuli and motor processes leading to the reaction are established. So, a nonconscious MEMORY is built, and this is responsible for the perceptual IDENTIFICATION of objects and words and can explain the influence of past experiences on STIMULUS processing without any recollection of earlier stimuli. Even an idea can initiate an overt act. This is known as an ideomotor action (*ideo* being Greek for "idea").

According to Armin Kibele, once the associations have been encoded, the mere PERCEPTION of a movement activates the previously established perceptual-motor representation, so that the motor reaction is automatic. This version has the advantage of not relying on genetic predetermination or intuition and bases its argument on learning processes.

Further reading

Kibele, Armin (2006). Non-consciously controlled decision-making for fast motor reactions in sports: A priming approach for motor responses to non-consciously perceived movement features. *Psychology of Sport and Exercise*, 7, 591–610.

Hogarth, Robin M. (2001). *Educating intuition*. Chicago, Ill.: University of Chicago Press.

See also: AUTOMATICITY; IMAGERY; INFORMATION PROCESSING; MEMORY; NERVOUS SYSTEM; PERCEPTION; PROPRIOCEPTION; REACTION TIME; SKILL; SKILL ACQUISITION; SKILL EXECUTION

MUSCLE DYSMORPHIA

James Leone et al. define muscle dysmorphia (or dysmorphism) as "an anatomical malformation [in which] the primary FOCUS is not on how thin a person can get but rather on how large and muscular." The prefix *dys* is used, especially in medicine, to denote a bad or troublesome condition, such as dyspepsia (indigestion) or dysphasia (a speech disorder). It derives from the Greek *dus*, for difficult. *Morphe* is Greek for form, or shape.

Research on the subject suggests that this definition is both limiting and normative. People displaying the symptoms of muscle dysmorphia are "preoccupied, to the exclusion of much else, with increasing muscle mass," according to Antonia Baum, "Athletes particularly susceptible to muscle dysmorphia include body-builders and weight-lifters. This is a population particularly susceptible to anabolic steroid abuse." Baum's study indicates a prevalence of EATING DISORDERS among this predominantly male group.

This and other studies suggest that muscle dysmorphia is less an anatomical malformation—which is a structural deformity or abnormality of the body—and more a cognitive condition, in which males are dissatisfied with their BODY IMAGE, believing they are too thin, too fat, or in some other way deficient, and in which their RESPONSE is to train, perhaps compulsively, and supplement their frequently Spartan diets with substances, some of which are proscribed by sports governing organizations. This definition carries no assumption of standards or norms of "proper" body shape and hangs on how perceptions lead to discontentment and how attempts to ameliorate this discontentment may be ultimately self-defeating.

As well as being associated with eating disorders, muscle dysmorphia has been likened to them in its etymology, development and effects. Leone et al. detect that they share common sources: "As society bombards people at younger ages with images of what the 'ideal' body looks like MDM [muscle dysmorphia] will likely continue to increase in the general population." Interestingly, Leone at al. argue: "Body image dissatisfaction has been a concern throughout the ages." So, muscle dysmorphia, on this account, is not new; though its *sequelae* (consequences of a disease or injury), as they put it, clearly are.

As with many body dissatisfactions, perceptions are usually at variance with the perceptions of others. People with muscle dysmorphia might see themselves as flabby or frail, while others see them as toned and sinewy. It is this pursuit of the grail of somatic perfection, which, however misguided, affects the individual's behavior. That behavior is reinforced by cultural influences.

"The sport environment may provide a breeding ground for the disorder," write Leone et al., presumably including gyms and health clubs in this definition. Exchanging evaluative comments, notes on diet and training regimes, and so on provide support for the muscle-dysmorphic person. In this kind of environment where appearances are paramount, dependencies can flourish. The "weightlifting dependency" studied by K. J. Munroe-Chandler bears close resemblance to muscle dysmorphia. As does EXERCISE DEPENDENCE and ANOREXIA ATH-LETICA. All are maladies that have cultural origins, as Munroe-Chandler et al. observe: "In today's CULTURE, images of ideal physiques saturate the media." Yet, all have psychological consequences.

Further reading

Baum, Antonia (2006). Eating disorders in the male athlete. *Sports Medicine*, 36, 1–6.

Hallsworth, Lisa, Wade, Tracey, and Tiggemann, Marika (2005). Individual differences in male body-image: An examination of self-objectification in recreational body builders. *British Journal of Health Psychology*, 10, 433–65.

Lantz, C., Rhea, D., and Mayhew, J. (2001). The drive for size: A psycho-behavioral model of muscle dysmorphia. *International Sports Journal*, 5, 71–86.

Leone, James E., Sedory, Edward J., and Gray, Kimberley A. (2005). Recognition and treatment of muscle dysmorphia and related body image disorders. *Journal of Athletic Training*, 40, 352–9.

Munroe-Chandler, K. J., Kim, Arvin J., and Gammage, Kimberley L. (2004). Using imagery to predict weightlifting dependency in men. *International Journal of Men's Health*, 3, 129–39.

See also: ANOREXIA ATHLETICA; ANOREXIA NERVOSA; BODY DISSATISFACTION; BODY IMAGE; BULIMIA NERVOSA; EATING DISORDERS; EXERCISE MOTIVATION; OBESITY; OBSESSIVE-COMPULSIVE; PERCEPTION; PERFECTIONISM; REINFORCEMENT; SELF-AWARENESS; SOCIAL PHYSIQUE ANXIETY; WEIGHT CONTROL

NEGATIVITY

If a person consistently contradicts, disproves, rejects or refuses to accept positive, assuring advice or counsel, he or she is said to exhibit negativity, from Latin *negare*, "deny" (*neg* = not). There are several dimensions to this: the person's COGNITION (including beliefs and opinions), emotions, interpretations of events, and dispositions to act will all be influenced by a negative orientation. An athlete's negativity can initiate what S. G. Ziegler once called a "negative thought-ANXIETY cycle," in which the experience of STRESS prior or during a COMPETITION leads to above-optimal AROUSAL and an increase in ANXIETY. These in turn lead to further physiological changes, such as muscular tension or "tightening," which contribute toward an error. The experience of making an error cycles back in the form of even more anxiety, which precedes decrements in CONCENTRATION, a loss of COMPOSURE, and the probability that more errors will follow. The process resembles a SELF-FULFILLING PROPHECY.

On the other hand, there is evidence that induced negativity can have team-building properties. The imposition of humiliating tasks as part of a program of rigorous physical training and initiation is known as hazing, and research by Caroline Keating et al. into this very process revealed its effects. "The heightened negativity of the experience is apparently transformed as devotion to the collective," observe Keating and her colleagues, revealing how MOOD change can give rise to group and task COHESION.

Negativity is close in meaning to *passive negativism*, which is an attitude characterized by a resistance to the suggestions of others. It should be distinguished from active negativism, which is a tendency to behave in ways contrary to rules or directions, even when there is no obvious reason for doing so. In REVERSAL THEORY, this is known as proactive negativism, aimed at achieving excitement only. It counterpoints reactive negativism, which is an emotional reaction to frustration or disappointment.

Further reading

Keating, C. F., Pomerantz, J., Pommer, S. D., Ritt, S. J. H., Miller, L. M., and McCormick, J. (2005). Going to college and unpacking hazing: A functional approach to decrypting initiation practices among undergraduates. *Group Dynamics: Theory, Research and Practice*, 9, 104–26.

Ziegler, S. G. (1980). An overview of anxiety management strategies in sport. In W. F. Straub (Ed.), S*port psychology: An analysis of athlete behavior* (pp. 257–64). Ithaca, N.Y.: Mouvement Publications.

See also: CHOKE; COGNITIVE-BEHAVIORAL MODIFICATION; DEPRESSION; EMOTIONAL INTELLIGENCE; INDIVIDUAL ZONES OF OPTIMAL FUNCTIONING; MOOD; SELF-FULFILLING PROPHECY; SELF-HANDICAPPING; STRESS; STRESS-INOCULATION TRAINING

NERVOUS SYSTEM

The physical arrangement of neural tissue in vertebrates is the nervous system, and its basic function is to receive information about the environment, to process, store, retrieve, and respond to it in appropriate ways. In all forms of physical activity, responses to change in the environment, to be effective, have to be swift and definite. Possessing a SKILL means being able to respond relevantly to surrounding changes and maintain CONTROL over one's body.

The human nervous system comprises: (1) the central nervous system (CNS), which is the control center of the brain, and its message conduit, the spinal cord; and (2) the peripheral nervous system (PNS), which is the network of nerves originating in the brain and spinal cord and which is responsible for picking up messages from the skin and sense organs (sensory nerve cells) and carrying messages from the CNS to muscles (motor nerve cells).

While humans exert a large degree of control over their bodies through the CNS, many vital activities, such as heartbeat, peristalsis, and functioning of the kidneys are not under conscious control. Regulating these is a secondary system of nerves called the autonomic nervous system (ANS). Many of the cell bodies of the ANS lie outside the brain and spinal cord and massed together in bunches called ganglia, which receive information from receptors in the various organs of the body and then send out appropriate instructions to muscles, such as the heart and glands, for example, salivary glands. Activation of organs and mechanisms under the control of the ANS will affect levels of AROUSAL, which are crucial to athletes.

The ANS is divided into two strata: the sympathetic system (more centrally located in the body and responsible for changes associated with arousal) and the parasympathetic system (more dispersed). The parasympathetic system constricts the pupils of the eyes, increases the flow of saliva, expands the small intestine and shrinks the large intestine; the sympathetic system has the opposite effect and is much slower. This is why bodily changes that occur after a sudden fright are rapid, but the process whereby they resume normal functioning is gradual.

The term AUTONOMIC NERVOUS SYSTEM implies that it is independent and self-regulated, whereas, in fact, the centers that control ANS activity are in the lower portions of the brain and usually below the threshold of conscious control. In sport, the appeal of bringing ANS functions under conscious control is obvious: the potential, particularly in the areas of RELAXATION, recovery from INJURY and perhaps even SKILL ACQUISITION (among others) is great.

Further reading

Wilmore, J. H. and Costill, D. L. (1999). *Physiology of sport and exercise*, 2nd edn. Champaign, Ill.: Human Kinetics.

See also: ADRENALINE RUSH; ANGER; AROUSAL; AUTOMATICITY; BIOFEEDBACK; ELECTROENCEPHALOGRAM; INFORMATION PROCESSING; INJURY; KNOWLEDGE OF RESULTS; LEFT-HANDEDNESS; MOTOR REACTION; NERVOUSNESS; PAIN; PROPRIOCEPTION; REACTION TIME; SKILL EXECUTION; VISUOMOTOR

NERVOUSNESS

Originally used to describe conditions and disorders connected with the NERVOUS SYSTEM, the noun "nervousness" was later used to capture any set of symptoms with emotional rather than organic sources. Nervousness has tended to slip out of popular usage, being replaced by STRESS (an all-purpose term to describe almost any form of discomfort), ANXIETY (as in anxiety attack) or hyper (agitated or excited), as well as other imprecise but commonplace expressions, such as highly strung (irritable or touchy) and panicky (usually meaning liable to sudden, uncontrollable apprehension). The term has evolved from the Latin *nervus* and the Greek *neuron* (a word now used for the cell that constitutes the basic unit of the nervous system).

In sport and exercise, as in other areas of social life, nervousness is actually a useful and relevant concept describing a proneness to agitation or alarm when confronted by an intimidating task. While the adjective "nervous" is typically reserved for persons with a propensity to become tense as they approach such tasks, to CHOKE as they face victory, or even those who deliberately try to become nervous before COMPETITION, it can affect practically anyone who is alarmed at a daunting prospect. Yet, practice often eliminates it. In their discussion of AUTOMATICITY, John Bargh and Tanya Chartrand observe how different forms of nervousness supersede each other as automatic processes take effect: "One sees the teenager go from being an overwhelmed tangle of nerves at the first attempts to drive a car to soon being able to do so while conversing, tuning the radio, and getting nervous instead over that evening's date."

In this example, competence, or SKILL ACQUISITION, gradually removes nervousness. There are shorter-term methods of alleviating nervousness. Pornratshanee Weerapong et al. report on "a reduced pre-participation anxiety (nervousnessness) after massage," possibly, they anticipate, as a result of the drop in saliva cortisol levels, which is an indirect measure of parasympathetic activity (saliva cortisol is known as the "stress hormone"). Research by Sarah Rausch et al. concluded that group MEDITATION and progressive muscle RELAXATION decreased nervousness. Various studies, including that of Claire Calmels et al., have revealed the ameliorative impact of IMAGERY. Most surprisingly, Daniel Bailis's study indicated that SELF-HANDICAPPING can relieve the nervousness induced by the knowledge that one's performance is seen and evaluated by others.

The State Anxiety Inventory, an instrument to evaluate state or transitory anxiety levels, includes "nervousness," along with apprehension, tension, and worry, as one of its indicators.

While nervousness has tended to disappear from the contemporary vocabulary, "nervous" prefixes terms that are still used popularly, such as nervous breakdown, which covers a variety of emotional disorders—many severe enough to incapacitate—and nervous habit, again covering a variety of tendencies, some relatively harmless (nail-biting, nose-scratching), others symptoms of a DEPENDENCE.

Further reading

Bailis, Daniel S. (2001). Benefits of self-handicapping in sport: A field study of university athletes. *Canadian Journal of Behavioural Science,* 33, 213–23.

Bargh, John A. and Chartrand, Tanya L. (1999). The unbearable automaticity of being. *American Psychologist,* 54, 462–79.

Calmels, C., Holmes, P., Berthoumieux, C., Singer, R. N. (2004). The development of movement imagery vividness through a structured intervention in softball. *Journal of Sport Behavior,* 27, 305–20.

Rausch, Sarah M., Gramling, Sandra E., and Auerbach, Stephen M. (2006). Effects of a single session of large-group meditation and progressive muscle relaxation training on stress reduction, reactivity, and recovery. *International Journal of Stress Management,* 13, 273–90.

Weerapong, Pornratshanee, Hume, Patria A., and Kolt, Gregory S. (2005). The mechanisms of massage and effects on performance, muscle recovery and injury prevention. *Sports Medicine,* 35, 235–56.

See also: ANXIETY; FEAR; IMAGERY; NERVOUS SYSTEM; RELAXATION; SELF-HANDICAPPING; STEREOTYPE THREAT; STRESS; YIPS

NOMOTHETIC

From the Greek *nomos*, meaning laws, and *etic*, which denotes an approach to study that is general and objective in perspective, nomothetic theories or conceptual approaches strive for abstract knowledge that can be generalized across a range of phenomena. In effect, the knowledge generates laws that apply not simply to one situation but to a great many.

Much of the output of sport and exercise psychology is oriented toward generating knowledge that is widely applicable. SOCIAL FACILITATION theory or REVERSAL THEORY are examples. One famous

INVERTED-U theory of AROUSAL included *law* in its name (the YERKES–DODSON LAW). Even theories that rely on the central role of COGNITION strive for enlightenment which is not confined to one particular case or even cluster of situations, but which may be used generally. Lisa Van Landuyt et al. warn against use of nomothetic approaches, arguing that, while they have "intuitive appeal," they "provide poor accounts of the diversity encountered in real-life."

Michael Bar-Eli et al., in their study of swimmers, guarded against this by using complementary methods: "In addition to the nomothetic quantitative methods employed in this study, ideographic [...] and qualitative methods should also be used, such as case studies and applied behavior analysis."

The reference to "ideographic" or IDIOGRAPHIC RESEARCH highlights the tradition with which nomothetic research is often compared and, indeed, contrasted. Idiographic research concentrates on particular cases, often studying in a way that accentuates uniqueness rather than generalizability. This is an example of an *emic,* as opposed to *etic,* approach to study, that is, investigating particular, unique or distinct elements and the manner in which they work (*etic* approaches strive for generalizable conclusions).

There is disagreement about whether the two research styles are compatible. Sarah Baker combined both in her study of social problem solving. Her term "idiothetic" conveyed the use of self-report records and to CONSTRUCT a theoretical MODEL. But Chris Harwood is more wary regarding what he sees as "the potential misuse of nomothetic measures for quantitative individualized or idiographic assessment."

Further reading

Baker, Sarah R. (2006). Towards an idiothetic understanding of the role of social problem solving in daily event, mood and health experiences: A prospective daily diary approach. *British Journal of Health Psychology,* 11, 513–31.

Bar-Eli, Michael, Dreshman, Blumenstein, and Weinstein, Yitzhak (2002). The effect of mental training with biofeedback on the performance of young swimmers. *Applied Psychology: An International Review,* 51, 567–81.

Harwood, Chris (2002). Assessing achievement goals in sport: Caveats for consultants and a case for contextualization. *Journal of Applied Sport Psychology,* 14, 106–19.

Howard, George S. and Myers Paul R. (1990). Predicting human behavior: Comparing idiographic, nomothetic, and agentic methodologies. *Journal of Counseling Psychology,* 37, 227–37.

Van Landuyt, L. M., Ekkekakis, P., Hall, E. E. and Petruzzello, S. J. (2000). Throwing the mountains into the lakes: On the perils of nomothetic conceptions of the exercise–affect relationship. *Journal of Sport and Exercise Psychology*, 22, 208–34.

See also: CONCEPT; CONSTRUCT; IDIOGRAPHIC; INDIVIDUAL ZONES OF OPTIMAL FUNCTIONING; META-ANALYSIS; MODEL; PHENOMENON; PROFILE OF MOOD STATES; PROFILING; SOCIAL FACILITATION; THEORY; YERKES–DODSON LAW

OBEDIENCE

Submitting to rules, norms, orders, commands, directions, prescriptions, mandates, wishes or any other kind of injunction is an act of obedience. In many respects the equivalent of compliance, obedience carries the additional implied meaning that the person behaving obediently does so without actually believing in or understanding what he or she is doing. They do it because they feel obliged to do so; this is an acknowledgment of the *authority* of the person or organization dispensing the orders.

The application in sports is transparent: athletes are frequently charged by coaches to perform tasks for which they see no purpose, logic, or meaning. Sometimes, they may violently disagree with coaches' or managers' instructions. Ideally, coaches or others with comparable responsibilities want athletes to agree with their operational decisions. In practice, methods must be found of exacting obedience, regardless of whether they agree or disagree. (The word is from the Latin *obedientia*.)

Compliance 1: Authority. Interestingly, obedience is not as difficult to institute as common sense might suggest. Studies by Muzafer Sherif (1906–88), in the 1930s, and, later, Solomon Asch (1907–96) showed how relatively easy it was to create conditions under which conformity to norms occurred. Sherif took subjects into a darkened room individually and asked them to make judgments about how far and in what direction a light was moving. The evaluations were wildly diverse. When the subjects were taken back in, this time, in a group, the judgments converged, indicating that individuals tended to conform to the judgments of the group. Asch took the ambiguity out of the situation by making subjects decide which of several lines was longer. Although, the correct answer was obvious, Asch planted subjects, instructing them to give an obviously wrong answer, just to discover whether the genuine subjects would provide manifestly wrong answers. They did: Asch concluded that the forces to conform to others overpowered a person's ABILITY to make simple sensory judgments. Dissenting from majority opinions was too much for Asch's subjects.

These and lesser-known studies highlighted the force of collectivities in influencing both the thought and behavior of individuals, even in the face of often bizarre, conflicting evidence. Individuals were more comfortable when conforming to group norms than they were in challenging majority views. The study that brought out the more ominous implications of these finding was Stanley Milgram's *Obedience to Authority*. In her 1963 thesis, *Eichmann in Jerusalem*, Hannah Arendt (1906–75) had argued that the atrocities of World War II were not brought about by "monsters" but by ordinary people who were following orders. Influenced by this, Milgram's experiments in the 1970s involved "ordinary" people who were asked to perform monstrously cruel deeds.

Participants were told they were being paid to participate in learning experiments: "Learners" were strapped into an electrically wired chair and had electrodes attached to their bodies. The subjects were told to test them and administer electric shocks when the learners got their answers wrong. Actually, the learners were "insiders" and did not receive the shocks; they just reacted dramatically to convince the subjects that the situation was real. Milgram's important finding was that the so-called ordinary people were quite prepared to keep upping the electric shocks, even when the learners were thought to be in considerable pain. Each time the subject would object, a researcher would snap back: "Please continue" or "You *must* go on." Milgram (1933–84) found that 65 percent of the subjects obeyed, progressing all the way to the maximum voltage of 450 volts. Subjects surrendered their autonomy to the experiment, believing it to be conducted in the spirit of "science," which, in this case, functioned as an overarching ideology. One presumes, the state and military imperatives function similarly in times of mass conflict, supplying the individual with a "greater good" to justify immediate evils.

Outside of the laboratory, exacting obedience is more problematic, though there are echoes of Milgram in the research of Caroline Keating et al. on initiation rituals at college: "Contrived threats are likely to empower leaders and groups by stimulating the kinds of attitudes, social perceptions, and affiliative bonds that breed group IDENTITY and inspire obedience and devotion among new members of face-to-face groups."

Compliance 2: Credibility. There are several mediating factors to consider when we consider the relevance of these findings to sport and exercise. The more direct the person's experience with the victim, the less the obedience. In other words, obedience is enhanced when there are several buffers. For example, a coach who tells a football player to try to injure a rival team's key player will have only a limited chance of getting his player to carry out the instruction. The player would have direct physical contact with the opponent and would witness firsthand the effects of the INJURY.

Also, the credibility of the communicator is vital. If players in a team doubt the wisdom of the coach or manager, they are unlikely to obey commands. Similarly, if exercisers have little faith in the expertise of their instructor, they are unlikely to adhere to his or her instructions if they cannot understand the logic behind them.

If, on the other hand, they have implicit faith in the coach or instructor, they will follow instructions, even if they do not know the reason for them. They may not even like the coach: what matters is that they believe the authority figure's judgments can be trusted. This may explain why coaches rarely seek to be liked and, in some cases, seem to go out of their way to be disliked. Credibility is a more potent resource when trying to establish obedience among players.

Many advertisers sign athletes to endorse their product: because consumers trust their judgment, they think they are credible. Another reason is that they *identify* with them. This too affects obedience. People often seek to identify with or be like people whom they like and admire, though they will not necessarily obey that person in defiance of their own principles (buying a sports drink or pizza is unlikely to raise inner conflicts).

A further factor is ATTRIBUTION. Often in sports, athletes interpret success and failure in terms of internal and external factors. In team sports especially, relinquishing a degree of personal CONTROL and judgment to an external source serves to protect SELF-ESTEEM, an idea that has been developed by Tom Pyszczynski et al. A defeat can be explained as due to the coach's faulty tactics rather than the athlete's ability, while a success can be understood as a triumph for both the coach's tactics and the individual's ability to operationalize them perfectly. In both cases, obedience affords the individual athlete something of a shield.

One further point on obedience is the human propensity to predict inaccurately that we will resist it. Kristina Diekmann et al. discovered that people exaggerate either their ability or willingness to confront authority and refuse to obey people or organizations. They do so because of what Diekmann et al. call "attributional errors for the future self": When they make forecasts about their own behavior, they become observers, neglecting the subjective experience of taking orders:

> When making forecasts one is likely to overlook the situational forces and constraints that will emerge in the actual situation one is forecasting. People rarely accurately perceive the situational constraints that will propel their behavior and do not make adequate allowance for the uncertainties of situational construal [their particular interpretation] that will actually guide their behavior.

Further reading

Asch, Solomon (1955). Opinions and social pressures. *Scientific American*, 193, 31–5.

Diekmann, Kristina A., Tenbrunsel, Ann E., and Galinsky, Adam D. (2003). From self-prediction to self-defeat: Behavioral forecasting, self-fulfilling prophecies and the effect of competitive expectations. *Journal of Personality and Social Psychology*, 85, 672–83.

Keating, C. F., Pomerantz, J., Pommer, S. D., Ritt, S. J. H., Miller, L. M., and McCormick, J. (2005). Going to college and unpacking hazing: A functional approach to decrypting initiation practices among undergraduates. *Group Dynamics: Theory, Research and Practice*, 9, 104–26.

Milgram, Stanley (1974). *Obedience to authority: An experimental view.* New York: Harper & Row.

Pyszczynski, T., Solomon, S., Greenberg, J. Arndt, J., and Schimel, J. (2004). Why do people need self-esteem? A theoretical and empirical review. *Psychological Bulletin*, 130, 435–68.

Sherif, Muzafer (1936). *The psychology of social norms.* New York: Harper & Row.

See also: COACH–ATHLETE RELATIONSHIP; COMMITMENT; DISCIPLINE; EXERCISE BEHAVIOR; EXTRINSIC MOTIVATION; IDENTIFICATION; IDENTIFIED REGULATION; INTEGRATED REGULATION; INTERNALIZATION; LEADERSHIP; REINFORCEMENT; RELATIONAL

OBESITY

From the Latin *obesus*, meaning having eaten till fat, obesity describes the condition of having an excess of body fat, not simply being overweight. It is possible for a 250-pound (114-kilogram) weightlifter or heavyweight boxer to be overweight, but, as this is probably due to muscle rather than fat, they would not be obese. Someone who scores 30 on BODY MASS INDEX (BMI), on the other hand, is obese. The BMI is calculated by dividing one's weight (in kilograms) by the square of one's height (in meters), to establish categories ranging from "normal" to "obese class III" (40+).

There are several different types of obesity. *Endogenous* obesity describes a condition in which the causes of the obesity originate internally, for example, from an endocrinal imbalance or a metabolic abnormality. Ovarian obesity is identified mainly in females who have sex hormonal imbalances, particularly later in life. There is some dispute over whether there is a "fat gene," which instructs the body to develop fat cells and which would suggest a genetic form of obesity.

Exogenous obesity, by contrast, is caused by external factors; for example, overeating, particularly high fat, high carbohydrate foods, and lack of exercise. This is responsible for what Andy Miah and Emma Rich have called an "obesity epidemic." According to Steven Joyal, the prevalence of obesity has increased dramatically over the past twenty years, doubling in the USA alone. There has been a sharp rise of 20–30 percent in the 2002–6 period.

In his comprehensive review of the treatments available for obesity, Joyal writes: "Although the contribution of aerobic exercise to obesity prevention is well-known, the importance of strength training for effective weight control is also at least as important."

Obesity is cited by Paul Lloyd and Sandra Foster as one of the leading "lifestyle diseases," others including inactivity and cigarette-smoking, their argument being that the main influences on obesity are exogenous—environmental and behavioral in this instance.

In the 1990s, research suggested links between obesity and downward social mobility, a prevalence among women, particularly black women, and DEPRESSION as well as low SELF-ESTEEM. There was also evidence of a degree of ignorance of obesity among coaches. None of these have been supported by more contemporary research. Indeed, it is difficult to imagine anyone involved in sport and exercise not being aware of obesity and the wide range of disorders with which it is associated, including type-2 diabetes, hypertension, and certain types of cancer. The form of obesity linked with these is often known as *morbid* obesity.

Among the more interesting findings on obesity is that of Greg Atkinson and Damien Davenne, who note the parallel growth of reports of SLEEP restriction (i.e., short, or interrupted patterns of sleep, much induced by lifestyle change) and the prevalence of obesity since the 1960s, especially since 2002. The neuroendocrinal abnormalities resulting from restricted sleep "may affect appetite, increasing the RISK of overeating and an increase in body mass index."

FEAR of obesity has been cited as one of the propulsions behind the number of EATING DISORDERS, particularly ANOREXIA NERVOSA.

Further reading

Atkinson, Greg and Davenne, Damien (2006). Relationships between sleep, physical activity and human health. *Physiology and Behavior*, 90, 229–35.

Joyal, Steven V. (2004). A perspective on the current strategies for the treatment of obesity. *Current Drug Targets—CNS and Neurological Disorders*, 3, 341–56.

Lloyd, Paul J. and Foster, Sandra L. (2006). Creating healthy, high-performance workplaces: Strategies from health and sports psychology. *Consulting Psychology Journal: Practice and Research,* 58, 23–39.

Miah, Andy and Rich, Emma (2006). Genetic tests for ability? Talent identification and the value of an open future. *Sport, Education and Society*, 11, 259–73.

See also: ANOREXIA NERVOSA; BODY IMAGE; BULIMIA NERVOSA; EATING DISORDERS; GENDER; MIMESIS; MUSCLE DYSMORPHIA; PHYSICAL SELF-PERCEPTIONS; PHYSICAL SELF-WORTH; SOCIAL PHYSIQUE ANXIETY; WEIGHT CONTROL

OBSESSIVE-COMPULSIVE

There are two components to this condition. (1) Obsessive is an adjective of the noun "obsession," which is a state in which a thought or idea persists unreasonably in the consciousness of someone. The thought might be about someone or something; it is sometimes known as an *idée fixe*, that is, a fixed idea. (2) This idea often leads to irresistible urges to behave in certain ways, frequently against one's wishes, and this action is known as a compulsion (from the Latin *compellere*, to force). Hence, *obsessive-compulsive* relates to a condition in which a person feels compelled to perform actions repeatedly, sometimes in a sequence, to alleviate obsessive and intrusive thoughts. The term is sometimes used as a noun, referring to a person characterized by such obsessive behavior. The root of obsessive is the Latin *obsessio* for "haunt."

There are misconceptions about obsessive-compulsive conditions. "When they hear the term obsessive-compulsive, many people conjure images of excessive hand washing or bizarre daily rituals," observe James Leone et al., in their research report on MUSCLE DYS-MORPHIA and related disorders. "When applied to the framework of BODY IMAGE, the obsession becomes the body, or, more specifically, the level of muscularity and leanness. The compulsion is to achieve the desired levels of muscularity and leanness."

This condition is closely associated and, on occasion, synonymous with EXERCISE DEPENDENCE in which the exerciser feels obliged to work out, sometimes to the point where it endangers his or her health. When this manifests itself in an obviously dysfunctional fashion, we talk in terms of ANOREXIA ATHLETICA.

These are among a range of obsessive-compulsions that have sources in cultural standards and which find expression in exercise and sometimes sport. H. G. Pope et al. write of the "male body obsession," suggesting that Western CULTURE promotes a standard of beauty and a FOCUS on being physically attractive. They argue that many body-related obsessive-compulsions are a response to the attempt to reach ideals of attractiveness. This has also manifested in, as K. J. Munroe-Chandler et al., observe, a weightlifting DEPENDENCE.

There is also what Antonia Baum calls a "crossover of obsessive compulsive symptoms and eating disorders, the latter being the manifestation of either the obsessions or compulsions." For example, studies have found that women who enrolled on exercise programs primarily to lose weight developed obsessional concerns about their weight, which, in turn, triggered a more diffuse dissatisfaction with their bodies. Exercise became a method, though a futile method, of pursuing of idealized BODY IMAGE, or, in some instances, unrealistic levels of workout performance.

Sport FANS sometimes manifest behaviors that indicate obsessive-compulsions. There are several known cases of obsessional fans. Günther Parche, an unemployed lathe operator from Germany, was obsessed with the tennis player Steffi Graf. He manifested what Lynne McCutcheon et al. call "over-IDENTIFICATION." At his home, he built an altar in her honor so that he could worship the object of his obsession. When Monica Seles replaced Graf as the world's leading female player and met her rival in the German Open of 1993, Parche ran onto the court and stabbed Seles.

William Lepeska tracked Ann Kournikova to within three doors of her Miami Beach residence and waited for her, naked. When police apprehended him, he implored the tennis pro, "Anna, save me!" and later explained: "I had all kinds of delusional assumptions about Anna's feelings toward me." He seems to have had a delusion known as *erotomania*, in which someone believes that another, usually of higher social status (sometimes older), is in love with him or her. As David Giles notes: "The obsessive fan who camps on the star's doorstep has the potential to become either a murderer or a marriage partner."

While there is clear evidence of obsession in these cases, we should guard against presuming the behavior was compulsive. It might have been the product of an irresistible urge; it might have been irresistibly interesting or exciting. But was it necessarily against the conscious wishes of the fans in question? This raises questions about the applicability of obsessive-compulsive. For example, S. Bratman and D. Knight write of an "obsession of healthy eating," while, in fact, a strict observance of health foods, while persistent, is unlikely to be so intrusive that it interferes with daily functioning. A particular type of GAMBLING is often called compulsive, though, in fact, the habitual gambler derives satisfaction and perhaps an agreeable EUSTRESS from gambling. In this sense, it may be a compulsion but not if the gambler has some degree of CONTROL over the habitual behavior.

Further reading

Baum, Antonia (2006). Eating disorders in the male athlete. *Sports Medicine*, 36, 1–6.

Bratman, S. and Knight, D. (2001). *Health food junkies—orthorexia nervosa: Overcoming the obsession of healthy eating.* New York: Bantam Doubleday Dell.

Draeger, John, Yates, Alayne, and Crowell, Douglas (2005). The obligatory exerciser: Assessing an overcommitment to exercise. *The Physician and Sportsmedicine*, 33, 13–23.

Giles, D. (2000). *Illusions of immortality: A psychology of fame and celebrity.* New York: St. Martin's Press.

Leone, James E., Sedory, Edward J., and Gray, Kimberley A. (2005). Recognition and treatment of muscle dysmorphia and related body image disorders. *Journal of Athletic Training*, 40, 352–59.

McCutcheon, Lynn E., Ashe, Diane D., Houran, James, and Maltby, John (2003). A cognitive profile of individuals who tend to worship celebrities. *Journal of Psychology*, 137, 309–14.

Munroe-Chandler, K. J., Kim, Arvin J., and Gammage, Kimberley L. (2004). Using imagery to predict weightlifting dependency in men. *International Journal of Men's Health*, 3, 129–39.

Pope, H. G., Phillips, K. A. and Olivardia, R. (2000). *The Adonis complex: The secret crisis of male body obsession.* New York: Free Press.

See also: ANOREXIA ATHLETICA; BODY DISSATISFACTION; BULIMIA NERVOSA; CELEBRITIES; DEPENDENCE; EATING DISORDERS; EXERCISE DEPENDENCE; FANS; GAMBLING; IDENTIFICATION; MUSCLE DYSMORPHIA; PERFECTIONISM; PSYCHOPATHOLOGY; SUPERSTITIOUS BEHAVIOR

OUTPERFORMANCE

Outperformance is the carrying out or accomplishment of an action or task in a way that is demonstrably superior to that of rivals. An individual can derive feelings of SELF-CONFIDENCE from outperforming others, though this will depend to a large degree on the CONTEXT in which the outperformance takes place.

MOTIVATIONAL CLIMATE is an important factor. As Blake Miller et al. point out:

> A perceived MASTERY motivational climate refers to a setting in which learning and SKILL development are salient and valued, and the prospect of outperforming others is not of direct interest to the individual [...] In contrast, athletes who play for a coach who stresses winning and outperforming the opponent and their own teammates as important for success perceive a performance motivational climate.

In such a performance-motivational climate, the emphasis is on normative success and outperforming others. But the consequences of this on learners can be detrimental, as Theresa Thorkildsen and Lisa White-McNulty argue: "Encouraging students to become preoccupied with outperforming others facilitates a degree of disengagement from learning."

It also facilitates deviant propensities, according to Maria Kavussanu et al.: "Because ego-oriented athletes' perceptions of competence are dependent on outperforming others, these individuals are more likely to break the rules and behave in an unsportspersonlike fashion, especially when winning is at stake."

While this type of athlete typically exhibits competence and might take pride in the achievement, the research of Julie Juola Exline and Marci Lobel discloses how outperformance might occasion ambivalence, discomfort, and even distress for the outperformer. They studied what they call "outperformance-related strain": outperformers often become "targets for upward comparison," which means others are envious of them, or deflated by the apparent prowess. Research has shown that gifted children camouflage their own academic achievements, and women who progress in male-dominated settings experience a status discrepancy, prompting them to disguise their prowess. Whether or not the outperformed groups actually do grew resentful and lose self-confidence is less relevant than what the outperformer believes. The question is, why would the outperformer care?

Exline and Lobel advance three answers. (1) Like anyone else, the outperformer has *affiliative needs*: as social animals, they need to feel socially connected and the kind of ostracism brought about by outperforming others is a kind of punishment for success. (2) Only the most severe ego-oriented performer will lack concern for the WELL-BEING *of rivals*: basic human empathy might have no place in the ruthless world of professional sport, but at lower levels it can dampen the euphoria that comes from winning. (3) There is also the risk of being widely *disliked*. High achievers are typically respected, but rarely regarded with fondness. In fact, outperformers are aware that others take a malicious pleasure from the misfortunes of the overachievers; it is called *Schadenfreude*. The outperformer often suspects that envious others will conspire to hasten his or her downfall.

Outperformers' responses are variegated. They range from deliberately easing up in training and COMPETITION to interpreting the credit afforded them as unjustified. The latter case gives rise to the IMPOSTOR PHENOMENON. Another response is to try to please others in an effort to win their approval; this is particularly pronounced among highly sociotropic individuals, who "rely heavily on others for support" and who fear rejection.

Cultural factors are likely to influence the frequency and intensity of the strain of being an outperformer, according to Exline and Lobel. Referring to 1960s research on FEAR OF FAILURE, they note that, even in the twenty-first century, women are still more liable to experience outperformance strain, if only because "men are typically socialized to value competition and individualistic achievement [. . .] whereas women are taught to inhibit aggressive and competitive impulses."

American CULTURE emphasizes individualistic achievement and self-enhancement, while East Asian cultures with collectivist climates are more likely to promote interdependency. The potential for outperformance strain is higher in the latter cultures, or among competitors socialized in such cultures.

Further reading

Exline, Julie Juola and Lobel, Marci (1999). The perils of outperformance: Sensitivity about being the target of a threatening upward comparison. *Psychological Bulletin*, 3, 307–37.

Kavussanu, Maria, Seal, Alistair, and Philips, Daniel (2006). Observed prosocial and antisocial behaviors in male soccer teams: Age differences across adolescence and the role of motivational variables. *Journal of Applied Sport Psychology,* 18, 1–19.

Miller, Blake W., Roberts, Glyn C., and Ommundsen, Yngvar (2004). Effect of motivational climate on sportspersonship among competitive youth male and female football players. *Scandinavian Journal of Medicine and Science in Sports,* 14, 193–202.

Thorkildsen, Theresa A. and White-McNulty, Lisa (2002). Developing conceptions of fair contest procedures and the understanding of skill and luck. *Journal of Educational Psychology,* 94, 316–26.

See also: AVOIDANCE; CELEBRITIES; DEPENDENCE; DEVIANCE; FEAR OF FAILURE; GENDER; GIFTEDNESS; IMPOSTOR PHENOMENON; MORAL ATMOSPHERE; MOTIVATIONAL CLIMATE; PEER LEADERSHIP; SELF-ESTEEM; SOCIALIZATION; SOCIOTROPY; STEREOTYPE THREAT; STRESS

OVERLEARNING

This describes an excess of repeated practices intended to lead to the acquisition of SKILL or knowledge but leading to debilitation. The CONCEPT has been used in research on STRESS and stress-related disorders. Teri Saunders et al., for example, suggest that "STRESS INOCULATION TRAINING has been recommended as a method of reducing the debilitating effects of overlearning."

In sport and exercise, overlearning is often associated with the stress of PERFECTIONISM. Mark Anshel and Hossein Mansouri report on an "overlearned set of emotions associated with performance under stressful conditions," meaning that repeated attempts to master a skill without positive reactions and only critical FEEDBACK, or none at all, can produce acute stress in a learner.

While not related to sport or exercise, a study of post-traumatic stress patients by Brett Litz et al. offers an illustration of how habits, beliefs, and lifestyles not immediately resulting from the post-traumatic stress, but developing out of it can be overlearned unless very early interventions are made. In other words, new responses that did not directly arise from the stress were overlearned.

Further reading

Anshel, Mark H. and Mansouri, Hossein (2005). Influences of perfectionism on motor performance, affect, and causal attribution in response to critical information feedback. *Journal of Sport Behavior,* 28, 99–125.

OVERREACHING

Langer, E. and Imber, G. (1979). When practice makes imperfect: Debilitating effects of overlearning. *Journal of Personality and Social Psychology*, 37, 2014–24.
Litz, B. T., Bryant, R., Williams, L., Wang, J. and Engle, C. C. (2004). A therapist-assisted internet self-help program for traumatic stress. *Professional Psychology: Research and Practice*, 35, 628–34.
Saunders, T., Driskell, J. E., Hall Johnston, J., and Salas, E. (1996). The effect of stress inoculation training on anxiety and performance. *Journal of Occupational Health Psychology*, 1, 170–86.

See also: AVOIDANCE; DEPENDENCE; EMOTION; EMOTIONAL CONTROL; EXERCISE DEPENDENCE; INTERVENTION; LEARNED HELPLESSNESS; PARALYSIS BY ANALYSIS; PERFECTIONISM; SKILL ACQUISITION; STRESS; STRESS-INOCULATION TRAINING

OVERREACHING

Sometimes called "short-term overtraining," this "refers to training that involves a brief period of overload, with inadequate recovery, that exceeds the athlete's adaptive capacity," according to Lawrence Armstrong and Jaci VanHeest. "This process involves a temporary performance decrement lasting from several days to several weeks."

David Smith observes that the "transient performance incompetence [. . .] is reversible within a short-term recovery period of 1–2 weeks and can be rewarded by a state of supercompensation."

This means that, while overreaching is often an unplanned and unwelcome consequence of persistent, strenuous training, it can also be deliberate. As explain Armstrong and VanHeest: "If a plateau or decrease in performance is reversed within a few days or weeks, and is followed by a performance that exceeds the level previously experienced," that is, a supercompensation.

Further reading

Armstrong, Lawrence E. and VanHeest, Jaci L. (2002). The unknown mechanism of the overtraining syndrome. *Sports Medicine*, 32, 185–209.
Smith, David J. (2003). A framework for understanding the training process leading to elite performance. *Sports Medicine*, 33, 1103–26.

See also: BURNOUT; COMEBACK; COMMITMENT; DEPRESSION; INJURY; OVERTRAINING SYNDROME; PAIN; RETIREMENT; SELF-HANDICAPPING; STRESS; STRESS-INOCULATION TRAINING; STRESS-MANAGEMENT TRAINING

OVERTRAINING SYNDROME

When the INTENSITY and frequency of training exceeds the body's capacity to respond positively to it, overtraining occurs. Performance decrements and chronic maladaptations occur consistently and are characterized by a set of associated symptoms. "Known as overtraining syndrome (OTS), this complex condition afflicts a large percentage of athletes at least once during their careers," according to Lawrence Armstrong and Jaci VanHeest.

A *syndrome* is a set of symptoms that persistently occur together. In this case, they include, according to Julia Dalgleish and Stuart Dollery:

> Tiredness, decreased immune system efficiency, nausea, excessive weight loss, aching joints and muscles, nausea, repetitive loading injuries (such as shin splints), reduction in bone density and an increased length of time to reach fitness goals (the 'plateau effect'). At least the first four of these symptoms may be described as psychophysiological in character, having both psychological and physical components.

While overtraining syndrome is commonly accepted as a feature of competitive life, "the underlying mechanism is not known," according Armstrong and VanHeest. Jonathan Metzler argues that overtraining is part of the training STRESS syndrome: "Athletes who have training stress greater than their ABILITY to adapt to that stress may experience a plateau or a decrease in performance."

For instance, competitors across a wide range of sports include weight training in their preparations. A 158-pound rower may bench press 225 pounds one week and increase this to 235 pounds three weeks later. Buoyed by this, the rower might expect comparable improvements and be disappointed when, after a further six months, there has been no betterment. "Initially, athletes also may observe increases in SELF-CONFIDENCE and MOTIVATION to train; this may catalyze further increases in training STRESS imposed by the athletes themselves," writes Metzler.

A combination of overenthusiasm and determination to improve produces more strenuous labors to maintain progress but, as anyone who has worked with weights has discovered, training gains do not accrue at a steady pace. The plateau arrives, and the athlete experiences a type of law of diminishing returns, or even a law of nonexistent returns: expenditures of effort beyond a certain point do not yield proportionate returns.

The experience leads to a decline in motivation and a corresponding drop in CONFIDENCE; in other words, the athlete becomes *stale*. Metzler warns: "Staleness should not be confused with being in a SLUMP" (which happens when there is a decrease in performance). Staleness arrives when an individual is no longer able to perform well or creatively because of having done something for too long. Among the adaptations available to an athlete in a condition of staleness is to rest, change, or to train even more. The final option produces overtraining and, possibly, even BURNOUT among some athletes; OVERREACHING, by contrast, is temporary. Another maladaptive strategy is to consume less: EATING DISORDERS are common among athletes trying to combat staleness.

Dalgleish and Dollery represent the process as a *dose–response curve*, each dose of training generating a positive response, but only up to a certain point. "As the level of exercise becomes excessive the body fails to adapt positively to the stress placed on the body," they observe. "When this optimal level is exceeded, the risks overtake the benefits and overuse injuries and reduced immune system efficiency results in illness."

Etiologically, overtraining syndrome has been compared to that of DEPRESSION. Armstrong and VanHeest suggest: "OTS and depression share neuroendocrine pathways and brain structures that restore homeostasis in response to stressors." (Neuroendocrine involves both nervous stimulation and endocrine secretion, the latter relating to glands that discharge hormones into the blood; stressors are environmental factors that disturb the brain's equilibrium).

Further reading

Armstrong, Lawrence E. and VanHeest, Jaci L. (2002). The unknown mechanism of the overtraining syndrome. *Sports Medicine*, 32, 185–209.

Dalgleish, J. and Dollery, S. (2001). *The Health and Fitness Handbook* Harlow: Pearson Education.

Metzler, J. (2002). Applying motivational principles to individual athletes. In J. M. Silva and D. E. Stevens (Eds.), *Psychological foundations of sport* (pp. 80–106). Boston, Mass.: Allyn & Bacon.

Raglin, J. S. and Wilson, G. S. (2000) Overtraining in athletes. In Y. L. Hanin (Ed.), *Emotions in sport* (pp. 191–108). Champaign, Ill.: Human Kinetics.

Smith, David J. (2003). A framework for understanding the training process leading to elite performance. *Sports Medicine*, 33, 1103–26.

See also: ANOREXIA NERVOSA; BULIMIA NERVOSA; BURNOUT; COMMITMENT; COPING STRATEGIES; DEPRESSION; EATING DISORDERS; NERVOUS SYSTEM; OVERREACHING; STRESS; STRESS-INOCULATION TRAINING; STRESS-MANAGEMENT TRAINING

PAIN

From the Latin *poena*, for penalty, pain refers to suffering in its generic sense. While physical pain is cited most commonly, artists may suffer for their art, lovers may suffer for their loved ones, and prisoners may suffer for their deeds or, perhaps, their conscience. In sport and exercise, pain most frequently refers to the physical feelings experienced because of INJURY or the sensation of crossing certain *thresholds* of endurance, that is, the pain barrier. FANS sometimes talk of the painful experience of witnessing their teams lose, though this metaphorical use is in jest (mostly).

Crossing the pain barrier relates to pain tolerance; and training for endurance events particularly is geared to instilling in an athlete the ABILITY to tolerate pain for long periods. The pain in question is not chronic, of course; but it is a dispersed discomfort that distance runners especially have to assimilate (chronic pain is long-lasting and intractable). Tolerance to pain may have a biological component, but its variability and susceptibility to change indicate that its also has a significant psychological component. In training, athletes are implored to "bite the bullet" or similar when approaching the pain threshold. Bodybuilders famously remind others of the "no pain, no gain" principle. The Gracie dynasty of jiu-jitsu fighters prepared its members for contests by a type of pain inoculation, inducing pain in training so as to safeguard against it during COMPETITION.

In his review article on training processes leading to elite athletic performance, David Smith includes "the aptitude to tolerate pain and sustain effort" as part of the "solid psychological platform" that an athlete needs to build, suggesting that the resistance is acquired.

Mark Anshel examines the manner in which the construction is done: "Elite athletes tend to use one of two mental techniques in coping with physical discomfort, *association* and *dissociation*." The GOAL of the first is to remain "in touch with one's body" and maintain the necessary MOTIVATION to meet challenges. Weight lifters "associate with" their muscles as they lift; runners concentrate on planting their feet with each stride. This strategy can backfire if the athlete's CONCENTRATION wavers and he or she begins focusing on the area of pain rather than the bodily functions that enhance performance. Dissociation entails externalizing projecting feelings and sensations outward to surrounding events rather than inward to internal experiences. Both are examples of pain endurance.

John Draeger et al. suggest that pain can take on a compulsive character. In their study of exercise DEPENDENCE, they note how some individuals experience physical pain as a habitual part of their compulsion yet feel obliged to endure it to continue exercising.

Further reading

Anshel, M. H. (1997). *Sport psychology: From theory to practice* 3rd edn, Scottsdale, Ariz.: Gorsuch Scarisbrick.

Draeger, John, Yates, Alayne, and Crowell, Douglas (2005). The obligatory exerciser: Assessing an overcommitment to exercise. *The Physician and Sportsmedicine*, 33, 13–23.

Smith, David J. (2003). A framework for understanding the training process leading to elite performance. *Sports Medicine*, 33, 1103–26.

See also: DEPENDENCE; EMOTION; HEDONIC TONE; HYPNOSIS; INJURY; KINESIO-PHOBIA; MENTAL TOUGHNESS; NERVOUS SYSTEM; PERCEPTION; PROPRIOCEPTION; REINFORCEMENT; STRESS-INOCULATION TRAINING; YOGA

PARALYSIS BY ANALYSIS

This describes the debilitating loss of effectiveness occasioned by over-analyzing one's own performance. Paralysis, in this sense, is used in a figurative sense for loss of function or cognitive processes (rather than a complete loss of ability to move or feel anything in part or most of the body; from the Greek *paralusis*, meaning "disabled at the side").

"When individuals attempt to consciously control aspects of their performance that they normally execute automatically, this change in their performance routine often results in sub-par performance," write Harry Wallace et al. "If performance pressure leads a veteran track hurdler to start thinking about the positioning of his feet during the race—something the hurdler does not normally think about—it is unlikely that this new attention to detail will benefit his performance."

Jin Wang et al. found that, under pressure, "'approachers' are more likely to become distracted from the task by becoming immersed in a process of explanation" (APPROACH response-coping directs efforts toward reducing the threat, as opposed to AVOIDANCE, which directs activities away).

Further reading

Wallace, Harry M., Baumeister, Roy F., and Vohs, Kathleen D. (2005). Audience support and choking under pressure: A home disadvantage? *Journal of Sports Sciences*, 23, 429–38.

Wang, Jin, Marchant, Daryl, and Morris, Tony (2004). Coping style and susceptibility to choking. *Journal of Sport Behavior*, 27, 75–93.

See also: ANXIETY; APPROACH; AROUSAL; AVOIDANCE; CHOKE; FEAR; FOCUS; HOME ADVANTAGE; OVERLEARNING; SELF-AWARENESS; SELF-HANDICAPPING; SLUMP

PARAMETERS

Originally a mathematical term, parameter is now commonly used to denote the limits of an activity within which that activity can be performed satisfactorily. It derives from the Latin *para*, for "beside," and *metron*, for "measure," and, strictly speaking, a parameter should have a numerical value. But "parameters" is popularly used synonymously with scope or boundaries (perhaps because it sounds so much like perimeters); as Zella Moore writes in her discussion of sport psychologists' ethical dilemmas, "practice parameters aid practitioners in finding 'the ethical path that will assist them'."

In sport and exercise, *performance parameters* are often cited as the limits within which a satisfactory competitive performance is conducted. They might be measured in terms of times, number of assists, rounds won; or, in an exercise CONTEXT, number of minutes on the treadmill, weights lifted and so on. The accent is on output. *Training parameters* are typically different and refer to input, such as numbers of repetitions, hours trained, that is, what someone has put into an activity, rather than how they have performed.

FITNESS parameters can include several limits, for example: metabolic parameters, which measure the chemical processes needed to maintain life; hematological parameters, which represent the physiology of the blood; or lipid parameters, which refer to the fatty acids and their derivatives. Anyone attending a gym regularly aims at remaining within certain *cardiovascular* parameters (as well as perhaps achieving muscle tone); this indicates that their heart and blood vessels are functioning satisfactorily. The aim of a fitness program is to bring the exerciser into optimal fitness parameters.

Adrian Taylor and Ken Fox refer to "fitness and anthropometric parameters," which include both the functioning and the measurement and proportions of the body. They report that systematic "engagement in physical activity" lead to changes in these.

Further reading

Moore, Zella E. (2003). Ethical dilemmas in sport psychology: Discussion and recommendations for practice. *Professional Psychology: Research and Practice*, 34, 601–10.

Taylor, Adrian H. and Fox, Ken R. (2005). Effectiveness of a primary care exercise referral intervention for changing physical self-perceptions over 9 months. *Health Psychology*, 24, 11–21.

See also: ETHICS; FITNESS; GOAL; GOAL ORIENTATION; NERVOUS SYSTEM; PEAK PERFORMANCE; PROFILING; SOCIAL PHYSIQUE ANXIETY; SOCIALIZATION; WEIGHT CONTROL

PARASOCIAL INTERACTION

A RELATIONSHIP that one party experiences as reciprocal, even though they have never met the other; for example, between FANS and the people they follow.

See also: CELEBRITIES; FANS

PARTICIPATION MOTIVATION

Participant motivation is the collective term given to the explanations of children for being involved with or withdrawing from sports. Studies in participant MOTIVATION typically use a SELF-RATING approach, inviting young people to address the reasons why they became interested in, continued in, or left sports. The FOCUS is on the personal dispositions of the individuals rather than on external factors that may affect MOTIVATION and COMMITMENT.

Reasons typically given for participating include: achievement, challenge, companionship, fun, health and WELL-BEING, SKILL ACQUISITION, and motives associated with a task–GOAL ORIENTATION and intrinsic motivation. While intuitively reasons such as fun and enjoyment might appear to be constant across all groups, Diane Gill offered a more complicated scenario with differences related to GENDER, age, parents' education, and geographic region: "the relevance of motivational dimensions varies according to sociocultural and geographic factors."

This was reinforced in a British study, using a Participation Motivation Inventory. Motives differed according to gender and age: intrinsic factors were more important between the ages of eleven and fifteen, less so after that age. Females were more motivated by team affiliation and achievement than males.

Further reading

Daley, A. and O'Gara, A. (1998). Age, gender and motivation for participation in extra-curricular physical activities in secondary school adolescents. *European Physical Education Review*, 4, 47–53.

Gill, Diane L. (2000). *Psychological dynamics of sport and exercise*, 2nd edn. Champaign, Ill.: Human Kinetics.

Sit, Cindy H. P. and Lindner, Koenraad J. (2006). Situational state balances and participation motivation in youth sport: A reversal theory perspective. *British Journal of Educational Psychology*, 76, 369–84.

See also: ACHIEVEMENT MOTIVE; ATHLETIC IDENTITY; COACH–ATHLETE RELATIONSHIP; EXERCISE MOTIVATION; EXTRINSIC MOTIVATION; GENDER; INTRINSIC MOTIVATION; MASTERY CLIMATE; MOTIVATION; MOTIVATIONAL CLIMATE; ROLE MODEL; SOCIALIZATION; TEAM PLAYER

PEAK PERFORMANCE

A peak performance is one of the highest value or quality, the word peak probably being a variation on the Middle English *pike*, meaning the top of a hill or a wooden shaft with a pointed metal head. Athletes are sometimes said to be "hitting a peak," or "peaking." The inference is the same: a maximum level feat. There are three ways in which peak performance is used:

(1) subjectively: a feat that is *experienced* as maximal, even though objectively it may not be at or even near the athlete's best effort in quantifiable terms;

(2) physiologically: which, as David Smith puts it, "represents a point in time where FITNESS and fatigue differences are maximised in favour of the overall performance outcome";

(3) cognitively: peak performances that require cognitive SKILL typically occur only after extensive training, but the peak period may last several years, as studies of chess players indicate.

Peak 1: Subjective. Abraham Maslow (1908–70) used the term "peak experience" to describe a moment in people's lives when they feel in harmony with all things about them and momentarily lose track of time and space. Similarly, Karen Lee Hill states that "the importance of other people to the outcome of the [peak] transaction is relegated to the background of the athlete's attention." So, outside evaluations, measurable or otherwise, are not important; experience is. While there is often congruence between feelings of peaking and actually peaking objectively, there is no necessary RELATIONSHIP. Athletes have been known to report a peak subjective performance, even though their measurable performance was not their best. (And vice versa. Athletes often reflect on how they did not feel themselves to be playing well, when observers considered them to be performing at or near a peak.)

By definition, peaking in sport is not an everyday occurrence; nor is it long-lasting. While athletes and coaches work sedulously at "peaking at the right time," there is no formula for achieving a peak. Preparation can only establish the conditions under which peaking is both possible and probable; it cannot guarantee it. In fact, if the work of Kenneth Ravizza is to be accepted, once the conditions are established, the athletes "must surrender the usual thinking-evaluating SELF to the experience."

Ravizza's interpretation of peaking is a highly subjective one and accentuates the "intrinsic satisfaction" rather than the objective referents. But, the conditions he stipulates seem applicable to both senses: CENTERING; keeping ATTENTION tightly focused, "being totally involved in the task at hand" and losing FEAR appear to be conducive to producing exceptional performances in an objective way. Mark Anshel adds to the desirable conditions: "feelings of being in an envelope"; states of physical and mental RELAXATION; an acute awareness of one's body; SELF-CONFIDENCE; and encouraging "no sense of imposing CONTROL"; that is, AUTOMATICITY. These, he suggests, form a "mental game checklist," which is "very helpful in preparing the athlete for COMPETITION." These are culled from the subjective reports of athletes after feelings of peak performance. Anshel's checklist is an instrument designed to replicate them in other athletes.

Peak 2: Physiological. The physiological peak performance studied by David Smith is far from spontaneous. It is a carefully planned process achieved through periodization and tapering. The former means breaking training periods into phases, each with its own goals, with a view to reaching a peak at a predetermined moment in the future. "A taper is a period where training volume is reduced before competition, since residual fatigue may mask or attenuate fitness gains that have occurred through overload training."

The preparation is the result of an interaction between the body's long-term increase in fitness, which is stimulated by training, and the opposing short-term fatigue. Smith argues that, with DELIBERATE PRACTICE, "the chances of making a workhorse more like a thoroughbred are increased and with correct peaking, a workhorse may also be highly competitive."

Reaching a peak at the requisite time is a matter of fine judgment. It is practically impossible to remain at a physiological peak for more than a few days. This is why, as Lawrence Armstrong and Jaci vanHeest observe: "Athletes at their peak [...] are also on the threshold of OVERTRAINING."

Peak 3: Cognitive. Peak performance in sports where COGNITION and MEMORY are more important than physiological factors is typically less fragile. "There is significant evidence to argue that the peak age of competitive chess performance occurs in the mid-to-late thirties," write Neil Charness and his colleagues in their study of chess players. Players' peaks arrive after painstaking practice lasting several years; the peak performances can extend over another several years; and the decline is slow, gradual and sometimes hardly perceptible.

Further reading

Anshel, Mark H. (1997). *Sport psychology: From theory to practice*, 3rd edn, Scottsdale, Ariz.: Gorsuch Scarisbrick.

Armstrong, Lawrence E. and VanHeest, Jaci L. (2002). The unknown mechanism of the overtraining syndrome. *Sports Medicine*, 32, 185–209.

Charness, N., Tuffiash, M., Krampe, R., Reingold, E., and Vasyukova, E. (2005). The role of deliberate practice in chess expertise. *Applied Cognitive Psychology*, 19, 151–65.

Hill, Karen L. (2001). *Frameworks for sport psychologists*. Champaign, Ill.: Human Kinetics.

Ravizza, Kenneth (1984). Qualities of the peak experience in sport. In J. M. Silva and R. S. Weinberg (Eds.) *Psychological foundations of sport* (pp. 452–61). Champaign, Ill.: Human Kinetics.

Smith, David J. (2003). A framework for understanding the training process leading to elite performance. *Sports Medicine*, 33, 1103–26.

See also: AROUSAL; ATTENTION; AUTOMATICITY; CENTERING; CONTROL; DELIBERATE PRACTICE; FOCUS; GATING; HYPNOSIS; ICEBERG PROFILE; INDIVIDUAL ZONES OF OPTIMAL FUNCTIONING; INTENSITY; MOMENTUM; OVERTRAINING SYNDROME; SELF-CONFIDENCE; SELF-FULFILLING PROPHECY; SKILL EXECUTION; ZONE

PEER LEADERSHIP

This describes the patterns of authority and status assignment that develop among young people as their parents lose significance as sources of support and influence and their peers assume more sway in either shaping or guiding their thought and behavior. Peers are contemporaries who are equals with respect to function, SKILL, or standing. The peer group is a collection of members who have roughly equal status.

While athletic groups typically have formal team leaders, there may be other individuals who, according to Todd Loughead et al., "offer leadership to a fewer number of teammates. While their influence may not be as widespread as team leaders, this type of leadership still can exert influence on its group members; which we have labeled peer leadership."

Acceptance of such peer leaders is determined by, for example, popularity, friendship, or interpersonal attractiveness, though, as Molly Moran and Maureen Weiss advise: "Within the sport CONTEXT, a certain amount of EXPERTISE and SKILL also tends to tip the scale in favor of peer leaders."

Further reading

Loughead, Todd M., Hardy, James, and Eys, Mark A. (2006). Nature of athlete leadership. *Journal of Sport Behavior,* 29, 142–59.

Moran, Molly M. and Weiss, Maureen R. (2006). Peer leadership in sport: Links with friendship, peer acceptance, psychological characteristics, and athletic ability. *Journal of Applied Sport Psychology,* 18, 97–113.

See also: COACH–ATHLETE RELATIONSHIP; COHESION; GROUP DYNAMICS; LEADERSHIP; OUTPERFORMANCE; RELATIONAL; ROLE MODEL; TRANSACTIONAL LEADERSHIP; TRANSFORMATIONAL LEADERSHIP

PERCEPTION

From the Latin *perceptio*, for seize or understand, perception is the facility to see, hear, or be aware of stimuli through the senses. It is sometimes used to denote a process of becoming, or just being aware, as in, for example, the perception of threat; in this sense, it involves interpretation of stimuli. While the perception of threat is usually occasioned by an external stimulus, perception can take place with an external agency or any kind of intervention, as when an internal stimulus prompts a perception of PAIN. The whole range of stimuli of which an individual is aware at one time is known as the *perceptual field*.

The perceptual field is not the sum total of stimuli available to the senses, but the ones of which the individual is aware. In other words, the physical objects that populate the environment around us do not determine the objects of perception. These are products of COGNITION, MEMORY, and several other factors, including the CONTEXT of the perception. This alerts us to the centrality of perception to sport and exercise psychology. Nearly every aspect of study involves becoming conscious of and making sense of stimuli. How someone perceives an event, a person, or a process is affected by the person's own qualities, whether acquired or inherent. It is also affected by the context in which the perception takes place. And the perception will affect the manner in which he or she responds. We can illustrate this, by comparing two previously mentioned perceptions of threat and of pain.

For example, the quality of MENTAL TOUGHNESS is used by Andrew Levy et al. to show how similar injuries can be perceived differently: "Mentally tough individuals have positive perceptions of their INJURY compared to lesser mentally tough individuals."

They are better able to cope with physical pain, particularly during the REHABILITATION period. Less mentally tough individuals are more likely to perceive the injury as a catastrophe. Sarah Pressman and Sheldon Cohen issue the reminder: "Pain is a perception."

But the setting in which perception takes place is also influential. Nickolas Smith et al.'s study of volleyball players "highlighted how performance context, particularly settings in which evaluation by others and social comparison form a part, may heighten perceptions of threat." The changing context provoked anxiety among players. So, for instance, as the MOMENTUM of a game swung against them, so the perception of threat and the attendant worry it brought on heightened.

The perception of a threat may be rational and, in a particular context, appropriate. But, if it persists then, as the research of Giulia Buodo et al., reveals, then the perception can lead to ANXIETY and other forms of unpleasant conditions—all triggered by the initial perception. So, individual qualities and surrounding context are both determinants of perception, while perceptions themselves can affect cognitive and behavioral responses that last long after the original stimulus has been removed.

Perception features in what we might call subgenres of sport and exercise psychology. For instance, perceptions of success or failure will impact on an individual's ADHERENCE to a program or the decision to drop out. Perceptions of COHESION, or the cohesiveness of one's team influence LEADERSHIP relations. Leaders in themselves can affect the MOTIVATIONAL CLIMATE and MORAL ATMOSPHERE of a group and thus promote particular kinds of perceptions. These include practically every kind of STIMULUS, including the rightness or wrongness of individual behaviors, ranging from breaking the rules to sticking too resolutely to rules.

These types of behaviors might, on occasion, be based on a "distorted" perception. For example, Anthony Papathomas and David Lavallee discovered that "athletes' perceptions of weight pressures interact with actual emphasis on weight in increasing eating disorder risk." Athletes perceived the dietary practices required to achieve PEAK PERFORMANCE, but sometimes in a way that precipitated EATING DISORDERS.

Research into ATTRIBUTION pays close attention to the pattern of perceptions of controllability. Those who perceive their performances and results as within their own CONTROL have an internal locus of causality; their perception is of a situation under their own command.

In a very different context, perceptions of seemingly insignificant items like a training partner's gym gear or an opponent's footwear can have profound effects on impressions and expectations, as the work of Iain Greenlees et al. indicates.

Self-perception, as the term suggests, is the awareness a person has of him or herself. Some schools of thought argue that we can only be aware of what we can observe of ourselves; so self-perception implicates us in regarding ourselves objectively. When self-perceptions concern the body, its presentation, effectiveness, and our satisfaction with it, the term "PHYSICAL SELF-PERCEPTION" is used. Standing in front of a mirror is just one source of stimuli for this perception. More critically, it is based on a person's perceptions of other people's responses and evaluations of his or her body. The relevance of this to the previously mentioned eating disorders and clothing effects, as well as a great many other aspects of sport and exercise psychology, are obvious. The perceptions people have of their own bodies are based in large part on *their* perceptions of *other's* perceptions.

Further reading

Buodo, Giulia, Sarlo, Michela, and Palomba, Daniela (2002). Attentional resources measured by reaction times highlight differences within pleasant and unpleasant, high arousing stimuli. *Motivation and Emotion*, 26, 123–38.

Greenlees, Iain, Buscombe, Richard, Thelwell, Richard, Holder, Tim, and Rimmer, Matthew (2005). Impact of opponents' clothing and body language on impression formation and outcome expectations. *Journal of Sport and Exercise Psychology*, 27, 39–52.

Levy, A. R., Polman, R. C. J., Clough, P. J., Marchant, D. C. and Earle, K. (2006). *Journal of Sport Rehabilitation*, 15, 246–54.

Papathomas, Anthony and Lavallee, David (2006). A life history analysis of a male athlete with an eating disorder. *Journal of Loss and Trauma*, 11, 143–79.

Pressman, Sarah D. and Cohen, Sheldon (2005). Does positive affect influence health? *Psychological Bulletin*, 131, 925–71.

Smith, Nickolas C., Bellamy, Mark, Collins, David J., and Newell, Danny (2001). A test of processing efficiency theory in a team sport context. *Journal of Sports Sciences*, 19, 321–32.

See also: ATTENTION; ATTRIBUTION; BODY IMAGE; BODY LANGUAGE; COGNITION; COHESION; DROPOUTS; LIFE COURSE; LOCUS OF CONTROL; MOMENTUM; PHYSICAL SELF-PERCEPTIONS; RECIPROCITY; SELF-EFFICACY; STIMULUS; VISUAL PERCEPTION

PERFECTIONISM

Perfectionism is an unwillingness to accept any standard or condition that is other than absolutely faultless and free from defects. The term is from the Latin *perfectio*, meaning "complete." It follows that a perfectionist is a person who tries to reach the desired state and refuses to settle for less. Perfectionists are characterized by a "striving for flawlessness and setting of excessively high standards for performance accompanied by tendencies for overly critical evaluations of their behavior," according to Joachim Stoeber and Anna Rambow.

While these might appear to be commendable qualities, particularly in an athlete, they give rise to aversive reactions, including symptoms of DEPRESSION, a PERCEPTION of parenting pressure, and an acute FEAR OF FAILURE that can undermine MOTIVATION and physical WELL-BEING. Perfectionists also "exhibit an excessive concern about mistakes, strong self-doubts, and perceive parents as being critical," suggest Daniel Gould et al. Correlations have been found between perfectionism and EXERCISE DEPENDENCE, though, as Amy Hagan and Heather Hausenblas record in the conclusion to their study, "the CAUSE and effect of this relationship is unknown." In other words, the dependence could cause the perfectionism, or vice versa.

Perfectionists' responses to criticism or milder forms of negative FEEDBACK, such as that which invariably follows sub-par performance are to perceive a threat and experience state anxiety. Even a prospective COMPETITION can prompt AVOIDANCE because, as Mark Anshel and Hossein Mansouri point out: "They [perfectionists] perceive evaluative situations as opportunities for failure."

Yet there is a paradox, Stoeber and Rambow's conclusions being that "not all aspects of perfectionism are neurotic, unhealthy or maladaptive. On the contrary, striving for perfection can form part of a healthy pursuit of excellence" (neurotic is an adjective relating to neurosis, which is a relatively mild mental disorder not caused by any known neurological or organic dysfunction, and which can involve ANXIETY, DEPRESSION, OBSESSIVE-COMPULSIVE tendencies and hypochondria). The findings are reinforced by Stoeber et al. who argue that, among the benefits of perfectionist strivings were an improvement in SELF-CONFIDENCE.

Some scholars separate two forms of perfectionism, adaptive and maladaptive, though much of the relevant research casts doubts on such a clear division and suggests more of a superimposition, both adaptive and maladaptive tendencies being evident in the same people at the same time.

Further reading

Anshel, Mark H. (2004). Sources of disordered eating patterns between ballet dancers and non-dancers. *Journal of Sport Behavior,* 27, 115–34.

Anshel, Mark H. and Mansouri, Hossein (2005). Influences of perfectionism on motor performance, affect and causal attributions in response to critical information feedback. *Journal of Sport Behavior,* 28, 99–125.

Gould, Daniel, Dieffenbach, Kristen, and Moffett, Aaron (2002). Psychological characteristics and their development in Olympic champions. *Journal of Applied Sport Psychology,* 14, 172–204.

Hagan, Amy L. and Hausenblas, Heather A. (2003). The relationship between exercise dependence symptoms and perfectionism. *American Journal of Health Studies,* 18, 133–7.

Stoeber, Joachim and Rambow, Anna (2007). Perfectionism in adolescent school students: Relations with motivation, achievement, and well-being. *Personality and Individual Differences,* 42, 1379–89.

Stoeber, Joachim, Otto, Kathleen, Pescheck, Eva, Becker, Claudia, and Stoll, Oliver (2007). Perfectionism and competitive anxiety in athletes: Differentiating striving for perfection and negative reactions to imperfection. *Personality and Individual Differences,* 42, 959–69.

See also: ANOREXIA ATHLETICA; ANOREXIA NERVOSA; BODY IMAGE; DELIBERATE PRACTICE; DEPRESSION; EATING DISORDERS; EXERCISE DEPENDENCE; FEAR OF FAILURE; MASTERY; OVERLEARNING; OVERTRAINING SYNDROME; SELF-CONFIDENCE; WEIGHT CONTROL

PERFORMANCE ENHANCEMENT

While the term "performance enhancement" has migrated into popular usage as a synonym for DOPING, it actually refers to any method, legal or illegal, of heightening, intensifying, or exaggerating the qualities or value of an athlete's performance (the term is derived from a combination of the Old French *parfourmer*, from *par*, for "to completion," and *fournier*, "to furnish" or "provide," and *enhauncer*, meaning "to exaggerate"). To be pedantic, a more accurate term would be training enhancement because most aids are ergonomic in effect: they help athletes work more efficiently in their environments. Most performance enhancers enable an athlete to train harder and longer.

The concept of performance enhancement has its origins in the late nineteenth and early twentieth centuries when biomedical scientists took an interest in competitive athletes. John Hoberman argues that science was specifically interested in studying athletes who were pushing their bodies to what were then assumed to be the boundaries of physical exertion. While there was no intention to use science to assist performance, the possibility of augmenting sport with science and technology was an attractive one. Some sports, particularly cycling, were already making use of pharmaceuticals to assist performance. As early as 1886, a cyclist named Arthur Linton collapsed and died after taking stimulants, though the most famous early case of a drug-related case was that of Thomas Hicks, a marathon winner at the 1904 Olympic games who took strychnine during the race (while known principally as a poison, the vegetable alkaloid was also used as a stimulant).

From the 1920s, the increasing emphasis on results rather than participation changed the ethos of competitive sports in a way that invited efforts to enhance training methods and performances. Dianabol, an anabolic steroid first produced in 1958, was used by the US weightlifting team in the 1950s and 1960s. Other sports also used drugs which were quite permissible at the time. The CONCEPT of performance enhancement was later to become synonymous with doping, but, from the 1960s, several other methods of expediting peak performances were introduced, most importantly in preparation.

Many athletes turned to AUTOGENIC and related forms of progressive RELAXATION, including HYPNOTISM. APPLIED SPORT PSYCHOLOGY is a resource used widely by athletes. It could even be argued that believing in god became a type of performance enhancement. After all, a devotee of a RELIGION who believes he or she is being guided toward victory by an omniscient being enjoys a competitive edge!

Sports apparel and footwear became more explicitly oriented to enhancing performance in the 1970s: Nike launched its "Tailwind" range in 1978. This incorporated air-inflated soles to cushion the impact of the striking the ball of the foot. While the technology behind it seems primitive by today's standards, it signaled the beginning of a RIVALRY among sportswear manufacturers producing ergonomic clothing. Aerodynamic body suits for sprinters and swimming outfits made from a synthetic fiber modeled on sharkskin (which has striations to allow rivulets of water to run across it) became commonplace.

Technologies of the body, while not specifically designed to enhance competitive performance, were tailored to suit the requirements of athletes. Laser surgery to correct vision, replacement joints, and prosthetics were among the many items available to general populations that were refined to meet athletic needs.

While it stretches the point unreasonably, training itself is performance enhancement and a form which, at times during the nineteenth century just before the rise of organized sport, would be tantamount to cheating. It was suggested that athletes who trained were trying to procure an advantage over those who chose not to train.

Further reading

Hoberman, John M. (1992). *Mortal engines: The science of performance and the dehumanization of sport*. New York: Free Press.

Kilpatrick, Marcus, Bartholemew, John and Riemer, Harold (2003). The measurement of goal orientations in exercise. *Journal of Sport Behavior*, 26, 212–136.

Russell, William, Pritschet, Brian, Frost, Beth, Emmett, John, Pelley, T. J., Black, Judy, and Owen, Jill (2003). A comparison of post-exercise mood enhancement across common exercise distraction activities. *Journal of Sport Behavior*,26, 368–83.

See also: ADRENALINE RUSH; AROUSAL; BIOFEEDBACK; CENTERING; DOPING; EXPECTANCY; GOAL ORIENTATION; HOPE; MOOD; MOTIVATIONAL CLIMATE; PSYCHING; SELF-CONFIDENCE; SELF-ENHANCEMENT; SUPERSTITIOUS BEHAVIOR

PERIPHERAL NERVOUS SYSTEM

Nervous system outside the brain and spinal cord.

See also: NERVOUS SYSTEM; SKILL EXECUTION

PERSONALITY

The singular, unique, and distinguishing character of a sentient being is personality. Beyond this most rudimentary definition, there is no agreement on what constitutes a personality, what purposes it serves, what consequences it has, and, indeed, whether it exists at all. Against this absolute lack of accord on a definition, it is impossible to draw a coherent statement on the question of what impact personality has on sport and exercise. Are certain personality types attracted to exercise? Do some personalities excel at sports? Will some personality types inevitably drop out or fail? An APPROACH to these and related questions is to consider how the term "personality" has been conceptualized in various theories. These theories cluster into four main groups: psychodynamic; trait; behaviorist; and constructivist.

Theory 1: Psychodynamic. These derive from the classic work of Sigmund Freud (1856–1939) and Carl Gustav Jung (1875–1961) and have been refined by the likes of Alfred Adler (1870–1937), Erich Fromm (1900–80), Karen Horney (1885–1952) and R. D. Laing (1927–89) among many others. Basic differences forbid a neat summary, though there is agreement on the existence of an entity called the personality that develops over time and is significantly affected by childhood experiences. Conflicts below the threshold of consciousness are a considerable motivating force in psychological development and how the individual deals with such conflicts contributes toward the integration of the distinct personality. In a sense, the way we repress, displace, or, in other ways, adapt to opposing desires and controls shapes the personality.

Theory 2: Trait. Assumptions about the existence of a personality structure (id, ego, and superego) were anathema to later psychologists who insisted on studying only observable phenomena. Trait theorists, in particular, concentrated on how personality is expressed through behavior. Stable patterns observed over time revealed consistent properties, or traits, that collectively provided a picture of an individual's personality. The guiding idea behind the trait approach was to formulate a matrix of identifiable personality factors. Hans Eysenck's THEORY of universal personality types exemplifies this. According to Eysenck (1916–97), everyone can be located somewhere on his schema, which includes the now-famous introvert–extravert dimensions. Eysenck's theory is firmly in the hereditarian tradition in that personality traits are inherited rather than produced through social exchange.

Theory 3: Behaviorism. Both theories 1 and 2 hypothesized that there was an entity called a personality, something that affected the way subjects thought and behaved; it was a permanent feature of a person's psychological makeup. By contrast, other theoretical approaches either cast doubt on the existence of a personality, or regarded it as a protean CONCEPT, changing constantly to suit different environments.

Behaviorists in particular, spurned any reference to what they regarded as an obscure internal entity, the existence of which could only be inferred from observable behavior. Consistent patterns of behavior, tendencies, and tastes were the outcome of contingencies of reinforcement. In other words, the environment determines who we are and what we become. There are variations on this, one being that we are originally *tabula rasa*, blank tablets on which experience is inscribed. In this view, humans have a largely passive role. "Softer" versions of the approach assign a greater role for COGNITION: human beings, unlike other creatures, can actively select stimuli in their environments and choose how he or she will respond to them.

Theory 4: Constructivist theories. The behaviorist approach broke from the conventional wisdom that personality originates in individuals and remains, in some form, with them for life. Constructivist approaches accepted the emphasis on environment or CONTEXT but explored the pivotal role of social interaction. Our personality, or, more accurately, personalities (we may have several), is constructed through day-to-day, moment-to-moment exchanges with others, who function as audiences. Subjects are actors, envisioning themselves as they imagine others see them and adjusting their language and behavior in such a way as to pull off a successful impression. This impression management is made possible by *reciprocity of perspectives*: Humans constantly try to see themselves not only as others see them but also as others see them imagining how they see them. This is what we mean when we refer to SELF-AWARENESS—not just awareness of ourselves but of how others are seeing and thinking about us. Personality, in this theory, is not a fixed entity but a process that is forever being negotiated between subjects and the people they mix with (their audience) in a process of RECIPROCITY.

Performance implications. Even this extremely brief and undeveloped summary of the main theoretical groups suggests profound differences in the concept of personality. The differences militate against any conclusions on whether it has an effect on recruitment, involvement, and performance in sport and exercise. If personality is a relatively permanent entity that produces certain patterns of thought and behavior, then there is a possibility that it affects participation in sports. In fact, Thomas Miller et al. believe personality is one of the three key concepts, which must be considered: "Preparing an athlete for an athletic career requires at least three areas of CONCENTRATION: first an extensive examination of the personality the athlete brings to sport and COMPETITION is needed." (The others are the athlete's "learning style," and a practical program that maximizes the athlete's potential.)

Other scholars, such as Heather Deaner and John Silva, cast doubt on the importance of personality. They dismiss many of the mooted relationships, including "the idea that certain individuals are born with psychological characteristics that predispose them to select into certain sports."

Deaner and Silva consider a number of other approaches, including Silva's own *personality and performance pyramid* that proposes that all sorts of personality types enter sport. But as athletes move up the pyramid toward elite levels, only those with "adaptive personality characteristics" advance. Physical abilities are more evenly matched at higher levels, so personality becomes significant. The authors argue that those athletes with patience, EMOTIONAL CONTROL, and SELF-CONFIDENCE are better able to make the transition upwards because their personalities equip them well when making adjustments, even after setbacks. Athletes who clearly lack patience as well as CONTROL but still make it to the top are exceptions, according to Deaner and Silva. This theory as well as several others is based on mapping features of personalities. The ICEBERG PROFILE, for example, predicts that athletes who have low scores on tension, DEPRESSION, ANGER, fatigue, and confusion but high on vigor are likely to be successful. The premise of both theories is the trait MODEL of personality.

Nor has personality proved a reliable indicator in the study of exercise behavior. For instance, K. E. Milton's study of women in an exercise program concluded that personality did not moderate exercise-induced MOOD enhancement. Yet, Ryan Rhodes and Kerry Courneya examined the effect of personality on exercise INTENSITY and concluded that personality played a strong role in the exercise domain and one that insisted on further attention.

There is so little agreement on what personality actually is that it would be astonishing if any link could be found. While the trait theory is serviceable and lends itself to research on personality and performance, a constructivist account would contend that the personality is actually in a process of construction during an athlete's career in sports or exercise and that, far from being a fixed entity, the personality is a negotiated process that continues through a career and beyond. Such is the disparity between conceptions of personality. Inadequate as it seems, the only safe and credible conclusion is that sports and exercise attract a diversity of personalities and, while those that ascend to elite levels may exhibit certain consistent features, or traits, it remains uncertain whether they possessed them at early stages or acquired them as they progressed.

Further reading

Deaner, H. and Silva, J. M. (2002). Personality and sport performance. In J. M. Silva and D. E. Stevens (Eds.) *Psychological foundations of sport* (pp. 48–65). Boston, Mass.: Allyn & Bacon.

Hampson, S. (1996). The construction of personality. In A. M. Colman (Ed.), *Companion encyclopedia of psychology* (Vol. II, pp. 602–21). London and New York: Routledge.

Miller, Thomas W., Ogilvie, Bruce, and Adams, Jeanine (2000). Sports psychology: Issues for the consultant. *Consulting Psychology Journal: Practice and Research*, 52, 269–76.

Milton, K. E., Lane, A. M., and Terry, P. C. (2005). Personality does not influence exercise-induced mood enhancement among female exercisers. *Journal of Sports Medicine and Physical Fitness*, 45, 208–13.

Rhodes, Ryan E. and Courneya, Kerry S. (2003). Relationships between personality, an extended theory of planned behaviour model and exercise behaviour. *British Journal of Health Psychology*, 8, 19–36.

See also: ATHLETIC IDENTITY; COGNITION; EXERCISE BEHAVIOR; EXERCISE IDENTITY; GOAL ORIENTATION; IDENTITY; MENTALITY; MOOD; PROFILING; RELATIONSHIP; SELF; SELF-AWARENESS; TEAM PLAYER; THEORY OF PLANNED BEHAVIOR; TYPE A

PERSONALITY ASSESSMENT

While there is historical and contemporary debate about what exactly constitutes a PERSONALITY, attempts have been made to appraise, evaluate, and measure this elusive concept by means of instruments known collectively as personality assessment. Matt Jarvis believes that, when we examine "such topics as attitudes, AGGRESSION, MOTIVATION and ANXIETY, what we are really interested in is how and why people differ in these aspects, and how we can modify these to improve athletic performance." In other words, the search for answers should begin with an assessment of the personality (and Jarvis's chapter "Personality Characteristics and Sporting Behaviour" provides an effective introduction to this).

Many personality assessments are based on an INVENTORY: a list of items to which the subject is asked to respond by indicating those that apply to him or herself, for example, "Yes," No," "Questionable." Or, the subject is presented with two pairs of statements and invited to choose which one best applies to him or her. Likert Scale testing involves asking subjects to reply to statements, usually with choices such "agree," "uncertain," "strongly disagree," and so on.

First used in 1942, the Minnesota Multiphasic Personality Inventory became one of the most popular personality assessments, consisting originally of 550 statements about feelings and behavior. Subjects were asked to indicate the ones with which they agreed/disagreed. Several different scales, each designed to assess different personality facets were spawned from the original test. The Cattell Sixteen Personality Factor Questionnaire (16PF) used a factor analysis that facilitated the identification of the sixteen "first order" factors of personality. From these, "second order," or surface traits could be traced. These included ANXIETY, independence and several other traits that appeared to be important to success in sports.

This APPROACH was adapted for sports. The Athletic Motivation Inventory attempted to measure personality traits associated with sports performance. Aggression, DRIVE, LEADERSHIP, EMOTIONAL control, and MENTAL TOUGHNESS were among the traits used in the instrument, though the results were inconclusive, underscoring the fact that, if there is a cluster of personality traits linked to success in sports, a way of discovering them has not yet been found.

"Sport personology" is the term used by William Morgan to characterize the search for a personality that provides a predictor of athletic performance. There is a basic disagreement between those who continue the search and those who believe it is futile. Many contemporary researchers take the middle ground, accepting that evidence from personality assessment reveals that there are certain personality features shared by successful athletes. But, these cannot be used to identify those who will ultimately become successful because personality is only one of a great many factors that contribute to athletic success.

Further reading

Jarvis, Matt (2006). *Sport psychology: A student's handbook*. London and New York: Routledge.

Morgan, W. P. (1980). Sport personology: The credulous–skeptical argument in perspective. In W. F. Straub (Ed.), *Sport psychology: An analysis of athlete behavior*, 2nd edn (pp. 330–9). Ithaca, N.Y.: Mouvement.

See also: AGGRESSION; ANXIETY; EMOTIONAL CONTROL; LEADERSHIP; MENTAL TOUGHNESS; PERSONALITY; PROFILE OF MOOD STATES; TEMPERAMENT

PERSONALITY DISORDER

Umbrella term to cover range of maladaptive behavior patterns.

See also: PSYCHOPATHOLOGY

PHENOMENON

The word is from the Greek *phainomenon*, meaning a thing appearing to view, and this is still basically the main sense in which it is used—with reference to an apparent fact or situation, especially one that invites or even demands an explanation, such as the IMPOSTOR PHENOMENON, or the SELF-HANDICAPPING phenomenon. Sometimes a CONSTRUCT is described as, for example, a psychological phenomenon, or a social phenomenon, describing the source of its causes, though the provenance of many phenomena is a matter of dispute and something like AROUSAL can be simultaneously a physiological, emotional, and psychological phenomenon, depending on how it is investigated.

In popular parlance, a phenomenon often describes something fantastic or extraordinary. Similarly, in sport, the abbreviation, *phenom* is an athlete with extraordinary, prodigious TALENT, usually a young person who outperforms older and more experienced colleagues—a *wunderkind* (from the German for wonder child, of course). *Epiphenomenon* means a byproduct.

Further reading

Hanoch, Yaniv and Vitouch, Oliver (2004). When less is more: Information, emotional arousal and the ecological reframing of the Yerkes-Dodson law. *Theory and Psychology*, 14, 427–52.

Kumar, Shamala, and Jagacinski, Carolyn M. (2006). Imposters have goals too: The imposter phenomenon and its relationship to achievement goal theory. *Personality and Individual Differences*, 40, 147–57.

See also: ADHERENCE; APPLIED SPORT PSYCHOLOGY; CONCEPT; CONSTRUCT; IDIOGRAPHIC; IMPOSTOR PHENOMENON; META-ANALYSIS; NOMOTHETIC; SELF-FULFILLING PROPHECY; SELF-HANDICAPPING; TALENT; THEORY; YERKES-DODSON LAW

PHYSICAL SELF-PERCEPTIONS

Physical self-perceptions refer to the awareness we have of our own bodies: specifically, the way we imagine them, our satisfaction or dissatisfaction with them, how we rate our physical competence, our capacity to perform specific tasks, and how we regard our health and FITNESS. It has clear repercussions in our eating habits, exercise patterns, and overall physical maintenance. Compare this with PHYSICAL SELF-WORTH, which emphasizes a changing evaluative process affecting overall conceptions of SELF-ESTEEM.

Physical self-perceptions are often related to mental WELL-BEING, according to Adrian Taylor and Ken Fox, whose study into the effects of an exercise program revealed that exercise resulted in significant improvements in physical self-perceptions, especially in middle-aged and older people. Interestingly, the changes were associated with reductions in body fat but not with improvements in fitness PARAMETERS.

The way we perceive our own physical bodies is not a straightforward process, but rather like standing in a hall of mirrors: Our perceptions are reflections of how we believe others are perceiving and judging us. So physical self-perceptions are in many respects our perceptions of others' perceptions.

Further reading

Taylor, Adrian and Fox, Ken R. (2005). Effectiveness of a primary care exercise referral intervention for changing physical self-perceptions over 9 months. *Health Psychology,* 24, 11–21.

See also: ATTRIBUTION; BODY IMAGE; BODY LANGUAGE; COGNITION; EXERCISE DEPENDENCE; EXERCISE MOTIVATION; PERCEPTION; PHYSICAL SELF-WORTH; SELF-EFFICACY; SOCIAL PHYSIQUE ANXIETY; VISUAL PERCEPTION

PHYSICAL SELF-WORTH

This represents that aspect of a person's overall SELF-ESTEEM that is reliant on physical appearance. As such, it is more susceptible to change than the combined, overall or "global" self-esteem, which is how we value ourselves in all dimensions, not just in terms of physical appearance.

Martin Hagger and Nikos Chatzisarantis envision physical self-worth at the lower levels of a hierarchy of self-esteem, in a way suggested in the 1980s by K. R. Fox and C. S. Corbin. Experiences at this level "effect [bring about] change in upper levels, while the upper levels are used as a source of information for motivational decisions in specific exercise experiences."

So, for example, a person's overall evaluation of him- or herself will influence decisions whether or not to APPROACH an exercise or diet regimen, and the resultant changes in strength, body shape, and physical competence will trigger modifications in his or her global self-esteem. If the changes are agreeable, then the person's physical self-worth is likely to influence further involvement in exercise. In other words, there is interaction between the various levels.

Determining physical self-worth is not just a perceptual process; it is judgmental, sometimes incorporating excessive criticism, which can lead to maladaptive responses, including EATING DISORDERS and EXERCISE DEPENDENCE.

Katherine Bond and Joanne Batey argue, perhaps contentiously that physical self-worth is especially pertinent to the exercise experiences of women: "Exerciser SCHEMA may be more strongly related to exercise intentions and behavior for women than men, because of the importance of physical attractiveness/self-worth for women."

A study of aerobic instructors by Cecilie Thøgersen-Ntoumani and Nikos Ntoumanis built on the view that exercise leads to improved levels of physical self-worth but added the qualifying reminder that this was likely only if the exercise was intrinsically motivated. The research pointed up the centrality of autonomy to physical self-worth. If the exercise is, in some measure, regulated through external means, then the impact is not so beneficial.

If an individual is prone to comparing his or her body with some cultural ideal, such as a size-zero model, or a muscular 22 body mass index, and sees a persistent discrepancy that elicits a negative EMOTION, then BODY SHAME is said to result.

Further reading

Bond, Katherine A. and Batey, Joanne (2005). Running for their lives: A qualitative analysis of the exercise experience of female recreational runners. *Women in Sport and Physical Activity Journal*. 14, 69–73.

Fox, Kenneth R. and Corbin, C. B. (1989). The physical self-perception profile: Development of preliminary validation. *Journal of Sport and Exercise Psychology*, 11, 408–30.

Hagger, Martin and Chatzisarantis, Nikos (2005). *The social psychology of exercise and sport*. Maidenhead: Open University.

Thøgersen-Ntoumani, Cecilie and Ntoumanis, Nikos (2007). A self-determination theory approach to the study of body image concerns, self-presentation and self-perceptions in a sample of aerobic instructors. *Journal of Health Psychology.* 12, 301–15.

See also: ANOREXIA NERVOSA; BODY IMAGE; BODY SHAME; BULIMIA NERVOSA; EATING DISORDERS; EXERCISE BEHAVIOR; EXERCISE MOTIVATION; EXTRINSIC MOTIVATION; INTRINSIC MOTIVATION; OBESITY; PHYSICAL SELF-PERCEPTIONS; SELF-DETERMINATION THEORY

POSITIVE AFFECT

In psychology, an affect refers to an EMOTION or desire that influences behavior. The word is from the Latin *afficere,* meaning "to influence." Hence, a positive affect is an affirmative or constructive emotional state that disposes someone to act in a certain way. Sarah Pressman and Sheldon Cohen unpick this as "the feelings that reflect a level of pleasurable engagement with the environment [...] such as happiness, joy, enthusiasm, and contentment."

On this view, there two forms: *trait* positive affect, which is a relatively stable disposition, and *state* positive affect, which is a short-term bout of positive emotions. Negative affect describes the opposite set of dispositions.

Martin Seligman and Mihaly Csikszentmihalyi speculate that "optimism and HOPE affect health [...] positive affective states may have a direct physiological effect that retards the course of illness." The evidence, however, is more equivocal, as Pressman and Cohen point out. Positive affect may directly influence changes in health practices, including better SLEEP, diet, and exercise; it encourages restorative practices, such as RELAXATION and "spending time in natural environments," which, in turn, help reduce STRESS and negative affective responses to stress. But there is no concrete evidence of a direct connection between positive affect and the propensity to exercise, less still to adhere to exercise programs and realize the manifold benefits.

Further reading

Pressman, Sarah D. and Cohen, Sheldon (2005). Does positive affect influence health? *Psychological Bulletin*, 131, 925–71.

Seligman, Martin E. P. and Csikszentmihalyi, Mihaly (2000). Positive psychology: An introduction. *American Psychologist*, 55, 5–14.

See also: EXERCISE BEHAVIOR; FITNESS; FLOW; HEDONIC TONE; HOME ADVANTAGE; HOPE; LUCK; MOOD; NEGATIVITY; RELAXATION; STREAKS; WELL-BEING

PRACTICE

Regular and routine application of a GOAL-directed procedure.

See also: DELIBERATE PRACTICE

PREGNANCY

Pregnancy describes the condition of having children or young developing in the uterus. The word combines the Latin *prae*, meaning "before," and *gnasci*, "be born," and is sometimes used figuratively to suggest "full of" (for example, full of meaning or significance, as in "a pregnant pause").

Until relatively recently, physical activity was not prescribed for women during pregnancy; in fact, in the late nineteenth and early twentieth centuries, it was stringently discouraged. Women were warned that concerted physical activity would damage their chances of ever becoming pregnant.

Menstruation was seen as a form of invalidity, as Patricia Vertinsky observes: "Puberty for boys marked the onset of strength and enhanced vigor; for girls it marked the onset of the prolonged and periodic weaknesses of womanhood."

Sport and exercise were unsuitable areas of activity for all women, who, according to medical opinion, possessed a finite amount of energy and, unlike men, were "taxed" biologically with special energy demands necessitated by menstruation and reproduction. Vertinsky quotes from prescriptive article in an 1892 edition of *Popular Science Monthly* which recommended just one form of exercise for women—"homely gymnastics," that is, housework.

Improbably, research in 2007 by Lisa Chasan-Taber et al. found that "household activity comprises a substantial portion of physical activity and, over the course of pregnancy, accounts for a larger proportion of total activity as exercise and occupational activity decrease." So, in the absence of other forms of exercise, vacuuming and dusting still provided a decent workout, especially during pregnancy.

Just being pregnant has several similar effects to exercise, as Don-Louise Martens et al. point out: "Physiological changes resulting from pregnancy are similar to cardiovascular and respiratory adaptations to exercise." While other research has indicated that there are losses in strength and, VO^2_{max} in the six week postpartum, or post-natal, period, the reasons for this are, as E. P. Roetert suspects, "probably a reflection of the changes in the mother's responsibilities when becoming a parent."

Echoing a great many other research findings, Martens et al.'s results utterly contradict the earlier cautions about the dire consequences of physical exertion: "Exercise during pregnancy can benefit both the mother and the fetus in a normal, uncomplicated pregnancy."

One of the specific ways is to shorten the often-prolonged second stage and prevent urinary incontinence through training the pelvic-floor muscles. Research by, among others, Kjell Salveson and Siv Mørkved defuses early warnings that strong pelvic floor muscles can obstruct labor and, according to Sandra Hines and her colleagues, can actually help build SELF-EFFICACY. This is an important finding: it indicates how exercise during pregnancy can induce psychological changes that complement the physiologically beneficial ones.

For example, a parturient woman can gain over 30 pounds (13.6 kilograms), one effect of which is to stretch the skin. Post-natal exercise assists WEIGHT CONTROL and skin tone, perhaps leading to a sense of fulfillment. "The favorable changes in body satisfaction [...] attest to the positive role exercise may play in contributing to maternal health and psychological well-being," report Sylvia Marquez-Sterling et al., who studied both the physical and psychological changes in primigravidae (women who are pregnant for the first time) after exercising.

"Women who exercise during pregnancy report less STRESS, ANXIETY, and increased SELF-ESTEEM in comparison to women who do not exercise regularly," the research team points out, though without specifying the mechanisms. Clearly, the enhanced body satisfaction is a strong mediating factor, but so too are the "sense of CONTROL" afforded by exercise and the social interactions at the gym.

This conclusion squares the circle. It does something considered impossible perhaps as recently as fifty years ago, by providing evidence that exercise, far from being detrimental, brings positive physical and psychological effects to pregnant women.

Further reading

Chasan-Taber, L., Freedson, P. S., Roberts, D. E., Schmidt, M., and Fragala, M. S. (2007). Energy expenditure of selected household activities during pregnancy. *Research Quarterly for Exercise and Sport*, 78, 133–6.

Hines, Sandra H., Seng, J. S., Messer, K. L., Raghunathan, T. E., Diokno, A. C., and Sampselle, C. M. (2007). Adherence to a behavioral program to prevent incontinence. *Western Journal of Nursing Research*, 29, 36–55.

Marquez-Sterling, S., Perry, A. C., Kaplan, T. A., Halberstein, R. A., and Signorile, J. F. (2000). Physical and psychological changes with vigorous exercise in sedentary primigravidae. *Medicine and Science in Sports and Exercise*, 32, 58–62.

Martens, DonLouise, Hernandez, Barbara, Strickland, George, and Boatwright, Douglas (2006). Pregnancy and exercise: Physiological change and effects on the mother and fetus. *Strength and Conditioning Journal*, 28, 78–82.

Polman, R., Kaiseler, M. and Borkoles, E. (2007). Effect of a single bout of exercise on the mood of pregnant women. *Journal of Sports Medicine and Physical Fitness*, 47, 103–11.

Roetert, E. Paul (2005). Fitness and pregnancy. *Strength and Conditioning Journal*, 27, 21–2.

Salvesen, Kjell Å. and Mørkved, Siv (2004). Randomized controlled trial of pelvic floor muscle training through pregnancy. *British Medical Journal*, 329, 378–80.

Vertinsky Patricia (1990). *The eternally wounded woman: Women, doctors and exercise in the late nineteenth century.* Manchester: Manchester University Press.

See also: AEROBIC/ANAEROBIC; ANXIETY; BODY IMAGE; DEPRESSION; EXERCISE MOTIVATION; FITNESS; SELF-EFFICACY; SOCIAL PHYSIQUE ANXIETY; WEIGHT CONTROL; WELL-BEING

PREMACK PRINCIPLE

A proposition advanced in the 1950s by David Premack (1925–), stating that if any two behaviors differ in their probability of occurrence, the more probable will reinforce the less probable. REINFORCEMENT is relative, not absolute. While reinforcers were conventionally regarded as stimuli which, when presented, strengthened the preceding response, Premack postulated that it was more helpful to conceptualize reinforcers as the responses or activities themselves. So, for example, an English football player may be contracted to receive a cash bonus of £1,500 per GOAL (not an uncommon arrangement). It is not the cash incentive (a stimulus) that reinforces the player's scoring of goals, but the spending of the money (an activity). Any activity a human, or, for that matter, any organism, performs can reinforce any other activity the organism engages in less frequently.

Premack arrived at his conclusions after an experiment in which he offered children the choice of operating a pinball machine or eating candy. The children who liked candy increased their rate of operating the pinball machine if playing the machine led to eating candy. So, eating candy reinforced playing the machine; one behavior reinforced the other. But the children who preferred playing pinball to eating candy ate more candy only if this enhanced their chances of playing pinball.

Among Premack's conclusions was that there was a hierarchy of reinforcement and, for any given subject, any activity in the hierarchy may be reinforced (that is, made more probable) by any activity above it and may *itself* reinforce any activity below it. Parents intuitively and, perhaps, unwittingly, subscribe to the principle when they allow their children to play computer games or watch DVDs only after they have completed homework.

The hierarchy is not static. Premack discovered that the children who liked playing pinball more than candy eventually became hungry, at which point the "reinforcement relation" reversed itself. Eating candy reinforced playing pinball. Another experiment involved rats. Food reinforced running for a hungry rat, but running reinforced eating if the rats were fully fed but had been locked up and unable to run around for a long time. Our football player may eventually become so wealthy that he becomes like the satiated rat; but his scoring rate tails off, causing his pride to suffer. The example is strained, but he might seek the private counsel of a professional yogi with expensive fees to help him rediscover the goal touch. Scoring goals would then reinforce spending money.

Further reading

Premack, David (1959). Toward empirical behavior laws: I. positive reinforcement. *Psychological Review,* 66, 219–33.

Premack, David (1962). Reversibility of the reinforcement relation. *Science,* 136, 255–7.

See also: APPLIED SPORT PSYCHOLOGY; EXTRINSIC MOTIVATION; INCENTIVE; INTRINSIC MOTIVATION; MOTIVATION; REINFORCEMENT; REWARD; TASK/EGO ORIENTATION

PREPERFORMANCE ROUTINES

Sequences of action that, as David Foster et al. put it, "involve cognitive and behavioral elements that *intentionally* help regulate AROUSAL

and enhance CONCENTRATION [...] and thus induce optimal physiological and psychological states."

The stress on *intentionally* is to distinguish such routines from rituals
that unintentionally activate arousal states immediately before a
competitive situation. These include SUPERSTITIOUS BEHAVIOR, which,
according to Michaéla Schippers and Paul Van Lange, is effective
in "regulating psychological tension," and can be "an inherent part of
mental and physical preparation to an important match in which
the outcome is rather uncertain." But the causal mechanisms of
superstitions are not known and cannot be understood as intentionally directed, on Foster et al.'s definition.

Preperformance ANXIETY is a common condition and it can manifest in, for example, FEAR OF FAILURE. This may be deactivated by a
variety of measures, including CENTERING and SELF-TALK. Those with
no FEAR and abundant SELF-CONFIDENCE, on the other hand, usually
manifest preperformance COMPOSURE. Harry Prapavessis et al. note a
preperformance strategy conspicuous among particular athletes: "SELF-
ENHANCEMENT via the generation of pre-performance handicaps is
most characteristic of individuals with high SELF-ESTEEM."

Further reading

Foster, David J., Weigand, Daniel A., and Baines, Dean (2006). The effect of
removing superstitious behavior and introducing a pre-performance routine
on basketball free-throw performance. *Journal of Applied Sport Psychology*,
18, 167–71.

Prapavessis, Harry, Grove, J. Robert, and Eklund, Robert C. (2004). Self-
presentational issues in competition and sport. *Journal of Applied Sport
Psychology*, 16, 19–40.

Schippers, Michaéla C. and Van Lange, Paul A. M. (2006). The psychological benefits of superstitious reiturals in top sport: A study among top
sportspersons. *Journal of Applied Social Psychology*, 36, 2532–53.

See also: ANXIETY; AROUSAL; CENTERING; COMPOSURE; EMOTION; NERVOUSNESS;
SELF-ENHANCEMENT; SELF-HANDICAPPING; SELF-TALK; SUPERSTITIOUS BEHAVIOR;
VISUOMOTOR

PROFILE OF MOOD STATES (POMS)

Originally designed by D. M. McNair et al. in 1972 to assess the
psychological states of psychiatric patients, this sixty-five-item self-

report questionnaire has been widely used in sport and exercise psychology to gain a representation of athletes' moods before and during COMPETITION.

The research instrument is used in real situations. This is important, as Matt Jarvis points out: "An athlete's mood at any one time is a product of both PERSONALITY and situation; therefore, [POMS is] a much more valid measure of their psychological state during performance."

There are six mood dimensions, or graduated ranges of values for: tension, DEPRESSION, ANGER, vigor, fatigue, confusion. Athletes report their scores on each of these. Several studies indicated that a particular pattern of scores emerges for successful athletes. They score low at each end of the scale and high in the middle ranges, so that graphically their moods resemble an iceberg. Tracey Covassin and Suzanne Pero's results were consistent with several other studies over the years. They concluded: "Winning tennis players in this study exhibited higher vigor scores than losing tennis players [. . .] Not only did the winning tennis players exhibit the ICEBERG PROFILE, but they also had lower total mood disturbance scores than losing tennis players."

This meant that, when faced with an adverse situation, such as serving at break point, a successful player would, as the authors put it, "shake it off" that is, their MOOD remained undisturbed. By contrast, less successful players were susceptible to significant and potentially damaging mood changes.

Further reading

Covassin, Tracey and Pero, Suzanne (2004). The relationship between self-confidence, mood state, and anxiety among collegiate tennis players. *Journal of Sport Behavior*, 27, 230–9.

Jarvis, Matt (2006). *Sport psychology: A student's handbook*. London: Routledge.

LeUnes, Arnold and Burger, Jolee (1998). Bibliography on the profile of mood states in sport and exercise psychology research, 1971–98. *Journal of Sport Behavior*, 21, 53–71.

McNair, D. M., Lorr, M. and Droppelman, L. F. (1972). *Profile of mood states manual*. San Diego, Calif.: Educational and Industrial Testing Service.

See also: ICEBERG PROFILE; INDIVIDUAL ZONES OF OPTIMAL FUNCTIONING; INVENTORY; MOOD; NEGATIVITY; NOMOTHETIC; PERSONALITY ASSESSMENT; PROFILING; RELAXATION; SELF-RATING; TELIC DOMINANCE

PROFILING

The process of selecting salient psychological characteristics of a person and integrating these into a coherent image that can guide inquiry and enable predictions. The person in question may be hypothetical. Police profilers who construct representations of criminals from evidence of their crimes and behavioral traits to assist investigations are often featured in television shows and films, though, as Angela Torres et al. point out, "the main goal of profiling in real investigations is to narrow the scope of a suspect pool rather than to identify a single guilty criminal."

In sports, the effort is to assess the capabilities of someone in a particular sphere of activity or to assist in identifying a specific sub group from which certain types of people might be drawn. The origins of the term "profile" are obscure but probably lie in the Italian *profilare*, to draw in outline.

The purpose of profiling in sports is to build a metaphorical sketch of an athlete based on his or her physical, technical, tactical, and psychological competencies and moods and applies this in several ways, all designed to enhance performance. Profiles have been used to interesting effect in the assessment of EMOTION. For example, the PROFILE OF MOOD STATES (POMS) was used to build a representation of an athlete's EMOTIONAL state just before COMPETITION. The subject would be asked to describe his or her state in terms of: tension, DEPRESSION, ANGER, vigor, fatigue, and confusion.

In one of the more successful applications of PERSONALITY ASSESSMENT research, W. P. Morgan used POMS with Olympic wrestlers and found members typically exhibited an ICEBERG PROFILE. They tended to score highly on vigor, lower on anger and fatigue and much lower on tension, depression, and confusion. Expressed graphically, with the states defining a horizontal axis, an iceberg shape surfaces. Aspiring or less proficient athletes would probably show other variations, such as having too much tension or too little vigor. Profiles help establish a representation of an optimal set of states, moods or properties. From this, deviation can be measured to assess how far individuals need to change before they APPROACH the desired profile.

A different approach to profiling is to study the development of the key psychological characteristics shared by certain groups, for example, Olympic champions. Daniel Gould et al. were interested in how profiles are nurtured, particularly by family and coaches. Their effort was to study "a complex system made up of a variety of factors of influence," rather than a static picture. Identifying these factors is a retrospective study, reflecting back on experiences.

But, as a predictive device, profiling has limitations. For example, there have been extensive attempts to investigate suicide bombers using profiling methods. After extensively reviewing them, Meytal

Grimland et al. conclude: "Psychological profiling of suicide bombers has not yet been successful." Instead, Grimland et al. suggest "a shift to the study of the processes of propagation, screening, and training of suicide terrorists and selection of individuals for LEADERSHIP roles"—in other words, how ideas are disseminated and promoted and how individuals are assessed for suitability, then trained and prepared for specific roles: a resocialization (as in religious conversations or similar revelatory experiences).

Further reading

Gould, Daniel, Dieffenbach, Kristen, and Moffett, Aaron (2002). Psychological characteristics and their development in Olympic champions. *Journal of Applied Sport Psychology,* 14, 172–204.

Grimland, Meytal, Apter, Alan, and Kerkhof, Ad (2006). The phenomenon of suicide bombing: A review of psychological and nonpsychological factors. *Crisis,* 27, 107–18.

Morgan, W. P. (1979). Prediction of performance in athletics. In P. Klavora and J. V. Daniels (Eds.), *Coach, athlete and the sport psychologist* (pp. 173–86). Champaign, Ill.: Human Kinetics.

Torres Angela N., Boccaccini Marcus T., and Miller Holly A. (2006). Perceptions of the validity and utility of criminal profiling among forensic psychologists and psychiatrists. *Professional Psychology: Research and Practice,* 37, 51–8.

See also: CONSTRUCT; EMOTION; ICEBERG PROFILE; INVENTORY; NOMOTHETIC; PERSONALITY; PROFILE OF MOOD STATES; SOCIALIZATION; TYPE A

PROPRIOCEPTION

This refers to stimuli produced and perceived within an organism; it describes the actions of sensory systems involved in providing information about the position, location, orientation, and movement of the body. The main groups of proprioceptors are: (1) in the vestibular system of the inner ear and (2) the somatosenses, comprising the kinesthetic (associated with muscles and joints) and cutaneous (relating to skin) systems.

Interoceptive stimuli are produced from within, particular in the viscera and other internal organs, whereas exteroceptive stimuli are external to the organism. Teleceptive stimuli are from distant environments.

KINESTHESIA is often used interchangeably with proprioception, though it specifically describes the awareness of the position and movement of parts of the body by means of sensory organs in the joints and muscles.

"Proprioceptive awareness of postures and movements is most required during the learning of new skills," writes Barry Stillman, who provides the example of touch-typing.

> By being conscious of what is happening an individual can more readily (that is, consciously) change how it is happening. As learning proceeds and the typing movements are refined, afferent FEEDBACK signals from the participating body segments are systematically stored in the brain as templates of properly executing typing movements.

(Afferent means conducted toward, for example, the central NERVOUS SYSTEM.)

Paul Ford et al. studied the execution of a soccer skill, observing, "There is evidence that with extensive practice a performer's reliance on sensory information, such as response-produced visual feedback, decreases." They call proprioception "an online source of feedback" and suggest that, in skilled performers, it operates independently without the need for information such as KNOWLEDGE OF RESULTS. This is why players often report on knowing they have scored a goal from the moment they kicked the ball, or boxers knowing they have scored a knockout the instant their punch landed.

Further reading

Ford, P., Hodges, N. J., Huys, R. and Mark Williams, A. (2006). The role of external action-effects in the execution of a soccer kick: A comparison across skill level. *Motor Control*, 10, 386–4–4.

Stillman, Barry C. (2002). Making sense of proprioception: The meaning of proprioception, kinaesthesia and related terms. *Physiotherapy*, 88, 667–646.

See also: BIOFEEDBACK; CONCENTRATION; FEEDBACK; INFORMATION PROCESSING; KNOWLEDGE OF RESULTS; MEMORY; MOTOR REACTION; NERVOUS SYSTEM; PAIN; SELF-AWARENESS; SKILL; SKILL ACQUISITION; SKILL EXECUTION

PSYCHING

Preparing mentally for a competition or any kind of challenging task is known as psyching. There are two varieties: *psyching up* typically involves heightening AROUSAL to an optimum state in an effort to enhance performance; *psyching out* means intimidating a rival, usually by exuding SELF-CONFIDENCE or by behaving in an overbearing manner before COMPETITION.

"Psyching-up refers to self-directed cognitive strategies used immediately before or during SKILL EXECUTION," write David Tod et al. in their 2003 article. Techniques are extremely varied. They can involve listening to pep talks, GOAL SETTING, SELF-TALK, and even, according to one study, reading information on posters. Strong vocal support from FANS is often thought to confer a home field advantage in competition, though the value of this as pre-competition psyching is in doubt.

Personal accounts of psyching up in sport are many. They range from listening to music or doing breathing exercises to punching teammates. Such accounts, as Aidan Moran points out, "are useful in highlighting the importance of arousal CONTROL to athletes." The empirical support, however, is more equivocal. The value of psyching up is strongest in sports or training that involve gross motor skills, weight-lifting and weight-training being obvious examples; though, even here, the research results are contested (compare, for instance, O. A. Adegbesan's study of competitors at the Nigerian University Games with Michael McGuigan et al.'s study of squat exercisers).

Evidence for psyching out is entirely anecdotal (rather than based on systematic research). BODY LANGUAGE can be an unintentional psyching out tactic: just appearing relaxed and ebullient can send out daunting nonverbal signals. Deliberately seeking to gain an advantage by either overawing, discouraging, or intimidating an opponent before a competition by fair (if occasionally disputable) means has been practiced for decades, though it has been called psyching out only since the 1960s, the heavyweight boxer Sonny Liston pioneering a method of staring opponents down during preliminaries. Liston's famous EYE MOVEMENT virtually challenged opponents to glare back or, as was often the case, avert their gaze. Even Muhammad Ali, who took the world title away from Liston in 1964 and gave the impression of being brash, later admitted, "Just before the fight, when the referee was giving us instructions, Liston was giving me that stare. And I won't lie; I was scared."

Perhaps the finest example of a psyching strategy that backfired was that of Butch Lewis, manager of boxer Michael Spinks, who, in 1988, prepared to fight Mike Tyson. As is customary in world title match-ups, a representative of the opponent is permitted to watch as a fighter bandages his hands. In his book *Tyson*, Peter Heller recounts how Lewis noticed a lump in Tyson's bandage and insisted the whole hand be unwrapped and rebandaged. It was a tactic Lewis believed would irritate Tyson and gain an advantage for Spinks. Instead, Tyson grew furious. After Lewis left the locker room, Tyson promised "I'm gonna hurt this guy." He did. With barely controlled ANGER, Tyson dismantled his opponent in only ninety-one seconds.

Further reading

Adegbesan, O. A. (2001). Analyses of psyching-up techniques used with athletes in Nigerian universities. *Journal of the International Council for Health, Physical Education, Recreation, Sport and Dance*, 37, 50–2.

Hauser, T. (1997). *Muhammad Ali: His life and times*. London: Pan Books.

Heller, Peter (1990). *Tyson*. London: Pan Books.

McGuigan, Michael R., Ghiagiarelli, Jamie, and Tod, David (2005). Maximal strength and cortisol responses to psyching-up during the squat exercise. *Journal of Sports Sciences*, 23, 687–94.

Moran, Aidan P. (2004). *Sport and exercise psychology: A critical introduction*. London and New York: Routledge.

Tod, David, Iredale, Fiona, and Gill, Nicholas (2003). "Psyching-up" and muscular force production. *Sports Medicine*, 33, 47–58.

Tod, D. A., Iredale, F. K., McGuigan, M. R., Strange, D. E. O., and Gill, N. (2005) "Psyching-up" enhances force production during the bench press exercise. *Journal of Strength and Conditioning Research*, 3, 599–604.

Tosches, Nick (2000). *Night train: The Sonny Liston story*. London: Hamish Hamilton.

See also: AGGRESSIVENESS; ANGER; AROUSAL; AUTOGENIC; BODY LANGUAGE; CENTERING; EYE MOVEMENT; FEAR; HOME ADVANTAGE; HYPNOSIS; IMAGERY; MOTIVATION; PEAK PERFORMANCE; PERFORMANCE ENHANCEMENT; PREPERFORMANCE ROUTINES; SANDBAGGING; SELF-TALK; VISUOMOTOR; YOGA

PSYCHOLOGICAL SKILLS INVENTORIES

Instruments designed to measure the psychological expertise associated with sports are psychological skills inventories, an INVENTORY being a detailed list of properties (from *inventorium*, Latin for things discovered). As the name suggests, the skills to be discovered are not, for example, deftness, footwork, timing, and so on, but ACHIEVEMENT MOTIVATION, CONTROL, CONCENTRATION, CONFIDENCE, MOTIVATION, team orientation, and so on.

Many of the inventories measure how well athletes cope with ANXIETY and STRESS, while others assess receptivity to coaching advice and ability to fit into a coherent team structure (that is, becoming a TEAM PLAYER rather than remaining an individual). Among the most discussed are M. J. Mahoney et al.'s Psychological Skills Inventory for Sports, R. E. Smith et al.'s Athletic Coping Skills Inventory and P. R. Thomas et al.'s Test of Performance Strategies (TOPS). TOPS was one of the most ambitious instruments that assessed athletes in COMPETITION as well as in training. The eight factors that measured psychological behavior during practice were: activation, attentional CONTROL, AUTOMATICITY, EMOTIONAL CONTROL, GOAL SETTING, IMAGERY, RELAXATION, and SELF-TALK. More specific measures include the Sport Competition Anxiety Test, which, as its name suggests, was devised to measure the tendencies to become anxious during competition.

As with other forms of SKILL, psychological skills can be studied and learned, and athletes can become adept at INTERVENTION techniques that help him or her adjust levels of AROUSAL, use IMAGERY and GATING procedures.

Further reading

Mahoney, M. J., Gabriel, T. J., and Perkins, T. S. (1987). Psychological skills and exceptional athletic performance. *The Sport Psychologist*, 1, 181–99.

Smith, R. E., Schultz, R. W., Smoll, F. L. and Ptacek, J. T. (1995). Development and validation of a multidimensional measure of sport specific psychological skills: The athletic coping skills inventory—28. *Journal of Sport and Exercise Psychology*, 17, 379–98.

Thomas, P. R., Hardy, L. and Murphy, S. (1996) Development of a comprehensive test of psychological skills for practice and performance. *Journal of Applied Sport Psychology*, 8, supplement S119.

See also: ACHIEVEMENT MOTIVE; AROUSAL; AUTOMATICITY; COGNITIVE-BEHAVIORAL MODIFICATION; CONCENTRATION; CONTROL; DELIBERATE PRACTICE; EMOTIONAL CONTROL; GATING; GOAL SETTING; IMAGERY; INVENTORY; MOTIVATION; PSYCHOLOGICAL SKILLS TRAINING; SELF-CONFIDENCE; SELF-TALK

PSYCHOLOGICAL SKILLS TRAINING

As the term suggests, psychological skills training (PST) means inculcating or educating people in the minor and largely hidden competences rather than the major conspicuous tasks associated with success in sport, or any field of endeavor.

In 1987, Michael Mahoney et al. identified ANXIETY management, CONCENTRATION, SELF-CONFIDENCE, MOTIVATION, mental preparation (PSYCHING up), and team orientation as critical psychological skills.

Over the years since, these have been included in several psychological skills inventories. Other psychological skills include the abilities to maintain attentional FOCUS, to keep emotions under CONTROL, and to combat irrational FEAR.

The premise of PST is that excellence in sport is not based primarily on TALENT or quantitative changes in training but, rather, the result of many small psychological skills that are incorporated into training routines. This was the view of D. Chambliss as presented in his paper "The Mundanity of Excellence" in 1989. In other words, he argued, the key to achieving excellence was in honing psychological skills. This was an unexciting prospect, but outstanding performance came through dull routines rather than exciting breakthroughs. More recent studies by, among others, Richard Thelwell et al. demonstrate the efficacy of PST in effecting small, incremental improvements, rather than dramatic changes in performance.

From this perspective, GIFTEDNESS, which is assumed to be an inherent quality and thus not learnable, is far less important than attending to instruction and undertaking painstaking practice over a period to gain the requisite mental skills. This is conveyed in the root of the word training: *trahere*, which is Latin for "draw," and which was used in the sense of causing a plant to grow in a desired shape.

Further reading

Chambliss, D. (1989). The mundanity of excellence: An ethnographic report on stratification and Olympian swimmers. *Sociological Theory*, 7, 70–86.

Mahoney, M. J., Gabriel, T. J., and Perkins, T. S. (1987). Psychological skills and exceptional athletic performance. *The Sport Psychologist*, 1, 181–99.

Thelwell, Richard C., Greenlees, Iain A., and Weston, Neil J. V. (2006). Using psychological skills training to develop soccer performance. *Journal of Applied Sport Psychology*, 18, 354–270.

See also: COGNITIVE-BEHAVIORAL MODIFICATION; CONCENTRATION; DELIBERATE PRACTICE; EMOTIONAL CONTROL; GIFTEDNESS; INTELLIGENCE; INVENTORY; OVER-LEARNING; PSYCHOLOGICAL SKILLS INVENTORIES; SELF-CONFIDENCE; SELF-TALK; SKILL ACQUISITION; SOCIALIZATION; TALENT

PSYCHOPATHOLOGY

The term is used to describe the investigation of maladaptive patterns, or abnormalities, which have no known biological agents in their etiology but which have causes in what used to be known as "mental disorders"; these are now particularized as, for instance, personality disorders. *Patho* is Greek for suffering, or disease, and *ology* denotes a branch of knowledge or study. So, neuropathology, for example, studies and treats disorders of the NERVOUS SYSTEM. There are analogous pathologies, such as plant pathology, which, as its name implies, is dedicated to the specialized study of diseases in trees, shrubs, and mosses and so on. Social pathology involves the investigation of, as Mihaly Csikszentmihalyi instances, "tripling of violent crimes, family breakdown" and other conditions that precipitate social conflict.

In the 1980s, W. P. Morgan proposed "that success in sport is inversely correlated with psychopathology," a suggestion that gave rise to the MENTAL HEALTH MODEL of sport. Subsequent attempts to test this NOMOTHETIC theory provided little support and found no presence of psychopathology among unsuccessful athletes. Psychologists tended to emphasize the more positive aspects of sport and exercise, according to Charles Brown, who, in 2001, wrote: "Sport psychology focuses on strengths and solutions rather than pathology."

Despite this, sport and exercise psychology increasingly addresses conditions that were previously beyond its remit. Not only do several psychopathological states intersect with pathways of direct concern but some pathological conditions have origins, if not in sport and exercise, in cognate areas.

When Richard M. Ryan and Edward Deci write that, "Social contexts that engender conflicts between basic needs set up the conditions for alienation and psychopathology," they suggest how cultural and psychological factors combine to produce pathologies that can manifest in issues of direct concern to sport and exercise psychology. For example, there is a close RELATIONSHIP between sport, exercise, and what Donald Williamson et al. call "pathological eating concerns and habits." EATING DISORDERS share many features with other compulsive behaviors that occupy sport and exercise psychologists, EXERCISE DEPENDENCE and ANOREXIA ATHLETICA being the most obvious.

When Thomas Miller et al. report that, "Pathological GAMBLING among athletes may also reflect characteristics of OBSESSIVE-COMPULSIVE disorder," they highlight another problematic pattern of behavior which may have origins in "conflicts between basic needs," but which is catalyzed by involvement with sport.

Participation in competitive sport can also conceal pathologies. Andrew Roffman's discussion of ANGER approaches this issue: "Whether the behavior is deemed acceptable, pathological, or criminal is dependent on the CONTEXT of appraisal." Assaulting someone on a football field may appear to be a manifestation of frustration and may be condemned but comprehended as part of the game. It could also be an expression of a player's underlying psychopathological condition and one that also manifests in other contexts.

Further reading

Brown Charles H. (2001). Clinical cross-training: Compatibility of sport and family systems psychology. *Professional Psychology: Research and Practice*, 32, 19–26.

Csikszentmihalyi, Mihaly (1999). If we are so rich, why aren't we happy? *American Psychologist*, 54, 821–7.

Miller, T. W., Adams, J. M., Kraus, R. F., Clayton, R., Miller J. M., Anderson, J., and Ogilvie, B. (2001). Gambling as an addictive disorder among athletes. *Sports Medicine*, 31, 145–52.

Morgan, W. P. and Johnson, R. W. (1978). Psychological characteristics of successful and unsuccessful oarsmen. *International Journal of Sport Psychology*, 11, 38–49.

Roffman, Andrew E. (2004). Is anger a thing-to-be-managed? *Psychotherapy: Theory, Research, Practice, Training*, 41, 161–71.

Ryan, Richard M. and Deci, Edward L. (2000). Self-determination theory and the facilitation of intrinsic motivation, social development, and well-being. *American Psychologist*, 55, 68–78.

Williamson, Donald A., White, Marney A., York-Crowe, Emily, and Stewart, Tiffany M. (2004). Cognitive-Behavioral Theories of Eating Disorders. *Behavior Modification*, 28, 711–38.

See also: ANGER; ANOREXIA ATHLETICA; ANOREXIA NERVOSA; APPLIED SPORT PSYCHOLOGY; BULIMIA NERVOSA; DEPRESSION; EXERCISE DEPENDENCE; KINESIOPHOBIA; MENTAL HEALTH MODEL; OBSESSIVE-COMPULSIVE; PERSONALITY; REHABILITATION; STRESS; THERAPY

RACE

Once accepted as an objective biological category, the concept of race, or "race" as many prefer (quotation marks denoting its indefinite status), is now usually considered as a belief held by those who consider the world's human population divisible into discrete, natural units. The units are known as "races" and the inference is that they are ordered hierarchically, some "races" occupying a position of preeminence over others—such a belief and the action it precipitates is racism. This is a definition that avoids the controversies over the ontology of race. Accepted by some as a fact and rejected by others as a fiction, the CONCEPT has engaged scholars and politicians for decades, even centuries.

One thing is certain: that the belief in race has been one of the great motivating and bedeviling doctrines of modern times. "We do not define races because biological data compels us so to do," writes Kenan Malik in his *The Meaning of Race: Race, History and Culture in Western Societies*. "Rather society begins with an a priori division of humanity into different races for which it subsequently finds a rationale in certain physical characteristics." In sports, as well as elsewhere, beliefs about the existence and effects of races and the guiding rationale behind such beliefs have precipitated debates and conflicts.

Racial issues 1: Prejudice and intelligence. In an essay published in 1973 to introduce his edited volume *Psychology and Race*, Peter Watson identified two central areas of interest to the psychologist: (1) prejudiced attitudes and discriminatory behavior; (2) INTELLIGENCE and race. Even now, the basic questions remain. Why does racism persist in a CONTEXT where it is discouraged and condemned? Are some populations designated races, endowed naturally with less intelligence than others? Both questions have relevance in sports. Stanley Eitzen adds a third: "Does sport reduce or exacerbate racial tensions?"

Psychology, sociology, political science, and the panoply of other disciplines that have tried to answer why prejudice exists have concluded that it is learned through childhood SOCIALIZATION and peer-group interaction, which are, in turn, influenced by the overall social context. Some arguments suggest that, as a species, we are predisposed to discriminate, if only for purposes of adaptive survival. Exactly *how* we discriminate, for example, because of skin color or other phenotypical (observable) characteristics, is learned, often from an early age. This may be reinforced if we move in circles that prevent or limit actual experience of groups/things that are the object of prejudice. Remember, the word prejudice means literally that: a judgment made before (pre-) experience.

Debates over whether INTELLIGENCE is inherited rather than learned have a history that dates back to the early twentieth century. In the 1960s and 1970s, the research of Arthur Jensen (1923–) in the USA and Hans Eysenck (1917–97) in Britain linked this to race by asserting that "Negroes" scored less well than whites in IQ tests and that this was due primarily to genetic, rather than social, factors. The argument gained fresh impetus in the 1990s with the publication of Richard Herrnstein and Charles Murray's *The Bell Curve: Intelligence and Class Structure in American Life* (Simon & Schuster, 1994).

Both these issues were reflected in sports. Arguments about "stacking," or allocating certain ethnic minorities to particular playing positions, came to the fore in the 1970s. It was argued by many that teachers, coaches, administrators, and other, mainly white, groups assigned black players to playing positions that required speed and power rather than tact and ingenuity. Basing evaluations on *stereotypes* (images based on false or incomplete information) rather than first-hand knowledge, those responsible for DECISION-MAKING would "ghettoize" African Americans and Britain's African Caribbeans on the sportsfield.

A justification for this was the "natural ability" argument. Black people had for long been known to possess sporting prowess and its source was presumed to be natural. The symmetry between this and the race–IQ argument is readily apparent. As Marek Kohn writes: "One consequence of admitting that human groups may have significant bodily differences [. . .] is that it implies the possibility of differences in the brain." The assumptions underlying this argument were racist; they were based on the premise that races existed and that some races were naturally suited to some tasks rather than others.

Racial issues 2: Myths and compensation. John Hoberman's book *Darwin's Athletes* bears the subtitle "How sport has damaged black America and preserved the myth of race". In it, he unravels the racist logic that maintains that blacks are natural athletes. He also shows how this entraps all but the few black athletes who make it to elite levels, in low-level jobs *and* provides continuing evidence for the view that blacks are ill equipped for more intellectual activities. Black athletic achievement is "haunted by the Law of Compensation," as Hoberman calls it, "an inverse relationship between mind and muscle, between athletic and intellectual development."

Hoberman supplies an answer of sorts to Eitzen's question about whether sport reduces or exacerbates racial tensions: it glosses over them. Every new black superstar appears to be a triumph for black people, but, in reality, just conforms to the Law of Compensation. Most black people continue to struggle.

Because race has been such a contested concept, its meaning has changed and will, according to Kohn, continue to change. It is "malleable." Contemporary scientists who subscribe to beliefs in distinct genetic distributions continue to lend credibility to the notion that there are races. Other analysts emphasize the power of culture in shaping population differences. Approaching the concept of race as a culturally sustained belief does not deny the possibility of actual variations, variations that may have genetic sources. It acknowledges that there is a RELATIONSHIP between biological varia- tion and cultural belief, at the same time suggesting that it is the belief rather than difference that makes most impact on human con- duct.

This has not prevented the term "race" appearing in research lit- erature, usually as a synonym for African Americans or African Car- ibbeans. Herbert Simon, for example, in his discussion of verbal and nonverbal behaviors, contends, "deeply analogous behaviors by athletes of different races receive different interpretations and different sanctions."

In a separate argument, Steven Philipp proposes that the "STRESS of day-to-day living means Blacks may not secure the same degree of benefit from their leisure as White, or that this stress remains present even while engaged in leisure activities," which leads to the conclu- sion, "race and gender are defining features of adolescent leisure experience."

In the latter sense, it is not race as an objective entity that defines the experience, but the subjective impact of being perceived and treated as a member of a different, and possibly inferior, race.

Further reading

Eitzen, D. S. (1999). *Fair and foul: Beyond the myths and paradoxes of sport.* Lanham, Md.: Rowman & Littlefield.

Hoberman, J. (1997). *Darwin's athletes: How sport has damaged black America and preserved the myth of race.* New York: Houghton Mifflin.

Kohn, M. (1996). *The race gallery: The return of racial science.* London: Vintage.

Malik, K. (1996). *The meaning of race: Race, history and culture in western socie- ties.* London: Macmillan.

Philipp, Steven F. (1998). Race and gender differences in adolescent peer group approval of leisure activities. *Journal of Leisure Research*, 30, 214–32.

Simon, Herbert D. (2003). Race and penalized sports behaviors. *International Review for the Sociology of Sport*, 38, 5–22.

Watson, Peter (1974). *Psychology and Race.* Chicago: Aldine.

See also: COMMITMENT; DEVIANCE; GIFTEDNESS; IDENTITY; INTELLIGENCE; SELF- ESTEEM; SELF-FULFILLING PROPHECY; SOCIAL PHYSIQUE ANXIETY; SOCIALIZATION; STEREOTYPE; STEREOTYPE THREAT; TALENT; TEAM PLAYER

REACTION TIME

The minimum time that elapses between the moment an unexpected STIMULUS is presented and the beginning of a motor RESPONSE to it is known as the reaction time (RT). It includes the time of the cognitive processes that link stimulus to response plus the time of noncognitive sensory and motor processes. RT is a generic term to cover several different types, which we will discuss first, before moving on to consider influences on reaction time, such as exercise and age, as well as MENTAL PRACTICE.

Disjunctive reaction time is relevant to most activity-based pursuits as this covers situations in which there are complex stimuli and responses available. It includes *choice* reaction time. In many competitive situations, athletes are presented at unpredictable times, not simply with a single STIMULUS and one response, but also a variety of distinct, fast-changing stimuli and a range of possible responses. The athlete has decisions to make; he or she must select an appropriate response to each of the stimuli. The choice reaction time describes how long it takes the athlete to make and implement the appropriate selections.

Closely related to this is the *discrimination* reaction time. In some situations, an individual must respond to some auditory or visual stimuli and desist from responding to the others. In other words, a rapid discrimination between the various stimuli must be made. In most sports, deception or faking is so commonplace that skilled athletes need to be able to refrain from responding needlessly to dummy stimuli.

Another variant of RT applicable to sports is *complex* (sometimes called *compound*) reaction time where two or more stimuli are available and two or more responses are employed in quick succession or simultaneously. This is common in ball sports where the release or the contact with the ball usually corresponds with other responses.

When the term RT is not qualified by any of the above, it usually refers to *simple* reaction time, in which a single stimulus requires a single response and describes the times between the two. These are rare in sports: a tip-off in basketball in which a tossed ball works as a stimulus for a single response might serve as an example. The starter's gun at the start of a sprint is another—though this is the subject of some dispute, as we will see.

In the early 1950s, research by W. E. Hick found that the more choices we are presented with, the more time we need to react appropriately. Alternatively, P. M. Fitts indicated that, if RT remained constant when the volume of stimuli went up, then accuracy was sacrificed. It was thought that humans had a "capacity-limited INFORMATION PROCESSING channel" and that there would inevitably be a sort of trade-off: speed for accuracy or vice versa.

More recently, other accounts of SKILL EXECUTION have indicated that RT is not so fixed and can be changed through extended repetition in training as well as other means. For instance, research has focused on the impact of aerobic exercise on age-related slow-downs in RT. While the evidence that exercise programs can ameliorate decline in cognitive function is mixed, Courtney Hall et al. indicate the possibility of exercise-induced cognitive improvements, specifically in EXECUTIVE CONTROL functions in the elderly. Executive control is a high-level function associated with the frontal lobe of the brain.

Even mental practice (that is, in the complete absence of motor response) has been shown to be effective in improving reaction time and not only among the elderly, according to George Grouios.

As if to warn against setting finite limits for RT, research has cast doubt on the International Association of Athletics Federation's standard that the fastest possible auditory reaction time is 100 milliseconds (100 × one-thousandth of a second) and that anything quicker is a false start. Matthew Pain and Angela Hibbs dispute this, demonstrating that simple auditory reaction times of under 85 milliseconds are possible.

Further reading

Buodo, Giulia, Sarlo, Michela, and Palomba, Daniela (2002). Attentional resources measured by reaction times highlight differences within pleasant and unpleasant, high arousing stimuli. *Motivation and Emotion*, 26, 123–38.

Fitts, P. M. (1954). The information capacity of the human motor system in controlling the amplitude of movement. *Journal of Experimental Psychology*, 47, 381–91.

Grouios, George (1992). Mental practice: A review. *Journal of Sport Behavior*, 15, 42–59.

Hall, Courtney, D., Smith, Alan L., and Keele, Steven W. (2001). The impact of aerobic activity on cognitive function in older adults: A new synthesis based on the concept of executive control. *European Journal of Cognitive Psychology*, 13, 279–300.

Hick, W. E. (1952). On the rate of gain information. *Quarterly Journal of Experimental Psychology*, 4, 11–26.

Pain, Matthew T. G. and Hibbs, Angela (2007). Sprint starts and the minimum auditory reaction time. *Journal of Sports Sciences*, 25, 79–88.

See also: AEROBIC/ANAEROBIC; AGING; ATTENTION; AUTOMATICITY; COGNITION; CONCENTRATION; DECISION-MAKING; EXECUTIVE CONTROL; EXERCISE BEHAVIOR; INFORMATION PROCESSING; INTELLIGENCE; MEMORY; MENTAL PRACTICE; MOTOR REACTION; NERVOUS SYSTEM; RIVALRY

RECIPROCITY

Mutual exchange, for example, of *perspectives* (points of view or approaches to something); of *feelings* (affection or dislike).

See also: COACH–ATHLETE RELATIONSHIP; PERSONALITY; RELATIONSHIP

REHABILITATION

The process by which someone, or something, is restored either to effectiveness or to a previous condition by training is rehabilitation, a term that comes from the Latin *re*, for again, and *habilitare*, ABILITY. In sport and exercise psychology, the restoration to effectiveness, rather than previous condition is usually the implied meaning. Rehabilitation's associations with recovery from substance abuse and forms of DEPENDENCE are commonplace, though, in sport and exercise, the restoration of FITNESS following INJURY is also rehabilitation.

Allen Cornelius cautions, "After an injury, athletes experience a wide range [of] serious disturbances in MOOD, including DEPRESSION, ANGER, frustration and tension." Every injury is accompanied by some degree of psychological upheaval, and the recovery process necessarily involves restoring, for example, the inclination to compete with INTENSITY rather than ritualistically (that is, to prevent a recurrence of the injury). So psychological INTERVENTION is necessary.

It might be assumed that injured athletes or enthusiastic exercisers would be highly motivated to follow treatment to recover, though, as Marcia Milne and her colleagues reveal, non-adherence rates are in the range of 30–70 percent.

How an individual interprets the injury and the expectations he or she has affect the process, as do environmental and personal factors (such as fellow recovering patients and the PAIN experienced). Milne et al. report that psychological strategies, including GOAL SETTING, HYPNOSIS, RELAXATION, and SELF-TALK, have increased ADHERENCE, though their particular interest is in the impact of IMAGERY and SELF-EFFICACY, which can be linked: "Cognitive imagery is used to rehearse rehabilitation exercises, and motivational imagery is used to CONTROL AROUSAL and increase SELF-CONFIDENCE."

"Imagery can also serve a healing function," state Milne et al. Healing is used here as meaning to make whole (from the Old English *hælen*). Rehabilitating patients can use healing imagery to restore their belief in their own capabilities.

Often injuries result in loss of capacities and a diminution of SKILL or physical capacities. Setting goals for the recovery of skill is often used in conjunction with others, such as acquiring new skills relating to judgment and strategy. These are also helpful attributes in the rehabilitative process itself.

While their study concerned the rehabilitation of coronary patients, Falko Sniehotta et al. stressed the importance of planning, which "may help individuals transform their intentions into behavior and to cope successfully with difficulties." The research team advocates the use of "*in situ* action control," meaning a form of SELF-REGULATION "activated when a behavioral intention has been formed."

To these interventions, we might add BIOFEEDBACK training, RELAXATION and the STRESS-MANAGEMENT TRAINING suggested by D. D. Cupal.

Further reading

Cornelius, A. (2002). Psychological interventions for the injured athlete. In J. M. Silva and D. E. Stevens (Eds.), *Psychological foundations of sport* (pp. 224–46). Boston, Mass.: Allyn & Bacon.

Cupal, D. D. (1998) Psychological interventions in sport injury prevention and rehabilitation. *Journal of Applied Sport Psychology*, 10, 103–23.

Milne, Marcia, Hall, Craig, and Forwell, Lorie (2005). Self-efficacy, imagery use, and adherence to rehabilitation by injured athletes. *Sport Rehabilitation*, 14, 150–67.

Sniehotta, F. F., Scholz, Urte, Schwarzer, R., Fuhrmann, B., Kiwus, U., and Völler, H. (2005). Long-term effects of two psychological interventions on physical exercise and self-regulation following coronary rehabilitation. *International Journal of Behavioral Medicine*, 12, 244–55.

See also: ADHERENCE; AGING; BIOFEEDBACK; DEPENDENCE; DEVIANCE; GAMBLING; HYPNOSIS; INJURY; INTERVENTION; LIFE COURSE; MENTAL TOUGHNESS; SELF-EFFICACY; SELF-REGULATION; SELF-TALK; STRESS-INOCULATION TRAINING; STRESS-MANAGEMENT TRAINING; THERAPY

REINFORCEMENT

The process of strengthening or supporting behavior is reinforcement, a term that is embedded in learning THEORY. As such, the use of the concept implicitly harbors assumptions about the mechanisms involved in learning and ultimately the nature of the human animal. Its application in sport and exercise is diffuse. Most coaches use rewards to reinforce SKILL ACQUISITION and punishment to deter improper behavior; whether they know it or not, they are using reinforcement. EXERCISE BEHAVIOR is often reinforced by the reactions of others to changes in appearance; this has been called social reinforcement, and it is one of several types of reinforcement, the most basic types being positive and negative.

Positive reinforcement describes stimuli that, when presented following a response, increase the probability that the same response will be repeated; the rewards accruing to successful athletics performances are examples. Related to this is *negative* reinforcement, including painful stimuli, like electric shocks or deafening noise, which, when withdrawn emit the desired response. Negative reinforcement is not the same as punishment. The former involves an active deterrent, such as removing the physical distress resulting from a shock, while the latter entails denial of, or withdrawal from access to rewards and decreases the probability of a RESPONSE. For example, giving an animal an electric shock every time it presses a lever will weaken not reinforce the response—this punishes pressing the lever.

Conditioning 1: Classical. The term "reinforcement" has origins in Ivan Pavlov's early twentieth-century experiments with dogs that were inadvertently conditioned to salivate in response to a signal as much as they did to the presence or smell of food. At first, the dogs salivated only when their food arrived—what Pavlov (1849–1936) called an unconditioned response (UR) to an unconditioned STIMULUS (US)—but the continual accompaniment of food with the signal forged an association, so that, even in the absence of food, the dogs salivated when the signal sounded. This was a *conditioned* response: the food (US) functioned as a reinforcer of the response to the conditioned stimulus (CS). Take the food away, and, eventually, the UR becomes extinct. The food satisfies a need or a desire.

In this sense, the reinforcer is a REWARD. Later experiments demonstrated that similar simple rewards could be used to induce rats to push levers and pigeons to perform often elaborate behavior, like "playing" table tennis. The conditioning process described is instrumental, and it works on the basic idea that the reinforcer is *contiguous* to the action. In other words, the reinforcement must take place quickly after the appropriate response. When every response is reinforced in sequence, there is a *schedule* of reinforcement. This is a little too straightforward, however.

Some human behavior does appear to operate according to the same principle. Fan adulation, cash, and sincere congratulations from a coach reinforce an athlete's successful performance, as do compliments about body shape. These may seem like functional equivalents of food for rats: the rats continue to press the right bar, while the athlete or exerciser attempts to reproduce the same behavior that brought him or her rewards—though, of course, they might not. Building cash incentives into contracts, raising prize monies, or awarding medals and extravagant gifts to those who reach goals work as reinforcers. Humiliation, exclusion from honors, and the EMOTION associated with failure may negatively reinforce, or punish, the behavior that brought defeat. Obviously, reinforcement does not work in this regular and predictable fashion.

Conditioning 2: Operant. Athletes do not win every COMPETITION; exercisers do not always hit their targets and draw applause; gamblers do not win every bet. Yet, athletes continue to play, exercisers continue to work out, and gamblers continue to gamble, at least until the losses are so consistent or punishing that they can no longer be sustained. While schedules of reinforcement are effective in developing, modifying, and maintaining many types of behavior, complex human behavior is more difficult. B. F. Skinner (1904–90) experimented with variable interval, compound, and other sorts of variations in schedules of reinforcement. His operant conditioning is one of the most comprehensive explanations available. An *operant* is any instance of behavior that effects a change in the environment, whether it is a rat pushing a lever or a football player scoring; when the operant is brought under the control of a specific stimulus or combination of stimuli, operant conditioning has happened. This is different from simple respondent behavior, which is a direct response to a stimulus, such as Pavlov's dogs' salivation. Operant behavior is controlled by its own consequences (the word *operant* is Latin for "at work"). For instance, left alone, a baby may kick out or cry spontaneously in the absence of stimuli. Once the behavior occurs, the likelihood that it will be repeated depends on the consequences. So, a tennis player who inadvertently changes grip and immediately hits a series of winners is likely to use the same grip again.

One of the premises of this APPROACH is that the human being is plastic, capable of being molded (the Greek *plastikos* means precisely this). Behavior can be modified as long as the necessary schedules of reinforcement can be identified—and, technically, they can be; though, in practice, they are not. Skinner, in particular, has been characterized as basing his theories on the view that the human is a passive receptor of stimuli rather than an active creator of his or her own environment. The tradition dates back to the seventeenth-century philosopher John Locke (1632–1704) and his *tabula rasa* conception of mind, as a "blank tablet" with no innate ideas. Yet, in Skinner's theory and, for that matter, Locke's, the human being is far from passive: in responding to stimuli in the environment, subjects *operate* actively, discriminating, comparing, and combining.

For Skinner, understanding human and, indeed, any animal behavior requires no reference to internal states, such as COGNITION, consciousness, motive, or PERCEPTION. All behavior is subject to the same principle of stimulus–response: As long as the pertinent stimuli and the appropriate schedules are known, any type of behavior is subject to operant conditioning. The emphasis for Skinner and for all those who subscribe to the explanatory power of reinforcement is on the environment—that which lies outside the organism.

Applications in sport. Accordingly, applications of reinforcement theory have focused on changing environmental contingencies, or circumstances, as a way of shaping and maintaining behavior. Desirable behavior is palpable; the chances of making it happen repeatedly can be enhanced by reinforcing it. The results are observable. Inner states, by contrast, are neither palpable nor observable, so followers of reinforcement theory are not interested. Instead, they concentrate on encouraging expedient and discouraging inexpedient behavior. Many coaches, perhaps intuitively, do this: Even something as simple as congratulating athletes after good moves and reprimanding them after errors is reinforcement. More extreme negative reinforcements include benching or not selecting players in team games; punishments might include fining athletes for misdemeanors on or off the province of play. Positive reinforcements are many, of course. Besides the obvious ones already mentioned, there are the less direct rewards that accrue from successful performance: endorsement deals, celebrity status, and the media exposure coveted by so many athletes.

Suppose a successful basketball player is offered the opportunity to host a television show due to start in eight weeks' time at the season's end. His contract with his club stipulates that he needs permission and the club allows him to do the television work, but only if he can finish with 3,000 points, a tough though not impossible task to which he rises splendidly, producing some of his best performances ever. Without realizing it, our player is demonstrating the PREMACK PRINCIPLE. Named after David

Premack (1925–), it states that reinforcement is a relative not absolute PHENOMENON. Chocolate will reinforce a child with a sweet tooth, but if they need to run around the block as fast as they can to get the chocolate, they will run hell for leather. Eating chocolate reinforces running. One activity works as reinforcement for another. The activity of having one's own television show reinforces points scoring for the basketball player.

Unlike this example, much of reinforcement's application in sports has been geared toward the learning of desirable behavior, such as SKILL, and the maintenance of habits that will either improve or preserve that skill. "When a particular goal-directed behavior is repeated frequently and consistently in a similar situation, with positive reinforcement, it eventually becomes automatic or habitual," write Tracey Brickell and her colleagues, outlining the process through which skills become "second nature" and require little attention, only the appropriate contingencies. The skilled behavior "can be elicited by environmental cues without conscious guidance."

In 1997, D. Scott et al. disclosed how a laser beam that let off a beep functioned as a positive reinforcer, signaling a successful pole vault, which eventually led to a modification of vaulting technique. Rewards were used to great effect in a study of golfers' performances by T. Simek et al. (1994). In this study, the golfers behaved rather like satiated rats. After responding to rewards with good play for a while, they came to expect the rewards, and their performance deteriorated abruptly when they were withdrawn.

Sometimes, reinforcement is not immediately apparent. For example, Dave Clarke asks, "Why do problem gamblers continue to gamble when the rewards are few and the consequences such as lack of internal CONTROL are unfavorable?" He argues that excitement, the release of tension, and the approval of others are reinforcements, which, when combined with periodic winning provide variable-ratio schedules of reinforcement; that is, where the ratio between responses and reinforcement varies in some random fashion.

While Skinner might not approve of the migration of reinforcement, the term *social reinforcement* has been used in several contexts, perhaps most effectively in the study of EATING DISORDERS. Donald Williamson et al. for instance, found, "social reinforcement for the thin ideal from family, peers, and the media was correlated with the onset of bulimic symptoms."

The CONCEPT of *vicarious reinforcement* has also been offered to describe the repetition of behaviors that people observe being rewarded when performed by others. This has clear relevance to the understanding of AGGRESSION, observational MODELING, and VICARIOUS

AGENCY, where stimuli and response are inferred. This involves cognitive processes and, as such, is far removed from the purer concept of reinforcement favored by Skinner.

Further reading

Brickell, Tracey A., Chatzisarantis, Nikos L. D., and Pretty, Grace M. (2006). Using past behavior and spontaneous implementation intentions to enhance the utility of the theory of planning behaviour in predicting exercise. *British Journal of Health Psychology*, 11, 249–62.

Clarke, Dave (2004). Impulsiveness, locus of control, motivation and problem gambling. *Journal of Gambling Studies*, 20, 319–45.

Scott, D., Scott, L. and Goldwater, B. (1997). A performance improvement program for an international-level track and field athlete. *Journal of Applied Behavior Analysis,* 30, 573–5.

Simek, T., O'Brien, R., and Figlerski, L. (1994). Contracting and chaining to improve the performance of a college golf team: Improvement and deterioration. *Perceptual and Motor Skills,* 78, 1099–105.

Skinner, B. F. (1938). *The Behavior of Organisms.* New York: Appleton-Century-Croft.

Williamson, Donald A., White, Marney A., York-Crowe, Emily, and Stewart, Tiffany M. (2004). Cognitive-behavioral theories of eating disorders. *Behavior Modification,* 28, 711–38.

See also: AGGRESSION; AUTOMATICITY; CAUSE; CONTROL; FEAR; GAMBLING; INCENTIVE; LEARNED HELPLESSNESS; LOCUS OF CONTROL; MODELING; MOTOR REACTION; NOMOTHETIC; PREMACK PRINCIPLE; REWARD; SKILL; SKILL ACQUISITION; THEORY; VICARIOUS AGENCY

RELATIONAL

Concerns the manner in which two or more persons (and sometimes other things) are connected. It is often used to accentuate how many of the qualities commonly assumed to have an inherent nature or essential property that determines their CHARACTER are, on closer inspection, *emergent,* that is, in the process of becoming and not analyzable simply as a single entity. They emerge as a result of changing combinations of constituent parts. So, studying a COACH–ATHLETE RELATIONSHIP by examining each figure (the coach and the athlete) individually will not allow the insights of an APPROACH that focuses on the connection between the two and perhaps others. For example, Nicole LaVoi suggests how *relational dialectics*—"a system best described by the tug-of-war metaphor"—is a continuously changing tension between the athlete's longing for autonomy and the dyadic connection he or she has with the coach. Focusing on this rather than the individuals concerned enables the analyst to understand why even apparently solid and successful partnerships disintegrate.

LaVoi documents another emergent PHENOMENON, *relational expertise*, which has four dimensions: engagement, empowerment, authenticity (to be open to influence), and conflict and difference. Unlike in traditional approaches, expertise does not lie with one party who passes it on to another but rather expands through the developing relationship.

Similarly, Sophia Jowett and Melina Timson-Katchis write of parent–child *relational transitions*, when they analyze the changing character of a key relationship. The same authors specify that "the three main relational properties that define the coach–athlete relationship" are closeness, COMMITMENT, and complementarity. In a separate study, Pamela Smith and Jennifer Paff Ogle suggest that personal relationships can be used as a *relational currency*, so that people can position themselves as agents of influence among peers.

A *relational base*, as understood by Richard Ryan and Edward Deci, is necessary for the expression of INTRINSIC MOTIVATION in any endeavor. In other words, any individual must have a matrix of relations with others with whom he or she can share the value they take from an activity.

When used as a verb, *to relate to* means to identify or empathize with someone or group and perhaps express concern about that someone or group's position. This process appears in many relational phenomena.

Further reading

Jowett, Sophia and Timson-Katchis, Melina (2005). Social networks in sport: Parental influence on the coach–athlete relationship. *The Sport Psychologist*, 19, 267–87.

LaVoi, Nicole M. (2007). Interpersonal communication and conflict in the coach–athlete relationship. In Sophia Jowett and David Lavalle (Eds.), *Social Psychology in Sport* (pp. 29–40). Champaign, Ill.: Human Kinetics.

Ryan, Richard M. and Deci, Edward L. (2000). Self-determination theory and the facilitation of intrinsic social development, and well-being. *American Psychologist*, 55, 68–78.

Smith, Pamela M. and Paff Ogle, Jennifer (2006). Interactions among high school cross-country runners and coaches: Creating a cultural context for athletes' embodied experiences. *Family and Consumer Sciences Research Journal*, 34, 276–307.

RELATIONSHIP

There are several senses in which the term relationship is used in sport and exercise psychology, all of them based on some kind of bond, connection, or COMMITMENT between two or more constructs, types of behavior, or people. For purposes of clarity, we can APPROACH them in terms of (1) conceptual and (2) human relations.

Relationship 1: Conceptual. Most commonly a relationship between two concepts conveys the way in which they are associated. For example, several studies have concluded that there is a relationship between PERFECTIONISM and procrastination. A type of behavior, for example, GAMBLING, might be related to a CONSTRUCT, such as LOCUS OF CONTROL. In both cases, the relationship is an invisible link that ties the two phenomena together in such a way that change in the one will result in change in the other. This gives rise to different possible types of relationship.

If change in the one always leads to change in the other and this feature remains invariantly under all conditions, then it is assumed that it acts as a CAUSE, in which case there is a *causal relationship*. Donald Williamson et al. for instance, write of the need "to empirically test the extent to which individual traits are causal in the development of EATING DISORDERS." Where there are several possible causal factors to be studied, multicausal relationships are said to exist. When Ann Boggiano describes a "causal relationship among perceived competence, motivational orientation, attibutional style, and achievement processes," she suggests the possibility of several relationships affecting each other, or several combining to produce one causal outcome. There are, as we know, several known causes of cancer, and several more as-to-yet-unknown causes.

Where there is a mutual connection with no clear indication that one causes the other, a CORRELATION is said to exist; as in, for instance, a correlation between pre-game ANXIETY and poor performance. If changes in the one are accompanied by changes in the other, there is a suggestion that changes in one will produce changes in the others, though this is not necessarily implied. For instance, a study might find a correlation between EXERCISE BEHAVIOR and MOOD state. These may well be correlated, but statistics can only suggest this.

When two more phenomena are mutually related, we refer to an *interrelationship*. So, for instance, at a relatively simple level, there is an "interrelationship between physical fitness and activity and cognitive functioning," according to George Rebok and Dana Plude. C. K. John Wang and Stuart Biddle's research, on the other hand, supported a MODEL of several "interrelationships between ABILITY beliefs, GOAL orientations, perceived competence and INTRINSIC MOTIVATION."

Relationship 2: Human. An INTERPERSONAL RELATIONSHIP usually describes the way in which two or more people communicate with each other; this will be affected by the thoughts and feelings they have about the others. *Inter* is Latin for "between." Such relationships often involve RECIPROCITY, that is, the practice of exchanging ideas or goods that affect the GROUP DYNAMICS.

These are often divided into *primary relationships*, which are the kind of durable, lasting relationships a person has with parents, and which are formed during early SOCIALIZATION, and *secondary relationships*, which cover a very wide spectrum of relationships with, for instance, teachers, coaches, mentors, and so on. It is possible that the latter can become the former. For example, an athlete might develop his or her relationship with a coach to the point where there is a strong COMMITMENT that endures beyond the COACH–ATHLETE RELATIONSHIP. While coaches are technically replaceable, the athlete might become so close that the coach becomes, in his or her eyes, irreplaceable.

Relatedness refers to interpersonal relationships that provide feelings of security and comfort and is an integral feature of SELF-DETERMINATION THEORY.

Further reading

Boggiano, Ann K. (1998). Maladaptive achievement patterns: A test of a diathesis–stress analysis of helplessness. *Journal of Personality and Social Psychology*, 74, 1681–95.

Magueau, Geneviève A. and Vallerand, Robert J. (2003). The coach–athlete relationship: A motivational model. *Journal of Sports Sciences*, 21, 883–904.

Rebok, George W. and Plude, Dana J. (2001). Relation of physical activity to memory functioning in older adults: The memory workout program. *Educational Gerontology*, 27, 241–59.

Wang, C. K. John and Biddle Stuart J. H. (2003). Intrinsic motivation towards sports in Singaporean students: The role of ability beliefs. *Journal of Health Psychology*, 8, 515–23.

Williamson, Donald A., White, Marney A., York-Crowe, Emily, and Stewart, Tiffany M. (2004). Cognitive-behavioral theories of eating disorders. *Behavior Modification, 28*(6), 711–38.

RELAXATION

From the Latin *re*, "once more," and *laxis*, "loose," relaxation involves a series of responses to stimuli, including a reduction of ANXIETY and an improvement of MOOD states. Somatically, there is an absence of activity in voluntary muscles, a slowing down of respiratory rate and a reduction of body temperature when the individual is relaxed. The changes in parasympathetic activity are matched by a change in hormonal levels.

The benefits of relaxation have been recognized either as part of an athlete's preparation for a contest or as winding-down technique after COMPETITION, and, less often, a way of restoring COMPOSURE during a contest. It can both enhance performance and reduce the risk of injury. More generally, relaxation has been integrated into workout programs, especially those incorporating YOGA techniques into exercise. Involuntary relaxation may be a troublesome condition for anybody; for it to be effective, it must be a voluntarily induced EMOTIONAL and bodily state.

Relaxation may be active or passive, the former meaning that participants can carry out procedures by themselves. Someone else administers a passive technique. For example, massage is a passive relaxation, as it requires a masseur or masseuse. There are six basic techniques for inducing active relaxation: (1) progressive muscle relaxation (PMR); (2) AUTOGENIC; (3) breathing exercises; (4) hatha yoga stretching; (5) IMAGERY, and (6) MEDITATION. PMR is perhaps most preferred among health professionals, though hatha and other styles of yoga have become popular workout routines at gyms and at home (there are instructional books and DVDs available).

PMR was devised in the 1929 and modified in 1938 by Edmund Jacobson (1883–1983). The procedure involves thinking of muscle groups separately, contracting and tensing the muscles, holding for a few seconds then relenting so that the tension disappears and the muscles go lax and limp. Thought then transfers to other muscle groups—for example, from the left arm to the right—so that groups of muscles are relaxed progressively. As muscle tension is released, so heart and breathing rates decline.

The technique is methodical and needs practice, though experienced exponents can progress through the muscle groups so quickly that, within minutes, they are unable even to grip something as light as a golf tee between their fingers. Relaxing before a COMPETITION or perhaps an important interview is often seen as a method of reaching optimal performance. There are instances of athletes consciously relaxing during a contest. Tennis players, for example, are sometimes seen with their eyes closed or with a towel draped over their heads during changeovers.

Starting in the latter part of the twentieth century, massage became one of the most popular relaxation techniques. Its effects on mood, using a profile-of-mood-states questionnaire, have been documented, and its manifold benefits are widely reported. Exactly how massage works is the subject of some discussion. Pornratshanee Weerapong et al. suggest that the limited research on the subject has led to only inconclusive results. Athletes and exercisers extol the virtues of massage. In particular, "A large number of studies of massage have reported the psychological benefits of massage between events," observe Weerapong et al.

Shahyad Ghoncheh and Jonathan Smith observe how research has concentrated on the *effects* of relaxation on the reduction of non-specific reduced sympathetic arousal. The positive psychological consequences are less uniform across all methods. Ghoncheh and Smith found that different techniques evoke different psychological states and at different intervals. For instance, PMR evoked particular levels of relaxation states (R-states) only after at least four weeks of training, and a further different effect would occur from the fifth week onwards. Yoga stretching evoked R-states at the outset, as well as post-training. There is not a "one-size-fits-all" relaxation method. Even when the somatic effects appear similar, there are significant differences psychologically, raising similar suspicions to the ones Weerapong et al. have about massage. While the researchers do not dispute the reported benefits, they point out that the "mechanisms" through which they work are not completely clear. In other words, relaxation works; we just do not know exactly *how* it works.

Further reading

Ghoncheh, Shahyad and Smith, Jonathan C. (2004). Progressive muscle relaxation, yoga stretching, and ABC relaxation theory. *Journal of Clinical Psychology*, 60, 131–6.

Jacobson, E. (1974). *Progressive relaxation*, 2nd edn. Chicago, Ill.: University of Chicago Press.

Rael Cahn, B. and Polich, John (2006). Meditation states and traits: EEG, ERP, and neuroimaging studies. *Psychological Bulletin*, 132, 180–211.

Weerapong, Pornratshanee, Hume, Patria A., and Kolt, Gregory S. (2005). The mechanisms of massage and effects on performance, muscle recovery and injury prevention. *Sports Medicine*, 35, 236–56.

See also: ANXIETY; AUTOGENIC; BIOFEEDBACK; DEPRESSION; ELECTRO-ENCEPHALOGRAM; ENDORPHINS; EUSTRESS; HYPNOSIS; IMAGERY; MEDITATION; OVERTRAINING SYNDROME; PROFILE OF MOOD STATES; SLEEP; STRESS; YOGA

RELIGION

A religion is an internally coherent system of beliefs that binds a believer to a pattern of worship, OBEDIENCE to a superhuman controlling power, and COMMITMENT to a specific doctrine purporting to explain problems that are germane to the human condition. Its root word *religionis* is Latin for "obligation" or "bond." While religions typically include belief in a transcendental entity, for example, a deity or divinely ordained prophets, some religions, such as Buddhism, do not.

Sport has been considered as a type of religion in the sense that it embodies, as Tara Magdalinski suggests, "shared moral ideals as well as behaviors, and emerges from daily life experiences to provide a means to integrate society." It also provides a sense of unity and belonging and even IDENTITY. But, for many, Magdalinski points out, "the contention that sport is a religious experience is problematic. [There] is a difference between having a religious experience when playing sport and playing sport for the actual purpose of glorifying god."

Both possibilities have psychological implications, which we will consider in sequence.

Sport 1: As spiritual experience. Sport, like religion, offers the opportunity to affirm a sense of IDENTITY and consolidate a presence in a particular group and this has suggested a convergence to several writers. Writing in 2005, for *The Futurist* magazine (January–February, pp. 31–6), Robin Gunston, in his article "Play Ball! How Sports Will Change in the 21st Century," predicted: "Religiosport [as he called it] will have its shrines (stadiums), costumes (uniforms), services (games and events), rituals (chants and songs), high priests (star athletes), and piety (fan loyalty)."

"Religiosport" is probably much older than Gunston imagined. In fact, Nigel Spivey and other historians have revealed that the history of sport itself is colored by *religiosity* (that is, a participation in, or expression of religion). Sporting contests dating from 2000 BCE formed part of religious festivals. Greek culture incorporated COMPETITION into civic and religious life (there was no hard and fast distinction between the two). The Greeks' pursuit of *agôn,* as it was called, was not simply a striving for athletic supremacy, but a quest for recognition in the eyes of the gods. Victory was an accomplishment of literally heroic proportions. We can only imagine what impact this made on MOTIVATION. Religious rituals incorporated practices that resembled COMPETITION in the Mayan culture of Central America: Priests oversaw ball games played near their temples. In Japan, sumo is suffused with religious elements, though Shinto, which dates from the early eighth century, has had the most enduring influence on Japanese sport.

The tradition of linking competition with religion persisted through the eighteenth century. English folk games, which were precursors to football, were played on designated holy days. In the nineteenth century, sports and exercise in Britain and North America were regarded as godly activities, united by the creed of muscular Christianity, a development documented by Tony Money.

Some contemporary scholars—most notably, Michael Novak, in 1976, and Shirl Hoffmann in 1992—have analyzed sport as if it were a functional equivalent of a religion. Its FANS are like body of believers, its symbols and rituals resemble religious ceremonies, and, perhaps most importantly, its meaning to worshippers.

Kathleen Dillon and Jennifer Tait operationalized this type of argument empirically in an attempt to discern the transcendent qualities of experiences when involved in sporting competition. They were especially interested in what happens to athletes when in the ZONE, or experiencing what Mihaly Csikszentmihalyi (1934–) called FLOW. "In this study then spirituality or religiosity will be defined as experiencing the presence of a power, a force, an energy, or a God close to you."

While they found that "being more spiritual in sports is related to being in the zone more often [. . .] the direction of RELATIONSHIP was not known." They found a CORRELATION rather than a causal relationship: "Spirituality may lead to more experiences in the ZONE, or experiences in the zone may lead to more experiences of spirituality."

Even a gym workout can be an occasion for experiencing worthiness, purity and the high moral standards demanded by many religions. As Cheryl Hansen et al.'s study revealed: "aerobic exercise may provide a sense of virtuousness similar to the work ethic demanded by traditional religion."

The research dovetails with that of Richard Ryan and Edward Deci, who argue that religion shares with physical exercise a capacity to satisfy "three innate psychological needs—competence, autonomy, and relatedness—which, when satisfied yield enhanced self-motivation and mental health and when thwarted lead to diminished MOTIVATION and WELL-BEING." So, while research has not revealed experiences of Damascene proportions, there is evidence that a profound sense a belonging and spiritual uplifting can emerge from participating in competitive sport or just exercise.

Sport 2: As glorification. Since the ancient Greek games, religion has continued to inspire athletes. Today, countless winners, when interviewed after a contest, still acknowledge the role of god in their victory; losers typically cite more mundane factors when apportioning blame. Evander Holyfield, a Christian, rarely missed the opportunity to praise god for guiding him safely through contests. Goran Ivanisevich entered Wimbledon 2001 as a wild card and emerged as champion, pronouncing throughout that his progress was guided by God.

Whether or not deities intervene in the earthly matter of sports cannot be known, of course. What can be known is the motivating power of *believing* that a god is "in your corner," so to speak. This can work in several possible ways, not all of them helpful. In Ivanisevich's case, he became convinced after his unlikely successes in the opening rounds of the competition. This enhanced his SELF-CONFIDENCE, so that, by the time he reached the final, he was certain of victory. He was even able to quell his short burst of ANGER midway through the final. The benefits of believing that victory is preordained are that the athlete can APPROACH a competition with an EXPECTANCY of winning; RELAXATION levels will be appropriate, and ANXIETY may not mar the performance. The dangers are that an athlete may become over-confident and lack INTENSITY; when the MOMENTUM of the contest swings against him or her, a trailing athlete may have difficulty getting FOCUS and lose MOTIVATION as the match drifts away. Some rivals of Ayrton Senna, a Roman Catholic, say his belief in an afterlife influenced his devil-may-care style which won him four world motor Formula 1 championships, but was also responsible for his death in 1994, when aged thirty-four.

Fighting in the name of god has a sporting counterpart. The first serious outbursts of fan VIOLENCE, or HOOLIGANISM were witnessed in Glasgow, where fans of the Protestant club, Rangers, clashed with the

Catholic fans of Celtic in the 1960s. Similar sectarian patterns emerged in Liverpool when rival fans of the city's two main clubs, Liverpool and Everton, fought. These fights were among the first instances of a PHENOMENON that was to spread and continue for the following decades.

Some coaches have famously discouraged appeals to god whether as an inspiration or a guiding power. In John Feinstein's *A Season on the Brink*, the onetime Indiana Hoosiers coach Bob Knight confronts player Steve Alford, a believer:

> Steve, you always talk about God. Well, I'm gonna tell you something, Steve, God is not going to provide any LEADERSHIP on this basketball team. He couldn't care less if we win or not. He is not going to parachute in through the roof of this building and score when we need points.

As an afterthought, Knight, who had been raised in a Methodist home and had gone to church every Sunday, asks, "Do you really think that God is going to help a team that *I'm* coaching?'

Further reading

Hansen, Cheryl, Stevens, Larry C., and Coast, J. Richard (2001). Exercise duration and mood state: How much is enough to feel better? *Health Psychology*, 20, 267–75.

Dillon, Kathleen M. and Tait, Jennifer L. (2000). Spirituality and being in the zone in team sports: A relationship? *Journal of Sport Behavior*, 23, 91–100.

Feinstein, John (1989). *A Season on the brink: A year with Bob Knight and the Indiana Hoosiers*. New York: Fireside.

Hoffman, Shirl J. (Ed.) (1992). *Sport and religion*. Champaign, Ill.: Human Kinetics.

Hubbard, S. (1998). *Faith in sports: Athletes and their religion on and off the field*. New York: Doubleday.

Magdalinski, Tara (2007). Sports and religions. In George Ritzer (Ed.), *The Blackwell encyclopedia of sociology* (pp. 4690–3). Oxford: Blackwell.

Money, Tony (1997). *Manly and muscular diversions: Public schools and the nineteenth-century sporting revival*. London: Duckworth.

Novak, Michael (1976). *The joy of sports*. New York: Basic Books.

Ryan, Richard M. and Deci, Edward L. (2000). Self-determination theory and the facilitation of intrinsic motivation, social development, and well-being. *American Psychologist*, 55, 68–78.

Spivey, Nigel (2004). *The ancient Olympics*. London: Oxford University Press.

See also: ATHLETIC IDENTITY; ATTRIBUTION; CELEBRITIES; COMMITMENT; DISCIPLINE; FANS; FLOW; INTRINSIC MOTIVATION; MORAL ATMOSPHERE; SELF-DETERMINATION THEORY; SELF-FULFILLING PROPHECY; SUPERSTITIOUS BEHAVIOR

REM

Rapid eye movement during SLEEP.

See also: SLEEP

RESPONSE

From the Latin *responsum*, for something offered in return, response has several meanings, the principle one in sport and exercise psychology being behavior elicited in reaction to particular circumstances. For example, an EMOTIONAL and physiological AROUSAL might be a response to the threat of painful experience, while the striving for SELF-ESTEEM might be one of a number of self-focused responses. The arrival of a new coach or gym instructor might elicit any number of responses. Literally, any situation can give rise to a response. Typically, those responses are grouped together by the similarity of their effects. This is why we are able to identify, for instance, AVOIDANCE responses as a relatively homogeneous class of behaviors, even though the circumstances that evoked them might be varied.

There are other meanings, the most popular being the excitation of any organism to, or in the presence of, a STIMULUS. Some wish to restrict this to motor or glandular reactions, that is, to eliminate COGNITION from the response. In this sense, response is mechanical; it is involuntary and does not require thinking. This is not the usual sense in which response is used in sport and exercise, which are areas in which no two responses are identical and vary in frequently subtle ways, depending on how individuals interpret circumstances. Think of different versions of a music track. "Toxic," for example, is popularly associated with Britney Spears but has been covered by several other artists, including Mark Ronson and Local H, each of whom has given it their own interpretation, without losing the distinctness that makes the number recognizable. Now, think of sneezing, which is a reflexive, involuntary expulsion of air in response to mild irritation of the nostrils. In sport and exercise, a response is more like a version of "Toxic" than sneezing.

To a survey researcher, a response is likely to refer to the answers—written or verbal—to items on a questionnaire.

Further reading

Buodo, Giulia, Sarlo, Michela, and Palomba, Daniela (2002). Attentional resources measured by reaction times highlight differences within pleasant and unpleasant, high arousing stimuli. *Motivation and Emotion*, 26, 123–38.

Eatough, Virginia and Smith, Jonathan (2006). "I was like a wild wild person": Understanding feelings of anger using interpretative phenomenological analysis. *British Journal of Psychology*, 97, 483–98.

Hale, B. S., Koch, K. R., and Raglin, J. S. (2002). State anxiety responses to 60 minutes of cross training. *British Journal of Sports Medicine*, 36, 105–7.

See also: ANGER; APPROACH; AROUSAL; AVOIDANCE; COGNITION; DEPRESSION; FEAR; PERCEPTION; PERFECTIONISM; POSITIVE AFFECT; REINFORCEMENT; STIMULUS; VIOLENCE

RETIREMENT

Withdrawal from active participation is retirement, a word taken from *re*, "again," and the French *tirer*, "to draw." Every retirement from work involves a loss of some sort. In many cases, it is a welcome loss of obligation, COMMITMENT, and responsibility after several decades and at an age when putting one's feet up appears desirable. But retirement from sport is different. It typically happens after a relatively short period and often at an age when workers outside sport still have plenty of yet-unrealized ambitions. Far from being welcome, the losses can be distressing and occasionally traumatic. But why? Research has suggested it is because of loss of IDENTITY and a forced withdrawal from an addictive lifestyle. We will deal with these before moving to consider the research on the sporting afterlife.

Loss 1: Identity. Considering an athletic career typically begins in childhood and may end, possibly because of INJURY, or erosion of SKILL, any time from the early twenties, an athlete invests a substantial portion of time and dedication in a relatively short period. During that time, an athlete acquires an ATHLETIC IDENTITY, shaped in large part by peers, coaches and managers, and FANS. Departure from sport often means that several of those relationships the athlete has with these groups will disappear.

William Webb et al. suggest that the loss of athletic identity is one of two special factors that distinguish retirement from sport from other sorts of retirement, the other being "the special circumstances of 'early' forced retirements." Webb's research team focused on athletic identity, which has a "unique public nature" in the sense that it carries role obligations to perform in front of a public. "This sort of performance pressure, a defining characteristic of the athlete role, is rarely encountered in other social role enactments," argue Webb et al.

The study was published in 1998, and, it could be argued that it is a lot less rarely encountered in the celebrity-struck twenty-first century, but the overall point is a strong one: that an athlete's identity is "joined to a larger community [and] the collective esteem of this larger community can rise and fall as a result of his/her athletic performance."

Retirement is inevitably disruptive to identity and, as Webb et al. point out, to overall life satisfaction, though a voluntary, as opposed to injury-forced retirement, affords the athlete a measure of CONTROL, and that in itself is a source of some satisfaction and SELF-ESTEEM. The study emphasized the importance of a PERCEPTION of CONTROL over one's destiny and, by implication, the "traumatic and unexpected" loss of control experienced by those who have active careers forcibly terminated.

The sense of loss experienced by retiring athletes is compounded for disabled athletes, according to Jeffrey Martin, who maintains that the psychological depletion is accompanied by a breakdown in social support and the relative inactivity that inevitably follows a departure.

Loss 2: Adulation. When Jay Coakley suggests that "an element of both psychological and physical addiction may also be present," in the athlete's life, he might well refer to the addictive power of having an adulatory audience. This is particularly acute for celebrity athletes who have become inured to media attention and the idolatry of a worshipful fandom. Jeff Pearlman comments of ex-NFL player Dexter Manley's DEPENDENCE: "Addicted to the perks that come with athletic success, he developed an unhealthy dose of narcissistic entitlement."

Even athletes who do not succumb to narcissistically entitled tendencies often have troublesome periods of adjustment. Certainly, the number of athletes who embark on at least one COMEBACK (often more) after announcing their retirement provides at least inferential evidence of dependence.

Loss 3: Structure. Only a minority of retirees transfer seamlessly into media jobs and maintain a highly visible profile. Of the others, many stay in sports, as, for example, managers, coaches, and scouts and, less often, owners. A fulltime career in sports equips its participants with specialist knowledge but only limited applications.

For those who do not succeed in gaining jobs in sport, or who fail in their new capacities, or who simply do not want to stay in sport, the consequences can be grim, according to Barry McPherson, who argues that "PERSONALITY disorders appear as reflected in attempted or successful suicides, alcohol or drug addiction and a general orientation to the past rather than to the present or future."

McPherson also points out that DEVIANCE of one kind or another is not uncommon among ex-pros. Apart from the obvious lack of skills, their SELF-ESTEEM has been structured around athletic performance. Once detached from a culture that has been such a source of identity cues, the retiree approaches an uncertain future in which horizontal or downward mobility are likely. Most athletes earn less and experience a drop in status in retirement. Even those that transfer to movie careers are usually best known for past athletic deeds.

McPherson writes of *skidding*, in which athletes who rarely if ever think about their futures extend their competitive careers for as long as possible, far beyond their peak years, simply because they have no conception of life outside sports. Eventually, they are involuntarily taken out of sports and undergo an abrupt decline in status and earning capacity. Often, they have mismanaged their earnings and have little emotional support from peers or employers once they retire.

Loss 4: Status. The drop in standing following retirement has prompted some writers to call it a social death, meaning that an athlete's status degrades, either suddenly or slowly—some star athletes are allowed longer periods to rediscover form, like a patient given a realistic chance of recovery. Stars are encouraged to indulge in illusions about their career longevity, while less distinguished athletes are simply discarded.

Research on college and amateur athletes, on the other hand, indicates that their retirement is less troublesome. In fact, many look forward to the relief from STRESS and pressure to perform involved in sports. Their adjustment is "mild" rather than severe, according to research by Susan Greendorfer and Elaine Blinde in 1987. Jay Coakley complicates this picture by arguing that: "Leaving sport is not inevitably stressful or identity-shaking, nor is it the source of serious adjustment problems."

Obviously, adjustments are necessary, but most ex-athletes eventually negotiate them. The more serious problems are experienced by those athletes who have not sought credentials outside sport, have restricted their relationships to other athletes, whose families have provided little support for them in nonsports activities. and/or who lack gratifying relationships and activities away from sports. Ethnic and class backgrounds and GENDER all factor into the equation, according to Coakley. For an extreme example, black athletes from poor backgrounds who have not handled their earnings wisely and who have restricted friends and contact to within sports circles are likely to have a problematic adjustment.

Further reading

Coakley, Jay J. (1987). Leaving competitive sport: Retirement or rebirth? In A. Yiannakis, T. D. McIntyre, M. Melnick, and D. P. Hart (Eds.), *Sport Sociology: Contemporary themes*, 3rd edn (pp. 311–17). Dubuque, Iowa: Kendall/Hunt.

Greendorfer, Susan L. and Blinde, Elaine M. (1985). Retirement from intercollegiate sport: Theoretical and empirical considerations. *Sociology Sport Journal*, 2, 101-10.

Martin, Jeffrey J. (1999). Loss experiences in disability sport. *Journal of Personal and Interpersonal Loss*, 4, 225–30.

McPherson, Barry D. (1987). Retirement from professional sport: The process and problems of occupational and psychological adjustment. In A. Yiannakis, T. D. McIntyre, M. Melnick, and D. P. Hart (Eds.), *Sport sociology: Contemporary themes*, 3rd edn (pp. 293–301). Dubuque, Iowa: Kendall/Hunt.

Pearlman, Jeff (2004). After the ball. *Psychology Today, 37*(May/June). Available online at http://psychologytoday.com/articles/pto-20040514–000001.html.

Webb, William M., Nasco, Suzanne A., Riley, Sarah, and Headrick, Brian (1998). Athlete identity and reactions to retirement from sports. *Journal of Sport Behavior*, 21, 338–63.

See also: ATHLETIC IDENTITY; CELEBRITIES; COACH–ATHLETE RELATIONSHIP; COMEBACK; DEPENDENCE; EXERCISE IDENTITY; EXPECTANCY; FANS; IDENTITY; INJURY; RELATIONSHIP; SOCIALIZATION; STRESS

REVERSAL THEORY

Reversal THEORY focuses on how the needs and desires that guide human behavior alternate from one psychological state to another and then back again, reversing to and fro as individuals engage in action throughout the course of a day. In recent years, its application to sport has become influential, posing an alternative to psychological theories that STRESS consistency and stability in human behavior. Reversal theory presumes humans are inconsistent, unstable, and in the process of constant change.

The theory is concerned centrally with MOTIVATION and experience, the latter referring specifically to "how one interprets and responds emotionally to, a given situation," according to Kurt Frey, who gives an example of reversal. In a particular state, a person may want to feel aroused, while, in another state, that person may want to feel calmness or RELAXATION. "However, if one desires to experience high AROUSAL, but does not, one will feel anxious," Frey observes. "Thus different states represent opposite ways of experiencing the same level of a particular psychological variable, such as arousal."

A person's motives can change throughout the course of activity, a process described as METAMOTIVATION. According to reversal theory, metamotivational states occur in pairs of opposites, involving opposite desires and subjective responses. There are four pairs and, at any given time, a person is experiencing a total of four states, one from each pair, though normally one state is "salient." The four active states determine the relationship between their HEDONIC TONE and AROUSAL level; or, expressed another way, what the person wants, how he or she thinks and acts, and the kinds of EMOTION he or she experiences.

The first two pairs of metamotivational states are *somatic* and refer to the process of experiencing one's own body. These consist of the *telic* and *paratelic* states. A football player at the kickoff would be in a state of TELIC DOMINANCE: narrowly GOAL-oriented with a specific aim in mind. In training, or perhaps playing with children, the same person will be much more playful and unfocused, attaching little importance to what he or she is doing, and so experiencing a paratelic state. In a serious game, the competitors may start intimidating each other to the point where players experience ANXIETY. In a casual pickup game, the action may become so slow and placid that they become bored.

The second pair of somatic states is *conformist* and *negativist*, and these relate to means versus ends—in other words, how a person regards rules and conventions that guide behavior in particular circumstances. In a conformist state, people wish to stick within the rules of a game; in a negativist state, they want to break free of any restrictions at all. During COMPETITION, they need to observe rules or RISK censure, of course; at the same time, they commit fouls and perhaps infringe other points of etiquette.

The other two pairs of states are known as *transactional* and describe a person's interactions with the immediate environment, including people. The first pair comprises MASTERY and sympathy states. A person in mastery state interprets an interaction as conflictual power struggle. In any competitive sport, this would be the salient state of athletes. When an athlete is generous, considerate, even caring toward an opponent or teammate (for example, after an INJURY), there is evidence of a sympathy state. More usually, the sympathy state manifests in the *esprit de corps* and cooperation of teammates. Perhaps the most famous example of a sympathy state expressing itself in an otherwise aggressive sport came in 1980 when Larry Holmes, then heavyweight champion of the world, battered the thirty-eight-year-old Muhammad Ali for ten sickeningly one-sided rounds. Over the final rounds, Holmes visibly eased up, at times inviting the referee to intervene to spare his opponent the punishment.

The other pair of transactional states is called *autic* and *alloic*, both concerned with outcomes. In an autic state, an individual is concerned with his or her own outcomes from an interaction, whereas, in a alloic state, the individual is concerned with others' outcomes.

The metamotivational reversal refers to the switch from any one state to its opposite in any one pair; the result is often a dramatic change in outlook and emotional experience. During a racquetball game at the gym, players may jostle, then jokingly make up, suggesting a movement from telic–paratelic reversal; as competitive action resumes, players reverse once more to telic states. Frustration at the failure to achieve one's goals can precipitate a reversal: Mike Tyson's astonishing switch from conformist to negativist states involved his taking a bite from Evander Holyfield's ear in their 1997 fight.

The premise of reversal theory is that any form of behavior, including competitive behavior, needs to be analyzed in terms of the motivations that underlie it. This is complicated by the fact that there is never a one-to-one correspondence between motivation and behavior, nor a direct link between behavior and experience. Identical behavior may be observed in two individuals, yet those individuals may be in contrasting metamotivational states and have totally different experiences. Reversal theory is based on a conception of human beings as inconsistent, self-contradictory, and capable of sometimes paradoxical changes during short periods of time.

Reversal theory's applications vary from Cindy Sit and Koenraad Lindner's study of Hong Kong school pupils to John Kerr and Hilde de Kock's analysis of HOOLIGANISM in Holland. Sit and Lindner found "that individuals' situational state balances correspond to different perceptions about their motives for sport and physical activity participation [. . .] an individual's combination of situational state balances is representative of the basic psychological motives underlying their specific personal needs and goals."

In a completely different context, Kerr and de Kock demonstrated how "the paratelic-negativistic fun and excitement that can be gained from engaging in hooligan activities" was central to VIOLENCE: "Hooligans' feelings of excitement, thrill, and positive affect are enhanced through fighting."

Further reading

Apter, M. J. (1989). *Reversal theory: Motivation, emotion and personality.* London and New York: Routledge.
Frey, Kurt P. (1999). Reversal theory: Basic concepts. In J. H. Kerr (Ed.), *Experiencing sport: Reversal theory* (pp. 3–17). Chichester: Wiley.
Kerr, John H. and de Kock, Hilde (2002). Aggression, violence, and the death of a Dutch soccer hooligan: A reversal theory explanation. *Aggressive Behavior*, 28, 1–10.
Sit, Cindy H. P. and Lindner, Koenraad J. (2006). Situational state balances and participation motivation in youth sport: A reversal theory perspective. *British Journal of Educational Psychology*, 76, 369–84.

See also: AGGRESSION; ANXIETY; AROUSAL; CONSTRUCT; EMOTION; HEDONIC TONE; METAMOTIVATION; MOTIVATION; RISK; SELF-CONFIDENCE; STRESS; TELIC DOMINANCE; THEORY; VIOLENCE

REWARD

As a noun: an appropriate return for agreeable behavior, such as a prize or other recognition for effort or accomplishment. As a verb: to express appreciation of an action by making a gift.

See also: DISCIPLINE; GOAL ORIENTATION; HEDONIC TONE; INCENTIVE; MOTIVATION; REINFORCEMENT

RINGELMANN EFFECT, THE

When individual performances are inhibited by the presence of others, the Ringelmann effect is said to have transpired. The implications in sport are evident. Individuals' performances should decrease as the size of the team in which they are competing increases.

Interest in the way in which individual performances are affected negatively by the presence of others was sparked by an experiment conducted by an engineer named Max Ringelmann (1861–1931), who worked at the French National Institute of Agronomy. His research focused on the relative work efficiency of oxen, horses, and men and involved elementary tasks such as rope pulling, measuring the amount of force exerted per person. As each new person was added to the group, so the amount of force for each individual diminished. It was found that, as the number of participants in a work task increased, so the individual performances decreased. For example, if one individual standing on a track, and told to exert maximum effort at pulling a rope, could be reasonably expected to pull 200 pounds (or 91 kilograms), then three should pull 600 pounds, five 1,000 pounds, and so on.

Contrary to expectations, there was a steady, progressive shortfall in the effort expended by the individuals as the size of the group increased. At first, Ringelmann thought that this was because of a loss of teamwork and coordination. In any cooperative task, members of groups have to coordinate their efforts to achieve maximum joint output. As with any team effort, there were person-to-person links that needed to be coordinated. The number of links increased exponentially with every added member: two people—one link; three people—three links; four people—six links; five people—ten links; eight people—twenty-eight links and so on. The formula is $(n^2 - n) \div 2$.

Coordination links helped explain the performance loss in some group activities, but not others. In some team games, especially ball games, cooperative operations are central and performance has to be socially organized throughout a COMPETITION. By contrast, the cooperative links in a relay race occur only between two members at a time and only at the handover of the baton. Later studies, including that of A. G. Ingham et al., minimized the coordination losses and still found decrements in performance with additional group members. The suspicion was that mechanical problems were not the source of the Ringelmann effect. The cause may be motivational loss.

Ringelmann's original research was conducted before, though not published till after Norman Triplett's 1897/8 studies of cyclists who pedaled with greater speed when they rode in teams rather than individually. While Triplett (1861–1931) had found a SOCIAL FACILITATION of MOTIVATION in which performance was enhanced by the presence of others, Ringelmann found that it was inhibited. Under some conditions, the presence of others led to motivational gains, while, under others, it produced motivational losses.

Impressionistic corroboration for Ringelmann's study comes from soccer and hockey: When a player is given a red card or sent to the sin bin, the team is reduced and fellow team players typically respond by sinking more effort into their play, often making it tough for the opposition to capitalize. While this does not constitute direct support for Ringelmann, the inference is that reducing group size delivers greater MOTIVATION and performance from individuals. The added value of the performance of fewer players is what Ivan Steiner, in his *Group Process and Productivity*, called the "assembly bonus."

David Kravitz and Barbara Martin argue that: "Ringelmann's work is still relevant to contemporary theory and research [on] SOCIAL LOAFING [a process in which performance is inhibited by the presence of others]."

Further reading

Ingham, A. G., Levinger, G., Graves, J. and Peckham, V. (1974). The Ringelmann effect: Studies of group size and group performance. *Journal of Experimental Social Psychology*, 10, 371–84.

Kravitz, David A. and Martin, Barbara (1986). Ringelmann rediscovered: The original article. *Journal of Personality and Social Psychology*, 50, 936–41.

Ringelmann, M. (1913). Recherches sur les moteurs animés: Travail de l'homme. *Annales de l'Institut National Agronomique, 12*(2),299–343.

Steiner, Ivan M. (1972). *Group process and productivity.* New York: Academic Press.

Triplett, N. (1898). The dynamogenic factors in pacemaking and competition. *American Journal of Psychology*, 9, 507–33.

See also: APPLIED   SPORT   PSYCHOLOGY;   CONTEXT;   GROUP   DYNAMICS; RELATIONAL; RELATIONSHIP; SOCIAL FACILITATION; SOCIAL LOAFING; TEAM PLAYER

RISK

From the Italian *risco*, for "danger," risk means exposure to jeopardy. It is a word that crops up a lot. In all sports, athletes often *run risks*; in some, they put their lives *at risk*. Gamblers *take risks* and, occasionally *risk losing* their shirts. People often exercise to *reduce the risk* of heart disease and quit smoking, which is a known *health risk*. Exercise itself is a form of health *risk management*. So, sport and exercise are full of *risk factors*.

Paradoxically, the effort to minimize the element of danger in mainstream sports over the past century has been accompanied by attempts to invent competitive activities that are unsafe by design. The proliferation of sports in which risk is paramount suggests a desire to seek out perilous situations combined with a wish to escape what some writers regard as an over-safe CULTURE in which personal security, public protection, and environmental management have become priorities. This contradicts the commonly held view that people avoid taking risks, even when they carry a potential gain, and submit to them only when trying to avert a certain loss—a phenomenon known as *risk aversion*.

Whole societies have become risk aversive. Mike McNamee's philosophical APPROACH to what he calls "safe society" is premised on the observation that, all over the world, people have become preoccupied by safety and that dangerous sports are a quest for excitement and elation; they heighten our awareness of unpredictability in a world in which nothing that is potentially controllable is left to chance.

As safety has gained MOMENTUM, the ways to escape it have become more ingenious. Established practices, like mountain climbing, stunt cycling, and potholing continue as newer adaptations flourish. Zorbing, bungee-jumping, whitewater rafting and other EXTREME SPORTS contain ersatz dangers. They offer thrills, though under controlled conditions, while other pursuits, such as hang-gliding, and kayaking off waterfalls are less amenable to CONTROL. Participants appear to be motivated by a DEATH WISH, though Matt Pain and Matthew Pain argue, "Risk taking cannot [...] be explained away as a self-defeating psychosis."

They offer an alternative explanation: "Engaging in risky sports leads to an increase in CONFIDENCE and SELF-ESTEEM, much like people who take financial risks in the workplace tend to be more successful." They assert that there is "strong evidence to suggest that the inclination to take risks is hard-wired into the brain and intimately bound to AROUSAL and pleasure mechanisms."

While Pain and Pain do not present this evidence, John Adams' book *Risk* does, and it leads the author to believe that we have inside us a *risk thermostat*, which is adjusted according to our own particular tastes and culture. "Some like it hot—a Hell's Angel or a Grand Prix racing driver, for example; others like it cool," writes Adams. "But no one want absolute zero." Most people would not go to a restaurant declared unsafe by state sanitary inspectors, but some of those same people might ski off-piste, scuba, or go on survivalist expeditions.

Michael Schrader and Daniel Wann advance on this argument. Human survival was predicated on our INTELLIGENCE, but with the development of intelligence came an ABILITY to think existentially, specifically about the possibilities of death. "One method used to achieve CONTROL (or at least the illusion of control) over one's mortality is cheating death," write Schrader and Wann. "It seems logical that participation in high-risk recreation may provide one method." In other words, risky ventures are designed to achieve control over mortality.

Sports present manufactured methods that are actually constructed to preserve natural dangers or build in new ones. Frank Furedi cites the example of rock-climbing which had some of its risks reduced by the introduction of improved ropes, boots, helmets, and other equipment: "The fact that young people who choose to climb mountains might not want to be denied the *frisson* of risk does not enter into the calculations of the safety-conscious professional, concerned to protect us from ourselves."

If the imperative behind risk-taking is, as Schrader and Wann and the Pains argue, to gain a measure of control, then the introduction of safeguards limits the utility and perhaps undermines the purpose of dangerous sports and denies the POSITIVE AFFECT they elicit.

Further reading

Adams, John (1995). *Risk*. London: U.C.L. Press.

Furedi, Frank (1997). *Culture of fear: Risk-taking and the morality of low expectation*. London: Cassell.

McNamee, Mike J. (Ed.) (2007). *Philosophy, risk and adventure sports*. London and New York: Routledge.

Pain, Matt T. G. and Pain, Matthew A. (2005). Essay: Risk taking in sport. *The Lancet*, 366, S33–S35.

Schrader, Michael P. and Wann, Daniel L. (1999). High-risk recreation: The relationship between participant characteristics and degree of involvement. *Journal of Sport Behavior*, 22, 426–42.

See also: ADRENALINE RUSH; AROUSAL; CONTROL; DEATH WISH; ENDORPHINS; FEAR; GAMBLING; HEDONIC TONE; INSTINCT; INTELLIGENCE; LIFE COURSE; LUCK; POSITIVE AFFECT; SENSATION-SEEKING; TYPE A

RIVALRY

A competition for scarce resources between two or more entities (people, groups, nations, and so on) is known as a rivalry, the term stemming from the Latin *rivalis*, for a person using the same stream as another (*rivus* "stream"). Sport is predicated on different individuals or teams vying for superiority in the same field of activity, though the term "rivalry" is usually reserved for particularly intense COMPETITION that may date back several decades. Liverpool vs. Manchester United would be an example. On an individual level, boxing's Muhammad Ali's rivalry with Joe Frazier in the 1970s, basketball's Larry Bird's with Magic Johnson in the 1980s, and tennis's Roger Federer's with Rafael Nadal in the 2000s were notable.

Paul Turman's research revealed how coaches can use rivalry to their advantage: "Often, focusing on the potential rivalry that existed between the two teams was identified as one clear technique to help promote the COHESION and unity team members." In this study, coaches created an "us" versus "them" feeling: "This technique was an extremely effective tool for bonding the athletes together and progressing toward one common GOAL."

There are other consequences, some of them revealed by Barry Kirker and his colleagues, who found that, when rivalry forms part of what they call the "natural environment" of a contest, the terms of engagement tend to change. Kirker et al. focused on basketball and observe that, when rivalry was a factor, "there were expectations for high levels of AGGRESSION, aggression toward officials was not uncommon, and there existed a high acceptance of aggression in sport."

Especially fierce competition such as that stirred by a rivalry always abounds with cues for violent behavior, and this is not confined to competitors. *Intergroup rivalry* (sometimes called "inter-team rivalry") typically refers to competition between FANS rather than players. John Kerr and Hilde de Kock focus specifically on the bitter rivalry that exists between football fans in Europe. Intergroup rivalry is like a set of Russian dolls, each of which sits inside one another: inner allegiances to the individual club nest inside an outer allegiance to the country. So, Liverpool and Manchester fans are rivals when they face each other, but, as Kerr and de Kock point out, "club allegiances and intergroup rivalry are frequently set aside for international matches."

When the England national team plays Holland, Liverpool and Manchester fans will unite in the face of, for example, Ajax and PSV Eindhoven fans, who will be similarly united. In a different CONTEXT, the rivalry will turn inwards, and fans of each club will localize their allegiances.

Sibling rivalry, as its name implies, describes competition between two or more children who have parents in common, though its usual connotation is of a particularly intense or even aggressive competition that can prove productive for one or both siblings if only because they strive so hard to succeed. Some feel sibling rivalry is a departure from the standard relations between brothers and sisters. Others, like the anthropologist Ernst Becker (1929–74) believed differently: "Sibling rivalry [. . .] is too all-absorbing and relentless to be an aberration, it expresses the heart of the creature: the desire to stand out, to be the *one* in creation."

Becker is quoted approvingly by Tom Pyszczynski et al. who argue that people are motivated to compete in the pursuit of SELF-ESTEEM, which "provides a buffer against the omnipresent potential for ANXIETY engendered by the uniquely human awareness of mortality."

Whether this is sufficient to account for the prodigious number of sibs who achieve, perhaps overachieve, in the same sport is doubtful. But anecdotal evidence from recent history may suggest sibling rivalry played some part in the motivational mix of the likes of Venus and Serena Williams, Peyton and Eli Manning, and baseball's Molina brothers, Bengie, Jose, and Yadier (interestingly baseball's sib trinities also include the DiMaggio and Alou brothers).

Binocular rivalry is a perceptual phenomenon occurring when different images are presented to the two eyes. PERCEPTION alternates such that each image is visible for a few seconds at a time. "This binocular rivalry phenomenon is usually understood as a competition between neuronal responses, so at a given time one representation is dominant and the other is suppressed," write Diego Fernandez-Duque and Mark Johnson (neuronal relates to cells transmitting nerve impulses).

Further reading

Fernandez-Duque, Diego and Johnson, Mark L. (2002). Cause and effect theories of attention: The role of conceptual metaphors. *Review of General Psychology*, 6, 153–62.

Kerr, John H. and de Kock, Hilde (2002). Aggression, violence, and the death of a Dutch soccer hooligan: A reversal theory explanation. *Aggressive Behavior*, 28, 1–10.

Kirker, Barry, Tenenbaum, Gershon, and Mattson, Jan (2000). An investigation of the dynamics of aggression: Direct observations in ice hockey and basketball, *Research Quarterly for Exercise and Sport*, 71, 373–87.

Pyszczynski, T., Solomon, S., Greenberg, J. Arndt, J., and Schimel, J. (2004). Why do people need self-esteem? A theoretical and empirical review. *Psychological Bulletin*, 130, 435–68.

Turman, Paul D. (2003). Coaches and cohesion: The impact of coaching techniques on team cohesion in the small group sport setting. *Journal of Sport Behavior*, 26, 86–104.

See also: ABILITY; AGGRESSION; DELIBERATE PRACTICE; GIFTEDNESS; INSTINCT; INTELLIGENCE; INTRINSIC MOTIVATION; MASTERY CLIMATE; MODELING; MOTIVATION; MOTIVATIONAL CLIMATE; PERCEPTION; PERSONALITY; SKILL; VICARIOUS EXPERIENCE; VISUAL PERCEPTION

ROLE MODEL

For all its popularity in everyday idiom, the term "role model" has rarely been defined. A role refers to any pattern of behavior involving expectations, obligations, and duties. Unlike a stage role (from which the term originates: the French *rôle* was a script from which actors read their lines), the role, in this sense, is not defined but is a more flexible assembly of semi-permanent presumptions or conjectures of how to behave and perhaps what values to hold. The person occupying the role has probably internalized others' expectations to the point where he or she enacts the role without constantly reflecting. Yet, the role is actually being created anew at every second. It is never a mold into which an individual actor can fit and, as such, is always open to negotiation.

The term "model," like "role," is used in a variety of ways. In this sense, it refers to something which is observable and which is emulated, or imitated. So, a good or positive role model stands as an ideal person who is worthy of copying. Some schools of thought suggest that role models, as defined in this way, perform important functions since a part of SOCIALIZATION involves simulation of others' speech and behavior, acceptance of their beliefs and values, and repetition of their mannerisms and even affects, or at least how they express them. The process through which this takes place is known as MODELING, and there is a body of research on this subject.

In her analysis of EATING DISORDERS, Antonia Baum asserts, "prominent athletes frequently become role models." An athlete whose desired GOAL is to lose weight would be a poor role model; as would one who succumbs to a GAMBLING habit, as Thomas Miller *et al.*, discuss. Douglas Kellner suggests an additional caution: "Although it is positive for members of the underclass to have role models and aspirations to better themselves, it is not clear that sports can provide a means to success for any but a few."

Even allowing for the uncertainty of whether it actually is "positive" for members of the so-called "underclass" to have role models, Kellner presents a case for discouraging young people from using sports figures as exemplars, except perhaps in the emulation of hairstyles, tattoos, jewelry, and other types of adornment. But, at deeper levels, research indicates that less glamorous figures have a more beneficial impact. For example, Bradley Cardinal concluded that leaders in health, physical education, recreation and dance (HPERD) "have the power to profoundly affect children's attitudes and behaviors."

Cardinal's use of *role modeling* suggests his emphasis is on the emulators or followers who observe and attempt to arrange their behavior, form opinions, develop their values or structure their ambitions on those of their teachers.

Further reading

Baum, Antonia (2006). Eating disorders in the male athlete. *Sports Medicine*, 36, 1–6.

Cardinal, Bradley J. (2001). Role modeling attitudes and physical activity and fitness promoting behaviors of HPERD professionals and preprofessionals. *Research Quarterly for Exercise and Sport*, 72, 84–90.

Hagger, Martin and Chatzisarantis, Nikos (2005). *The social psychology of exercise and sport*. Maidenhead: Open University Press.

Kellner, Douglas (1996). Sports, media culture, and race: Some reflections on Michael Jordan. *Sociology of Sport Journal*, 13, 458–67.

Miller, T. W., Adams, J. M., Kraus, R. F., Clayton, R., Miller J. M., Anderson, J., and Ogilvie, B. (2001). Gambling as an addictive disorder among athletes. *Sports Medicine*, 31, 145–52.

See also: AGGRESSION; CELEBRITIES; COACH–ATHLETE RELATIONSHIP; DEVIANCE; EATING DISORDERS; FANS; LEADERSHIP; MODELING; MORAL ATMOSPHERE; PEER LEADERSHIP; SOCIALIZATION; VICARIOUS AGENCY

SANDBAGGING

To underperform deliberately in a COMPETITION, usually to gain an unfair advantage. Sandbagging is a strategy employed by proficient performers who wish to hide their skills from others. This can be deployed, as Harry Wallace et al. point out, "in reducing the expectations of supportive audiences" and alleviating the pressure of performing maximally. Or it can be used in the early phases of a contest as a way of inducing overconfidence and a drop in the AROUSAL level of an opponent. Another sense of the term is to coerce or persuade someone or something by harsh methods, such as hitting them with a bagful of sand; hence the term.

Further reading

Wallace, Harry M., Baumeister, Roy F., and Vohs, Kathleen D. (2005). Audience support and choking under pressure: A home disadvantage? *Journal of Sports Sciences*, 23, 429–38.

SCHEMA

"A schema is a cognitive generalization about the SELF that helps the individual organize and process information concerned with the individual's social experience," write Brian Gallagher and Frank Gardner, "a lens through which the individual sees the self and his or her relation to the world."

Expressed another way, a schema is framework or THEORY that serves as both a MODEL for interpreting information about both the self and society and a guide for future action. Typically, a schema is elaborate and adaptable enough to cope with changing situations. It can also offer a way of retrospectively interpreting events that have passed. As such, it should not be confused with a scheme, which is designed with a particular aim; they both derive from the Greek *skhema*, for "form," or "figure."

"Schemas can reduce working MEMORY load, because once they have been acquired and automated, they can be handled in working memory with very little conscious effort," observe Tamara van Gog et al. A schema can be used for "screening, coding, and evaluating the stimuli that impinge on the organism," according to Aaron T. Beck, whose writing in the 1960s influenced a school of thought known as *schema theory*, which is organized around the investigation of enduring cognitive structures that are part of an individual's PERSONALITY.

In sport and exercise, schema theory has been used for understanding the RELATIONSHIP between coping style and the RESPONSE to INJURY and to highlight how maladaptive schemas (or schemata, as they are sometimes known) can impede recovery. The theoretical APPROACH has also been employed to understand how predispositions can activate FEAR OF FAILING or FEAR OF SUCCESS, in specific situations. Schemas are also integral to COGNITIVE LOAD THEORY.

Donald Williamson et al.'s research on EATING DISORDERS uses *body-self schemas* about body size and shape to discover cues, both external and internal, which can direct a person's ATTENTION "to body- and food-related stimuli and to bias interpretations of self-relevant events in favor of fatness interpretations."

Similarly, the constructs *exercise schemas*, or exercise-self schemas, have been used by many researchers, including Katherine Bond and

Joanne Batey to understand the exercise experience and assess how ADHERENCE and SELF-ESTEEM are impacted by EXERCISE BEHAVIOR.

Further reading

Beck, A. T. (1967). *Depression: Causes and treatment*. Philadelphia, Pa.: University of Pennsylvania Press.

Bond, Katherine A. and Batey, Joanne (2005). Running for their lives: A qualitative analysis of the exercise experience of female recreational runners. *Women in Sport and Physical Activity Journal*, 14, 69–73.

Gallagher, Brian V. and Gardner, Frank L. (2007). An examination of the relationship between early maladaptive schemas, coping, and emotional response to athletic injury. *Journal of Clinical Sport Psychology*, 1, 47–67.

van Gog, Tamara, Ericsson, K. Anders, Rikers, Remy M. J. P., and Paas, Fred (2005). Instructional design for advanced learners: Establishing connections between the theoretical frameworks of cognitive load and deliberate practice. *Educational Technology, Research and Development*, 53, 73–81.

Williamson, Donald A., White, Marney A., York-Crowe, Emily, and Stewart, Tiffany M. (2004). Cognitive-behavioral theories of eating disorders. *Behavior Modification, 28*(6), 711–38.

See also: ATTENTION; COGNITION; COGNITIVE LOAD THEORY; CONSTRUCT; FEAR OF FAILURE; FLOW; INFORMATION PROCESSING; MEMORY; MENTALITY; MODEL; PERCEPTION; SOCIALIZATION; THEORY; THERAPY

SELF

The part of a person's experience that defines who he or she is as distinct from all others is known as the self, a word that has Germanic origins in *selbha*. The term self is usually used in a way that suggests reflexivity. When we are aware of the self, we are, by necessity, considering it as an object—we are aware of *something*. We express this reflexive action in our speech: "I wasn't my real self today"; or about others, "He spends so much time looking after others that he neglects his own self." (*Reflexivity*, in this sense, means referring back to oneself, rather than performed without conscious thought, as in a reflex action).

While "self" is commonly employed, it is rarely defined, many scholars assuming the word's pervasiveness in language suggests a common understanding. There are, however, slight differences, Arthur Reber detecting six uses of self:

(1) an inner agent or force with controlling and directing functions;

(2) an inner witness to events—this is basically the sense in which the philosopher/psychologist William James (1842–1910) used it when he distinguished between the *I* (the knowing self) and the *me* (the self known);

(3) the totality of personal experience and expression, which makes it comparable if not synonymous with ego, person, individual and other inclusive terms;

(4) an integrated synthesis of everything the person is (a definition that is very close to PERSONALITY);

(5) consciousness, or personal conception (who we think we are);

(6) an abstract goal or endpoint, as envisaged in the later work of Carl Jung (1875–1961), who saw the self as final expression of spiritualistic development; this is similar to Abraham Maslow's version of SELF-ACTUALIZATION.

Julie Juola Exline and Marci Lobel invoke use (2) in their research on OUTPERFORMANCE, where they suggest that "comparisons against those faring better than the self should lead to negative affect": the self is an object being thought about. By contrast, when Molly Moran and Maureen Weiss study "LEADERSHIP among adolescent athletes from the standpoint of self, coach, and peers," they implicitly refer to use (3). In discussing how athletes cope with injuries, Leslee A. Fisher and Craig Wrisberg use a conception that lies somewhere between uses (5) and (6) when they advise, "the healthier option is to grieve and let go of one's 'old self' so that the 'new self' can be ushered in."

As a reflexive prefix, self- (with a hyphen) is used in myriad ways. The fifteen entries that follow this provide some examples. The terms usually express a characteristic directed toward oneself, such as self-contempt (a loathing for oneself) or relating to oneself, like self-control (the ABILITY to CONTROL one's own behavior or emotions).

Further reading

Exline, Julie Juola and Lobel, Marci (1999). The perils of outperformance: Sensitivity about being the target of a threatening upward comparison. *Psychological Bulletin*, 3, 307–37.

Fisher, Leslee A. and Wrisberg, Craig (2005). The "Zen" of career-ending injury rehabilitation. *Sport Psychology and Counseling*, 10, 44–5.

Moran, Molly M. and Weiss, Maureen R. (2006). Peer leadership in sport: Links with friendship, peer acceptance, psychological characteristics, and athletic ability. *Journal of Applied Sport Psychology*, 18, 97–113.

Reber, Arthur (1995). *Dictionary of psychology*, 2nd edn. Harmondsworth: Penguin.

See also: ATHLETIC IDENTITY; ATTRIBUTION; BODY IMAGE; EXERCISE IDENTITY; IDENTITY; MOTIVATION; PERSONALITY; PHYSICAL SELF-PERCEPTIONS; PHYSICAL SELF-WORTH; REHABILITATION; SELF-ACTUALIZATION; SELF-AWARENESS; SELF-CONCEPT; SELF-DETERMINATION THEORY; SELF-ENHANCEMENT; SELF-HANDICAPPING

SELF-ACTUALIZATION

A term introduced by Kurt Goldstein (1878–1965) to describe fulfilling one's potentialities; "actualize" is from the Latin *actualis*, for "active," and means making into a reality. Goldstein conceived of this as a DRIVE or motivating need in all human beings, that is, to develop their latent ABILITY. It was the mother lode of all other motivations: All others were manifestations of it. (Goldstein's approach was *holistic*: the human being was an organic whole and could not be understood by analyzing constituent parts separately.)

The "concept" was adapted by Abraham Maslow (1908–70) to form the final level of his hierarchy of needs MODEL of human MOTIVATION. For Maslow, self-actualization can only be achieved after all basic and other needs have been satisfied. There is great similarly between the two uses of the term, though Maslow regarded it as a tier in a hierarchy of needs rather than an all-purpose source of MOTIVATION.

The CONSTRUCT has been used in several contemporary contexts. Karla Henderson, for example, describes "leisure as a self-actualizing process" when she examines women's involvement in physical activities, such as walking or even RELAXATION classes. In a similar vein, Katherine Bond and Joanne Batey, after studying recreational runners, conclude, "achievement in sport (at whatever level) can facilitate the development of a more competent SELF and contribute to enhanced self-actualization."

One of the more interesting applications by Galen Trail and Jeffrey James yielded the finding that just watching sport can serve as a self-actualizing experience for FANS.

Further reading

Bond, Katherine A. and Batey, Joanne (2005). Running for their lives: A qualitative analysis of the exercise experience of female recreational runners. *Women in Sport and Physical Activity Journal*, 14, 69–73.

Goldstein, Kurt (1995). *The organism: A holistic approach to biology*. New York: Zone Books. First published 1934 *Der Aufbau des Organismus*, 1934; first English translation 1959.

Henderson, Karla A. (2003). Women, physical activity, and leisure: Jeopardy or wheel of fortune? *Women in Sport and Physical Activity Journal*, 12, 113–25.
Trail, Galen and James, Jeffrey D. (2001). The motivation scale for sport consumption: Assessment of the scale's psychometric properties. *Journal of Sport Behavior*, 24, 108–28.

See also: ACHIEVEMENT MOTIVE; ATHLETIC IDENTITY; DRIVE; EXERCISE IDENTITY; INCENTIVE; INTRINSIC MOTIVATION; LIFE COURSE; MASTERY CLIMATE; MOTIVATION; PARTICIPATION MOTIVATION; SELF; SELF-DETERMINATION THEORY; SELF-EFFICACY

SELF-AWARENESS

Being conscious of oneself as both a subject and an object that is liable to appraisal and criticism is known as self-awareness. While some other animals have demonstrated an awareness of themselves, only humans reflect on EMOTION and MOTIVATION as well as on their own existence.

Becoming self-aware, if only momentarily, leads to comparisons, as influential research in 1972 by T. S. Duval and R. A. Wicklund pointed out. Once we are prompted to FOCUS on ourselves, we become self-aware and attend to both our sensations and an ideal standard, which serves as a kind of exemplar. We then evaluate ourselves against the standard. Typically, this leads to attempts to reduce the discrepancy between the self and the standard.

Subsequent research focused on how people try to effect the reduction, whether by changing themselves or by somehow adjusting the standard. Whichever option they choose depends on how they attribute the blame for the discrepancy. If a person attributes failure to conform to the standard to the self, then they will attempt to change. If, as work by Jeffrey Katula and Edward McAuley suggests, they attribute the CAUSE to the standard, they will try to change that.

Katula and McAuley agree with C. S. Carver and M. F. Scheier's earlier prediction that one's PERCEPTION of capabilities is the critical mediator of the effects of self-awareness. In other words, "Those with high perceptions of capabilities should respond positively to self-awareness, whereas those with lower perceptions of capabilities should respond negatively."

Katula and McAuley set up a project in which they positioned a mirror so that exercisers were forced to watch themselves. As the exercisers worked out, they became aware of their physical abilities and BODY LANGUAGE. "It is plausible to suggest that the mirror caused participants to become more aware of feelings of MASTERY resulting from the completion of their exercise bout, resulting in enhanced perceptions of capabilities," they reasoned, adding that the mirror "may have increased the saliency of efficacy-relevant information." The information contributed toward the enhancement of SELF-EFFICACY.

Despite its positive impact in exercise, self-awareness can impede competitive performance, as Paul Silvia notes: "FLOW experiences are characterized in part by reduced self-awareness—ATTENTION is wholly devoted to ongoing activity." During PEAK PERFORMANCE, competitors become unaware of time, the environment and even themselves. "Yet, when SELF re-enters the picture, the flow state is disrupted."

Further reading

Carver, C. S. and Scheier, M. F. (1998). *On the self-regulation of behavior.* New York: Cambridge University Press.

Duval, T. Shelley and Wicklund, R. A. (1972). *A theory of objective self-awareness.* New York: Academic Press.

Katula, Jeffrey A. and McAuley, Edward (2001). The mirror does not lie: Acute exercise and self-efficacy. *International Journal of Behavioral Medicine*, 8, 319–26.

Silvia, Paul J. (2002). Self-awareness and emotional intensity. *Cognition and Emotion*, 16, 195–216.

See also: ATTENTION; AUTOMATICITY; BODY LANGUAGE; EMOTION; EXERCISE BEHAVIOR; FEEDBACK; FLOW; FOCUS; INTERNALIZATION; MASTERY; MASTERY CLIMATE; PARALYSIS BY ANALYSIS; PERCEPTION; PROPRIOCEPTION; SELF; SELF-EFFICACY

SELF-CONCEPT

As the term suggests, this is the mental picture we have of ourselves, formed by assembling information and ideas about ourselves summoned from the responses of other people as well as our own thoughts. In other words, how we see ourselves and how we think others see us.

Unlike SELF-ESTEEM, self-concept is descriptive and not judgmental. For example, an athlete approaching RETIREMENT might face a transformation of self-concept as he or she moves away from the kind of activity that has influenced the way he and many others visualize him. As William Webb et al. observe, "an internalized athlete IDENTITY likely dominates the individual's overall self-concept."

So, the items we assemble in constructing our self-concept are not indiscriminately gathered: the "self-surveillance," as Lisa Hallsworth et al. call it, is selective. Hallsworth et al. provide an example: "Bodybuilders placed a relatively greater emphasis on the importance of appearance with respect to their self-concept, whereas weightlifters and controls rated competency as being more important to their self-concept."

Each group was likely to pay more attention to information about the particular facet of themselves they regarded as salient—salient, in this CONTEXT, meaning prominent or conspicuous.

Further reading

Hallsworth, Lisa, Wade, Tracey, and Tiggemann, Marika (2005). Individual differences in male body-image: An examination of self-objectification in recreational body builders. *British Journal of Health Psychology,* 10, 453–65.

Webb, William M., Nasco, Suzanne A., Riley, Sarah, and Headrick, Brian (1998). Athlete identity and reactions to retirement from sports. *Journal of Sport Behavior,* 21, 338–63.

See also: ATHLETIC IDENTITY; AUTOTELIC; BODY IMAGE; BODY LANGUAGE; BODY SHAME; COGNITION; FANS; GENDER; IDENTIFICATION; PERCEPTION; PERFECTIONISM; PHYSICAL SELF-PERCEPTIONS; PHYSICAL SELF-WORTH; SELF-AWARENESS; SELF-ESTEEM; SELF-HANDICAPPING; SELF-TALK; SOCIAL PHYSIQUE ANXIETY; SOCIALIZATION

SELF-CONFIDENCE

From the Latin *con*, meaning for, and *fidere*, trust, self-confidence is typically understood as an attribute possessed by people who trust their own abilities and judgment, are self-reliant and assured and, perhaps, on occasion, bold. In other words, it is a state or feeling of self-assurance that derives from an appreciation of one's own qualities or ABILITY. While much research has concentrated on the role of self-confidence in sport, it does not usually encompass the particular form of self-confidence that relates to exercise. We will deal with both forms.

Form 1: Sport. Self-confident athletes enter COMPETITION certain in the knowledge that they will achieve their GOAL. Resolute and secure, confident competitors approach contests with "the belief or degree of certainty," as Robin Vealey puts it, "about their ability to be successful in sport." Accurate as this statement is, it does not convey the unstable feature of self-confidence: It can be built, damaged, and sometimes destroyed by events and personalities.

William Moore argues that self-confidence enables an athlete to move from conscious CONTROL to AUTOMATICITY—the automatic execution of tasks needed for PEAK PERFORMANCE. In other words, the confident performer does not think about the job at hand. He or she just does it. Persuading an athlete to surrender conscious effort to motor control involves trust, and this involves a belief in one's own capacities, or what Albert Bandura called SELF-EFFICACY. Repeated successes enhance self-efficacy to the point where occasional defeats are insignificant and have little impact on a performer's self-confidence. Vealey's research suggested that *sport confidence* may be transferable, so self-confidence in one discipline may carry over to others if the athlete has a particular kind of personality trait.

The effects of an infusion of self-confidence can also be spectacular. Going into her 100 meters semifinal at the 2001 World Track and Field Championships, Zhanna Puntusevich-Block faced the forbidding prospect of Marion Jones, who was undefeated in fifty-four straight races. Unexpectedly, the Ukrainian ran a 10.93 to squeeze Jones into second place. Both qualified for the final, and, while observers may have dismissed Jones's loss as irrelevant, Puntusevich-Block used it as evidence of Jones's vulnerability and her own prowess. In the final, she repeated her win over Jones, recording 10.82 to take the gold medal. "The semi gave me a lot of psychological confidence," she said after the final. "I realised that I could beat Marion" (quoted in *Athletics Weekly*, 55, 34, August 22, 2001).

Instilling self-confidence in an athlete can involve affirmations, "strong, positive statements about something that is believable and has a realistic potential for becoming true," as Moore defines them. It may also involve the athlete in IMAGERY: to visualize a favorable scenario before competition. But, the "as if" approach is one of the most effective ways: encouraging athletes to put themselves in the shoes of another whom they wish to emulate. What begins as a fake display, or perhaps an attempt at MODELING, may develop into self-confidence.

For instance, Muhammad Ali, in his early career, modeled himself on Gorgeous George, a brash and boastful wrestler in the 1960s. Ali later confessed that he was so apprehensive about his first title fight with Sonny Liston that he needed an act to hide it. His success in this and subsequent title fights increased his self-confidence to the point where he genuinely believed he could never lose. On occasion, Ali, like many other athletes allowed his self-confidence to become insolent pride, or presumption; in other words, *over-confidence*.

Other dangers to self-confidence include *pressing*, or trying too hard, which leads to tension, and *controlling* in which athletes concentrate on the mechanics of what they are doing. Self-confidence allows the competitor to let go of conscious CONTROL and trust his or her SKILL, so that their performance feels "instinctive." Arrogant, or bombastic athletes are not necessarily confident. It is possible that their bold appearance is manufactured to mask *self-abasement*, which develops from excessively critical self-evaluation and the debasement of their own abilities (that is, belittling oneself).

Effective LEADERSHIP in sport often depends on the self-confidence athletes have in another for example, a coach or manager. If they trust that figure and believe in his or her ABILITY to guide them, they will accept decisions, follow instructions and respect that person's judgment. Once a leader-figure loses the self-confidence of players, leadership breaks down and resignation or dismissal usually follows.

Form 2: Exercise. According to Carolyn Vos Strache et al., *exercise confidence* depends on self-evaluation, which is linked to the physical SELF. A working definition is: the state of feeling self-assurance about displaying one's own body and certainty about one's own competence in the performing exercise tasks.

Someone can conceal poor reading ability, or the fact that he cannot hold down a job, but, if they are overweight or too skinny, this is conspicuous and open to public purview. ("Self-evaluation," in this CONTEXT, appears to be approximate SELF-ESTEEM.)

While there is sense in the familiar advertising for gyms that suggests self-confidence is enhanced by exercise, the RELATIONSHIP is not quite so straightforward, and those with ANXIETY about their physical self, for example, are likely to avoid situations in which their bodies are under the scrutiny of others. This includes pools and aerobic areas. This group is likely to protect self-confidence by using alternative COPING STRATEGIES, such as dismissing the media's accentuation of slimness or priding themselves on their good health despite a lack of regular exercise and a sedentary lifestyle.

These resemble what Stephen Mellalieu et al. call *confidence management* strategies "to protect against debilitative anxiety"; while their research focused on a competitive environment, the results can be generalized. For example, strategies, such as SELF-TALK, rationalization of thoughts and images, use of IMAGERY, building robust perceptions of "enactive MASTERY" were all found to assist in increasing self-confidence and reducing anxiety levels.

This does not completely preclude anxiety. Even self-confident performers experience anxiety symptoms, though, as Sheldon Hanton and Declan Connaughton have shown: "Self-confidence moderates the effects of anxiety."

This means that exercisers as well as athletes with high levels of self-confidence typically respond to anxiety with an APPROACH, rather AVOIDANCE: They are more likely to persist with a task, not disengage from it, possibly redoubling efforts to complete an action. Hanton and Connaughton note the importance of CONTROL as a kind of antidote to panic. RELAXATION, imagery, and other psyching procedures have all been shown to be useful ways of stabilizing self-confidence, particularly before undertaking a program or starting a competition.

Further reading

Hanton, Sheldon and Connaughton, Declan (2002). Perceived control of anxiety and its relationship to self-confidence and performance. *Research Quarterly for Exercise and Sport*, 73, 87–97.

Manzo, L. (2002). Enhancing sport performance: The role of self-confidence and concentration. In J. M. Silva and D. E. Stevens (Eds.) *Psychological foundations of sport* (pp. 247–71). Boston, Mass.: Allyn & Bacon.

Mellalieu, Stephen D., Neil, Richard and Hanton, Sheldon (2006). Self-confidence as a mediator of the relationship between competitive anxiety intensity and interpretation. *Research Quarterly for Exercise and Sport*, 77, 263–70.

Moore, W. (1998). Self-confidence. In M. A. Thompson, R. A. Vernacchia, and W. E. Moore (Eds.) *Case Studies in applied sport psychology: An educational approach* (pp. 63–88). Dubuque, Iowa: Kendall/Hunt.

Vealey, R. S. (1986). Conceptualization of sport-self-confidence and competitive orientation: Preliminary investigation and instrument development. *Journal of Sport Psychology*, 8, 221–46.

Vos Strache, Carolyn, Strong, Alana, and Peterson, Cheree (2004). The female physique: Motives guiding self-evaluation. *Women in Sport and Physical Activity Journal,* 13, 5–17.

See also: ANXIETY; APPROACH; AUTOMATICITY; AVOIDANCE; BODY IMAGE; BODY SHAME; COMPOSURE; CONTROL; EXERCISE BEHAVIOR; IMAGERY; MENTAL TOUGHNESS; PEAK PERFORMANCE; PHYSICAL SELF-PERCEPTIONS; PHYSICAL SELF-WORTH; SELF-EFFICACY; SELF-ESTEEM; SELF-TALK; SOCIAL PHYSIQUE ANXIETY; STREAKS

SELF-DETERMINATION THEORY

Self-determination is the process by which people CONTROL their own behavior, acting on the basis of personally held beliefs, values, and commitments rather than externally imposed norms or rules.

Some scholars, such as Richard Ryan and Edward Deci theorize that it is "essential for facilitating optimal functioning of the natural propensities for growth and regulation, as well as for constructive social development and personal well-being."

Ryan and Deci identify three "innate psychological needs": competence, relatedness, and autonomy. Relatedness, in this CONTEXT, refers to interpersonal relationships that provide feelings of security and comfort. Humans strive to learn, extend themselves, master new skills, and apply their TALENT. This is taken as given. Self-determination THEORY, or SDT, attempts to specify the conditions that elicit and sustain rather than subdue and diminish the innate propensity and, in this sense, is closely aligned with COGNITIVE EVALUATION THEORY. SDT has become "the most widely cited theory relevant to INTRINSIC MOTIVATION processes, in part because of its elegance in accounting for MOTIVATION and performance" according to Ann Boggiano.

Threats, deadlines, directives, and imposed goals are among the factors that bring about a perceived external LOCUS OF CONTROL and so diminish intrinsic motivation. Money is a classic mechanism of EXTRINSIC MOTIVATION, and a powerful one too. *Amotivation* describes an absence of both intrinsic and extrinsic motivation; people do not value an activity or believe that engaging in it will produce any meaningful outcome.

So, while intrinsic motivation is not the only type of motivation explained by SDT, one of its aims is to address the processes through which nonintrinsically motivated behaviors become self-determined and acquire value as regulators. For example, someone can *internalize* (or "take in," as Ryan and Deci put it) others' values or rules. The ways in which the social environment influences these processes is of central interest to SDT. SOCIALIZATION is always in FOCUS: SDT looks closely at the agents responsible for imparting beliefs and regulations and the circumstances in which they are internalized and experienced as catalysts for autonomous action.

Cecilie Thøgersen-Ntoumani and Nikos Ntoumanis' study concluded "that aerobic instructors who are motivated to exercise mainly because their SELF-WORTH is contingent upon exercise and its associated outcomes (such as improved physical appearance) are more likely to have high levels of BODY IMAGE concerns and SOCIAL PHYSIQUE ANXIETY, as well as lower levels of PHYSICAL SELF-WORTH."

Yet, it seems feasible to suggest that working in an exercise environment can lead to an assimilation of the values and attitudes of other workout-oriented trainers, that is, INTERNALIZATION. A further transformation might come through INTEGRATED REGULATION, when what were initially other people's values and attitudes are experienced as their own and express their sense of self. For instance, a salesman, who spends most of his working day behind a steering wheel, might begin exercising after a colleague bets him he cannot lose 20 pounds in two months. He discovers that the exercise experience itself is rewarding. Extrinsic motives are derailed, as the salesman is reinforced with positive feelings and improved psychological as well as physical health.

John Maltby and Liza Day studied this type of integration in their research on EXERCISE MOTIVATION. Their findings support the SDT view that motives change with experience and, under certain conditions, intrinsic replace extrinsic motives. Maltby and Day did not assume that intrinsic exercise motives CAUSE psychological WELL-BEING. As they point out, "It is perhaps more likely that a more integrative relationship occurs, whereby exercise motive and psychological well-being interact, through REINFORCEMENT of positive feelings, and exercise becomes more rewarding."

Those who challenge self-determination theory regard the CONCEPT of self-determination as illusory and insist that humans are ultimately respondents to stimuli.

Further reading

Biddle, Stuart, Soos, Istvan, and Chatzisarantis, Nikos (1999). Predicting physical activity intentions using goal perspectives and self-determination theory approaches. *European Psychologist*, 4, 83–9.

Boggiano, Ann K. (1998). Maladaptive achievement patterns: A test of a diathesis-stress analysis of helplessness. *Journal of Personality and Social Psychology*, 74, 1681–95.

Hagger, Martin and Chatzisarantis, Nikos (Eds.) (2007). *Intrinsic motivation and self-determination in exercise and sport*. Champaign, Ill.: Human Kinetics.

Maltby, John and Day, Liza (2001). The relationship between exercise motives and psychological well-being. *Journal of Psychology*, 135, 651–60.

Ryan, Richard M. and Deci, Edward L. (2000). Self-determination theory and the facilitation of intrinsic motivation, social development, and well-being. *American Psychologist*, 55, 68–78.

Thøgersen-Ntoumani, Cecilie and Ntoumanis, Nikos (2007). A self-determination theory approach to the study of body image concerns, self-presentation and self-perceptions in a sample of aerobic instructors. *Journal of Health Psychology*, 12, 301–15.

See also: ADHERENCE; COGNITION; COGNITIVE EVALUATION THEORY; COMMITMENT; CONTROL; DROPOUTS; EXERCISE BEHAVIOR; EXERCISE MOTIVATION; EXTRINSIC MOTIVATION; IDENTIFIED REGULATION; INTEGRATED REGULATION; INTERNALIZATION; INTRINSIC MOTIVATION; LOCUS OF CONTROL; MASTERY CLIMATE; MOTIVATION; REINFORCEMENT; SELF-ACTUALIZATION; SOCIALIZATION; THEORY

SELF-EFFICACY

Albert Bandura's CONSTRUCT to describe a person's or a team's belief in their capacity to produce a desired or intended result under specific conditions is self-efficacy. It is a cognitive mechanism that affects behavior. As conditions change, so might someone's belief in their competence to bring about the result might change, as might the strength of their COMMITMENT. So, self-efficacy is specific to situations and changeable.

Marcia Milne et al. identify three specific types of self-efficacy: (1) *task*, involving judgments about capabilities in specific contexts; (2) *barrier*, about the capability to overcome personal and social constraints; and (3) *scheduling*, meaning planning strategies. The word "efficacy" shares a common root with efficiency, the Latin *efficax*, which means creating a desired outcome.

Unlike SELF-CONFIDENCE, which suggests trust and assurance in oneself across a range of endeavors, self-efficacy relates to particular tasks, which might include, for example, a particular physical activity, REHABILITATION from INJURY, or recovering from ALCOHOLISM or another kind of DEPENDENCE. It also relates to conditions. A recovering alcoholic might experience self-efficacy, but only if he steers clear of his old drinking friends; a marathon runner might believe she excels in most weathers, apart from when the temperature drops below 32 degrees Fahrenheit (0 degrees Celsius).

It differs in another important respect, pointed out by Jeffrey Katula and Edward McAuley: "Self-efficacy is a form of self-evaluation in which several sources of information (for example, performance accomplishments, interpretations of physiological arousal) are appraised to form perceptions of capabilities." Self-confident individuals are unlikely to rely on such "efficacy-relevant mastery information"; their self-assurance is usually implicit. Katula and McAuley's study examined the impact of a mirror in a gym studio: "Participants reported significantly greater exercise self-efficacy in the mirror condition as compared to the no mirror condition."

Steven Bray's research implemented methods designed to develop self-efficacy include vicarious experience, verbal persuasion (for example, seeing and hearing about others' success), and guided MASTERY (exposure to enjoyable forms of physical activity). The conclusion was that self-efficacy can be built independently of actually achieving intended goals. Complementary research though in a completely different CONTEXT by Bradley Cardinal and Maria Kosma, on muscular fitness training, pointed out ways in which self-efficacy is instilled using behavioral and cognitive strategies, some of them quite minor, such as subscribing to a FITNESS magazine or learning how to perform certain exercises.

The effects of self-efficacy as both a determinant and a consequence of EXERCISE BEHAVIOR are well documented (and reviewed by McAuley and Blissmer). The exercise environment, physical and social, can also affect the development of self-efficacy, as can the GENDER of other trainers. Gender is relevant to self-efficacy, as is RACE, according to the research of Zan Gao and Louis Harrison, who revealed that men experienced significantly more self-efficacy than women.

In the same study, African Americans scored higher than whites on self-efficacy, but not in their physical task performances. The self-efficacy differences were consistent with other research on EXPECTANCY, and perceived physical ABILITY as well as on STEREOTYPE THREAT and the SELF-FULFILLING PROPHECY.

Self-efficacy is valuable in understanding why performers are motivated to continue performing in a domain where they have experienced success yet tend to avoid activities they perform poorly. It is not so useful in explaining engagement in areas of activity where individuals might initially have difficulties and might even continue to struggle, yet persist with DELIBERATE PRACTICE and ultimately improve.

Further reading

Bandura, Albert (1997). *Self-efficacy: The exercise of control.* New York: W. H. Freeman.

Bray, Steven R. (2007). Self-efficacy for coping with barriers helps students stay physically active during transition to their first year at a university. *Research Quarterly for Exercise and Sport*, 78, 61–70.

Cardinal, Bradley J. and Kosma, Maria (2004). Self-efficacy and the stages and process of change associated with adopting and maintaining muscular fitness-promoting behaviors. *Research Quarterly for Exercise and Sport*, 75, 186–97.

Katula, Jeffrey A. and McAuley, Edward (2001). The mirror does not lie: Acute exercise and self-efficacy. *International Journal of Behavioral Medicine*, 8, 319–26.

McAuley, Edward and Blissmer, B. (2000). Self-efficacy determinants and consequences of physical activity. *Exercise and Sport Sciences Reviews*, 28, 85–8.

Milne, Marcia, Hall, Craig, and Forwell, Lorie (2005). Self-efficacy, imagery use, and adherence to rehabilitation by injured athletes. *Sport Rehabilitation*, 14, 150–67.

Gao, Zan and Harrison, Louis (2005). Examining the role of physical self-efficacy as a function of race and gender (research note). *Research Quarterly for Exercise and Sport*, 76, A72.

SELF-ENHANCEMENT

This is sometimes viewed as a tendency shared by a great many
people, at other times, a strategy employed by those possessed of high
SELF-ESTEEM seeking further boosts. In the first meaning, there is an
inclination shared by all humans to compare themselves with others,
specifically with others who are less accomplished or skilled or appear
deficient in some way. The *downward comparison*, as it is called, permits a
favorable impression of the person making the comparison. "In daily
life, we do not always have the luxury of confining social comparisons
to the realm of imagination, manipulating them to serve our needs for
self-evaluation and self-enhancement," reflect Julie Juola Exline and
Marci Lobel. But, in sport, competitors can do exactly that.

Self-enhancement typically occurs after success: it involves augmenting one's own performance by referring to, for example, how
one was suffering from a bad lane draw yet still won, or was out
drinking the night before, while rivals were in bed early. In a study
by Harry Prapavessis et al.: "Self-enhancement was restricted to
individuals with high self-esteem who claimed handicaps."

By contrast, those experiencing failure sometimes strive for SELF-
PROTECTION by discounting their performance as, for instance, an
"off-day" or "not the real me out there, today."

It has been suggested that self-enhancement is affected not only by
PERSONALITY, disposition, and other personal attributes, but also by
SOCIALIZATION in particular cultures. Concluding their research, Jerry
Burger and Amy Lynn allude to the more general meaning of the
term, though with qualifications: "These observations are consistent
with investigations that find a tendency for self-enhancement among
Americans but not among Japanese citizens."

Further reading

Burger, Jerry M. and Lynn, Amy L. (2005). Superstitious behavior among
American and Japanese professional baseball players. *Basic and Applied
Social Psychology*, 27, 71–6.

Exline, Julie Juola and Lobel, Marci (1999). The perils of outperformance: Sensitivity about being the target of a threatening upward comparison. *Psychological Bulletin*, 3, 307–37.

Prapavessis, Harry, Grove, J. Robert and Eklund, Robert C. (2004). Self-presentational issues in competition and sport. *Journal of Applied Sport Psychology,* 16, 19–40.

See also: ACHIEVEMENT MOTIVE; APPROACH; ATTRIBUTION; BODY LANGUAGE; INTERVENTION; LOCUS OF CONTROL; OUTPERFORMANCE; PERCEPTION; PREPER-FORMANCE ROUTINES; SELF-CONFIDENCE; SELF-HANDICAPPING; SELF-SERVING BIAS

SELF-ESTEEM

'The concept of self-esteem generally refers to a person's evaluation of, or attitude toward, him- or herself," write Tom Pyszczynski et al. Its source is the Latin *æstimare*, to estimate.

Historically, there have been several formulations of different types of self-esteem, though, as Pyszczynski et al. indicate, all are underpinned by two points:

(1) It refers to an evaluation.
(2) Humans are motivated to sustain high levels of it, even if that MOTIVATION leads to undesirable behavior.

Pyszczynski et al. argue that the pursuit of high self-esteem is motivated by the need to reduce existential anxiety, that is, reminders about human mortality.

Pamela Smith and Jennifer Paff Ogle summarize several research findings when they point out, "athletic participation is associated with increases in self-esteem and positive feelings about the body." William Russell's work suggests that this probably relates to one "dimension" or aspect of self-esteem—the physical (that is, how we judge our own bodies compared with others' bodies). Other dimensions of self-esteem might be intellectual, competitive, congenial (whether others like you, for instance), all, in some way, rating how we value aspects of ourselves.

Robert G. LaChausse's research revealed that the pursuit of self-esteem is a powerful motive behind marathon runners, cyclists, and other exercisers. A great many studies have documented self-esteem's positive association with EXERCISE BEHAVIOR, while others have noted the RELATIONSHIP between low self-esteem and EATING DISORDERS,

OBESITY, and several forms of DEPENDENCE. Self-esteem is popularly used interchangeably with self-evaluation and high self-esteem with, among other terms, self-respect, self-assurance, and dignity, though its closest neighbor conceptually is PHYSICAL SELF-WORTH; for many scholars, the CONSTRUCT has become too inflated to be useful.

Further reading

LaChausse, Robert G. (2006). Motives of competitive and non-competitive cyclists. *Journal of Sport Behavior*, 29, 304–15.

Pyszczynski, T., Solomon, S., Greenberg, J. Arndt, J., and Schimel, J. (2004). Why do people need self-esteem? A theoretical and empirical review. *Psychological Bulletin*, 130, 435–68.

Russell, William D. (2002). Comparison of self-esteem, body satisfaction and social physique anxiety across males of different exercise frequency and racial background. *Journal of Sport Behavior*, 25, 74–90.

Smith, Pamela M. and Paff Ogle, Jennifer (2006). Interactions among high school cross-country runners and coaches: Creating a cultural context for athletes' embodied experiences. *Family and Consumer Sciences Research Journal*, 34, 276–307.

See also: BODY DISSATISFACTION; BODY SHAME; CHARACTER; DEPRESSION; EXPEC-TANCY; FITNESS; OBESITY; PHYSICAL SELF-WORTH; SELF; SELF-DETERMINATION THEORY; SELF-ESTEEM; SOCIAL PHYSIQUE ANXIETY; TYPE A; WEIGHT CONTROL

SELF-FULFILLING PROPHECY

"The self-fulfilling prophecy is, in the beginning, a *false* definition of the situation evoking a new behavior which makes the originally false conception come true." This is how Robert K. Merton (1910–2003), in 1948, first defined the process by which false ideas are converted into practical realities. Merton's seminal argument was inspired by the axiom, "If men define situations as real, they are real in their consequences."

In the 1960s, a study by Robert Rosenthal and Lenore Jacobson illustrated this: they selected 20 percent of children on San Francisco school rolls completely at random and informed the relevant authorities, including teaching staff, that these children were intellectually promising, in their terms, "bloomers." Returning to the schools later, the researchers found that the children in the 20 percent were excelling, not, they concluded, because of their own capacities or efforts, but because of the schools' heightened expectations of them and the extra ATTENTION they were afforded. Teachers had accepted the researchers' initial, deceptive observations and had adjusted their behavior toward the "bloomers" in such a way as to create conditions under which they could achieve good results.

One can easily imagine the experiment in reverse, with specific groups of pupils falsely defined as "slow learners" and a reality being created to fit the beliefs; or some young athletes labeled as GIFTED by coaches. T. S. Horn and C. Lox, in 1993, showed how coaches' expectancies of athletes affect the attention they pay to them and their overall coaching behavior in a way that confirms their initial impressions, however misguided those impressions might have been. Other research has highlighted how referees respond to prejudicial information—for example, about one player or team having a reputation for AGGRESSION—by officiating in a way that confirms original preconceptions.

It is probable that initial beliefs become the raw material of EXPECTANCY, which influences teachers', coaches', or referees' behavior and, in turn, affects the outcome of an interactive activity or sequence of activities. It is probable that the initial preconceptions affect the information that is sought and attended to, the way in which the person encodes the information, remembers it, and uses it to interpret and judge others' behavior. For example, a referee might focus on a particular player about whom he holds preconceptions and interpret his or her behavior as being consistent with his image (perhaps as someone who slyly annoys and prompts opponents toward VIOLENCE; what the British call a "niggling" player). The way in which the referee understands the player's actions and dispenses judgment on him or her will serve to bolster the first impression and thus fulfill his original "prophecy."

There are, however, unintended consequences, as the research of Kristina Diekmann et al. evinces. Individuals who expected opponents to be very competitive became less competitive themselves, encouraging their rivals to rise to the occasion and ultimately confirm their expectations. "They had gone from a self-fulfilling prophecy to a self-defeating one," conclude Diekmann and her colleagues. They "ended up creating a reality that they possibly wished they had not created."

In confirming the power of the self-fulfilling prophecy in competitive situations, the research also highlighted its unreliability as an accurate guide to outcomes. There are innumerable situational contingencies that cannot be known before COMPETITION. Crowd noise, the MOTIVATION of an opponent and even sheer LUCK are among the myriad factors bearing on the outcome of a competition. Even the most self-confident athlete cannot possibly know about all of them.

Further reading

Diekmann, Kristina A., Tenbrunsel, Ann E., and Galinsky, Adam D. (2003). From self-prediction to self-defeat: Behavioral forecasting, self-fulfilling prophecies and the effect of competitive expectations. *Journal of Personality and Social Psychology,* 85, 672–83.

Horn, T. S. and Lox, C. (1993). The self-fulfilling prophecy theory: When coaches' expectations become reality. In J. M. Williams (Ed.), *Applied sport psychology: personal growth to peak performance* (pp. 68–81). Mountain View, Calif.: Mayfield.

Jacobson, Lenore and Insel, Paul M. (Eds.) (1975). *What do you expect? An inquiry into self-fulfilling prophecies.* Menlo Park, Calif.: Cummings.

Jones, R. (1977). *Self-fulfilling prophecies: Social, psychological and physiological effects of expectancies.* Hillsdale, N.J.: Lawrence Erlbaum.

Merton, Robert K. (1948). The self-fulfilling prophecy. *Antioch Review,* 8, 193–219. Reprinted in R. K. Merton (Ed.), *Social theory and social structure.* New York: Macmillan, 1968, and in several texts, including E. McDonagh and J. Simpson (Eds.) (1969), *Social problems,* 2nd edn, New York: Holt, Rhinehart & Winston.

Rosenthal, Robert and Jacobson, Lenore (1968). *Pygmalion in the classroom* New York: Holt, Rhinehart & Winston

See also: ATTRIBUTION; BODY LANGUAGE; CHOKE; DEFENSIVE ATTRIBUTION; EXPECTANCY; FEAR OF FAILURE; HOME ADVANTAGE; HOPE; IMAGERY; IMPOSTOR PHENOMENON; NEGATIVITY; RACE; RELIGION; SEX TYPING; STEREOTYPE; STEREOTYPE THREAT; SUPERSTITIOUS BEHAVIOR

SELF-HANDICAPPING

Claiming or actually creating impediments to sabotage one's own effective ability to function is known as self-handicapping, the word "handicap" evolving from "hand-in-cap," which refers to a seventeenth-century form of betting in which players drew money from a cap, and which then gave its name to a type of horseracing, the *handicap* referring to extra weight carried by the faster horses.

Many people tend, consciously or not, to behave in ways that undermine or subvert their own ABILITY to function optimally whether competing, training, or executing a task. While it may seem a wholly destructive maneuver, research suggests it serves several purposes.

Purpose 1: Threat reduction. The self-handicapper provides him or herself with a convenient subsequent explanation, or perhaps excuses for failure and so affords a degree of SELF-PROTECTION. Failure to beat a rival or complete a gym class can be discounted, being attributable to, for example, adverse weather conditions or an INJURY.

Andrew Elliot and M. A. Church suggest that self-handicappers are motivated by the need for a ready-made excuse for failure. The function of the self-imposed handicap is, "to reduce a threat to esteem," according to R. M. Arkin and A. H. Baumgardner.

In this way, self-handicapping can help preserve SELF-EFFICACY by attributing a defeat or lackluster performance on factors other than one's own ability—an external LOCUS OF CONTROL, in other words.

This is supported by research away from sport and exercise, which also highlights the importance of self-handicapping in image-maintenance.

Purpose 2: Self-presentation. A Norwegian research team observed that students purposely postponed study so that they could attribute failure to lack of preparation rather than limited ability or other explanations that challenge SELF-WORTH. For Yngvar Ommundsen et al., self-handicapping represents "a self-presentational strategy to protect and enhance SELF-ESTEEM."

Extending this, Harry Prapavessis et al. argue self-handicapping is "an attempt at impression management and self-presentation." The Australian research team gives the hypothetical example of an athlete who, before COMPETITION, tells teammates he has a sore arm, then, during competition, massages it in full view of the crowd. "Is he doing so because he wishes to provide *himself* with a ready-made excuse [. . .] or because he wishes to provide *others* with a viable reason not to denigrate him [. . .] ?" they ask, answering affirmatively to both.

Purpose 3: Avoidance. Andrew Elliot et al. have investigated the role of self-handicapping as a mediating link between achievement goals and performance, the CONSTRUCT achievement goals representing the aims of individuals in an evaluative CONTEXT. "Self-handicapping emerges from AVOIDANCE forms of MOTIVATION," conclude Elliot et al. "Indeed self-handicapping appears to be a thoroughly AVOIDANCE-based strategy, in that it is grounded not only in performance-avoidance goals, but also in FEAR OF FAILURE and avoidance temperament."

Purpose 4: Emotions and performance. Self-handicapping appears to be an inadequate or inappropriate adjustment to a competitive environment in which performance is open to the evaluation of a crowd; it also contravenes established psychological advice on PREPERFORMANCE

ROUTINES, such as CENTERING, GOAL SETTING, IMAGERY and so on But these are techniques designed to enhance performance rather than protect SELF-ESTEEM. A study of Canadian university athletes disclosed that self-handicappers suffered no precompetition ANXIETY, nor loss of MOTIVATION. In fact, as researcher Daniel Bailis points out: "Over four months of observations, this research found no consistent evidence of possible negative consequences, but reliable evidence of positive ones, for athletes' emotions and performance during competition."

Purpose 5: Situational relief. Iain Greenlees et al.'s study of judo players brings out the importance of "situational self-handicapping," a process activated only in response to specific circumstances and which does not necessarily indicate a PERSONALITY characteristic: "Self-handicapping should be studied in a social CONTEXT (situational self-handicapping) besides being examined as a personality trait."

While neither this research nor the previously quoted Bailis and Prapavessis et al. studies were concerned with exercise, the results combined indicate how situational self-handicapping has relevance in, for example, a gym, an environment alive with potential for evaluation. Any apprehension, nervousness or other forms of inhibiting emotion can be "relieved" (to use Bailis's term) with self-handicapping, which can also assist in the impression management that operates in exhibiting one's body and indeed one's competence before an audience. The context of a gym, or, for that, matter any public exercise environment, can occasion the self-handicapping response.

Further reading

Arkin, R. M. and Baumgardner, A. H. (1985). Self-handicapping. In J. H. Harvey and G. Weary (Eds.), *Attribution: Basic issues and applications* (pp. 169–257). Orlando, Fla.: Academic Press.

Bailis, Daniel S. (2001). Benefits of self-handicapping in sport: A field study of university athletes. *Canadian Journal of Behavioral Science*, 33, 213–24.

Elliot, Andrew J. and Church, M. A. (2003). A motivational analysis of defensive pessimism and self-handicapping. *Journal of Personality*, 80, 501–19.

Elliot, Andrew J., Cury, François, Fryer, James W. and Huguet, Pascal (2006). Achievement goals, self-handicapping, and performance attainment: A mediational analysis. *Journal of Sport and Exercise Psychology*, 28, 344–61.

Greenlees, Iain, Jones, Simon, Holder, Tim, and Thelwell, Richard (2006). The effects of self-handicapping on attributions and perceived judo competence. *Journal of Sports Sciences*, 24, 273–80.

Ommundsen, Yngvar, Haugen, Richard and Lund, Thorleif (2005). Academic self-concept, implicit theories of ability, and self-regulation strategies. *Scandanavian Journal of Educational Research*, 49, 461–74.

Prapavessis, Harry, Grove, J. Robert, and Eklund, Robert C. (2004). Self-presentational issues in competition and sport. *Journal of Applied Sport Psychology*, 16, 19–40.

See also: ACHIEVEMENT MOTIVE; APPROACH; ATTRIBUTION; CHARACTER; COHESION; HOME ADVANTAGE; HOPE; LEARNED HELPLESSNESS; LOCUS OF CONTROL; NEGATIVITY; NERVOUSNESS; OVERREACHING; PREPERFORMANCE ROUTINES; SELF; SELF-ENHANCEMENT; STEREOTYPE THREAT

SELF-PROTECTION

Method of interpreting an event in a way that prevents harm or INJURY to one's SELF-CONFIDENCE.

See also: SELF-ENHANCEMENT

SELF-RATING

This is a research instrument that allows an individual to assess him- or herself with respect to specified qualities, such as LEADERSHIP—as in the study by Molly Moran and Maureen Weiss. They directed their participants: "For the following items, read each word and make an 'X' through the dash mark which best reflects how you would describe yourself." The INVENTORY listed descriptors, such as *determined, organized*, and *respected*, and players were asked to assess whether these were *not like me, always like me, occasionally like me* and so on.

By contrast, George Rebok and Dana Plude employed a more open-ended approach when studying the effects of exercise on elderly people. Their instructions were to "Track your progress" with the request to provide "a personal history of performance and self-ratings on both physical and cognitive activities and exercises."

David Bergin and Steven Habusta used dual self-ratings of GOAL ORIENTATION, asking both hockey players and their parents to complete self-ratings to compare the assessments.

The INDIVIDUAL ZONES OF OPTIMAL FUNCTIONING approach uses self-rating to CONSTRUCT its MODEL of performance-related states and specify how these change throughout a COMPETITION or exercise. Self-rating is used in the analysis of PHYSICAL SELF-PERCEPTIONS, self-ratings of health being consistent predictors of EXERCISE BEHAVIOR.

Self-rating is typically used in IDIOGRAPHIC studies.

Further reading

Bergin, David A. and Habusta, Steven F. (2004). Goal orientations of young male hockey players and their parents. *Journal of Genetic Psychology*, 165, 383–98.

Hanin, Yuri L. (2003). Performance related emotional states in sport: An analysis. *Forum: Qualitative Research*, 4, 1–29. Available online at http://www.qualitative-research.net/fqs-texte/1–03/1–03hanin-e.htm.

Moran, Molly M. and Weiss, Maureen R. (2006). Peer leadership in sport: Links with friendship, peer acceptance, psychological characteristics, and athletic ability. *Journal of Applied Sport Psychology*, 18, 97–113.

Rebok, George W. and Plude, Dana J. (2001). Relation of physical activity to memory functioning in older adults: The memory workout program. *Educational Gerontology*, 27, 241–159.

Taylor, Adrian H. and Fox, Ken, R. (2005). Effectiveness of a primary care exercise referral intervention for changing physical self-perceptions over 9 months. *Health Psychology*, 24, 11–21.

See also: ABILITY; CONSTRUCT; GOAL ORIENTATION; IDIOGRAPHIC; INDIVIDUAL ZONES OF OPTIMAL FUNCTIONING; INTENSITY; INVENTORY; LEADERSHIP; PARTICIPATION MOTIVATION; PEER LEADERSHIP; PROFILE OF MOOD STATES; STRESS

SELF-REGULATION

As the term suggests, this refers to any effort intended to alter one's own behavior without intervention from external bodies. In sport and exercise psychology, it typically involves a set of techniques, which in Michael Bar-Eli's study were, "AUTOGENIC training, IMAGERY, and BFB [BIOFEEDBACK]," this being "one of the most powerful techniques for facilitating learning of AROUSAL self-regulation."

Self-regulated learning is typically supported by DELIBERATE PRACTICE, though, as Tamara van Gog et al. point out, a learner only becomes capable of self-assessment after mastering basic skills, so self-regulation presumes a degree of MASTERY.

Falko Sniehotta et al.'s study of a cardiac REHABILITATION program highlighted how improving self-regulatory skills enables patients to make intended lifestyle changes. The study focused particularly on one facet of self-regulation: ACTION CONTROL, which involves attempts to control intentional behavior by recognizing a baseline of, in this case, physical FITNESS, planning a method of changing this (through, for example, three forty-five-minute gym sessions per week) and learning how to identify and reduce discrepancies and between expected and actual changes.

Further reading

Bar-Eli, Michael (2002). The effect of mental training with biofeedback on the performance of young swimmers. *Applied psychology: An international review,* 51, 567–81.

Carver, C. S. and Scheier, M. F. (1998). *On the self-regulation of behavior.* New York: Cambridge University Press.

Sniehotta, F. F., Schotz, Urte, Schwarzer, Ralf, Fuhrmann, B., Kiwus, U., and Völler, H. (2005). Long-term effects of two psychological interventions on physical exercise and self-regulation following coronary rehabilitation. *International Journal of Behavioral Medicine,* 12, 244–55.

van Gog, Tamara, Ericsson, K. Anders, Rikers, R. M. J. P., and Paas, Fred (2005). Instructional design for advanced learners: Establishing connections between the theoretical frameworks of cognitive load and deliberate practice. *Educational Technology, Research and Development,* 53, 73–81.

See also: ADHERENCE; AUTOGENIC; BIOFEEDBACK; CONTROL; FEEDBACK; MASTERY; OVERLEARNING; REHABILITATION; SELF-AWARENESS; SELF-TALK; THEORY OF PLANNED BEHAVIOR

SELF-SERVING BIAS

A characteristic form of behavior in which people attribute poor performance following failure to external causes, such as bad LUCK, and good performance following success to internal causes, like ABILITY—sometimes known as DEFENSIVE ATTRIBUTION.

It is what Tom Pyszczynski et al. call "a well-established SELF-ESTEEM maintenance strategy," the use of the word "strategy" suggesting it is designed to achieve an overall aim. "Contrary to the view that a self-serving pattern of internal attributions for success and external attributions for failure reflects attempts to manage the impression of an audience rather than one's own self-esteem, a clear pattern of self-serving attributions was observed in both public and private and was actually somewhat stronger in private than in public," Pyszczynski et al. concluded after their study.

There are other interpretations. Peter De Michele et al., for example, argue: "Stability plays the most significant and predictable role in the self-serving bias [...] the higher the perceived success, regardless of actual performance, the more stable the attributional interpretation."

Other research on self-serving bias has shown it to operate inconsistently. For example, publicly declared attributions are less self-serving than private attributions. They also change over time, when attributors have time to reflect and assimilate more information on the factors affecting the performance. And it simply does not occur in some areas at all, particularly in self-paced events (like free-throwing in basketball). Perhaps surprisingly, away from sport, self-serving bias does not operate among smokers who fail in their attempts to quit smoking: They tend to blame themselves, whatever the circumstances.

Self-serving bias should not be confused with the complementary though distinct concept SELF-ENHANCEMENT.

Further reading

De Michele, Peter E., Gansneder, Bruce, and Solomon, Gloria B. (1998). Success and failure attributions of wrestlers: Further evidence of the self-serving bias. *Journal of Sport Behavior*, 21, 242–56.

Pyszczynski, T., Solomon, S., Greenberg, J. Arndt, J., and Schimel, J. (2004). Why do people need self-esteem? A theoretical and empirical review. *Psychological Bulletin*, 130, 435–68.

Rees, Tim, Ingledew, David K. and Hardy, Lew (2003). Attribution in sport psychology: Seeking congruence between theory, research and practice. *Psychology of Sport and Exercise*, 6, 189–204.

Van Raalte, J. L. (1994). Sport performance attributions: A special case of self-serving bias? *The Australian Journal of Science and Medicine in Sport*, 26, 45–8.

See also: APPROACH; ATTRIBUTION; AVOIDANCE; CHARACTER; DEPENDENCE; EXPECTANCY; LEARNED HELPLESSNESS; LOCUS OF CONTROL; LUCK; MIND ATTRIBUTION; SELF-ENHANCEMENT; SELF-HANDICAPPING; SUPERSTITIOUS BEHAVIOR

SELF-TALK

A method of verbalizing or silently affirming to oneself before or during a contest or, indeed, any kind of event, self-talk has several intended uses: to allay ANXIETY, achieve optimal AROUSAL, invoke feelings or empowerment and SELF-CONFIDENCE, and assist in RELAXATION. It can be used in isolation, or in conjunction with IMAGERY, BIOFEEDBACK, CENTERING, and other PREPERFORMANCE ROUTINES. But it can also misfire, as we will see shortly.

Typically, performers will FOCUS inwardly, listing strengths and deflecting ATTENTION away from others. The LOCUS OF CONTROL can be identified in phrases such as: "You CONTROL your own destiny," or "It's in your own hands now."

John Malouff and Colleen Murphy examine the specific effects of *self-instruction*. Golfers use this type of self-talk: for example, "body still" before putting. A tennis player might utter "high toss" before serving. Exercisers too can use this, mixed with *self-exhortations*. Spinners might encourage themselves with "dig in" or "keep a tight grip." Malouff and Murphy, however, were interested in self-instruction and found they "were more effective than positive self-talk for fine motor movements, but not for strength or endurance tasks."

They suggest three possible reasons:

(1) Self-instructions facilitate focusing on the immediate task at hand.
(2) They serve as quality instruction.
(3) THE HAWTHORNE EFFECT: the awareness of being observed led to an alteration of behavior.

This final reason is important: The original Hawthorne experiments found that participants in the study changed their behavior due to their consciousness of being watched. Using self-talk, whether to instruct or exhort can induce this type of consciousness and it can cut both ways, as Melissa Day et al. detected.

In their research on *lost move syndrome* (that is, when a well-learned SKILL cannot be performed), Day et al. note how its onset is marked by a switch from AUTOMATICITY to conscious processing, a switch that can be instigated by self-talk and scrutiny. Mike Voight endorses this: "Most competitors' performances will suffer when their thoughts and self-talk turn negative and self-defeating. This occurs because this NEGATIVITY can increase INTENSITY levels or adversely affect confidence levels." So, while one of the purposes of self-talk is to reflect and analyze during a performance, this can lead to PARALYSIS BY ANALYSIS.

Negative self-talk has a self-perpetuating quality. For example, a golfer might feel positive about all aspects of his or her game, apart from putts just outside the "gimme" range. "I hate these 3-feet shots," the golfer may say silently as he or she approaches the hole. "Such self-talk reinforces a negative, ineffective SELF-CONCEPT and evokes images and emotions that reinforce the fear," writes Jack Lesyk, suggesting that similar situations will begin to evoke the same negative self-talk, so that each successive outcome will be unfavorable. Positive affirmations can help break this cycle, argues Lesyk, who recommends cue cards plastered with messages such as: "I can putt successfully from this range."

Although it is hard to imagine a pro golfer being handed index cards by a caddie, the point is a valid one. The words are intended to evoke a specific, practiced response in competitive situations. This is an example of COGNITIVE-BEHAVIORAL MODIFICATION: using mental dexterity to change the way the athlete approaches material situations and producing actual changes in the way he or she executes a putt, or any other maneuver, for that matter. Self-talk is designed to alter not only the way competitors view a task but also the way they respond to it—which, in turn, controls arousal levels and, ultimately, thoughts. The negatively self-perpetuating cycle is broken and replaced by an affirmative loop.

As well as having potentially both constructive and destructive effects, self-talk is also unpredictable, as former tennis pro Pat Rafter confirmed when reflecting on his second successive Wimbledon final in 2001. Rafter used self-talk the previous year, when he lost to Pete Sampras. Despite exhorting himself to "relax, relax," he tightened. "So, this time, I'll be saying "CHOKE, choke," said Rafter before his second final. He lost in five sets to Goran Ivanisevich!

Further reading

Day, Melissa C., Thatcher, Joanne, Greenlees, Iain, and Woods, Bernadette (2006). The causes of and psychological responses to lost move syndrome. *Journal of Applied Sport Psychology*, 18, 151–66.

Lesyk, Jack L. (1998). *Developing sport psychology within your clinical practice: A practical guide for mental health professionals.* San Francisco, Calif.: Jossey-Bass.

Malouff, John M. and Murphy, Colleen (2006). Effects of self-instructions on sport performance. *Journal of Sport Behavior*, 29, 159–68.

Voight, Mike (2005). Integrating mental-skills training into everyday coaching. *Journal of Physical Education, Recreation and Dance*, 76, 38–48.

See also: AUTOGENIC; AUTOMATICITY; CENTERING; CHOKE; COMPOSURE; CONTROL; EMOTIONAL CONTROL; GATING; MENTAL PRACTICE; NEGATIVITY; PARALYSIS BY ANALYSIS; PREPERFORMANCE ROUTINES; REHABILITATION; SELF-CONCEPT; SKILL EXECUTION; VISUOMOTOR; ZONE

SENSATION-SEEKING

A sensation is a physical feeling or PERCEPTION that results from something that happens to, or comes into contact with the body. All functioning organisms have some capacity for sensations; from the Latin *sensus*, for "sense." Sensation-seeking is a scale along which we can measure individuals' propensities to search out and participate in activities or experiences that allow various levels of sensation. It has been described as a conceptual relative of the extraversion–introversion personality scale.

Everyone seeks some level of sensory stimulation. *High-sensation seekers* search for high levels. Manrin Zuckerman describes high-sensation seekers as those with "the need for varied, novel, and complex sensations and experiences and the willingness to take physical and social risks for the sake of such experience." The salient features of this group are: pursuit of thrills and new experiences, "disinhibition" (that is, lack of hesitance or reservation), and a susceptibility to boredom.

Unsurprisingly, these characteristics were found among high RISK sport enthusiasts in a study by S. J. Jack and K. R. Ronan; but were absent among aerobic exercisers in a study by T. Babbitt et al. The latter study suggested that the group-based, regimented, and structured approach of the exercise class suited low-sensation seekers.

While such studies might give the impression that status seeking is a trait or an individual property, P. Ekkekakis and S. J. Petruzzello point out that "sensation seeking can also manifest itself as a state," suggesting that it can be triggered or perhaps shaped by the circumstances in which the individual finds him- or herself.

Further reading

Babbitt, T., Rowland, G., and Franken, R. (1990). Sensation seeking and participation in aerobic exercise classes. *Personality and Individual Differences*, 11, 181–3.

Ekkekakis, P. and Petruzzello, S. J. (1999). Acute aerobic exercise and affect: Current status, problems and prospects regarding dose-response, *Sports Medicine*, 28, 337–74.

Jack, S. J. and Ronan, K. R. (1998). Sensation seeking amongst high and low risk sports participants. *Personality and Individual Differences*, 25, 1063–83.

Zuckerman, M. (1979). *Sensation seeking: Beyond the optimal level of arousal*. Hillsdale, N.J.: Lawrence Erlbaum.

SEX

Biological differences between males and females are subject to classification, and the main way in which contemporary CULTURE determines differences is according to sex, a term derived from the Old French *sexe*. Distinctions between men and women that have a natural, as opposed to social, origin which relate to reproductive capabilities and hormonal characteristics as well as anatomical structures are sexual differences—as contrasted with GENDER differences, which involve the cultural responses to biological distinctions. (Note: Sex is often used synonymously with gender though there is a difference, the latter referring to cultural meanings attached to the former.)

Difference 1: History. Humans are a sexually dimorphic species, that is, there are two distinct forms, each with distinct physical and behavioral characteristics. While common sense advises that this is self-evident, history suggests otherwise. Thomas Laqueur's studies of historical medical texts indicate that the male/female dichotomy is a product only of the past 300 years. For 2,000 years before, bodies were not visualized in terms of differences. This means that there were people, some of whom could have children, others of whom could not. Sexual difference was not a CONCEPT, so it was impossible to conceive of a distinct dimorphism. Even physical differences that today seem obvious were not so obvious without a conceptual understanding of sexual difference. In some periods, a woman's clitoris was thought to be a minuscule protuberance, an underdeveloped version of a penis. This vision complemented a male-centered worldview in which, as Laqueur puts it, "man is the measure of all things, and woman does not exist as an ontologically distinct category."

The tradition of physical similarities came under attack, particularly from anatomists who argued that sex was not restricted to reproductive organs but affected every part of the body. Londa Schiebinger's medical history traces how nineteenth-century anatomists searched for the sources of women's difference and apparent inferiority. In the process, the concept of sexual difference was integrated into the discourse; so that, by the end of the century, female and male bodies were understood in terms of opposites, each having different organs, functions and emotions.

In the eighteenth and early nineteenth centuries, intellectual curiosity centered on the dissimilarities between men and women. In what respects were they different? While this may seem perfectly clear, the fact that it was not illustrates just how dramatically understandings of sex have changed. Nelly Oudshoorn's research on how sex hormones were discovered shows how the female body only became conceptualized in terms of its unique sexual character in the 1920s and 1930s. In these decades, sex endocrinology created a completely new understanding of sex based on hormones. Eventually hormonal differences became accepted as natural facts.

Once women were perceived as different from men in a sexual and so most categorical and unchangeable way, they were discouraged from all types of practices, including sports (they were also encouraged in others, such nurturing and domestic duties), which were considered harmful to their reproductive capacities and liable to affect their sexual characteristics. One THEORY held that any woman who competed strenuously risked damaging her reproductive abilities or even developing male physical characteristics such as body hair and a deep voice, a process known as *virilization*.

Even in the late twentieth century—and possibly to the present day—questions of sex differences persisted in sports. The CONCEPT of psychological ANDROGYNY dispelled the idea that EMOTION, INTELLIGENCE, PERSONALITY, and other features were not linked to biological sex. Despite the grand explanatory power conventionally attributed to sex, many of the differences—particularly psychological differences—ascribed to men and women owe more to cultural than to natural processes, though the interplay between the two has prompted several lines of inquiry.

Difference 2: Responses. Evolutionary psychology—which is an APPROACH based on the gradual development of the species from simple to complex forms and which emphasizes how genetic and biological imperatives respond to changing contexts—suggests that sex differences can explain differences in behavior, including EXERCISE BEHAVIOR. If, as evolutionary psychologists propose, sex differences are the means by which men and women select one another as mates, then we should expect sex-specific EXERCISE MOTIVATION, men working out their upper bodies and women working out their lower bodies to gain an advantage in the COMPETITION for mates. "In an evolutionary paradigm, individuals are motivated to engage in behaviors that attract mates," states Peter Jonason, adding that his study "indicates the possibility that there are pronounced sex differences in exercise behaviors that are driven primarily by intrasexual COMPETITION" (that is, within rather than between sexes). Men and women strive to enhance their attractiveness to others and increase the probability of finding mates, or getting a "higher quality mate."

Marita McCabe and Lina Ricciardelli gathered broadly similar results from their research, though their interpretation of them is pitched at a different level. "Being thin is highly valued within our society, particularly among women, for whom thinness is often equated with attractiveness," they declare. "Being muscular is also highly valued in our society, particularly among men." Their interpretation is predicated on "societal messages," as they call them, rather than biological imperatives.

These are just two examples of investigations in which sex and the multiple differences that are organized around it, bifurcate populations in a way that implies that biological difference itself is the *primum mobile*—the central source of action. This implication has been challenged by research accentuating the human RESPONSE to the PERCEPTION of sex differences as a more important starting point. Returning to the earlier distinction, investigation continues to ask which has greater explanatory power, sex or gender?

Further reading

Hausenblas, Heather A. and Symons Downs, Danielle (2002). Relationship among sex, imagery, and exercise dependence symptoms. *Psychology of Addictive Behaviors*, 16, 169–72.

Jonason, Peter K. (2007). An evolutionary psychology perspective on sex differences in exercise behaviors and motivations. *Journal of Social Psychology*, 147, 5–14.

Laqueur, T. (1990). *Making sex: Body and gender from the Greeks to Freud*, Cambridge, Mass.: Harvard University Press.

McCabe, Marita P. and Ricciardelli, Lina A. (2003). Body image and strategies to lose weight and increase muscle among boys and girls. *Health Psychology*, 22, 39–46.

Oudshoorn, N. (1994). *Beyond the natural body: An archaeology of sex hormones*. London and New York: Routledge.

Schiebinger, L. (1989). *The mind has no sex: Women in the origins of modern science*. Cambridge, Mass.: Harvard University Press.

See also: ANDROGYNY; ANOREXIA NERVOSA; BEM SEX ROLE INVENTORY; BODY SHAME; EATING DISORDERS; EXERCISE BEHAVIOR; EXERCISE DEPENDENCE; FITNESS; GENDER; GENDER VERIFICATION; INSTINCT; MASTERY; MODELING; OBESITY; SELF-ENHANCEMENT; SELF-FULFILLING PROPHECY; SEX TYPING; SOCIALIZATION; VIOLENCE

SEX TEST

Examination of parts of the body to determine someone's SEX.

See also: GENDER VERIFICATION

SEX TYPING

This refers to the categorization of people, their appearance or behavior, according to expectations and perceptions of what is considered typical of each SEX. The expectations are frequently, perhaps always, based on a particular kind of STEREOTYPE.

Much research has strongly advanced the idea that, while there is nothing inherent or natural about boys opting for robust and aggressive pursuits and girls favoring reflective and nurturing pastimes, they are still regarded as such. For example, some activities, such as collision or combat sports, are seen as "masculine," while reading and playing with dolls are still regarded as "feminine."

Sex typing affects the entire SOCIALIZATION of children, so that, by the time they reach adolescence, they are likely to engage in sex-typed behavior and experience this as "natural." But this is changing, as the research of Susan McHale et al. indicates. The researchers studied the sex typing of children and teenagers, noting particularly how it affects adolescents much more than children and how males are more susceptible to sex-typed activities than females. The study reinforced the conclusion of earlier work, that children's schemas about sex-appropriate activities affect their choices but, crucially, that "the role of contextual forces in affording opportunities and setting constraints on children's daily activities" is pivotal.

Perhaps the most revealing finding of the McHale et al. study was the resistance of young women to sex-typed roles and their preparedness to spend time in "masculine activities." The study, which was published in 2004, deviated from earlier research, especially in highlighting the degree to which young women engaged in "counterstereotypical activities."

The research combines interestingly with a study of the masculine-dominated culture of French soccer by Geneviève Coulomb et al. Female players committed fewer aggressive infringements than their male counterparts, yet were penalized more by male referees. "GENDER stereotypes could be relevant explanations for such results," concluded the researchers.

There is also a biological meaning of sex typing: it is determining the sex of a person, or some other organism, particularly in ambiguous cases where sex tests are necessary.

Further reading

Beale, C. R. (1994). *Boys and girls: The development of gender roles.* New York: McGraw-Hill.

Coulomb, Geneviève, Rascle, Olivier, and Souchon, Nicolas (2005). Player's gender and male referees' decisions about aggression in French soccer: A preliminary study. *Sex Roles.* 52, 547–53.

Koivula, Nathalie (1999). Sport participation: Differences in motivation and actual participation due to gender typing. *Journal of Sport Behavior,* 22, 1–22.

McHale, Susan M., Kim, Ji-Yeon, Whiteman, Shawn, and Crouter, Ann C. (2004). Links between sex-typed time use in middle childhood and gender development in early adolescence. *Developmental Psychology,* 40, 868–81.

See also: ANDROGYNY; ANOREXIA NERVOSA; BEM SEX ROLE INVENTORY; BODY IMAGE; BULIMIA NERVOSA; CONTEXT; CULTURE; EATING DISORDERS; GENDER; GENDER VERIFICATION; IDENTITY; INSTINCT; MODELING; PHYSICAL SELF-WORTH; SCHEMA; SELF-FULFILLING PROPHECY; SEX; SOCIALIZATION; STEREOTYPE

SIBLING RIVALRY

COMPETITION for the same objective between two or more children, or offspring having common parents.

See also: RIVALRY

SKILL

The competence to perform elaborate planned sequences of behavior efficiently and repeatedly to achieve a predetermined objective with economy of effort is known as a skill. The word is from the Old Norse *skil*, meaning distinction or knowledge. In contrast to what some regard as natural ABILITY, skill is achieved through learning, development, and refinement. Skill is obviously central to sport, though its relevance to exercise is less apparent. A closer examination of the exact types of skill required in each area will reveal a variety of skills, all of which are learned in their own specific CONTEXT.

Context 1: Sport. There are three basic types of skill, all referring to the capacity for carrying out motor activities, which is the commonsense understanding of a skill; for example, controlling a ball or executing a dive:

(1) motor skills, which are responsible for the production of complex sequences of physical movement;
(2) perceptual skills, which involve receiving information about the environment by way of the senses, and which are particularly important in many sports and activities where, for instance peripheral vision is called for;
(3) cognitive skills, which relate to thinking, again important skills in many sports, particularly chess, bridge, and sports in which superior performance depends on anticipation and DECISION-MAKING.

In all three types, extended DELIBERATE PRACTICE reduces the need for involvement as performance becomes automatic. Different enterprises demand different permutations of the three types of skill, an activity such as lifting weights requiring few perceptual or cognitive skills but a lot of motor skills to perform a task successfully. Success in golf depends on choosing and carrying out strokes that are appropriate to particular conditions and so involves all three types of skill. Skill in this instance lies as much in the strategy of the game as in the making of accurate individual strokes, or in muscular strength.

There is a relationship between skill, aptitude, and ability. For example, an individual's potential to perform a task is *aptitude*. This describes the possibility that an individual may be trained. If an individual can perform a certain task without any training at all, we refer to his or her ability—the unlearned qualities, faculties, or talents that enable them to complete the task without instruction or practice. Training will enhance their ability to perform the task with greater degrees of proficiency. In other words, skill is made possible by a person's aptitude and builds on their ABILITY (TALENT is a somewhat uncertain property).

Returning to weightlifting, this is an activity that involves *gross motor* abilities, including dynamic strength (in exerted force), explosive strength (short bursts of muscular effort), and gross body coordination (while the lift is in motion). Other sports involve *psychomotor* abilities, for example, manual dexterity in manipulating objects, aiming at targets, and rapid reaction to stimuli, such as the bang of a starter's pistol. A person's aptitude is the potential they have to convert these abilities into skills.

The skill developed through training in weightlifting is clearly very different from the skills honed by a chess player, golfer, gymnast, or many other types of athletes. Whereas weightlifting involves a *discrete* skill with a sharply defined beginning and end, other sports, such as cycling or rally driving, are *continuous* and progress in long cycles without a clear finish. The latter involves the performer in continually varying responses to continuously varying stimuli. Beyond this basic bifurcation of skills, there are many ways of subdividing types of athletic skills. Competitive and exercise environments often determine the precise manner in which we classify skills.

Time is an important criterion. In some situations, where a person might operate in an environment which affords him or her plenty of time, *self-paced* skills are called for. A basketball player many stand and compose him- or herself when preparing to take a free shot or just practicing alone; there is no interference from other players and he or she has complete CONTROL over the pace at which the skill is brought about. That same person will then employ *externally paced* skills. His or her movements will be affected by the speed and direction of the ball and other players, both teammates and rivals— these constitute the external factors that will impinge on the execution of skills and introduce pressure to move quickly. While basketball players need to employ both self- and externally paced skills, some sports, such as golf, require self-paced skills exclusively. Most sports that need externally paced skills include an element for self-paced skills; even fast sports like soccer and hockey have interludes when self-pacing is essential.

The competitive environment will also dictate whether the athlete can use *closed* skills. The exact conditions under which the skill is to be performed are established in advance for all competitors and incalculable factors are minimized. Typically, closed skills are exhibited in sports that emphasize aesthetic as well as athletic qualities. Synchronized swimming, ice dancing, and gymnastics are obvious cases. By contrast, *open* skills are practiced in environments in which change, inconsistency, and indeterminacy are the norm. All sports in which confrontation or collision are ingredients need open skills: athletes have to make quick decisions and react to movements, either of other athletes or of missiles, to perform the skill. Open skills typically incorporate all three basic skills: motor, perceptual, and cognitive.

Most sports, whether competitive or recreational, do not involve one distinct skill but a great many that are linked together in the execution of an athletic performance. Coaching skills usually involve digesting sequences of activity, reducing them to a convenient number of small movements. Sprint coaches often make their athletes work exclusively on their starts before switching to the pickup and then moving to finishing. The skills that contribute to a 100-meters sprint are linked together in an unbroken chain, so that the whole motion is continuous.

Context 2: Exercise. David Peterson and Jennifer Millier itemize "a dozen skill areas: delegating, coaching, prioritization and time management, leadership, communication, networking, managing upward, influencing, listening skills, organizational politics, stress management, coping with ambiguity."

All of these might not qualify as individual skills, but by *skill areas* the authors presumably mean they each provide a specific context in which skill can be performed. Skill, in this sense, is not confined to motor activity: it covers other areas of competence where complex patterns of behavior and thought are carried out. Exercising routinely in a goal-directed manner requires such skills.

In their study of exercise as part of an ALCOHOLISM rehabilitation program, Jennifer Read and Richard Brown observe: "Skills can include time-management skills, such as balancing exercise and recovery commitments, or anger-management skills, such as using physical exercise to work through painful or unpleasant emotions."

Similarly, George Rebok and Dana Plude's research on the effects of exercise on the elderly concluded:

> The proposed program will equip older adults with the skills needed for maintaining and increasing daily physical, as well as daily cognitive activity levels, for improved perceived efficacy for participating in an activity enhancement program, and for monitoring the effects of increased activity on everyday cognition, memory, and functional performance.

In this sense, a skill has a kind of multiplier effect. It combines with other skills and qualities to produce new skills that help ADHERENCE, enhance SELF-EFFICACY, sharpen PERCEPTION, and so on.

Exercise environments are typically social milieus, which both promote and encourage what Caroline Keating et al. call *group-relevant skills.* These reinforce a group's status hierarchy and stimulate "forms of social DEPENDENCY in group members." While this sounds rather like surrendering one's autonomy to a collectivity with a pecking order, Keating et al. argue that that it serves to heighten the importance of the group, tighten COHESION, build comradeship, and foster mutual support.

This inclusive APPROACH to skill is symptomatic of an inflation of the concept. It is further distended by Leslee Fisher and Craig Wrisberg's study of REHABILITATION from INJURY, which necessitates developing the "Buddhist skills of 'taking the middle path.' This includes learning how to grieve and let go, accepting what happens and learning from it, having a 'you win some, you lose some' attitude, allowing natural PAIN to occur and working through it, and speaking up when one has been hurt."

If these are to count as skills, or even (taking a cue from the earlier comments) skill areas, they might properly be collected under the rubric of *coping skills*, which are conscious and rational methods of responding to ANXIETY and STRESS by directing efforts at the source. Someone who senses other aerobic-class members are sneering at them because of their clumsy maneuvers might experience anxiety and learn a coping skill, such as taking additional classes or hiring a private trainer. If they just dropped the class, they would be avoiding the source of anxiety and thus taking a defensive option.

Finally, skill in sport's analogous sphere of GAMBLING has been studied by, among others, Michael Cantinotti et al., who expose it as a "cognitive distortion," providing betters with the misapprehension that they have refined their competence and knowledge to be able to predict the outcome of competitions. Cantinotti and his colleagues' research indicates that "perceived skills in sports betting are only a manifestation of the illusion of CONTROL often found in most gambling activities."

Further reading

Cantinotti, Michael, Ladouceur, Robert, and Jacques, Christian (2004). Sports betting: Can gamblers beat randomness? *Psychology of Addictive Behaviors*, 18, 143–7.

Fischman, M. G. and Oxendine, J. B. (1998). Motor skill learning for effective coaching and performance. In J. M. Williams (Ed.), *Applied sport psychology: Personal growth to peak performance,* 3rd edn (pp. 13–27). Mountain View, Calif.: Mayfield Press.

Fisher, Leslee A., and Wrisberg, Craig A. (2005). The "Zen" of career-ending-injury rehabilitation. *Athletic Therapy Today*, 10, 44–5.

Griffin, L. L., Mitchell, S. A. and Oslin, J. L. (1997). *Teaching sport concepts and skills.* Champaign, Ill.: Human Kinetics.

Keating, C. F., Pomerantz, J., Pommer, S. D., Ritt, S. J. H., Miller, L. M., and McCormick, J. (2005). Going to college and unpacking hazing: A functional approach to decrypting initiation practices among undergraduates. *Group Dynamics: Theory, Research and Practice*, 9, 104–26.

Peterson, David B. and Millier, Jennifer (2005). The alchemy of coaching: "You're good, Jennifer, but you could be *really* good." *Consulting Psychology Journal: Practice and Research*, 57, 14–40.

Read, Jennifer P. and Brown, Richard A. (2003). The role of physical exercise in alcoholism treatment and recovery. *Professional Psychology: Research and Practice*, 34, 49–56.

Rebok, George W. and Plude, Dana J. (2001). Relation of physical activity to memory functioning in older adults: The memory workout program. *Educational Gerontology*, 27, 241–59.

See also: ABILITY; ADHERENCE; AGING; ALCOHOLISM; ANGER; ANXIETY; APPLIED SPORT PSYCHOLOGY; APPROACH; AUTOMATICITY; AVOIDANCE; CHOKE; COACH–ATHLETE RELATIONSHIP; COGNITION; COGNITIVE LOAD THEORY; DECISION-MAKING; DELIBERATE PRACTICE; FEEDBACK; GOAL; GOAL SETTING; LEFT-HANDEDNESS; MEMORY; MENTAL PRACTICE; MODELING; NERVOUS SYSTEM; PEAK PERFORMANCE; PROPRIOCEPTION; REHABILITATION; SELF-CONFIDENCE; SELF-EFFICACY; SKILL ACQUISITION; SKILL EXECUTION

SKILL ACQUISITION

As conventionally understood, skill acquisition refers to the process through which we experience the environment and learn to perform activities that are refined into skills. This suggests that *acquired* skills depend on critical experiences rather than innate, species-specific properties; the Latin root *acquirere* means to "gain in addition."

Experience 1: Adaptation. Some scholars doubt whether we possess skills at all. For instance, Lucien Malson's study of feral children "reveals the absence of these dependable *a priori*, of adaptive schemata peculiar to the species." Deprived of human contact and reared in the wild by animals in their formative years, feral children who had been discovered by humans were mute quadrupeds, who began to stand erect only after painstaking tutoring. Some eventually spoke, though not competently. One boy could use his hands only for picking up objects between his thumb and index finger. Yet, many were adept at tree climbing and other dexterous acts not usually associated with humans, such as lapping up water or fighting with hands and teeth.

Their perceptual skills were also different. Some had acute senses of smell and hearing, while others could not judge distance or even distinguish between paintings and reality. Children who had been raised by nocturnal animals had photophobia, an extreme sensitivity to light. Malson encouraged a conception of humans as having "an *acquired nature* [...] a structure of possibilities [...] which are only realized in some specific social CONTEXT."

Experience 2: Stages. Any analysis of skill acquisition should be informed by this observation: Even the most elementary of tasks, ones that are commonly regarded as "natural" are learned. Some are adaptations to the environment; others are developed through imitation and tuition. P. M. Fitts and M. I. Posner formulated an early MODEL that identified three stages to the acquisition. The *cognitive stage* involves understanding a task and its demands. Lack of familiarity means that there will be clumsiness and plenty of errors. Progressing to an *intermediate and associative stage*, the learner begins to identify strategies that allow quick PERCEPTION and retrieval of information pertinent to the task at hand; the subject learns appropriate responses; errors decrease and speed increases. The final stage is *late or autonomous*: The skilled performer is able to execute the SKILL, or skills, efficiently and with the minimum of errors without much cognitive involvement.

Experience 3: Practice. But the question this raises is: Precisely how does the acquisition process work? Several theories, including COGNITIVE LOAD THEORY, have purported to answer this, many resting on the idea that, initially, we learn through observation of others who have already acquired a skill. While this is intuitively appealing, research by Spencer Hayes et al. indicates that: "Physical practice is proposed to be the critical variable for scaling [controlling motions]." Observation, imitation and, most importantly, practice are the keys to the successful execution of a planned action.

During practice, the results of our engagement with the material world feeds back to us in the form of valuable information, which we, in turn, use to modify our behavior. KNOWLEDGE OF RESULTS accomplished through previous actions is fed back to the individual; the more precise and direct, the more effective. In the early cognitive stage, the information needs to be exact and detailed, but, as the practicing individual improves and reaches the associative stage, he or she is able to modify behavior in accordance with the knowledge fed back. Eventually, less conscious attention needs to be paid and the performance of the skills becomes automatic.

At this autonomous stage, when the basic skills have been conquered, each item of MEMORY-stored information covers a larger unit of performance. For example, a cricket batsman will not need FEEDBACK on grip, posture, and positioning, as he does not need to be consciously aware of these features. He may still require information on how to play a particular type of bowler on a particular type of surface, and that information may result in his using a mixture of unorthodox reverse sweeps and pulls with conventional driving. Because fewer units of performance need to be adjusted, the modification will appear smoother. Highly skilled performers are not only efficient but also versatile. An efficient, yet inflexible batsman may have acquired technique but may be unable to adapt to unusual conditions. And, as Matt Jarvis points out, individual differences complicate the model: "Some athletes are more dependent on their visual sense; others on PROPRIOCEPTION. Some of us are extremely analytic, while others like to 'just do it'." Jarvis is suspicious of one-size-fits-all models of skill acquisition.

Experience 4: Transference. Skill acquisition is often very specific and does not transfer to other skills, though it can carry the potential for transference to related domains. This means that the strategies and knowledge picked up in acquiring one skill may be applied to other areas. Mathematics students famously apply the skills acquired during their studies to chess-playing. COGNITIVE LOAD THEORY has demonstrated how there are common mechanisms of learning, the acquisition of SCHEMA (for storage of appropriate knowledge and modes of implementation) being a crucial one. Bo Jackson and Dennis Compton were both adept at ostensibly very different sports, in Jackson's case football and baseball, in Compton's, soccer and cricket. But each pair of sports shared perceptual and cognitive skills, if not motor skills. The strategies employed to master one of the sports were presumably used to master the other. Or, for cognitive load theorists, the transfer was made possible by the schema.

Typically, improvements in skill acquisition are rapid at first, then slow down to a gradual pace. Simple repetition and REINFORCEMENT is the key mechanism at first, but improvement requires new knowledge and strategies. An improvement in accuracy and coordination is not achieved by performing the same skill over and over again but by introducing new, related skills. Athletes improve by taking on new and possibly unfamiliar challenges. This does not mean that highly proficient performers will lose their original skills. Quite the contrary: once the skill has been attained, it is secure for many, many years, though, of course, fine edges may be dulled without continual practice. Even after prolonged inactivity, enforced by INJURY, athletes can usually recapture skills in a relatively short period. Injury, loss of ambition or lack of physical condition rather than the erosion of skill end careers.

Further reading

Fitts, P. M. and Posner, M. I. (1967). *Human performance*, 2nd edn, Belmont, Calif.: Brooks/Cole.

Hayes, S. J., Hodges, N. J., Scott, M. A., Horn, R. R., and Mark Williams, A. (2006). Scaling a motor skill through observation and practice. *Journal of Motor Behavior*, 38, 357–66.

Jarvis, Matt (2006). *Sport psychology: A student's handbook*. London and New York: Routledge.

Malson, Lucien (1972). *Wolf children and the problem of human nature*. New York: Monthly Review Press.

van Gog, Tamara, Ericsson, K. Anders, Rikers, Remy M. J. P., and Paas, Fred (2005). Instructional design for advanced learners: Establishing connections between the theoretical frameworks of cognitive load and deliberate practice. *Educational Technology, Research and Development*, 53, 73–81.

See also: AUTOMATICITY; BIOFEEDBACK; COGNITION; COGNITIVE LOAD THEORY; DELIBERATE PRACTICE; EXECUTIVE CONTROL; FEEDBACK; INFORMATION PROCESSING; LEARNED HELPLESSNESS; LIFE COURSE; MASTERY CLIMATE; MEMORY; MENTAL TOUGHNESS; MODELING; OVERTRAINING SYNDROME; PROPRIOCEPTION; SCHEMÁ; SKILL; SOCIALIZATION

SKILL EXECUTION

Putting learned expertise into effect under testing conditions is skill execution, from the Latin *exsequi* for "carry out," or "punish." Execution involves both sensory and motor functions, that is sensorimotor actions, and these can be broken into three components: (1) memorizing features of previous performances, or rehearsals (such as in training)—including sensory input (how the body felt); (2) interpreting information from the present environment; and (3) exercising judgment in choosing actions appropriate to particular circumstances, which may change suddenly.

So, skill execution involves the three tenses of past, present, and future. It requires the performer to draw on experiences accumulated from practice and *past* performance and combine these with knowledge of *immediate* situations, while *anticipating* the probable results of lines of action. All the time, adjustments must constantly be made to take account of FEEDBACK from the here and now. An obvious example: a golfer might discover midway through a round that a strong wind necessitates a modification of technique. Information from the present environment impels a change, familiarity with similar past situations influences the decision and an evaluation of the likely outcomes of the decision informs the response. Other situations in different sports may demand that the performer responds more quickly than a golfer, but the components of the process are likely to be similar.

While execution is kinetic in the sense that it results from motion, the observable motions conceal several important responses.

Response 1: Nerves. The successful performance of SKILL usually depends on responding to swift and definite changes in the environment. Both components of the NERVOUS SYSTEM—the central nervous system (CNS) and the PERIPHERAL NERVOUS SYSTEM (PNS)—need to direct changes and issue instructions to relevant parts of the body in order that they react quickly. The quickest communication system is based on electrical impulses. Simply put, the CNS comprises the CONTROL center of the brain and its message conduit, the spinal cord and the PNS is the network of nerves originating in the brain and spinal cord which is responsible for picking up messages from the skin and sense organs (sensory nerve cells) and carrying messages from the CNS to the muscles (motor nerve cells).

Response 2: Cognition. It is probable that athletes and nonathletes alike can pick up roughly equivalent quantities and qualities of information from the environment. Sense organs enable us to take in information through eyes, ears, and other body parts. What separates highly skilled performers from others is how they interpret information and adjust their behavior accordingly. Interpreting information received through the senses involves several cognitive processes. Very briefly, data received, whether visual, auditory, or tactile, is stored before it is either sent to the short-term, or working MEMORY, or discarded.

For example, a basketball player will momentarily store the sound of the official's whistle before attempting a free shot; or a quarterback will fleetingly hold the image of a moving wide receiver before releasing a pass. In both these and myriad other cases in sports, the athlete is busy screening out irrelevant information and selectively attending to the job at hand. It is for this reason that Rob Gray suggests, "attentional mechanisms would seem to be one of the most prominent behaviors that distinguish experts from novices." Skilled executors (not executioners, which is something different!) operate fast, efficient CONTROL procedures that can, as Gray points out, "function largely without the assistance of working memory or attention." (AUTOMATICITY is the process at work at this level of execution.) "Largely" but not *completely* without the assistance of working memory and, in stressful, competitive situations, as Sian Beilock and Thomas Carr point out: "Pressure creates mental distractions that compete for and reduce working memory capacity that would otherwise be allocated to skill execution." This why even extremely skilled performers occasionally CHOKE.

Athletes often interpret, or make sense of sensory input in highly specialized ways. A cricketer can use tactile information about the surface of a cricket ball; a tennis player will hit the heel of a hand with the racket to assess the tension of the strings. Disabled athletes often compensate for the loss of sense organs with others that are highly developed, such as a sense of equilibrium or an acute sense of hearing. In all cases, initial movements provide sensory feedback, which facilitates adjustment and control of future actions—which, in turn, provide further information.

Response 3: Decisions. Perhaps the most critical component in the performance of skill is DECISION-MAKING. Once information from the environment has been received and understood, an athlete is faced with a range of possibilities about what to do. Skilled athletes typically make appropriate choices. How do they arrive at their decisions? It is tempting to imagine that they consider the various actions available to them, project ahead to possible outcomes and assign probabilities and utilities to these outcomes. In other words, this would be a completely rational decision-making process based on systematic principles. In practice the process is less rational.

In the 1980s, an influential collection of research by Daniel Kahneman et al. indicated that we make use of experiences to devise rules of thumb, or HEURISTICS. For instance, an experienced, skilled boxer might base a provisional fight strategy against southpaw opponents on his (or her) recollection of previous similar opponents and, assuming the memory is sound and that the experiences were representative, then there is sufficient for a judgment. This may serve the boxer well in this fight, but it may also lead to error if the opponent is unlike previous southpaw opponents (that is, unrepresentative), or if the boxer has fought so few southpaws that previous experiences are not readily available. Heuristics may prove reliable in most circumstances, but they are imperfect, especially in circumstances filled with uncertainty—as sports are, of course. Highly skilled performers are those who can estimate the probabilities of outcomes and respond appropriately regularly, though not on every single occasion.

More recently, research interest has centered on *metacognition*, which Michael Martinez defines as "the monitoring and control of thought" and analogizes with a toolbox. The conceptual tools at our disposal enable us not only to think about our own thoughts but also the factors that are influencing—or might influence—those thoughts.

Matt Jarvis emphasizes that "experts make more use of metacognitive knowledge [than less skilled performers]."

Further reading

Beilock, Sian L. and Carr, Thomas H. (2005). When high-powered people fail: Working memory and "choking under pressure" in math. *Psychological Science*, 16, 101–5.

Gray, Rob (2004). Attending to the execution of a complex sensorimotor skill: Expertise differences, choking and slumps. *Journal of Experimental Psychology: Applied*, 10, 42–54.

Jarvis, Matt (2006). *Sport psychology: A student's handbook*. London and New York: Routledge.

Kahneman, Daniel, Slovic, Paul, and Tversky, Amos (Eds.) (1982). *Judgement under certainty: Heuristics and biases*. Cambridge: Cambridge University Press.

Martinez, Michael E. (2006). What is metacognition? *Phi Delta Kappa*, 87, 696–9.

See also: AGING; ATTENTION; CHOKE; COGNITION; CONCENTRATION; DECISION-MAKING; EXECUTIVE CONTROL; FEEDBACK; FLOW; FOCUS; INFORMATION PROCESSING; INTELLIGENCE; MEMORY; NERVOUS SYSTEM; PEAK PERFORMANCE; PERCEPTION; PERFORMANCE ENHANCEMENT; PROPRIOCEPTION; REACTION TIME; SELF-TALK; SKILL

SLEEP

Sleep is the condition in which the NERVOUS SYSTEM is relatively inactive, eyes closed, postural muscles relaxed, and consciousness temporarily suspended. It derives from the Old English noun *slæp*.

There are two main types of sleep: REM and non-REM, sometimes called NREM. REM is an acronym for rapid eye movements, which characterize the stage of sleep when the eyeballs move in the sockets and there is a relative absence of delta brainwaves (the slow, large-amplitude electrical impulses, as measured on an ELECTRO-ENCEPHALOGRAM), flaccid musculature, fluctuating heartbeat, erratic respiration, genital changes, and, in the vast majority of cases, vivid and emotional dreaming. REM sleep typically occurs in cycles every ninety minutes.

NREM sleep is divided into four stages based on the proportion of delta waves. The third and fourth stages can have 50 percent or more delta waves, and they are referred to collectively as short-wave sleep: heartbeat is regular, respiration rhythmic, and metabolic activity low. This is deep sleep.

Sleep has been linked beneficially to exercise, as Greg Atkinson and Damien Davenne observe: "It is generally thought that exercise constitutes a non-pharmacologic behavior which promotes sleep, and so regular bouts of physical activity are recommended as therapy for individuals who are having difficulty in sleeping."

The recommendation is supported by the research of F. Mougin et al., which focused on how sleep deprivation affects athletes' recovery process when working out the following day.

During sustained physical activity, energy is expended and tissue broken down. As sleep conserves energy and restores tissue, it seems reasonable to conclude that there is a complementary relationship between the two. There is also the obvious fact that exercise is physically fatiguing and sleep is restitutive (though fatigue is not the same as sleepiness).

Yet, studies suggest other variables that complicate the picture. Shawn Youngstedt highlights four:

(1) People who sleep better show a greater willingness and ABILITY to exercise.
(2) Better health and less STRESS are associated with better sleep and a greater willingness to exercise.
(3) Exercisers tend not to smoke or drink excessively and so sleep better.
(4) Outdoor exercisers receive several times more natural daylight than the average, which is about twenty minutes per day, or 2,500 lux (the unit of luminance), and exposure to light is associated with better sleeping.

Then, there is the possibility that sleep is affected not by exercise per se, but by the rise in body and brain temperature it induces. Passive body heating by way of a sauna or a soak in the bathtub increases slow-wave sleep. Even a bout of exercise shortly before retiring can raise body temperature, without being arousing enough to disrupt sleep, and so promote sleep.

The impact of exercise on MOOD has been documented and, as ANXIETY and DEPRESSION are commonly cited causes of insomnia, it seems plausible to suggest a CORRELATION, though evidence has been, perhaps surprisingly, inconclusive.

Can exercise actually have unfavorable consequences on sleep? "While most people have assumed that exercise promotes sleep, the potential adverse effects of exercise on sleep have received little ATTENTION," writes Youngstedt, noting anecdotal evidence that

OVERTRAINING SYNDROME leads to disturbed sleep. We should also consider the deleterious impact of EXERCISE DEPENDENCE, perhaps obliging the dependant to work out at the expense of sleep. Youngstedt and Christopher Kline question the reliability of assertions about the RELATIONSHIP between exercise and sleep, believing most arguments to be simplistic. They argue for the inclusion of social variables, such as socioeconomic status and level of education as well as physical variables, such as BODY MASS INDEX, all of which have the potential to affect the RELATIONSHIP.

Other research has focused on the other direction of the relationship. In particular, Cheri Mah's research (reported by Jennifer Warner) found that athletes performed significantly better and reported improvements in mood states and higher energy levels after extra sleep over several nights.

Further reading

Atkinson, Greg and Davenne, Damien (2006). Relationships between sleep, physical activity and human health. *Physiology and Behavior*, 90, 229–35.

Mougin, F., Bourdin, H., Simon-Rigaud, M. L., Nguyen Nhu, U., Kantelip, J. P., and Davenne, D. (2001). Hormonal responses to exercise after partial sleep deprivation and after a hypnotic drug-induced sleep. *Journal of Sports Sciences*, 19, 89–97.

Youngstedt, Shawn D. (1997). Does exercise truly enhance sleep? *The Physician and Sportsmedicine*, 25, 72–82.

Youngstedt, Shawn D. (2005). Effects of exercise on sleep. *Clinics in Sports Medicine*, 24, 355–65.

Warner, Jennifer (2007). More sleep boosts athletic performance. June 13. Available online at http://www.webmd.com/sleep-disorders/news/20070613/more-sleep-boosts-athletic-performance.

Youngstedt, Shawn D. and Kline, Christopher E. (2006). Epidemiology of exercise and sleep. *Sleep and Biological Rhythms*, 4, 215–21.

See also: BIOFEEDBACK; DEPENDENCE; ELECTROENCEPHALOGRAM; EXERCISE DEPENDENCE; HYPNOSIS; MEDITATION; OBESITY; OVERTRAINING SYNDROME; POSITIVE AFFECT; RELAXATION; STRESS; YOGA

SLUMP

A sudden decline or a gradual subsidence in form that extends beyond normal fluctuations is known as a slump, a word that may have origins in the German *schlump,* for wet, muddy ground.

In the 1990s, J. Taylor's research suggested that potentially anything can CAUSE a slump and basically concurred with the orthodox view that INJURY, *pressing* (trying too hard), OVERREACHING (training too much), and PARALYSIS BY ANALYSIS (thinking too deeply) are among the common sources of a performance decrement that can then become self-perpetuating. So, ANXIETY over a poor performance can affect the next performance, which feeds more anxiety, and so on. Pressure builds as performers take conscious CONTROL over what are ordinarily automatic skills, suggesting an inverse RELATIONSHIP between the level of performance and the amount of skill-focused ATTENTION.

More recently, however, research has cast doubt on this. Focusing attention on the procedural aspects of SKILL execution "will likely hurt current real time performance in the short term," according to Rob Gray. Yet, "it may serve to improve SKILL EXECUTION in the long run [. . .] skill-focused ATTENTION in experts should no longer be considered a negative trait that must be avoided at all costs."

Further reading

Goldberg, A. (1998). *Sports slump busting: 10 steps to mental toughness and peak performance.* Champaign, Ill.: Human Kinetics.

Gray, Rob (2004). Attending to the execution of a complex sensorimotor skill: Expertise differences, choking and slumps. *Journal of Experimental Psychology: Applied,* 10, 42–54.

Taylor, J. (1988). "Slumpbusting: A systematic analysis of slumps in sports" *The Sport Psychologist,* 2, 39–48.

See also: AUTOMATICITY; CAUSE; CHOKE; MENTAL TOUGHNESS; MOMENTUM; OVER-REACHING; OVERTRAINING SYNDROME; PARALYSIS BY ANALYSIS; PEAK PERFORMANCE; SELF-CONFIDENCE; SKILL EXECUTION; STREAKS

SOCIAL FACILITATION

The presence of others has the effect of making an action or process easier; in other words, it facilitates it. For example, fully fed chickens carry on eating when surrounded by other chickens which are eagerly devouring feed; children will play more enthusiastically when their friends are around. The effect is known as social facilitation, and, in sport, it was first documented in the pioneering research of Norman Triplett (1861–1931), who, in the late nineteenth century, observed the differences in cycling records set under different conditions. Facilitate is from the Latin *facilis* for "easy" or "unconstrained," and the research suggested that company can have the effect of removing constraints on performance (it is also related to *facile*, meaning "neat," but lacking recognition of complexities).

Triplett compared cyclists riding alone with those paced by the clock and those racing against each other. There was a pronounced improvement across the three situations, leading Triplett to conclude: (1) The presence of others aroused the "competitive instinct" which, in turn, released hidden reserves of energy; (2) the sight of others' movements had the effect of making the subject speed up.

Speed was important to the research tradition started by Triplett. In the 1920s, Floyd Allport (1890–1978) argued that the presence of others facilitated enhanced quantity or quickness of movement, but that it also led to decrements in precision or quality of performance. Greater speed came at the cost of accuracy. In this and subsequent research, the role of others' presence in facilitating behavioral changes in athletes, whether individuals or in teams, became ever clearer.

Robert Zajonc (1923–) is credited with providing most clarity to social facilitation with his 1965 research. A follower of the variant of learning theory advanced by Clark Hull (1884–1952), known as DRIVE reduction hypothesis (which maintains that GOAL-motivated behavior is directed toward the reduction of drive states), Zajonc argued that the sheer presence of others, either as spectators or fellow participants (co-actors), increased DRIVE or AROUSAL level. If the participant is well practiced and has command over a SKILL, or the skill itself is relatively simple, then the increased DRIVE benefits performance and the appropriate response is dominant. If, on the other hand, the participant is a beginner or the skill is difficult, then the performance will be hindered. This would account for why young or inexperienced athletes sometimes "freeze" in their first outing at a big venue.

Contradictory research findings followed. For example, some studies showed that rookies were less affected by audiences than experienced competitors and that their performance did not suffer; other studies showed that social facilitation worked for simple skills but not always where complex skills were needed. There were also conceptual criticisms leveled at Zajonc. Whereas Hull had used drive as a theoretical CONSTRUCT to explain motivated behavior, Zajonc conflated it with AROUSAL, which may be operationalized empirically, using palmar sweating, heart rate increases, self reports, and so on. In this way, Zajonc produced a THEORY that could be tested and challenged. (In using "drive" to explain behavior, Zajonc used a precise operational definition and specified quantifiable behavioral referents as measures of the construct.)

Doubts were raised about the "mere presence factor". Is the mere presence of others enough to arouse athletes, or are there other causal factors, such as the type of crowd or the athletes' awareness of the crowd? For instance, if athletes interpret the spectators as having the potential to evaluate them, then this may give rise to ANXIETY, which leads to decrements in performance. If nothing turns on the performance and the consequences of the crowd's evaluation is of no significance, then there is unlikely to be any apprehension.

There have been several attempts to modify Zajonc's formulation, one of the most interesting by Leonard Wankel, whose 1984 essay moved beyond what he called the "mechanistic drive theory" toward "more complex models which place greater emphasis on COGNITION and how the individual interprets the information in the social situation." "It is this subjective social situation that constitutes the reality to which the individual reacts," wrote Wankel, who introduced features such as age, GENDER, previous experience, and PERSONALITY into the mix to show that there are many surprising findings in social facilitation.

Less experienced competitors experience less STRESS and distraction at big championship events than more experienced athletes, presumably because they feel they have "nothing to lose." Audience effects on female competitors were changing when Wankel wrote his paper. The gender of the audience and that of the competitor, as well as the nature of the task, were all factors. But values have changed, and it is less likely that the gender of performers or observers has as much influence.

The composition, size, density, expectations, and general character of the crowd also have relevance: bellicose and boisterous fans urging competitors to play more aggressively may influence performance. Crowds are often thought to "get behind" teams, especially when at home. This is one among other factors in HOME ADVANTAGE, though we should also allow for the possibility that officials as well as athletes are subject to social facilitation and their performance will affect outcomes.

The famous HAWTHORNE EFFECT operates when people are aware of being watched and improve their performance accordingly.

Further reading

Allport, Floyd H. (1924). *Social psychology*. Boston, Mass.: Houghton Mifflin.

Triplett, Norman L. (1898). The dynamogenic factors in pacemaking and competition. *American Journal of Psychology*, 9, 507–33.

Wankel, Leonard (1984). Audience effects in sport. In J. M. Silva and R. S. Weinberg (Eds.), *Psychological foundations of sport* (pp. 293–314). Champaign, Ill.: Human Kinetics.

Zajonc, R. B. (1965). Social facilitation. *Science*, 149, 269–74.

See also: AROUSAL; CHOKE; CONTEXT; DRIVE; FEEDBACK; GROUP DYNAMICS; HOME ADVANTAGE; NOMOTHETIC; RELATIONAL; RINGELMANN EFFECT; SOCIAL LOAFING; TEAM PLAYER; VICARIOUS AGENCY; YIPS

SOCIAL LOAFING

Not to be confused with just loafing—spending time idly or acting at a leisurely pace—*social* loafing is the inclination to reduce effort when working toward a common GOAL with others. In other words, individuals tend to slacken off when trying to accomplish something with a group. This is by no means confined to sports; it has implications for any collective endeavor. Yet, it does have particular effects in team sports where the potential for individuals to reduce effort under some conditions is high.

A research team led by B. Latané in 1979 questioned the adage "Many hands make light work." The team discovered that there was a "motivational loss" when individuals worked in groups, and this led to a decrease in performance. Exploring what had previously been called the RINGELMANN EFFECT, the team was interested in the apparent loss in MOTIVATION of group members as the size of the group increased. The tasks assigned were relatively simple, clapping and shouting, but the finding was significant: people who thought they could get "lost in the crowd" did not try as hard as they would if they thought they could be identified as individuals. A comparison would be people singing hymns in a church: if the church is relatively empty, they might sing more vigorously than if it was crowded. The potential for being identified and appraised decreases with increases in the size of the group.

So, social loafing is unlikely to occur when performers know or suspect their performances are being evaluated or even compared with those of others. Research by S. G. Harkins and J. M. Jackson indicated that social loafing is least likely to happen when individual performances can be clearly monitored, giving rise to ANXIETY about evaluation. The potential for social loafing is highest when all team members are not only trying to achieve a common goal but also performing the same task. A tug-of-war is the most obvious example because every team member is doing exactly the same thing—pulling the rope. Rowing is another sport in which all members of the crew, apart from the cox, are working in unison. Athletes are unlikely to believe they are accountable for their individual performances in these kinds of contests.

In 1983, N. L. Kerr argued that this creates two types of competitor. The *free rider* thinks there is a good chance that other members of the group will perform better than him or her and he or she will still get the same amount of credit. So the cost–benefit equation is simple. Do less work for the same approval. The problem is that the others will get the same idea, and, rather than being the *suckers* who do all the work while others slack off, they reduce their own efforts as a way of balancing out what might otherwise be an unequal distribution of effort. In this light, social loafing appears to be less the result of a reduction in motivation and more an avoidance of doing more than one's fair share of the work for only the same amount of credit.

Minimizing social loafing in team sports is obviously crucial, and S. G. Harkins and K. Szymanski provide a clue as to how coaches might do this: merely reminding individuals in a group of a personal performance standard was enough in itself to stop social loafing. In most team sports, there is a division of labor that ensures that individual performances can be monitored. In baseball and cricket, two team sports in which statistics are tabulated on individuals' batting, fielding, and so on, the possibilities for social loafing are slim.

After reviewing recent research, Matt Jarvis asks how we recognize when social loafing or SOCIAL FACILITATION will occur. In the latter, the presence of others encourages better performance. He answers that GOAL ORIENTATION will determine which. Task-oriented individuals will strive hard in all conditions, while ego-oriented people will save their best performances for when they can be assessed, that is judged.

Further reading

Harkins, S. G. and Jackson, J. M. (1985). The role of evaluation in eliminating social loafing. *Personality and Social Psychology Bulletin*, 11, 456–65.

Harkins, S. G. and Szymanski, K. (1989). Social loafing and self-evaluation with an objective standard. *Journal of Experimental Psychology Bulletin*, 11, 456–65.

Jarvis, Matt (2006). *Sport psychology: A student's handbook.* London and New York: Routledge.

Karau, S. J. and Williams, K. D. (1993). Social loafing: A meta-analytic review and theoretical integration. *Journal of Personality and Social Psychology*, 65, 681–706.

Kerr, N. L. (1983). Motivation losses in small groups: A social dilemma analysis. *Journal of Personality and Social Psychology*, 45, 819–28.

Latané, B, Williams, K., and Harkins, S. G. (1979). Many hands make light the work: The causes and consequences of social loafing. *Journal of Personality and Social Psychology*, 37, 822–32.

See also: CONTEXT; GOAL; GOAL ORIENTATION; GROUP DYNAMICS; INCENTIVE; MOTIVATION; RELATIONAL; RINGELMANN EFFECT; SANDBAGGING; SOCIAL FACILITATION; TASK/EGO ORIENTATION; YERKES-DODSON LAW

SOCIAL PHYSIQUE ANXIETY

"This occurs when individuals are concerned that other people are negatively evaluating their physiques or bodies," observe Vikki Krane and her colleagues.

Social physique anxiety (SPA) is closely related with BODY IMAGE dissatisfaction. Exercise domains are places where, as Marcus Kilpatrick et al. point out, "individuals actively engage in the construction and management of their image and impression projected to others." Gyms, in particular, present a CONTEXT in which all manner of people will appear to each other, often disclosing parts of their body they might otherwise conceal and moving their bodies in ways that would be considered unusual, if not inappropriate, in other surroundings. They also offer, as Christopher Lantz et al. put it, "situations where their bodies may be evaluated negatively."

Even if fellow exercisers are not actually judging someone's body, the PERCEPTION that they are can produce SPA. There is irony in the fact that, although exercise has a proven positive effect in diminishing SPA, those who experience ANXIETY about exhibiting their bodies will tend to avoid group exercise situations like gym classes and opt for just one same-sex training partner.

SPA does not affect everyone uniformly, of course. Harry Prapavessis et al. suggest that reference groups make a difference. For example, physically disabled persons may not agree with, or even be aware of the evaluations of their fully abled counterparts. African American males have lower BODY DISSATISFACTION than many other groups, according to research by William Russell, who argues, "Cultural ideals have been shown to shape individuals' body-image experiences and the extent to which one utilizes dieting, exercising, and other measures to manage body-image experiences."

The point is that groups internalize specific expectations rather than a single, homogeneous ideal body shape, though a formidable body of work has documented the acceptance of what Heather Hausenblas and Kathleen Martin call "the aesthetic ideal of a thin physique."

This has become something of a cultural default setting for a great many young women. Hence, "Social physique anxiety is considered a RISK factor in the development of EATING DISORDERS," according to the research of Cecilie Thøgersen-Ntoumani and Nikos Ntoumanis. It has been speculated that SPA is characterized by a desire to CONTROL the appearance of one's body, though Thøgersen-Ntoumani and Ntoumanis point out that this is not supported by evidence. Being preoccupied with one's body and, perhaps more relevantly, how others judge one's body, is unsurprisingly a feature of the motivational mix behind eating disorders.

Further reading

Hausenblas, Heather, A. and Martin, Kathleen A. (2000). Bodies on display: Female aerobic instructors and social physique anxiety. *Women in Sport and Physical Activity Journal*, 9, 1–14.

Kilpatrick, Marcus, Bartholomew, John, and Riemer, Harold (2003). The measurement of goal orientations in exercise. *Journal of Sport Behavior*, 26, 121–7.

Krane, Vikki, Waldron, Jennifer, Michalenok, Jennifer, and Stiules-Shipley, Julie (2001). Body image concerns in female exercisers and athletes: A feminist cultural studies perspective. *Women in Sport and Physical Activity*, 10(1), 17–33.

Lantz, Christopher D., Hardy, Charles J., Ainsworth, Barbara E. (1997). Social physique anxiety and perceived exercise behavior. *Journal of Sport Behavior*, 20, 83–94.

Prapavessis, Harry, Grove, J. Robert, and Eklund, Robert C. (2004). Self-presentational issues in competition and sport. *Journal of Applied Sport Psychology*, 16, 19–40.

Russell, William D. (2002). Comparison of self-esteem, body satisfaction, and social physique anxiety across males of different exercise frequency and racial background. *Journal of Sport Behavior*, 25, 74–90.

Thøgersen-Ntoumani, Cecilie and Ntoumanis, Nikos (2007). A self-determination theory approach to the study of body image concerns, self-presentation and self-perceptions in a sample of aerobic instructors. *Journal of Health Psychology*, 12, 301–15.

See also: ANOREXIA ATHLETICA; ANOREXIA NERVOSA; BODY DISSATISFACTION; BODY IMAGE; BODY SHAME; BULIMIA NERVOSA; EATING DISORDERS; EXERCISE BEHAVIOR; EXERCISE DEPENDENCE; EXERCISE MOTIVATION; FITNESS; MUSCLE DYSMORPHIA; OBESITY; PARAMETERS; PERFECTIONISM; PHYSICAL SELF-PERCEPTIONS; PHYSICAL SELF-WORTH; PREGNANCY; SELF-CONCEPT; SELF-DETERMINATION THEORY; SELF-ESTEEM

SOCIALIZATION

The process by which humans learn to become members of a culture is socialization, from the Latin *socius*, "company," and *izare*, meaning "method." Defined in its broadest sense, CULTURE is everything that is learned, rather than inherited genetically; it is transmitted from one generation to the next primarily through language, changed for future transmission, then changed again, so that it never actually stands still. Socialization has two main phases, primary and secondary; in some cases, there is resocialization; anticipatory socialization refers to preparing for what might happen in future.

Phase 1: Primary. This is the initial phase in which language, personality, and basic cultural competence are achieved. As humans develop in groups of other humans, they learn the characteristics that actually make them human, for example, their PERSONALITY, values, and behavioral traits. Obviously, human development depends on a combination of biological, psychological, and social factors, and much of the argument on the precise balance of influences in the socialization process involves the nature versus nurture debate. Recognizing that there are biological PARAMETERS does not preclude the substantial impress of culture in, for example, cognitive development, including INTELLIGENCE, IDENTITY formation, and SELF-CONCEPT.

Phase 2: Secondary. This involves the learning of specialist skills and capacities. Clearly, certain aspects of us are not conferred by nature. We have no biological predisposition to speak English rather than Punjabi any more than we have to like rock more than classical music. Even GIFTED artists are not literally "gifted," as in having natural endowments but may have basic propensities that are nurtured and shaped. MODELING enables a person to refine his or her abilities by imitating and, perhaps, innovating on the accomplishments of others. This has obvious applicability in a domain where someone acquires a new vocabulary, a new circle of significant others, and, probably, a new set of goals as well as a new repertoire of behavioral habits. For instance, Chris Harwood's IDIOGRAPHIC research on athletes from a variety of sports, including soccer, swimming, and tennis, was designed, "to facilitate an in-depth investigation of those factors underpinning the socialization of both task and ego orientations."

People *learn* achievement orientations and the kind of goals at which they are aiming as well as the methods they use to pursue them and, in this sense, the sport CONTEXT involves *anticipatory* socialization: learning a future role to which an athlete aspires, whether it is that of a champion or a routine healthy competitor.

Phase 3: Resocialization. This means learning sometimes the most basic "facts" over again. For instance, converts to a new RELIGION sometimes question domain assumptions, such as loving one's parents and believing in god. The biographical hiatus jolts individuals into interpreting their "former life" so that they can look back and render their lives intelligible in terms of the new conceptual framework, or SCHEMA. To a lesser extent, being imprisoned or joining the armed forces both involve a resocialization of sorts, because new values, codes, and behaviors are imposed and need to be learned. While the changes are not so dramatic, converts to exercise sometimes acquire an EXERCISE IDENTITY as they immerse themselves in a culture that can facilitate SELF-ACTUALIZATION. They might be using exercise as a part of REHABILITATION from ALCO-HOLISM or some other form of DEPENDENCE and experience the exercise environment as a liberating resocialization into new values and behavior.

Agents of socialization are varied. While family, close peers, and sometimes the church are instrumental in primary phases, the media, particularly television, and the school become more prominent later. In secondary socialization, any number of agencies can figure. This is not to suggest that the various agencies exert a one-way influence: the socialization process should be understood as negotiated, that is, a productive interaction between the person and the agencies involved. All socialization takes place in face-to-face interaction, yet, at the same time, both primary and secondary socialization relate the individual to the wider world. "The attitudes which the individual learns in socialization usually refer to broad systems of meaning and of values that extend far beyond his immediate situation," wrote Peter and Brigitte Berger in what remains one of the most thorough examinations of the process.

Claudia Kernan and Patricia Greenfield's study illustrates this perfectly. The authors use the idea of *value lenses*, which affect how each member of two basketball teams in Los Angeles saw themselves in a common environment. All had different principles and standards of behavior, which were gradually remodeled through their INTER-PERSONAL RELATIONSHIP with the others. Gradually, a "team culture" was created by the participants, though this was never actually complete because such cultures "are not static essences; instead they are dynamic adaptations to real-world situations."

Further reading

Berger, Peter and Berger, Brigitte (1981). *Sociology: A biographical approach*. New York: Penguin.

Harwood, Chris (2002). Assessing achievement goals in sport: Caveats for consultants and a case for contextualization. *Journal of Applied Sport Psychology*, 14, 106–19.

Kernan, Claudia L. and Greenfield, Patricia M. (2005). Becoming a team: Collectivism, ethnicity, and group socialization in Los Angeles girls' basketball. *Ethos*, 33, 542–66.

McHale, Susan M., Kim, Ji-Yeon, Whiteman, Shawn, and Crouter, Ann C. (2004). Links between sex-typed time use in middle childhood and gender development in early adolescence. *Developmental Psychology*, 40, 868–81.

See also: ABILITY; AGGRESSIVENESS; ATHLETIC IDENTITY; BURNOUT; COACH–ATHLETE RELATIONSHIP; COGNITIVE LOAD THEORY; CONTEXT; CULTURE; EXERCISE BEHAVIOR; EXERCISE IDENTITY; EXPECTANCY; GENDER; GOAL ORIENTATION; GROUP DYNAMICS; IDENTITY; INTERNALIZATION; LEFT-HANDEDNESS; LIFE COURSE; MASTERY CLIMATE; MENTALITY; MODELING; MORAL ATMOSPHERE; MOTIVATIONAL CLIMATE; OUT-PERFORMANCE; PARTICIPATION MOTIVATION; RELATIONAL; SELF-CONCEPT; SELF-DETER-MINATION THEORY; SELF-ENHANCEMENT; SEX TYPING; SKILL; STEREOTYPE; TEAM PLAYER; VISUAL PERCEPTION

SOCIOTROPY

The state of exhibiting "a strong desire for approval, acceptance and nurturance from others, greater sensitivity to interpersonal criticism or rejection, and greater effort to please others to maintain inter-personal relatedness," as Tina Oates-Johnson and David A. Clark describe it, sociotropy can manifest in behavior designed to impress or please others (at the gym or on the playing field), or in personal habits, such as dieting. "Socio" is from the Latin *socius*, for compa-nion, and "tropy" is from the Greek *trope*, meaning turning toward (as in, for example, psychotropic drugs that affect mental states, and heliotropic, directed toward the sun).

Julie Juola Exline and Marci Lobel's study of OUTPERFORMANCE indicated that there is a RELATIONSHIP between sociotropy and what they call "sensitivity about being the target of a threatening upward comparison." In other words, people who wanted to please others felt anxious about beating them in competitive events.

Sociotropy is also prevalent in younger women who have heigh-tened concerns with physical appearance, body weight, and image. Social disapproval from others due to weight and physical appearance has been found to be a significant predictor of elevated *dysphoria*—generalized lack of ease with life—in dieting women.

Further reading

Exline, Julie Juola and Lobel, Marci (1999). The perils of outperformance: Sensitivity about being the target of a threatening upward comparison. *Psychological Bulletin*, 3, 307–37.

Oates-Johnson, Tina and Clark, David A. (2004). Sociotropy, body dissatisfaction and perceived social disapproval in dieting women: A prospective diathesis-stress study of dysphoria. *Cognitive Therapy and Research*, 28, 715–31.

See also: BODY IMAGE; BODY SHAME; DEPRESSION; EMOTIONAL TONE; OUTPERFORMANCE; RELATIONSHIP; SOCIALIZATION

STEREOTYPE

Derived from the printing term for a plate cast from a mold (originally from the Greek *stereos*, for solid), a stereotype is a popular, oversimplified or distorted impression of a particular group or type of person. Gordon Allport (1897–1967) wrote of the stereotype in his 1954 classic *The Nature of Prejudice*: "An exaggerated belief associated with a category. Its function is to justify (rationalize) our conduct in relation to that category."

Stereotypes are, almost by definition, easy to grasp and reliable as a guide to conduct, even if that conduct impacts unjustly and unfairly on the group to which the stereotype is applied. Negative and unfavorable generalizations are usually emphasized, though even positive attributions can be damaging.

"Stereotyped beliefs about Black and White athletes can influence perceptions of an athlete's performance," write Jeff Stone and his colleagues. "Specifically, Black athletes are perceived to have natural athletic ABILITY (which is a positive sports attribute) but are thought to be less intelligent, even in a sports CONTEXT (a negative sports attribute)."

Stereotypes can give rise to a SELF-FULFILLING PROPHECY: They sometimes contribute to the creation of conditions under which it is difficult for the stereotyped group to act in a way that undermines the popular image. Stone et al. suggest that, in excelling, black athletes confirm the stereotype of them as naturally GIFTED, while whites become concerned and perform poorly. In living up to the stereotype, black athletes inadvertently validate beliefs about their lack of INTELLIGENCE, and, in the process, as Matthew Soar detects, "they may provide dominant groups with a means to contain, CONTROL and exploit these imagined cultural and physical dispositions." In Soar's view, there is a link between psychological and political realms: "The phenomenal—and radically *atypical*—success of Michael Jordan as an enormously wealthy, black basketball star and media celebrity, for example, can be attributed at least in part to the successful preclusion of these particular associations [with lack of intelligence]."

One of the prominent features of the stereotype is its degree of permanence. Once fixed in the popular imagination, it is extremely difficult to damage even in the presence of evidence that contradicts it.

Stereotyped behavior is persistent, repetitive behavior that conforms to a fixed pattern, though for no apparent purpose. The behavior may be physical or verbal; it can manifest in gestures, such as repetitive rubbing of hands or touching.

Further reading

Allport, Gordon W. (1979). *The Nature of Prejudice*, 25th anniversary edn. New York: Perseus.

Soar, Matthew (2001). Engines and acolytes of consumption: Black male bodies, advertising and the laws of thermodynamics. *Body and Society*, 7, 37–55.

Stone, Jeff, Lynch, Christian I., Sjomeling, Mike, and Darley, John M. (1999). Stereotype threat effects on Black and White athletic performance. *Journal of Personality and Social Psychology*, 77, 1213–27.

See also: GENDER; GOAL ORIENTATION; HOME ADVANTAGE; INTELLIGENCE; OUT-PERFORMANCE; RACE; ROLE MODEL; SELF-FULFILLING PROPHECY; SEX TYPING; SOCIALIZATION; STEREOTYPE THREAT; YIPS

STEREOTYPE THREAT

A STEREOTYPE refers to an image of a group that is popular but based on distorted, or clichéd information, and a threat is, of course, a warning of danger or RISK. In sport, stereotype threat "occurs when PERCEPTION of a negative stereotype about a social group leads to less-than-optimal performance by members of that group, according to Sian Beilock and Allen McConnell.

Stereotypes abound in sports, especially ones with racist connotations: white people do not have natural ABILITY; black people are GIFTED in certain sports. These can influence competitors' own perceptions, not only of others but also of themselves. Similarly, women have been stereotyped as "not fast, strong, or athletic," according to Beilock and McConnell. Left-handers can also be included; southpaw baseball pitchers are subjects of negative stereotypes, especially when facing right-handed batters.

The manner in which people think of and classify themselves can significantly alter the impact that performance stereotypes have on their SKILL EXECUTION, or indeed on their involvement in sports. White sprinters who remain aware of the supposed natural prowess of black opponents might induce a self-fulfilling cycle in which they self-handicap themselves and fail. Or a prospective black golfer might interpret the limited number of African American professionals as evidence of their lack of suitability and withdraw his or herself from the sport completely.

Research indicates that the stereotype threat exerts at least two different effects: (1) it fills working MEMORY with worries; (2) it entices the competitor to attend explicitly to the execution of well-learned motor skills, such as golf putting, skills that would ordinarily have been performed automatically. It can also work in the other direction, to enhance performance. The "white men can't jump" stereotype might be threatening to white players, but it might actually improve the performance of blacks by raising SELF-CONFIDENCE and SELF-EFFICACY in task performance so that they can concentrate on high-level skills, such as devising and executing tactics. This is known as *stereotype lift*.

Further reading

Beilock, Sian L. and McConnell, Allen R. (2004). Stereotype threat and sport: can athletic performance be threatened? *Journal of Sport and Exercise Psychology*, 26, 597–609.

Walton, G. M. and Cohen, G. L. (2003). Stereotype lift. *Journal of Experimental Social Psychology*, 39, 456–67.

See also: ANXIETY; APPROACH; CHOKE; GENDER; HOME ADVANTAGE; LEFT-HANDEDNESS; NEGATIVITY; NERVOUSNESS; OUTPERFORMANCE; PERCEPTION; RACE; SELF-CONFIDENCE; SELF-EFFICACY; SELF-ESTEEM; SELF-FULFILLING PROPHECY; SELF-HANDICAPPING; STEREOTYPE

STIMULUS

Event or occurrence that evokes behavioral responses from an organism; from the Latin *stimulare*, animate.

See also: ANXIETY; ATTENTION; COGNITION; COGNITIVE-BEHAVIORAL MODIFICATION; DECISION-MAKING; EXECUTIVE CONTROL; EYE MOVEMENT; FEAR; FOCUS; IMAGERY; INFORMATION PROCESSING; MOTOR REACTION; PERCEPTION; PREMACK PRINCIPLE; REACTION TIME; REINFORCEMENT; RESPONSE; VISUAL PERCEPTION

STREAKS

Uninterrupted sequences of recent results are known as a streaks, from the Old English word *striks*, meaning strokes (for example, of pens or swords). A popular notion in sports is that winning or losing streaks affect ensuing contests. Going into a match-up on a five-game hot streak is preferable to coming off five straight defeats, for example. The idea is that the rise in SELF-CONFIDENCE and SELF-ESTEEM that accompanies a succession of good results affects the positive MOMENTUM of an individual or entire team. Yet, in contrast to accepted wisdom, Roger Vergin found that the statistical chances of winning are not dependent on the results of recent contests, and so the streak has no causal connection with future outcomes.

Vergin's findings tend to undermine athletes' own commonsense ideas about the impetus precipitated by winning runs and the self-perpe-tuating qualities of a SLUMP: "The probability of winning a game is independent of the results of recent games"—though it should be pointed out that much of the research on MOMENTUM focuses on athletes' PERCEPTION of the impetus rather than its objective effects.

Further reading

Vergin, Roger C. (2000). Winning streaks in sports and the misperception of momentum. *Journal of Sport Behavior*, 23, 181–97.

See also: CAUSE; FLOW; GAMBLING; HOPE; LUCK; MOMENTUM; PERCEPTION; SELF-CONFIDENCE; SELF-ESTEEM; SLUMP

STRESS

Although it is commonly associated with almost any form of dis-comfort, stress is, strictly speaking, a constraining or propelling force or pressure that causes a significant change in a system; alternatively, it may be approached as the RESPONSE of a system to force; or even the RELATIONSHIP between the two. Robert Gatchel captures aspects of all three when he defines stress as "the process by which environmental events threaten or challenge an organism's WELL-BEING and by which that organism responds to this threat." The term "stress" is taken from distress, originally *destresser,* an Anglo-French word meaning to vex or make unhappy.

Stress is one of the most overused and misunderstood terms in the lexicon. People complain of being "stressed-out" by their work, their domestic situation, and even their leisure activities. In this sense, stress is considered an effect or consequence of, or RESPONSE to underlying forces, rather than the forces themselves. This still fits in with the above definition, though scholars have tried to be more precise in examining the RELATIONSHIP between stress as an antecedent of effects and stress as a reflection of other conditions.

Richard Lazarus, for example, has argued that stress should properly be examined as a transaction between the human being and the environment, the force being produced by their interaction rather than residing in either one or the other. This moves away from more straightforward CAUSE-effect models in which stress is the causal agent. For Lazarus, the process is *recursive*, the individual and the environment affecting and changing each other in a sort of rebounding interaction. (The word recursive is from the Latin *re*, as in "again," and *curs*, "run.") So far then, we see that stress is a response to conditions but a response that can boomerang and prompt further changes that can exacerbate the sources of the stress. We will now examine the implications of this, first in sport, then in exercise.

Context 1: Sport. Tim Woodman and Lew Hardy echo the thoughts of many: "It is the individual's cognitive appraisal of the situation within the work environment that is central to this organizational stress process." Their IDIOGRAPHIC study concerned *organizational stress* in athletes, which they "conceived as an interaction between the individual and sport organization."

Again, the emphasis is on the response to demands. Those demands might seem onerous to one person, a piece of cake to another, and these differences in interpretation defy any simple solutions. "The coping process in sport is influenced by the athlete's PERCEPTION of the event," write Mark Anshel et al. after concluding that there can be no single effective response to what they call "acute stress," which is brought about by the appraisals of others. In this instance, appraisal is a *stressor*, that is the source of the emotional strain. If the concept of recursive stress is accepted, the stressor is actually a relationship, or a response of an individual to a situation that can rebound back into that situation. This is why responses to what might be potentially stress-inducing situations are crucial.

Athletes recovering from INJURY often have prolonged periods of enforced inactivity. Some might use the time productively, involving themselves in new pursuits, while others might find the lack of sti-mulation intolerable and experience what Hans Selye calls *hypostress* (we have all probably felt something similar when waiting for hours with nothing to do at an airport). In the results–oriented environment of professional sport, *hyperstress*, which results from an overload of responsibility, or *distress*, which manifests in tension and apprehension, are most common. Selye's other main type is EUSTRESS, which we have all experienced, if only by watching a game of foot-ball, which can be stressful, though in a pleasant and perhaps fulfilling and maybe even euphoric way.

Context 2: Exercise. "The benefits of exercise to psychological WELL-BEING have been well documented. In particular, exercise is thought to reduce DEPRESSION [. . .] and stress." This is the conclusion of John Maltby and Liza Day, though they add a qualification: "Extrinsic motives for exercise are thought to lead to stress in individuals, whereas intrinsic motives for exercise are thought to lead to a release of stress."

Influenced by SELF-DETERMINATION THEORY, Maltby and Day argue that, while motives for taking up exercise might begin as extrinsic, they are likely to change to intrinsic as time passes. After six months, SELF-RATING revealed a rise in SELF-ESTEEM and a reduction in stress levels. While the results were consistent with those of a great many other studies, the motivational shift is crucial to under-standing how exercise can relieve stress and, again, this alerts us to the importance of COGNITION. Someone might join a gym with a utilitarian MENTALITY. A friend has told him it will be useful for meeting business contacts. While this proves well founded, the gym encounters do little to alleviate the stress he has been experiencing, at least until he starts actually enjoying his sessions for themselves rather than what he can get out of them. Intrinsic motives replace the extrinsic.

If our networking gym member had not just been looking for contacts and had opted for an outdoor exercise regimen, research indicates that he would have found it enjoyable, stimulating, and energizing, though not as relaxing as his gym sessions. And if he had been a *she*, she would have been more susceptible to the environment and would have found outdoor experience more enriching. These were the findings of Thomas Plante et al. whose findings concurred with the others about the stress-reducing effects of exercise, while disclosing how men and women favor different stress reducing—a finding supported by Jon Hammermeister and Damon Burton.

Further reading

Anshel, Mark H., Jamieson, John, and Raviv, Shula (2001). Cognitive appraisals and coping strategies following acute stress among skilled competitive male and female athletes. *Journal of Sport Behavior*, 24, 128–44.

Gatchel, Robert (1996). Stress and coping. In A. M. Colman (Ed.), *Companion encyclopedia of psychology*, (Vol. I, pp. 560–77). London and New York: Routledge.

Hammermeister, Jon and Burton, Damon (2004). Gender differences in coping with endurance sport stress: Are men from Mars and women from Venus? *Journal of Sport Behavior*, 27, 148–64.

Lazarus, R. S. (1993). From psychological stress to the emotions: A history of changing outlooks. *Annual Review of Psychology*, 44, 1–21.

Maltby, John and Day, Liza (2001). The relationship between exercise motives and psychological well-being. *Journal of Psychology*, 135, 651–60.

Plante, Thomas G., Cage, Cara, Clements, Sara, and Stover, Allison (2006). Psychological benefits of exercise paired with virtual reality: Outdoor exercise energizes whereas indoor virtual exercise relaxes. *International Journal of Stress Management*, 13, 108–17.

Selye, Hans (1983). The stress concept: Past, present and future. In C. L Cooper (Ed.), *Stress Research* (pp. 1–20). New York: Wiley.

Woodman, Tim and Hardy, Lew (2001). A case study of organizational stress in elite sport. *Journal of Applied Sport Psychology*, 13, 207–38.

See also: ADHERENCE; AEROBIC/ANAEROBIC; ALCOHOLISM; ANXIETY; BURNOUT; CHOKE; COPING STRATEGIES; DEPENDENCE; DEPRESSION; EMOTION; EUSTRESS; EXTRINSIC MOTIVATION; FEAR OF FAILURE; INJURY; INTRINSIC MOTIVATION; MENTAL TOUGHNESS; MOOD; NEGATIVITY; NERVOUSNESS; OVERLEARNING; OVERREACHING; OVERTRAINING SYNDROME; RELAXATION; RETIREMENT; SELF-DETERMINATION THEORY; SLEEP; STRESS-INOCULATION TRAINING; STRESS-MANAGEMENT TRAINING; WELL-BEING; YOGA

STRESS-INOCULATION TRAINING

As its name suggests, stress-inoculation training is a COGNITIVE-BEHAVIORAL MODIFICATION that involves the use of STRESS itself to protect against its more serious attacks. To inoculate is to treat a person or animal *with* the agent of a disease to induce a milder form of it (from the Latin *in*, "into," *oculus*, "eye": The original meaning was grafting a shoot onto a plant). Pioneered by Donald Meichenbaum, the training exposes individuals to situations of progressively greater stress, the idea being that this will eventually work as a safeguard.

There are three phases.

(1) Conceptualization phase: This involves encouraging the person to recognize and address the character of his or her stress and the effects it has on his or her performance.
(2) Skills acquisition phase: RELAXATION, deep breathing, IMAGERY, problem solving, and other COPING STRATEGIES are developed. The emphasis is on controlling negative thoughts and reinforcing effort.
(3) Application and follow-through phase: The person translates the coping skills into practical action.

The inoculum (substance used for an inoculation) is stress; so, modest amounts of whatever stresses the patient are introduced. For example, an athlete may be induced into a relaxed state, then encouraged to imagine stressful encounters before rehearsing ways of coping with them. Role-playing and videos of imaginary situations are used. The main effort is to create extremely high levels of emotional AROUSAL in subjects by urging them to imagine a situation of maximum stress while practicing coping skills. Once this is well practiced, the athlete may be plunged into a real stressful situation so that he or she can experience firsthand a low level of stress. As the athlete becomes skilled at coping, the level of stress is upped and a more intimidating situation is created. This continues until the athlete is adept at coping in even highly stressful circumstances. Ultimately, the athlete is able to confront and overcome the original problem in actual COMPETITION.

While it was limited to white, male, amateurs, Michael Ross and R. Scott Berger's study indicated that stress–inoculation training "significantly reduced self-reported ANXIETY and PAIN in athletes during their postsurgical REHABILITATION of a knee INJURY." The researchers claimed that the training sped up the return to full functioning, a claim supported by the META-ANALYSIS of Teri Saunders et al. in 1996, and, by research of Brett Litz et al. in 2004. The latter employed a modified version of stress inoculation administered by way of the Internet on patients recovering from *post-traumatic stress disorder* (this refers to the syndrome arising from emotional disturbances and can involve ANGER, DEPRESSION, guilt, and other symptoms following a trauma).

Further reading

Litz, B. T., Bryant, R., Williams, L., Wang, J., and Engel C. C. (2004). A therapist-assisted internet self-help program for traumatic stress. *Professional Psychology: Research and Practice*, 35, 628–34.

Meichenbaum, D. (1977). *Cognitive behavior modification: An integrative approach*. New York: Plenum.

Meichenbaum, Donald (1985). *Stress inoculation training*. New York: Pergamon Press.

Meichenbaum, Donald (1997). *Treating post-traumatic stress disorder: A handbook and practice manual for therapy*. Brisbane: Wiley.

Ross, Michael J. and Scott Berger, R. (1996). Effects of stress inoculation training on athletes' postsurgical pain and rehabilitation after orthopedic injury. *Journal of Consulting and Clinical Psychology*, 64, 406–10.

Saunders, Teri, Driskell, James E., Hall Johnston, Joan, and Salas, Eduardo (1996). The effect of stress inoculation training on anxiety and performance. *Journal of Occupational Health Psychology*, 1, 170–86.

See also: COGNITIVE-BEHAVIORAL MODIFICATION; CONTROL; COPING STRATEGIES; DEPENDENCE; DEPRESSION; IMAGERY; INTERVENTION; MENTAL TOUGHNESS; MOOD; NEGATIVITY; OVERTRAINING SYNDROME; REHABILITATION; STRESS; STRESS-MANAGEMENT TRAINING

STRESS-MANAGEMENT TRAINING

Aimed at equipping subjects with the ability to cope with ANXIETY, stress-management training is predicated on the view that there must be active cognitive involvement from the person experiencing STRESS. Whereas other approaches to ANXIETY reduction involved subjects passively, the cognitive–affective orientation of stress-management training means that "the client plays a far more active role and assumes more personal responsibility for developing and applying new modes of thinking about problem situations," according to Ronald Smith.

While method advanced by Smith in the 1980s resembled that of STRESS-INOCULATION TRAINING, it differed in an important respect: rather than practicing under low levels of stress, a technique known as induced affect is employed to allow rehearsal of coping responses while experiencing strong EMOTION. Individuals are typically encouraged to imagine an intensely stressful situation, then to experience the feelings that the scene elicits in them. By conjuring a worst-case scenario, individuals are imaginatively immersing themselves in a worse situation than they will actually encounter. When they reach a very high state of AROUSAL, they are told to "turn it off," using COPING STRATEGIES, such as deep breathing or task-relevant SELF-TALK, that induce physical RELAXATION.

The premise of the method is that learning to manage high levels of stress ensures that lower levels can also be managed in real situations;

stress inoculation proceeds from the other direction. For example, an ice skater was asked vividly to imagine a scene in which she skated onto the ice and fell down during her routine. This would be unlikely to happen in actuality. Having generated a high level of AROUSAL, the skater was then advised to go through her repertoire of coping strategies, such as deep inhalation and mental commands ("I can do no more than give my best, so relax") during exhalation. After perfecting this, the skater discovered that she could use the strategies to reduce high levels of anxiety both in training and in COMPETITION. The long-term benefits of the approach include a continuing ABILITY to CONTROL high arousal and an enhancement in SELF-EFFICACY. There is also the possibility of generalizing the results from sports-specific situations. For instance, the skater, having developed a capacity for managing competitive stress, may be able to use coping strategies to deal with a wide range of other potentially stressful situations and grow in CONFIDENCE as a result.

Like other forms of cognitive-affective training, stress management seeks to influence new patterns of behavior by introducing subjects to the value of relaxation, IMAGERY, SELF-TALK, and other cognitive techniques. Although some of these techniques are used in behavioral approaches, they are conceived rather differently—as silent behaviors. The GOAL of behavioral approaches is to modify the subjects' behavior, not necessarily to equip him or her with the cognitive ability to control the anxiety.

Two areas of particular interest to sport and exercise psychology are the role of exercise as stress management resource and GENDER differences in coping with stress. Several studies have reported a positive role for both exercise in itself and the physical FITNESS it produces in managing stress. Indeed, interventions in industry have integrated exercise programs into their management strategies. Exercise has been demonstrated to have favorable effects on PHYSICAL SELF-IMAGE and SELF-ESTEEM, leading to greater SELF-CONFIDENCE and diffuse enhanced MOOD. Yet, the impact is not uniform. Not only do women respond differently to similarly stressful situations but they do not experience personal fitness as such a valuable resource in managing stress.

Further reading

Guszkowska, M. (2005). Physical fitness as a resource in coping with stress among high school students. *Journal of Sports Medicine and Physical Fitness*, 45, 105–12.

Hammermeister, Jon and Burton, Damon (2004). Gender differences in coping with endurance sport stress: Are men from Mars and women from Venus? *Journal of Sport Behavior*, 27, 148–64.

Lloyd, Paul J. and Foster, Sandra L. (2006). Creating healthy, high-performance workplaces: Strategies from health and sports psychology. *Consulting Psychology Journal: Practice and Research*, 58, 23–39.

Smith, R. E. (1980). A cognitive-affective approach to stress management training for athletes. In C. Nadeau, W. Halliwell, K. Newell, and G. Roberts (Eds.) *Psychology of motor behavior and sports—1979* (pp. 54–72). Champaign, Ill.: Human Kinetics.

Smith, R. E. (1984). Theoretical and treatment approaches to anxiety reduction. In J. M. Silva and R. S. Weinberg (Eds.) *Psychological Foundations of Sport* (pp. 157–70). Champaign, Ill.: Human Kinetics.

See also: ANGER; ANXIETY; COGNITIVE-BEHAVIORAL MODIFICATION; COPING STRATEGIES; DEPRESSION; EUSTRESS; EXERCISE BEHAVIOR; STRESS; STRESS-INOCULATION TRAINING

SUPERSTITIOUS BEHAVIOR

A practice thought to influence events but in a way that defies logical, causal explanation is superstitious behavior. The word "superstitious" (the adjective of superstition) is from the Latin *super* denoting "above" and *stat* for "stand." Anthropological studies confirm that ritualistic and superstitious practices have existed in situations of uncertainty among all cultures and in all ages. Believing in the ABILITY to influence events without any physical understanding of why has been called *magical thinking* and, according to Emily Pronin et al., "glimmers of magical thinking appear even in ordinary people [. . .] when they are faced with a combination of uncertainty about an outcome and a desire for CONTROL over that outcome."

A football fan might wear his underpants inside out to go to a football game and privately take credit every time his favorite team wins. The inference is based on the PERCEPTION that there is a RELATIONSHIP between the underwear and subsequent events—which either is or can become a superstition. People come to believe in the effectiveness of their own thoughts and behaviors on actual events.

The way superstition comes into being may be explained in behaviorist terms. Say the first time the fan inadvertently puts on his underpants inside out, he watches his team have its best win of the season. Only later, does he discover the reversed underpants and resolves to wear them like that for subsequent games, some of which his team wins, others it does not. Winning the first game when the underpants were worn strengthened the likelihood that he would wear them like this again. In other words, the behavior was reinforced. This raises the frequency of the behavior during the next several games, so that, next time the team returns a good win, the probability is that he will be wearing his underwear the same way. That serves as the next REINFORCEMENT, which, in turn strengthens the frequency of the underpants being worn in future. Over time, the fan will probably display a superstitious inside-out undergarment-wearing RESPONSE, even though the response has no direct relationship to the reinforcement being received. The underwear does not CAUSE good performances but is merely reinforced adventitiously and irregularly. If FANS are superstitious, athletes are probably more so. Peculiar charms, complex dressing routines, and bizarre procedures form parts of athletes' superstitions. Common to them all is the complete absence of anything resembling what others would recognize as adequate evidence that they work. Their power lies in the fact that the individual athletes believe they work. As such, they can help reduce ANXIETY, build SELF-CONFIDENCE, and provide the impression of control in an uncertain situation. In this sense, superstitious beliefs might assist in engaging an internal LOCUS OF CONTROL. Research on this is equivocal, Judy Van Raalte et al. finding athletes who attributed control over events to themselves (that is, internally) were more likely to indulge in superstitious behavior, presumably believing that they could exert further control. Later research by Melissa Todd and Chris Brown contradicted this: "Athletes who tend to believe that events occur due to chance, LUCK, or the influence of other people were more likely to practice superstition in sport competition."

The latter research linked superstitious behavior to TYPE A behavior patterns, part of which is the DRIVE to maintain control over uncertain situations. It also highlighted a link with ATHLETIC IDENTITY. A strong identification with the athlete role can help build self-confidence as competence improves; it can also increase susceptibility to trauma following INJURY or unexpected reversals of fortune and, for these reasons, inclines athletes toward superstitions, if only as a way of trying to ward off misfortune. Jerry Burger and Amy Lynn's 2005 study of American and Japanese baseball players disclosed "widespread superstitious behavior" among professionals who train assiduously to minimize the intrusions of luck, chance or any other kind of random variable and, yet continue to understand their sport as being at the mercy of "uncontrollable forces." The research indicated that Americans used superstitious behavior in an effort to assist their personal performance, while Japanese players used it to help their teams.

A Dutch research project by Michaéla Schippers and Paul Van Lange concluded that, for all the seeming irrationality of performing superstitious rituals, "at least one important outcome is likely to be obtained: regulating psychological tension." Accordingly, they advise treating superstitious behavior "as an inherent part of mental and physical preparation."

Once the superstition appears to bring desired results, athletes' self-confidence may be affected, their COMPOSURE may improve and their expectancy may change; reductions in ANXIETY may follow. The athlete's feelings of control over performance may offer a perceived way of minimizing the uncertainty inherent in COMPETITION. In this sense, the superstition can function as a placebo.

Superstitions are not unalloyed in their benefits to believers. Serena Williams once admitted: "I have too many superstitious rituals and it's annoying. It's like I have to do it and if I don't then I'll lose." Superstitious behavior is voluntaristic, or freely willed; if the same behavior becomes irresistible it is OBSESSIVE-COMPULSIVE.

Further reading

Burger, Jerry M. and Lynn, Amy L. (2005). Superstitious behavior among American and Japanese professional baseball players. *Basic and Applied Social Psychology*, 27, 71–6.

Pronin, Emily, Wegner, Daniel M., McCarthy, Kimberly and Rodriguez, Sylvia (2006). Everyday magical powers: The role of apparent mental causation in the overestimation of personal influence. *Journal of Personality and Social Psychology*, 91, 218–31.

Schippers, Michaéla C. and Van Lange, Paul A. M. (2006). The psychological benefits of superstitious rituals in top sport: A study among top sportspersons. *Journal of Applied Social Psychology*, 36, 2532–53.

Todd, Melissa and Brown, Chris (2003). Characteristics associated with superstitious behavior in track and field athletes: Are there NCAA divisional level differences? *Journal of Sport Behavior*, 26, 168–87.

Van Raalte, Judy, Brewer, Britton, Nemeroff, Carol, and Linder, Darwyn (1991). Chance orientation and superstitious behavior on the putting green. *Journal of Sport Behavior*, 14, 41–50.

See also: FANS; GAMBLING; HOME ADVANTAGE; LOCUS OF CONTROL; MENTAL PRACTICE; OBSESSIVE-COMPULSIVE; PERFECTIONISM; PREPERFORMANCE ROUTINES; RELIGION; SELF-FULFILLING PROPHECY; TYPE A; VICARIOUS AGENCY

TALENT

The possession of special desirable gifts, faculties or aptitude.

See also: ABILITY; GIFTEDNESS

TASK/EGO ORIENTATION

Task orientation describes the position and direction of someone who strives to improve their SKILL or overall proficiency, while ego orientation is characteristic of those who organize their thoughts and behavior on developing the appearance of competence and protecting their ego. The Latin *orient*, meaning rising, or east, is the most likely source for the contemporary verb to orient, for aligning, or finding one's position, and the noun "orientation."

When an individual utilizes a task orientation, "perceptions of ABILITY are self-referenced; improving one's performance or performing better than one had expected results in feelings of competence and perceived success," Dawn Stephens concludes from her study of female soccer players. "In contrast, an individual utilizing an ego orientation will use a normative reference for perceptions of ability and success; the individual's FOCUS is on demonstrating superior ability in relation to others."

Using personal standards of success, the former typically focus on long-term goals, while the latter, measuring success by comparison with others, employ short-term goals. Task and ego *involvement* refer to the corresponding goal states.

Among the most frequently used instruments in measuring these is the Task-and-Ego-Orientation in Sport Questionnaire and the Perceptions of Success Questionnaire.

Further reading

Duda, Joan L. and Nicholls, J. G. (1992). Dimensions of achievement motivation in schoolwork and sport. *Journal of Educational Psychology*, 84, 290–9.

Roberts, G. C., Treasure, D. C., and Balague, G. (1998). Parental goal orientation and beliefs about the competitive sport experience of their children. *Journal of Applied Sport Psychology*, 24, 631–45.

Stephens, Dawn E. (2000) Predictors of likelihood to aggress in youth soccer. *Journal of Sport Behavior*, 23, 311–26.

TEAM PLAYER

A person who plays or works well as a member of a collectivity rather than as an individual, the team player is assimilated into what Claudia Kernan and Patricia Greenfield call "a superordinate group IDENTITY" (superordinate means something of superior rank or status). An individual is willing to surrender self-interest, or egotism, in service to the team.

There is no necessary incompatibility between being a team player and an individual. In fact, individual excellence is often realized in the CONTEXT of a team—a point made by basketball coach Pat Riley in his *The Winner Within: a Life Plan for Team Players.* Another prominent basketball coach, Phil Jackson, once observed of arguably the best individual ever to play basketball: "I had to convince Michael [Jordan] that the route to greatness was in making others better."

Both accounts stress that team players are shaped and this is confirmed in the Kernan/Greenfield study of high school sports teams in L.A. The conclusions included the finding that people's sometimes-incompatible values, perspectives and interests are never once and for all and can be "recreated" in a way that reflects current circumstances. One of the methods used was to encourage players to express openly their implicit values, and "foster a respect for both individualism and collectivism." Again, the emphasis is on individual excellence *through* the collectivity.

Further reading

Kernan, Claudia L. and Greenfield, Patricia M. (2005). Becoming a team: Collectivism, ethnicity, and group socialization in Los Angeles girls' basketball. *Ethos*, 33, 542–66.

Riley, Pat (1994). *The winner within: A life plan for team players.* New York: Berkeley.

TELIC DOMINANCE

"Telic" describes action, or attitude directed toward a definite final GOAL; it is from the Greek *telikos*, meaning "end." Telic dominance describes a serious, plan-oriented state, in contrast to *paratelic dominance*, which is playful and spontaneous.

Further reading

Kerr, J. H., Wilson, G. V., Svebak, S., and Kirkcaldy, B. D. (2006). Matches and mismatches between telic dominance and type of sport: Changes in emotions and stress pre- to post-performance. *Personality and Individual Differences*, 40, 1557–67.

See also: AGGRESSIVENESS; EMOTION; EMOTIONAL TONE; EUSTRESS; FLOW; HEDONIC TONE; IDIOGRAPHIC; METAMOTIVATION; MIMESIS; MOOD; PROFILE OF MOOD STATES; REVERSAL THEORY

TEMPERAMENT

"Stable individual differences in how people experience and express emotions," is how Peter Crocker et al. define "temperament." It reflects dispositions to react to particular types of stimuli and becomes manifest in childhood, as Geneviève Mageau and Robert Vallerand point out: "From a very early age, individual differences in temperament can be observed."

Michael Sheard and Jim Golby concur, suggesting young people with "an easy temperament" are capable of adjusting to changes in circumstances. By "easy" they mean they can adapt to environments without great effort and experience no emotional upheaval.

Temperamental is an adjective typically used to describe people prone to exhibit an unusual sensitivity to certain stimuli. As such, they are often described as erratic, impetuous and, sometimes, aggressive.

Further reading

Crocker, P. E., Kowalski, K. C., Graham, T. R. and Kowalski, N. P. (2002). Emotion in sport. In J. M. Silva, and D. E. Stevens (eds) *Psychological Foundations of Sport* (pp. 107–31). Boston, Mass.: Allyn & Bacon.

Mageau, Geneviève A. and Vallerand, Robert J. (2003). The coach–athlete relationship: A motivational model. *Journal of Sports Sciences*, 21, 883–904.

Sheard, Michael and Golby, Jim (2006). The efficacy of an outdoor adventure education curriculum on selected aspects of positive psychological development. *Journal of Experiential Education*, 29, 187–209.

See also: ANGER; EMOTION; MOOD; PERSONALITY; PERSONALITY ASSESSMENT; SELF-HANDICAPPING

THEORY

From the Greek *theoros*, for "contemplation," theory has three related meanings: (1) a series of linked concepts or ideas that purport to explain a set of known findings (for example, THEORY OF PLANNED BEHAVIOR); (2) a set of principles that prescribes an activity (pedagogic theory; that is, how teaching should be done); (3) an abstraction used to describe what should happen if certain conditions are met ("in theory, this should work").

The most common in sport and exercise is (1): Theories are advanced to make sense of a PHENOMENON in terms of known principles, but in a way that clarifies or demystifies rather than establishing truth. In his classic 1963 treatise, the philosopher Karl Popper (1902–94) argued that knowledge proceeds through conjectures and refutations, theories being the incomplete information conjectured, and research being attempts to refute, or prove them wrong. If the theory is not refuted by the research, then it stands corroborated, though not proven.

While good theories, for Popper, are those that are amenable to empirical testing, the clarifying power of some theories is self-contained. For example, the theories of Sigmund Freud (1856–1939) and Charles Darwin (1809–82), while thorough, cogent, and illuminating, do not lend themselves to rigorous testing, yet they have transformed the manner in which we understand ourselves.

Further reading

Lox, Curt L., Martin Ginis, Kathleen A., and Petruzzello, Steven (2006). *The psychology of exercise: Interpreting theory and practice,* 2nd edn. Scottsdale, Ariz.: Holcomb Hathaway.

Popper, Karl (1963). *Conjectures and refutations.* London and New York: Routledge & Kegan Paul.

Weinberg, Robert S. and Gould, Daniel (2007). *Foundations of sport and exercise psychology,* 4th edn. Champaign, Ill.: Human Kinetics.

See also: ACHIEVEMENT MOTIVE; AGGRESSION; ANGER; ANXIETY; AROUSAL; ATTRI-
BUTION; BURNOUT; CATHARSIS; COGNITIVE EVALUATION THEORY; COGNITIVE LOAD
THEORY; COHESION; CONCEPT; CONSTRUCT; DELIBERATE PRACTICE; DRIVE; EXPEC-
TANCY; FEAR OF FAILURE; FEEDBACK; FLOW; GOAL SETTING; IDIOGRAPHIC; IMAGERY;
INSTINCT; INTERNALIZATION; LEADERSHIP; LEFT-HANDEDNESS; LOCUS OF CONTROL;
META-ANALYSIS; METAMOTIVATION; MIMESIS; MOMENTUM; MOTIVATION; NOMO-
THETIC; PERCEPTION; PERSONALITY; PHENOMENON; REINFORCEMENT; REVERSAL
THEORY; SCHEMA; SELF-AWARENESS; SELF-DETERMINATION THEORY; SELF-ESTEEM;
SKILL ACQUISITION; THEORY OF PLANNED BEHAVIOR

THEORY OF PLANNED BEHAVIOR

This influential THEORY has guided research on why people are
motivated to initiate EXERCISE BEHAVIOR. Central to the theory is the
CONCEPT that the performance of any behavior is determined by a
combination of intention and CONTROL. *Intentions* are expressions of
plans of action and make known motivations to behave. *Perceived
behavioral control* represents how hard or easy a person feels it will be
to carry out a particular behavior.

The theory's propositions can be summarized: (1) The strength of a
person's *intention* to perform (or not perform) a certain type of behavior
(for example, a workout) is a reliable predictor of their behavior; (2)
Intention is determined by *attitudes* toward the type of behavior and
subjective norms (how significant other people think about the behavior);
(3) Intention and behavior are additionally affected by *perceived behavioral control*, which is basically how hard or easy it is to perform the
behavior—these are related to the person's experience, SKILL, ABILITY,
SELF-CONFIDENCE, as well as the amount of time and money they have.

The theory is an outgrowth of the theory of reasoned action which
was originated by Martin Fishbein and Icek Ajzen in the 1970s and
has been used across a variety of contexts; for example, attempts to
quit smoking, recycling waste, as well as starting exercise programs.
In all cases, the attempt is to understand the link between intention
and behavior. The theory is based on a MODEL of the human being as
rational, calculating, and aware of social pressures from people they
regard as important. But John Arnold and his colleagues argue that
humans behave in ways that "promote the collective good" and not
just their own interests. He also suggests that the theory ignores
IDENTITY, which is influenced by how we see others seeing us and
how we align ourselves with causes that are not attached to our personal circumstances.

In Arnold et al.'s study of occupational choice in the health sector, differences between individuals and groups in prior behavioral commitments and ease of implementing occupational decisions were factors affecting behavior, as were external obstacles independent of perceived behavioral control. In other words, the theory needed expanding to include factors other than those suggested by the theory.

Tracey Brickell et al. found the theory worked in predicting exercise, though past behavior interacted with "spontaneous implementation intentions"; in other words, if people had exercised in the past, their current intentions did not count for as much as those who were starting to exercise for the first time. Past behavior was also a concern of Christopher Armitage, whose study was otherwise supportive of the theory: "The perceived behavioral control component of the theory of planned behavior is predictive of both initiation and maintenance of actual exercise attendance, which seems to reflect general exercise behavior, and sheds light on the likely genesis of exercise habits."

In an unusual application of the model, Amy Latimer and Kathleen Martin Ginis studied individuals undergoing REHABILITATION for spinal cord INJURY and discovered that, while personal behavioral control (PBC) did not predict "leisure time physical activity" (LTPA) among the rehabilitees, intentions were strong mediators and "these findings suggest that to bolster intentions among individuals with poor intentions, health practitioners should target subjective norms (for example, encourage physicians to recommend LTPA), attitudes (for example, highlight benefits of participation), and PBC (for example, provide detailed 'how to' information)."

Further reading

Armitage Christopher J. (2005). Can the theory of planned behavior predict the maintenance of physical activity? *Health Psychology,* 24, 235–45.

Arnold, J., Loan-Clarke, J., Coombs, C., Wilkinson, A., Park, J., and Preston, D. (2006). How well can the theory of planned behavior account for occupational intentions? *Journal of Vocational Behavior,* 69, 374–90.

Brickell, Tracey A., Chatzisarantis, Nikos L. D. and Pretty, Grace M. (2006). Using past behaviour and spontaneous implementation intentions to enhance the utility of the theory of planned behaviour in predicting exercise. *British Journal of Health Psychology,* 11, 249–61.

Fishbein, M. and Ajzen, I. (1975). *Belief, attitude, and behaviour: An introduction to theory and research.* Reading, MA: Addison-Wesley.

Latimer, Amy E. and Martin Ginis, Kathleen A. (2005). The theory of planned behavior in prediction of leisure time physical activity among individuals with spinal cord injury. *Rehabilitation Psychology,* 50, 389–96.

THERAPY

From the Greek *therapeia*, for "healing," therapy is the treatment of any form of disorder. Psychological therapy refers to treatment by psychological rather than biological or physical means. The term serves as an umbrella for many different types of techniques, all of which are intended to assist individuals in modifying their behavior and COGNITION and perhaps their emotional responses to particular circumstances. Therapy for athletes may be directed at any source of ANXIETY or STRESS experienced by a performer at any level of COMPETITION.

Different types of therapy rest on different assumptions. For example, some believe that the modification of behavior is dependent on a person's understanding of his or her motives, while others feel that subjects can learn COPING STRATEGIES without exploring motives and just by changing their behavior. Still others APPROACH therapy through a combination of techniques, sometimes known as COGNITIVE-BEHAVIORAL MODIFICATION.

Beyond differences, most therapy is predicated on the alliance between the principals: the therapist and the client. The client is expressly reminded that, to be effective, the alliance relies on his or her total honesty. In return, a nonjudgmental atmosphere is maintained as the therapist offers guidance designed to support the client and promote independence rather than indefinite reliance.

Exercise has become part of the spectrum of therapeutic behaviors, the term *therapeutic exercise* describing the specific treatment for both physical and psychological conditions. In fact, an Italian study found that "8 weeks of AT [aerobic training] may be more effective than NR [neurological rehabilitation] in improving maximum exercise tolerance and walking capacity in patients with MS [multiple sclerosis] and mild to moderate disability."

Further reading

Gallagher, Brian V. and Gardner, Frank L. (2007). An examination of the relationship between early maladaptive schemas, coping, and emotional response to athletic injury. *Journal of Clinical Sport Psychology*, 1, 47–67.

Huber, F. E. and Wells, C. L. (2006). *Therapeutic exercise: Treatment planning for progression*. St Louis, Miss.: Saunders.

Lesyk, Jack L. (1998). *Developing sport psychology within your clinical practice: A practical guide for mental health professionals.* San Francisco, Calif.: Jossey-Bass.

Rampello, A., Franceschini, M., Piepoli, M., Anetnucci, R., Lenti, G., Olivieri, D., and Chetta, A. Effect of aerobic training on walking capacity and maximal exercise tolerance in patients with mulitiple sclerois: A randomized crossover controlled study. *Physical Therapy,* 87, 545–55.

See also: ANXIETY; APPROACH; AVOIDANCE; COGNITIVE-BEHAVIORAL MODIFICATION; COPING STRATEGIES; DEPRESSION; INJURY; INTERVENTION; KINESIOPHOBIA; MEDITATION; MOOD; REHABILITATION; SLEEP; STRESS; STRESS-MANAGEMENT TRAINING

TRANSACTIONAL LEADERSHIP

This describes a style in which leaders and followers negotiate a kind of contract stipulating which assignments will be carried out in exchange for commensurate compensation, such as recognition, or rewards. The leader of a group typically outlines tasks and expectations, sets out the contingent REWARD and monitors how the group members perform. Group members are responsible for carrying out the tasks, using whatever resources they have available.

Behaviorist assumptions about the way in which organisms react to rewards and punishment underpin transactional LEADERSHIP. For instance, a coach or captain's RELATIONSHIP with the rest of the team would hinge on the clear exchange of information followed by the consequent performance. Once the exchange is completed and the rewards or punishments discharged, the contract is at an end. Transactional leadership is usually contrasted to TRANSFORMATIONAL LEADERSHIP.

Transaction comes from the Latin *transire* meaning go across. While popularly used in business, where a commercial transaction usually refers to buying and selling, its applications extend into several areas of psychology in which actors meaningfully interact and exchange with each other. *Transactional analysis* is an APPROACH to psychotherapy practiced in groups; transactional PERCEPTION refers to a THEORY that holds that perception results from our engagement with the environment; in the transactional MODEL of STRESS, cognitive appraisal mediates the intensity of the stressful events; and in transactional *problem-solving*, problems are seen as the products of the transaction between individuals and their environment rather than arising from a single source.

Further reading

Burns J. M. (1988). *Leadership*. New York: Harper & Row.

See also: COACH–ATHLETE RELATIONSHIP; GROUP DYNAMICS; INCENTIVE; LEADER-
SHIP; PEER LEADERSHIP; REINFORCEMENT; REVERSAL THEORY; REWARD; TRANSFOR-
MATIONAL LEADERSHIP

TRANSFORMATIONAL LEADERSHIP

As the name implies, this refers to a form of LEADERSHIP that involves
thorough and dramatic changes. "This inspirational process," as Jens
Rowold describes it, "relies on emphasizing task-related values and a
strong COMMITMENT to a mission [...] followers are stimulated to
view their tasks or challenges from new perspectives."

There are five factors in transformational leadership: (1) *inspirational
MOTIVATION*: followers should share a vision of the future; (2) *idealized
influence-attributed*: followers attribute positive values and characteristics to a leader; (3) *idealized influence-behavior*: a collective sense of
mission and set of common values are emphasized; (4) *intellectual stimulation*: followers are tasked to find novel solutions to familiar problems and question their own beliefs; (5) *individualized consideration*: all
individuals' needs are recognized and their strengths developed.

While the leader and his or her behavior is a component of this
type of leadership, there are several other variables, including cognitive
ones—for example, the way followers perceive and evaluate and the way
they react to him or her. In other words, transformational leadership
describes a developing relationship in which all parties are changed.

In this sense, transformational leadership shares characteristics with
transformational grammar, which describes the process by which elements in an underlying deep structure of language are converted to a
set of rules for rewriting those structures on surface forms in a way
that allows humans to become generative, or creative language-users.

Transformational leadership is often contrasted with TRANSAC-
TIONAL LEADERSHIP.

Further reading

Bass, Bernhard M. (1998). *Transformational leadership: Industrial, military, and
educational impact*. Mahway, N.J.: Lawrence Erlbaum.
Rowold, Jens (2006) Transformational and transactional leadership in martial
arts. *Journal of Applied Sport Psychology*, 18, 312–25.

See also: COACH–ATHLETE RELATIONSHIP; COHESION; GROUP DYNAMICS; LEADER-
SHIP; OBEDIENCE; PEER LEADERSHIP; RELATIONAL; RELATIONSHIP; TEAM PLAYER;
TRANSACTIONAL LEADERSHIP

TRANSGENDERED

Adjective describing a person who identifies with, or feels emotionally that they belong to, the opposite SEX.

See also: GENDER VERIFICATION

TRANSSEXUAL

Someone who has undergone surgery and hormone treatment to
acquire the physical characteristics of the opposite SEX.

See also: GENDER VERIFICATION

TRANSTHEORETICAL MODEL

A MODEL of behavior change that is used to promote health behavior,
the transtheoretical model (TTM) integrates elements from several
other theoretical approaches; hence the name—the prefix *trans* means
"across." Its principal CONSTRUCT is stages of change plus independent
variables, processes of change and outcome measures, such as decisional balance and temptation scales. It has been used to explain
EXERCISE BEHAVIOR, delineate the stages of change, and predict future
lifestyle changes.

TTM is predicated on sequential *stages of change*. The transitions
between stages are affected by *processes of change* with intervening
variables, such as *decisional balance* (weighing up the costs and benefits
of change) and SELF-EFFICACY (to resist the temptation to relapse). The
five stages of readiness each have different perceptual properties
regarding undertaking or completing exercise, and these remain relatively consistent across individuals. They are: (1) precontemplation,
when people have no intentions about changing; (2) contemplation,
when they are intending to change during the next six months and
are aware of the costs and benefits of change; (3) preparation, when
they seek advice from others as they prepare to start changing; (4)

action, when they make substantial lifestyle changes; (5) maintenance, when the temptation to relapse recedes and they grow more CONFIDENT about continuing to change.

Regression is always possible, though studies indicate that only about 15 percent of people revert to stage (1). The point is that the model is in constant flux, changes happening constantly with no end state, even during the maintenance stage. For example, ceasing to smoke, or drink or overeat are not seen as events but stages of change in behavior.

Clearly, maintenance is important to all forms of behavior change, though, in the case of smoking cessation, there is a declining relevance for what the MODEL identifies as decisional balance; eventually, the decision whether or not to have a cigarette becomes redundant. In exercise, the exerciser often needs to make a series of decisions—if only because not smoking becomes a case of *not* doing something, whereas exercise always requires action.

Self-efficacy is also integral to the model. For behavioral change to continue, the individual will have to face temptations, and heightened self-efficacy enables him or her to resist. During the changes, individuals engage with experiential processes, such as rewarding themselves for each bout of exercise, or displaying posters on the benefits of exercise in their offices. But Ralph Maddison and Harry Prapavessis question whether this is a determinant or a consequence of changed behavior. Their study indicated a "reciprocal" effect: "stage of readiness [to exercise] and self-efficacy are intertwined [. . .] a person with greater self-efficacy to overcome barriers to exercise is more likely to be active, and greater activity is, in turn associated with greater self-efficacy."

TTM has been used extensively to explain various behavior changes, the studies of Kelly Juniper et al. and Bradley Cardinal and Maria Kosma providing contrasting examples of the versatility of the model. But Aidan Moran presents four shortcomings:

(1) It fails to specify the precise psychological mechanisms facilitating transitions.
(2) It neglects individual differences that might account for relapses.
(3) There is only "poor" empirical validation.
(4) Most applications have been on middle-aged rather than young populations, which are "increasingly sedentary."

Martin Hagger and Nikos Chatzisarantis doubt the value of TTM's central concept: "The stages of change adhere very closely to measures of intention and in this respect the stages themselves are merely a reflection of the different levels of intention toward engaging in the behavior."

Further reading

Cardinal, Bradley J. and Kosma, Maria (2004). Self-efficacy and the stages and process of change associated with adopting and maintaining muscular fitness-promoting behaviors. *Research Quarterly for Exercise and Sport*, 75, 186–97.

Hagger, Martin and Chatzisarantis, Nikos (2005). *The social psychology of exercise and sport*. Maidenhead: Open University Press.

Juniper, Kelly C., Oman, Roy F., Hamm, Robert M., and Kerby, Dave S. (2004). The relationships among constructs in the health belief model and the transtheoretical model among African American college women for physical activity. *American Journal of Health Promotion*, 18, 354–7.

Maddison, Ralph and Prapavessis, Harry (2006). Exercise behavior among New Zealand adolescents: A test of the transtheoretical model. *Pediatric Exercise Science,* 18, 351–63.

Moran, Aidan (2004). *Sport and exercise psychology: A critical introduction.* London and New York: Routledge.

See also: ADHERENCE; ALCOHOLISM; COMMITMENT; CONSTRUCT; DECISION-MAKING; DISCIPLINE; EXERCISE BEHAVIOR; EXERCISE MOTIVATION; HOPE; MODEL; NOMOTHETIC; SELF-DETERMINATION THEORY; SELF-EFFICACY; THEORY; THEORY OF PLANNED BEHAVIOR

2 × 2 ACHIEVEMENT GOAL FRAMEWORK

A theoretical model for analyzing achievement motivation, this developed the traditional conceptual approach that proposed a GOAL dichotomy: MASTERY and performance. It comprises mastery–APPROACH, mastery–AVOIDANCE, performance–approach, and performance–avoidance, and attempts to reveal empirical profiles for each.

Further reading

Elliot, Andrew J. and McGregor, Holly A. (2001). A 2 × 2 achievement goal framework. *Journal of Personality and Social Psychology,* 80, 501–18.

See also: ACHIEVEMENT MOTIVE; APPROACH; AVOIDANCE; CONSTRUCT; GOAL; GOAL ORIENTATION; MASTERY; MASTERY CLIMATE; MOTIVATION; MOTIVATIONAL CLIMATE; RESPONSE; TASK/EGO ORIENTATION; THEORY

TYPE A

A PERSONALITY type characterized by excessive DRIVE, intense competitiveness, high ambition, an exaggerated sense of time urgency, an unwillingness to tolerate criticism, an inability or extreme reluctance to make self-evaluation, and a tendency to prioritize quantity over quality. It follows that *Type A Personality Behavior*, or TABP, is a pattern, or complex, described by M. Friedman and R. H. Rosenman, in 1974, as "an action–EMOTION complex that can be observed in any person who is aggressively involved in a chronic, incessant struggle to achieve more in less time, and if required to do so, against the opposing efforts of other things or other persons." Type A is thought to be a RISK factor in susceptibility to STRESS and coronary heart disease.

Because Type A individuals are intemperately competitive, they have been shown, by, among others Kevin Masters et al., to APPROACH exercise activities with an inappropriate attitude and do not benefit from the enhanced MOOD or several of the other benefits deriving from exercise, unless in specifically noncompetitive environments (for example, using a cycling machine for twenty minutes and being told "Go ahead," as opposed to " Go as far as you can. Your distance will be recorded and compared to that of other participants").

Further reading

Friedman, M. and Rosenman, R. H. (1974). *Type A behavior and your heart.* New York: Alfred Knopf.

Masters, Kevin S., Lacaille, Rick A., and Shearer, David S. (2003). The acute affective response of Type A behavior pattern individuals to competitive and noncompetitive exercise. *Canadian Journal of Behavioral Science,* 35, 25–34.

See also: AGGRESSIVENESS; APPROACH; EMOTION; EXERCISE BEHAVIOR; GOAL ORIENTATION; IDENTITY; MASTERY CLIMATE; MOOD; PERSONALITY; SELF-ESTEEM; STRESS

VICARIOUS AGENCY

"Feelings of authorship for the actions of others," is how Daniel Wegner and his colleagues define vicarious agency, the word "vicarious" deriving from the Latin *vicarius*, for substitute, and agency, a person or thing that produces a result—from *agentia*, doing. ("Vicar" shares the same root as vicarious: It originally meant a priest or clergyman deputizing for another.)

For Wegner et al., "Vicarious agency may be most evident in everyday life when we are placed in conditions that invite us to confuse our actions with those of others." The research team gives examples of when we are performing the same or complementary actions as others, or, "because we have an interest in the GOAL or outcome, or even because the action simply occurs in our presence."

Such situations are common in sport. FANS imaginatively experience success through their team or favored individual and take both credit and satisfaction from the achievement of the right result. Emily Pronin et al. call this "magical thinking" and relate it to the abundant SUPERSTITIOUS BEHAVIOR among FANS.

Parents feel similarly when their children win awards, not because they want to claim credit but because of what Wegner et al. term their "anticipatory thoughts of the glory." This has clear relevance to a generation of parents emerging in the 1990s which William Nack and Lester Munson once dubbed *parentis vociferous*! These are a species of "loud, intrusive moms and dads" who vigorously encourage their children to achieve in youth sports, and, on occasion, engage in VIOLENCE with each other.

The "anticipatory thoughts of glory" override rational judgments of authorship and youths are burdened with the expectations of their elders. On the account of Wegner et al., this is not due only to a displacement of the parents' own thwarted sporting ambitions but to a kind of empathic entrapment. The parents are unable to separate their emotions (of elation, frustration, despair, and so on) from the experiences of their children. They have invested so much of their own time, money, and other personal resources in cultivating their children's prowess that disengagement is impossible.

Another aspect of this parental vicariousness has been disclosed by Rachel Bachner-Melman, whose testimonies from people with EATING DISORDERS included accounts of parents who compensated for their own lack of achievement by way of their children and inadvertently hastened the children toward ANOREXIA NERVOSA.

Finally, we should note the role of vicarious agency in AGGRESSION, particularly that of FANS, who engage in MODELING, that is, replicating the violent behavior of players they observe. While the players might be penalized by referees, they are rewarded with kudos in the macho culture of many sports, thus prompting a vicarious REINFORCEMENT of the behavior.

Further reading

Bachner-Melman, Rachel (2003). Anorexia nervosa from a family perspective: Why did nobody notice? *American Journal of Family Therapy*, 31, 39–50.

Nack, William and Munson, Lester (2001). Out of control. *Sports Illustrated*, 93, 86–95.

Pronin, Emily, Wegner, Daniel M., McCarthy, Kimberly, and Rodriguez, Sylvia (2006). Everyday magical powers: The role of apparent mental causation in the overestimation of personal influence. *Journal of Personality and Social Psychology*, 91, 218–31.

Wegner, Daniel M., Sparrow, Betsy, and Winerman, Lea (2004). Vicarious agency: Experiencing control over the movements of others. *Journal of Personality and Social Psychology*, 86, 838–48.

See also: CELEBRITIES; COACH–ATHLETE RELATIONSHIP; INTERNALIZATION; RELATIONSHIP; SOCIAL FACILITATION; SOCIALIZATION; SUPERSTITIOUS BEHAVIOR; VIOLENCE

VIOLENCE

Behavior involving the exercise of physical force intended to hurt, injure or disrespect another human, or property, is violence—from the Latin *violentia*, which has essentially the same meaning. In sports, as in many other areas, violence is equated with the unlawful use of force or intimidation, though many sports either tacitly condone or exhibit violence. Hockey is an example of the former and boxing the latter, of course. In both sports, however, the transgression of boundaries is still punishable, as this constitutes a rule *violation* (from the same Latin root).

Violence should be distinguished from AGGRESSION, which is behavior, or a readiness to behave, in a way that is either intended or carries with it the possibility that a living being will be harmed, though no action or harm *necessarily* materializes. Aggression is considered legitimate under many conditions. AGGRESSIVENESS is not only legitimate but a requirement of many sports. Only combat sports officially approve of violence and, even then, within strictly determined frameworks of rules that ostensibly protect competitors from sustaining unnecessary punishment.

Even retaliation to acts of violence, which may be justified as self-defense in many quarters, is punishable in sports. In COMPETITION, much aggressive behavior is instrumental rather than hostile (that is, intended to procure an advantage through intimidation). "The closest parallels may be found between athletes and military personnel, who also follow strongly institutionalized regulatory structures," argues

Kevin Young, perhaps overlooking the more spontaneous eruptions of violence that lack any calculation.

Young's overview of the types of violence in sport encompasses player and fan violence. Explanations of their causes often link the two, spectators MODELING their behavior on that of competitors. Gershon Tenenbaum et al. observed in the 1990s: "Winning has become an essential part of sport [. . .] when athletes place a strong emphasis on beating others (in contrast to focusing on personal improvement and their own performance), they are more likely to [. . .] perceive intentionally injurious acts as more acceptable."

On this influential account, violence in sport became not only quotidian but also more acceptable from the perspective of the athlete and, if modeling is operational, from the perspective of the fan. The role of the media in disseminating and sometimes sensationalizing accounts of player violence has also had an impact on fan violence, if not in directly stimulating it, in legitimizing it.

Soccer HOOLIGANISM, in particular, has proved the most resilient and enduring type of fan violence that has resisted all attempts to eradicate it. Clampdowns on player violence throughout the world made little impact on violent disorder among crowds. Soccer violence embodies elements of spontaneity and calculation. While the actual episodes may be catalyzed by unexpected events, confrontations are frequently planned beforehand.

Hooliganism has been approached as a ritualistic pattern of fighting behavior, as, for example, wildebeests defend their territory in a stylized horn-locking standoff. There are certainly rituals involved in fan violence, as there are in many other forms of violent behavior in and out of sports. Even the seemingly unpremeditated and impulsive rages common in public places have formulaic elements that suggest the presence of MIMETIC processes. There also appears to be a propensity for perpetrators of violence to repeat their actions, presumably because they experience REINFORCEMENT. To understand the appeal of violence—and we should consider the VICARIOUS AGENCY of fans of ultraviolent sports, such as cage-fighting—we might examine what happens to those who engage in violence.

An assailant, in and out of sports, experiences AROUSAL that has been likened to sexual excitement. Individuals have reported responses that resemble an ADRENALINE RUSH when engaging in a violent act. Often there is a dehumanization of the target person. The perpetrator either involuntarily loses or abandons the ABILITY to empathize and treats the victim as an object. This is consistent with a binary mode of thinking in which the antagonist conceives the action only in terms of right/wrong, good/bad, justifiable/unjustifiable, and so on. The violence is typically understood as right, good and justifiable. Perhaps most interestingly, subjects recount feelings of empowerment and CONTROL while attacking, at the same time sensing they are *out* of control ("I just snapped"). This squares with an argument first advanced by Andreas Fontana in 1978 in which even impetuous displays of violence are rendered comprehensible in terms of an increasingly fragmented and impersonal society. Fragmentation prompted a "return to primitive sensation," violence being a way of reasserting individuality and personal distinctness. Far from being at the mercy of uncontrollable impulses the perpetrator uses violence as a resource to restore a subjective feeling of power.

Further reading

Fontana, Andreas (1978). Over the edge: A return to primitive sensation in play and games. *Urban Life*, 7, 213–29.

Tenenbaum, Gershon, Stewart, Evan, Singer, Robert N., and Duda, Joan (1996). Aggression and violence in sport: An ISSP position stand. *International Journal of Sport Psychology*, 27(2), 229–36.

Young, Kevin (2000) Sport and violence. In J. Coakley and E. Dunning (Eds.) *Handbook of Sports Studies* (pp. 382–407). London: Sage.

See also: AGGRESSION; AGGRESSIVENESS; ANGER; APPROACH; CATHARSIS; DEVIANCE; DRIVE; EMOTIONAL TONE; FANS; HEDONIC TONE; INSTINCT; MIMESIS; RELIGION; RESPONSE; REVERSAL THEORY; RIVALRY; VICARIOUS AGENCY

VISUAL PERCEPTION

Visual perception refers to the processes by which we see and become aware of objects, qualities, or other items of sensory input and organize them into coherent units of experience. This is an inclusive definition of a term that stems from the Latin *visus*, for sight, and *perceptio* for seize or understand.

Visual perception covers the entire series of actions, from the physical presentation of STIMULUS to the subjective sensations. Although sensory content is always present in visual PERCEPTION, the process is not passive or automatic: STIMULI do not impress themselves on consciousness. Rather, visual perception is an active operation in which MEMORY, expectations, and surroundings are influences.

This can be illustrated by the way we perceive distance, or DEPTH PERCEPTION. Stereoscopic vision is the term to describe how each of our eyes picks up slightly different information. The eyes work to compare the images and the slight lack of correspondence between them produces an experience of distance and depth. But, several studies have indicated that such perception is not innate in humans and probably not in other animals: perception can be modified by experience, a phenomenon known as perceptual plasticity.

Research on previously blind people who, having had their sight restored, had initial difficulty in their perception of distance, length, and color showed that, only over time were they able to perceive "normally." In another case, a member of an Equatorial African tribe who had lived most of his life amid trees and foliage, when taken into open country, mistook a distant herd of buffalo for insects and a boat some way offshore as a piece of wood. Again, it took time before normal perceptual functioning occurred. The point is that visual perception is learned through experience, at first through SOCIALIZATION and, later, through training.

Athletes train in perception, particularly depth perception. A bowler in cricket or a baseball pitcher needs an acute perception of depth to be able to deliver accurately and consistently. Fielders in both games need perception of distance and motion to be able to retrieve balls and return them without hesitation. Once struck by the bat, the ball appears as a tiny speck traveling through space. To field it successfully, a player needs to judge its variable distance, its speed and its likely direction. In this sense, perception is a SKILL and is refined by much the same processes as other skills. As in any sport, perceptual cues in the environment are used; this is especially intricate in fielding because of the lack of physical coordinates as the ball moves at great speed through space and the player is looking upwards.

In such situations, the size of the retinal image (the image of the visual scene formed on the retina at the back of the eye) depends on the distance between eye and the ball. Of course, the perceived size does not vary markedly: The ball does not suddenly appear to be the size of a meteor. While the retinal image may grow, the player's actual experience (the phenomenology) of it does not. This *perceptual constancy*, as it is called, occurs not only for size, but also for shape, color, brightness, and so on. So, a cricket ball or a baseball does not appear to the players to change color as the darkness falls and floodlights are switched on, even though the stimulation reaching the retina is different. The perceptual world remains stable, especially to athletes who must judge distance, trajectory, and so on, in markedly different environmental conditions. The stability is a result of the fact that most of our percepts (objects of perception) are *overdetermined*, meaning that visual, auditory, tactile, and other types of cues about the environment mutually reinforce each other, yielding information that provides a consistent representation of the world.

Not all perception is immediately apparent. *Subliminal* perception (from *sub*, beneath, and *limen*, threshold) involves a STIMULUS of very short duration that can be shown to have been perceived without conscious awareness. So, it is possible to perceive an image, or any other kind of information from the environment without actually being aware of it. Fears about the misuses of this, by, for instance, advertisers and politicians (to manipulate tastes and change opinions) have been largely unfounded.

Further reading

Buodo, Giulia, Sarlo, Michela, and Palomba, Daniela (2002). Attentional resources measured by reaction times highlight differences within pleasant and unpleasant, high arousing stimuli. *Motivation and Emotion*, 26, 123–38.

Davids, Keith, Williams, John, and Williams, Mark (Eds.) (1998). *Visual perception and action in sport*, London and New York: Routledge.

Turnbull, C. M. (1961). Some observations regarding the experiences and behavior of the Ba Mbuti Pygmies. *American Journal of Psychology*, 74, 304–8.

See also: ATTENTION; BODY LANGUAGE; CENTERING; COGNITION; EYE MOVEMENT; FOCUS; IMAGERY; MEMORY; MENTAL PRACTICE; PERCEPTION; PHYSICAL SELF-PERCEPTIONS; RIVALRY; STIMULUS; VISUOMOTOR

VISUOMOTOR

This relates to motor processes linked to VISUAL PERCEPTION by the brain, for example, the coordination of movement. *Visuomotor behavior rehearsal* is a COGNITIVE-BEHAVIORAL MODIFICATION technique that encourages the experiencing of, for example, PEAK PERFORMANCE as a way of reducing ANXIETY, leading to enhanced actual performance. IMAGERY is a favored method.

Further reading

Davis, Paul A. and Sime, Wesley (2005). Toward a psychophysiology of performance: Sport psychology principles dealing with anxiety. *International Journal of Stress Management*, 4, 363–78.

Gray, S. W. (1990). Effects of rehearsal with videotaped modeling on racquetball performance of beginner players. *Perceptual and Motor Skills*, 70, 379–85.

See also: ANXIETY; CENTERING; COGNITIVE-BEHAVIORAL MODIFICATION; ELECTRO-ENCEPHALOGRAM; FEEDBACK; HYPNOSIS; IMAGERY; MODELING; MOTOR REACTION; NERVOUS SYSTEM; PREPEFORMANCE ROUTINES; PSYCHING; RELAXATION; SELF-TALK; VISUAL PERCEPTION

WEIGHT CONTROL

Using a variety of activities, techniques or appliances to maintain body weight within certain limits is known as weight control, or weight management. The practice dates back to the ancient Romans who built *vomitoria*, which were passages in their amphitheaters where they would go deliberately to spew back their food—a practice not dissimilar to symptoms of what we now call BULIMIA NERVOSA. In fact, of the variety of weight control behaviors now employed, several involve EATING DISORDERS or analogous forms of PSYCHO-PATHOLOGY.

Much of the impetus behind contemporary forms of weight control is cultural, whether the sedentary lifestyle that contributes a variety of conditions associated with inactivity, including OBESITY, or the ideal of thinness that fosters BODY DISSATISFACTION and the often-maladaptive behaviors it triggers, especially among women.

One of the effects of sedentariness is obesity, which is described by Ethan Berke et al. as an epidemic and which "has been associated with many health problems, including cardiovascular disease, diabetes, some cancers, DEPRESSION, and arthritis. Physical activity is believed to be an important determinant of health and body weight."

Physical exercise is a type of physiological compensation. It acts as a STIMULUS contributing to body functionality and has been shown to be a successful INTERVENTION in the treatment of obesity. So, the benefits of exercise extend beyond weight loss and, according to Robert Dachs, exercise "appears to play an important role in maintaining long-term weight loss and in preventing weight regain."

It is not a panacea, however. Angelo Tremblay and Fanny Therrien's research carries a caution:

> Even if one displays an exemplary DISCIPLINE in the implementation of a healthy lifestyle, the resulting impact is not unlimited [...] we have not been able to promote mass losses exceeding 12%–15% of the initial level without having induced metabolic and behavioral changes compromising the ABILITY to maintain subsequent long-term mass stability.

In other words, the body biology can only tolerate so much exercise-induced change.

There is a cultural source, though of a different kind, for weight control methods with deleterious effects. "Societal messages are so pervasive that the values and views related to thinness as an ideal are already advocated by children as young as 7 years of age," suggest Marita McCabe and Lina Ricciardelli. Their evidence indicates that "children learn from their families, teachers, friends, and the media that fat is 'bad' and thin is 'good' [...] children as young as 8–9 years of age are engaging in dieting and strategies to increase muscles."

The results of this English study are consistent with those of American research, which revealed BODY IMAGE as related to SELF-ESTEEM and, as such, a potential precursor to attempts to CONTROL weight. Adrian Furnham et al. point out that in many countries, "eating disorders appear to start soon after puberty and persist through secondary school years." Even in adulthood, concerns over weight persist, as Paula Ziegler et al. point out: "Most healthy women (50% to 60%) wish to lose weight although they might be judged normal or below normal weight by medical standards."

As obesity is an "epidemic," eating disorders are "a universal issue," according to Furnham et al. Sonya Elder and Susan Roberts' META-ANALYSIS revealed that exercise, despite its "modest but consistent dose-response effect on body fatness," can mediate the effects of both obesity and eating disorders: "Long-term decreases in hunger associated with improved insulin sensitivity contribute to loss of body fat." (Note: insulin is the hormone which regulates the amount of glucose in the blood.)

In recent years, research has focused on the influence of SELF-EFFICACY on weight control. In particular, the work of Jennifer Linde et al. disclosed that CONFIDENCE in following an eating plan and confidence in following an exercise plan were "significantly associated with weight loss program monitoring behaviors, such as days of tracking ADHERENCE to diet or physical activity plans."

While this might not sound surprising, it signals the importance of trying to "use this confidence to motivate the performance of an effective set of weight control practices," rather than just concentrating on the weight loss behavior itself.

Further reading

Berke, E. M., Koepsell, T. D., Vernez Moudon, A., Hoskins, R. E., and Larson, E. B. (2007). Association of the built environment with physical activity and obesity in older persons. *American Journal of Public Health*, 97, 486–92.

Dachs, Robert (2007). Exercise is an effective intervention in overweight and obese patients. *American Family Physician*, 75, 1333–4.

Elder, Sonya J. and Roberts, Susan B. (2007). The effects of exercise on food intake and body fatness: A summary of published studies. *Nutrition Reviews*, 65, 1–19.

Furnham, Adrian, Badmin, Nicola, and Sneade, Ian (2002). Body image dissatisfaction: Gender differences in eating attitudes, self-esteem, and reasons for exercise. *Journal of Psychology*, 136, 581–96.

Linde, Jennifer A., Rothman, Alexander J., Baldwin, Austin S. and Jeffrey, Robert W. (2006). The impact of self-efficacy on behavior change and weight change among overweight participants in a weight loss trial. *Health Psychology*, 25, 282–91.

McCabe, Marita and Ricciardelli, Lina A. (2003). Body image and strategies to lose weight and increase muscle among boys and girls. *Health Psychology*, 22, 39–46.

Tremblay, Angelo and Therrien, Fanny (2006). Physical activity and body functionality: Implications for obesity prevention and treatment. *Canadian Journal of Physiology and Pharmacology*, 84, 149–56.

Ziegler, P. J., Kannan, S., Jonnalagadda, S. S., Krishnakumar, A., Taksali, S. E., and Nelson, J. A. (2005). Dietary intake, body image perceptions, and weight concerns of female US international synchronized figure skating teams. *International Journal of Sport Nutrition and Exercise Metabolism*. 15, 550–66.

See also: ADHERENCE; ANOREXIA ATHLETICA; ANOREXIA NERVOSA; BODY DIS-SATISFACTION; BODY IMAGE; BODY SHAME; EATING DISORDERS; EXERCISE BEHAVIOR; EXERCISE DEPENDENCE; OBESITY; PARTICIPATION MOTIVATION; PERFECTIONISM; PHY-SICAL SELF-PERCEPTIONS; PHYSICAL SELF-WORTH; SELF-CONFIDENCE; SELF-EFFICACY; SELF-ESTEEM

WELL-BEING

Often used synonymously with health, well-being encompasses physical health, happiness, comfort, and all-round satisfaction. In sport and exercise psychology, three main subtypes of well-being occur: *mental, psychological,* and *emotional,* all of which are positively related to physical activity. For example, M. J. Rotheram et al. discovered that: "Adolescents that are more active had significantly better values in mental wellbeing," which is measured by such indicators as "positive attitude to life," "SELF-ESTEEM," and "joy of life."

Antonia Baum discerned the value of *psychological well-being* as a protection against the EATING DISORDERS that can affect (in her study, male) athletes. Psychological well-being is reflected in SELF-CON-FIDENCE and SELF-EFFICACY. Research by Sarah Donaldson and Kevin Ronan disclosed the positive impact of participation in physical activity particularly on PHYSICAL SELF-PERCEPTION, which enhanced *emotional well-being*, this being assessed on the absence of STRESS, DEPRESSION or other forms of ANXIETY.

Further reading

Baum, Antonia (2006). Eating disorders in the male athlete. *Sports Medicine,* 36(1), 1–6.

Donaldson, Sarah J. and Ronan, Kevin R. (2006). The effects of sports participation on young adolescents' emotional well-being. *Adolescence,* 41, 369–94.

Rotheram, M. J., Bawden, M. A., Maynard, I. W., Thomas, O. T., and Scaiffe, R. (2006). An exploratory investigation of the "yips" using a mixed methodological approach. In P. Hassmen and N. Hassmen (Eds.), *Yearbook, 2006 of the Swedish Sport Psychology Association* (pp.1–22). Laholm: Trydells Tryckeri AB.

See also: AEROBIC/ANAEROBIC; AUTOGENIC; EMOTIONAL CONTROL; EMOTIONAL INTELLIGENCE; EMOTIONAL TONE; ENDORPHINS; EUSTRESS; FITNESS; FLOW; HOPE; PHYSICAL SELF-PERCEPTIONS; POSITIVE AFFECT; SELF-CONFIDENCE; SELF-EFFICACY

YERKES–DODSON LAW

First published in 1908, the "law" framed by Robert M. Yerkes (1876–1956) and John D. Dodson (1879–1955) stated that, as performers approach a highly desirable GOAL, their level of AROUSAL increases. Research indicates that when a supportive audience is present, arousal can increase beyond the point at which optimal performance is likely. So, there is a relationship between arousal and task performance that, when plotted on a graph, defines an INVERTED-U shape.

On intricate tasks, low levels of arousal improve performance relative to high levels, but on straightforward tasks the reverse holds. High arousal levels facilitate performance relative to low levels. Golf putting, for example, requires considerably less arousal than weight lifting, which is sometimes improved when the lifter experiences ANGER.

The "law" (in this sense, a NOMOTHETIC statement deduced from observation that specifies that, under certain conditions, a PHENOM-ENON always occurs) continues to generate research. For example, in 2004, Yaniv Hanoch and Oliver Vitouch revised it, suggesting that arousal affects both ATTENTION and the amount of information someone is capable of processing: "High emotional arousal states can be viewed as a vital mechanism allowing humans, despite their naturally limited resources and computational capabilities, to cope with the unpredictability and complexity of the environment."

In other words, arousal restricts the amount of information we can take in but facilitates DECISION-MAKING speed by narrowing the range of cues and forcing us to FOCUS on only GOAL-relevant information. Options are reduced and the body is mobilized to react to specific contingencies only.

In a completely different CONTEXT, Daniel Voyer et al. applied the law, studying the effect of HOME ADVANTAGE during the National Hockey League's playoffs. They hypothesized that, "when a supportive audience is present, arousal can increase beyond the point at which optimal performance is likely."

Further reading

Hanoch, Yaniv and Vitouch, Oliver (2004). When less is more: Information, emotional arousal and the ecological reframing of the Yerkes–Dodson law. *Theory and Psychology*, 14, 427–52.

Voyer, Daniel, Kinch, Stephen, and Wright, Edward F. (2006). The home disadvantage: Examination of the self-image redefinition hypothesis. *Journal of Sport Behavior*, 29, 270–79.

Yerkes, R. M. and Dodson, J. D. (1908). The relation of strength and stimulus to rapidity of habit formation. *Journal of Comparative and Neurological Psychology*, 18, 459–82.

See also: AROUSAL; CHOKE; CONSTRUCT; CONTEXT; HOME ADVANTAGE; INFORMATION PROCESSING; INVERTED-U; NOMOTHETIC; PHENOMENON; SOCIAL FACILITATION; SOCIAL LOAFING; THEORY

YIPS

Extreme NERVOUSNESS that affects individuals when they are performing finely controlled motor skills, the yips are associated mainly with golf, particularly putting, and manifest in involuntary movements.

A New Zealand research team led by C. M. Stinear used physiological and behavioral measures to identify two types of yips: (1) where there is "muscle activity during putting and greater errors and less inhibition of the anticipated response task"; (2) where there are changes in cognitive ANXIETY.

Using a different methodological approach based on the subjective experience, Mike Rotheram et al. revealed that not only golfers, but cricketers, darts players as well as athletes from other sports reported physical disruptions in the muscles during SKILL EXECUTION, involuntary movements, a lack of CONTROL, FEAR of the environment and a lack of SELF-CONFIDENCE at crucial stages. "These symptoms go beyond the simplistic description that the 'yips' involve a choking mechanism," the team concluded. "All participants reported fear of the environment, a characteristic [...] linked with sports performance phobias."

In this sense, the yips appear to be closer to the kind of phobias (extreme aversions) of musicians who have *dystonia*—abnormal muscle tone resulting in muscular spasm. Rotheram et al. found high levels of self-consciousness among "yippers," as they called people who suffered from yips. *Self-consciousness* is an awareness of one's presentation and actions and how they appear to others. Unlike some other forms of ANXIETY, the yips, on this account, arise from a heightened state of knowledge of oneself, particularly in the presence of others.

Further reading

Bawden Mark and Maynard Ian (2001). Towards an understanding of the personal experience of the "yips" in cricketers. *Journal of Sports Sciences*, 19, 937–53.

Rotheram, Mike, Bawden, Mark, Maynard Ian, Thomas, Owen and Scaife, Robert (2006). An exploratory investigation of the "yips" using a mixed methodological approach. In P. Hassmen and N. Hassmen (Eds.), *Yearbook 2006 of the Swedish Sport Psychology Association* (pp. 1–22). Laholm: Trydells Tryckeri AB.

Stinear C. M., Coxon J. P., Fleming M. K., Lim V. K., Prapavessis H. and Byblow W. D. (2006). The yips in golf: multimodal evidence for two subtypes. *Medicine and Science in Sports and Exercise,* 38, 1980–9.

See also: ANXIETY; AROUSAL; AUTOMATICITY; BODY LANGUAGE; CHOKE; CONCENTRATION; FEAR; NERVOUSNESS; SELF-AWARENESS; SOCIAL FACILITATION; STEREOTYPE THREAT

YOGA

Originally a Hindu spiritual and ascetic discipline, yoga has been adapted and popularized into a set of practices that assist RELAXATION and contribute to WELL-BEING. Those practices include breath CONTROL, prescribed body postures, and basic MEDITATION. The word "yoga" is Sanskrit for union.

The most popular form of yoga in the West is *hatha* yoga, which has been integrated into exercise programs. *Ashtanga* yoga, sometimes known as power yoga, has also been popularized at gyms around the world. This is a faster, more physically demanding form and has been adapted to suit aerobics. *Kundalini* is another form, the GOAL of which is to release the latent energy believed to lie coiled at the base of the spine ("kundalini" means snake). The basic belief behind kundalini is that breathing can release the energy. Claims for this particular form of yoga include the amelioration of OBSESSIVE-COMPULSIVE disorders, ANXIETY, DEPRESSION, and dependences as well as enhancement of SELF-ESTEEM.

Other varieties include Bikram yoga, which is practiced in hot environments, and Iyengar yoga, which uses blocks and straps. Like other yoga forms, these have become popular as workouts.

Jennifer Daubenmier's research concludes that practicing yoga yields another range of favorable results, including satisfaction with one's own body and fewer EATING DISORDERS. Other studies, for example, that of Sung Lee et al., reported, "fewer depressive symptoms, less trait anxiety, and greater SELF-EFFICACY."

Hatha yoga has been used in conjunction with COGNITIVE BEHAVIORAL MODIFICATION, or interventions which often involve writing down or expressing thoughts, some of which are deeply unpleasant (posttraumatic stress has been treated with this technique). Yoga complements this when exercisers are "paying ATTENTION to the way their emotions are expressed in their bodies," says Zindel Segal (quoted in Weintraub).

Despite the cumulative findings of minor studies and the documented physical benefits of yoga in, for example, muscular flexibility and VO^2_{max}, the largest, controlled trial of yoga "demonstrated that a 6-month yoga program did not produce any improvements in cognitive function." Barry Oken et al.'s research urged caution about the panacean qualities of yoga.

Further reading

Daubenmier, Jennifer J. (2005). The relationship of yoga, body awareness, and body responsiveness to self-objectification and disordered eating. *Psychology of Women Quarterly*, 29, 207–19.

Lee, Sung W., Mancuso, Carol A. and Charlson, Mary E. (2004). Prospective study of new participants in a community-based mind-body training program. *Journal of General Internal Medicine*, 19, 760–5.

Mishra, M. and Sinha, K. R. (2001). Effect of yogic practices on depression and anxiety. *Journal of Projective Psychology and Mental Health*, 8, 23–7.

Oken, Barry S., Zajdel, Daniel, Kishiyama, Shirley, Flegal, Kristin, Dehen, Cathleen, Haas, Mitchell, Kraemer, Lawrence, Julie and Leyva, Joanne (2006). Randomized, controlled, six-month trial of yoga in healthy seniors: Effects on cognition and quality of life. *Alternative Therapies in Health and Medicine*, 12, 40–47.

Shannahoff-Khalsa, David (2007). *Kundalini yoga meditation: Techniques for psychiatric disorders, couples therapy, and personal growth*. New York: Norton.

Weintraub, Amy (2000). Yoga: It's not just an exercise. *Psychology Today*, 33, 22–4.

See also: AUTOGENIC; BIOFEEDBACK; BODY IMAGE; ELECTROENCEPHALOGRAM; HYPNOSIS; MEDITATION; PAIN; PSYCHING; RELAXATION; SLEEP

ZONE

The metaphor of the zone is used to describe a mental state in which athletes believe they can perform to peak levels. In this conceptual space, athletes acquire an enhanced capacity to FOCUS and, in some cases, a level of consciousness that facilitates exceptional COMPOSURE. They also report blissful feelings and an agreeable loss of their sense of time and space, complemented, on occasion, by almost otherworldly sensations that have been likened to a spiritual experience. While the term "zone" is commonly used in sporting circles, it has also been appropriated by followers of the IZOF (INDIVIDUAL ZONES OF OPTIMAL FUNCTIONING) approach to studying the relationship between AROUSAL, emotions and athletic performance.

When in the zone, athletes have related passages of peak experience (a term originally used by MOTIVATION theorist Abraham Maslow), or PEAK PERFORMANCE, when they abandon all FEAR and inhibition and perform to the best of their ABILITY, at the same time enjoying a sharpness of PERCEPTION. This is a subjective experience and may or may not coincide with an objectively verifiable peak performance.

Reports of this altered state of consciousness or transcendence have led some writers, including A. Cooper, to suggest that being in the zone is akin to a spiritual experience, meaning that its effects go beyond material or physical changes. Kathleen Dillon and Jennifer

Tait put this idea to the test, concluding that there was a RELATION-SHIP between spirituality and the zone, though without knowing its direction: "Spirituality may lead to more experiences in the zone, or experiences in the zone may lead to more experiences of spirituality, or a third variable like propensity to altered states of consciousness [. . .] may account for this relationship."

Whatever the source, the overall point is complemented by Kenneth Ravizza's research on peak performance which includes accounts of "focused awareness, complete CONTROL of SELF and the environment and transcendence of self." While Ravizza does not cite the zone, his reference to an athlete's ability "to exclude external variables (for example, the crowd)" suggests that he was studying the same phenomenon under a different name.

For Ravizza, the individual has a *centered present focus*, meaning that "consciousness is channeled into the present moment" and outside distractions are eliminated. CONCENTRATION yields a *narrow focus of attention* exclusively on the object of the individual's PERCEPTION. There is also *complete absorption* in the task at hand and, often, individuals lose track of time and space.

Ravizza's participants reported feelings of *harmony and oneness* in which "total SELF is integrated physically and mentally" and fatigue and PAIN disappear. The experiences are *noncritical* and *effortless,* meaning that they surrendered themselves to the experiences, rather than exerting themselves. Participants were in a "higher state of consciousness."

The emphasis on awareness, AUTOMATICITY, effortlessness and bliss suggests strong comparisons with the concept of FLOW, a state in which athletes lose self-consciousness, self-judgment and self-doubts and just allow themselves to be carried along by the performance—they just go with the flow. In these senses, getting in the flow shares characteristics with both the zone and peak performance. We can add one more shared characteristic: evanescence—they fade quickly. Being in the zone may be a lustrous and vivid encounter; but it is a short-lived one. Whether or not it is possible to create conditions under which athletes can enter zones is an open question. Some believe RELAXA-TION, SELF-TALK and related strategies can maximize the chances of zone entry. HYPNOSIS has also been used as a route to the sought-after zone. Subjects in Susan Jackson's 1992 study of flow believed that, while the state was not available on demand, it could be approached through physical preparation and MENTAL PRACTICE (reported in Jackson and Csikszentmihalyi).

Entering the zone requires uncommon CONCENTRATION, yet without great exertion; feelings of WELL-BEING, power and potency are concomitant, that is they naturally accompany the transition to the zone. And, of course, they all leave the athletes with the—often-inaccurate—sense that they have performed to their highest level.

Sometimes, however, the two do coincide. Consider this account: "It felt like your whole mind, your whole body, was either in space or in the middle of the ocean, with no traffic, with no noise. Everything was as calm and quiet as could be." The words were those of Ben Johnson, reflecting on his 9.79 seconds 100 meters at the Seoul Olympics of 1988. The time was subsequently expunged when Johnson was found guilty of DOPING. But the singular experience he described is as lucid a depiction of being in a zone as imaginable. Of course, his passage into the zone was chemically assisted. (Johnson recounted his experience on BBC2/A&E television's *Reputations: Lost Seoul*.)

Further reading

Cooper, A. (1998). *Playing in the zone: Exploring the spiritual dimensions of sport*. Boston, Mass.: Shambhala.

Dillon, Kathleen M. and Tait, Jennifer L. (2000). Spirituality and being in the zone in team sports: A relationship? *Journal of Sport Behavior*, 23, 91–100.

Jackson, S. A. and Csikszentmihalyi, M. (1999). *Flow in sports: The keys to optimal experiences and performances*. Champaign, Ill.: Human Kinetics.

Ravizza, Kenneth (1984). Qualities of the peak experience in sport. In J. M. Silva, and R. S. Weinberg (Eds.) *Psychological Foundations of Sport* (pp. 452–61). Champaign, Ill.: Human Kinetics.

See also: ADRENALINE RUSH; AUTOGENIC; AUTOMATICITY; CENTERING; COMPOSURE; CONCENTRATION; ENDORPHINS; FLOW; FOCUS; GATING; HEDONIC TONE; HYPNOSIS; INDIVIDUAL ZONES OF OPTIMAL FUNCTIONING; METACOGNITION; PEAK PERFORMANCE; PREPERFORMANCE ROUTINES; RELIGION

INDEX